PSYCHOLOGY for TEACHERS

PRAISE FOR THE LAST EDITION

'Written in a very accessible style, this book makes the links between underpinning psychological theory and practice easy for the reader to relate to.'

John Luker, Glyndwr University

'A very accessible text which demonstrates how theory can be effectively applied within the classroom. The companion website provides a very useful source of information and resources.'

Jean Bourne, Herefordshire & Ludlow College

'This is a thorough and readable introduction to educational psychology. It deals with historical approaches as well as emerging ones in a lucid manner. Practising teachers looking to extend their knowledge will find the reflective questions at the end of each section valuable.'

Louise Campbell, University of Edinburgh

'*Psychology for Teachers* provides a comprehensive introduction to the application of key ideas from Psychology to Education from an inter-disciplinary perspective.'

Jonathan D. Reid, Oxford Brookes University

PSYCHOLOGY *for* TEACHERS

PAUL CASTLE
SCOTT BUCKLER

2nd Edition

Los Angeles | London | New Delhi
Singapore | Washington DC | Melbourne

Los Angeles | London | New Delhi
Singapore | Washington DC | Melbourne

SAGE Publications Ltd
1 Oliver's Yard
55 City Road
London EC1Y 1SP

SAGE Publications Inc.
2455 Teller Road
Thousand Oaks, California 91320

SAGE Publications India Pvt Ltd
B 1/I 1 Mohan Cooperative Industrial Area
Mathura Road
New Delhi 110 044

SAGE Publications Asia-Pacific Pte Ltd
3 Church Street
#10-04 Samsung Hub
Singapore 049483

Editor: James Clark
Assistant editor: Rob Patterson
Production editor: Rachel Burrows
Marketing manager: Lorna Patkai
Cover design: Sheila Tong
Typeset by: C&M Digitals (P) Ltd, Chennai, India
Printed in the UK

Library of Congress Control Number: 2017951048

British Library Cataloguing in Publication data

A catalogue record for this book is available from
the British Library

ISBN 978-1-5264-1354-3
ISBN 978-1-5264-1355-0 (pbk)

At SAGE we take sustainability seriously. Most of our products are printed in the UK using responsibly sourced
papers and boards. When we print overseas we ensure sustainable papers are used as measured by the PREPS
grading system. We undertake an annual audit to monitor our sustainability.

CONTENTS

LIST OF FIGURES

LIST OF TABLES

NEW TO THIS EDITION

Psychology for Teachers has been updated extensively for this second edition with a range of new content.

The major additions to this edition include eight new chapters divided into three entirely new parts on Mental Wellbeing (Part 4), Psychological Skills Training (Part 5), and Evidence-based Teaching (Part 6). The new chapter topics include Mental Wellbeing, Coaching Psychology and Developing Resilience (Part 4), Goal-Setting, Mental Imagery, Self-Talk and Cognitive Restructuring, and Relaxation (Part 5) and Doing Research and Analysing Data (Part 6). The addition of this new content is in response to current and topical developments in educational psychology and educational research and practice more widely.

Chapter 9 (Understanding Special Educational Needs and Disabilities) has also been thoroughly revised to include coverage of the SEND Code of Practice (Department for Education/Department for Health, 2015), and there is a more critical perspective applied to the discussion of Learning Styles in Chapter 20.

We've also taken the opportunity to include additional further reading in a selection of the new chapters as well as fully revised references throughout this new edition.

ACKNOWLEDGEMENTS

This book would not have been possible without the contributions of many others.

From SAGE Publishing we would specifically like to express our gratitude to the commissioning editor, James Clark, whose original vision promoted the first edition of this book and who had the timely foresight to consider a second edition. Our thanks also extend to Robert Patterson at SAGE whose meticulous attention to detail has helped take the manuscript through to publication. Furthermore, for the copy-editing by Gemma Marren whose attention to detail has helped immeasurably; along with Rachel Burrows, the Senior Production Editor whose support was extremely welcome in the final stages. We similarly appreciate the support from the many others 'behind the scenes' at SAGE who contribute to such a wonderful experience for authors, in turn ensuring that SAGE is the beacon of academic excellence when it comes to publishing.

Paul would especially like to thank Professor Jo Smith, along with Briony Williams, Jo Augustus and Dawn Goodall, for providing inspiration at appropriate moments during the writing of the new section on mental wellbeing, and also Mick Donovan, Gareth Jones and Lerverne Barber for supporting the initiative within the Institute of Sport and Exercise Science at the University of Worcester. Thanks go to all of the teachers I have had the pleasure of supporting through their own challenging times and who have inspired much of the material presented here. Additionally I would like to thank staff at the Droitwich Spa Lido, one of the few remaining inland, open-air saltwater pools for the 'early morning swim' sessions, which helped clear my 'writing head'. Finally, as always, my thanks go to Nikki Castle for her love, humour and infallible support. Always smiling! Always happy! We grow older together! Je t'aime à mourir ma chérie!

Scott would like to thank Genea Alexander from the University of Worcester for the many professional discussions to ensure that the content is relevant to all those progressing with their careers in teaching. I would also like to thank Professor Alison Kington, similarly from the University of Worcester, for her academic support and advice. Additionally, I would like to thank all the staff at Hindlip First School, Fernhill Heath, Worcester, for simply being superb models of what teaching should be and an outstanding school. Finally I would like to thank Chloe and Cameron, for challenging everything I thought I knew about children and education.

PUBLISHER ACKNOWLEDGEMENTS

The publishers would like to extend their thanks to the following individuals for their invaluable feedback that has shaped this second edition:

Professor Anna Lise Gordon, St Mary's University, Twickenham
Russell Grigg, freelance editorial consultant
Sian Templeton, University of Gloucestershire
Sue Wilkinson, Cardiff Metropolitan University

ABOUT THE AUTHORS

Paul Castle joined the University of Worcester as a senior lecturer in September 2004. He is a Chartered Sport and Exercise Psychologist, Associate Fellow of the British Psychological Society and is registered with the Health & Care Professions Council. As an active practitioner, with almost 20 years' experience, Paul provides applied psychology consultancy to clients in a wide array of disciplines, with a particular emphasis on providing individual- and small-group support to teachers and lecturers, to ameliorate the effects of stress, depression and burnout. As Mental Health and Wellbeing (MHWB or MWB) Lead for the Institute of Sport & Exercise Science at Worcester, Paul has embraced the emerging issue of MWB in students and staff within primary, secondary and tertiary education. He is an advocate for reducing the stigma associated with MWB and provides applied psychological support in guiding students through their own 'personal challenges' by a combination of sport, physical activity and psychological skills training. Paul is trained in Mental Health First Aid (MHFA) and Applied Suicide Intervention Skills Training (ASIST), in conjunction with his professional grounding. He is an active member of the 'Suicide Safer' Project Group at the University of Worcester, which aims to promote 'suicide safer communities' both regionally and nationally.

Scott Buckler has worked extensively in education since 1995 as a teacher and university lecturer. He has led degree programmes at undergraduate and postgraduate level, and lectured predominantly on applied educational psychology, inclusive education and leadership in schools. He is a Chartered Psychologist with a specific interest in transpersonal psychology. Other SAGE publications Scott has co-authored are *Your Dissertation in*

Education (2016 with Nicholas Walliman) and *How to Be a Successful Teacher: Strategies for Personal and Professional Development* (2009 with Paul Castle). He is currently writing *Responsible Radical Teaching* with Pie Corbett, and runs a CPD consultancy.

FOREWORD

As we write this foreword, it is raining. Rain, we have realised, is good for writing. It is rhythmic. It reduces the distractions otherwise associated with writing in the summer months. It provides a contrasting backdrop to the creative process required to write. In this respect, we have been unlucky. Much of our writing has taken place in the heat, so we have had to utilise our contingency plan: good coffee … and lots of it! Of course, since coffee is a diuretic, we have also had to ensure that we remained adequately hydrated in order to remain focused. We have had to adapt to ever-changing pressures and forces conspiring against us. Likewise, this is quite normal within the education system. Things change! Often! They change again and after a while, some things travel full circle and the wheel is reinvented, with a new label.

It is not change that is the difficulty: change is inevitable. Rather, it is how we all adapt to this change that is the key, transforming a multitude of thoughts into a coherent whole. With this is mind, we hope that the following chapters provide you with a convenient structure to assemble your own thoughts. The indivisible relationship between psychology and education in facilitating positive learning behaviour will become apparent as each section develops. It will also become apparent that a range of perspectives need to be considered by the teacher in order to promote best practice in the classroom. Since the first edition, we have updated where necessary, but we have also added three new sections as a result of emerging trends.

The issue of mental health and wellbeing (MHWB or MWB) has entered the public domain in the last two years and is an area of such concern that it was mentioned in the Queen's speech (21/06/17). Both Princes William and Henry (Harry) are instrumental in the roles they play in promoting MWB in society. Equally, some high-profile celebrities are campaigning to reduce the stigma associated with diminished MWB. Moreover, we see these challenges emerge in our schools, colleges and universities every day, and in order for aspiring teachers to consider how best to educate and guide their students, it makes sense to consider their own MWB. This part, in combination with the second new part on Psychological Skills Training, will enable you to explore and develop MWB, with guidance provided here.

The third new part is on research methods. Many people avoid these two 'dirty words'. Dry, dull, tedious, difficult, incomprehensible, pointless, meaningless! If you subscribe to this view, you are hindering yourself. Rather, look at research methods as a vehicle to explore your thoughts and ideas. In the education system, recording information, monitoring progress, achieving results and keeping track are inescapable … they happen anyway! Think in terms of data and suddenly you have a diverse amount of information at your fingertips, ready to answer your questions. Yet, if you don't have the knowledge to do something with it, it is not working for you. The teacher of tomorrow, implicit in the Teachers' Standards, is expected to formulate ideas, design studies, conduct research and report the results scientifically, in order to reach valid conclusions. The new section will facilitate this.

Finally, we hope that the theories and perspectives within this book can be embraced to further enhance your classroom practice. Throughout your career, keep an open mind and keep searching for the peer-reviewed evidence when a new initiative is suggested, or in the absence of any evidence, propose investigating it formally. It is your job not only to promote thinking within your learners, but also to promote a critical, questioning attitude across the profession: only then can we, as teachers, ensure that the very best of practice is adopted, and if necessary, adapted. Be mindful of striving to achieve the work–life balance that will enable you to remain resilient on your exciting journey and seek out challenges to make you stronger and more effective as your teaching evolves.

Paul Castle and Scott Buckler
January 2018

PREFACE

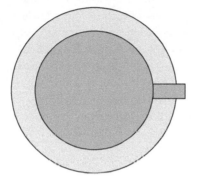

What do you see?

What do you see in this picture? Is it a tea cup viewed from above? Is it a washing-machine door? A duck? Is it just two circles and a rectangle? Or can you see something different?

As a profession, teaching requires us to question our perspective. We are swayed by what we believe to be best practice, what the theory says about best practice, what we perceive about our own teaching, our thoughts and feelings, the thoughts and feelings of others, and so on. We are continually considering this array of perspectives as we develop our teaching and as we develop our profession.

Perspective is fundamental within psychology and we believe that psychology is of fundamental importance within teaching. Although the term 'psychology' can be simply defined as the 'scientific study of people, the mind and behaviour' (British Psychological Society, 2017), the focus on 'behaviour' raises a number of differing perspectives. For example, what is behaviour? Can behaviour be influenced or controlled? What is the best way to modify behaviour: medication, rewards or punishment? Is behaviour the result of processes internal to the individual or externally influenced? What do we define as 'misbehaviour'? A number of other questions could similarly be raised in relation to any aspect within the teaching profession. This book encourages you to consider a range of psychological perspectives and how these relate to teaching.

As the cover of this book demonstrates, the ladder acts as a 'vehicle' or 'tool' to encourage this ascent. The ascent is analogous to your professional development. No two people will take the same ascent and this is a core reason why education is deemed a profession. Although we are informed of best practice, such practice can only be developed by taking the initial steps, gaining confidence along the way and continually asking if there are new ways that can be developed to enhance our teaching further.

Within this book you are provided with current theoretical perspectives and encouraged to consider how these perspectives relate to your practice and, on this basis, what makes (or even enhances) best practice within the profession. Each chapter provides explicit links to the most relevant Teachers' Standards (Department for Education, 2013), demonstrating how psychology and education explicitly relate. Fundamentally the book encourages you to explore current theoretical perspectives, analysing and evaluating how these perspectives relate to your practice through structured reflections and activities. Through this approach, we encourage you to develop your personal teaching philosophy, which enhances best practice.

Let this exploration of the clouds of perspective begin!

ONLINE RESOURCES

The second edition of *Psychology for Teachers* is supported by a range of online and downloadable resources available at: **https://study.sagepub.com/castlebuckler2e**
   Resources include:

- lecturer PowerPoint slides
- downloadable activity sheets
- selected SAGE journal articles

Part 1
PSYCHOLOGICAL PERSPECTIVES ON EDUCATION

This part contextualises the theme of the book by inviting the reader to examine classical approaches (Chapter 1) and emerging psychological approaches (Chapter 2) to perspectives on education. These perspectives inform the developing teacher and provide frameworks upon which newly acquired knowledge can be 'attached', while providing a discussion about the qualities of the effective teacher (Chapter 3). These perspectives will also enable the teacher to develop their own philosophy on and psychology of professional practice (Chapter 4).

1
CLASSICAL APPROACHES TO PSYCHOLOGY

CHAPTER OBJECTIVES

- Consider the defining features of a variety of psychological perspectives.
- Develop an understanding of how various psychological perspectives have influenced education.
- Evaluate how psychology can be applied within education.

TEACHERS' STANDARDS

A teacher must:

4   Plan and teach well-structured lessons

- reflect systematically on the effectiveness of lessons and approaches to teaching

5   Adapt teaching to respond to the strengths and needs of all pupils

- have a secure understanding of how a range of factors can inhibit pupils' ability to learn, and how best to overcome these
- demonstrate an awareness of the physical, social and intellectual development of children, and know how to adapt teaching to support pupils' education at different stages of development

1.1 INTRODUCTION

Perspective is the central focus of the book: by appreciating that there is a wide variety of approaches to teaching, the teacher who continually reflects on their own approach should place themselves in a position of achieving their best practice. The concept of perspective is discussed before exploring various psychological perspectives spanning the past century. This chapter will provide an overview of the 'classic' approaches (psychodynamic, behaviourist, cognitive, humanistic, psychobiological) and their relevant contributions to learning. We then introduce and discuss the importance of the evolutionary perspective in psychology.

1.2 PERSPECTIVES IN PSYCHOLOGY

The world does not exist! That sounds like a very strange statement to make, given that we are all present in a world that is revolving (literally) and that in our daily lives we interact with our world, or our immediate environment. There is therefore a multitude of evidence to show that the world *does* exist. Of course it does. Yet, not too long ago, the world was flat. Or at least that was the accepted wisdom of the day, held to be correct by many people. Throughout the history of humankind, people have held a set of beliefs, attitudes and opinions on anything and everything that affected them.

These beliefs, attitudes and opinions may not be shared by everyone though. Some people may question and challenge the accepted wisdom. 'The world is not flat and I shall prove it to you' (or words to that effect) led to the intrepid explorer Ferdinand Magellan (1480–1521) embarking on a voyage of discovery that could have ended either in success or failure of the highest order. Fortunately, for Magellan, and for cartographers and globe manufacturers, evidence for a round world was found and a new set of beliefs was formed. A new perspective on how the seas did not simply fall off the edge of the world came into existence, became accepted and the previous perspective of a flat world was dismissed. Interestingly, children of today would find the view of a flat world absurd. A recent example is that the discovery of stone megaliths at Göbekli Tepe in Turkey demonstrate civilisation existed from the tenth to eighth millennium BCE, pre-dating the earliest accepted civilisation of Mesopotamia by at least 5000 years.

Artists talk of perspective within paintings. By this they mean the arrangement of objects within the painting in such a way as to give the illusion of depth. Of course, we could discuss classical paintings such as Constable's *Hay Wain*, or the work of the Impressionists of the late nineteenth and early twentieth centuries. However, perspective is perhaps best reflected in the work of M.C. Escher (1898–1972). Escher's lithograph *Relativity* (1953) sums up perspective in a visual sense perfectly (see Figure 1.1). If one looks closely at the lithograph it becomes apparent that the perspective doesn't make sense. It does not work. Yet, on the surface, the image looks perfectly normal. Escher has used perspective to provide depth, by placing objects in front of or behind each other in a way one would expect in artistic work. However, he has then created a twist in reality; to produce an image that simply could not work in the real world. Indeed, this lithograph is similar to the flat world view mentioned above. If you were to try to walk up or down all of the stairs in Escher's image, you would simply fall off, because they do not all ascend or descend as they appear.

The lithograph fools us into seeing something that is not all that it seems. Equally, if we look at Escher's symmetry drawings, we 'see' what we want to see first because of the perspective we adopt. This is not perspective as in the 'depth' sense of the term, but rather, perspective in the sense of the prior knowledge and experience we bring to the viewing of the drawing. Your perspective changes, possibly very quickly, but nevertheless it shifts so that you take on a new view of the image. The content of the image hasn't changed, but the way in which you see it has.

Artwork takes many forms, some quirky, some not, but it does provide us with excellent examples of how perspective can be used to great effect and how we as humans will fall for something that is not quite as it seems. In the next example (Figure 1.2), one can obviously see a house, woodland, a bridge and a river. Certain objects appear in

Figure 1.1   Escher's *Relativity*

the foreground; certain objects in the background. Some trees are taller than others, reflecting their age. The water appears to be flowing, reflected in the direction of the foliage under the surface. Yet in reality, it is not under the surface, the trees do not display age and the image is a two-dimensional representation of a three-dimensional scene that has been recreated by the human brain.

Perspective is important in psychology because it provides us with a conceptual standpoint from which we can begin to make sense of the world around us. Perspective enables us to look at something from one point of view and, hopefully, to see the same thing from another's point of view. This is important and is something that we encourage children to do all the time. 'How do you think John feels when you tease him?' A child learns how others may be affected by the actions of another by adopting the perspective of that child. In the classical developmental psychology of Jean Piaget (1896–1980) this is known as perspective-taking and is illustrated by showing a child a doll and then placing that doll in another room, before asking the child what the

Figure 1.2   An example of perspective (from R.G. Smith, reproduced with permission)

doll can see in that room. In order to answer, the child must adopt or take the perspective of the doll.

In discussing the role of perspective in helping humans to understand and interpret the world around them, we have shown that perspectives can change and that adopting the perspective of another may provide a completely different interpretation of the world under scrutiny. Having established the importance of perspective, we cannot simply launch into the perspectives in psychology without providing a historical 'road-map' showing from where these perspectives have derived. The next part of this chapter explores the roots of psychology but we will be mindful throughout to make links to practical application and relevance to you as teachers.

1.3 THE ROOTS OF PSYCHOLOGY AND PARADIGM SHIFTS

This part will provide as close to a chronological history of psychology as possible and begins with relevant philosophical underpinning. It is far easier to understand the nature, scope and diversity of psychological perspectives when one can see how psychology itself has evolved to its current stature in science. In adopting a chronological approach, not only you will see where psychology has derived from, but also you will experience the various paradigm shifts that have taken place

(Hergenhahn, 2009). A paradigm is an orientation towards something using a particular focus, for example a behaviourist perspective, discussed later in this chapter. A paradigm is therefore the accepted wisdom of the time. Paradigms change over time, as evidence accrues and academic thinking changes. This change in thinking leads to the development of paradigm shifts, usually when a critical mass of like-minded thinkers agree on the emergent development. Not only will you see where psychology has come from, but you will also be able to see where the pendulum of science has swung throughout the centuries to arrive at our current paradigm, which by definition is only favoured today; in five, fifty or one hundred years, the existing paradigm may have been replaced.

1.4 ANIMISM

An early paradigm was animism, whereby every object capable of moving possesses a soul, comprising the ability to think and feel, whether the object is animate or inanimate. Of course, while this is logical for animals it is hardly likely for an inanimate object capable of motion, such as a car tyre. Animism, therefore, has no place in this book. That is until one considers the phenomenon in developmental psychology, where children ascribe feelings and thought processes to inanimate objects such as dolls or teddy bears.

1.5 RATIONALISM OR CARTESIAN DUALISM

René Descartes was a French mathematician (1596–1650) credited with being the founder of modern philosophy. Essentially, Descartes postulated that the body is a physical entity, a machine subject to the physical laws of mechanics, whereas the mind was non-physical and therefore not subject to such laws. Descartes' work was known as rationalism, or the pursuit of truth through reasoning. Cartesian (from Descartes) dualism is such that the mind and body are separate entities and should be treated as such. However, Descartes did advocate interactionism: the mind and body interact with each other. Today we talk in terms of voluntary and involuntary movements of the body. Voluntary movements are subject to conscious processing and are based, to a large extent, on free-will or choice (you can choose whether to walk, run, skip or hop), whereas involuntary movements are devoid of conscious processing (you do not have to think about breathing or digesting lunch, it just happens).

Interestingly, the source of the interaction between brain and body, according to Descartes, was the pineal gland, located in the centre of the brain. Descartes would not have been aware at the time that the pineal gland is an important neuroendocrine structure involved in hormone regulation in childhood. More importantly, this focus on interactionism has been a significant factor in the growth of modern psychology.

1.6 EMPIRICISM

Traditionally, empiricism replaced Descartes' rationalism, with the focus shifting away from a search for truth through reasoning, in favour of the search for truth through experience and observation. The English philosopher John Locke (1632–1704) postulated that new-born children enter this world as a blank slate, or *tabula rasa*, upon which knowledge is imprinted. Interestingly, today we talk about learner-centred learning, an approach that places the learner at the centre of the learning experience and educational focus. The roots of this 'new' idea on education lie firmly in the philosophies of academics such as Locke, David Hume and George Berkeley 400 years ago.

Of course, empiricism would not be advocated wholeheartedly today, since the wealth of evidence collected on a number of developmental stages in childhood (for example, cognitive development, development of sensory and motor systems, emotional development, to name but some) points to genetic influences or genetic predisposition in favour of such behaviours occurring. Here, an interaction between person and environment is now seen as the accepted norm.

Today, if empiricism is viewed as a method, rather than a philosophy, it is of far greater benefit to us as scientists. On this basis, empiricism entails investigation of a research question, or hypothesis, on the basis of existing theory. It is testable and involves the collection and analysis of data, followed by an interpretation of results, culminating in supporting or refuting the hypothesis. We hope you can see that you probably use empiricism as a technique many times in a classroom situation. For example, if you believe that a child is badly behaved in a lesson when he or she is with a particular group of children, you might move them to another, observe and note any differences and use this data to support or refute this hypothesis. Equally, if another member of staff comments that a child is 'always aggressive', you might seek to explore a range of circumstances where you observe the child to look for emerging patterns. For example, perhaps aggressive behaviour only takes place during the first lesson of the day and only on a particular day, or just after lunch after other children have been taunting him or her in the playground during the lunch break. Testing hypotheses about the behaviour is empiricism.

1.7 STRUCTURALISM VERSUS FUNCTIONALISM

Structuralism was the beginning of modern psychology as we now know it. Wilhelm Wundt (1832–1920) is credited with being the father of modern, scientific psychology. His approach, known as structuralism, explored the 'science of immediate experience' of the mind through introspectionism (looking inwards). Data was obtained by observing stimuli and recording around 10,000 introspective experiences (it is interesting that sportspeople talk about the 'magical 10,000 hours' of practice required to become elite). Wundt's systematic study of structure of the mind was the first attempt at experimental psychology and was successful in separating psychology from philosophy.

Whereas structuralism focused on the conscious experience of ideas and sensations, functionalism emerged as a new trend, focusing instead on the processes of perception and learning as conscious activities. William James (1842–1910) was the leading advocate of functionalism. Functionalism was based to some extent on the work of Charles Darwin, who was advocating the function, or biological significance, of occurrences in nature (survival of the fittest). In the same *modus operandi* of Darwinism, functionalism relies on adaptation, examining the functioning organism within its existing or changing environment. Indeed, elements of functionalism are still in existence in modern psychology. One only needs to look at journals reporting functional advances in language, memory or sensory processing to notice that science is seeking to explain function. It has long since been interested in reporting and understanding physical structures. Houdé et al. (2010) provide an excellent meta-analysis of functional magnetic resonance imaging (fMRI) studies in numerical processing, reading and executive functions in the developing brain, comprising more than 800 children between 1999 and 2008. Bandettini (2009) examines the mindset of fMRI research around this time, while Muckli (2010) examines fMRI evidence in relation to the processing of visual information.

It may help to draw upon an analogy here. In medicine, we have computerised tomography (CT) scans and fMRI scans. CT scans are able to display structural anomalies whereas fMRI scans do not detect structural anomalies, but are able to display functional processes, such as when a patient is asked to perform a linguistic task. This analogy highlights the difference between structuralism and functionalism. It is not always sufficient for us to know about the structure of something, since that does not necessarily provide the whole picture of what is happening. If you have a child who is poor at paying attention to your instructions, you would benefit from investigating the functional nature of information processing, rather than looking at a picture of the child's ear (unless of course, this was an X-ray or CT scan showing signs of physical anomaly).

REFLECTION

Functionalism is about adaptation to an environment. As children pass through the education system, they are faced with having to adapt to new environments. This can be observed, for example, as the oldest class in a primary school becomes the youngest class in a secondary school. Different children will adapt at different rates so it is up to us as educators to facilitate the smooth transition at each important stage of the educational system.

Consider transitions that have affected you.

- Can you remember your first day of school? Your first day of secondary school? Your first day at college or university?
- How do you adapt to change on a daily basis?

1.8 PSYCHODYNAMIC PERSPECTIVE

The psychodynamic perspective is synonymous with the combined works of Sigmund Freud (1856–1939), the father of psychoanalysis. Indeed, Freud is single-handedly responsible for the commonplace belief today that 'psychologists can read minds' and that all we ever do is 'psychoanalyse people'. Of course, this is not the case. Neither of the authors can read minds and neither of us possesses a couch (as in, 'lie on my couch and I'll tell you what you're thinking'). Returning to the psychodynamic perspective, which in fact is based on more than Freud alone, this perspective seeks to explore the central elements of motivations and drive for human behaviour, which are formed during the critical early childhood years between the ages of three and five.

Freud proposed the existence of three structural concepts of the mind. In explaining each one it is beneficial for you to think of an iceberg. What you see of the iceberg above the surface of the water is only part of the overall structure of the iceberg. Two of Freud's concepts are equivalent to being above the surface, or conscious, and the other is equivalent to being below the surface, or unconscious. These concepts are the ego, superego and id, depicted in Figure 1.3.

We should begin under the surface by explaining the id. The id was seen by Freud as the 'pleasure component' of the mind, that part of personality requiring immediate hedonic gratification, regardless of the appropriateness of the act being sought, rather like the mind's 'naughty child'. The id was also seen as an unconscious part of the mind, surfacing or showing itself under situations of disturbance.

Competing with the id, the ego was seen by Freud as the 'self' and is derived from the Latin for 'I'. It is the part of the mind that serves to control behaviour, through perception, cognition and memory. This aspect of the mind tries to obey the 'reality principle', which aims to placate unconscious demands and desires by remaining realistic about whether such demands and desires can be satisfied immediately, or whether delayed gratification is necessary.

The superego, for Freud, comprises two elements: the ego-ideal and the conscience. The ego-ideal is the part of the superego that we would like to achieve, and the conscience is, as the modern interpretation suggests, the voice in our head that

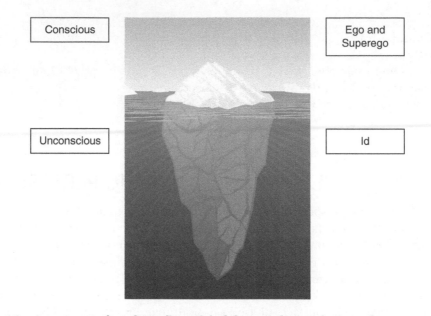

Figure 1.3   A representation of Freud's model of the conscious and unconscious

Source: iStock.com/Big_Ryan

differentiates right from wrong and influences whether we feel guilty or not. The superego provides us with a moral code of accepted standards of behaviour.

The constant competition between the id, ego and superego may ultimately lead to conflict in the mind. Indeed, it would be difficult to see how conflict-avoidance is possible according to Freud's conceptualisation of the mind. Conflicts influence the activity of one or both of Freud's hypothesised 'primary drives': the sexual drive and the aggressive drive. In short, these instinctual drives are constantly in a state of fluctuation, being kept under control by the prohibitive nature of the superego (the conscience), with a compromise being reached between the id and the superego. For Freud, dreams were the place in the human mind that desires of the id could be played out in the safety and security of the mind, while the person was sleeping. In this way, sexual and aggressive acts could remain undetected and therefore go unpunished by society. Conflicts emerged when these undesirable or inappropriate acts sought to display themselves outside of sleep.

Children had the difficult task of repressing desires of the id and learning the rules of appropriate behaviour, which influenced the development of their personalities in later life. Errors were inevitable and can be seen in such examples today as the child in the middle of a supermarket aisle having what we all tend to call a 'tantrum'. For Freud, this behaviour would be a display of the conflict between the id requiring immediate gratification ('I want those sweets *now*') and the under-developed super-ego, or an under-developed version of 'I should not lose control here'. We are sure you will have examples of your own from the classroom.

REFLECTION

A child's personality forms during early childhood and this shapes their adulthood. Behaviour is influenced by three concepts:

- perception of reality
- consciences
- immediate gratification of desires.

Can you explain how the ego, id and superego relate to the way in which behaviour is influenced?

1.9 BEHAVIOURIST PERSPECTIVE

Whereas structuralism fell from favour, functionalism underwent metamorphosis and was subsumed by behaviourism. Essentially, behaviourism ignored the elements of introspectionism, which, by its very nature, was subjective and could not be measured. Behaviourism, which began with John Watson (1878–1958) during the 1910s and was later developed by B.F. Skinner (1904–90), focused instead on that which is observable and thus measurable. Unlike Watson (1930), who paid attention to observable acts of behaviour, Skinner (1938, 1953) focused his attention on the effects of those acts, something we recognise today in part when we talk of the ABCs in the classroom: antecedents, behaviour, consequences (see Chapter 14 for a further discussion in relation to behaviour). Although behaviourism as a paradigm fell out of favour in psychology after the late 1950s and in the strict 'reward and punish' era in education up to the 1980s, around the time of the abolition of corporal punishment in schools, certain elements of this paradigm remain today. The notion of 'behaviour-shaping' is based on principles of behaviourism: situations in which a desired behaviour is required necessitate reinforcement of closer and closer approximations towards that behaviour. Integral to behaviourism are the concepts of classical and operant conditioning. Classical conditioning is based on stimulus–response principles and was first demonstrated, using dogs, by Ivan Pavlov (1849–1936). As Figure 1.4 demonstrates, if a stimulus is presented, a response will occur. So, in the case of Pavlov's dogs, the stimulus is a bowl of food and the response will be salivation. If the bowl of food is presented at the same time that a bell is rung, over a period of time, the dog will begin to associate the sound of the bell with the food, and salivation will take place. Consequently, the sound of the bell becomes the new stimulus and will elicit salivation every time it is rung, even if food is not presented. The desired response (salivation) is produced at the sound of the stimulus (the bell). You can try this with the family pet, although you have probably already done so not using a bell, but using the sound of the tin as it opens. Our pets are convinced that the sound of opening a tin of chickpeas or soup means tuna. You will then start to wonder who is conditioning whom. Are you conditioning your pet by the sound of the tin, or are they conditioning you by meowing or barking for food, to which you then respond?

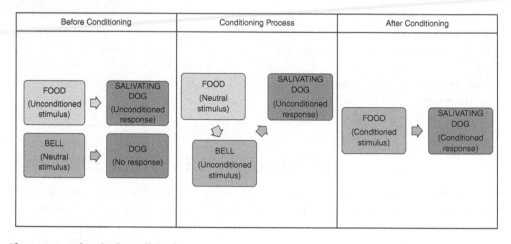

Figure 1.4   Classical conditioning

In essence, behaviour can be elicited in one of three ways: through positive reinforcement, as in the example of a teacher rewarding a learner for good behaviour by moving him or her 'up the zone board'; through punishment, as in the example of a teacher giving a detention to a learner for a misdemeanour; or through negative reinforcement, as in the example of a learner handing in a piece of homework on time in order to avoid a punishment. In these examples, instrumental learning, or operant learning, takes place. Operant conditioning, therefore, differs from classical conditioning in two ways. Whereas an unconditioned stimulus is always presented regardless of whether the behaviour occurs or not during the conditioning stage in classical conditioning, it is not necessary in operant conditioning. Secondly, reinforcement is made on the basis of a desired response emanating from choice: the person produces the desired behaviour out of volition and the behaviour is subsequently reinforced. In the classroom, this perspective is widely adopted today, especially with younger children. For example, if a teacher wishes to foster the behaviour of younger children not shouting out the answer, which may otherwise potentially create acoustic chaos, he or she may reinforce the desired behaviour of responding only to children with their hands up. A child with their hand up will receive attention and be allowed to give their answer. Every time this happens, the behaviour, 'Don't shout, put your hand up and you will receive attention', becomes reinforced and the child learns that this is the most effective way of receiving attention from the teacher. For the child who shouts out, the teacher ought to ignore the behaviour wherever possible, sending out the message, 'Shouting out does not elicit the teacher's attention.' There is one caveat to bear in mind. Conditioning only works as long as the reward continues to be available. The response will become extinguished relatively quickly in the absence of the reward, because the association between stimulus and response is broken. However, it is possible to re-establish the association by reintroducing the stimulus.

Once the desired behaviour has been learned, the teacher should focus on varying the reinforcement schedule. By this, we mean that the reward, such as attention in the example above, should not be available every time the desired behaviour is elicited. Rather, it might be elicited on every third occasion until the children realise that a pattern is emerging, in which case, it might be elicited every third, fifth, eighth and fourteenth occasion. Of course, we are not asking you to employ a specific mathematical formula here. That would be far too unwieldy and time-consuming in keeping track. Instead, we are merely suggesting that you keep them guessing so that the children know that reinforcement will be coming, but they don't know exactly when.

In this way, all behaviour is goal-directed. The goal is to receive positive reinforcement, something that we probably all like to receive, or to avoid punishment. Although psychology has moved far beyond the principles of behaviourism, these seemingly inescapable facets of behaviourism remain. Psychologists today acknowledge that behaviourism in its strict form is untenable as a perspective explaining human behaviour, but that certain elements, such as learning through operant conditioning, are powerful tools in promoting desirable behaviour, especially in the classroom. In this way, the volitional aspects of operant conditioning sit comfortably with the newly prevailing notion of learner-centred learning and learner-centredness, albeit one perhaps where 'higher authorities' (teachers) are manipulating the volitional aspect of choice.

REFLECTION

- Consider a desired behaviour you would like to be evident in your classroom.
- Identify a series of smaller steps that would be required to evidence this desired behaviour.
- Consider how each appropriate step could be rewarded as there is progress towards the behaviour.

1.10 HUMANISTIC PERSPECTIVE

Humanistic psychology developed in the 1950s and 1960s as a backlash against the inadequacies of the psychodynamic approach, with its 'unhealthy' emphasis on disturbances and neuroses. Similarly, humanistic psychologists, such as Abraham

Maslow (1908–70), Carl Rogers (1902–87) and Eric Fromm (1900–80), were disillusioned with the overly mechanistic theorising of the behaviourist approach. Instead, the humanistic approach considered so-called higher human motives and the journey of self-development towards a state of existence known as self-actualisation. Humanism therefore favours positive growth, through experience and choice. According to Maslow, we are all capable of achieving positive growth and it is our experiences and choices made during our lives that direct us towards this growth. Maslow is synonymous with the 'hierarchy of needs', usually depicted as a pyramid, where solid foundations at the bottom of the pyramid allow for development and progress above it (see Figure 1.5). The hierarchy varies between five and eight layers as people have developed this over time: what is important to note is that it is a conceptual model, not an exact model.

Being Needs (for growth)	*Self-actualisation* (achieving full potential)
	Aesthetic (pleasure and satisfaction in harmony)
	Cognitive (understanding of the world)
	Self-esteem (accomplishment and recognition)
Deficiency Needs (for stability)	*Emotional* (love, friendship, belonging)
	Safety (personal security, health, wellbeing)
	Physiological (air, water, food, warmth)

Figure 1.5   Maslow's hierarchy of needs

Maslow places physiological needs at the base of the pyramid. These needs are of major importance. If an organism cannot satisfy its basic physiological needs for food, water and oxygen, it will not survive, either in the Darwinian or indeed any other sense. So humans strive to secure life by securing these basic needs. Above these needs are those of safety, in seeking shelter and security, where danger is removed, or at least minimised. Motivation to strive further can be met once these first two needs are secured. Maslow then discusses the motivation to strive for emotional needs, or social needs, specifically the need to love and be loved, and to obtain a sense of belonging. This is evident today with the widespread phenomenon and popularity of social networking sites. Humans need to be needed by each other. Next, Maslow proposes self-esteem needs. These are the need to be competent within one's field and to be recognised as being competent; in the modern day this is usually through certificates and qualifications, but does not exclude competence through experiences that do not necessarily produce pieces of paper. After self-esteem needs, the satisfaction of cognitive needs is sought, through exploration of problems or questions. This leads to an increased understanding of the world in which we find ourselves and helps us to find solutions to the challenges we face throughout our lives. As we journey closer towards self-actualisation, Maslow proposed that we strive to acquire aesthetic needs, such as beauty and harmony. The beauty found in a flower or in a natural landscape provides us with a sense of pleasure and satisfaction. Equally, the harmony we may experience when we seek out and listen to a piece of music or when viewing a piece of art are examples of the human desire to meet aesthetic needs. Once each of these needs has been fulfilled, Maslow proposes that we enter, or indeed have already entered, the state of self-actualisation, whereby we have achieved our full potential as a human being. This drive to achieve self-actualisation is, according to Maslow, innate and all humans possess it. The extent to which each of us strives to achieve it is, as we are sure you will see from the daily news, rather questionable to say the least. It is important to note that Maslow evolved the hierarchy throughout his writing and many permutations exist. Ultimately the hierarchy can be summarised as containing deficiency needs (aspects that if lacking cannot enable a human to function effectively), and being needs (for the individual to thrive and achieve their full potential).

Carl Rogers differed from Maslow in that he did not advocate a hierarchical approach to human growth. Rather, Rogers advocated the importance of the self-concept in each of us. According to Rogers, this is the opinion we and others have of ourselves. It is a need to be held in high esteem by others and to feel a sense of positive regard for who each of us is as an individual. Our personality develops as a product of each of us striving to satisfy the need for approval by others and it is this approval that provides our own happiness or unhappiness. This approach would seem to place each of us in a rather shallow position, doing things on the basis of what others think. Rogers' position should not be interpreted in this way. Instead, Rogers discussed the concept of unconditional positive regard. This can be explained using the example of children within (we would like to think most) families. Parents talk in terms of unconditional love – doing anything for their children, regardless of the 'wrongs' or misdemeanours the children may have done. Parents don't 'give love to receive love': their love is unconditional. Rogers proposed that, if a context of unconditional positive regard is fostered, then each of us as individuals is presented with the opportunity to grow, develop and strive to achieve our potential regardless of what others think of us. The opinions others have of us become a by-product of what we are striving to achieve, rather than our reason for striving to achieve it.

Whether the concepts and processes or drives postulated by the humanistic approach can be investigated scientifically is questionable and so humanistic psychology in the past has not had a large impact on the science of psychology. Nevertheless, in recent years, with incidents of stress, anxiety and depression on the increase, people are beginning to see something appealing in the tenets of the humanistic approach. There does indeed seem to be a desire to search for the things in life that make one a better person, not in a materialistic or financial sense, but in a 'quality of life' sense.

This is noticeable within psychology, with the emergence of transpersonal psychology since the 1960s and positive psychology since 1998.

The humanistic perspective is appealing in the school setting, on the basis that it is everything that teachers would wish for the children in their charge to aspire towards. The notion of reaching one's full potential has been seen on school reports for many years and no doubt will continue long into the future. 'Could do better' was a phrase from the past, although interestingly is still in use today (Beadle, 2008). 'Is not reaching his or her potential' is another. In the same way that teachers are striving for their children to achieve, teachers are also striving to better themselves. We talk in modern phraseology of CPD, or continuing professional development. There does not appear to be a time when we are not seeking to improve on our personal development, raise our standards and seek out challenges requiring us to self-reflect and implement solutions. The peak of Maslow's hierarchy may always seem out of reach if we are constantly seeking to go higher, but this is not a bad thing. Imagine sitting at the top of Maslow's pyramid, wondering where to go next. In the absence of goals and aspirations, there is little else to foster the sense of challenge and exploration that, as humans, keeps us going. Of course, in the modern day, it may seem like we are being overwhelmed by the sheer amount of development that we are expected to make, by those in positions of authority above us. This is where we need to seek a balance between expectations, of ourselves and of others, and the practical implications of doing too much. Indeed, a phrase used regularly nowadays is the 'work–life balance'.

REFLECTION

Once basic physiological and safety needs have been secured, it becomes possible to explore and understand our immediate (and wider) world to solve problems and achieve successes. Considering the way that education is prevalent in all societies and cultures as long as food, water and shelter are provided, why do you think that education is such a fundamental aspect of human culture?

1.11 COGNITIVE PERSPECTIVE

Whereas the brain was not important in the observation-laden approach of behaviourism, the cognitive perspective placed the brain, or rather its functions, firmly at the centre of human behaviour. Although the two approaches appear to be at extreme ends of the spectrum, the emergence of cognitive psychology attempted to fill a gap in behaviourist theory. The cognitive perspective emphasises the importance of explaining behaviour in terms of internal events, the meaning of concepts and processes, beliefs, attitudes and intentions. It is not a return to the introspectionism of Wundt (1896), or to the meanings inherent in the psychodynamic approach. Rather, cognitive psychology attempts to explain 'cognitions' – thoughts, language, memory, decision-making, attention and information processing – that inform our everyday lives. These are the very processes that behaviourism neglected to investigate because they were not observable. In emphasising information processing, cognitive psychology developed the computer analogy. The human mind was seen as being similar to a computer, acquiring information at the stimulus-input point (the sensory organs), processing information (the sensory systems and structures within the brain) and producing a subsequent 'output' or behaviour (usually generated by the motor system). A monitoring and safety process was seen to be inbuilt (the feedback loop), which provides the organism with a constant stream of information, and this becomes part of the new 'input'. Back in the 1990s, the computer analogy was replaced by the concept of neural networks. A neural network was considered to be akin to a set of 'nodes', each one responsible for a specific thing or containing a particular piece of information. Each of these nodes is connected to other nodes within a similar 'network' and each network is connected to other networks. Furthermore, each node is either excitatory or inhibitory and, when a node is activated, this will lead to the activation of like minded nodes in the system. If these are excitatory, activation will lead to a process taking place, such as the processes involved in the linguistic function of asking a question (including movement of the lips, vibration of the larynx and regulation of lung function). In contrast, if the nodes are inhibitory, activation will lead to a process ceasing, for example, the processes involved in stopping speech production at the point when you need to listen to the answer to the question that has just been asked (Bechtel and Abrahamsen, 1990).

Although the replacement of 'computer' with 'neural network' was considered a development in cognitive psychology and it has indeed enabled psychologists to look at human behaviour in a different way, it really does seem to be nothing more than a change in semantics. What we have described above as a network is not really very different from the way one might describe the internet today. It is a network of computers, linked in like-minded ways. We place controls on what should or should not be viewed by subscribing to websites, forums (or as we prefer, fora) and groups as members, hence these become inhibitory if one is not a subscriber. At the heart of this 'connectionism' is the computer, so we return to our starting point of the computer analogy. Nevertheless, the human mind as a network has been fruitful in advancing psychology.

Today, certainly in applied and in therapeutic settings, psychology may be considered as a blend of both cognitivism and behaviourism. Many applied practitioners adopt what is known as a cognitive behavioural approach to problems or, as we would prefer to say, challenges. We explore thought processes with our clients as well as observing them in their own environments. For example, the elite sportsperson may be observed before an important competition, or the trainee teacher may be observed in the lead-up to an important lesson-observation. As practitioners, we may be looking for signs of anxiety (or anxiety-regulation), confidence or self-belief. Any observations may be followed up with a discussion to see what the person's perceptions of the event were, or we may precede an observation with this discussion, in order to guide us about what we should be looking for in advance of an observation.

REFLECTION

If the human mind is viewed as a network of like and unlike nodes, then our job in the classroom is to find ways of activating' the network in such ways that learning takes place. As a teacher, you will be helping children to acquire packets of information or knowledge, assemble them into sub-networks and begin to forge links between concepts within the ever-increasing network. Your role now is to consider *how* you might facilitate this within the classroom.

1.12 PSYCHOBIOLOGICAL PERSPECTIVE

Huge advances in the field of neurobiology in the latter part of the twentieth century have had a significant effect on our understanding of the human brain. Much is now known about the intricate structures within the brain, about the systems and interrelationships between these structures from a functional point of view and about electrochemical communication between neurons within the human brain. None of this would have been possible without advances in other areas of science that have helped to provide us with the necessary equipment to assist in our voyage of discovery.

These advances have spawned a wide variety of specialist subdivisions, such as cognitive neuroscience, neuroendocrinology and psychobiology. Psychobiology is an umbrella term that explores psychological processes from a biological or physiological point of view (Carlson, 2012). Consequently psychobiology, biological psychology, physiological psychology and psychophysiology are used interchangeably. Although there are nuances that do distinguish them from each other, a discussion of them here would be neither necessary nor indeed fruitful.

Essentially, the psychobiological perspective takes reductionism as its starting point. This means that the human being is viewed as a set of interacting systems, rather than holistically. The focus may be on the central nervous system, the limbic system or the endocrine system. This may be reduced further, to a focus on the visual system or, even further, to a set of neurons that may contribute to what we call learning or memory. This perspective, therefore, explores psychological processes by considering systems within the human body and causal or correlational factors within those systems (Pinel, 2010). For example, an understanding of the limbic system (a set of structures within the human brain) helps us to understand the associated behaviour of aggression, or complements a behavioural observation of mood and emotion. You might ask why such knowledge would be useful, until you are faced with a behaviour-management issue in your classroom that you are struggling to find an explanation for. Your knowledge of how the brain functions, even if it is limited, may help you to understand the behaviour that you see in front of you.

Similarly, an understanding of how the human brain develops during childhood will help you to appreciate why, for example, children struggle with acquiring fundamental movement skills, such as catching a ball in PE. Your knowledge of how the brain executes movement or how depth perception is not sufficiently developed in children until approximately 12 years of age (Gallahue and Ozmun, 2011) helps to inform your observations of displayed behaviour.

REFLECTION

Having at least some knowledge of psychobiology will help you to appreciate the processes taking place in children's brains. In order to decide what to learn about, you should start from your current knowledge of the learning disabilities you have seen within schools: dyslexia, dysgraphia, dyspraxia, attention deficit/ hyperactivity disorder (ADHD) and so on. Ask yourself one question, 'What is happening in the brain?', for any of these disabilities and then explore the literature to build your knowledge base.

1.13 EVOLUTIONARY PERSPECTIVE

Evolutionary theory looks at how species have evolved to fill a niche in their environment. An evolutionary perspective considers how humans adapt to their environments and it is this word, 'adapt', that holds a vital key to why an understanding of evolutionary psychology is important for the remainder of this book. Evolutionary psychology is based on elements derived from the seminal *Origin of Species* by Charles Darwin (1859) and behavioural genetics (Plomin et al., 2008). It is this combination that enables humans as a species to occupy the privileged niche that we do.

In essence, Darwin (1809–82) espoused the view that, genetically, only the fittest survive: 'Survival of the fittest'. Genes are carried on through the generations of those animals who are the most successful at adapting to their environment. Don't think for one minute that we are suggesting that only the fittest, most successful teachers survive to pass their genes on to their offspring and create a new breed of 'super-teacher'.

Rather, hold this as a controversial thought for discussion later in the chapter, while we return to the evolutionary perspective.

Evolutionary psychology focuses on three important elements: inclusive fitness, kin selection and differential parental investment. Inclusive fitness is the strategy of promoting one's own genes, in such a way that they continue in the gene pool. We are now talking in terms of genetic survival, as opposed to person survival. If Darwin's natural selection favours survival of the fittest, then it is important to ensure that our own genes are part of the process, a 'got to be in it to win it' concept. Inclusive fitness is aimed, therefore, at ensuring that the direct replication of genes occurs first and foremost. Linked to this is the notion of kin selection, whereby not only are one's own genes favoured, but also the genes of related, if indirect, wider family members. The third strategy, differential parental investment, is the notion that females take a greater parental investment in rearing offspring (remember we are talking about various species, not only humans) and consequently, become more selective when it comes to seeking a mate. By the nature of child-rearing, the father takes less of a hands-on role and consequently also takes less of a role when it comes to mate-selection, in the sense of natural selection.

The impetus to satisfy the demands of natural selection is not necessarily a conscious one. We do not necessarily go about daily life thinking about procreating with all and sundry in an attempt to have a greater opportunity in the gene pool. Rather, we get on with the process of living. Certainly, the concept of altruism would not exist if we were only to favour our own genetic survival. Altruistic acts, by their very nature, are not necessarily gene-driven, especially if the person towards whom we are acting altruistically does not share any of our genetic material. Yet altruism takes place on many occasions, on a daily basis. This may be viewed, perhaps, in a reciprocal manner. Reciprocal altruism is the notion, coined by the sociobiologist Robert Trivers in 1971, that one should act and behave towards others in the same way that one would wish others to act and behave towards oneself. So, a child shares some of his or her lunch with a friend, who is genetically unrelated, because that friend is hungry. There is no benefit to the benefactor and no advantage gained in depriving themselves of the food, but there is a potential reciprocal benefit. The beneficiary may be more likely to reciprocate this gesture at some point in the future (Kenrick, 2001). Of course, we all view this as a normal action of everyday life; surely we would all share lunch if a friend found themselves without food. But, in this part, we are explaining this act from an evolutionary psychology perspective. If we were to explain it from a humanistic perspective, we might talk instead of the altruistic act being performed in order to satisfy our self-esteem needs (refer to the discussion of Maslow's hierarchy of needs and Figure 1.5). In terms of relevance to this book, the evolutionary approach helps us to appreciate the role of social and cognitive factors in the way in which children adapt to their environment. It goes without saying that it would be ridiculous to talk about the genetic consequences of successful adaptation to the school environment. If, however, one views this in microcosm, as part of the continuous process of adaptation throughout one's lifespan, then any adaptive experience should help to promote a longer life, and more potential opportunity to add to the gene pool, or protect offspring to maturity so that they can then add to the gene pool.

REFLECTION

Rather than thinking of the evolutionary perspective as being synonymous with genetic propagation, think more in terms of the school or classroom environment and ask yourself, 'How can I provide a stimulating environment for the children, and how can I help them to adapt to changes and foster reciprocal altruism within that environment?' Understanding the role of social and cognitive factors will guide you in exploring these questions.

1.14 SUMMARISING INTERACTIONISM FROM AN APPLIED PERSPECTIVE

We have already discussed the interaction between genetic predispositions and environmental opportunities, or influences. In applied terms, children interact with and are products of their environment; this is why certain undesirable behaviours that occur at home are brought into school. If these undesirable behaviours are not tolerated and are punished, this leads to confusion because there is disparity in the message between home and school. As you will be aware, teachers spend a large proportion of their time in school explaining why such behaviours are inappropriate, whether inside or outside of school, in the hope that the child will take the message and apply it to their home circumstances as well as within school. This is not always successful, but always necessary for teachers as educators in wider sociobehavioural issues.

Returning to the interaction discussion, not only does the child interact with the school environment and other children, but also the group dynamic includes an interaction with the teacher, or a range of teachers. If we add the physical environment, within which interaction occurs throughout the school day, week, term and indeed academic year, we are experiencing what Descartes spoke about when he postulated the interaction between the physical and the mental. 'The physical', in Cartesian terms, is akin to motivational climates in modern terms. If children are to interact with their environment in an enriching way, then it goes without saying that the classroom and wider school environment must be equally enriching and vibrant. That is why we put displays up and refine seating arrangements to suit the needs of all those who interact within that environment. We will return to the issue of motivational climate in Chapter 10.

1.15 CONCLUSION

In this chapter we have introduced the notion of perspective and discussed how it is possible to adopt different perspectives. Psychologists tend to favour a perspective or, especially in the case of some applied practitioners, will adopt a combination of perspectives to suit the needs of their clients. We favour this approach, since it complements the idea of constantly striving to adapt to an ever-changing environment, both in the Darwinian sense, as well as in a practical day-to-day sense. You should reflect on the contents of this chapter, to explore your own needs and the needs of those who you will be interacting with (don't forget to include other adults as well as children). You will begin to discover (or adapt to) a perspective, or elements from different perspectives, that sit comfortably with you.

In the next chapter, we examine more recent (post-behaviourism) psychological approaches in more detail, providing an evaluation of their potential contribution to education, aimed at developing a more holistic approach to education than the classical approaches have previously offered.

1.16 FURTHER READING

Beaver, B.R. (2008) 'A positive approach to children's internalizing problems', *Professional Psychology: Research and Practice*, 39 (2): 129–36.
Beaver's research paper provides a clear discussion of a positive, strength-based approach to respond to the increased prevalence of childhood anxiety and depression.

Eysenck, M.W. (2009) *Fundamentals of Psychology*. Hove: Psychology Press.
This book is recommended as a theoretical overview of psychology, which provides a very well-rounded resource on the subject.

Maslow, A.H. (1962/1999) *Toward a Psychology of Being* (3rd edn). Chichester: John Wiley & Sons.
This book sets out the fundamental basis of Maslow's theories, providing an insight into the depth and scope of his work.

2
DEVELOPING APPROACHES TO PSYCHOLOGY

CHAPTER OBJECTIVES

- Build an understanding of developing psychological perspectives that are influencing education, specifically positive psychology and transpersonal psychology.
- Consider the relationship between humanistic psychology and the branches of positive psychology and transpersonal psychology.
- Appreciate the contribution of 'flow' and the conditions to promote flow.
- Evaluate how developing perspectives of psychology relate to education.

TEACHERS' STANDARDS

A teacher must:

4   Plan and teach well-structured lessons

- reflect systematically on the effectiveness of lessons and approaches to teaching

5   Adapt teaching to respond to the strengths and needs of all pupils

- have a secure understanding of how a range of factors can inhibit pupils' ability to learn, and how best to overcome these
- demonstrate an awareness of the physical, social and intellectual development of children, and know how to adapt teaching to support pupils' education at different stages of development

2.1 INTRODUCTION

Consider the message from Chapter 1: there are a number of perspectives, or ways of looking at things. Additionally, although no one perspective provides the full picture, we tend to adopt a perspective that resonates deeply inside of us. Sometimes what resonates inside one person may not resonate with another and a tension is formed. For example, consider popular approaches to discipline for younger children (often advocated on the television): 'the naughty step' or 'time-out cushion' may well bring about a desired result through a behaviourist approach. However, such an approach may diminish a child's sense of self (see Chapter 8), if they perceive that their core being is being ignored, that they have to conform and suppress what makes them unique, that they will be a clone with a diminished sense of self (functionalism). If just one such incident becomes suppressed in the subconscious this in turn can be a foundation for a neurosis (psychodynamic theory). If a child has been punished for talking out of turn about an exciting discovery they have made within their learning, being told to 'keep quiet', this could for example cause the child to progress into an adult who never really expresses what they feel, or is afraid to speak in front of others.

These previous fields of psychology have developed since 1887: Myers (2000) analysed over 100,000 abstracts published in *Psychological Abstracts*, suggesting that 90 per cent of these focused on psychopathology, the treatment of mental illness, for example, depression and anxiety, while the remaining articles focused on the positive aspects of psychology, such as altruism and life satisfaction. An assumption has been made that, if individuals are treated for existing problems through clinical practice, this will in turn lead to optimal levels of wellness (as discussed by Greenspoon and Saklofske, 2001). However, Frisch (1999) questions this, reporting that many adults continue to experience dissatisfaction long after they have been treated. Consequently, Huebner and Gilman (2003) suggest an inclusive approach, where psychopathology is supported through research, which helps to understand the factors that contribute to, and enhance, positive psychological wellbeing.

The enhancement of positive psychological wellbeing has a tradition of research within psychology. Indeed, a group of psychologists, notably Abraham Maslow and Carl Rogers, highlighted the negative effect that teaching can have on the individual, advocating humanistic psychology as a way of enabling the positive attributes within the individual. It is these positive attributes, and how to facilitate a positive approach to enabling these within the individual, which provide the focus for this chapter. Specifically, this will be achieved through analysing two further psychological perspectives: positive psychology and transpersonal psychology.

2.2 POSITIVE PSYCHOLOGY

WHAT IS IT?

Maslow (1954/1987) first used the term 'positive psychology' (which he also called 'orthopsychology') as an approach focusing on fully functioning and healthy human beings. However, the term has become associated specifically with the work of Martin Seligman, since the turn of the millennium, as research in the area has burgeoned (Gillham et al., 2002; Hart and Sasso, 2011; Wong, 2011). Indeed, according to Yen (2010), positive psychology is the most popular course at Harvard University. Despite this recent reinterpretation and development of positive psychology, Beaver (2008) suggests that the interpretation is informed by many decades of previous research, and in essence the concept is not necessarily new. Indeed, the focus of this interpretation of positive psychology still resonates with the work of Maslow and Rogers, in that it focuses on the positive features of human beings, and the experiences that make life worth living. Hart and Sasso (2011), however, warn that positive psychology has become as much a popular culture movement as it has a fledgling academic subject, which in turn has caused individuals to consider the field as 'happiology' or the science of happiness. Consequently, a more refined, academic definition is provided below to define the field further.

Many attempts have been made to define positive psychology, which suggests that the term remains a lucid concept with a variety of definitions (Linley et al., 2006). For example, Sheldon and King (2001: 216) suggest it is 'the scientific study of ordinary human strengths and virtues', a definition similar to Engler's (2013) assertion that it focuses on the positive features of human beings that make life worth living. Such positive features are classified by Robbins (2008) as positive subjective experience (including flow, joy and optimism), personality traits of thriving individuals (character strengths and virtues) and enhancing social institutions to sustain and develop positive subjective experience (Cowen, 2000; Rich, 2001; Robbins, 2008). Seligman and Csikszentmihalyi (2000) refer to these areas as the three pillars of positive psychology, each of which should serve as a foundation from which research in the field should develop. These are summarised in Figure 2.1.

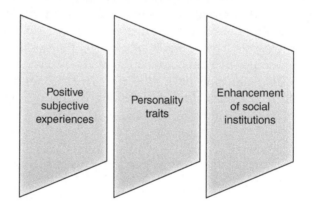

Figure 2.1   The three pillars of positive psychology

Further attempts at defining positive psychology have focused on the range of constructs central to the field. Such an attempt is provided by Huebner and Gilman (2003) who suggest the following areas: self-concept, hope, socially responsible behaviour and emotions, flow, emotional competence, life satisfaction and positive school attitudes. Hart and Sasso (2011) conducted further analysis of definitions to examine how positive psychology had been interpreted and redefined over the preceding decade. From their research, they conclude that the majority of research has focused on the first two pillars, (1) positive subjective experience and (2) personality traits, with limited research into the third pillar of enhancing social institutions. Indeed, the third pillar appears to be the most problematic given the lack of research to support it (Gable and Haidt, 2005; Martin, 2006).

From this brief introduction to positive psychology, the area can be summarised as aiming to enhance individuals and institutions, specifically focusing on enhancing our natural resources as opposed to addressing deficits. Needless to say, as teachers, focusing on the positive is central to our practice.

REFLECTION

Consider positive psychology applied to the classroom.

- What are the positive experiences children have demonstrated in one of your lessons?
- What are the positive attributes you would see in a child who is enjoying your lesson?
- What are the positive attributes demonstrated by a teacher who enjoys teaching?
- What character attributes would you expect to see in a positive learner?
- What makes a happy classroom?
- What makes a happy school?

REFLECTION

What would you deem to be the positive qualities fundamental to the growth of children?

2.3 SCHOOL-BASED RESEARCH WITHIN POSITIVE PSYCHOLOGY

One of the core features of positive psychology is the focus on empirical research: specifically Seligman and Csikszentmihalyi (2000) asserted that research is required to ensure the field is a scientific contribution to psychology as a subject, while also distancing positive psychology from humanistic psychology, which they claimed lacked a research tradition.

Many research studies have been reported adhering to the different pillars of positive psychology and associated themes and concepts outlined above. As an indicative example of such research findings, Lyubomirsky et al. (2005) reported that optimistic or happy people perform better, are less depressed, have fewer health problems and have better relationships. Danner et al. (2001) noted that people who report more positive emotions tend to have longer, healthier lives. Additional research into the subjective experiences of flow, optimism and happiness have similarly reported positive results (Carr, 2011; Linley and Joseph, 2004; Lopez et al., 2014).

In reference to children many researchers have advocated positive psychology as a significant approach for future development. Specifically, Gillham et al. (2002) observe that interventions to promote inner strengths within children have long been sought by parents, teachers and community leaders, to ensure children are more resilient to a variety of problems associated with modern life such as depression, substance abuse, risky sexual behaviour or violence. Despite their assertions about promoting such strengths, Gillham et al. (2002) comment that the majority of research focuses on remediation of existing problems as opposed to the development of positive qualities in children. Furthermore they comment that such research produces varied findings, with the effects of various studies seldom being replicated.

There are four strands that unite the research on the positive development of school-aged children, identified through existing literature (Baker et al., 2003; Noddings, 2003; Park and Peterson, 2003).

These are:

1. Resilience (the process of adapting positively to adversity)
2. Developmental assets (developing positive relationships, competencies, self-perceptions and values to succeed)
3. Social-emotional learning (promoting social and emotional wellbeing)
4. Subjective wellbeing (the individual's experience of the positive qualities of their life).

Although various authors have suggested that research is limited within the third pillar of positive psychology, enhancing social institutions (Gable and Haidt, 2005; Hart and Sasso, 2011; Martin, 2006), a number of publications have sought to address this criticism through conducting research to strengthen this pillar (Delle Fave and Bassi, 2009; Donaldson and Ko, 2010; Korunka et al., 2009). Specifically within education, for example, Baker et al. (2003) suggest that schools can function as psychologically healthy environments if they address and in turn challenge children's developmental needs.

2.4 FLOW

One significant area of positive psychology is Csikszentmihalyi's concept of flow (Csikszentmihalyi, 1993, 1996, 2000, 2002), which he defines as 'a panhuman, species-specific state of positive psychic functioning' (Csikszentmihalyi, 1988: 364). What does this actually mean? (And how do you pronounce Csikszentmihalyi? Working backwards, thankfully the man himself informs readers of his books that his name is sounded as 'chick-sent-me-high-yi'.) As for his definition of flow, it would be worth asking you to consider a time when you have been lost in the moment while engaged with an activity: this is a state of flow. Indeed, Csikszentmihalyi (2000) characterises flow as a state where one is absorbed, where there is a sense of control but loss of self-consciousness, where action and awareness merge and a transformation of time occurs.

By being able to recognise flow within your own life, in turn, this should enable you to help others experience flow. Although flow appears to happen spontaneously, Csikszentmihalyi (2000) offers a model that provides the 'antecedents' or conditions for flow, the behaviour or characteristics of being in the state of flow and the consequences or outcomes of flow. These are summarised in Figure 2.2.

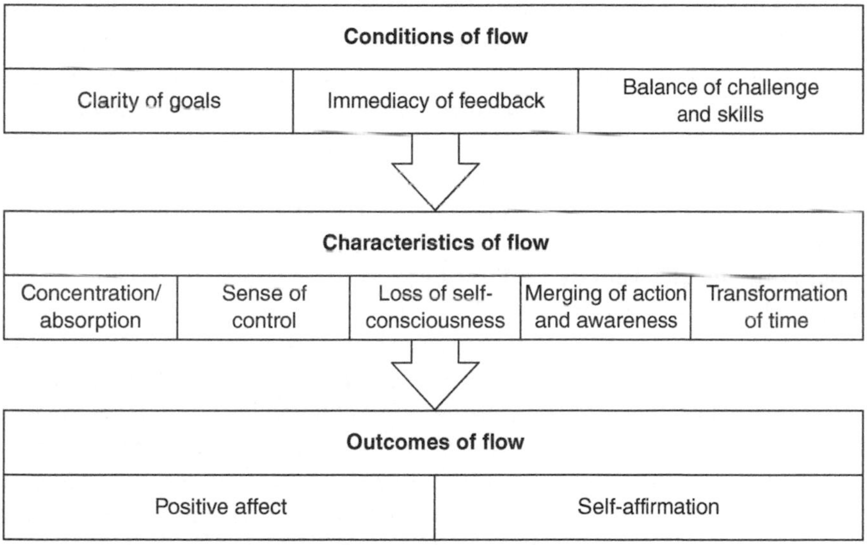

Conditions of flow		
Clarity of goals	Immediacy of feedback	Balance of challenge and skills

Characteristics of flow				
Concentration/ absorption	Sense of control	Loss of self-consciousness	Merging of action and awareness	Transformation of time

Outcomes of flow	
Positive affect	Self-affirmation

Figure 2.2   The conditions, characteristics and outcomes of flow (adapted from Csikszentmihalyi, 2000)

Looking through these characteristics, consider a time when you were totally lost in an engaging activity, where time seemed to slow down (a common feature in a staff meeting!) or speed up (how quickly does Monday morning come after a Friday afternoon?). Such an example could be when driving on an open, undulating stretch of road, being lost in a computer game or some other sport or hobby, perhaps even when a lesson you have been teaching has gone really well and all the elements just came together. Such states of flow can occur in a multitude of contexts as described, and indeed, 90 per cent of people recognise the flow experience, an experience that is intrinsically motivating and enjoyable, and an experience that has an end in itself rather than some other end product (Boniwell, 2006).

What is the purpose of this state? Csikszentmihalyi and Csikszentmihalyi (1988: 367) report that 'the function of flow … seems to be to induce the organism to grow … fulfilling the potentialities of the organism.' Additionally they discuss (1988: 367) that the outcome of flow is pleasure; that 'pleasure ensures that the organism will be motivated to repeat the behaviour necessary to maintain its homeostatic balance.' Consequently, if you can recall one lesson that went perfectly, you are likely to want to bring about that feeling again and again, developing and refining your teaching to bring about such optimum conditions. This concept of continually wanting to make improvements relates to reflection, as discussed in Chapter 4.

2.5 DEVELOPING FLOW IN THE CLASSROOM

There will be times when you can recognise the flow state within the children you work with, when they are so engrossed in an activity that they do not appear to be engaged in the lesson or their wider surroundings. Many a female teacher has experienced being called 'Mum' by a child fully engaged with their work: indeed, this is a widely reported phenomenon among colleagues we have worked with. However, do you allow the child to continue in this state, or do you end it abruptly because you need to move on with the lesson?

By ending the lesson abruptly for that child, you are robbing them of a fundamental experience which may be pivotal to their education: an experience that in years to come they may still remember as their most wondrous learning experience. What if they have been 'robbed' of such an experience and realise that their learning is not intrinsically motivated and that they have to be continually answerable to what the curriculum demands at that point of time on a Thursday afternoon? This in turn creates a dilemma for the teacher in what they consider to be the purpose of teaching: is it to facilitate the curriculum to the best of their abilities? Alternatively, is it to engage children with the joy of learning, and through so doing equipping them with an insatiable thirst for further study?

In recognising the state of flow in a child, as a teacher you can thus aim to ensure that you provide the antecedents or conditions to encourage the flow state, not only for one child but for the class. By working through Csikszentmihalyi's model, specifically the three conditions of flow, it is possible to structure lessons that facilitate the flow experience.

1. *Clarity of goals*: What are the objectives for the lesson? Do the children know exactly what they have to do? Do they have the right resources to engage? What are the children expected to do? Do they know (and understand) what they need to do?

2. *Immediacy of feedback*: How does a child know that they are correctly engaged with the lesson? How do they know that they are advancing, or getting things right? Being able to provide immediate feedback is the optimum condition here; this is not easy when you have 30 in the room. As such, consider activities that either have no right or wrong answer, or activities that implicitly enable the child to know that what they are doing is correct.

3. *Skill/challenge balance*: This is perhaps the hardest condition to establish given the multitude of individuals in the class. There are four potential scenarios for ensuring the skills of the child meet the challenge of the lesson, as demonstrated in Table 2.1.

Table 2.1   The skill/challenge balance (adapted from Whalen, 1998)

		Skills	
		Low	High
Challenge	High	'It's too difficult!' or	'This is great!' or
		'I don't think I can do this!'	'I'm really enjoying this!'
		(Anxiety)	(Flow)
	Low	'Why do we have to do this again?' or	'This is too easy!' or
		'Why should I bother?'	'I'm bored with this!'
		(Apathy)	(Boredom)

Although the skill/challenge balance appears to be an important element in facilitating flow, according to Voelkl et al. (2003), the skill/challenge balance has been over-emphasised in research and other factors may account for higher incidents of the flow experience.

In addition to these criteria, Shernoff et al. (2003) discuss three further conditions for flow: concentration, interest and enjoyment. In relation to concentration, flow experiences are developed through setting a learning context that requires deep absorption in an activity. As Shernoff et al. (2003) report, gifted and talented teenagers concentrate more than their peers during learning activities, but less while watching television or when engaged in social activities. They suggest that being able to concentrate for more complex mental tasks upon demand may in turn lead to achievement and talent development.

Additionally, interest in an activity is a characteristic to promote flow, which in turn provides a foundation for continued motivation and the subsequent engagement with learning. In relation to self-determination theory, if a learner is interested in an activity, they will invest more resources to develop their learning, through self-directed study (for example, reading around the subject, working with others, discussing the subject).

Finally, enjoyment is fundamental in promoting flow. If a learner enjoys their work, this promotes feelings of satisfaction and accomplishment, which in turn encourages the learner to engage further with their learning (Shernoff et al., 2003).

Consequently, there are six areas as discussed above to promote flow in the class-room. These are summarised in Table 2.2.

Table 2.2 Conditions to promote flow

Teacher		Student	
1	Clarity of goals	2	Concentration
3	Immediacy of feedback	4	Interest
5	Skill/challenge balance	6	Enjoyment

To what extent are all of these elements the responsibility of the teacher? Can you be responsible for promoting concentration, interest and enjoyment within your learners? Surely interest and enjoyment are subjective aspects: we are all interested in different things, and we all enjoy different things. However, this is a superficial statement. As a teacher, within our practice we should ensure that we aim to provide interesting and stimulating lesson content, perhaps taking the driest of topics and finding a way to make these as engaging as possible. Taking science as an example, specifically the force of gravity, a number of activities can be introduced into a lesson. For example:

- Making paper helicopters and comparing how the wing span affects gravity through the increase of air resistance (equal and opposite forces). This could be extended through adding varying numbers of paperclips to the helicopter and predicting, then recording, what happens.
- Illustrating how the centre of gravity operates through using a 'plumb line' with different two-dimensional shapes, before progressing to make a balancing par-rot, and perhaps extending the lesson to see if the learners can make different balancing animals (for example, a monkey balancing from its tail, a snake and so on).
- Encouraging the learners to sit upright in a chair, with their back touching the back of the chair, their feet on the floor and their arms crossed, then asking them to stand without leaning forward. This reinforces where the centre of gravity is in ourselves, and could be extended with trying to balance in different ways in a gym class.
- Experimenting with a ball of malleable material (Blu Tack or Plasticine) to make an object that floats, thus demonstrating a different opposing force to gravity, that of upthrust.

There are countless other examples you could consider with gravity, and the same can apply to any aspect you are responsible for teaching. Obviously developing such creative lessons demands time for planning and obtaining the resources, yet the reward for the learners, and in turn, the teacher, outweighs such demands. In addition, the sixth element listed in Table 2.2, enjoyment, may be a by-product of such engaging lessons.

How can the teacher promote concentration? This is an aspect addressed fully in Chapter 6, although in brief, if mental fitness is the same as physical fitness, both need to be trained with increasing demands. By concentrating fully on one stimulus (such as breathing), concentration can be improved. This relates to the concept of 'mindfulness', which is discussed below.

2.6 CLASSROOM STUDIES ON FLOW

A number of studies have been conducted in relation to flow in the classroom. According to research, flow has been shown to promote learning and development among secondary school learners (Parr et al., 1998; Whalen, 1998) and primary school learners (Sun et al., 2017). Specifically, the research by Sun et al. (2017) analysed flow states through game playing, identifying the need to ensure flexible difficulty levels based on learners' flow states to maintain the skill/challenge balance. The role of technology has similarly been reported by Theodoulou et al. (2015) who assert that the role of computer games in education to engage learners requires further development to enhance learning through evoking interest and creating a flow state while playing the game.

Other such studies into flow have been conducted by Butzer et al. (2016) who identified a positive relationship between yoga and psychological states of flow and mindfulness through a two-month programme for young musicians. From their research, those engaged with the programme reported significant decreases in confusion while increasing dispositional flow, leading to enhanced musical performance. Indeed, music has similarly been reported to develop dancers' experience of flow, specifically through the merging of action and awareness, autotelic experience, and the loss of self-consciousness as reported by Panebianco-Warrens (2014).

While these studies demonstrate the link between the flow state and creative subjects, further research is required into how flow could be applied more widely across the curriculum. One such example was the research of Egbert (2003) who investigated flow states in a secondary language classroom, and although she highlighted that flow can and does exist, she could not fully explain why flow existed. She was unable to report whether one element is more substantial in promoting flow than other elements. Egbert (2003: 517) adapted a previous questionnaire to assess flow states, which is reproduced here.

PERCEPTIONS QUESTIONNAIRE

Participants responded to each of the following items on a scale from 1 (strongly disagree) to 7 (strongly agree). Questions 3, 4, 10 and 12 were reverse-scored.

1. This task excited my curiosity.
2. This task was interesting in itself.
3. I felt that I had no control over what was happening during this task.
4. When doing this task I was aware of distractions.
5. This task made me curious.
6. This task was fun for me.
7. I would do this task again.
8. This task allowed me to control what I was doing.
9. When doing this task, I was totally absorbed in what I was doing.
10. This task bored me.
11. During this task, I could make decisions about what to study, how to study it, and/or with whom to study.
12. When doing this task I thought about other things.
13. This task aroused my imagination.
14. I would do this task even if it were not required.

According to Meyer and Turner (2006), flow integrates cognition, motivation and emotion. Their research indicates that learners are likely to report more non-flow experiences when the lesson does not engage them fully, and the teacher dominates most of the lesson through talking as opposed to the learners actually being engaged in activity. Such non-flow activities are characterised by apathy or boredom. In addition, their research indicated that, where learners' skills outweigh the demands of the lesson (culminating in boredom), learners actually reported higher levels of happiness, although they did not report pride in their achievements. This is an important highlight, in that lessons that have a high degree of challenge and a high degree of learner involvement do not necessarily equate to positive learning experiences for learners.

Many of these studies outlined above focus on secondary school pupils and there appears to be a limited range of literature relating to flow in the earlier years of education.

2.7 THE FUTURE OF POSITIVE PSYCHOLOGY RELATED TO EDUCATION

By the very nature of teaching, and the sense of inherent and integral professionalism, teachers are seldom happy: there is always something else they could have done, should have done or would have done, if they had the time or more resources. Arguably, such self-criticism (or reflection) spurs teachers to achieve their best within the classroom, yet a fine balance needs to be sought to prevent over-reflection where the teacher is unable to operate effectively due to self-doubt. Consequently, if a group of inspectors told you (and your setting) to be happier, or indeed measured your happiness with suggestions on how to improve, how would you react? If the following day everyone was wearing fixed smiles, and telling you how wonderful you look, would you feel that this was sincere, or the outcome of the inspection?

Indeed, this scenario demonstrates one of the fundamental criticisms against positive psychology: that it has an inherent value system which calls into question the impartiality of the empirical research tradition advocated within positive psychology (Held, 2002; McDonald and O'Callaghan, 2008; Miller, 2008; Sundararajan, 2005). Furthermore, the ideals of positive psychology have been discussed as being ethnocentric, with the suggestion that positive psychology is informed through American ideals, which may not be equally shared by other cultures (McDonald and O'Callaghan, 2008).

McDonald and O'Callaghan (2008: 128) similarly discuss how positive psychology has produced and defined what a 'positive' human experience is. In turn they suggest that positive psychology has established a prescriptive set of constructs, which in turn can refute alternative perspectives within psychology. Additionally, Miller (2008) questions whether one's life should necessarily be governed through setting and achieving goals, and whether a person's traits, emotions, thoughts and feelings can be consciously managed or controlled through the approaches advocated by positive psychology. If flow is taken as an example, Boniwell (2006: 28) warns that the pursuit of flow may not necessarily be desirable, that 'activities in which flow is found can be morally good or bad', specifically highlighting addiction to flow. Take, for example, the workaholic who never spends time with family or friends because they enjoy working so much to bring about the flow. Consider compulsive gambling, serial killers, or indeed any activity taken to extremes that may harm oneself or others. Consequently, as opposed to the field of positive psychology, such hedonism could actually be deemed to be a negative psychology, where growth is not the ultimate goal, yet the thrill of the flow experience is.

Furthermore, Martin (2006: 308) questions whether positive psychology is actually any different from educational psychology, commenting that both focus on 'creating conditions for optimal human learning and development'. Finally, Leontiev (2006: 50) states that 'positive psychology today is an ideology rather than a theory … There is no unified theoretical explanatory model behind them at this moment.' Perhaps analysis of other related disciplines within psychology can help provide such a unified theoretical model.

Consequently, although positive psychology may continue to receive attention, the reader should be critically aware of some of the tensions that exist in the field and possible future directions. Among these future directions, Linley et al. (2006) suggest that the field may be embedded within different areas of psychology, in turn redressing the balance of the predominant focus that psychology has previously had on the negative side of human beings. Alternatively, it may revisit earlier psychological perspectives, such as humanism, and analyse these earlier perspectives through a new lens. Additionally, positive psychology may engage in a more active dialogue with other academic disciplines (such as sociology, economics, science). Needless to say, further work in relating positive psychology to education is similarly required.

2.8 TRANSPERSONAL PSYCHOLOGY

Transpersonal psychology can be dated to the mid-1960s when work by Carl Jung, Roberto Assagioli, Stanislave Grof and Abraham Maslow among others was gaining popularity (Chinen, 1996). This culminated in the publication of the *Journal of Transpersonal Psychology* in 1969. However, Daniels (2011) suggests that the actual field of the transpersonal dates to William James and his Gifford Lectures delivered at the University of Edinburgh in 1901–2, which concluded in the publication of *The Varieties of Religious Experience* (1902/1999). Since its inception, transpersonal psychology has remained relatively obscure, despite its many inherent themes dating back to the foundation of psychology's conception (Daniels, 2005; Fontana, 2005).

What is transpersonal psychology? Simply defined, the transpersonal has been interpreted as 'beyond the person' (Daniels, 2005; Ferrer, 2002; Fontana and Slack, 2005), although this is a limited definition that does not really convey the focus of the field. Some suggest that the field is the psychology of spirituality (Daniels, 2005); others that it is a combination of elements blending Western psychology with Eastern contemplative traditions (Ferrer, 2002; Fontana and Slack, 2005; Miller, 1991). Indeed, perhaps the greatest criticism of transpersonal psychology is the multiplicity of definitions and the conceptual uncertainty about the content of the field; it has come to mean different things to different people (Cunningham, 2006).

Through an analysis of 35 years of research into transpersonal psychology, Hartelius et al. (2007) identified three encompassing themes: beyond-ego psychology, integrative/holistic psychology and the psychology of transformation. Beyond-ego psychology relates to examining the ego (the realistic sense of the 'self', or the part of the mind that controls behaviour through perception, cognition and memory, as discussed in Chapter 1), the aspects that can impact on the ego and exploration beyond the ego. Integrative/holistic psychology relates to the development of a single, unified field of psychology that examines the whole person, for example, explaining how our thinking, emotions and physical self relate to one another. The third theme is concerned with understanding how we can cultivate growth as individuals and as communities. Hartelius et al. (2007) respectively refer to the themes as the content (the actual transpersonal states), the context (through which human experience is studied, for example, the beliefs, attitudes and intentions) and the catalyst (where such growth relates to personal and social transformation), as demonstrated in Figure 2.3.

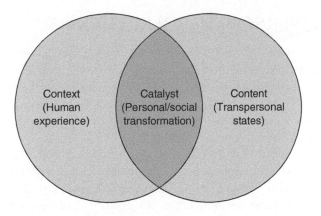

Figure 2.3   The themes of transpersonal psychology (based on Hartelius et al., 2007)

Succinctly defined, the field of transpersonal psychology examines what it means to be an integrated, fully functioning human, while seeking to continually improve and refine ourselves (individually and collectively) through a process of personal transformation (Hartelius et al., 2007). Areas within transpersonal psychology include meditation, intuition, inspiration, altered states of consciousness, compassion, developing a moral code, promotion of inner harmony (Fontana, 2003); creativity, peak experience (Rowan, 2005); states of absorption or experiences of deep connection (Daniels, 2005); and examining values and beliefs about the meaning of life and the nature of reality (Jankowski, 2002) – in other words, a sense of transcending the individual's sense of everyday reality. How can such an approach relate to education?

Hartelius et al. (2007) assert that the themes within transpersonal psychology can be applied to many areas, including education, to promote a more inclusive society, for example through promoting social action. At a time of exponential global change, being centred and in control, while working for the greater good of ourselves and humanity, may indeed be a vision for the future to tackle the problems caused by greed or anger. Indeed, certain authors advocate that education is perhaps the most significant area of future enquiry and exploration within the field of transpersonal psychology (Cunningham, 2006; Rothberg, 2005); however the area has remained significantly dormant. Indeed Maslow's writings seldom discuss education, despite every learner teacher being aware of how the hierarchy of needs relates to motivation. To date, only two books have been written on the subject, both of which date back to the 1970s, although Buckler has made an attempt to ignite further debate in this area, revisiting the themes within existing research and revisioning them for the present day (Buckler, 2011a, 2012, 2014).

2.9 TRANSPERSONAL EDUCATION

Transpersonal education may be deemed as an approach to education that explores three interacting domains, where a domain is an area of 'development' and these domains develop at different rates. So, the cognitive (intellectual), affective (emotional) and psychomotor (physical) domains combine to facilitate personal transformation to enable the child to become a healthy, self-actualised or, indeed, self-transcended adult, in turn transforming society (Buckler, 2011a).

Taking the component parts of this definition further, an integration of the various personal domains has been proposed by a variety of authors to promote healthy development of the individual (Moore, 1975; Roberts and Clark, 1976; Rothberg, 2005). The concept of personal transformation relates to personal change and development to elevate the individual beyond their self-centred existence towards a more satisfying or valuable condition (Daniels, 2005). Through the process of transformation, the individual can achieve their highest potential (self-actualisation) and even progress beyond this, achieving greater heights of being (self-transcendence). The term 'self-transcendence' has lacked a clear definition (as discussed by Daniels, 2005; Friedman, 2002), although Buckler (2011b) has referred to Maslow's original interpretation, which is characterised by the themes of developing a sense of calmness or serenity, mindfulness and an appreciation of the interconnectedness of life, while acknowledging one's own mortality. Consequently, the concept of self-transcendence can be seen as an awakening, similar to the themes often portrayed in the 'Hero's Journey' (Campbell, 1949/2012), displayed in such films as *Star Wars*, *The Matrix*, *Harry Potter* and *Lord of the Rings*. To illustrate this concept further, Bach (1977/1998: 134) writes, 'What the caterpillar calls the end of the world, the master calls a butterfly.' As a result of such personal transformation, the individual can make a more positive contribution to society, and subsequently, the more individuals can work together beyond their personal sense of self, the greater the development of that society.

How should such an educational approach be developed practically? Ralph Tyler identifies four fundamental areas in his principles of curriculum design:

1. What educational purposes should the school seek to attain?
2. What educational experiences can be provided that are likely to attain these purposes?
3. How can these educational experiences be effectively organized?
4. How can we determine whether these purposes are being attained? (Tyler, 1949: 1)

In essence, these can be summarised as relating to the policies that identify and establish the purpose of the curriculum, the principles that inform how the curriculum should be organised and the practices that inform the educational experiences which enable the curriculum to be fulfilled.

In relation to the policies governing transpersonal education, the original definition previously discussed provides the justification: that the focus should be on integrating the cognitive, affective and psychomotor domains to facilitate personal transformation.

The focus shares a similar emphasis to the areas of humanistic and positive psychology, that of personal growth, yet whereas the former areas do not make direct reference to educational practices, transpersonal education has educational practice as the foundation from which to develop the integral dimensions of the child.

In facilitating such transformative practices, Maslow (1971/1993) asserts the need for both parents and teachers to continue with their own personal development in order to prevent their own patterns of behaviour being conveyed to the child. For example, if a parent feels that their toddler is testing the boundaries by dropping food on the floor, rearranging the furniture, removing cushions, throwing objects, along with a multitude of other such behaviours, the parent may get cross with them, perceiving the child to be naughty, and therefore enforce a range of discipline measures (for example, the 'time-out' step as discussed in the introduction to this chapter). Yet the behaviours exhibited by the toddler are all examples of 'play schemas', or patterns of play, where the child is exploring and making sense of their world (Nutbrown, 2011). For example, dropping food or throwing objects relates to the trajectory schema; rearranging furniture can be explained through the transporting, positioning or enclosure schema. Understanding schemas explains the developing child's behaviour. Consequently, if a parent gets cross with a child for such behaviour, aiming to diminish rather than encourage the pattern of play, the child is being denied a chance to develop and make sense of their world.

A further example of how a parent's behaviour may be conveyed to a child is through driving: if a parent is 'precious' about the stretch of road they are currently driving on and the driver in front is going too slowly, the parent may display signs of frustration. Or perhaps a minor misdemeanour from another road user manifests in the parent providing a sign of agitation, for example some form of gesture. The child travelling in the car may in turn believe that it is fine to lose their temper with others in an aggressive way. Yet if the parent does not feel threatened by other road users and is in control of their cognition (how they perceive other road users), their emotions (whether or not they feel personally threatened by other road users) and their subsequent psychomotor displays (whether they indicate the error of another road user's ways through some form of gesticulation), then the developing child can see a calm and collected adult as a model for their own behaviour.

REFLECTION

Consider how teachers you have experienced in the past may have limited their learners.

How should transpersonal education be organised? In other words, what are the guiding principles central to such an educational approach? Buckler (2012, 2014) asserts that there are a series of general themes that can be derived

(Continued)

through the transpersonal psychology literature – themes that may resonate with educational practitioners as they serve as models of effective practice. For example, such principles include: that learning should be joyful (Maslow, 1971/1993; Moore, 1975); that learning should be promoted through developing the learner's intrinsic curiosity (Maslow, 1971/1993); and that the learner should develop autonomously through a process of self-discovery (Deci and Ryan, 1985; Kirchschenbaum, 1975; Rogers, 1961). Furthermore, such an educational approach should be value-free and promoted by the teacher in the role of a facilitator (Kirchschenbaum, 1975; Maslow, 1971/1993; Rogers, 1961), and education should promote lifelong learning (Maslow, 1970). These are summarised by the outer circle on Figure 2.4.

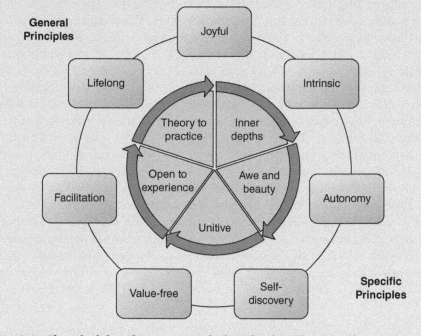

Figure 2.4   The principles of transpersonal education (Buckler, 2011a)

There are similarly a number of specific principles that outline the operational considerations for transpersonal education. One central feature is that education should relate to the discovery of the inner depths of the individual, in an attempt to explore the essential human nature (Maslow, 1970). Indeed, this theme resonates throughout transpersonal psychology: what does it mean to be human, and how can we develop our own and others' inner resources to become the best we can be? In addition, such an educational approach should encourage the consideration of the interconnectedness of various elements (Moore, 1975; Rothberg, 2005), what Maslow (1971/1993) calls a 'unitive experience'. An example of this theme is illustrated by O'Brien (2008) in her discussion of 'sustainable happiness' and how this relates to education. O'Brien (2008) asks the reader to consider drinking a cup of coffee: the process of drinking the coffee and the direct relationship to this process can be related to mindfulness (Kabat-Zinn, 2001, 2004), although the wider relationship to the process should also be considered. For example, is the coffee Fair Trade (where the coffee plantation has been grown with respect to the environment and the workers on the plantation have been paid fairly)? in other words, the emotional impact at the expense of drinking the coffee with regard to other people and the environment? Taking this further, did the person who boiled the kettle use just enough water to make the cup, or was energy wasted through overfilling the kettle?

A further specific principle of transpersonal education is that of the importance of experiential learning (Roberts and Clark, 1976; Rogers, 1961). Being open to experience means that learning is contextualised and brought to life; learning does not just exist in the classroom environment but in our wider surroundings. The development of 'Forest Schools' and the 'Outdoor Curriculum' are testament to how such a principle is currently being put into practice. A final associated principle suggests that theory should be linked to practice whenever and wherever possible, again to contextualise the learning (Rothberg, 2005).

Although the guiding policies and practices of transpersonal education have been outlined, what are the actual practices to promote the transpersonal? Buckler (2011a, 2014) provides a representative series of practices, which he warns are indicative and not meant to be an exhaustive or prescribed list.

One area that has received a lot of attention in recent years is the development of 'mindfulness', which relates to any practice where a person concentrates fully on a physical task, such as breathing, eating, drinking, exercising, or a cognitive task, for example watching one's thoughts without judging them, just allowing them to arise without any subsequent attention. Such mindful practice is an attempt to synthesis the mind and body to be here in the present moment (Kabat-Zinn, 2001, 2004; Rothberg, 2005). Arguably, mindfulness is not a new concept: the effects of other practices, such as meditation, have an established research tradition (Roberts and Clark, 1976). Indeed mindfulness has its roots in various Eastern and Western contemplative practices.

Mindfulness research with school-aged children is currently gaining momentum. For example, mindfulness has been used as a form of therapy with children (Bell, 2009) while mindfulness-based cognitive therapy has been discussed by various authors (Lee et al., 2008; Wisner et al., 2010). In addition, further studies have used mindfulness as a way of reducing stress in primary teachers (Gold et al., 2010).

Roger Walsh has also identified a series of 'perennial practices', which he suggests are found globally to promote transpersonal development. These practices are summarised as: redirecting motivation, transforming emotions, living ethically, developing concentration, refining awareness, cultivating wisdom, and practising service and generosity (Walsh, 1999).

In summary, the policy central to transpersonal education is that it should unite the cognitive (intellectual), affective (emotional) and psychomotor (physical) domains to facilitate personal transformation to enable the child to become a healthy, self-actualised or, indeed, self-transcended adult, in turn transforming society.

The principles behind a transpersonal education should be value-free and joyful, promoting learner autonomy through a process of self-discovery. Additionally, transpersonal education should encourage exploration of the essential human nature and the way in which the person relates on a larger scale to other people and nature, whereby a sense of awe and beauty can be promoted. Such experience should capitalise on linking theory to practice through experience.

In practice, a transpersonal education can be promoted through a range of practices advocated by Walsh, for example, developing concentration through mindfulness. How could such a transpersonal education be utilised within the education context? Moore (1975) provides three suggestions: (1) apply the transpersonal to existing subjects; (2) select activities and studies that lead to an awareness of the transpersonal; and (3) incorporate many new areas into the curriculum.

2.10 CONCLUSION

The themes identified above are not new: arguably many of the individual elements have been advocated and utilised within education previously; for example, Rudolf Steiner considered the role of spirituality within education and the interplay between the cognitive, emotional and behavioural development of children (McDermott, 2010). Yet transpersonal education attempts to synthesise such past and present elements into a coherent framework for the twenty-first century. Such a framework has been absent from alternative perspectives on psychology, such as positive psychology, although many of the themes discussed within this chapter demonstrate how positive psychology and transpersonal psychology overlap. Indeed, Kantor (1975) suggested that a thorough investigation of our inner world is required to rival and surpass space exploration in interest and importance: given the current monumental social, economic and political changes, one could question the exponential budgets invested in particle accelerators and the theoretical musings on the edges of the universe at the expense of the wonder of being human.

This chapter has, however, sought to provide an indication of how education may develop in the coming years and to keep an open mind about such developments: can we really still adhere to a curriculum model that provides the same 'diet' of subjects as prescribed in 1905 yet, in England and Wales, was only formalised in 1988? How do you see the curriculum developing over your lifetime as a teacher (which could be another 40 or more years)? What changes would you like to implement to ensure that the children of today are equipped to be the adults of tomorrow?

Having progressed through the first two chapters, which provide the theoretical basis for various psychological perspectives, the following chapters focus on the practicalities of using psychological approaches within your practice. Fundamental to your teaching is you, and although this chapter has discussed themes of personal growth, what are the core attributes of a successful or effective teacher? This will be explored in Chapter 3.

2.11 FURTHER READING

Csikszentmihalyi, M. (2000) *Beyond Boredom and Anxiety: Experiencing Flow in Work and Play*. San Francisco, CA: Jossey-Bass.
This summarises Csikszentmihalyi's concept of flow and how it may be applied in different contexts.

Grenville-Cleave, B. (2012) *Positive Psychology: A Practical Guide*. London: Icon Books.
This book provides a clear, coherent overview of positive psychology and how it may be applied.

Hartelius, G., Caplan, M. and Rardin, M.A. (2007) 'Transpersonal psychology: Defining the past, divining the future', *The Humanistic Psychologist*, 35 (2): 135–60.
This research paper provides an overview of transpersonal psychology including the defining trends within the area.

3

THE EFFECTIVE TEACHER

CHAPTER OBJECTIVES

- Develop an understanding of the core attributes required by a teacher to engage learners successfully.
- Critically evaluate the components of an effective teacher from a learner perspective and a research perspective.
- Consider how effectiveness can be enhanced professionally.

TEACHERS' STANDARDS

A teacher must:

4   Plan and teach well-structured lessons

- reflect systematically on the effectiveness of lessons and approaches to teaching
- contribute to the design and provision of an engaging curriculum within the relevant subject area(s)

5   Adapt teaching to respond to the strengths and needs of all pupils

- have a secure understanding of how a range of factors can inhibit pupils' ability to learn, and how best to overcome these

8   Fulfil wider professional responsibilities

- take responsibility for improving teaching through appropriate professional development, responding to advice and feedback from colleagues

3.1 INTRODUCTION

What makes an effective teacher? Can an effective teacher really be summarised through a few bullet points? A number of research reports have been published that discuss the composition of an effective teacher (some of which will be reviewed in this chapter). However, this chapter will progress beyond merely presenting what others have said and indeed tap into you as a resource: after all, you have been one of the most recent successes of the education system, no doubt experiencing brilliant and not-so-brilliant teachers over the years. So, having succeeded and in turn being of a new generation of inspirational teachers, let's start with you and your experience.

REFLECTION

Consider a couple of teachers who have been instrumental to your development and success. What attributes made them stand out as an excellent teacher?

Consider other teachers, outside of school, who have had some impact on you in some way. For example, a sports coach, a relative or a friend. What attributes did they have?

On an outline of the human figure, note down these attributes.

Can these attributes be grouped in any way?

Having completed the reflection activity, consider whether the teacher would be deemed successful from a different person's perspective. For example, did you have any friends who didn't get on well with the teacher? Would an inspector see the positive attributes you highlighted? Indeed, as discussed in Chapter 1, perspectives vary from individual to individual; as a result different people have different perspectives. Is it possible that this teacher 'echoed' your learning style, that you perceived them as being successful because they taught in a way that suited you? Consequently we will look at what makes an effective teacher from two perspectives: (1) the learner, and (2) the researcher.

Although a number of studies will be reviewed, what we present here is a series of combined themes evident within this work. Needless to say, this is an ongoing area of research, which in time may reveal additional themes. Furthermore, we have grouped these themes from our perspective: different people may perceive the groupings differently, an aspect we would encourage any reader to do in order to make sense of and take responsibility for their own learning.

3.2 WHAT IS MEANT BY 'EFFECTIVE'?

'Effective' can quite simply be defined as 'getting the job done', so an effective teacher is one who can engage with the full range of expected activities, for example, planning the lesson, preparing the resources, facilitating the learning experience and determining whether the learning experience was of benefit through assessment and feedback. Arguably more time is devoted to the initial stages than the latter – for example, it may take three hours to plan a one-hour lesson. Indeed, the lesson may well be very effective, yet what has been the cost to the teacher? If each lesson takes three hours to prepare and there are four lessons in the day, the teacher would need to find 60 hours per week in order to plan before the actual teaching, assessment and other assorted elements of the school week. Although each lesson may be 'effective', a balance needs to be sought: to prevent exhaustion the teacher needs to develop an efficient approach to their work. Indeed, although research frequently discusses what makes an effective teacher, little credit is given to efficiency, as cutting corners is often seen as bad practice.

In an attempt to redefine efficiency, as you progress with your teaching career, you will identify elements that work for you, activities that can be adapted, which in turn will result in higher productivity. This approach can be likened to a trainee chef cutting carrots: at first each slice will take time, with different-sized slices of carrot, resulting in some being over- or under-cooked, yet when a chef becomes practised, chopping a carrot looks effortless, with each slice being of a uniform size. A similar analogy can be made with learning to walk, drive a car, indeed any skills where practice makes perfect. Consequently, within your teaching career, becoming efficient, while balancing this with effectiveness, is something to strive for.

Taken to an extreme, a teacher may be very efficient at planning a lesson, perhaps only spending 20 minutes on this (approximating to seven hours of planning for a week), yet the lesson may not be effective: the lesson may be too simple or too complex, it may not cover the recommended objectives, and so on. Indeed, the balance between effectiveness and efficiency can be as presented in Figure 3.1.

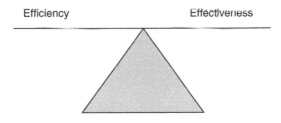

Figure 3.1   The balance between efficiency and effectiveness

This balance of efficiency and effectiveness can be summarised in relation to the Confucian philosophical approach, specifically the Doctrine of the Mean, dating back over two thousand years, which can be seen as doing the right thing at the right time to achieve a desired outcome (Fung, 1976).

ACTIVITY

As carefully as you can, draw a perfect circle.

Now, as quickly as you can, draw another circle.

How do they compare? Are they both circle-ish in nature? If you were to draw a circle in the classroom, which one would you opt for?

(Continued)

This in turn relates to handwriting. Consider when you have been in a lecture room or a seminar and have had to make notes. No doubt this has not been in your perfectly precise handwriting style, but sufficient to record what is relevant for you.

How would this compare to writing on a pupil's work?

In returning to the focus of this chapter, as previously mentioned, very little research has been conducted on efficiency within teaching, with the predominant focus being directed towards effectiveness, as discussed in the next section.

3.3 AN EFFECTIVE TEACHER: WHAT DO LEARNERS THINK?

Several studies have asked learners what they think makes an effective teacher. From reviewing these studies, there are three key areas that appear as themes across the research: (1) effective teachers are able to develop good learning relationships; (2) effective teachers have a good subject background; and (3) effective teachers have good organisational skills.

EFFECTIVE TEACHERS ARE ABLE TO DEVELOP GOOD LEARNING RELATIONSHIPS

Within this element there are three strands: understanding, communication and enjoyment. These three areas can overlap as will become evident below.

In relation to understanding, according to Check (1986), an effective teacher understands learners and their problems. Such examples in practice relate to a teacher who has an appropriate judgement and expectations of what a learner can do, while similarly encouraging the learner to raise their own expectations (Brown and McIntyre, 1993). Additionally, such understanding is demonstrated by being able to help learners with difficulties through spending time with them and focusing on their needs (Brown and McIntyre, 1993; Santrock, 2001; Upton and Taylor, 2014). Understanding is also demonstrated through being able to relate well with learners while treating them with respect (Upton and Taylor, 2014). Check (1986) similarly discusses respect through being able to relate well with learners while demonstrating an interest in them, and Santrock (2001) examines the need to be fair to all learners.

The second strand, communication, is closely aligned to the third strand of enjoyment. Consider a time when you have enjoyed your teaching and the effect this has had on the learners you worked with, as opposed to a time when you have not enjoyed a lesson, perhaps continually checking the time to see when you could escape and progress to a more fulfilling lesson. Given that, as teachers, our aim is to communicate increasingly more complex concepts in a manner that all learners will understand and actually engage with on a personal level, communication is central to our role. Indeed, consider any incidents of your teaching career so far where you have worked with a learner and seen their proverbial 'eyes light up' as they have understood a concept, a time when your communication was explicit in nature, clear to the learner and at an appropriate level to ensure their learning progressed. Again, this may be seen as a balance, a central theme within this book, where you were working in tune with the ability of the learner.

REFLECTION

Consider a recent occurrence when you have enabled a learner (or learners) to succeed with learning a concept. What was the objective of the lesson? How did you help the learner(s)? What indicated to you that the learner(s) had understood the concept based on your communication? Note down a couple of words about the occurrence to summarise your thoughts/feelings.

Now consider a time when you, as a learner, understood a concept for the first time. How did you feel? What was it about the situation that enabled you to understand? Sum up your feelings in a couple of words.

Finally, consider a time when you were completely lost in a learning situation, a time when the information was too abstract, too confusing or even too boring. Sum up your feelings in a couple of words.

Reviewing the words you have noted, consider how these relate to, and how these can be manifested within, your teaching.

As discussed, communication relates closely to enjoyment: if you are working at your optimum level, you will not only communicate efficiently and effectively, you should also be enjoying the lesson unfolding somewhat seamlessly. In such a lesson, your learners too should reap the benefits, in turn enjoying the learning experience. There will, however, be times when a lesson may not be the most awe-inspiring; perhaps due to your confidence in the subject matter, or because learners are not as inspired by the focus of the lesson. Consequently, balancing the demands of the curriculum with the demands of the learners is an area to consider, as is echoed throughout this book. The aim is to find something inherent in the lesson that will captivate and engage the learners, often finding unique and novel ways to stimulate such learning. Ultimately, being able to communicate with learners on a number of levels is of paramount importance (Check, 1986).

Yet what does this mean in practice? Simply defined, this may relate to working with the learners at class level (when communicating the core ideas of the lesson), group level (when leading a discussion) or individual level (providing one-to-one support). Alternatively this may relate to the teaching cliché of being able to communicate the same idea or concept in a hundred different ways for a hundred different learners. Consequently, there is a holistic theme (the concepts of the lesson), combined with an atomistic theme (ensuring the individual learner is able to understand the concept at their level in a manner suitable for them), and the continuum between these polarised points is summarised in Figure 3.2.

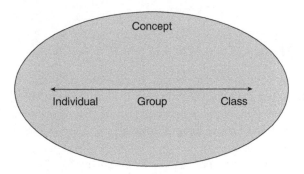

Figure 3.2   The holistic/atomistic continuum of communication

To illustrate this figure, imagine the focus of the lesson is based on floating and sinking. Take the widely used approach to planning in primary education, whereby all children should understand that different objects float or sink; some may be able to group objects that float or sink; while a few may be able to progress to describe the properties of objects that float. A whole-class introduction to the lesson may be provided through discussing a story or observing the difference between certain objects, before progressing to allow the learners to experiment with a range of objects. The lesson may involve categorising different objects according to whether they float or sink, where discussion with certain groups may help in establishing common properties of the range of objects that float. During the lesson, one child may question why some objects do not fully float on the surface of the water, or do not fully sink to the bottom of the tank. From this, you may engage them on an individual basis to explore this concept, perhaps introducing new terms such as surface area, opposing forces and so on. Indeed, you may even provide the learner with a ball of play-dough to see if they can make it float. Such experimentation may develop their learning on an individual level where, from trial and error, the ball is flattened, then curved, increasing the surface area of the object creating a resultant greater force where upthrust outweighs gravity.

ACTIVITY

Using Figure 3.2, consider a lesson that involves class, group and individual work. Monitor the lesson as it develops, being attentive to your changing communication in the different contexts.

One of the most significant areas highlighted through Santrock's (2001) work, and echoed by others, is the need for a sense of humour. Santrock highlights this as the key factor learners have expressed as an attribute of an effective teacher. Does this mean that the teacher needs to be a stand-up comedian alongside all of the other roles encompassed by the term 'teacher'?

The use of humour that Santrock identifies may relate to approaching all situations with a light-hearted manner, for example turning around a negative situation with a timely joke or witty remark as discussed by Check (1986). Of course, such remarks should not be aimed at any one learner but at the situation, as it is never nice to be on the receiving end of a joke. A more general approach is being able to divert a situation through a kind, positive word, or a light-hearted remark. Indeed, creating a relaxed, enjoyable atmosphere is highlighted by Brown and McIntyre (1993), and we are sure you would agree that such an atmosphere is the most conducive for learning.

Such enjoyment is similarly discussed by Ruddick et al. (1996) and Check (1986), whereby learners commented that an effective teacher enjoys their teaching, both of the learners and of their subject. This enjoyment and enthusiasm links to the second element, that effective teachers have a good subject background.

EFFECTIVE TEACHERS HAVE A GOOD SUBJECT BACKGROUND

An effective teacher is unlikely to work to the best of their abilities without having a sense of enjoyment and enthusiasm for teaching: such enthusiasm is displayed through a teacher who has a strong subject background. Indeed, learners have reported that an effective teacher has a good knowledge of their subject (Check, 1986; Santrock, 2001) and that this knowledge enables the teacher to present stimulating work (Brown and McIntyre, 1993; Santrock, 2001; Upton and Taylor, 2014).

Of course, the very nature of teaching means that the subject content will continue to be redefined over a teacher's career; similarly very few teachers will be versed in the intricacies of their subject (or a range of subjects) before qualifying, or indeed for a few years after. However, a teacher's commitment to ensuring the continual improvement of their knowledge and skills is paramount, which in turn ensures that teaching is viewed as a profession and not just a job.

To this extent, there is little separating teaching and learning; teaching is a continual process of developing subject expertise, then being able to share this with learners so that they can develop their own knowledge and understanding. The process is never-ending: new knowledge, newly defined changes to the curriculum, the role of learning technologies, among many other variables, continue to ensure that teachers will never become complacent. Such complacency is an important issue to address, given the discussion about profession: once a teacher becomes complacent, without the continual drive for perfection through continually improving their knowledge and skills, can such a teacher be deemed a professional? As can often be the case, others can probably see what such a teacher is unable to: that there may be failings in their practice. This relates to what is termed the 'conscious competence' learning model.

The conscious competence learning model is frequently reported to have been developed by Noel Burch from Gordon Training International (Flower, 1999). The model describes four stages of development for learning any new skill, behaviour or knowledge (Figure 3.3).

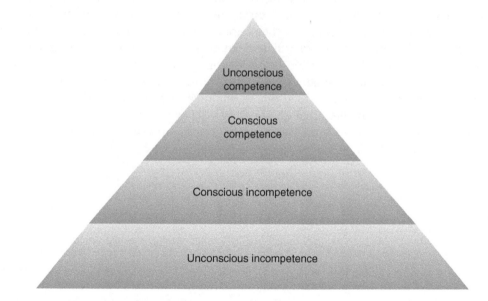

Figure 3.3   The four stages of conscious competence

The first stage of the model relates to unconscious incompetence. This is where the person is unaware that they may be lacking the skills or knowledge within a particular area: this may arise from their ignorance of the area, their ignorance of their limitations or their denial of the relevance or usefulness of the skill. The second stage of the model is conscious incompetence. Within this stage, the individual progresses through being aware of the skill to be developed, alongside the relevance of the skill to complement their existing attributes. By acknowledging the need to develop the skill, the individual will appreciate that they are at a start point of continual refinement. This in turn leads towards the third stage, conscious competence. At this level, the individual is able to perform the skill when required, although they will need to concentrate on performing the skill in order to internalise the skill further, so that practice makes perfect. The final level is unconscious competence: this is where the skill has become internalised, where the skill can be performed automatically.

The reason for providing this model is to reiterate that, when developing our professional skills, we may at times feel frustrated with our progression (or lack of it). With time and effort, what seems difficult will become second nature; consequently the model can serve as a reminder not to be too hard on ourselves. Furthermore, the model is not only useful to provide teachers with an understanding of their personal development; it is also usefully applied when working with learners to consider the level from which they may be operating. As with most models, other authors tend to make the simple more complicated by including additional stages, for example teaching the skill to another person, or restructuring the model into a new shape: indeed, the conscious competence model has been presented as a ladder, a series of concentric circles and as a matrix.

REFLECTION

Consider a recent skill you have developed, for example, learning to drive, or learning how to use a new piece of software. How did the four stages of conscious competence manifest as you developed this skill?

Consider a skill that you can now perform with unconscious competence. Revisit this skill through the four stages listed above. How would you teach this skill to another person?

EFFECTIVE TEACHERS HAVE GOOD ORGANISATIONAL SKILLS

A teacher may be able to develop great learning relationships and be extremely well-versed in their subject, yet without organisation supporting these other elements, the teacher will not be effective. It is this last element that combines the others. Such organisation is demonstrated through well-prepared, clearly structured lessons (Check, 1986; Ruddick et al., 1996). Additionally, such lessons have a specific focus with an engaging content where there is a variety of pace and activity (Ruddick et al., 1996). Given the attributes relating to organisational skills, how do these transform to your specific planning? Indeed, this very much relates to the age range of the learners you are working with, alongside the area of the curriculum you are covering. Certain subjects are clearly structured (for example, numeracy or literacy), while others have less refined structures (for example, history or music). What may be appropriate in one subject may not be appropriate in another, therefore it is worth reflecting on a lesson you delivered that has worked really well.

ACTIVITY

Consider one of your most memorable lessons. Using the organisational attributes listed below, review your lesson, making a few notes against each attribute as evidence for the lesson's organisation.

Attribute	Evidence
Specific focus	
Appropriate preparation	
Clear structure	
Engaging content	
Variety of pace	
Variety of activity	

Now consider how effective the lesson was. How did you assess this?

Although organisation has been discussed in relation to lesson planning, in returning to the theme of this chapter, two words were initially discussed: effectiveness and efficiency, specifically in relation to balancing the two elements. As noted, if it takes 60 hours to plan for the week, you may have developed the most awe-inspiring, creatively fantastic lessons but, when it comes to teaching these, you may be exhausted. Consequently, organisation relates equally to the management of the most fundamental resource in the teaching arsenal: you! (A book about personal management for teachers has been written by Castle and Buckler, 2009.) The second most important resource for any teacher is time, an aspect discussed below.

In a study by Zhang and Fishbach, research participants were asked to estimate how long it would take them to complete a specific task, then record how long the task actually took. The results were hardly surprising, in that participants took longer to complete the task than they had originally estimated, an area commonly referred to as planning fallacy. However, the aspect important to note is that those who had been overly optimistic with their estimated time completed the task earlier than those who were less optimistic (Zhang and Fishbach, 2010). The self-imposed standard of over-estimating thus appears to relate to optimism. Indeed, if there is a task that appears onerous, an individual can often impose barriers to prevent the task being completed, yet if an individual can focus on the positive elements of having the task completed, they can lessen the time (and often the effort) required to achieve the desired result. As an example, consider the end of the school week. Friday afternoon comes quickly and, along with the final bell, you load yourself up with marking and planning to occupy your weekend. Perhaps you leave the planning and marking until Sunday when you know you have a clear day, yet can you actually switch off and relax on Saturday, in the knowledge that your working week is six days long? By reframing the situation, perhaps you are disciplined to complete most of your marking on the Thursday evening, thus lessening your marking load over the weekend. From this, you have one day's worth of marking on Friday, some of which you may be able to complete during lunchtime, or straight after school. You may also decide to ensure that your planning has been completed on the Friday by spreading this over some of the preceding days. Ultimately, you would have freed the weekend for yourself: you can relax!

REFLECTION

Are you an optimist with your marking and planning, or a pessimist?

Do you attempt to complete such tasks immediately, or are they seen as things to put off because you dread them?

How can you reframe aspects that you least enjoy so that you accomplish these quickly, effectively and efficiently?

3.4 AN EFFECTIVE TEACHER: WHAT DO RESEARCHERS THINK?

A number of researchers have similarly explored what makes an effective teacher. Although this looks at the issue through a different perspective, the same three themes as those from the learner's perspective are apparent: (1) effective teachers are able to develop good learning relationships; (2) effective teachers have a good subject background; and (3) effective teachers have good organisational skills.

EFFECTIVE TEACHERS ARE ABLE TO DEVELOP GOOD LEARNING RELATIONSHIPS

The importance of developing good learning relationships has been highlighted through the work of Langlois and Zales (1992) and Wray et al. (2000), whereby the development of a supportive, cooperative environment is paramount to learning. Establishing such an environment in turn enables learners to develop their independence (Galton et al., 1980), an environment where learners are able to explore concepts, appreciating their role within the learning process. Such independence is developed when learners are constantly praised for their efforts (Rutter et al., 1979), which in turn develops a motivational climate. Rutter et al. (1979) similarly discuss the need to be able to engage and interact with the whole class. Indeed, ensuring learners are continually motivated to achieve when they are clear about the expected academic standards has been discussed by Wray et al. (2000).

Although research has highlighted factors that promote good learning relationships, how are these related in practice? How for example is a supportive, cooperative environment established? How can you ensure that your classroom and your lessons are structured in a way that enables every individual learner to achieve? If this element is effective, arguably independence and motivation will fall into place. What follows is a way in which you can consider how to develop all of these elements using an analogy from establishing a business.

Consider yourself as a consultant, one who is responsible for selling exciting and stimulating ideas to your clients (or your learners). How will you encourage your clients to buy into what you are selling? First off, let's go to an empty room, your room. Initially in this room are the four walls, you and nothing else: no learners, no furniture, no resources, and no displays. How are you going to turn the place into a successful venture? Fundamentally the key feature in this room is you.

As a learner (or established) teacher, at some point you will have gone through the process of selection, perhaps an interview to be accepted onto a teacher training course, or an interview for your first job. You and you alone had to 'sell' why you should be the chosen one above all others. What attributes could you bring to teaching? What experience have you already had? Why should you be invested in? Within business, this is referred to as the 'USP' or unique selling point. Why you?

Taking this one stage further, another business term commonly used is the 'elevator pitch': this is where all attention is directed your way for up to one minute to sell your idea. The rationale behind this is that, if you have been met at the reception desk by the chief executive before being led to their office (which is probably on the top floor of the building), you have a minute to share an elevator with them to sell your idea. Indeed, Boothman (2008) discusses how the first few moments of an encounter are extremely important as to whether you will get on well with someone.

ACTIVITY   Elevator pitch

Consider your elevator pitch, a one-minute period where you need to sell yourself as a teacher.

Write down all your defining features as a teacher. You could use the W5H1 questions (who, what, why, when, where, how?) as a frame of reference. For example, why did you become a teacher? Who has influenced your teaching?

From this, consider what is fundamentally unique about you. What is your unique selling point?

Consider who you are selling to. For example, is it the headteacher and governors, the parents or the learners? Is it all three groups?

Structure your elevator pitch into a couple of paragraphs, no more than 150 words.

From this activity, you will have appreciated your uniqueness as a teacher. Yet what supports your sense of identity in relation to your appearance? Obviously your best interview outfit may not be appropriate for the classroom, so consider your day-to-day appearance.

Having established your professional identity, let us direct our attention to your classroom. The age range you work with will influence the way in which you structure your classroom (or in keeping with the business analogy, your 'shop front').

ACTIVITY   Classroom

Take a mental walk through the classrooms you have previously experienced. Consider the layout of the room, where the board was located, how the tables and seats were arranged, the resources, the displays.

Make a list of the key features a classroom has to have.

Next to each item on this list, note down the attributes that influence how the item should best be situated, then in the third column, note what you need to do to ensure that the feature is appropriate. For example:

Feature	Key attributes	What I need to do
Board	Central to the classroom High enough so learners can see the full board yet not so high as to cause neck strain	Sit in each learner's place to see if I can view the board without straining my neck

(Continued)

Taking this one example, you will appreciate how seating arrangements are influenced by the location of the board. Of course, your teaching may not necessarily be board-based, so is there a different central feature to the room that establishes a sense of orientation for the learners (in the same way a fireplace is located in a living room)?

ACTIVITY   Logo

Who designs the logo for schools, or the colour scheme used throughout a school? Taking the logo, some are established and have been for over a hundred years, some may have been designed by learners, others by the headteacher, local education authority, committee or a graphics design company. It would certainly be an interesting question to ask the headteacher of a school you may be working at, or visiting on placement.

Yet consider the market appeal of a logo. Think of a famous soft-drink manufacturer. Think of the logo used by fast-food companies. The power of the logo as establishing a sense of identity is paramount within businesses, so by analogy why shouldn't this apply within the education sector?

Although your school's logo may be out of your control, let's return to your classroom and you. Spend a few moments jotting down symbols that resonate with you as a teacher. Perhaps a tree, whereby you are taking seedlings, providing the right nourishment for growth and establishing their roots of learning as they work with you over the year. Perhaps an outstretched hand.

Is there a motto that could be included with your logo?

This activity is designed to help you consider the uniqueness of you and your classroom – a place learners want to be. A place that offers the learners a sense of identity and purpose, or perhaps comfort in the same way any recognised logo appeals. Even if you haven't engaged with this activity, it could certainly be one of those ideas you store for the next time you need a quick space-filling lesson or are asked to cover a class at short notice.

EFFECTIVE TEACHERS HAVE A GOOD SUBJECT BACKGROUND

A theme discussed from the learner's perspective is that an effective teacher needs to know their subject. Yet as research indicates, it is more than just being a walking encyclopaedia of knowledge: the art of teaching is in being able to communicate this knowledge (and strategies for learners to develop this knowledge) at an appropriate level. Rutter et al. (1979) highlight the importance of being able to provide stimulating learning experiences within a work-centred learning environment. Taking the focus as work-centred, Langlois and Zales (1992) and Wray et al. (2000) advocate that an effective teacher should maximise time for learning. To focus on the purpose of learning, consider how much time can be wasted in a classroom when dealing with administration, or the after-effects of a wet playtime.

Consequently, the subject background again relates to organisational skills, so that a lesson can be structured in a way in which less time is spent by the teacher in talking, and more time is spent by the learners on their work.

EFFECTIVE TEACHERS HAVE GOOD ORGANISATIONAL SKILLS

Organisation is the third strand evident from researchers' perspectives about effective teaching. Rutter et al. (1979) and Galton et al. (1980) both highlight the need for clear, strong organisation. Such organisation is apparent through the development of established routines (Langlois and Zales, 1992; Wray et al., 2000).

The effective teacher is able to constantly scan the classroom and is aware of the progress of the class as a whole, and also individual progress and achievement (Langlois and Zales, 1992; Wray et al., 2000). Associated with monitoring progress is the use of feedback to learners, informing them of their progress while also being able to monitor how learners are achieving (Ursano et al., 2007). Wray et al. (2000) highlight the need for timely feedback, yet it is important to note that 'feedback' is different from 'marking'. Informing learners of their progress within a lesson, reminding them of what they should be doing, and helping those who may need further elaboration or explanation, while ensuring learners reach a desired outcome, is different from marking unless such marking takes place in situ with the learner where you can explain what you are looking for. Thus providing feedback can be short, spoken comments in the context of the lesson to an individual, a group or the whole class. This enables the learner to appreciate how well their efforts are meeting criteria, either your own, or theirs.

Feedback must also be constructive (Galton et al., 1980). Merely commenting 'You should be working harder' or 'Well done' to a learner provides little information. Does the phrase 'should be working harder' relate to the amount of effort a learner needs to invest or the amount of output? Does the phrase consider whether the learner is having problems with the work or has misunderstood some element of the lesson? Perhaps a better phrase would be, 'I see that your work is limited today; how are you progressing with your work?' or 'Is there anything you would like me to help you with so that you can achieve X by the end of the lesson?' Such use of questioning avoids value statements; for example, what does 'working harder' actually mean? What does, 'well done' mean? Does 'well done' mean: 'You have managed to sit quietly all lesson', or 'You have completed a full page of sums' (even if the sums are subsequently wrong)? Again, it may be better to comment, 'I can see that you have completed X. How do you feel you have progressed?', or 'What have you been able to achieve during this lesson?', or 'What were the easiest [or hardest] parts of the lesson?' The use of questioning relates to the previous theme on subject knowledge; however, such questioning in this context enables feedback to be provided through engaging in dialogue with a learner. Of course, such questions could be used individually, with a group or a whole class, either verbally or in written context. You could ask the group to note down one thing they found easy and one that they found hard, with an associated strategy to help improve on this to discuss at the end of the lesson.

Closely aligned to this scanning is being able to monitor behaviour, being proactive (avoiding behavioural issues escalating) and preventing problems before they arise; behaviour will be discussed in Chapter 20.

Although it is easy to advocate what teachers should be doing, it is more difficult to actually put this into practice: how does a teacher develop 'eyes in the back of their head', so to speak? Two different yet associated words are discussed below.

3.5 A SYNTHESIS BETWEEN THE LEARNER AND RESEARCHER PERSPECTIVES

Perspectives from both learners and researchers indicate that there are three themes that define an effective teacher: relationships, subject knowledge and organisation. If one element is missing the other two will not be supported. A simple way of portraying this is shown in Figure 3.4.

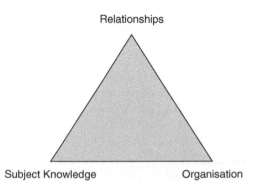

Figure 3.4   The effective teacher

This chapter has reviewed research into the area of an effective teacher, although as discussed at the start, research into effective teaching practices continues to evolve. Furthermore, the findings could be grouped differently if considered through alternative lenses. However, the chapter has illuminated a series of strategies for developing effectiveness within your teaching.

3.6 SEVEN HABITS OF HIGHLY EFFECTIVE TEACHERS

Despite specifically discussing the concept of effectiveness from a research-informed perspective, one pop-psychology book that has achieved a high degree of success is Steven Covey's *The Seven Habits of Highly Effective People* (2004). Covey's book provides a series of principles related to 'effectiveness' that, he suggests, are found globally, with such 'habits' having naturally developed among many highly successful people. These principles can be related to anyone and any profession: the following is an interpretation and adaptation of his habits applied to the teaching profession.

The first three habits relate to developing independence. The next three habits relate to interdependence or working with others. The final habit could arguably be central to the other six and has been represented as such in Figure 3.5.

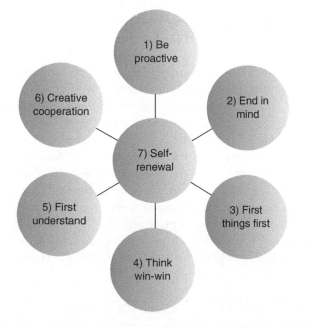

Figure 3.5   Seven habits of highly effective teachers (based on Covey, 2004)

HABIT 1: BE PROACTIVE

The only thing we can truly be in control of is ourselves: it is not possible to control all external dimensions to our day-to-day living; for example, we cannot control the weather, the traffic or when school inspectors decide to visit. All we can do is control our response to these situations. We can get very agitated if sitting in a traffic jam; alternatively we can reframe our perspective and enjoy the music on the radio, consider the actions for the day ahead or just watch other people scurrying about. In relation to the weather, we may understand the effect that a wet and windy day may have on our learners – that they may appear more lively than normal – consequently we can ensure that there is time at the start of the lesson to spend a few moments of mindful practice (see Chapter 2) to create a calm feeling before progressing with the lesson.

Furthermore, associated with themes discussed in Chapters 1 and 2, we operate on a cognitive, affective and psychomotor domain: our thinking, emotional and physical domains. If we are starting to feel agitated, that events appear to be spiralling out of control, we can regain a balance of the cognitive and affective domains through controlling our physical domain, for example, we can breathe more slowly, focusing solely on the breathing process (see Chapter 17).

By being proactive, not only can we control our responses to uncontrollable situations; we can consider the balance between those aspects that concern us, and those which we can influence. Many facets of our day-to-day teaching can cause us concern – grade results, changes to the curriculum, Class 7B – yet we have to consider these concerns against the aspects we can influence. We cannot control all areas of concern, yet we can control our areas of influence. Taking the aforementioned list, grade results may be of a concern and this is something we can target and influence through our teaching. The constantly changing curriculum may similarly be a concern yet outside our area of influence; however, we can be proactive in considering how to engage with such changes.

According to this habit, if we focus our efforts on those elements we are unable to control, we are being reactive in nature. Alternatively, if we focus our efforts on those aspects we can influence, which relate to areas of concern, then we are being proactive. Although it is acknowledged that some of our choices may result in negative outcomes, or so-called mistakes, we are unable to alter what has happened. From a proactive perspective, we can reflect on what has happened and why, then consider how we could make an alternative decision if such a future course of action happened again. Indeed, this relates to the concept of reflection, discussed in Chapter 4.

In summary, this first habit relates to taking responsibility for our choices and the subsequent consequences, with the realisation that you are in control.

HABIT 2: BEGIN WITH THE END IN MIND

What do we mean by the 'end'? Indeed, this is the central concept to this habit: being able to define this ultimate goal. Is retirement your ultimate goal or becoming a headteacher, or is there an alternative you have in mind? The reason for asking these questions is to prompt your thinking about what you really want from your career. Indeed, what would bring you the highest level of satisfaction within your teaching career?

Many teachers appear to be concerned with the short-term, day-to-day concerns, yet true success (however you want to define it) is related to a longer-term goal. Such goals may not be found with a few moments' reflection but may take far longer to identify. Indeed, it may be more than achieving a highly paid job: instead it may relate to fulfilling your personal philosophy. To this extent, the themes discussed in Chapter 4 should help you define these goals based on your personal philosophy of teaching.

In summary, the second habit relates to identifying your ultimate goal, a goal that resonates deeply within you. Once you have crystallised your goal, you can progress with the third habit – identifying the steps that need to be taken and putting first things first.

HABIT 3: PUT FIRST THINGS FIRST

What is the difference between completing tasks that are urgent, and those that are important? This habit encourages you to consider the difference between urgency and importance, with the emphasis on planning, prioritising and performing such tasks.

One helpful way Covey suggests in considering such tasks is through providing a 2×2 matrix which provides four quadrants to prompt you (Figure 3.6).

	Essential	Non-essential
High Priority	Quadrant 1 'Emergency: I need to do this before anything else!'	Quadrant 2 'i have time to do this and it is a priority for me'
Low Priority	Quadrant 3 'Someone else wants me to do something quickly but it isn't important. I should say 'no'!'	Quadrant 4 'Why is this even on my list?'

Figure 3.6   Quadrants of priority (adapted from Covey, 2004)

- *Quadrant 1:* Within this quadrant are the tasks that could be considered as emergencies. The problem with anything in this quadrant is that it tends to expand, draining your resources. The key to being effective is to limit the tasks that go into this first quadrant, instead focusing on those in the second quadrant.
- *Quadrant 2:* This is the true quadrant within which a person works effectively. If you have understood and internalised the first two habits, by having the strength of character to say 'no' to things while also realising your own goals,

you will have identified what is important to you, and in turn the tasks for you to engage with. The tasks within this quadrant have a high degree of impact on your working life.

- *Quadrant 3:* Within this quadrant a paradox exists: can a task really be urgent but not important? If effort is placed into completing such urgent tasks but they do not resonate with you as being important, a tension may exist where you seldom complete the tasks you really need to do, in the face of those that are demanding your immediate attention. One example of this is the use of emails, where often people will tend to check and then respond to emails as their working day begins, rather than getting on with the tasks they have really set themselves for the day. Indeed, most jobs that are classified as 'urgent' tend to have been imposed by other people to meet their deadlines. In returning to emails, every email that you open asks you to do something with it and places a demand on your time and resources: initially read it then decide, for example, whether to delete it, respond to it or store it for later action.
- *Quadrant 4:* Arguably anything not important and non-urgent can be ignored due to the pressing demands of those found in the other quadrants.

The ultimate aim of this model is to ensure that you limit the tasks in Quadrant 1 to allow more time to be spent on those in Quadrant 2, while staying away from Quadrants 3 and 4 because they are not important. Indeed, if this balance could be achieved, you would be in more control of your working and personal life. Alas it may take an investment of time to ensure that you can devote most of your resources to Quadrant 2: initially you would have to clear those in Quadrant 1 as these cannot be ignored, and then those in Quadrant 3.

HABIT 4: THINK WIN-WIN

This habit emphasises the need to find mutually beneficial solutions to interactions and long-term resolutions as opposed to other alternatives where only one person gets their way. The habit concerns developing interpersonal relationships that in the long run aid both sides. To illustrate this further there are five possibilities when working with others based on the concept of 'winning' or 'losing':

1. *I win, you lose*: This relates to an authoritarian style of interaction based on the concept of competition. An authoritarian makes a demand of someone and they fulfil this demand.
2. *I lose, you win*: This relates to a permissive style of interaction, where an individual seeks personal strength from being accepted by others through doing what is asked of them, even if this means they have to make a sacrifice.
3. *I lose, you lose*: This relates to when one person aims to make the other person lose, even if this means that they similarly lose.

4. *I win, you win* (deal): A mutually beneficial approach based on building relation-ships to ensure proactive future working patterns.
5. *I win, you win* (no deal): If a mutually beneficial solution cannot be obtained, the 'best' compromise is not to compromise and to take no further action together.

Relating this to an educational context, consider the role of developing effective parent partnerships to develop the reading levels within your class. You could hold a workshop for parents one evening at a time when most are able to attend, with the workshop focus-ing on promoting a range of reading strategies to engage fully with their child's reading development. Such a workshop may initially focus on the reasons for promoting reading, informed from a research perspective where reading has been shown to develop expo-nentially with full involvement of parents. From this, there might be a series of strategies on discussing various forms of literature with their child along with associated strategies to promote reading. With the child placed firmly as the focus of the workshop, both the teacher and the parents are working together for a mutually beneficial purpose: that the child develops their reading ability. This may improve reading levels within the class, which is of benefit to the teacher, but also ensures that reading is a valuable shared experience at home, which the child and parent together can enjoy.

HABIT 5: SEEK FIRST TO UNDERSTAND, THEN TO BE UNDERSTOOD

How much do we actually hear when another person is communicating with us? As teachers, we tend to solve problems and can be at fault by aiming to solve problems before we understand the full context of the situation. As an example, take behaviour management. Within our class, we may see an unwarranted behaviour and, in turn, enforce a consequence (a quiet or even a loud word with the miscreant); yet do we, the teacher, really know why such behaviour happened and how we can prevent it happening again? The only way to fully understand what has happened is to look at the antecedent: what happened before the behaviour was exhibited? Have we actually diagnosed what has happened before we prescribe a solution? As a different example, a pupil may have difficulty in starting the work the class has been assigned, and as teachers our first course of action should be to review what the pupil has understood from the lesson and the task at hand, diagnosing where the issue may have arisen. How often do we listen and, when we do, are we actually hearing what is being said?

There are five levels of listening: ignoring, pretending, selective, attentive and empathic. It is this last level of empathetic listening that we should engage with more fully, where we listen with intent to fully understand the other person, in essence hearing what is being said with our ears, seeing what the person is saying by reading their body language, and internalising their communication through 'listening with the heart'. Although a greater personal investment has to be made by the listener, this may actually save future investment to correct misunderstandings at a later stage.

HABIT 6: PRINCIPLES OF CREATIVE COOPERATION (SYNERGISE)

If the previous habits of mutual cooperation through advocating a win-win approach along with attentive listening to others are in place, the sixth habit capitalises on these through seeking synergy, or cooperating with others effectively. In management speak, this could be deemed 'team-building'. Yet as a manager of a group of people (your class), fostering such a cooperative approach within your classroom should be advocated. Through ensuring such a cooperative (or synergetic), approach, more can be achieved: indeed, the word 'synergy' means that the whole is greater than the constituent parts.

Central to fostering such cooperation is building an attitude of mutual respect by developing an inclusive approach, where everyone is valued and encouraged to work at and then exceed their optimal level.

HABIT 7: PRINCIPLES OF BALANCED SELF-RENEWAL (SHARPEN THE SAW)

The final habit is about personal development: renewing your personal resources to ensure you can be as effective as possible. This relates to a range of different dimensions, for example, your physical, mental and emotional wellbeing. For example, ensuring that you are eating the right foods, are sufficiently hydrated, have periods of relaxation and quality sleep, while maintaining a degree of fitness, can help prepare you for the physical demands of teaching.

3.7 KEY FINDINGS FROM EFFECTIVE TEACHER RESEARCH

Drawing together a range of literature, Kington et al. (2014: 18) highlighted core features of effective teachers, specifically that effective teachers:

- are clear about their teaching and learning goals;
- are knowledgeable about curriculum content and the strategies for teaching it;
- communicate to their students what is expected of them;
- make expert use of existing teaching and learning materials in order to devote more time to practices that enrich and clarify the content;
- are knowledgeable about their students, adapting teaching to their needs and anticipating misconceptions to their existing knowledge;
- teach students metacognitive strategies and give them opportunities to master them;

- address higher- as well as lower-level cognitive objectives;
- monitor students' understanding by offering regular appropriate feedback;
- integrate their instruction with that in other subject areas;
- accept responsibility for student outcomes.

Conversely, from previous studies, ineffective teachers are characterised by:

- inconsistent expectations for different learners that are lower for disadvantaged students from low-socioeconomic-status families;
- an emphasis on supervising and communicating about routines;
- low levels of teacher–student interaction;
- low levels of student involvement in their work;
- students' perceptions of their teachers as not caring, unhelpful and under-appreciative of the importance of learning and their work;
- more frequent use of negative criticism and feedback.

The research by Professor Kington and her colleagues significantly extends previous exploration into the area, while developing their previous investigation into the project, 'Variations in Teachers' Work, Lives and Effectiveness' (VITAE). This was a four-year, large-scale mixed-methods project that involved teachers from both primary and secondary schools across England (Day et al., 2007; Sammons et al., 2007). Through Kington and her colleagues' work, they took the original definition of effectiveness from the VITAE project, exploring further their investigation into teacher effectiveness. Specifically, they demonstrated how effectiveness was relational in nature, that teachers' overall effectiveness depended upon how they experienced and managed personal and professional fluctuations. This resonates with themes we identify in Chapter 13 on resilience.

Kington and her colleagues identified ten key features of an effective teacher (Kington et al., 2014: 98–9); they:

- are highly motivated and committed to their students;
- value professional development and look for opportunities to improve their subject knowledge and teaching practice;
- build strong relationships with their students and ensure they know them well, so that they can understand their needs;
- are firm but fair, positive, open and supportive;
- communicate clearly with students, particularly in terms of expectations and feedback;
- have high expectations of their students;
- give positive praise and feedback to students, carefully adapted to the individual's needs;
- are flexible with lesson plans and are able to adapt and enrich lessons in ways appropriate for their students;

- plan creative, enjoyable and stimulating lessons to engage students in learning, by considering a range of different learning styles;
- encourage students to take control of their own learning and ask questions to guide their own intellectual enquiry.

The work by Kington et al. (2014) must not be overlooked given their research pedigree, the extent of the research, and also their continued research in the field. An example of such research that Kington and Buckler are currently engaged with is the International Comparative Analysis of Learning and Teaching (ICALT), along with notable academics such as Professor Daniel Muijs from the University of Southampton, and international colleagues led by Professor Wim van de Grift from the University of Groningen. ICALT is research based on quantitative analysis of teaching, where a series of core criteria are being used to research teacher effectiveness worldwide. While PISA (Programme for International Student Assessment) league tables may compare students' results, the research through ICALT will allow comparisons of the key features that distinguish effective teaching. Additionally, ICALT highlights on an individual basis developmental areas for the teacher to focus on for their continued improvement.

3.8 CONCLUSION

This chapter has sought to explore what is meant by 'effectiveness': the term is often used but without contextualising what it means. From a psychological perspective, a series of skills have been identified to promote best practice, although we would like you to frequently revisit what the term means as you progress through your career and as swathes of new information, insights, policies and practices become available. Central to the discussion has been the process of reflection, an aspect we will discuss in Chapter 4.

3.9 FURTHER READING

Ginnis, P. (2001) *Teacher's Toolkit: Raise Classroom Achievement for Every Learner.* Bancyfelin, Camarthen: Crown House Publishing.
This book includes many practical strategies that may be implemented within the classroom context. It also provides audit tools to aid teacher reflection on practice.

Kyriacou, C. (2014) *Effective Teaching in Schools: Theory and Practice* (4th edn). Oxford: Oxford University Press.
This seminal publication further discusses teacher effectiveness and effective classroom practice.

4

THE PHILOSOPHY AND PSYCHOLOGY OF PROFESSIONAL PRACTICE

CHAPTER OBJECTIVES

- Consider the explicit links between philosophy and psychology.
- Critically evaluate a variety of perspectives and how this informs your educational philosophy.
- Evaluate the role of reflection in professional practice and how this can be enhanced.

TEACHERS' STANDARDS

A teacher must:

8 Fulfil wider professional responsibilities

- make a positive contribution to the wider life and ethos of the school
- take responsibility for improving teaching through appropriate professional development, responding to advice and feedback from colleagues

4.1 INTRODUCTION

The first part of this book has discussed the role of perspective, specifically how perspective is shaped and influenced by a number of decisions that are required within the course of teaching. In the preceding chapters, various activities have requested your active engagement with the theories and concepts explored, asking you to consider a variety of perspectives and decisions, for example, on what makes an effective teacher.

Despite government guidance, the inspection process, the demands of the curriculum and the setting within which you work, what is paramount within the teaching profession is you and your sense of individuality. Although there are agreed conventions, policies and practice with many topics that affect teaching, it is how you work alongside and within such structures that defines you and your professional identity. Is this to say that we're advocating either educational anarchists who do whatever they like, or a clone of the teaching profession? Taking these two points on a continuum (Figure 4.1), an adaptive approach may be required. You may have a wonderful idea or initiative you would like to try out, only to meet resistance from others. Being secure in your own mind is one element, being able to justify this to others is another.

Clone   Educational
                                         Anarchist

Figure 4.1   Where are you on this continuum?

The following chapter encourages you to develop your personalised educational perspective, one based on who you are, what values you uphold and, indeed, the core being of you as a teacher. However, what has this to do with psychology? This will be explored below.

4.2 PHILOSOPHY AND PSYCHOLOGY

You may have been fortunate enough to have studied philosophy or psychology either as subjects prior to becoming a teacher, or during your teacher training. Yet the appearance of philosophy within a psychology textbook may seem out of context: whereas psychology professes to be scientific in nature, philosophy tends to be considered as less defined, perhaps wrapped up in the process of thinking. Indeed, this is exactly what we have been asking you to do in this first part (and will in the subsequent chapters too): presenting you with the psychological theory so that you are able to decide the most effective course of action in applying the psychological principles – in other words, thinking about psychology or the philosophy behind psychology.

Arguably philosophy has served as the foundation to psychology, for example, as in Cartesian dualism, whereby the mind and body are treated differently, compared to monism, where the mind and body are integrated as a whole. Further exploration of what defines philosophy can help to explain how it is related to psychology.

Various authors interpret philosophy in different ways:

'What is philosophy? This is a notoriously difficult question' (Warburton, 2004: 1)

'Thinking about thinking' (Ho]nderich, 2005: 702)

'Some kind of values by which we live our lives' (Craig, 2005: 1)

'To question and understand' (Nagel, 1987: 5)

'A particular way of thinking' (Strangroom, 2006: 7).

From these interpretations, there appears to be one overarching theme: that philosophy is concerned with the nature of thinking through questioning. Three specific questions are fundamental to philosophy, each relating to a specific branch of philosophy as detailed in Table 4.1.

Table 4.1   The three questions and the three associated branches of philosophy

Three philosophical questions (Craig, 2005)	Three branches of philosophy (Honderich, 2005)
What is there?	Metaphysics (the theory of existence, or the general nature of the world)
How do we know?	Epistemology (theory of knowledge, or the justification of belief)
What should we do?	Ethics (theory of value, or the conduct of life)

According to Blackburn (1999), philosophy by itself is useless: it needs to be applied. For example, thinking about what you are actually doing affects whether you do it at all, or how you do it. This in turn enables individuals to seek a sense of direction, through analysing and evaluating competing beliefs and preferences in order to justify the approach they decide to make (Honderich, 2005). Unfortunately education is full of such competing beliefs and preferences, for example, the synthetic versus the analytic phonics debate, 'real' books versus reading schemes, alongside a multitude of other decisions and competing demands the teacher faces throughout their career. We used 'unfortunately' in the preceding sentence, but a change of perspective could drop the prefix 'un-' and say that, 'fortunately', education is full of issues that make constant demands on the teacher. Framed through this perspective, perhaps one of the joys of teaching is that nothing stays the same; that macro changes on a global scale may inform curriculum development, which in turn affects the micro changes in schools and within us. Indeed, as you consider how your future teaching career unfolds, are you likely to stay the same teacher that you are now, or constantly adapt to and even initiate change? To what extent can another's perspective inform your perspective? In other words, has someone who has spent more time in the teaching profession become stagnant, or inspirational? Should we conform to practice 'because that's how it's always been done here', or should we seek to create an innovative practice based on a wider perspective?

Consequently, being able to make a judgement is very much based upon your individual philosophy, and this will be informed through an array of perspectives. In turn, this relates to the focus of this book: providing you with a variety of perspectives from which to select as the most appropriate to inform your teaching. However, keeping to the philosophical discussion for the time being, education has continually been shaped by different philosophical approaches, as is discussed in the next section.

4.3 PHILOSOPHY AND EDUCATION

There are four key philosophies that have influenced education: essentialism, realism, progressivism and existentialism. Each of these is explored briefly below.

ESSENTIALISM (KNOWLEDGE)

An essentialist approach to education centres on the commodity of knowledge: that there is a common core of knowledge which schools need to transmit to learners in a systematic way. The purpose of education is based on ensuring learners have the knowledge and skills to enable them to function productively in society. This approach has been informed through the work of Plato, René Descartes, Immanuel Kant, Georg Hegel and William Bagley, among others.

The teacher is seen as the authoritative source of all knowledge, and their role is to prepare learners to conform to society's accepted standards, while maintaining a sense of order. Within this approach, teachers help learners to explore their ideas within the confines of a syllabus. This is achieved through discussing, analysing and synthesising issues before applying such principles in practice.

REALISM (RULES)

A realist approach focuses on the development of meaning through empirically proven facts; reality is constructed on the assumption of natural laws. The purpose of education is deemed to enable learners to understand and apply shared principles to help solve problems. Some of the philosophers who have informed this approach are Aristotle, Bertrand Russell, John Locke and Alfred North Whitehead.

Within the realist approach, teachers are similarly perceived as authoritative, directing learners to use tried and tested methods to achieve results. The teaching method consists of a scientific approach, for example, making observations and generalisations based upon such observations, testing ideas and verifying outcomes.

PROGRESSIVISM (EXPERIENCE)

The progressive approach places the learner at the centre of the educational process, specifically in encouraging learners to find their own processes that achieve a desired outcome. Such an approach is based on action that gives rise to experiences, which the learner makes sense of. The goal of a progressive education is to enable the individual learner to pursue their needs and interests within a course of study. Jean-Jacques Rousseau, William James and John Dewey all discussed such a progressive educational philosophy. Teaching consists in facilitating the content and skills of learning:

for example, problem-solving, enquiry, working with others and being in charge of their own learning. Progressive teachers facilitate the learning process through offering suggestions and encouragement, while questioning the learner and helping them plan their course of action.

EXISTENTIALISM (VALUES)

An existentialist approach highlights the importance of the individual experience. Specifically, the approach helps learners to focus on their values or their truth. Education is centred on the needs of the individual learner, which might seem similar to the progressive approach, but it differs in relation to the role of the teacher. Within the existentialist philosophy, teaching is facilitated through enabling the learner to make choices, to ask their own questions and establish their own conclusions. Philosophers central to existentialism are Jean-Paul Sartre, Edmund Husserl, Maurice Merleau-Ponty, Martin Heidegger and Søren Kierkegaard.

IDIOSYNCRATIC OR ECLECTIC (MIXTURE)

Having read through the four philosophical approaches to education, does any single approach resonate within you? Perhaps more than one resonates; alternatively you may appreciate that each approach is useful within certain contexts. For example, you may decide that all learners need to be able to read, write and use mathematical skills (thus an essentialist philosophical approach) or that learners need to be able to test ideas appropriately through a scientific method (realist). You may decide that the joy of education is in the autonomy to explore our own ideas (existentialist), or that learning should be supported or facilitated to enable a learner to pursue their own interests (progressive). Indeed, are you attracted more to any one approach than another?

A fifth philosophical perspective can be introduced, called the idiosyncratic or eclectic approach, which is a combination of the above. This approach implies that a teacher will rarely keep rigidly to a single educational philosophy – that they will be informed by the different approaches depending on the context. Consequently most teachers have an eclectic philosophy.

ACTIVITY

Reread the paragraphs on the four philosophies (essentialist, realist, progressive and existentialist). Which one appeals to you most as a teacher? Try to sequence the four philosophies from the one that resonates most with you through to the one that resonates the least.

What actually is the point to all this philosophical discussion? If you were faced with the favoured interview question, 'What is your educational philosophy?', would you really reply, 'Well I have an eclectic approach where I tend to favour progressive education to a greater extent, mixed with a sizeable dose of existentialism, and a touch of essentialist and realist for good measure'? What does this actually mean to anyone who is not well versed in philosophical thought? Perhaps your philosophy is something more than being able to cite a few big words. Talking about big words, let us introduce one more while your brain is awash with them: heuristics.

4.4 HEURISTICS

According to Dawes et al. (2005), heuristics is concerned with the process of personal discovery: it is a method of enquiry and a way of knowing. Simply put, you could refer to it as your 'gut reaction', or 'what your heart tells you is right'. Such an internal reaction is subconsciously based upon the collected experiences that have shaped you since you joined the human population and how such experiences, thoughts, and reflections have shaped your inner knowledge.

This inner knowledge is commented on by Moustakas (1990: 9) who defines heuristics as 'a process of internal search through which one discovers the nature and meaning of experience and develops methods and procedures for further investigation and analysis'. Taking these definitions in relation to education, the implication is that we operate as teachers according to what resonates within us, what we feel is right. Of course, there may be times when we undertake a course of action only to be proved wrong. Yet assuming we learn from the experience, we are continuing to develop in order to pursue what is right. Indeed, this could be deemed the foundation of any professional practice: being told what to do, or being shown what to do, only goes so far; we actually have to experience this for ourselves and then make sense of it. No doubt you have already realised that there is a strong link between heuristics and the existentialist philosophy, if you have been reading closely.

So what is right? Although tutors, colleagues and experts can share their perspectives on teaching, they are not you. You are unique – given your experiences and attributes. If asked to do something that does not resonate with you, you have the choice of reluctantly trying it out, committing yourself fully to it or indeed engaging somewhere in between these points, deciding on whether to use the advice or not. However, the need to adhere to best practice is essential in the decision that you undertake.

In establishing your personalised educational perspective, let's return to some of the themes already discussed in this first part as a review. A series of statements and questions is presented below relating to the preceding chapters. If you are able to share your thoughts with another teacher (ideally one who has read the first three chapters), then you may be able to appreciate how different perspectives influence education.

- Chapter 1: Psychological perspectives – classical approaches

  o   Is the behaviourist approach the predominant approach within education?
  o   Does the psychodynamic perspective have any relevance today?
  o   Can human behaviour be purely explained through analysing the structure of the brain?
  o   The brain is just an information-processing unit.

- Chapter 2: Psychological perspectives – developing approaches

  o   Flow should be encouraged within all lessons to ensure appropriate learning.
  o   Maslow's hierarchy of needs is still relevant today.
  o   Should themes within transpersonal education be developed within the curriculum?
  o   More investment should occur within education and allied disciplines, as opposed to scientific exploration of space.

- Chapter 3: The teacher's perspective

  o   What do you think makes an effective teacher?

Such questioning is fundamental to the sense of identity of the teacher in order to define their individual philosophy. However, the concept of questioning and examining a range of information before deciding on the best course of action is fundamental not only to the teacher but to anyone who classifies their occupation as a 'profession'. The central concept to such questioning is commonly referred to as 'reflection'.

4.5 REFLECTIVE PRACTICE

The concept of reflection has become synonymous with professional practice, for example, in the teaching or healthcare professions (Dimova and Loughran, 2009; Dymoke and Harrison, 2008; Ghaye, 2010; Kinsella, 2009). Indeed, McIntosh (2010) comments that, without reflection, people cannot be successful within their profession. Reflection can be simply defined as a process of acquiring new knowledge through considering practical experience (Cottrell, 2017; Dyke, 2006).

A reason for the development of reflection is that the knowledge economy is continuing to develop at an astounding pace. Whereas in the past, certain theories stood the test of time, with greater levels of communication through such media as the internet, it is almost impossible to remain on the cusp of new knowledge. Fish (1998) highlighted the need for a greater depth of knowledge by professionals due to advances in technology and the associated increase in competencies to be managed. If you consider teachers who trained 20 years ago, they may still hold onto theories and concepts they covered in their teacher training days. However, engaging in continual reflection ensures that their practice is kept up to date, while enabling the teacher to consider areas for potential change within their practice (Hillier, 2009).

Furthermore, Fish (1998) asserts that the process of reflection is essential for the development of professional practice.

According to Jordi (2011), there is no single, prescriptive formula for developing reflection within professional practice; as Black and Plowright (2010) discuss, this is due to the multi-dimensional nature of the concept. Many models of reflection have been advocated, although most tend to be a reinterpretation of Kolb's cycle of experiential learning.

KOLB'S CYCLE OF EXPERIENTIAL LEARNING

A classical model of reflection often used to discuss reflection within adults is Kolb's cycle of experiential learning (Kolb, 1984). We see from the name of the model that the emphasis is on experience: that we learn best through actually trying something out in practice. Indeed, Kolb was not the first person to raise this issue: a saying ascribed to Confucius is, 'I hear, I forget. I see, I remember. I do, I understand.' Consequently, direct experience of an event enables us to fully understand the situation (Figure 4.2). After a direct or concrete experience there is a process of reflective observation prompted by the feelings and impressions that have arisen. The third stage is called abstract conceptualisation, as the person attempts to make sense of the experience. This leads to a process of planning what to do the next time a similar situation occurs, or active experimentation.

Looking at your training to be a teacher, you can attend numerous lectures, read numerous books or papers, and write numerous lectures theorising about education, yet it is only when you stand in front of a class of learners for your first lesson that you really start to understand what it means to be a teacher.

According to Kolb and Fry (1975), learning can occur at any one of the four points in Figure 4.2, although most often reflection will be initiated through concrete experience.

'What has happened?'
The event/experience
Concrete Experience

'How do I feel about this?'
Feelings/impressions
Reflective Observation

'Why did that happen?'
Making sense of the experience
Abstract Conceptualisation

'How can I best deal with the situation next time?'
Planning what to do next
Active Experimentation

Figure 4.2   Kolb's cycle of experiential learning (adapted from Kolb, 1984)

Furthermore they point out that, despite the model being called a 'cycle', it should be considered more as a continuous spiral. A further point they raise is that effective learning occurs when an individual utilises all four elements of the cycle, although they do report that people tend to favour one particular dimension. This has subsequently been assessed through the Learning Styles Inventory (Kolb, 1976).

The Learning Styles Inventory (LSI) categorises learners into the following:

- *Converger*. Favours abstract conceptualisation and active experimentation. Such learners tend to prefer the practical application of knowledge, using deductive reasoning to approach problems, and tend to be unemotional.
- *Diverger*. Favours concrete experience and reflective observation. Such learners tend to use their imagination to develop ideas and consider alternate perspectives, and prefer working with other people.
- *Assimilator*. Favours abstract conceptualisation and reflective observation. Such learners tend to prefer developing their own theoretical models through inductive reasoning, preferring to work with abstract concepts rather than people.
- *Accommodator*. Favours concrete experience and active experimentation. Such learners prefer to take risks and actually do things, reacting well to immediate issues through use of intuition.

Kolb's work has received criticism, notably from Jarvis (1995), in relation to the limited research conducted on the validation of the questionnaire, as the model does not apply to all situations. A further criticism of Kolb's model is that it has been perceived as too predominantly focused on the individual, with little attention to the social factors, as reflection does not occur without social interaction (Dyke, 2006). The model was subsequently developed into other questionnaires, for example, the Learning Styles Questionnaire (LSQ) (Honey and Mumford, 2000).

The LSQ enables the individual to consider their learning style as it relates to Kolb's cycle. (An internet search will enable you to find the questionnaire, which you can complete for yourself.) There are subtle differences through the renaming of categories of the four quadrants of learners, along with slightly different interpretations of the categories. As such, the four categories they suggest are:

- *Reflectors*: A preference to learn from activities that allow time to think things through for themselves. Such learners prefer lectures and to use reflective journals.
- *Theorists*: A preference to solve problems in a sequential manner. Such learners prefer reading, lectures and analysing case studies.
- *Pragmatists*: A preference to apply theory to practice to evaluate whether things work. Such learners prefer practical work where there is an explicit link between a problem and the task.
- *Activists*: A preference for new experiences and working with others. Such learners prefer small group discussions and problem-solving.

Perhaps the most significant difference between Kolb and Honey and Mumford is that the latter suggest that learners can enter and exit the cycle at any point of choosing without necessarily following through all four steps.

BROOKFIELD'S CRITICAL LENSES

One of the greatest problems with reflection is that it is informed, and so influenced, by our personal perception. As discussed in Chapter 1 (and throughout this book), our perception can be influenced by a range of factors. Brookfield's (1995) model suggests that there are four perspectives we should use to facilitate our reflection. These are: our personal perspective, our learners' perspectives, our colleagues' perspectives and theoretical perspectives from literature.

Taking the perspectives in turn, Brookfield is keen to assert that our personal perspective is a fundamental tool we should use: we can ask for advice from others, yet if this advice does not resonate, we are unlikely to act because we need to internalise all information, no matter where it comes from. As professionals, we should develop an awareness about whether something has worked productively or not, and seek to find ways to either repeat (or not repeat) various situations that have occurred.

Learners' perspectives similarly contribute to providing an informed perspective on the learning situation. They are the recipients of your planning, teaching and assessment, and so they can gauge whether the learning has been effective or not. If you think of the amount of times you are asked to evaluate your modules or courses, you will appreciate that the learners' perspective has become increasingly significant. However, as teachers, how often do we ask the learners in our classroom for feedback when we have just taken them through a double mathematics lesson on algebra? (This is not to say that algebra is not a most riveting subject if taught by a creative and enthusiastic teacher. It's just one we had problems with at school.) Consequently, taking learner feedback from any group of learners you work with can provide some interesting insights.

Our colleagues' perspectives can provide a high level of insight from which we can benefit. Discussing professional issues is a common practice within education, where we share our problems (and hopefully solutions) with one another. Indeed, through your training days as a teacher, you have probably been observed numerous times by tutors and class teachers who can not only provide feedback, but in turn encourage you to reflect on the lesson through a mentoring approach. Similarly, there will be occasions where we ask someone about their ideas for a lesson or a strategy to try out.

From the perspective of literature, we are able to determine what may theoretically be best practice. Indeed, analysis of literature (critically questioning what we have read to see whether it resonates with our experience and whatever else we have read, then taking the best bits) and subsequent synthesis (comparing ideas from one source to another to generate meaning) allow us to develop an informed perspective. We may in turn test the theoretical perspective in practice, or engage in dialogue with others to assess their views on the topic.

In essence, the four lenses can be considered like cogs within a machine, whereby each contributes holistically to the smooth operation of the machine. At times, one cog may become more dominant than another; at other times, there may be a tension between the cogs, which needs to be resolved. For example, if we think we have presented an effective learning experience and ask learners what they thought, their feedback may be swayed by the environment (too hot, too cold, uncomfortable chairs, time of the day), or indeed a range of personal factors (amount of sleep, hydration, hunger). It may be some time before they reflect on the core message, internalise this, then put it into action: thus they may not be able to perceive the immediate benefits of sitting in the lecture. However, through utilising what may be perceived as 'best practice' from discussion with colleagues and from reading through numerous pages of literature on facilitating effective learning situations, the learning experience may have been exactly what was required. In returning to the analogy of the cogs, we then need to consider whether they are working together or not. Perhaps we can further question the learners about the learning situation in the subsequent weeks to see if their perspective has changed.

The culmination of reflection is a process of transformation due to the changes in the individual's schemas, or thoughts, and their persona, or their character (Ghaye, 2010; Ghaye and Lillyman, 2000). Furthermore, Boud and Walker (1998) report that the main benefits of reflective practice are that it:

- provides a deeper understanding for teachers about their own learning and teaching style
- enables the teacher to be more effective
- enables the teacher to challenge traditional practices through considering new or alternate approaches
- develops a greater respect for diversity in applying theory to classroom practice.

Simply put, reflection is the process of making an informed decision on educational practice.

4.6 PUTTING THE PIECES TOGETHER

If we were not prepared to take risks, our knowledge and understanding would become stagnant. Consequently this book aims to encourage you to consider how to utilise the theories and perspectives to develop a workable model individually tailored to you.

The following activities are ways in which to tap into your creative potential to bring various themes together.

ACTIVITY   Your dream school

Aim: To consider the qualities of effective teachers.

Rationale: In 2011, a reality television series was screened on Channel 4 (UK) called *Jamie's Dream School*. The series questioned whether learners who had, for whatever reason, became disengaged with the education system could be influenced by certain teachers to become re-engaged. The teachers on the programme were perceived experts in their fields, with few working in the school sector (for example, Olympic athletes for physical education and outdoor pursuits, academics from Oxford University to teach history and Latin, famous musicians).

Instructions: The following activity asks you to decide who would work in your dream school. What teachers would you select to teach various subjects? Your choice of teacher can be one from the present, or the past ... but should be someone who actually existed. Assign an individual for each of the subjects listed in the box below.

Headteacher	English
Mathematics	Science
Information and Communication Technology	Art and Design
Geography	History
Religious Studies	Music
Design Technology	Physical Education
Other?	

As an example, for science, we would choose Johnny Ball (ask your parents/ grandparents if you have never heard of him; you may know him as the father of Zoë). For music, we would choose Alexi Murdoch (whose music has the trinity of soul, passion and meaning!).

Having assigned an individual to each of the subjects, consider the attributes that they all have in common. Aim to list two or three attributes for the collected group.

Borrowing loosely from the psychodynamic approach, specifically the concept of transference, we would ask whether the attributes you have highlighted from your dream school are attributes you would aim to represent within your teaching.

ACTIVITY   Who am I?

Aim: To identify inherent qualities that characterise you and in turn your personal philosophy.

Rationale: Authenticity may be described as the times when you share your natural being, rather than when you are struggling to be something you feel you 'ought to be', or what others say you 'should be' (Barber and Bates, 2000, in Dawes et al., 2005).

Instructions: Close your eyes and relax for a few moments. Then try to complete the following phrases by writing the first three things that come into your head for each phrase without allowing your 'inner critic' to censor them before you get them onto paper.

What I like about myself is:

 i)
 ii)
iii)

The things I am good at are:

 i)
 ii)
iii)

My best personal qualities are:

 i)
 ii)
iii)

What other people like about me:

 i)
 ii)
iii)

The qualities I most admire in other people are:

 i)
 ii)
iii)

I want to be remembered for:

 i)
 ii)
iii)

Read back over the statements you have written about yourself.

- Do they reveal any unexpected sides of you?
- What, if any, new insights do they give you?

Pick out those that are an essential part of who you are and what is unique and important about you.

Finally, ask a friend or your family what they like, respect and value about you.

ACTIVITY   Values

Aim: To identify personal values that are integral to your developing philosophy.

Rationale: Values are active principles that underpin the choices you make about how you think and behave, and the way you view other people and events. Personal values reflect individual identity, while shared values reflect those of your culture and environment.

Instructions: Relax and centre yourself, allowing your thoughts and concerns to quieten down. Note down any responses to the following questions:

- What matters deeply to you? For example, it may be a place, quality, activity or relationship.
- What inspires, excites or enthuses you?
- What angers or upsets you?
- What do you see as your main guiding principle or responsibility in life?
- What is important to you in a close relationship?
- What do you like to give other people?
- What do you need for yourself?

Spend a while reflecting on your responses to these questions. Then list those values that matter most to you.

Gandhi said: 'My life is my message.' Imagine that your values are a unique expression of you. What message is being expressed? Try to find a word or short phrase that sums up your message. It might be something like honesty, integrity, wholeness or love.

4.7 CONCLUSION

In returning to the introduction to this chapter, and indeed this first part of the book, your educational approach will be unique, albeit influenced by the theories you have read, how you have applied these theories in practice and how these influence your beliefs. No doubt as you continue to develop as a teacher, your experiences will continue to influence your perspective, but the key message being presented is that, as long as you are secure in what you believe – and more importantly, why – then you will continue to develop as a teacher if you are prepared to keep an open mind to new perspectives while reflecting upon your experiences.

4.8 FURTHER READING

Lovewell, K. (2012) *Every Teacher Matters: Inspiring Well-being through Mindfulness*. St Albans: Ecademy Press.
As Lovewell notes, teachers are central to education, yet little is invested in ensuring that they remain effective within the classroom. This book combines insights and practices to help maintain your effectiveness.

Part 2
THE INDIVIDUAL LEARNER

This part examines the neurological and physical development of the learner and highlights the importance of extending a teacher's knowledge beyond the psychology of teaching and learning. In order to understand how children acquire knowledge, one should have a knowledge of the structure and development of various systems within the human body, especially the central nervous system, which houses the 'master organ', the brain (Chapter 5). With an understanding of brain structure and function, it then becomes possible to explore perceptual and cognitive development (Chapter 6), along with social and emotional development (Chapter 7).

5

NEUROLOGICAL AND PHYSICAL DEVELOPMENT

CHAPTER OBJECTIVES

- Develop an understanding of the core stages of neurological and physical development within the child.
- Consider the key functions of the brain and how these affect the developing child.
- Identify how brain development affects the child and the impact of education.

TEACHERS' STANDARDS

A teacher must:

2   Promote good progress and outcomes by pupils

- be aware of pupils' capabilities and their prior knowledge, and plan teaching to build on these
- demonstrate knowledge and understanding of how pupils learn and how this impacts on teaching

5   Adapt teaching to respond to the strengths and needs of all pupils

- have a secure understanding of how a range of factors can inhibit pupils' ability to learn, and how best to overcome these
- demonstrate an awareness of the physical, social and intellectual development of children, and know how to adapt teaching to support pupils' education at different stages of development

5.1 WHAT IS DEVELOPMENT?

In a general sense, 'development' is defined in the Collins English Dictionary as 'the act or process of growing, progressing or developing'. In the strict sense, the term 'development' refers to maturation from birth through to death. Certainly, developmental psychology as a discipline covers human development across the whole lifespan. The tendency today, however, is to constrain study to a narrower period – developmental psychologists examine the childhood years from infancy to the beginning of adulthood. If one is seeking a pertinent marker of when child development ceases and adulthood begins, then perhaps the physical maturation of the human organism, at approximately 21 years of age, is as good a marker as any. By this age, all physical growth has finished, the human brain has reached maturity, all sensory systems are fully mature and the human organism is sufficiently equipped to inhabit its environment. In order to reach physical maturity, a child undergoes sequences of development that are pre-programmed by genetics and are therefore hard-wired into our DNA, with critical periods during which certain specific physical events take place, as you will see in the following sections.

In another way, development is also acknowledged to be functional. Maturation of structure goes hand in hand with maturation of function. In essence, we are talking here in terms of the progressive unlocking of abilities as the systems controlling those abilities become increasingly more developed, and these are defined in part by the opportunities present in or absent from the immediate environment. Progress, by its very nature of increasing sophistication in developing systems, enables the organism to unlock functionality in a diverse array of areas. It becomes possible to talk in terms of social, emotional and cognitive, or intellectual, development from a functional point of view. Figure 5.1 uses slightly more specific terminology to provide more depth for exploration. We will consider each of these elements of development. As you will begin to understand, it is our interaction with the environment that shapes us, not only as a species, but also as individuals. For example, if certain opportunities such as nutrition and learning are unavailable, we can hardly expect development in the true sense of the term to be as effective or progressive as it would be if those opportunities were available. Without adequate nutrition, the human body will not develop in a way that its genes would wish. More importantly, inadequate nutrition has implications for brain development, which is

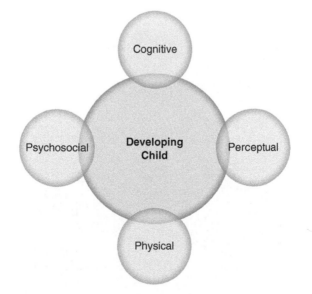

Figure 5.1 The components processes at work in the developing child

at the seat of functional development. This is why healthy eating programmes in schools are vital. It is clear that these are an attempt to combat the obesity problem that appears to be virulent, especially in Western societies. Yet few people stop to consider that healthy eating is equally important in helping our children's brains achieve their functional potential. But we digress.

5.2 PHYSICAL DEVELOPMENT IN THE DEVELOPING CHILD

There are several ways in which we can examine physical development. At the macro level, we can talk in terms of the overall growth of a child from infancy to late adolescence. We can relate this growth to somatotype or body shape, which has a tripartite classification system: mesomorphic (muscular appearance, narrow waist, broad shoulders), endomorphic (rounded, soft appearance) and ectomorphic (lean appearance, tall and thin). At the micro level, we can talk in terms of the maturation of numerous systems within the child's body. Essentially, we are examining structure, whether it is directly observable structure, such as height and weight (e.g. Mansur

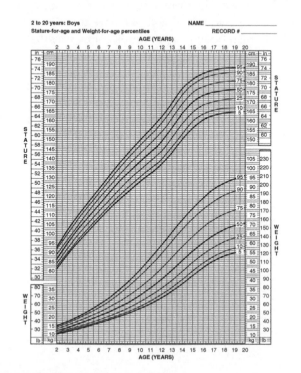

Figure 5.2a   Sigmoid curves or growth charts for boys

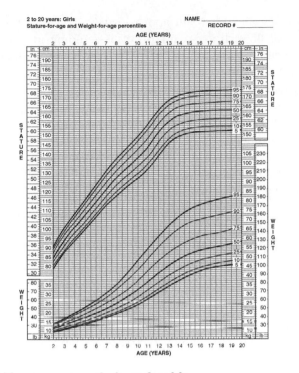

2 to 20 years: Girls
Stature-for-age and Weight-for-age percentiles

NAME _____

RECORD # _____

Figure 5.2b   Sigmoid curves or growth charts for girls

et al., 2015; Orden and Apezteguía, 2016), or whether it is indirect, unobservable, yet inferred, such as depth perception as an indicator of a developing visual system (e.g. Leisman et al., 2015).

A useful place to begin might be to look at what are termed 'growth spurts' in childhood (Towne et al., 2008). In order to do this we are able to draw upon existing, well-documented evidence. Figures 5.2a and 5.2b are known as 'growth charts', or sometimes, 'sigmoid curves' (referring to the shape of the curve, not as one of our learners once commented, because it was 'found by Sigmund Freud!').

These growth curves display the height and weight of both boys and girls, relative to their age throughout childhood. The approximately central bold line running through each of these reflects the average height and weight for children, and outer lines on both sides reflect the potential variability in height and weight. In this way, the growth charts show the complete spectrum of variation in children of different ages and the potential height and weight range within each year of childhood. We now have a set of norms that enables physical growth, by which we mean outward physical appearance, to be determined quickly, effectively and in relation to others of similar, or different, ages. It is possible to make predictions of height and weight in children, based on these growth charts. For example, looking at the chart for boys, an average 7-year-old boy should weigh approximately 22 kilograms and be approximately 1.2 metres tall. If such a 7-year-old boy is standing in front of us, we could fairly accurately predict that, by the age of 14, he will be approximately 52 kilograms in weight and approximately 1.7 metres tall. In contrast, looking at the chart for girls, an average 7-year-old girl should also weigh approximately 22 kilograms and be approximately 1.2 metres tall. Similarly, we could fairly accurately predict that, by the age of 14, she will be approximately 55 kilograms in weight and approximately 1.6 metres tall. While the differences between the ages of 7 and 14, for boys and girls, might not appear to be very distinct, there *is* a difference and the pattern is consistent. It is this pattern that helps researchers to explore functional aspects of development as a result of structural aspects of development.

5.3 DEVELOPMENT OF THE BRAIN

Strictly speaking, development of the brain could be subsumed into the section above on physical development. It could also be incorporated into the section on cognitive development later in this chapter. However, the brain, or to be more precise the central nervous system (CNS), which comprises the brain and spinal cord, lies at the core of our very existence. It is the organ that controls everything we do. If it gets damaged, we lose sometimes vital functions. As it develops, our capability to do more and more increases dramatically, especially during childhood (Reynolds and Horton, 2008). It is often said that children 'soak up' knowledge like a sponge. During childhood, brain development is fuelled by play, inquisitiveness, nutrition and rest/recovery (Anderson, 2015; Benton, 2010; Bergen, 2016; Pellis and Pellis, 2007; Piccolo et al., 2016; Tarullo et al., 2011).

As we will see in this section, having some knowledge of brain development is beneficial. To contextualise this for you, imagine that, as a teacher, you will have several dealings with an educational psychologist throughout your career. The educational psychologist may suggest observing the child-client in class, before chatting with the child to make an assessment. The educational psychologist will carry out a series of tests and assessments, some of which will be linked to the child's immediate needs, but some of which will be related to development of the brain. If a deficit can be traced to an anomaly in brain development, then we have an immediate link to a wealth of scientific literature on whichever functional area of brain development has been highlighted (Kolb and Whishaw (2015) is an excellent reference text in this area). Moreover, we then have access to a range of applied interventions that could be employed to assist the child (Minnis and Bryce, 2010). A teacher's knowledge of brain development, even if rudimentary, could prove useful in any discussions about these interventions (Hohnen and Murphy, 2016; Katzir and Paré-Blagoev, 2006). However, sometimes the advice and guidance given by those who are not directly involved with the child on a daily basis may not be as feasible as it sounds in theory. This can be seen, for example, in the culturally driven suggestion that epilepsy-sufferers in Ethiopia are better treated by seeking religious remedies and that a preferred alternative approach should be to provide special needs educational training courses for teachers (Gebrewold et al., 2016).

So, let's move on to understanding brain development at a level that may be all that you need, which of course does not preclude you from reading further and more widely outside of this book. In Chapter 1, we mentioned that, from the cognitive perspective, the brain has been likened to a computer. It is a storage device of epic proportions, greater than even the largest flash drive or memory stick that one could imagine. Indeed, its storage capacity appears endless (Huajin et al., 2010). The developing brain also has a wonderful propensity to repair itself. If damage is localised and the child is under approximately seven years of age, repair is generally rather effective, given adequate rehabilitation. This is known as neural plasticity, whereby the brain is sufficiently malleable for other regions to take over the functional aspect of the damaged area (e.g. Everts et al., 2010; Holland and Schmidt, 2015; Kolb and Gibb, 2011; Ortman et al., 2017). The same cannot be said for damage caused to the adult brain, which displays far less plasticity (Kleim and Jones, 2008). Sometimes there is little chance of restoring function after damage (Crews, 2008). Of course, neural plasticity is not an excuse to neglect protecting the brain in childhood. We have all witnessed countless children riding their bicycles without helmets. Until helmets become compulsory, we need to convince children that helmet-wearing is a cool thing (as proven by our Olympic cyclists), as one never sets out to receive a head injury and we can never know if a head injury is likely to occur on our child's next journey.

There are two key components to brain development: nutrition and stimulation. On one level, without appropriate nutrition the brain will not develop. But also, on a daily level, nutritional intake is the brain's fuel (Benton, 2010). Eating appropriate foods will provide the brain with glucose, which it needs to function properly. Hand in hand with nutrition is hydration, an often overlooked yet vital component of brain development. Increasingly, we see water-coolers in schools and children are allowed to bring water bottles into the classroom. Whereas the common view was that children could wait until break time for a drink, there is an increasing acceptance that adequate hydration aids learning (Johnston Molloy et al., 2008). Dehydration does not affect one immediately, but if allowed to develop it will affect all aspects of a child's performance, and may do so at the most inappropriate of times. To put this into perspective, if the human body becomes dehydrated by as little as 2 per cent, physical performance can be impaired by anything up to 20 per cent (Bar-David et al., 2009). If dehydration levels increase further, muscular strength is reduced and perception of effort is increased, which significantly increases fatigue (Judelson et al., 2007). This is how serious and important fluid intake is. In addition to these physical effects, dehydration directly impairs brain function – slowing down the decision-making processes, reducing skill and accuracy, reducing concentration and being detrimental to attention (Fadda et al., 2012; also see a review on the effects of hydration on health and wellbeing by Popkin et al., 2010), although perplexingly this may not be the same in developing countries familiar with water shortages (Trinies et al., 2016). It is this aspect of hydration that we can link to brain development in the wider sense of the term.

REFLECTION

Consider the importance of fluid intake for children in your charge. By advocating fluid intake you will be contributing to their brain development on a micro level. Also, make sure that you too drink as much as possible, even if you do not feel thirsty.

Brain development can be considered in two ways: from an evolutionary perspective and from a structural basis (Kolb and Whishaw, 2015). In evolutionary terms, the brain comprises three 'brains'. The oldest part of the brain is known as the 'reptilian brain'. It is the innermost part of the human brain as we know it today, situated at the top of the spinal column, and houses all the involuntary functions, such as respiration, that are vital to an individual's survival. From the reptilian brain, the palaeo-mammalian brain developed, so think of it as being built on top of the reptilian brain. This is the part of the brain that we know of today as the limbic system. It is a subcortical region (under the surface of the cerebral cortex) that houses emotion and contains 35 separate structures, interlinked by 53 tracts. The limbic system may have been the seat of Freud's id, the impulsive part of the personality that requires immediate gratification (discussed in Chapter 1). Interestingly, it is this part of the brain, in real terms, that comes to the foreground when under the influence of alcohol. We have all heard of someone who has embarrassed themselves at a party after having too much to drink. One could argue that it is the limbic system that is responsible for these unselfconscious, usually emotion-laden actions. The outer covering of the brain is known as the neo-mammalian brain, or cortex (which is Latin for 'bark' – as in tree, not dog). This is the newest part of the human brain; it houses cognition, memory, language, decision-making and many more of the processes that one takes for granted every day of one's life. We shall discuss the cortex in more detail later in this section.

To summarise brain development so far, we have explored the brain from the inside, or deepest region, outwards to the covering or cortex. This helps us to establish newer brain function from older brain function, but we would be doing an injustice to the story of the human brain if we left our exploration at that. There are at least three other ways of exploring the brain that may be useful in complementing this book: divisions of the nervous system, divisions of the brain, and structure and function of nerve cells.

It is important to understand where the brain fits into the nervous system as a whole. Humans have more than one nervous system, as depicted in Figure 5.3.

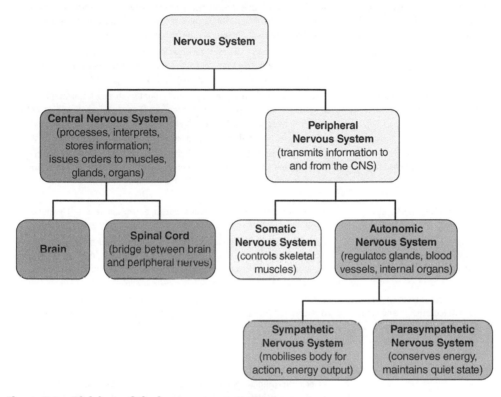

Figure 5.3   Divisions of the human nervous system

The significance placed on the central nervous system enables one to consider ten important principles of nervous system functioning (Kolb and Whishaw, 2015). These are summarised and adapted from Kolb and Whishaw. We have incorporated a column in Table 5.1 to provide applied examples for your use in this chapter.

We have already spoken about the central nervous system as comprising the brain and spinal cord. In addition there is the peripheral nervous system (PNS), consisting of the cranial and spinal nerves and peripheral ganglia, which are responsible for transmitting messages to the CNS and generated by the CNS. The PNS is also split into two divisions: the somatic nervous system and the autonomic nervous system (ANS). An easy way to remember what the somatic nervous system is responsible for is in the root of the word. 'Soma' is Greek for body and somatic means 'of the body'. The somatic nervous system is therefore concerned with the control of the body (not the brain), receiving input from sensory organs and executing movement.

Table 5.1   Ten principles of central nervous system functioning and their application to the developing child

Principle	Description	Example related to the child
Principle 1	The nervous system enables the brain to perceive the world and produce movement.	A child's behaviour is directly related to the way he or she perceives their world. No two children will perceive the world in exactly the same way. We might see the colour green, you might see the colour turquoise.
Principle 2	The nervous system is subject to neuroplasticity and is thus constantly changing.	A child's experience changes the organisation of their brain. Learning creates memory traces, which form connections to other memory traces. These connections are strengthened through practice.
Principle 3	A large number of circuits in the brain are 'crossed'.	A child has two brains! A left brain and a right brain, or a left hemisphere and a right hemisphere. Sensory information enters one hemisphere and crosses to the other hemisphere, e.g., if the child hears something with their right ear, the input will be transmitted to the left side of the brain for processing.
Principle 4	The central nervous system functions on multiple levels.	Children are able to control their behaviour on different levels. As brain development occurs, behavioural control increases as does the opportunity to refine behaviour, e.g., an infant's 'leg thrashing' motions are refined into walking or running.
Principle 5	The brain is symmetrical *and* asymmetrical.	The hemispheres may look identical but each hemisphere is also asymmetrical. Control of function, such as language, is localised to the left hemisphere.
Principle 6	Systems in the brain are organised hierarchically *and* in parallel.	Information entering the brain is processed at a basic level, before being sent onwards for further processing, hierarchically, elsewhere. At each processing point, the meaning of the sensory input is enriched by the integration of information about the stimulus from other, non-hierarchically linked regions of the brain.
Principle 7	The nervous system comprises segregated sensory and motor divisions.	In the central nervous system, sensory regions are located in a dorsal arrangement (upwardly on the cortex) and motor regions are located in a ventral arrangement (towards the front).
Principle 8	Sensory input is divided for motor control and for object recognition.	Perceiving information about objects is independent from perceiving information for movement. It is not as important to perceive that one will be hit by a car, a van or a lorry as it is to perceive that one is about to collide with a moving object. Perceiving for motor control is a basic evolutionary characteristic. Perceiving for object recognition is a more recent evolutionary characteristic.
Principle 9	Brain function is localised *and* distributed.	A child's language develops in many regions of the brain, i.e., it is distributed. Certain aspects of the umbrella term, language, can be traced to specific areas of the brain. Speech production, for example, is localised to Broca's area in the left hemisphere.
Principle 10	The nervous system juxtaposes excitation and inhibition.	The child's brain inhibits certain actions in order to produce other actions. For example, in order to pick a pencil up (excitatory action), the brain stops the hand from forming a fist or from clapping (inhibitory), hence this is juxtaposition.

Source: adapted from Kolb and Whishaw (2015)

It is a nervous system under conscious, voluntary control. In contrast, the ANS acts as its label implies. It is autonomic, involuntary and automatic. The ANS functions without us having to think about it and is responsible for activities such as regulating smooth muscle (skin), cardiac muscle (the heart) and glands (hormone release). The term 'regulation' also implies that something can increase or decrease, and the

ANS is further split into two divisions: the sympathetic branch and the parasympathetic branch.

Although the ANS generally functions effectively, the regulatory mechanism of the ANS is not always as accurate as one might like. This inaccuracy can sometimes lead to what is known as parasympathetic rebound – indeed, you may have already seen an example of this without realising it. Imagine the scene. A group of learners has been outside at break time, playing and larking around, perhaps in an out-of-bounds part of the school. They have got overly excited, or we may say that their sympathetic nervous systems are working above and beyond the call of duty. Adrenaline is rushing through the bloodstream as they are involved in prohibited activities. As the bell rings, signalling the end of break time, the learners return to the school building and, upon entering, one learner suddenly faints. The first aid procedures are followed and the learner regains consciousness fairly quickly. This is parasympathetic rebound in action. What has happened here is that the sympathetic nervous system has acted to stimulate smooth muscle, cardiac muscle and glands as a way of dealing with the requirements of the activity. Once the activity has ceased, it would be inefficient for the sympathetic nervous system to maintain its actions at this level, so the parasympathetic nervous system counteracts the actions of the sympathetic branch. It returns everything to its previously normal level, or to a state of homoeostasis (balance or equilibrium). Sometimes, the parasympathetic branch misjudges exactly where the previous level was and goes a little too far past it, hence the fainting episode.

Figure 5.4 shows the target organs of the ANS and their functions based on sympathetic or parasympathetic control. Some examples of sympathetic or parasympathetic control are readily observable. For example, dilation of the pupils is a sympathetic response, as is increased heart beat and perspiration. Each of these actions is survival-related (Carlson, 2012). They prepare the body for 'fight or flight', the in-built mechanism all species have to deal with a situation of danger or excitement. Less observable is relaxation of the bladder. Nevertheless, you now know that relaxation of the bladder is under sympathetic nervous system control. This won't help you when faced with a young child who may have wet themselves with excitement, but at least you will have a scientific explanation for it. Once the 'fight or flight' situation has ended or has been removed, pupils constrict again, heart beat slows and perspiration diminishes or ceases altogether (Bradley et al., 2008). The parasympathetic branch has regulated each of these processes to previous levels, and a state of homoeostasis returns, until next time.

Earlier, we discussed the structure of the brain itself from an evolutionary perspective (Hellige, 2006) and mentioned the reptilian, palaeo-mammalian and neo-mammalian brain(s). Using the accepted terminology of today, we can talk more in terms of the divisions of the brain as forebrain, midbrain and hindbrain, which correspond to the evolutionary divisions mentioned above. However, as Table 5.2 shows, these divisions can be further subdivided. You will notice that each subdivision includes the root

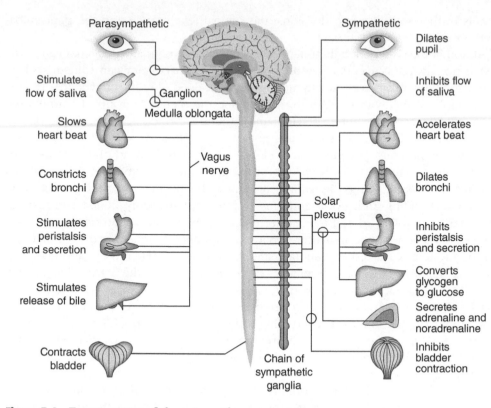

Figure 5.4   Target organs of the autonomic nervous system

Table 5.2   The major divisions and subdivisions of the human brain

Major division	Subdivision	Structure	Example behaviour
Forebrain	Telencephalon	Cerebral cortex	Language deficit
	Diencephalon	Thalamus, hypothalamus	Sensory filtering, aggression
Midbrain	Mesencephalon	Tectum, tegmentum	Auditory and visual processing
Hindbrain	Metencephalon	Cerebellum	Fine motor coordination
	Myelencephalon	Medulla oblongata	N/A. Deals with vital survival function

'encephal[on]', which simply means 'pertaining to the brain'. We have included the major divisions to contextualise the subdivisions. An example of relevant structures is also included. These will be related throughout the book to day-to-day observable behaviours so that you will gain an appreciation of which brain regions are responsible for or contribute to the behavioural issue you are observing.

5.4 HEMISPHERIC LATERALISATION AND LOCALISATION OF FUNCTION

Lateralisation, or laterality, is derived from the root 'lateral', which means 'of or relating to the side'. It moves away from the mid-line. So, when people talk of lateral thinking, they mean don't stick to the normal way of thinking (the mid-line) but instead focus elsewhere. If you take the phrase 'thinking outside the box' as being similar to the phrase 'lateral thinking', you will remember the directional nature of lateralisation. After this analogy, the term 'hemispheric lateralisation' becomes clear and it is simple to say that it refers to the left and right hemispheres of the brain, which are situated, by their very location, away from the mid-line, or corpus callosum: the bundle of interconnecting nerve fibres allowing for the transfer of information from left hemisphere to right hemisphere.

One might argue that we possess two brains, a left brain and a right brain (Springer and Deutsch, 1993). An ever-increasing body of evidence suggests that each brain, or hemisphere, is responsible for particular processes or functions (Behrmann and Plaut, 2015; Nowicka and Tacikowski, 2011; Spironelli and Angrilli, 2009; Xiao et al., 2016). At a very general level, we can say that the left hemisphere is the analytical, rational, sequential hemisphere. It is the hemisphere that has enabled us to structure this book in a logical sequence (we hope) for you to understand. The right hemisphere, in contrast, is synthetic, creative and holistic. It is the hemisphere that has enabled us to give life to this book so that it is not simply a boring volume of dry facts. The two hemispheres complement each other in allowing us to produce what you have in front of you now. Appreciation for music and art has been associated with right hemisphere function. Those in the neuroscience community would no doubt say that this distinction between the left and right hemispheres is overly simplistic and perhaps naive in its thinking, and of course we would agree. Compartmentalisation and segmentation is not as simple as that. However, for the purposes of acquiring a general understanding it will suffice. One does not need to know how a car works in order to drive it. Having a basic understanding of some of the functions of how that car works may improve the way in which one drives the car.

On this basis, let's compartmentalise and segment a little more. Using the correct terminology, we would say that language is lateralised to the left hemisphere (Geschwind and Levitsky, 1968; Xiao et al., 2016). For an interesting research paper questioning the idea of lateralisation, see Pinel and Dehaene (2010). We could also say, for example, that speech production, which is but one element of the term 'language', is localised to the left frontal lobe (Judas and Cepanec, 2007). So, we need to consider what is known as localisation of function. This principle is such that all functions can be located approximately within one or other of the four lobes of the brain. These are defined 'geographically' in the brain, based on specific landmark features, known as fissures and sulci (grooves in the cortex). As Figure 5.5 shows, the frontal lobe is situated at the front of the head, with the parietal lobe behind it, the temporal lobe underneath the parietal lobe and the occipital lobe at the very back. It is easy to remember the location of the occipital lobe because its primary role is vision and it is the furthest lobe away from the eyes, which is ironic and hence rather memorable.

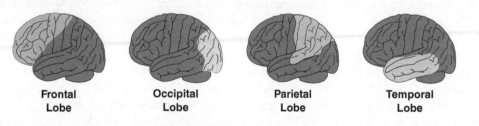

| Frontal | Occipital | Parietal | Temporal |
| Lobe | Lobe | Lobe | Lobe |

Figure 5.5   The four lobes of the brain

Table 5.3 serves as a quick reminder of some of the localised functions that may be useful in the context of teaching. We have mentioned vision already. Bringing this into the playground, it is not surprising to consider why children say that they can 'see stars' after they have just fallen over and bumped their heads. If the fall was backwards, then the occipital lobe would be the first point of contact with the ground. As a result, 'seeing stars' is quite a logical symptom of making contact with the ground at this point.

Table 5.3   Generic localised functions of the brain

Lobe	Example behaviour
Frontal	Speech production
Parietal	Integrating sensory information into unitary concepts
Occipital	Visual processing
Temporal	Auditory processing, memory, olfactory (smell) processing

In functional terms, information is transmitted from the senses to the primary sensory and motor cortex, so these areas are responsible for the initial sensation of stimuli. Perception, learning, memory, decision-making and responding to the sensory stimuli take place in what are known as association areas. If we accept that the occipital lobe contains both primary and association cortex, then this lobe is responsible for vision. For this reason, it can be considered as the visual cortex and is perhaps the reason for humans being a visually dominant species. The parietal lobe combines inputs from different senses into what is known as a single 'percept' (hence, perception). So, for example, the sensory systems responsible for the sight, sound, touch and smell of a dog are combined to inform us that we are in the presence of a dog.

The brain integrates the information into a single percept. It does not tell us that there are four unrelated pieces of incoming information. Of course, to everyone who knows what a dog is, this seems obvious. That is our point. We take for granted many of the functions that our brains perform. This chapter should help you to appreciate the complexities of what is taking place under the surface. The frontal lobe serves an executive function. It makes decisions, acts upon advice from other regions of the brain and has been linked to personality. In psychology we use the unfortunate case of Phineas Gage to highlight what can happen if the frontal lobes are damaged. In 1848, Phineas Gage worked as a construction worker for a railway company and suffered a horrific accident when some explosives ignited, causing an explosion (Harlow, 1848, 1868; Wilgus and Wilgus, 2009). A tamping iron (a type of iron rod) was propelled through Gage's skull, entering near his left eye and exiting through the top of his head, causing a significant amount of damage to both frontal lobes. Miraculously, Gage survived the accident and made an excellent physical recovery. However, Gage was no longer able to make long-term decisions. His personality also changed and he became more aggressive than before the injury. The temporal lobes are linked with auditory processing, memory, olfactory (smell) processing and object recognition as well as the limbic system, the structures underneath the layer of cortex responsible for regulating emotion.

An example will highlight temporal lobe function. Imagine walking through a woodland, or perhaps a Forest School setting. As you walk along the path, you encounter something scurrying across the path in front of you. What happens next? Your temporal lobes will be working out what you have just encountered. Let's analyse the process. The rustling sound you heard as the object moved across the path is processed in the auditory cortex. If you saw the object as it moved, the occipital lobe will already have processed basic information regarding the object, but the temporal lobes are now piecing the information together in greater detail to recognise the object, and this object recognition is an interaction between what you have seen and the material held in your memory (Neisser, 1976). Let's imagine that the object has now been recognised as a grass snake. What happens next will be determined largely by how you feel about encountering this creature. Those of us with a fear of snakes would undoubtedly begin to have some form of emotional panic reaction, whereas non-phobics might feel excited about seeing something interesting. Others may feel nothing and simply continue walking. The temporal lobes have put a lot of effort into this situation and they do this constantly during waking hours; indeed, they also perform certain functions during sleep, such as basic auditory awareness (Hamzelou, 2010; Wilf et al., 2016).

We have included this information not to confuse, but rather to get you to start thinking about day-to-day activities and behaviour that occur in the classroom or during the school day. This can range from the child who is acting aggressively, or the child who appears not to be concentrating (but in actual fact you suspect has a hearing deficit that may or may not be corrected), through to the child whose letter formation in handwriting lessons is progressing poorly, or the child who is experiencing linguistic difficulties. Each of these acts, behaviours or deficits may be linked back to your knowledge of how the human brain is structured and how it functions.

If we look at the right-hand column of Table 5.3 we can illustrate this nicely. A language deficit would be related to a deficit in the forebrain. It is difficult to pinpoint this exactly, since the term 'language deficit' is far too broad. But if you knew that a child had difficulties with speech production, a little further reading would point you in the direction of Broca's area (named after Paul Broca, in 1861). Alternatively, the educational psychologist assessing the child may reach the conclusion that the child is suffering from aphasia. Further reading will inform you that aphasia is a partial or complete loss of linguistic ability (Johnson and Cannizzaro, 2009). You will also discover from your reading that the specific form of aphasia known as Broca's aphasia is localised to the left frontal lobe. Alternatively, you may have a suspicion that a child may be experiencing difficulties in understanding what you say. This could be for one of a number of reasons. For example, the child may be suffering a hearing impairment, in the structures contained in the ear, or it may be neurological and the child may be suffering from a midbrain deficit, leading to an inability to process auditory information appropriately. The child may be suffering from a different type of aphasia, known as Wernicke's aphasia, named after Carl Wernicke in 1874, or conduction aphasia (see Martin (2006) for a review of research into sentence processing). Wernicke's aphasia is a neurological comprehension deficit, emanating from damage to Wernicke's area in the left temporal lobe, which as we mention elsewhere is partially responsible for storing memories. Equally, you may notice during the course of classroom activities that a child struggles to manipulate small objects, or continually drops a pencil. This may be further supported by receiving reports from parents that the child is clumsy. While this may simply be a normal motor-developmental characteristic of a younger child developing coordination skills (as we discuss in the section on motor development), it could be a symptom of a neurological deficit in motor coordination, such as developmental coordination disorder, otherwise known as dyspraxia (Carslaw, 2011; Jokic and Whitebread, 2011). If this is combined with the fact that there is evidence that the child received an injury to the back of his or her head at some time, perhaps in a car accident, you will know from your operational knowledge of the location of the cerebellum (at the back of the head just above the top of the neck area) that deficits in fine motor may (and we stress, only may) be a reasonable characteristic to observe.

One thing we should point out is that it is beneficial to compartmentalise structure and function in order for us to learn the material, almost in rote fashion, or perhaps by using a mental mind-map or spider figure. In reality, localising function, or to use the correct terminology, localisation of function to specific areas, is not as clear-cut as this. The brain functions as a system, the CNS (Pinel, 2010). Regions within the brain function as systems and these systems interact with other systems within the body, such as the endocrine system (hormones) and the immune system (fighting 'invaders'). It is not possible to say that certain areas house certain functions, because, as we explained when we discussed neural plasticity, other regions of the brain compensate for loss or damage. This compensation may not be complete and sometimes does not happen at all, but the brain's systems will endeavour where possible to replace the deficit.

This section has been especially complicated. We have endeavoured to explain it in an applied manner so that it is useful rather than off-putting. We are not expecting you to acquire the knowledge of a neurosurgeon or neuroscientist. What we are asking of you is to establish a working knowledge, something that will be useful to you as a teacher. We have spoken to many teachers who have had dealings with educational psychologists over the years and who have reflected on their lack of basic knowledge of the brain. Remember that one of best people to provide information on a child under these circumstances is the person who sees most of the child during the school day. That person is the class teacher. When we both started in our professions, we knew nothing about the brain. So we are testament to the fact that it is possible to build up knowledge of this seemingly complicated area, to a respectable point. The only *caveat* we would also offer is that we know our own limitations and would not expect to discuss issues beyond our operational knowledge.

5.5 COMMUNICATION BETWEEN NEURONS

Having explored the structure of the brain, we are now ready to take you further, by exploring the structure and function of nerve cells, or neurons, within the brain. When we talk about function, we can split the discussion further, into neural generation and neural propagation (Carlson, 2012). Neural generation is the process whereby a nerve cell, or neuron, activates a neural message. It is a starting point for neural communication and is where an action potential is triggered within the neuron, in response to a sensory stimulus. Once an action potential has been generated, the electrical signal is transmitted down the neuron to its end-point. Neurons do not touch each other, so the message cannot simply be transmitted from one neuron to another. The message has to cross a gap, known as a synapse or synaptic cleft. A chemical substance, known as a neurotransmitter, is released into the gap at the end of the neuron (the pre-synaptic neuron) and this neurotransmitter crosses the gap and stimulates the next neuron in line. In reality this does not take place on a neuron-by-neuron basis, but rather with many thousands of neurons in functional clusters acting together. Once this chemical has crossed the gap and stimulated the next neuron, this causes another action potential to be generated in that neuron (the post-synaptic neuron). The process continues until the message, the electrochemical signal, reaches its destination, whichever systems or regions in the brain have been activated by the stimulus. The result will be some form of action or behaviour in response to the stimulus, so one might answer a question, in response to the auditory stimulus requiring an answer, or one might shake hands, in response to the visual stimulus of someone putting their hand out on meeting for the first time. The examples we could use are endless and we are sure that you understand our point. If you struggle with the biological aspects of psychology, but understand the process of neural communication as we have described it above, then you will have gained a valuable foundation upon which you can begin to build as your knowledge increases (see Fellin, 2009). We take the view that if you wish to seek an explanation for a child's behaviour, there may be an underlying component that you cannot observe but that you might be able to understand by thinking about the behaviour from a biological perspective. For example, if you have been told that a child has been prescribed medication, such as methylphenidate (Ritalin) for ADHD, our introduction to neural communication here will help you to understand how Ritalin exerts its influence at the synapse and on resulting behaviour (Mercugliano, 1995). (See Agay et al. (2010) for behavioural effects in adults; or see Singh (2008) for a sociohistorical account of the diagnosis of ADHD and the prescription of methylphenidate.) In short, Ritalin acts on the neurotransmitter dopamine by preventing reuptake. From our explanation of synaptic transmission, this simply means that dopamine remains in the synaptic gap for longer, enabling it to continue stimulating the next neuron, or bundle of neurons. (For a further discussion of ADHD, please refer to Section 9.6.)

5.6 DEVELOPMENT OF THE MOTOR SYSTEM

As the brain develops, so to do aspects of the motor system (Haibach et al., 2011). This development unlocks the capability to execute an increasing range of movements as the infant progresses through childhood. The notion underlying this progressive unlocking of movement capability is that neonates embark on a journey of motor discovery, passing through a set of phases of motor development, as described by Gallahue and Ozmun (2011). In Gallahue and Ozmun's hourglass model (which can be freely found on the internet with the search term 'Gallahue's hourglass model'), the approximate age ranges can be seen on the left of the hourglass and corresponding phases in the centre. Each phase can be further subdivided into stages, which helps observers to differentiate movement developments within each of the approximate age ranges, or phases. We will explain each of these phases, together with their relative stages, in turn.

The first stage in motor development is known as the reflexive movement phase (in utero to one year old). During the initial part of this phase, the embryo starts to display reflexive movements. Pregnant mothers show great delight when they feel their unborn baby kicking for the first time. This is an example of a spontaneous movement and certainly in the infant (post-birth) is actually more than what we perceive as an individual kick. If we place an infant on his or her back (the supine position) the child will tend to display what is called supine kicking. This is the apparently spontaneous thrusting of their legs in a thrashing or kicking motion (Thelen, 1985, 1995).

However, this motion is far more complex than it appears and it has been suggested by Thelen that it is a precursor to walking. In breaking down the components of supine kicking, there are some surprising findings. Thelen and her colleagues discovered rhythm and coordination in the kicking actions. Instead of uncontrollable limb movements, the hip, knee and ankle joints move in cooperation with each other. Although reflexive, surely it is no coincidence that the hip, knee and ankle act in a similarly coordinated manner during walking from early childhood. During infancy, supine kicking can simply be a one-legged action, or it can be two-legged, which certainly would seem to be an appropriate practice exercise for later walking. It is worth remembering at this point that the infant is unable to stand or hold its own body weight, so the fact that he or she is in the supine position ensures that weight distribution and balance do not prohibit or restrict movement capability. The infant is adapting to their environment using the reflexive actions unconsciously available to them, and preparing for the attainment of motor milestones later in infancy and beyond. We will return to motor milestones later in this section. One *caveat* to remember here is that we are not suggesting that supine kicking is walking in a supine position. Although similarities exist, as mentioned above, they are just that: similarities, not exact blueprints. For example, in adult walking, the muscles involved in flexing (flexors) and extending (extensors) the limb are activated in an alternating manner. In contrast, in infants, the flexors and extensors are activated simultaneously. Equally, the infant tends not to move both limbs in sequence, as one would in walking, but rather in unison. Coordinated limb action begins to develop after around six months and it is this element of learning coordination that infants take into later stages and phases of motor development. Poor coordination in an earlier phase may lead to difficulties in acquiring more complex motor skills in later phases.

Reflexive movements do not occur randomly, but as a result of the presence of a stimulus. Reflexive movements are still involuntary – they manifest themselves in the absence of conscious control – but there is no processing of information taking place. Blinking is an example of a reflexive movement that we have made through our lives thus far and will continue to do until the day we die. Blinking is an excellent mechanism for providing the eye with sufficient moisture to function effectively, to remove particles that may have entered its surface, to provide a comfortable working environment for it. For those of you who wear contact lenses, you blink more frequently than people who don't, otherwise your eyes would feel dry and your contact lenses would become uncomfortable. Although you have to remind yourself to blink more when you first start wearing contact lenses, it quickly becomes the norm. Essentially, the reflexive action of blinking is not something that humans need or would wish to have to think about. Breathing is another example of a reflexive movement, and we are sure there is no need to explain why this should be so.

With the exception of breathing, which quite evidently is a prerequisite for life, these reflexive behaviours are species-specific and appear to be innate. These behaviours possess obvious benefits for members of the species and, if we adopt a Darwinian perspective, are just as much a part of natural selection for humans as they are for any other species. The only significant difference, perhaps, is that humans no longer need to learn to walk and then run, in order to avoid being eaten by predators from early infancy, in contrast, for example, to gazelles, which are seemingly pre-programmed to stand within minutes of birth. Rather, humans invest a huge amount of time in protecting their offspring for many years, before they leave the nest. This is quite uncommon in the animal kingdom and is rather cost-ineffective in Darwinian terms.

Reflexive movements can take one of three forms: primitive, postural and loco-motor. Primitive reflexes, unlike spontaneous movements, are simple reactions or responses to stimuli. Since they are responses to incoming stimuli, they are localised rather than generalised and can be observed in the sucking action of infants from birth to 6 months of age, in response to stimulation of the face by touch. Palmar grasping can be observed during the first 4 months: in response to stroking of the hand, the infant contracts their fingers around the person's hand who is stroking it. Similarly, plantar grasping can be observed during the first 12 months: in response to stroking of the foot, the infant contracts their toes around the hand of the person who is stroking it. Postural reflexive movements are those movements involving the gravity-based reflexes of maintaining posture in the infant's environment, whether this is maintaining an upright, seated position, or moving to help the infant roll over. Such postural reflexes become increasingly less significant as the infant progresses through childhood. Nevertheless, remnants of postural reflexes remain, as you will know if you are about to fall from a bicycle or a narrow rock ledge or path that you may be walking along. Humans are wired in such a way as to prevent damage to themselves, by correcting postural imbalances as far as is possible. Of course, we are not always successful, but we do have this period of the reflexive movement phase to assist us in times of need.

The final form of reflexive movement is locomotor reflexive movement and this comprises three distinct reflexes: crawling, stepping and swimming. Having established some degree of postural control, the infant begins to explore his or her surroundings in a much wider sense. No longer is there a restriction on distance in a basic sense. The immediate world has become a much larger place. No longer is the infant confined to the boundaries of a mat or baby chair. Crawling enables the infant to move from point A, usually the mat, to point B, wherever choice or parental control allows. Indeed, one could view crawling as being a precursor to bipedal locomotion; humans are bipeds since they have two legs. It is a motor milestone. Without the ability to crawl, or locomotor, from point A to point B, standing upright and unaided before walking is unlikely to happen. Equally, stepping is the reflexive action of moving for-ward in space and this also relies on postural stability. The swimming reflex can be observed if an infant is placed into, or over, water. This reflex, whereby the arms and legs perform a swimming action, emerges from approximately 11 days through to 5 months of age. Whether it is actually a swimming action or whether it is a pattern of movement that we interpret as swimming, because it occurs in the contextualised setting involving water, is not certain. However, if infants are placed into the water, they exhibit the basic movement pattern that one would associate with swimming. As with other reflexive movements, the swimming reflex tends to be extinguished a long time before the voluntary act of learning to swim occurs in children older than infants.

The reflexive movement phase gives rise to the rudimentary movement phase, which takes its name from the word 'rudiment', meaning a beginning or first emerging appearance of something (Reber et al., 2009). In this instance, it is the beginning of motor skill acquisition. It is the point at which involuntary, reflexive actions drop away and are replaced by voluntary movements under conscious control. Of course, we use the word 'control' loosely at this point, since there is much trial and error, many falls and knocks occur and the infant has not perfected the later-phase skills. Nevertheless, the rudimentary movement phase is where reflexive actions are transformed into something more meaningful for the infant. It is not known whether the reflexive actions are inhibited before rudimentary actions take over, or whether various physical changes, such as changes in body proportion or weight, serve as constraints to progress (Thelen, 1985). For example, if a change in limb weight is not accompanied by an increase in muscular strength to accommodate the now heavier limb, then functionally the change in limb weight will impede development rather than assist it, until the corresponding increase in muscular strength is present. Along with constraints in terms of both muscular and postural development, other constraints include the development of the central nervous system and a corresponding increase in the child's ability to process sensory information

In essence the younger the child, the greater the number of constraints there are. As the child matures, or more accurately, as the child's systems mature, the more these constraints are relaxed or removed and the more freedom the child has to move around in his or her environment. The constraints serve as 'rate controllers': mechanisms that control the extent to which children are able to move around safely and efficiently within their environment. From an evolutionary perspective, rate controllers may serve to keep the infant safe until bodily systems have developed sufficiently.

Karl Newell (1986) proposed that three types of distinct yet interrelated constraints exist, exerting influences over motor development: individual, environmental and task constraints (Figure 5.6). Individual constraints can be further categorised into structural and functional constraints. A structural constraint refers to physical attributes of a child's body. Height, weight, body mass and limb length are all examples of structural constraint. They are constraints relating to the architecture of the body and, although they change over time, we are unable to do much to change them (Malina et al., 2003). With the exception of eating food, which may affect body size widthways, we are powerless to get taller, for example. That is determined by our genetic code, or defined by our DNA. The other type of individual constraint, according to Newell, is known as a functional constraints. Functional constraints are non-structural aspects of the individual (revisit Section 1.7 about structuralism versus functionalism to see the similarities).

Examples of functional constraints include motivation, attention and concentration (Deci and Ryan, 2000; Wu et al., 2011). For instance, if a child is suffering from a lack of motivation to carry out required motor tasks, or is not paying sufficient attention to a set of instructions, this will constrain the way in which they actually perform the task. Examples of this can be seen during physical education lessons when a child is required to participate in an activity that they do not like participating in or have little interest in. Indeed, both lack of motivation and poor attention or concentration severely impede success in any task. They are significant functional constraints.

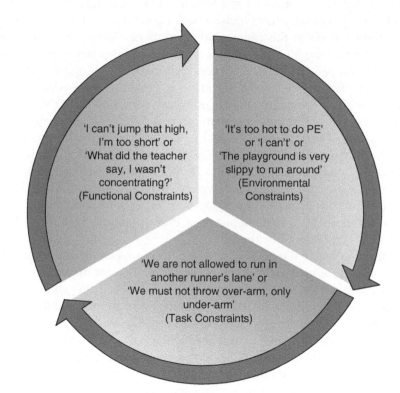

Figure 5.6   Applied example using an interrelated constraints model of motor development (adapted from Newell, 1986)

Environmental constraints, in contrast, are all those tangible constraints that are not part of the individual child. As one may anticipate, they are related to physical qualities of the environment in which children find themselves. By expanding what is covered under the term 'environmental', it becomes possible to incorporate other factors that might otherwise be disregarded as important contributors to motor development (Iivonen et al., 2011; Venetsanou and Kambas, 2010). Obvious examples of environmental constraints include terrain, surfaces, temperatures and light levels.

Combining each of these into an example will provide a clearer picture of how they serve to constrain motor behaviour. Walking on rough terrain, such as a gravel trail, may necessitate a change in walking behaviour to accommodate the unstable nature of the ground under foot. This would equally change depending on the individual's footwear. If the same gravel trail now became wet and slippery, the individual would have to adopt a different, perhaps safer style of walking; indeed we see this time and time again when people venture onto pavements in snow or ice, when walking patterns and posture can be quite humorous to watch and nothing like the walking behaviour of the same person on a dry, summer day. The same gravel trail may be far harder to traverse on a 35°C day where the sun is beating down, sapping energy and producing lethargy of movement, than it would be on a mild, pleasant day with a slight breeze blowing. Again, walking behaviour may change if light levels are beginning to drop away – less important on a gravel trail with no apparent dangers associated with it, but extremely important if the gravel trail is atop a mountain ridge or precariously close to a rocky cliff-top on the coast. The need to be surefooted suddenly becomes a priority and walking behaviour changes as a result. Perhaps we are being overly dramatic here. We think not. Environmental constraints can apply equally to the school environment.

Indeed, since the integration of Forest School as a concept into many schools today (Swarbrick et al., 2004), staff have been able to look at the terrain within which a school is situated and identify, for its location, an area that would be ideal, or at least as ideal as possible under the circumstances. Not only does an unused area of the school become useful, but also it may be able to fulfil this role with little structural change. How does this link with our discussion of environmental constraints? If environmental constraints influence motor development and we offer environmental conditions that help children experience differences in terrain, surfaces, temperature or light levels, then those children should find it easier to develop motor patterns that are successful within that environment. Moreover, the environment is safe, because health and safety issues will have been considered and a risk assessment is in place. The environment is educational, in the sense that it becomes a classroom outdoors. The environment is also a microcosm of the wider natural environment, so it provides children with a safe way of exploring their natural world, even if it has been carefully constructed and controlled, to the extent that child-centred learning can be controlled.

The third type of constraint is task constraints. In essence, task constraints can be summarised as the 'rules of engagement'. These are the aims, objectives, rules or instructions associated with particular tasks or activities. For example, the aim of a 100-metre sprint is to reach the finish line faster than any opponents. The person that does this wins the race. There are certain rules attached to this form of competition. One rule is that runners are required to remain in their designated lane for the duration of the race and are not allowed to change lanes. Another rule is that competitors are not allowed to start running until the gun has been fired or the claxon or whistle has been sounded. False starts are penalised by disqualification. Another task constraint is the necessity to start from the starting blocks. Finally, and perhaps less obvious, is the task constraint of having to stop running fairly soon after the finish at some venues due to lack of space, which could equally be seen as an environmental constraint.

Having passed through the rudimentary phase, the child enters the fundamental movement phase, between the approximate ages of two to seven years. Twelve widely accepted fundamental movement skills have been identified (Gallahue and Ozmun, 2011). These are listed as:

- Locomotor skills:

    1. running
    2. galloping
    3. hopping
    4. jumping
    5. leaping
    6. sliding.

- Object control skills:

    7. striking
    8. throwing
    9. kicking
    10. catching
    11. stationary dribbling
    12. underhand rolling.

As the child reaches the elementary and mature stages, they begin to experiment with combinations of these skills. So, for example, a child who is becoming increasingly successful at running and kicking or catching, in isolation, may begin to combine these skills. As adults, we may find it relatively easy to run and catch at the same time – think of rugby or cricket as examples of sports where proficiency in both skills at the same time may be useful. Children struggle with this combination during the earlier stages of the fundamental movement phase, but with practice become proficient, to a greater or lesser extent. Of course, we must be mindful that individual differences play a role here. Not every child will be equally successful, but they may be more successful at other combinations. Indeed, we have all observed this in the school environment, where children in the same class show a great diversity of sporting prowess. Clubs and academies are always on the lookout for talented children to coach and provide support for. As teachers, our role is equally to identify such talent, but it is also to nurture skills in children who may not be so proficient (Mukherjee et al., 2017; Tortella et al., 2016; Zuvela et al., 2011).

The fundamental movement phase can be further subdivided into three stages: initial, elementary and mature. We intend to use the fundamental movement skill of running to highlight each of the subdivisions. The initial stage, which usually occurs between two and three years of age, is where basic elements of a fundamental movement skill are displayed, such as the beginning runner holding his or her hands out in front to aid balance. During the elementary stage, which usually occurs between four and five years of age, arm action begins to become more coordinated, with arms swinging backwards and forward, but not in synchrony with the legs. During the mature stage of running, which usually occurs between six and seven years of age, the arms swing in an ipsilateral motion: as the left leg swings forward, so too does the left arm, and as the right leg swings forward, so too does the right arm. If we are only interested in the arm movement itself, then motion is contralateral: as the left arm moves forward, the right arm moves backwards and vice versa. This pattern of development, from initial to mature, is distinct and always sequential. The child is unable to enter the fundamental movement phase immediately at the mature stage. The process must begin with the basics, before developing and then refining.

We must reiterate at this point that the transition through the stages of the fundamental movement phase may be constrained by the development of the muscular and central nervous systems. Maturity is an indicator that these systems are acting as enablers to progressive movement. Acquiring fundamental movement skills is not defined by chronological age. So the age ranges claimed by Gallahue and Ozmun (2011) are only approximate. It is feasible that, if a child is not provided with the opportunity or resources to acquire any of the fundamental movement skills, they will not automatically acquire them. Experience and practice are key to acquisition of these skills. So, when Gallahue and Ozmun talk in terms of maturity, one should not consider this age-biased. Certainly, if a child is exposed to the opportunity to acquire skills earlier in childhood, chronologically speaking, then the only constraint to development would be whether the muscular and central nervous systems have sufficient capacity to produce mature movement. Of course, other systems should also be taken into consideration. In the next section, we will show how important perceptual development is in contributing to success in movement capabilities. For example, if a child is unable to catch a ball, one might say that he or she has not acquired that particular fundamental movement skill. However, the question should not be, 'Have they or haven't they acquired the skill?' That is quite evident from the child's performance. A more important question to ask might be, 'Why might they not have acquired the skill?' You might think that this is straightforward. Failing to catch a ball may be because coordinated grasping is poorly timed and the ball is slipping through the child's fingers. Alternatively, it may be because the child's arm action is not fast enough: it is not raised at the correct moment to facilitate the catch. Or, less obviously, is the possibility that the child's visual system is not sufficiently developed, specifically in relation to depth perception. The consequence of this would mean that the child fails to catch the ball because they misperceive where that ball is spatially at a given point in time – the point at which a catching action is required.

Having successfully negotiated the fundamental movement phase, children enter the specialised movement phase, which is also subdivided into three stages: transition, application and lifelong utilisation. During the transition stage, between the ages of seven and ten years, children begin to refine their fundamental skills, by incorporating them into the sport. Fundamental skills are mature in most children by this age and sport or physical activities provide the vehicle for refinement. Neurological structures are sufficiently developed also by this age, as is musculature, both of which have acted as rate limiters (constraints to development) previously. Perceptual systems are by and large equipped to assist, although they are not fully refined, as we discussed above, with depth perception. One caveat with direct relevance to the classroom, or we should say to PE lessons, is that if children have not reached the mature stage of the fundamental movement phase, then acquisition of specialised movement skills will be impeded. The implication of this is a lack of progression through the specialised movement phase. In short, teachers need to be vigilant in PE lessons, to identify those children who are not applying the fundamental movement skills, such as catching, throwing, striking and running, to a wide variety of situations (Zuvela et al., 2011). We often talk in education of common or transferable skills. Our learners should be able to transfer what they have learned in one situation to other situations. The application of motor skills to new situations is no different and it is in this transition stage that teachers will be able to observe effort, successes and challenges (we prefer not to use the term 'failures').

ACTIVITY

Devise a checklist to help you in observing and recording each of the 12 fundamental movement skills. Collect evidence over a period of time for each of the children in your class. You can be as detailed or as basic as you wish in your records. At the very least you should record a minimum of three successful sightings of each fundamental movement skill. You might also like to record the dates and then expand on your definition of what is being observed. So, for example, a child may produce three successful catches, but are these under-arm, over-arm, one-handed, two-handed, from a high or low trajectory or from a strong delivery or a weaker lob?

For ease, you might produce a sheet for each of these examples and collect the evidence over a longer period of time. It will be very useful when you come to write your reports on each child – and so will not be a waste of your time.

After the transition stage comes the application stage, between the approximate ages of 11 and 13. This stage is as one may expect. It is where the skills tested out in a wide variety of sporting activities are put in operation: they are applied. Application is largely but not exclusively determined by both the curriculum and by available resources. This is an example of where schools in the independent or private sector may be more successful in fostering mature fundamental skills and subsequent specialised movement skills because of their access to such resources. Indeed, we have seen facilities at some independent schools that some universities would be envious of. It would be very interesting to establish a database of our successful sportspeople, linking these to demographic information about their schools' facilities and opportunities for sporting activities. Of course, this is not the complete picture. Wider societal influences cannot be ignored. A school may not have sufficient resources to promote a wide variety of specialised movement skills, but this does not necessarily mean that a child will be prevented from applying these skills. Outside agencies, such as clubs, teams and coaches, all help in the practical element of the application stage. As an awareness of personal assets and limitations emerges, the child channels efforts into those areas of sport that he or she is more proficient in, and more than likely finds more enjoyable. Teachers and coaches should be able to provide guidance on whether the child is making full use of their personal assets and acknowledging their limitations.

Having made choices on the areas of sport that children are competent at, they reduce the number of activities in order to focus on those that they have chosen, or have been chosen for them, perhaps by eager parents. If children are encouraged to continue in their chosen sporting activities, their development of specialised movement skills will then tend to stay with them into adulthood, although drop-out during adolescence especially ages 10–13 is something of a concern (see Russell and Heck, 2008). This is known as the lifelong utilisation stage, from the age of 14 years onwards. It does what its title suggests. The skills are refined through increased training, refinement of technique and building an awareness of strategy for a particular sport. Personal interests, motivations, goals and ambitions play a large role in whether the chosen sport will continue long into adulthood or whether it will drop away. Indeed, later in life people often return to sports that they were competent at during school when they are seeking to incorporate more physical activity into their lives.

Having taken you through Gallahue and Ozmun's conceptual model of motor development, we now reach the point at which they suggest that the skills learned through formative childhood years are utilised in adulthood. This utilisation of skills can, according to Gallahue and Ozmun, take the form of utilisation for living, for recreation or for competition. One only needs to look around to see that competitive sport is not for everyone. Utilisation of skills for recreation gives the impression of exertion, perspiration and effort. Yet, this is not the case. Of course, utilising skills is an excellent way of promoting health through recreational sport and exertion, and perspiration or effort may be a part of that. However, utilisation of skills for recreation is more about enjoyment. It is taking advantage of the skills one does possess and using them to enhance daily life. Utilisation of skills for living cannot be avoided. We may not be competitive sportspeople. We may not enjoy recreational physical activity, but we are all required to negotiate through our daily environments. It is here that utilisation of skills learned during childhood is part of a lifelong process. For example, stepping off the kerb, running across the road to catch a bus or negotiating a flight of steps before alighting a train all involve an element of successfully acquired movement skills. This all begins in childhood.

The accepted contemporary view favours a link between movement and perception (Payne and Isaacs, 2011). In day-to-day terms, the sensory systems provide individuals with information about what is happening in the immediate environment, on a second-by-second basis. The person may select any one or more of these stimuli to attend to (we will discuss 'selective attention' in more detail in Chapter 6) and process. This processing is what we commonly understand as perception. Having perceived a sensory stimulus, an action usually follows. For example, a child who touches a hotplate in the kitchen will favour removing their hand with great speed.

5.7 CONCLUSION

This chapter may be used for reference purposes as and when required. Several complex topics have been housed in one location for you to make use of at appropriate junctures in your career. Arguably, there is little need to know this information. However, we would defend our position by proposing that one's continuing development may extend to the macrocosmic to provide contextualisation, or equally it may extend to the microcosmic. The microcosmic context of the developing brain – its neurons, systems and means of communicating with and interpreting the world of its developing host (the child) – is part and parcel of the wider themes of this book. There is little reason to fear the themes within this chapter. Rather, our advice is to use them as vehicles for your own discovery.

5.8 FURTHER READING

Bergen, D. (2016) 'Play, toys, learning, and understanding', *American Journal of Play*, 8 (2): 145–56. This paper provides an interview with Doris Bergen, giving an account of her knowledge through the prose of an interview transcript.

Gallahue, D.L. and Ozmun, J.C. (2011) *Understanding Motor Development: Infants, Children, Adolescents, Adults* (7th edn). Boston, MA: McGraw-Hill.
Gallahue and Ozmun's book has stood the test of time, providing a clear introduction to biological, affective, cognitive and behavioural aspects across various developmental stages.

Kolb, B. and Whishaw, I.Q. (2008) *Fundamentals of Human Neuropsychology* (6th edn). New York: Worth.
This is the textbook for a fully informed discussion of neuropsychology, in terms of anatomical organisation, higher functions and disorders. It is a fascinating reference book if you are looking to understand specific aspects of cortical and subcortical brain functioning.

Popkin, B., D'Anci, K. and Rosenberg, I. (2010) 'Water, hydration, and health', *Nutrition Reviews*, 68 (8): 439–58.
The importance of hydration and health is fully explored within this journal article.

6
PERCEPTUAL AND COGNITIVE DEVELOPMENT

CHAPTER OBJECTIVES

- Appreciate how the growing child develops perceptually and cognitively.
- Consider how the child's stage of development affects their ability in the classroom.
- Develop an increased awareness of how the child can be supported through their perceptual and cognitive development.

TEACHERS' STANDARDS

A teacher must:

2   Promote good progress and outcomes by pupils

- be aware of pupils' capabilities and their prior knowledge, and plan teaching to build on these
- demonstrate knowledge and understanding of how pupils learn and how this impacts on teaching

5   Adapt teaching to respond to the strengths and needs of all pupils

- have a secure understanding of how a range of factors can inhibit pupils' ability to learn, and how best to overcome these
- demonstrate an awareness of the physical, social and intellectual development of children, and know how to adapt teaching to support pupils' education at different stages of development

6.1 INTRODUCTION

This chapter explores the significance of perceptual and cognitive development in the child. It shows how perceptual systems are important in determining the child's interpretation of their environment and how this is influenced by and influences cognitive development.

6.2 PERCEPTUAL DEVELOPMENT

Perceptual development is extremely important in evolutionary terms, if an organism is to survive the rigours of natural selection. Of course, this is a rather dramatic statement, given the nature of this book. However, it is not as strange as one may think. Since humans as a species are visually dominant, we will focus in this section on the visual sensory system. As outlined in Chapter 5, the primary visual cortex is located in the occipital lobes at the back of the head, in various regions labelled V1–V8 (Zeki, 2003). Information passes from there to the visual association cortex in the temporal lobes and to the parietal lobes for integration. This is all very straightforward to explain in terms of the adult brain, but the developing brain in children is far from its adult state.

There are two main competing theories of perception: the information-processing theory and the ecological theory, otherwise known as direct perception. Information-processing theory (Gregory, 1980) is a reductionist theory and can be explained using an input–output computer analogy. In this way, incoming information (input) stimulates the senses and is processed, before an action (output) is produced. In contrast, Gibson (1966: 79) argues against information processing, in favour of direct perception. Direct perception, according to Gibson, does not rely on embellishments of cognition and inference. Rather, he argues that all the information one requires is present in the stimulus, and all one needs to do is 'attune to its affordances', or those aspects of the stimulus that hold meaning for us. An easy way to decode Gibson's terminology is to think of an old analogue radio, the type with a manual tuning knob. The signals from regional radio stations can be picked up by tuning in to them, until the signal becomes clear. When Gibson mentions 'attuning to the affordances of a stimulus', he is talking in similar terms. Although these competing theories may be worth exploring, further discussion would not enhance your reading of this chapter, so we will move on.

In considering visual perception, one may think we are simply talking about 'seeing'. Yet visual perception is so much more than that. As the child, or more specifically as the child's brain, develops, different visual abilities emerge. The list is longer than one might think and is worth setting out for that very reason. Visual abilities include visual acuity (sharpness), contrast sensitivity, colour vision, focus flexibility, depth perception, central–peripheral awareness, eye–hand–body coordination, visual adjustability (for example, night vision and reaction time, which is not necessarily always visual but is enhanced by cross-modality perception), the integration of input from different sensory systems in the parietal lobes (Coren et al., 2004). Given the extent of this list, it is not surprising that the child's brain is not fully equipped in early childhood. So when do these abilities emerge? It is not necessary to provide an exhaustive account here, so we will select some examples below.

A rapid improvement in visual acuity occurs between the ages of 5 and 7 and this plateaus until the next rapid improvement between the ages of 9 and 10. Visual acuity for static objects is mature by the age of 10, but the child must wait until the ages of 11–12 before achieving visual acuity for dynamic or moving objects.

Gibson and Walk's classic 'visual cliff' study highlights the apparent hard-wiring or survival-instinct of perceiving depth (Gibson and Walk, 1960). The 'visual cliff' involves a platform on one side and a deep step on the other side and hence visually is representative of danger. The whole area is covered in a chequerboard pattern. A sheet of glass extends from the platform, over the deep step so that there is in fact no step at all – it becomes a raised glass floor. Gibson and Walk placed 6-month-old infants (the age at which babies are generally able to crawl) on the platform side and situated their mothers at the opposite side. In order to reach their mothers, the babies had to crawl across the glass platform. It was found that the infants were reluctant and would stop crawling when they reached the 'drop zone', suggesting that they were able to perceive depth. From an evolutionary perspective, this makes perfect sense. After all, we don't really want our infants falling off cliffs, since it is not good for the survival of our species! Rudimentary depth perception is present in infants at 6–14 months. Evidence to support this ability was clearly revealed in meta-analyses of the data from 5-month-olds (475 infants, 5–5.5 months of age) who participated in preferential-reaching studies. Findings showed that the infants responded more consistently to depth relationships specified by pictorial cues under monocular than under binocular viewing conditions, indicating that 5-month-old infants respond to pictorial depth cues (Kavšek et al., 2012).

This may not be an issue in terms of identifying depth in pictures or in static objects placed in the environment, for example, placing a hoop on the floor at a distance from the 'throwing line' and asking children to throw bean bags into the hoop during a PE activity. There is little if any danger from participating in this activity, especially from an evolutionary perspective, so one might be forgiven for assuming that only survival-related depth perception is hard-wired and readily accessible when needed. Let's face it: if 6-month-old infants can use it to inform their actions, then we as humans should never make errors in perceptual judgement if the consequence reduces the odds of survival. This argument is not, however, as clear-cut as that. Children below the age of 3 find it extremely difficult to estimate perceptual depth. Children between 3 and 4 years of age make frequent errors of judgement in depth perception and it is not until 5 or 6 years of age that judgement errors begin to reduce. A rapid improvement occurs between the ages of 7 to 11, but depth perception does not reach maturity until approximately 12 years of age (Haywood and Getchell, 2014). There is great danger involved if a child who has not adequately acquired depth perception needs to cross a busy road. The objects (cars) are moving and apparently far away. Yet there are countless reports of children being knocked down by cars. The driver's response is commonly, 'The child just stepped out in front of me and I couldn't stop.' Let's give the driver the benefit of the doubt and assume that he or she was not speeding, under the influence of alcohol or drugs, or going too fast for the prevailing conditions. The child stepping out would not have been expected, unless one holds the view that all drivers should go past every child at below 5–10 mph, and consequently most people would argue that the accident was not the driver's fault. It is also common in these circumstances for witnesses to say that the child couldn't have looked or why else would they be hit by the car? In reality, the child may indeed have looked and, in fact, have seen the car. Yet, as a consequence of under-developed depth perception, the child was unable to judge distance and approach speed sufficiently to stop themselves from stepping out into the path of the vehicle.

Perception of objects follows a similar developmental progression through childhood. This can be illustrated through the concept of 'figure-ground'. Figure-ground is the ability to detect discontinuities or extremal edges in the visual display (Palmer and Ghose, 2008). Figure 6.1 shows a series of objects placed together. As adults, we find it a straightforward exercise to perceive which objects appear in the series, which objects do not and, more importantly, where these objects finish or start. This is figure-ground: the ability to distinguish what is object and what is background in the visual array.

Figure 6.1   A series of objects, with examples of objects that may appear in series

The figure is always in front of the ground. It may be behind another object but nevertheless, the adult human brain is able to separate the object from its background. In the developing child, this is not the case.

ACTIVITY

On the next school trip or visit, pick out a series of objects in the environment and ask the children if they can see them and then describe them. The answer you get will be dependent on the age of the child. Some children won't be able to detect the objects, let alone recognise exactly what they are. This is quite normal.

As adults, we find it easy to identify which objects from the set of options appear in Figure 6.1. Children do not find this process of object recognition as easy. A process of improvement, plateau and further improvement takes place.

ACTIVITY

Look again at the series of objects contained within Figure 6.1.

Now look underneath at the options and try to decide which of the objects appears in the series of objects above and which do not. Now ask a child to do the same. The younger the child, the harder it will be for them to identify the objects correctly.

Detecting these edges, or discontinuities, in the visual display begins to develop by 3 or 4 years of age, showing a rapid improvement up to 6 years of age. An additional spurt happens around 7 to 8 years of age and maturity of this ability comes into effect between the ages of 8 and 12 years, all dependent on exposure to and experience of object recognition (Bezrukikh and Terebova, 2009; Bova et al., 2007).

ACTIVITY

Look yet again at the series of objects contained within Figure 6.1.

Looking at the continuities and discontinuities of the lines, try to decide which of the objects is in front and which is behind another. This may sound easy, but is actually rather difficult to do (especially when you begin to think in 3D).

> So, object recognition is a combination of detecting where objects start and finish as well as what those objects are. We find it easy to identify the objects in Figure 6.1 because we can see where they start and finish but also because our memory is providing information about those objects based on past experiences. For example, we may not have seen exactly the same jug, hammer and key as those illustrated, but we have all seen jugs, hammers and keys before and are making a judgement based on those previous experiences.

Object recognition is also subject to developmental processes, when it comes to facial recognition. For example, young children (aged 5–7 years) are less accurate than older children (aged 9–11 years), adolescents (aged 13–16 years) and young adults when making facial age judgements (Brigham et al., 1986; Gross, 2015). Facial recognition is a complicated process, involving the checking of features against those stored in memory. Even as adults we sometimes get it wrong. Have you ever mistaken a complete stranger for a friend and had to say, 'Sorry, I thought you were … you look alike'?

As adults, we are also able to see things that aren't really there. Look at Figure 6.2 and consider what you can see.

Figure 6.2   What can you see?

You may see the shape of a heart, fish, face, scooter, person, or finally a rabbit. Of course, each of these is a fair and accurate description of the image in front of you. Yet, in actual fact none of them are correct. This is the intrigue of abstract perception.

The human brain tries to make sense of the world around it. It is so used to piecing together parts of the visual array that do go together, as in the example of facial features, that it often goes beyond what is actually there. The phrase, 'I can't believe my eyes' is sometimes rather true. If you show the same image to children you will find that they will struggle to see what is obvious to your adult brain.

ACTIVITY

Show Figure 6.2 to a selection of children within different age ranges. Ask them to tell you what they can see. Record your answers on a response sheet and reflect on which age group of children say what to you. Reflect on the children's responses and consider what it might mean for you as a teacher, when preparing visual materials for use in the classroom or on display boards around the school.

Everything we have spoken about so far regarding perceptual development has involved a single sensory system in isolation. We have not even begun to consider what happens when sensory systems are combined. This is known as cross-modality perception and we will only cover it briefly here. Cross-modal (or 'across modes') perception occurs when sensory input is integrated into a single percept (Levitin et al., 2000). Let's use an everyday example to explain this. You are standing at the edge of the pavement, at a pedestrian crossing, waiting to cross the road. After a short while you hear the signal to say that the light has changed to red and you see the green 'walk' signal light up. Both of these pieces of information have been processed in different sensory systems (visual and auditory) yet your experience is of a single act happening. This is an example of cross-modality perception. In the case of this example, it is cross-modal in terms of auditory-visual perception. Age-related development is also apparent, but the age ranges are more dependent upon environmental opportunities so, for example, a trend towards improved performance in auditory-visual perception occurs between the ages of 5 and 12 years, with maturity occurring thereafter.

In relating these developing elements of perception to Newell's model, we are again able to talk in terms of constraints being released as maturation of structural systems occurs. But we are also able to introduce the notion of perception–action coupling. Perception–action coupling is the relationship between perception and action (Gibson, 1979). If the purpose of perception is to inform oneself about what is happening at present, then a response or action will generally follow. One does not tend to happen without the other, even if the action is to do nothing. The two acts are therefore coupled or linked together. A stimulus is attended to, perceived and then acted upon.

Once this has taken place, we begin the process again, or rather, the process is cyclical. Once we have acted, we are possibly in a new position in the environment and, consequently, subjecting ourselves to new stimuli that require processing, perceiving and responding to action. This process continues on a daily basis every day of our lives. It even takes place when we are less aware of it. For example, during sleep, the visual system will generally not be receiving any input. However, the auditory system may become increasingly responsive to noises inside and outside the home. Sometimes even the ticking of a clock can appear very loud in the dead of night.

Loubser et al. (2016) explored children from disadvantaged backgrounds, finding that they would benefit from perceptual-motor interventions, both outside the classroom such as use of outdoor apparatus (jungle gyms, hoops, balls, etc.) and inside the classroom such as use of indoor apparatus (building blocks, drawing activities, puzzles and clay). Similarly, Bütün Ayhan et al. (2015) reported the use of well-chosen, daily activities, promoting conceptual development and the way in which it relates to visual perception.

6.3 COGNITIVE DEVELOPMENT IN THE DEVELOPING CHILD

Structurally speaking, at birth, the outward appearance of a newborn's brain is equivalent in size to that of an adult brain. Between 3 and 18 months there is a 30 per cent increase in weight, a further 10 per cent increase between 2 and 4 years, followed by 10 per cent increases between 6 and 8, 10 and 12, and 14 and 16 years (Carlson and Birkett, 2017). These increases in brain weight are indicative of the strengthening connections within the brain and are reasonably well linked with Piaget's stages of cognitive development (Piaget, 1955), Gallahue and Ozmun's phases of motor development (Gallahue and Ozmun, 2011) and development of perceptual abilities. As Table 6.1 shows, increases in cognitive capacity between the ages of 2 and 7 and then between 7 and 12 years are considerable. It would be a huge coincidence if this development was unrelated to the physical development of the brain during childhood. We will now discuss each of these stages in turn.

THE SENSORIMOTOR STAGE

In understanding the sensorimotor stage, we suggest breaking down the terminology into 'sensori-' and '-motor'. Immediately, this implies that the stage is characterised by the senses and motor activity, or movement. Think for a moment about the day-to-day capabilities of an infant under the age of two years. Cognitively speaking, this age group will not be complicated. Their needs are basic and immediate. Information impinges on their senses and an action is initiated. Reaching for an object is one example (Hemker et al., 2010). Opening one's mouth to receive a spoonful of food is another. There is a stimulus and there is a subsequent action. Or put another way, sensory receptors transmit afferent information to the central nervous system, which then sends efferent information to the muscles required to perform the task. The sensorimotor stage ends when the child begins to develop symbolic thought, for example, a toy doll which becomes 'Mummy', and object permanence – an understanding that objects still exist if they are out of sight (Bogartz et al., 2000).

Table 6.1   Piaget's stages of cognitive development

Cognitive stage	Achievement
Sensorimotor thought (0–2 years)	Symbolic thought begins to emerge
	Object permanence develops
Preoperational thought (2–7 years)	Mental representation in language, art and play develops
Concrete operational thought (7–12 years)	Logical thought becomes more objective
Formal operational thought (12> years)	Hypothetico-deductive reasoning and abstract thought develops

ACTIVITY

You will need access to an infant under the age of two, a toy and a sheet of A4 paper or a cushion.

Show the toy to the child so that you attract their attention. Next hold the piece of A4 paper up in landscape position in front of the infant, with the longest side horizontally. Move the toy from left to right (or right to left) so that it passes behind the paper for a short period of time.

Observe the expressions on their face when the toy disappears from view and then when it reappears. If the infant has not acquired object permanence their expression upon reappearance of the toy will be one of surprise, and perhaps excitement. In the child's mind two toys exist rather than the permanent, single toy that has been temporarily hidden.

THE PREOPERATIONAL STAGE

Beyond the sensorimotor stage, the child begins to develop an understanding of concepts. The preoperational stage reflects the emergence of early forms of symbolism and concept learning (Lourenco, 2003; Piaget, 1955). Thinking is not logical during this stage, but elements of language, art and play develop. Children in this stage are suddenly exposed to a wide array of linguistic opportunities, socially and through pre-school and school. They begin to experiment with words verbally and learn the conceptual elements of the alphabet, symbolising those words (Siegel, 1999). Whereas as adults we perhaps take the alphabet for granted, children have to learn and understand the conceptual workings of this symbolic code in order to fulfil their potential on their journey towards adulthood. During this stage, children acquire the ability to categorise. By this we mean that the ability to group certain things together develops. So, for example, objects in the kitchen can be categorised in terms of cooking-related or eating-related. Objects in the garden shed can be categorised in terms of garden-related, and objects in the bathroom can be categorised in terms of bath-time. Categorisation in this way is dependent upon an increasing capacity for memory, and this increasing capacity for memory is dependent upon the structural development of a child's brain (the hippocampus and temporal lobes) during this stage.

We have mentioned the emergence of linguistic symbolism during the preoperational stage. This stage is also characterised by symbolism in areas outside of language. So, for example, a child will perhaps be seen running around a playground, arms outstretched to the sides, symbolising an aeroplane. Similarly, a child may be galloping in circles, representative of being a horse, or perhaps making steering movements with their arms, representative of riding a bicycle. In each of these examples, the true nature of the action is symbolic and the child knows that it is symbolic. What is it that dictates the type of symbolic play that children display? As one might anticipate, environmental influences play a big role in the type of symbolism children adopt (Donaldson, 1978). A child living in a rural environment where horses are perhaps commonplace will more than likely be influenced by this and will display equestrian symbolic play. Yet for the child living in an inner-city environment, the likelihood of seeing this example of symbolic play would perhaps be rare. You notice that we do not say that it would be absent or non-existent, because that may not be the case. The inner-city child may have seen a television programme involving horses, have been excited by the programme and subsequently has incorporated this into their play. Equally, the rural child may be less likely to display 'I am a car' symbolism, but this again is not necessarily set in stone.

ACTIVITY

You will need access to a child between the ages of two and seven.

Observe the child at play over a period of one week, for let's say 15 minutes at a time. See if you can identify the behaviour that you see and make notes on the symbolism involved. Next, ask the child what they are doing. This will help you to confirm whether your observations (or more accurately, interpretations)

(Continued)

were correct. It is essential that you ask this question, because what you are seeing as an adult is not always the same as what is happening in the child's mind. Generally, however, if a child looks as if they are an aeroplane and making the sounds of an aeroplane, they will not tend to tell you that they are 'being a shark'. But one never knows!

Piaget also talks in terms of signs and signifiers. There is a subtle difference between them. We can explain this using road signs as a simple analogy. Think of a road sign: for example, twisty road, level crossing ahead or traffic lights. It is a sign that explains the physical object or road layout ahead. It is informative and meaningful and advises us of what we are approaching. As a signifier, it means far more than the sign itself. Each of the warning signs in a copy of the *Highway Code* signifies the same thing: danger. While the sign dictates what is ahead, as a signifier it is signifying the fact that, unless a particular course of action is adopted, usually involving slowing down, a driver will be exposing themselves to a particular danger.

Equally, far less dramatically and with far less severe consequences, children will begin to appreciate the signs that are relevant to their world, within pre-school, nursery or school. These signs will be common to all children and all children develop an understanding of what the signs mean; we do not mean that children always adhere to them though. A signifier, in contrast, within a child's environment will be more specific to the child and immediate family. We have known of a case where a young child would bang their fist, rather violently, on the floor at a particular time every day. To the untrained eye, the behaviour was inexplicable. Upon talking to the mother, it became evident that this behaviour was representative of or signified boredom.

THE CONCRETE OPERATIONAL STAGE

Marking the end of the preoperational stage, children are beginning to display signs of what Piaget called 'conservation' (Piaget, 1955, 1964). Conservation represents a move into the concrete operational stage where logical thought becomes more objective. Piaget used the term 'conservation' to explain a child's understanding of the quantitative nature of an object once it has been transformed. We can explain this more easily by describing Piaget's experiments in conservation of mass, length and number, but first we need to clarify what is meant by 'transformation'. Transformation is the change in visual but not quantitative appearance of a physical object. The three tasks below provide practical activities for you to observe conservation in action. It would be extremely useful to conduct each task and then return to the remainder of this section. If you are unable to do this now, don't forget to try it. You will find the experiment interesting and will be able to predict whether children can or cannot display conservation, which in turn indicates whether they are in the concrete operational or in the preoperational stage. It is also fun.

ACTIVITY   Conservation of mass

You will need access to children in the 2–7-year-old and 7–12-year-old age group. Try this task with a wide range of children so that you can collect some real data on conservation. This will help you to build up a clear picture of conservation within your sample of children.

You will also need two equally sized pieces of clay or Plasticine.

Place the two balls of clay in front of the child and ask if the balls contain the same amount of clay (which of course they do). Now, roll one of the balls into a sausage shape in front of the child and ask if they still contain the same amount of clay. Children who have acquired conservation of mass will tell you they still contain the same. Children who have not acquired conservation of mass will tell you that one has more clay (usually the sausage shape).

It is worth trying this with a 12-year-old child, just so that you can watch them look at you as if you have gone mad, when they think 'Of course the pieces have not changed ... you idiot!'

ACTIVITY   Conservation of number

Use the same children from your sample population as for conservation of mass.

You will also need ten counters or buttons.

Place the counters in two equal rows in front of the child and ask if the rows contain the same number of counters, which of course they do. Now, space the counters further apart in one of the rows, in front of the child, and ask if they still contain the same number of counters. Children who have acquired conservation of number will tell you they still contain the same. Children who have not acquired conservation of number will tell you that the 'longer looking' row contains more counters.

As they did with conservation of mass, the 12-year-old should again look at you as if you are stupid!

ACTIVITY   Conservation of volume

Use the same children from your sample population as for the previous conservation tasks.

You will need three beakers. Two must be the same size and the other must be taller and narrower. You will also need some water.

(Continued)

Pour equal amounts of water in the two equal-sized beakers and place them in front of the child. Ask the child if the beakers contain the same volume (you should perhaps use the word 'amount') of water, which of course they do. Now, pour the water from one beaker into the taller, narrower beaker, in front of the child, and ask if they still contain the same volume (or amount). Children who have acquired conservation of volume will tell you they still contain the same. Children who have not acquired conservation of volume will tell you that the taller, narrower beaker contains more water.

The 12-year-old should react in a similar way to the previous two conservation tasks.

The acquisition of conservation is not an all-or-nothing affair. Piaget discovered that children showed conservation of number by 6 years of age, yet conservation of volume tended not to emerge until 11 years of age. The acquisition of logical thought processing is therefore more or less objective, depending on whether the child is in the early or the late part of the concrete operational stage. It is the child's entry into adolescence, during which the ability forms to categorise, to empathise with the feelings of others and to investigate increasingly complex cause–effect relationships. Complex logical thought, however, is still under development.

THE FORMAL OPERATIONAL STAGE

By the time the child reaches 12 years of age, they will enter the formal operational stage of hypothetico-deductive reasoning and abstract thought (Piaget, 1955, 1964). This is the stage where the elements lacking from the concrete operational stage are now fulfilled. The task below exemplifies whether the child has successfully acquired hypothetico-deductive reasoning.

ACTIVITY   Hypothetico-deductive reasoning

You will need a group of 10–12-year-old children.
Write the following statement and question on the whiteboard:

Kianna is taller than Cameron and Cameron is taller than Chloe.

Who is taller: Kianna or Chloe?

The 10-year-olds will typically struggle in answering this question, whereas the older children should find it easier, because they have developed abstract problem-solving capabilities.

In preference to the term 'hypothetico-deductive reasoning' we suggest that 'abstract reasoning' is used, since it is far less wordy and works neatly in an applied sense. So abstract reasoning is the ability to test hypotheses and make deductions about a problem, both of which are abstract, in that they do not have a concrete basis (Knifong, 1974; Piaget, 1955: 64). It is this scientific thinking that contextualises the formal operations stage. Such thinking occurs during post-11-year-old education. Social and cultural influences impact on this stage. For example, a child obtaining an education in an independent or private school may be exposed to more opportunities for scientific thinking, partly due to smaller class sizes and adequately equipped classrooms and associated resources, in contrast with a child obtaining an education in an under-resourced school, where buildings, facilities and resources are scant in comparison.

It would be prudent to remind ourselves of other events taking place during this stage. As the child enters adolescence, they are undergoing significant cognitive development. Yet at the same time, the neurochemical maelstrom under way during adolescence is at the very least causing some impediment to progress. Of course, this is an understatement. The formal operational stage is perhaps the hardest stage in which to make progress. Not all children will acquire the necessary depth of skills during this stage. But then we all know that, from our experience of people. Some people are 'highly intelligent', 'intellectually competent', 'academically advanced' or whatever term suits you best. Other people are less so, but may be excellent in practical-based activities. Society puts great emphasis on academic success and appears to reject academic failure. Within schools, staff are required to facilitate academic learning and the acquisition of academic qualifications because they are under pressure to show that they have succeeded as schools. Whether the child achieves their full academic potential may actually be determined by the extent to which they are successful in progressing through the formal operational stage, combined with the extent to which they are able to overcome the neurochemical turmoil taking place during this time.

6.4 ATTENTION, CONCENTRATION AND MEMORY

If one accepts Newell's constraints model, attention and concentration become functional constraints, alluded to in Chapter 5. By its very nature, the familiar concept we know as memory requires attention, and concentration is its precursor. Without them, memory traces are less likely to be stored, or available for retrieval. In order to discuss these elements it is worth explaining memory before we go on to discuss how attention and concentration facilitate or impair the development of memory (or useable knowledge, if you prefer this term). Defining what memory is feels somewhat like defining what food is. Just as there are different types of food, there are different (albeit far fewer) types of memory. To provide a generic definition would not be helpful. As this section unfolds, the different types of memory will become apparent and these will overlap with attention and concentration.

At this point it is helpful to view memory in terms of its suggested component-processes. There are three important processes involved in memory: encoding, storage and retrieval (Figure 6.3). These are explained in more detail below with the use of examples and each of them is vital if a memory is to exist in the brain and become knowledge.

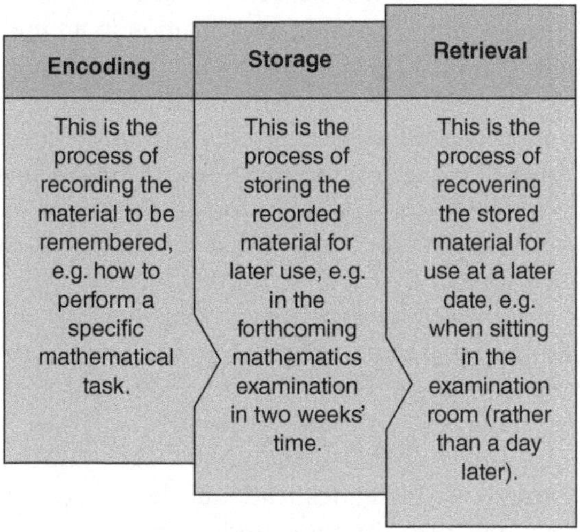

Encoding	Storage	Retrieval
This is the process of recording the material to be remembered, e.g. how to perform a specific mathematical task.	This is the process of storing the recorded material for later use, e.g. in the forthcoming mathematics examination in two weeks' time.	This is the process of recovering the stored material for use at a later date, e.g. when sitting in the examination room (rather than a day later).

Figure 6.3   Currently recognised components of memory

Having identified the components of memory it is now possible to examine two opposing models used to explain memory; the linear information-processing model and the connectionist parallel distributed processing (PDP) model. The information-processing model is based on a multi-store concept in psychology (Atkinson and Shiffrin, 1968). It starts with a stimulus from one or more of the sensory systems, such as the sound of a teacher's voice during a lesson. In a perfect world, multiple stimuli are held in sensory memory, which is an extremely large, brief storage facility (between 0.5 and 3–4 seconds depending on which sensory system is involved). There are mobile telephone applications available that enable users to send images to others that they would prefer not to exist as a permanent record (for reasons that we would perhaps leave to your imagination). Our learners tell us that it is possible to set the duration of the image so that it disappears within seconds of being opened. This is akin to a memory trace entering sensory memory for a brief moment before our brain moves on to processing the material at a deeper level. Information is transferred from here into working memory (sometimes called short-term memory) and is held for up to 30 seconds unless it is rehearsed. This is where you would store a telephone number just before dialling it;

by rehearsing it you are more likely to remember it, but failure to rehearse will mean that it is lost after 30 seconds. Information that is successfully rehearsed will enter long-term memory: the relatively permanent, relatively unlimited storage facility that houses our knowledge. Memory traces can, or should, be readily available for transfer back to

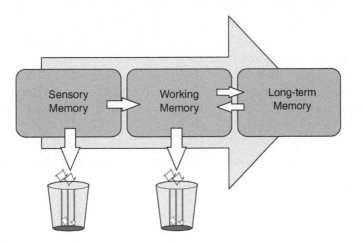

Figure 6.4   The information-processing model of memory

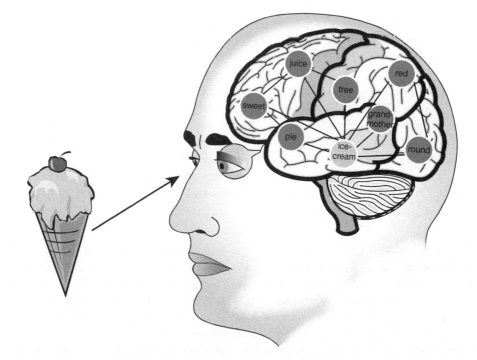

Figure 6.5   Depiction of a parallel distributed processing model for the memory of ice-cream

working memory when we need them. Figure 6.4 summarises the information-processing model of memory.

In contrast, the parallel distributed processing model (McClelland and Rummelhart, 1981) views memory as a process whereby sensory information is combined with existing knowledge held in memory in the form of a connected network of related information. So memories are distributed across a network and are accessible when one of the elements or nodes becomes activated. For example, the sight, smell or taste of an ice-cream may activate memories of a summer holiday at the beach. This initial stimulus will inevitably activate related nodes in the network, regarding the weather, emotions experienced (e.g. happiness) during the holiday, places visited, people who were present, what they were wearing and conversations that were taking place. This can be seen in Figure 6.5.

ACTIVITY

You are probably able to recall significant numbers (for example, car registration numbers, telephone numbers and so on), from many years ago because they were successfully stored and thus readily retrieved. Whether you subscribe to the information-processing model or the parallel distributed processing model, this activity will offer anecdotal support for either.

I (Paul Castle) can remember two registration numbers for cars that my father owned: EOK 61L (a dark blue Morris Marina) in 1973 and MDU 678P (a bright orange Austin Mini Clubman 1275GT) in 1976. I was 7 and 10 years old respectively and still remember these numbers 30 years later. I don't need to know them. They won't help my career, but they will simply not disappear from long-term memory.

Reflect on significant numbers of your own, write them down and then see what memories they hold for you. A good tip is to attach an emotional trigger if you can, in order to help unlock additional information.

If the children that we teach can remember what we have taught them (rather than car registration numbers), we will have been successful as educators.

Of course, we do not operate in an ideal world. Memory fails each of us – indeed, sometimes at the most inopportune moments – and this may be due to not paying attention at the encoding stage of processing. A clear distinction can be made between two types of attentional processing: automatic and effortful. Automatic processing is, as it suggests, automatic. It involves little, if any, conscious effort on behalf of the learner. For example, if you or your learners closed their eyes, they would still be able to negotiate their way slowly around the classroom to the exit if you asked them to.

None of them would previously have consciously memorised the classroom and its routes, but this information has been committed to memory via automatic processing. In contrast, effortful processing is, as it also suggests, making conscious effort. It is the processing teachers would expect to be taking place in any learning environment. It requires one to pay attention to specific aspects of the multitude of sensory stimuli, focusing in on what is important and what should be learned or remembered. This is exactly the point at which memory and attention converge.

In terms of effortful attentional processing, a further distinction should be made between two types: selective and divided. Selective attention is the conscious act of selecting those stimuli impinging upon the senses for further processing (Broadbent, 1958; Treisman, 1960). It is an active, effortful decision and is a precursor to what is commonly known as concentration (verbalised as 'paying attention'). Divided attention is, by definition, not focused. Rather, it is split between competing stimuli, vying for one's attention. Teachers will be aware of what this looks like in the classroom, when they see some learners looking at the teacher with 'blankness written all over their face'. Attention is divided between the drone of the teacher's voice, the sounds outside the classroom window and what is for dinner later that day. This, as one might expect, is not conducive to learning, or should we say, to encoding information for later retrieval.

WHAT IS HAPPENING WITHIN THE BRAIN?

Studies in neuroscience reliably inform us that there is no specific memory centre within the brain (Kolb and Whishaw, 2015). Instead, memories appear to be distributed across a variety of brain regions. As we saw in Chapter 5, the intimate links between systems in the brain would support this view. Consider the sensory systems (vision, audition, gustation, somatosensation) by which brain regions process initial information, before sending it to other areas of the brain for further processing in order for humans to act on the encoded information. Consider how the emotional brain (the limbic system) adds an additional dimension to that sensory information: how it makes the recipient feel. Consider how physical or physiological influences on those systems contribute to the resulting actions or behaviour and how each of these in turn provides feedback to the brain – and it is not surprising that memory exists in a single region of the brain.

Notwithstanding this *caveat*, experiments have identified prominent areas of the brain that appear to be strongly implicated in memory. For example, the hippocampus is a structure within the limbic system (emotion), which appears to store episodic elements of long-term memories (episodes that take place in the course of life) temporarily for additional processing in the neocortex. The prefrontal cortex has been shown to be involved in working memory (Deco et al., 2004; Deco and Rolls, 2003), which if you recall is the short-term storage facility where newly acquired information is processed or encoded. Visual information is processed in the occipital lobes; auditory and olfactory information is processed in the temporal lobes; and these are prominent senses where information becomes part of the memory trace. Accessing one element makes it easier to access other elements of that memory trace.

Memory deficits have been investigated in children on the autistic spectrum or with ADHD or dyslexia. Children with a diagnosis on the autistic spectrum have been found to have anomalies in the hippocampus, amygdala and temporal lobes, related to deficits in episodic memory but not in semantic memory (Salmond et al., 2005), displaying functional deficits in visuo-spatial processing efficiency in working memory (Zinke et al., 2010), and in a non-fMRI study, functional deficits in working memory for visual shapes (Salmanian et al., 2012; Stoicea et al., 2011). Children diagnosed with ADHD have been found to experience deficits in visuo-spatial aspects of working memory, especially when those children are off medication (Kibby and Cohen, 2008). The medication methylphenidate (brand name Ritalin), prescribed for children with ADHD, is a stimulant that increases the neurotransmitters dopamine and norepinephrine (see Chapter 5) in underactive brain regions that control attention and behaviour (Leung et al., 2017). The result is an increase in activity within these regions. Brain morphology is different between dyslexic and non-dyslexic children. Specifically, differences exist in the planum temporale and thalamus along with cortical malformations in dyslexic children (Wajuihian, 2012), and fMRI studies have revealed asymmetrical differences in cortical activity (Leonard and Eckhart, 2008). In terms of memory deficits, evidence suggests that dyslexics' working memory lags behind that of non-dyslexics, resulting in difficulties in encoding if material is presented too quickly (see Fostick et al., 2012).

CONTEXT-DEPENDENT AND STATE-DEPENDENT MEMORY

Both context-dependent (Godden and Baddeley, 1975) and state-dependent (Eich, 1980) memory are coloured by emotion (Eich and Macaulay, 2000; Goodwin et al., 1969). Context-dependent memory is the successful recall of learning that was encoded in a particular context. This can be illustrated using a simple example. A learner who sits an examination in the same room that they learned (encoded) the information will be more likely to retrieve the material because the context the room provides acts as a cue to effective recall. In reality, it is not always possible to sit examinations in the usual classroom (many examinations take place in assembly halls due to the space available). To overcome this, the teacher should explore the possibilities of conducting revision sessions in the examination room so that the room facilitates the retrieval process. It is interesting to note that olfaction (the sense of smell) plays a significant role in the emotional experiences associated with contextualised odour-evoked memories (Castle et al., 2000; Miles and Berntsen, 2011). Often parents comment, upon walking into the school buildings for parents' evenings, that the smell of the place triggers immediate, emotionally charged memories of their own school days years before. Usually it is the smell of varnished floors in the school hall or pencil shavings that evoke these memories of childhood. These memories are not triggered in teachers who frequent the buildings during the working week. Rather, the comments we have received from teachers usually relate to the odour of children's feet or of sweaty corridors. These undoubtedly become associated with the teacher's role and can trigger emotionally charged memories if they are experienced in an environment totally removed from the school. If a school hall has been used for physical education the day before an examination, it would be wise to open the windows to allow the odours to dissipate, purely to aid context-dependent recall, unless the material was encoded in a similarly odorous environment!

State-dependent memory is the successful recall of learning that was encoded under the same physiological state. Goodwin et al. (1969) found that retrieval of information was facilitated when participants who had consumed alcohol during encoding were in the same alcohol-induced state at recall. Our learners frequently remind us of this enlightening piece of research during examination periods, for obvious reasons. Our riposte usually reminds them that alcohol is a nervous system depressant and is therefore not a reliable strategy to adopt (for a multitude of reasons).

ACTIVITY   Memory aids

Split the class into three groups, A, B and C. Create a tray of 20 objects (or a PowerPoint slide depicting those objects). Their task is to memorise as many of the items as possible in a two-minute time period before the teacher removes/covers them from view.

Group A should be instructed to link the objects in pairs or threes while they are rehearsing.

Group B should be instructed to think of taking a mental journey around the school, 'placing' the objects in different rooms or areas.

Group C should be instructed to simply recall the items.

Next, test learners' memory by asking them to write down as many of the objects as they can remember. You might then set up a discussion to ask them how they managed to remember (or forget) the objects.

In the activity above, you should find that Group C perform poorly on the task because they are trying to remember all 20 objects as a list. The majority of these learners will be able to remember approximately seven items (Miller, 1956) and you will also notice that they will be more inclined to remember the first few and last few objects, but not those in the middle of their list. This is known as the serial position effect or primacy-recency effect (Murdock, 1962) and has implications for teachers. The message here is to avoid putting important material in the middle of whatever you require of your learners. If necessary, segment the lesson plan, so that important material that is unavoidably deliverable in the middle of a lesson is preceded by a short break, so that it then becomes the start of the next segment (so that a primacy effect will occur).

Groups B and C should perform equally better than Group A. For some learners, pairing objects by association (Group A) is beneficial and indeed cuts down the number of objects by 50 per cent, because the recall of the first object in the pairing triggers the recall of the second. Equally, learners who embark on a mental journey where they place objects in various rooms of a building will recall those objects if the learner re-embarks on the journey to retrieve them. This principle can be applied to semantic memory such as factual information. A mental journey around a familiar house could readily feature figures in history, depicting timelines, with ancient history being in the garden, the middle ages being in ground floor rooms and modern history being on the first or second floors (of course this could similarly be used to reflect significant people within a particular period in history).

OTHER WAYS TO ENHANCE ATTENTIONAL FOCUS

There are numerous other practical ways to help improve attentional focus, or shifting of attention away from distractors and back to the task at hand. The task outlined in the activity box illustrates how attention can stall or fixate when shifting of attention is required to complete the task (adapted from Harris and Harris, 1984).

ACTIVITY   Attention shifting

Part 1

Give your learners a copy of this activity (face down) and tell them what is required of them before you ask them to turn the sheet over to begin (otherwise learners might start looking for the sequence before you finish explaining the task).

The person completing the task should locate the square with 00 and cross that box, then 01, 02, etc. up to 99 within a two- or three-minute time restriction (in reality 99 will not usually be reached in the time given). The task therefore requires shifting of attention from the number just found to the next number in the sequence, something that requires fast and efficient scanning of information.

Learners should be instructed to stop after the designated time period.

32	10	57	02	83	22	47	24	63	06
51	25	88	43	15	91	68	89	12	49
65	59	17	38	85	74	34	09	62	70
20	75	52	30	50	42	56	77	84	92
03	82	28	07	71	69	95	46	98	26
11	48	78	35	64	93	37	80	76	16
86	45	58	19	97	61	99	33	23	40
67	31	73	08	90	21	72	94	04	14
41	79	01	00	39	87	81	29	66	44
96	60	54	13	27	55	05	53	36	18

Record the scores in a data set (that may perhaps be used in a mathematics lesson at a later date). This is a rudimentary measure of learners' attentional shifting ability.

Part 2

In pairs, one person will be the first to complete the task. The other will act as the 'distractor'.

The person completing the task should again locate the square with 00 and cross that box, then 01, 02, etc. up to 99.

The distractor should repeat random numbers at their partner to try and make it difficult for him or her to concentrate on the task. Alternatively they could repeat times-tables or any other mathematical distraction.

Learners should be instructed to stop after the designated time period and swap roles.

Record the 'distracted' scores in the original data set; and there is now an opportunity to compare attentional performance with and without distractions.

Intuitively, you might predict that learners will remember more with no distraction. We would tend to agree but have seen learners' record higher scores under distraction. Upon questioning, some learners have said that it is so noisy when they are trying to study at home that they are unable to concentrate unless it is equally noisy (see our discussion of context-dependent memory above). Although totally impractical we hope you can appreciate the implication of this during test or examination conditions where silence is expected.

CONCENTRATION AND HYDRATION

In Chapter 5, we highlighted the importance of adequate hydration to learning (Johnston Molloy et al., 2008). We discussed how dehydration directly impairs brain function, slowing down the decision-making processes, adversely influencing attention and reducing the ability to concentrate (Popkin et al., 2010). Now we are able to make the links between what is happening within the brain (Chapter 5) with difficulties in encoding information to be stored in memory. If a child is unable to concentrate at the encoding stage, the likelihood of their successfully storing the material will be bleak to say the least. A simple way of ensuring that all learners are hydrated (bearing in mind that an element of individual differences in fluid-intake will exist), the class teacher may set targets with the children regarding the amount of water that must be drunk before lunchtime or during the afternoon. A quick visual scan around the classroom will be an easy way to monitor hydration levels. Indeed, why not build in 'Take a sip or two from your bottles' into the lesson plan at various opportune points during a lesson. Of course, the only caveat to bear in mind is the balance between staying hydrated and 'Please Miss, I need the toilet'!

PHYSICAL ACTIVITY/EXERCISE AND CONCENTRATION

Research evidence suggests that physical activity or exercise enhances the learning of information (Barkley, 2004; Dolezal et al., 2017; Majorek et al., 2004) and this may reflect improved memory. For example, running prior to class may enhance attention in class (Bass, 1985). Exercise has been shown to reduce or buffer the effects of stress, depression and anxiety, facilitating academic performance (reflected in mid-year examinations), and research also suggests that learners who participate in exercise are more self-determined, and therefore more intrinsically motivated (Hashim et al., 2012). Similarly, a relationship between health-related physical fitness and mathematics academic achievement scores has been found (Eveland-Sayers et al., 2009), reflecting improved encoding and retrieval of knowledge. A 45-minute period of exercise on a daily basis has also been shown, as expected, to improve fitness and is perhaps linked to increases in fluid intelligence and perceptual speed (Reed et al., 2013). The provision of quality physical education programmes offers an opportunity to improve academic achievement through increases in exercise activity (Ryan and Panettini, 2011).

The rise in obesity levels has been in part adversely influenced by the increase in children's time spent playing video games. This of course is of concern. However, the very behaviour that is causing concern has been examined by incorporating elements of exercise into those games. 'Exergaming', as it is known, has been shown to influence working memory in children (Russell, 2009), and working memory, as we have discussed above, is a vital component of the encoding stage of knowledge acquisition.

A useful data collection exercise would be for teachers to monitor their learners' performance (in learning or memory terms) after a PE lesson, compared to beforehand. Of course, there may be extraneous variables to take into account, such as the 'post-prandial dip' that appears following lunch, which may influence subsequent performance in lessons. However, the data collected by the teacher monitoring their class can be used to help structure weekly lessons to capitalise on the timing of PE sessions, by designing lessons immediately after PE that take advantage of the learners' renewed concentration levels.

BRAIN GYM® AND EMERGENT STRATEGIES

Although we have discussed the role of exercise in promoting cognitive development, a number of other strategies and interventions have been proposed. Perhaps most significantly is the use of Brain Gym®, a series of movements proposed to advocate the necessary stimulation required for effective learning (Hannaford, 1996). The premise upon which Brain Gym® has been developed is that, through a prescribed series of movements, greater integration of the brain and the body can be coordinated, in turn promoting more efficient learning. The movements are based on developing three dimensions: laterality, or the coordination of the right and left hemispheres of the brain to integrate movement and thinking (for example, through speech, reading, writing and so on); focusing, or the ability to coordinate information between the front and back portions of the brain used for comprehension; and centring, or the coordination of the top and bottom halves of the brain to balance rational thought and emotions (Dennison and Dennison, 1994).

Brain Gym® has been widely adopted by a range of countries; however, there is a paucity of credible academic research to support its unsubstantiated claims (see Hyatt, 2007). There have been concerns raised about the 'lack of a research-supported theoretical foundation', whereby after an extensive literature review only five peer-reviewed journal articles about the effectiveness were addressed, with all of the articles published in the same journal, and methodological issues have also been identified (Hyatt, 2007: 120).

This has not prevented the wide adoption of Brain Gym® in schools, although Hyatt (2007: 123) warns that, 'If teachers are to use scientific, research-based practices to maximum extent, they must have adequate training for interpreting research and be aware of past fads that never seem to pass.'

Despite the critique of Brain Gym®, recent research has advocated a simpler process to enhance learning: doodling. This indicated that doodling (in the case of the research, shading in a variety of shapes on a sheet of paper) can enhance memory recall by 29 per cent more than not doodling (Andrade, 2009). Perhaps the last thing a teacher should say to their learners is 'Put your pencils down and listen to me.' If one adopts the principles underlying context-dependent memory, holding a pen or pencil at the encoding stage of learning would then mean that the same pen or pencil becomes a cue or trigger for effective retrieval when required. Of course, we would not advocate this with retractable pens, where our own experience in lectures has shown us that the incessant clicking is just downright distracting!

6.5 CONCLUSION

The physical development of the human nervous system, outlined in Chapter 5, unlocks functional capacity for the growth or development of perception and cognition. When the child embarks on this fascinating journey, the child's interpretation of their environment changes as new or refined functions emerge. A classroom may appear the same to an adult over a period of time, but one should not assume that the child experiences that classroom in the same way. As teachers, we should attempt to explore the world 'through a child's eyes' and by this we are referring to more than simply their ocular apparatus.

6.6 FURTHER READING

Baddeley, A.D. (2002) 'Is working memory still working?', *European Psychologist*, 7 (2): 85–97. Alan Baddeley is a prominent researcher in the field of memory. Any of his books or papers are worth exploring. This one is a straightforward, readable example.

Gibson, J.J. (1979) *The Ecological Approach to Visual Perception*. Boston, MA: Houghton Mifflin. Gibson's book is the classical text on perception and the way in which we process visual information.

Miles, A.N. and Berntsen, D. (2011) 'Odour-induced mental time travel into the past and future: Do odour cues retain a unique link to our distant past?', *Memory*, 19 (8): 930–40.
This fascinating paper highlights the powerful effects of odour-evoked memories and may stimulate ideas for teachers on the use of olfactory cues, or smells, to enhance active learning and recall in the classroom.

Mulrine, C.F., Prater, M.A. and Jenkins, A. (2008) 'The active classroom: Supporting students with attention deficit hyperactivity disorder through exercise', *Teaching Exceptional Children*, 40 (5): 16–22.
This is a readable article examining physical activity for students with ADHD. It offers practical advice on how to incorporate techniques into lessons to benefit all learners, not just those with ADHD, and is worth reading.

7

SOCIAL, EMOTIONAL DEVELOPMENT AND PERSONALITY

CHAPTER OBJECTIVES

- Develop an understanding of how the developing child develops socially and emotionally.
- Appreciate how the child's stage of development affects their ability in the classroom.
- Develop an increased awareness of how the child can be supported through their social and emotional development.

TEACHERS' STANDARDS

A teacher must:

2   Promote good progress and outcomes by pupils

- be aware of pupils' capabilities and their prior knowledge, and plan teaching to build on these

5   Adapt teaching to respond to the strengths and needs of all pupils

- have a secure understanding of how a range of factors can inhibit pupils' ability to learn, and how best to overcome these
- demonstrate an awareness of the physical, social and intellectual development of children, and know how to adapt teaching to support pupils' education at different stages of development

7.1 INTRODUCTION

Central to Chapter 7 are the themes of social and emotional development. These themes, together with those discussed in Chapter 6, are intimately interrelated. A learner's personality will shape and be shaped by their experiences, including the way in which they learn and retain knowledge. Thinking of these themes in isolation is restrictive and unproductive, since it is equally feasible that one's personality will be shaped by intelligence, memory and learning style.

7.2 SOCIAL DEVELOPMENT IN THE DEVELOPING CHILD

Social development is a complex process of observing, assimilating and reproducing behaviours that are acceptable in the society within which the child lives. It is important at this point to point out that one's definition of 'society' can be considered fairly flexible. Society, as we perceive it as adults, refers to the wider society we live in. It is a global society or a Western society for example. Yet we can consider society as being a much smaller concept. As a learner, you are part of a 'society' in microcosm at university. We do not mean any societies that you may have joined while at university. Instead, we mean that the university itself exists in its own world, with its own rules, regulations and codes of conduct or practice. The same can be said of school. Headteachers comment in assemblies about the 'school community' and by this are referring to the unique society in school. It is unique, because while the education system shares a common vision, each school is different in some way. It is the dynamic mixture of teaching staff, children and management that leads to subtle or to extreme differences between each school. The school community both is part of the wider geographical community and is a community that exists in its own right. It is also exclusive insofar as 'membership' is restricted to staff and pupils who attend.

Considering the school as a society or community, a child must learn the formal rules of the school, alongside the accepted codes of behaviour in that community. Indeed, sometimes a child may have to relearn those formal rules, in instances of migration from other countries, necessitating cultural readjustment (Purdy et al., 2014). In a wider sense, this is known as the socialisation process (Haralambos and Holborn, 2008). The socialisation process is lifelong, although the term is largely used to explain the process that children undergo to enable them to become integrated into society. It is about learning the values of society, acceptable attitudes (that are deemed acceptable at a point in time and subject to change themselves), social skills and sensitivity, together with knowledge of appropriate language in that society (evident in the 'no expletives' policy of schools). It could be said that a child will undergo the socialisation process in two places, once during the school day and then outside of school. Since children spend a large proportion of their childhood at school, it is unsurprising that much of their socialisation takes place within the school system. Teachers facilitate the socialisation process by ensuring, as much as is possible, that children are learning the rules of 'societal engagement' through the rules of the school. Consistent reinforcement of those rules, in a positive way where possible, should serve to foster familiarity with those rules, with the expectation, anticipation or at least hope that the child will adopt them as a code of good conduct outside of school hours. In acquiring the rules of socialisation, the child, and later the adult, will learn a societal role: the role that the person occupies within the society, for example, mother, father, solicitor, doctor or mechanic, and the responsibilities that are acceptable for and expected of that role.

The three major facets of the socialisation process are significant others, social situations and individual constraints. Significant others, or socialising agents, are those people in positions of influence who act as facilitators of the knowledge needed. We have been careful here not to use the term 'educators' because, although these people do educate the child in the acceptable workings of society (Ametepee et al., 2009), they are not confined to being qualified teachers. Anyone who imparts socialising knowledge could be considered a teacher of sorts, but we would prefer to avoid confusion, hence the word 'facilitator'. Social situations are 'environmental opportunities' in which socialisation may take place, be reinforced, refined or adapted. Socialisation cannot take place in the absence of the external situation. Social situations may influence the child in positive ways, but equally, negative social situations can have a detrimental effect on a child's socialisation, for example, if the child 'falls in with the wrong crowd'. Individual constraints are those specific to the child. For example, children on the autistic spectrum will generally have a tendency to vary considerably from others (Rose and Anketell, 2009). Some will display extreme agitation towards any form of social interaction and this will undoubtedly contribute to the way in which they travel through the socialisation process. When this is combined with sometimes rather severe cognitive and emotional deficits, the child's development becomes hindered in a variety of ways. We will return to this topic in Chapter 9.

Societal norms, values and attitudes are linked to the notion of social control. Having undergone the socialisation process, individuals internalise these societal norms, values and attitudes and adopt them as their own. Society dictates or controls that which is deemed acceptable and unacceptable and is therefore under the controlling influence of those people in society who have sufficient authority or 'voice' to promote, or change, these norms, values and attitudes. Societal control may therefore be imposed from above, but may change if sufficient like-minded people reflect the changing needs of a society. This can be seen in the example of the fall of the Berlin Wall (see Gaab, 2011), or the fragmentation of the former Eastern Bloc countries (see Kramer, 2011). Of far less significance and closer to home, the relaxation of a strict school uniform policy may perhaps be brought about by the increasing pressure of the learner, or parental, voice.

The instruments of social control can take one of two forms: negative and positive. Negative social control occurs, as one might expect, through punishment and the deterrent effect of punishment. If formal rules, regulations or laws are broken, a punitive sanction serves to correct the recipient. Whether this is a prison sentence for breaking a law, or a detention for breaking a school rule, the principle is the same. However, negative social control is not necessarily so formal. Its controlling influence could take place through disapproval, such as 'the teacher's glare' that we have all experienced – or given, at some point in our school careers – or through ridicule, such as the sometimes-cruel way in which other children (who have learned and internalised the societal norms) poke fun at us for having performed a socially unacceptable action.

In contrast, positive social control exerts its influence by offering or providing rewards, approval and benefit of some kind. The rather behaviourist word 'reward' conveniently acts as an umbrella term to describe all three. A reward may be financial, or it may be monetary in some other way by providing something of monetary value even if it is not specifically currency. The teacher who gives out sweets for good work in lessons is providing a 'monetary' reward, as is the teacher who gives small gifts to each child in the class at the end of the academic year, since they both have monetary value. Approval is a rewarding experience and as we saw in Chapter 1 links in to our pursuit of satisfying self-esteem needs. So, the teacher who gives praise for good progress, or even good application, is providing a reward. The third type of positive social control – other benefit – can be whatever we want it to be. The teacher who shows a movie for children whose behaviour has been exemplary during term is providing a benefit, or at least a benefit as perceived by the children who are watching a movie and hence not doing double maths.

Although social control is, by definition, controlling, this does not mean that it is exploitative and it does not exist so that individuals can obtain personal gain at the expense of less fortunate members of society, although unfortunately in some instances this is the case: consider the host of dictatorial regimes that have been over-thrown in recent years. Social control is the mechanism by which society 'polices' itself and socialisation is the process by which people learn the rules of that society. If individuals are to adapt to the society that they inhabit, it is vital to acquire and internalise these rules. One of the ways in which these rules are acquired and internalised in children is through play.

Play is an extremely important aspect of social and cognitive development. Indeed, play can be considered as a form of social behaviour. Young children imitate what they have seen, either from their parents or from television. The young child pretending to be 'mummy' or the seven-year-old child acting out a role as 'teacher' in a play scenario with friends is testing their understanding of how others are expected to act in accordance with the label attached to their role (Barbu et al., 2011). A teacher, in the eyes of a seven-year-old, is expected to act in a particular way. Indeed, that expectation is perhaps taken through to adulthood and remains for many years.

ACTIVITY

Ask children in your class to write a list of ten characteristics of an adult in a chosen profession. Give the children the following list to choose from: police officer, teacher, bus driver, sports coach, doctor. Of course, the children could always choose something not on the list.

If you are able to conduct this task with children in different age groups, you will be able to see how their lists change across age groups.

Next, select one or two children at a time (no need to inform the children of this), and ask the whole class to act out their chosen role during break time. Observe and record the behaviour that you see. Compare this with the list of characteristics the children produced in class. This will give you an insight into how well they understand the role of adults in that profession for their age.

Piaget did not view play as imitation, but rather as role adoption: the child is not acting out the role of the adult; rather they are, according to Piaget, actually taking on that role. For the duration of the play activity, the child 'becomes' the teacher or the fire-fighter. Day-to-day objects are then used to symbolise items considered to be part of the role. In this way, Piaget saw play as a cognitive activity, rather than a social activity, which requires children to make use of thought processes to enhance the quality of the play experience. Piaget called this symbolic play (Piaget, 1955). Whether play is cognitively underpinned or not, the fact remains that it still takes place in social settings and is a social activity. Socialising processes are therefore at work during play and we see little benefit here in arguing over whether play falls into the realms of cognitive or social development. In an applied sense, play can be utilised by teachers to probe children's knowledge and understanding of adult – or older child – roles. Essentially this is the basis for the contrast between Piaget's theory of cognitive development and that of Vygotsky, who espoused a sociocultural theory of cognitive development (Vygotsky, 1978). As we point out elsewhere in this chapter, the culture in which a child lives and grows up contributes to shaping their development. For Vygotsky, cognitive development is the result of an interaction between a child and their environment. This is similar to Newell's model of constraints discussed in the section on physical development. Both Piaget and Vygotsky saw cognitive development as the creation of internal representations of the world. Evidence to support the importance of Vygotsky's inclusion of sociocultural factors is provided if one examines whether lack of stimulation or opportunities adversely influences sociocognitive development. One would assume that a child raised in a stimulating environment, with many opportunities to see, hear and interact with parents, friends, peers, teachers and others, would develop far more socially and cognitively than a child raised in an environment lacking little or any stimulation (we are thinking here of examples such as children of the 1990s in Romanian orphanages) (Audet and Mare, 2011). Lack of stimulation, cognitively, socially and culturally, has a negative impact on a child's development. The presence of others would appear to help the child in mastering problem-solving situations. Vygotsky would argue that this is as a result of those others guiding the child through the problem. The same can be said for linguistic development, which essentially is another problem-solving situation – the problem being: how can the child make themselves understood by communicating their needs effectively?

In Chapter 1 we discussed the evolutionary perspective, Darwinism and the survival of the fittest. We would now like to introduce the concept of social Darwinism. In social Darwinist terms, society is seen as competitive, where conflict often occurs. Those individuals who are successful survive the competition and conflict, whereas those who do not become unsuccessful. Success breeds social desirability and this in turn breeds greater success, hence the term 'social Darwinism'. Equally, failure to succeed diminishes social desirability and this in turns guides the individual on a downward spiral.

ACTIVITY   Does social Darwinism display itself in the classroom?

Look at the register and give a 'social success' rating to each child (0–10, where 10 is high).

Next, look at each child's academic attainment and give them an 'academic success' rating (0–10, where 10 is high).

Plot these ratings on a scatterplot.

Next, produce a table figure of your classroom, containing the names of the children, and where they sit.

Is there a relationship between their 'social success' and 'academic success' in terms of who sits with whom? Reflect on what this means in social Darwinist terms. Do you need to change your classroom seating plan?

7.3 EMOTIONAL DEVELOPMENT IN THE DEVELOPING CHILD

In discussing emotional development it is first necessary to establish what is actually meant by the term. Is 'emotion' mood, is 'mood' emotion? Where does the term 'affect' fit in? The literature sometimes uses these terms interchangeably to mean the same thing, when actually there are subtle differences between them. Figure 7.1 outlines these subtleties.

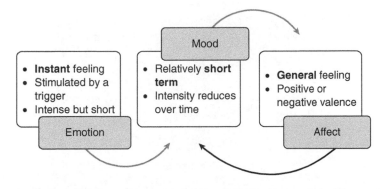

Figure 7.1   The nuances between emotion, mood and affect

As Figure 7.1 summarises, an emotion is an instant feeling created by some form of trigger, such as a car pulling out in front of you. It is a short, intense feeling that may cause a person's mood to change. No doubt we have all heard someone comment, '… and that put me in a bad mood for the morning.' A bad mood generally diminishes over time. On occasion, however, it remains and leads to a generalised negative feeling, or a positive feeling if the mood was positive. These distinctions are subtle but it is necessary to understand the difference between them, even if it does seem on the surface to be a matter of semantics.

So, now that we have established this difference, let's look at emotions in more depth. Our starting point should be: 'What exactly is an emotion?' There are only six basic emotions: anger, fear, sadness, surprise, excitement, joy (Niedenthal et al., 2006). Joy, excitement and surprise are deemed positive emotions, while anger or rage, fear or terror, and sadness or dejection are deemed negative emotions (Niedenthal et al., 2006). Dig a little deeper and one will find that these basic emotions have been expanded to include additional emotions. In the same way that two grape varieties may be blended to produce a different flavour of wine, Plutchik (2003) also talks of blending emotions to produce 'emotional variants'. Plutchik's emotional wheel can be seen in Figure 7.2 and the blends can be seen around the outer edge of the wheel.

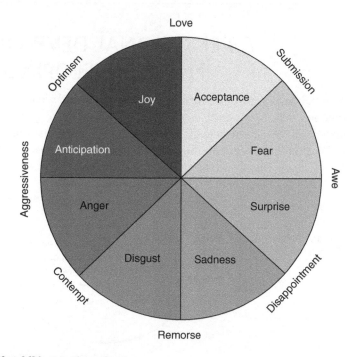

Figure 7.2   Plutchik's emotion wheel

As we can see, the basic emotions are contained within the wheel, along with the additional emotions: disgust, acceptance and anticipation. When two adjacent emotions are combined, a new emotional blend emerges. For example, a combination of anger and disgust produces contempt. Equally a combination of joy and anticipation produces optimism. By thinking of emotions in blended terms, we are now provided with a range of emotions that actually seem to make sense.

ACTIVITY   Identifying emotions in the classroom

Convert Plutchik's emotional wheel into a record sheet so that you can record instances where you observe a particular emotion.

As the opportunity arises during a normal school day, or lesson if you prefer, record any examples of emotions that appear on your record sheet.

If you feel that you are able to do the same for emotional blends then do the same.

A word of warning: you may need to establish what each emotion looks like before you start, in terms of the observable characteristics. If you cannot 'see' it you cannot record it.

Emotional development begins early on in an infant's life. A newborn infant bonds very quickly with its mother, followed by those family members closest to the infant. In evolutionary terms, John Bowlby (1969) advocates that this is a natural occurrence in the animal kingdom and, as humans, we are no different to many other species in this respect. Bowlby coined the term 'attachment'. By this, he proposed that the child forms a relationship with their mother that maximises the closeness of contact between them. This will be the child's first experience of a relationship with another person. All future emotional attachments will be based on elements of this first relationship.

There is also a strong link between cognition (cortex), emotion (limbic system, which is subcortical) and social development (see Figure 7.3). We have explored cognition and social development but it is apparent that to isolate any one of these is difficult, if not impossible, when considering a child's developmental years.

An alternative way to explore emotions is to consider them in terms of the interplay between hormonal influences, autonomic nervous system responses and behaviour. Each 'ingredient' is thrown into the mix and what emerges is a result of previous experience, current practice, the context in which the emotional response is portrayed and whether it is deemed by others to be appropriate or not. This 'mix' model may be further refined. Myers (2010) proposes that it is the interpretation of the physiological activation and expressive behaviour that defines the emotion experienced. This view is based on the classic model proposed by Schachter and Singer (1962) and is still accepted today. The importance of Schachter and Singer's model is that it espouses the significance of cognition in interpreting and experiencing emotions.

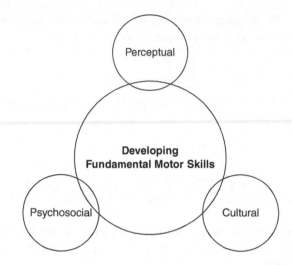

Figure 7.3   Schematic representation showing the triangulation of cognition, emotion and social development

While these schematic figures help us to understand emotion as a general theme, it is important to consider a model with greater scientific credibility. We have discussed the types of emotions and these can be borne in mind when one considers the cognitive relational model of emotion, espoused by Lazarus (1991, 1999) as summarised below:

System: emotion is an organised process.

Process: emotion can recur in same patterns within a stable person-environment.

Developmental: biological and social factors influence emotion.

Specificity: each emotional experience is distinct.

Relational meaning: emotional meaning is constructed through cognitive appraisal.

The cognitive relational model is based on five principles: system, process, developmental, specificity and relational meaning. The system principle holds that emotion is organised and structured. The process principle holds that if the person and their environment is stable, then displays of emotion will follow similar patterns. The developmental principle holds that emotion is influenced by biological and social factors. Both of these factors continually change as a person progresses through childhood and therefore learning is always a case of 'learning for the immediate future' and transferring skills if necessary as the next change takes place. The specificity principle holds that each emotional experience is distinct. We can refer back to the basic emotions and Plutchik's emotion wheel for support. Finally, the relational meaning principle holds that it is through cognitive appraisal and evaluation that emotional meaning is constructed. So the meaning of a particular emotion is based on an individual's interpretation of it.

There is evidence to suggest that newborns show awareness of their mother's breast milk over that of formula milk, or preferences for their mother's breast milk over that of another mother (Aoyama et al., 2010; Marlier and Schaal, 2005; Schaal et al., 1980). Such research concludes that the newborn is displaying signs of olfactory bonding, and that the smell of the mother's breast is more familiar to the newborn that that of a stranger. This behaviour is not unidirectional either. Mothers have been shown to be equally adept at identifying their own babies by odour alone. Whether this is a genetic predisposition or whether it is a result of familiarity and learning is less important here. What is interesting is that the mother–child bond is already forming. We shall consider bonding, or attachment, later in this section.

It is important to remind ourselves too of the structural part of the brain that plays a role in this process. We discussed the evolutionary divisions of the brain in Chapter 5 (reptilian, palaeo-mammalian, neo-mammalian) and commented on the palaeo-mammalian brain as being the emotional brain: the structures lying underneath the cortex that we now call the limbic system. The link between the emotional brain and the olfactory system is also very strong. The olfactory sense (the sense of smell) is an extremely powerful sense that links us almost immediately to memories and emotions (Castle et al., 2000). Humans are very good at associating particular smells with particular events or experiences. We can show this through the example in the following activity.

ACTIVITY

Go into your school environment, close your eyes ... and sniff! Be aware of the smells in different parts of the school, including your classroom at different points of the day. For example:

8.30am: Coffee – staffroom

11.30am: Body odour – school hall or gym after PE

12.00pm: Lunchtime smells

1.00pm: Damp coats hanging up if it has been raining

2.30pm: Chlorine – swimming baths for lesson

4pm: Disinfectant or other cleaning products

(Continued)

(Of course the examples used will be largely determined by the age range you work with. The science corridor in a secondary school could smell of sulphur. You may smell campfire smoke if you have been working with Forest Schools.)

Make a list of these odours.

Look at the list of odours you produced in the task. Can you recreate these in the privacy of your own home? This might involve bringing physical resources with you. For example, sit at home, sharpen a pencil and put it close to your nose to smell it. Close your eyes and think of the classroom. You should now mentally be in the classroom. The smell has acted as a cue to fool your brain into thinking that you were actually there.

REFLECTION

If you wish to enhance a classroom-based or other learning activity, think about whether you can use an odour to recreate the odour-context of that activity. For example, Nikki Castle, a teacher in Droitwich Spa, England, sought our assistance in using the sense of smell to enhance her English lessons. We guided her in the use of mental imagery and added everyday odours to this concept. Nikki would set the scene for an essay-writing task by reading a passage to contextualise the topic and have several objects available for her children to smell, such as a peeled orange, or a chocolate cake. She would then incorporate a link to the smell in her verbal delivery and encourage her learners to consider their evoked thoughts and emotions from the odour. This odour-fuelled contextualisation led her to unlock emotional aspects of the children's writing that had previously not been available. Consider how you could use odour to enhance lessons that you teach.

The interrelationship between cognitive, social and emotional development is further strengthened when one considers our earlier comment that memory, a temporal lobe function, is equally entwined in each of these developmental aspects (Kolb and Whishaw, 2015). Previous experiences are stored in memory, or at least they are if they are 'memorable', and current actions are based to a large extent on an individual's evaluation of what is expected in the current situation. Memory therefore guides future actions, whether these actions are purely cognitive or whether they are social. Emotions tend to colour one's actions; the emotional state an individual is in will influence what they do and how they do it. For example, a child in your class who is usually mild-mannered may suddenly display aggressive behaviour in response to a fellow child who accidentally knocks a water bottle onto a piece of work. This out-of-character action may have been caused by the child arriving at school in an angry state because of an event that happened at home, but which has had a negative influence since then and has not dissipated by the start of the school day.

Controlling one's emotions is sometimes difficult, even for adults. Not only are children expected to acquire emotional control, but society perhaps requires that they acquire it swiftly. Emotional intelligence (EI) is a recently emerging concept in psychology that guides us in applying a label to this emotional control (see Roberts et al., 2008, for a status update). EI can be considered as the ability to respond in emotionally inducing situations, to be able to manage oneself and adapt to such situations in an appropriate manner. It can be defined as: 'The ability to perceive emotion, integrate emotion to facilitate thought, understand emotions, and to regulate emotions to promote personal growth' (Salovey and Mayer, 1990: 185). In an applied sense EI entails understanding the triggers of emotional responses and adapting to the situation in such a way that responses may be reconsidered before acting.

In a similar way that Piaget talks about children acquiring skills as they progress through the stages of cognitive development, we must consider that children also face the need to acquire skills in EI during these formative years. Yet EI is not an all-or-nothing skill. It is not something that one doesn't possess on a Monday but does possess by the next day. The context for making use of EI in the adult world is relatively stable. As adults, we are expected to behave in certain societally predetermined ways in a varied range of relationships. But for children this is not quite so stable. Of course, children are expected to behave in certain ways and use EI to inform this behaviour. However, in reality, children might find it easy to imitate, and indeed we know that infants imitate adult behaviour long before they understand the meaning of that behaviour, but they do not necessarily possess the skills required for empathy. In a classroom situation, the teacher will generally be able to use EI to put themselves in the minds of the children, in order to anticipate how they will react to a given situation. Similarly, dependent on the age group, children will be able to use their growing knowledge of EI to anticipate how other children, or the teacher, may react to a given situation that they instigate. This understanding will become refined with increasing age or, to be more exact, with increasing experience, combined with age. However, children on the autistic spectrum lack some or all of this apparently natural ability to evaluate and interpret anticipatory behaviour in others. Geake (2009) draws attention to the discovery of 'mirror neurons' as a possible explanation, proposing that a mirror neuron system exists in the brain to enable humans to acquire information through imitation. Although evidence for mirror neurons exists (Heyes, 2010), whether this is a valid explanation of the process, or rather whether it can be explained within the standard explanations of memory and knowledge acquisition, remains to be seen.

What is clear is the relationship between emotion and cognition, which, as we have said, appears to be intimately interlinked. Having discussed the development of so many different facets during childhood, we would probably say that emotion and cognition are inseparable. Look at the next activity and consider how your emotions colour and are coloured by your cognitions.

ACTIVITY

Establish an occasion when you are in a good mood, and your emotions are positive and 'high'. For example, this might be just after a period of exercise, a pleasant walk or a social situation that you enjoyed. Next, mark a set of books, or some other work-related task that you know is on your 'to do' list. As you are carrying out this activity, be aware of your emotional state and see how it affects your performance of the activity. You will probably find it easier. Carry out the same procedure when you are in a negative emotional state. For example, you have had a particularly tiresome meeting, a stressful drive home or have to produce a document for the management team by tomorrow as well as marking those books. You will probably find the task much harder and your emotional state will influence the way in which you go about marking.

Of course, as we pointed out earlier, the cortical (cognitive) and subcortical (emotional) areas are housed within the same skull, so it would be unsafe to assume that they do not interact with each other. As a result of the limbic system emerging earlier in the evolutionary development of the brain, it may play second fiddle to the neocortex (or it may not) but it cannot be ignored. Emotional development taking place during the development of the brain from birth to adulthood must therefore be given greater prominence than perhaps it was given before the turn of this century. This translates to the classroom in an applied sense. How many times have you heard of a colleague being told to take five deep breaths or count to ten before selecting a course of action on something that has annoyed them? The immediate emotional response is the dominant response; evolution has given us that legacy. The rational, cortex-based response takes some thought, information processing and decision-making and these things take a little longer before they become clear. Hence the advice – 'five deep breaths' or 'count to ten' – provides a calming-down period. It is a behavioural no-man's land and should be used as just that: a time to remove oneself from the emotionality of the situation before responding. As a classroom management strategy, it is equally effective and something that no doubt we all endeavour to instil in the children within our charge.

The reason for your completing the task above is based around the following question: 'If you cannot identify your own emotional states and feelings, then how can you expect to be able to identify the emotional states and feelings in others?' In order to understand how these emotional states and feelings influence behaviour, one needs to be self-reflective. Being armed with an understanding of emotional states and feelings in oneself will help in putting oneself into another person's position and thus in empathising with that person's feelings. Again, we all ask children to do this when something inappropriate has happened at school: 'How do you think Jane feels about what you have done to her book?' We are teaching our children about emotional intelligence even if we have been unaware of the label placed on it. Interestingly, research evidence suggests that there is a link between EI and academic achievement (Mavroveli and Sánchez-Ruiz, 2011; Qualter et al., 2012).

REFLECTION

Development is a widely used yet extremely complex term. You should always ask the question, 'Development of what?' This will enable you to focus more clearly on the specific area, such as motor development. In a sense, it equates to your adopting a specific perspective.

With the exceptions of social and emotional development, this chapter has centred upon chronological development. We have placed time frames on the development of processes and emergence of actions or abilities. These time frames are arbitrary and although based on normative data or evidence are of course not set in stone. Individual differences play a huge role in developing systems, processes and abilities. So too, as we have discussed, do environmental opportunities. Nevertheless, thinking in terms of age-related development does help in understanding how abilities develop and mature. We would ask you also to consider the age-related divisions within the educational system currently in place. Of course this will differ depending on which country you are working in. The existing structure within England and Wales can be seen in Table 7.1.

Table 7.1 The National Curriculum Key Stages and associated age ranges, England and Wales

Key stage	School year group	Age range
1	Reception to Year 2	4–7
2	Year 3 to Year 6	7–11
3	Year 7 to Year 9	11–14
4	Year 10 to Year 11	14–16
5	Year 12 to Year 13	16–18

In Chapter 5 we explored how the individual learner develops, by considering the development of a wide array of physical systems and processes. It should have become apparent that each of these systems and processes influences and is influenced by one another in some way or other. Such changes in development lay foundations for the variety of unique attributes that characterise each learner. In the same way that no two fingerprints are identical, no two people are identical, not even identical twins. This will be explored through four components of the individual learner: personality, intelligence, memory and learning styles (Figure 7.4).

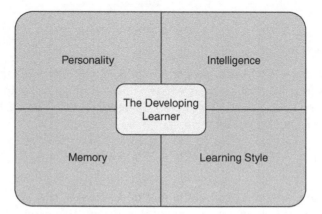

Figure 7.4   The influences on the individual learner

7.4 PERSONALITY

Everybody has a personality. It is part of what makes us who we are. Even if you have heard somebody talking about 'so and so, who has no personality', it does not actually mean that they have no personality. Rather, it means that the person being spoken about is perhaps not particularly vibrant or lively. People jokingly talk about accountants and librarians as having no personality. This of course is not the case. Such people may simply be quiet and restrained in their day job and may, or may not, continue this in their private lives. It still does not mean that they have no personality.

Children are not born with personality. Personality is something that is acquired, as a result of an interaction with the environment and people within that environment. Personality is therefore shaped from infancy. People talk in terms of infants having a personality. But equally people talk about a child's personality beginning to show through later in childhood. That same personality may, and usually does, change during adolescence. Any parent will have a story or two about their child's 'terrible twos' or their teenage years. These examples are not bad: they merely reflect the child's personality at a particular point in time. They are a personality snapshot that can change over time. As children enter adulthood, they establish a personality that often remains the same for many years, although sometimes life-events and stresses may cause, or contribute to, a change in personality.

None of this introduction to personality thus far provides an indicator of exactly what personality is. How can one be expected to establish a personality in light of such complexity? Our starting point must therefore be to provide a definition of personality so that we may explore the concept further. Let us make it clear that defining personality is extremely difficult. What should be included? What should be omitted? This is evident in there having been in excess of 50 definitions of personality by 1927 (Allport, 1927). Think back to Chapter 1, where we discussed perspectives. Any definition may possibly be coloured by one's perspective and thus may be inappropriate for use by theorists, or practitioners, who favour a different perspective. There are, however, some elements that one should include in a definition of personality. These include, but are not restricted to, the notion that whatever constitutes personality includes an element of stability: the characteristics of a person's personality do not change (much) over time. They are predictable because they happen consistently when the person is faced with different situations. Another element of personality is the notion of difference. It is apparent, looking around us, that people are different in their personalities. There is no single personality type. It is not an all-or-nothing concept. Indeed, if everyone were the same, life would be pretty mundane to say the least.

So we now have a simple definition of personality: 'A particular pattern of behaviour and thinking that prevails across time and situations and differentiates one person from another' (Carlson et al., 2004: 582). Michael Eysenck expands on Carlson et al.'s definition, using an earlier definition by Child (1968): 'The more or less stable, internal factors that make one person's behaviour consistent from one time to another and different from the behaviour other people would manifest in comparable situations' (Eysenck, 2009: 287). As Eysenck points out, the word 'internal' is significant because it identifies that personality is an internalised process that manifests itself in our externalised behaviour.

ACTIVITY   Identifying personality characteristics

Using your class, or teaching practice, compile a list of personality types from your existing knowledge of the children. Ask yourself how they differ from each other, and where they may be similar to each other.

Are any common themes emerging as you progress through the class list?

Does anyone have any personality characteristics that you admire?

Does anyone have any personality characteristics that you dislike?

Having completed this task, you will already have some appreciation of what we will discuss next. Did you find that you were able to group children on the basis of your evaluation of their personalities? Would it be prudent to put personality-alike children together within the classroom seating arrangement, or should you mix and match? Here is one example of how personality may influence the way in which the classroom operates. Our advice, rather than being prescriptive, would be to ask you to test your own hypotheses and see what works for you. Bear in mind that this may not work exactly the same for another teacher and, indeed, it may not work for you next year. So you will need to see how to use personality theory to inform the way in which you operate.

In returning to the list generated in the task above, you may have noticed a small number of themes, or characteristics, emerging. These characteristics are known as traits and it is to trait theories of personality that we shall turn next. We have moved a long way from early, pre-psychology days of theorists trying to explain personality characteristics. In the second century AD, the Greek physician Galen proposed a theory based on excesses of one of four fluids, or humours as he called them. These can be seen in Table 7.2, along with a description of their associated personality traits.

Although you may have used terms such as those found in Table 7.2 it is highly unlikely that you will have related them to the four humours and, of course, why should you? We know that personality is not related to excesses of these substances; it may though be influenced in part, in some people, on occasion by excesses or reduced amounts of neurotransmitters, neuromodulators or fluctuations in the neuro-endocrine system, but that is a different thing entirely. Unbeknown to him, Galen's contribution to psychology was to establish a list of personality types. Furthermore, the four humours were adopted by Rudolf Steiner as a way of differentiating the different needs of learners (Steiner, 2008). In modern psychology, however, we prefer to discuss the degree, or extent, to which these traits contribute to a person's personality. In looking at personality in this manner, it becomes possible to investigate personality while also acknowledging the wide variety of individual differences that exist between people.

Table 7.2   Galen's 'four humours' and their associated personality traits

Humour	Excesses of	Personality traits
Sanguine	Blood	Happy, cheerful and full of passion
Choleric	Yellow bile	Irritable and bad tempered
Phlegmatic	Phlegm	Unexcited, calm and lethargic
Melancholic	Black bile	Pessimistic and miserable

A trait therefore is a characteristic that can be observed or inferred in people. Height and weight are traits, albeit physical ones, as we saw in Figures 5.2a and 5.2b (Chapter 5). We would recommend that you revisit these briefly before reading any further. Why is this important?

It is important because it provides people with a valid and reliable method of being located somewhere on a continuum for height and weight. As such, with such traits as height and weight, while both are to some extent predisposed, aspects such as muscle mass can place a rugby prop-forward in the 'obese' category, despite being incredibly fit. Consequently, with any such trait, whether physical or psychological, there are extraneous influences that may affect a person at a specific point in time. Additionally, while psychometrics are used for psychological assessment, they are never used in isolation and should only be used to inform a wider discussion. Furthermore, the results of a psychometric test are only reliable for a six-month period before needing to be repeated.

Depending on which theorist we are discussing, there are between 3 and 16 personality traits. This is considerably fewer than the 4,000 generated by Allport and Odbert (1936) in a trawl of descriptors that related, in their view, to personality, and interestingly it supports our earlier point that personality is notoriously difficult to define. We will examine those factors of personality deemed traits by four personality theorists, Raymond Cattell, Hans Eysenck, and Robert McCrae and Paul Costa.

For each of these theorists, the statistical test of choice in determining personality traits was factor analysis. In order to explain factor analysis, we need to refer to questionnaires. Questions in questionnaires are usually grouped together under a handful of umbrella headings or themes. So, a 50-question questionnaire may actually be exploring five themes, because the questions can be collapsed into these themes. Factor analysis is a technique that establishes which of those questions collapse into those themes, and researchers who create questionnaires will spend time ensuring that the questions do actually collapse into these themes. So, factor analysis is a way of ensuring that the questionnaire does what it purports to do. Personality questionnaires are no different. Allport and Odbert (1936) did not have 4,000 factors. Equally, Cattell, Eysenck, and McCrae and Costa have collapsed many questions into between 3 and 16 themes or factors.

Raymond Cattell was the first person to produce a questionnaire that was considered at the time to reflect 16 personality traits, or so-called 'source traits' (rather than the less-significant 'surface traits'). Table 7.3 outlines the factors generated by Cattell's (1956a, 1956b, 1956c, 1956d) '16PF', which stands for 16 Personality Factors. The respondent, completing the questionnaire, will answer each question on a ten-point scale and when collapsed into the factors in Table 7.3, a profile will emerge for those factors. Once a profile has been generated, this can be compared with the profiles of other people. This is the essence of personality tests and personality testing. It is worth mentioning at this point that we have not said whether any of these factors

Table 7.3   Cattell's 16PF source traits

Cool	Warm
Concrete thinking	Abstract thinking
Affected by feelings	Emotionally stable
Submissive	Dominant
Sober	Enthusiastic
Expedient	Conscientious
Shy	Bold
Tough-minded	Tender-minded
Trusting	Suspicious
Practical	Imaginative
Forthright	Shrewd
Self-assured	Apprehensive
Conservative	Experimenting
Group-oriented	Self-sufficient
Undisciplined	Controlled
Relaxed	Tense

are positive or negative. For example, is 'submissive' a negative trait and 'dominant' a positive one? While one might prefer a police officer to be authoritative in the field, one might prefer a butler, or other member of a royal household, to be unassuming. Both qualities are pertinent to the situation the police officer and butler find themselves in. Equally, in the classroom, a teacher who is submissive to a dominant child will struggle to establish control. Taking another example, while one can see the merit of 'controlled', is 'undisciplined' a negative personality trait, or is it representative of a person not being afraid to step out from the crowd, being free from the constraints of authority?

Cattell's 16PF remains popular but in actuality should be viewed with some caution. As you will see from Table 7.3, some of the factors are closely allied with each other. For example, the relaxed continuum, the apprehensive continuum and the emotionally stable continuum would appear to be testing a more generalised, anxiety-related factor. The inconsistency in findings produced when using the 16PF has led to it falling out of favour among psychologists. Notwithstanding this problem, Cattell's approach has provided a focus for refinement by other theorists.

Hans Eysenck (1916–97) argued that personality could be collapsible into as few as three factors: extroversion, neuroticism and psychoticism. As was the case for Cattell's factors, each of these factors is bipolar in nature: they have two opposing ends. The Eysenck Personality Questionnaire (EPQ) (Eysenck and Eysenck, 1975) was produced by Eysenck and his wife to assess these personality traits.

As we can see in Figure 7.5, a person will fall at some point or other on each of these scales. Extroversion reflects the extent to which a person is highly outgoing while its polar opposite, introversion, reflects the extent to which a person is cautious, isolating (as opposed to isolated) and crowd-averse. Neuroticism reflects the extent to which a person is anxious. People who score high on neuroticism are highly anxious and suffer from tension and emotional instability. In contrast people who score low on neuroticism are relaxed and emotionally stable. A child in your class who you might say is 'highly strung' would probably score high on the neuroticism scale if you scored them on the questionnaire. The psychoticism dimension is centred on aggression, egocentricity and antisocial activity. People who score high on psychoticism are aggressive, impersonal, cold and egocentric (overly self-focused), while those on the polar opposite of the scale are non-aggressive, warm and caring for others. We must make the point here that Eysenck's use of the psychoticism scale does not refer to the same meaning as 'psychotic' in clinical psychology. Psychoticism is not what is commonly thought of as relating to a psychopath (someone with a severe mental disorder that may manifest itself through extreme violence). Rather, it takes the antisocial personality attributes and suggests that the person is averse to being social in a way that society finds acceptable. So, a recluse or hermit may score highly on this scale simply by the nature of their choice to avoid social contact.

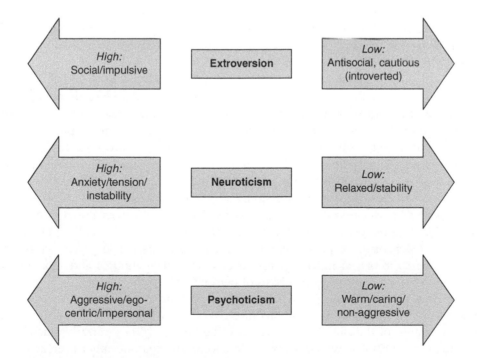

Figure 7.5   The polarised nature of Eysenck's personality traits

Eysenck's theory of personality is based on the premise that personality is biological in nature. By this he emphasises the importance of physiological arousal of the central nervous system, which we discussed in Chapter 5. For Eysenck, activation of the brain is responsible for personality. People who have higher levels of cortical arousal have little need to seek further arousal. According to Eysenck, these people would score highly on introversion. In contrast, people who have low levels of cortical arousal feel a need to seek out additional arousal-inducing activities in order to boost their levels of arousal. For Eysenck, these people would score highly on extroversion. This line of thinking has intuitive appeal and immediately throws a genetic basis into the theory. For Eysenck, our propensity to form an individualised personality is dictated by our genes, because it is our genes that determine where we all sit on the arousal continuum. Eysenck applied the same argument to the neuroticism scale: people who are high in neuroticism do not need to seek out any further activation. The reasoning behind the activation for psychoticism remains less clear. However, as a theory of personality, this explains why some people would favour seeking out extreme activities, such as bungee jumping or motorsport for example, while for other people, those activities would induce fear and dread.

The blend of emotions which make our unique personality are a blend of different aspects. For example, whether we like risk and excitement and are outgoing and sociable, compared to being sociable but more risk-aversive in nature. The 'blend' is akin to any recipe: an addition of slightly more of one ingredient can change the overall flavour of a meal. In a similar way, Eysenck's personality factors can be blended to form new combinations. For example, pessimism is a personality trait that we have all experienced in people at some point in our daily contact with others. Pessimism does not, however, appear in Figure 7.5. In fact it does, but one needs to look below the surface a little. According to Eysenck, pessimism is a blend of the extroversion and neuroticism scales. More specifically, a person whose responses on the EPQ place them higher on introversion and higher on the neuroticism scales, reflecting higher instability, would be associated with what we understand to be the traits of a pessimistic person.

There is, however, insufficient evidence to support Eysenck's proposal that genes are responsible for 67 per cent of the individual differences in personality among people. Indeed, as one comprehensive study has shown, the percentage is more likely to be in the region of 41 per cent for extroversion, and 31 per cent for neuroticism (Pederson et al., 1988). Nevertheless, Eysenck has collapsed Cattell's 16 traits down further into manageable units (or perhaps unmanageable by the small number) and has put forward a potential mechanism for personality through cortical arousal. The psychoticism scale does not appear to play as much of a role as Eysenck initially thought and, more importantly, support for the physiological basis of personality is sadly lacking.

In recent years, psychologists in general have tended to favour the 'Big Five' approach to personality (Costa and McCrae, 1985), albeit with some debate regarding the exact nature of the Big Five. So, what are the Big Five? They can be remembered using the word 'OCEAN', which is not a reference to the sea but rather is an acronym, explained in Table 7.4.

Table 7.4 The 'Big Five' personality traits identified by Costa and McCrae, 1985 (adapted from Eysenck, 2009)

Trait	Descriptor	Learner characteristic
Openness	Creativity/imagination/curiosity	Interest in a topic; going beyond what is expected; intrigue
Conscientiousness	Diligent (work ethic)/persistence/ambition	Attention to detail with the task; wanting to do one's very best
Extroversion	Sociability/optimism/talkative	Willing to share and discuss ideas with peers
Agreeableness	Cooperation/good-natured/helpful	Working together with other learners in a constructivist approach; helping other learners individually or collectively
Neuroticism	Anxiety/insecurity/emotional	Vulnerability; unsure of what is expected from the teacher or the task; emotional distress

These five traits have been collapsed from a 181-item questionnaire, the Neuroticism, Extroversion, and Openness Personality Inventory (NEO-PI), designed specifically for this purpose (McCrae and Costa, 1990), using a five-point Likert scale ranging from 'strongly agree' to 'strongly disagree'. The NEO-PI has been linked to social status in adults, with those people scoring highly on extroversion being correlated with higher social status in both men and women. Our point here is that the beginnings of these personality traits are formed during childhood and, as a teacher, you will be ideally placed to see personality develop before your very eyes. This surely is a privileged position to be in.

ACTIVITY   Can you see the 'Big Five'?

Select five children from your class. Using the descriptors in Table 7.4 above, see if you can establish whether your children display any or all of these personality traits (on a yes or no basis). Next, consider the extent to which the children display these traits. Use a 1–10 rating scale for ease of scoring.

We must stress that this procedure is not how the NEO-PI operates, but does help you to interpret these traits through the child's observable behaviour. Let's face it: administering a 181-item questionnaire would be at the very least impractical and totally inappropriate in terms of the data it may produce (the NEO-PI was not designed for use with children).

As with Cattell's and Eysenck's traits, the Big Five do contain an element of potential overlap, so while they offer a useable measure of personality, the factors are not necessarily as independent of each other as perhaps one might like them to be.

Whether this problem will ever be truly resolved, given the complexity of personality as a concept, remains to be seen.

Having looked at some of the many personality theorists, we are faced with something of a dilemma. Developing one's personality is quite evidently something very personal. We all have the freedom, within certain constraints, to develop our own unique personality. Or do we? Does society impose personality upon us? As we have seen in Chapter 6, there are many factors that come into play when 'sculpting' us as individuals. Opportunities are available to some people and not to others, or at least not to the same extent. These opportunities help forge the adults we become, as do the setbacks we face. The point we are making is that, while a list or set of personality traits can be generated, they are not sufficient on their own to be of any use, until the reason for finding people with those 'desired' traits is apparent. Personality testing, more generally subsumed under the banner of psychometric testing, has been utilised in industry for many years within many high-profile companies, such as Coca-Cola, the Metropolitan Police, Tesco and the National Health Service (NHS), among many others (Psytech International, 2013). Companies often employ people on the basis of whether those people fit in with the operations of the company, based partly on psychometric scores. Furthermore, in the *Importance of Teaching: The Schools White Paper*, section 2.11 discusses the use of 'assessments of aptitude, personality and resilience as part of the candidate selection process … as part of the selection process for teacher training' (Department for Education, 2010: 21). At the time of writing, this initiative has yet to be implemented nationally.

Within schools, children are labelled with particular personality traits from an early age (see Chapter 9). This is not necessarily a bad thing; it is simply human nature to categorise and compartmentalise everything we can, so that a sense of order can be achieved. As a teacher, you will have, or think you have, a good idea of which professions would be suited to which children in your class the further through childhood they get. There will no doubt be occasions where these predictions are way off the mark but, in the main, as a teacher, you will be in a position where you are instrumental in facilitating their progress towards adult careers.

Establishing specific traits is only one way of exploring personality. Whether people respond in the same way across different situations or the same situation on different occasions has yet to provide unequivocal evidence. We cannot simply say that people will respond in the same way, reflecting their personality. One might benefit therefore from exploring personality from a different angle. In previous chapters we have established a need to consider the person in relation to their environment and their own previous experiences: the person–environment interaction (remember Newell's model from Chapter 5, for example). The social learning approach to personality seeks not to establish specific traits. Rather, psychologists adhering to social learning theory seek to understand the effects of environmental and cognitive influences on personality, as shown in Figure 7.6.

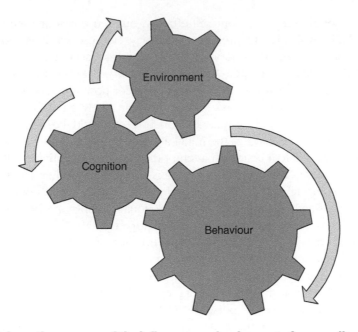

Figure 7.6 Schematic summary of the influences on development of personality

With this schematic figure in mind we are ready to explore Bandura's social-cognitive approach to personality (Bandura, 1986, 1999). For Bandura, reciprocal determinism plays a significant role in establishing personality. Reciprocal determinism is nothing new to you: Newell's model is an example, as is the diagram above. It can be thought of in terms of Heider's balance theory (Heider, 1958) – the notion that social attraction is a two-way or mutual concept. So, to put this in context, if child A likes child B, there is a greater likelihood that child B will also like child A. Equally, in Figure 7.6, cognition determines and is determined by behaviour and both are determined by their interaction with the environment. One without the influence or contribution from another would be lacking, in the same way that walking in the absence of having two fully functioning legs would be lacking – we do not use this in a derogatory sense, merely as a simple example to help you remember what the term 'reciprocal determinism' conveys.

Bandura also places emphasis on expectancy. By this he means that a person's expectations of success at a particular task or activity will determine whether or not the person will adapt to their changing environment or whether they will revert to how they usually behave in given situations. You may notice that certain children in your class behave consistently across many situations, and when you introduce a new situation, this causes confusion for them. Some will test out their skills while others will not. Those who refuse to test their skills may be doing so in order to avoid failure while those who agree to give it a go are prepared to accept this as a learning experience.

Both of these options feed in to our self-efficacy, our sense of our own abilities. The path of avoidance will serve to protect self-efficacy, because we have not failed, and hence have avoided appearing to look foolish. The path of acceptance will serve to test our limits and develop and acquire adaptive skills, which in the longer term may be far more beneficial even if we do initially fail. Consider how you feel when a child has tried but failed in a challenging task. You more than likely gave the child praise for attempting the challenge and commented on how it would be easier next time as things are never usually as hard as the initial attempt. Similarly, you will no doubt have observed situations where a child will attempt the challenging activity, but will give up very quickly. You might notice that this happens in a range of other situations and you may mentally attach a label to this behaviour in relation to the child's personality. Other children who constantly fail, yet persevere, are equally displaying behaviour that you would see as an asset ('X can't do it, but never stops trying').

Self-efficacy is developed on the basis of four factors: a child's previous experience (whether they were successful last time when performing the activity); transferable or vicarious experience (whether the child has seen another child perform the activity successfully – this is vital in terms of imitating observed behaviour of others: 'If they can do it then so can I'); verbal persuasion (if a child is convinced by someone else that they do actually possess the ability and skills necessary to complete the activity successfully); and physiological arousal (whether the child is at an appropriate level of physiological arousal to perform the activity). Too high a level of arousal will elicit feelings of tension and anxiety. The contribution from each of these factors will feed in to a child's self-efficacy. The motivation to succeed, or even simply to participate, will also play a role in determining the behaviour that a child will display.

A second important facet in determining behaviour, according to Bandura, is self-regulation. Self-regulation is linked closely with cognitive control mechanisms. Essentially, self-regulation 'does what it says on the tin'. It is a mechanism for regulating or controlling the self or individual and is based on internal rather than external sources. If you like, it is a 'cognitive conscience' comprising three internalised processes. First, self-observation is the process whereby a person observes themselves, not necessarily directly (which of course would be impossible without video recording facilities), but rather through observing the product derived from the activity, for example, a child's excellent essay or test score. Secondly, judgement is the way in which a person judges their performance or output on the basis of comparisons against others or against societal norms such as a child's ranking on a task against the rest of the class. Thirdly, self-reaction is the emotional component attached to the activity. It is displayed or reflected in self-satisfaction or pride in the quality of performance, compared with their own personal standards, for example, a child outperforming his or her anticipated result by a positive margin, raising the bar. Through self-regulation it becomes possible to set new targets. Self-efficacy is protected, motivation is high and the need to achieve the new level becomes internalised and formalised. We will examine the concepts of self-efficacy and self-regulation again in Chapter 8, when we discuss applied strategies for boosting self-efficacy and for enhancing self-regulation by thinking differently about the situation through employing cognitive restructuring (as discussed in Chapter 16).

Mischel (1984) also favoured the reciprocal determinism approach adopted by Bandura. However, Mischel argued that differences in cognition accounted for the individual differences found in personality across people. Mischel called these 'person variables', of which there are five, summarised below:

1. Competencies
2. Encoding strategies and personal constructs
3. Expectancies
4. Subjective values
5. Self-regulatory systems and plans.

For Mischel, competencies are the skill-sets we possess. They are a person's abilities to take on challenges based on these skill-sets. Encoding strategies and personal constructs are related to a person's processing of information. Mischel argues that people are different in the way they process incoming information, and the way in which they do this is linked to the way in which they perceive that information. One child may perceive a maths test as challenging and exciting while another child may perceive it as 'horrible'. The incoming information is the same; the perception of it is markedly different. Expectancies differ from competencies in that expectancies are the outcomes that a person expects to happen, based on previous knowledge and experience of similar situations. It is not about competence to be successful, but about the effect of one's expectation on behaviour. For Mischel, subjective values are related to a person's belief system. A person is more likely to seek out challenges that are linked to outcomes that the person places value on. In a sense, this is like pursuing situations that fall in line with one's perspective on the world (we use the word 'world' in a loose sense). Finally, Mischel's reference to self-regulatory systems and plans is a self-monitoring construct. As humans, we are keen to monitor our own progress; this is lucky given that we inhabit a society, especially in the teaching profession, where self-monitoring, alongside external monitoring, is highly valued. Accordingly, a person is likely to monitor personal progress, applying a subjective system of self-reward and self-punishment on the journey to achieving goals. Moreover, a person is likely to establish an action plan to achieve those goals. We will discuss the applied nature of this further in Chapter 14 when we cover goal-setting.

7.5 CONCLUSION

With the exceptions of social and emotional development, this chapter has been focused on chronological development. We have placed time frames on the development of processes and emergence of actions or abilities. These time frames are arbitrary and although based on normative data or evidence are of course not set in stone. Individual differences play a huge role in developing systems, processes and abilities. So too, as we have discussed, do environmental opportunities. Nevertheless, thinking in terms of age-related development does help in understanding how abilities develop and mature. We would ask you also to consider the age-related divisions within the educational system currently in place. Of course this will differ depending on which country you are working in.

It would be easy for us to incorporate this information into one large table, containing the relevant age ranges from all other material within this chapter. However, that would not necessarily be the most effective strategy in helping you to make connections yourself. We suggest that you revisit this chapter with an eye on age-related comparisons so that you can build a personal profile for your own needs. For example, you might wish to check the relationship between one of Piaget's stages of cognitive development, such as preoperational thought, the point at which visual acuity develops rapidly, acquisition of fundamental movement skills and which Key Stage a child is in when these abilities develop. There are a wide variety of combinations here, so it really does depend on your own curiosity to forge links.

7.6 FURTHER READING

Baker, J.A., Dilly, L.J., Aupperless, J.L. and Patil, S.A. (2003) 'The development context of school satisfaction: Schools as psychologically healthy environments', *School Research Quarterly*, 18 (2): 206–21.
This research paper suggests that schools can function as psychologically healthy environments if they address and in turn challenge children's developmental needs.

Mavroveli, S. and Sánchez-Ruiz, M. (2011) 'Trait emotional intelligence influences on academic achievement and school behaviour', *British Journal of Educational Psychology*, 81 (1): 112–34.
A research paper that provides strong support for the relationship between emotional intelligence, achievement and behaviour.

Niedenthal, P.M., Krauth-Gruber, S. and Ric, F. (2006) *Psychology of Emotion*. Hove: Psychology Press.
An engaging and accessible book, providing both a cognitive and a social approach to emotion.

Qualter, P., Gardner, K.J., Pope, D.J., Hutchinson, J.M. and Whiteley, H.E. (2012) 'Ability emotional intelligence, trait emotional intelligence, and academic success in British secondary schools: A 5 year longitudinal study', *Learning and Individual Differences*, 22 (1): 83–91.
This research paper provides a detailed study over an extended period of time in relation to how emotional intelligence can enable success.

Part 3

MEETING THE NEEDS OF THE LEARNER

This part examines the specific needs of the learner. Initially the concept of the self is explored, its various components and how the sense of self can be enhanced (Chapter 8). The next chapter looks at the way learners are classified, questioning whether this is appropriate, extending the discussion of the uniqueness of the individual. Next, the various needs of the learner are explored in relation to what has traditionally been called 'Special Educational Needs' (Chapter 9). The part progresses to explore motivation, discussing how this is central to promoting effective learning, examining traditional perspectives before introducing self-determination theory (Chapter 10). The final chapter in this part integrates the previous chapters, while introducing solution-based approaches for when the needs of the learner are preventing effective learning (Chapter 11).

8
UNDERSTANDING THE SELF

CHAPTER OBJECTIVES

- Develop an understanding of the different theories of the self, and that the concept of the self is still a developing area.
- Identify the components of the self and the uniqueness of the self.
- Consider how the sense of self can be affected, while identifying strategies to promote a sense of self.

TEACHERS' STANDARDS

A teacher must:

2   Promote good progress and outcomes by pupils

- demonstrate knowledge and understanding of how pupils learn and how this impacts on teaching
- encourage pupils to take a responsible and conscientious attitude to their own work and study

5   Adapt teaching to respond to the strengths and needs of all pupils

- know when and how to differentiate appropriately, using approaches which enable pupils to be taught effectively
- have a secure understanding of how a range of factors can inhibit pupils' ability to learn, and how best to overcome these
- demonstrate an awareness of the physical, social and intellectual development of children, and know how to adapt teaching to support pupils' education at different stages of development
- have a clear understanding of the needs of all pupils, including those with special educational needs; those of high ability; those with English as an additional language; those with disabilities; and be able to use and evaluate distinctive teaching approaches to engage and support them

8.1 INTRODUCTION

An essential element in teaching, as well as in life, is to achieve a balance between a constant interplay of competing elements. Take, for example, the decision as to what to eat for an evening meal. You may not be hungry now yet experience leads you to believe that you may be hungry later in the day. After deciding what you want to eat, a range of other decisions may need to be considered:

- What time do you plan to eat? (This will depend on your commitments during the day and even your evening commitments.)
- Do you have the ingredients to prepare the meal? (Are they in date, do you have the required amount, how many people will be eating, do you need to buy some ingredients? If so, what, when, where and do you have the required money?)
- Do you have the required time to prepare the meal? (If you prepare the meal too soon, you may not be hungry; if you leave your preparation until too late, you may have opted for something simpler or have started snacking.)
- Will you have something to drink with the meal?
- Will the calorific/nutritious value of the meal sustain you?
- Will you have a dessert?
- Would it be easier to buy a takeaway? If so, what type and where from?

Such decisions related to one meal demonstrate the complexity of decisions our brains compute often without too much attention. Now let us factor in how to obtain the relevant finances to pay for the meal. This will involve decisions about balancing our financial resources to ensure that there is enough money for the rest of the week. This leads into a wider cycle of decisions about how we obtain this money, for example, through employment. Employment in its own right leads to a multitude of further decisions. Factor in health, family, interests, home, even a social life, and hopefully you may appreciate the merry dance of life as these areas merge, evolve, diminish and flourish at different points in time.

To return to teaching, there are similarly many decisions that need to be balanced on a day-to-day basis, if not minute-to-minute. From long-term planning, to the medium term, to the actual short-term planning of the lesson and then to how the lesson evolves, it is no wonder, as teachers, that we are exhausted by the end of the day!

Yet how have we become this superbly functioning, multi-dimensional, information-gathering, decision-making, action-taking, evolved human being? From developing an understanding of how this has been accomplished in our lives, we can then apply this understanding with our learners.

In extending the themes from the last chapter, appreciating our individual uniqueness is a strong foundation from which many other themes throughout this book develop. What is so unique about our self?

8.2 THE SELF

'Self' is a wonderful word that means everything and nothing all at once. Psychologists often refer to the self as a hypothetical construct or theory that we personally develop about who we are and our place in society (for example, Hayes, 2010). To this extent, it is a theory 'we' make about our individual identity: yet, who actually are 'we' and how do 'we' differ from each other?

Through many textbooks, the actual definition for the word 'self' is avoided, instead linking it with a hyphen to a number of other words. After all, it prefixes a number of other psychological terms, among which include self-concept, self-identity, self-esteem, self-efficacy, self-motivation, self-actualisation, self-determination, self-awareness, self-image and self-affirmation. The next activity serves as an introduction to the extent of the self.

ACTIVITY   Speed dating interview

Imagine you are at a speed dating event where you need to portray who you are to another person in a limited amount of time so that they form a very positive image of you. You have one minute to answer this question:

'Tell me about yourself ...'

How much information did you convey? Did you include any of the following: place of birth, home town, hobbies, interests, musical preferences, food preferences, your previous work history, favourite subjects, least-favourite subjects, your current work, favourite books, holiday destinations, siblings, pets, other?

Would it be different if you were asked to complete the activity again but to make a strong first impression for a job interview? Even by being asked to provide a 'pen portrait' of your very own 'self', you may begin to appreciate that you could write a book on the subject. Yet, if you have read any autobiographies, how much information is left out? What is included or excluded to leave the reader with a favourable impression? What would you include or exclude in speed dating or an interview? Indeed this leads to the first element in discussing the self and its component parts.

In reviewing this activity, you will see that the terms you have used can be grouped in different ways. At the simplest level, there are the factual physical attributes that act as a point of reference about you, for example, sex, age or place of birth. An alternate way of grouping may involve the way you relate to others. Are you a sister or brother? Are you part of a group? Do you have a specific taste in music, food, shoes or television programmes? Consequently, the self is both 'you-as-an-individual' and 'you-as-a-social-entity'. Such duality was originally discussed by William James (1890), arguably the 'father of modern psychology'. He discussed the self-as-perceiver (the person who is the knower or the 'I') and the self-as-object of perception (the object that is known to others or the 'me') (Damian and Robins, 2012; Klein, 2012). Furthermore, James (1890) asserted that the self is the core concept within psychology: everything else revolves around this fundamental part of being human.

8.3 THE 'SELF-AS-I'

A child is born. Taking that first gasp of air, cleaned, checked over, bundled, then given to the mother to cuddle, the child has entered into the world for the start of their life's journey. Over the first few weeks, the parents are asked the same questions continually: girl or boy, weight, whether he or she is keeping well, how the mother is keeping and, of course, the name. With the wonders of modern technology the parents may even be able to decide upon a name before the child is born if they know what sex the child is; alternatively it may take a couple of days before a name is provided. The name is recorded with the Registrar of Births and Deaths and the child freely enters into the world. The child now has a developing sense of identity by being given a name. There is, however, a growing body of research to indicate that the child's sense of self starts to develop while in the womb, as previously discussed by several authors (Assagioli, 1968; Grof, 1985).

Our name is perhaps the single most defining attribute of who we are. Of course, other people share our name, as a quick name search on the internet would reveal. (As a side note, the author Dave Gorman even tracked down all of the 'Dave Gormans' he could find on the internet, as recorded in the book, *Are You Dave Gorman?*: Wallace and Gorman, 2001.)

ACTIVITY   What's in a name?

Consider your name. What does it say about you? What do you want it to say about you?

What does your name actually mean? Look this up on many of the name websites available.

Where does your surname come from?

How many people on any of the social media networking sites share your name? Were you the first person to have your name?

What makes you unique compared to others who share your name?

Our name initially serves as a point of reference. However, as opposed to saying a somewhat clumsy sentence such as 'Scott Buckler would like a cappuccino, please', we replace our name with the personal pronoun 'I'. Taking this further, the use of the word 'I' relates to our self-awareness, or the object of attention whereby we communicate our thoughts, feelings and desires (Damian and Robins, 2012). The self as 'I' can also be seen as having an executive function. By this, the self is more than just a 'being': it is also a 'doer', through responding to information, making choices and executing action (Baumeister, 2011).

ACTIVITY   Use of 'I'

A very simple task: for one day (or even one lesson) avoid using the word 'I'.

If you managed to complete this activity for even a couple of minutes, you have done extremely well. From a scientific perspective, there is no need for an 'I' as we are just a collection of cells and chemical processes. Such a position is proposed by Parfit (1984) who argues that people do not exist outside of their physical components of the brain and body, a position known as 'reductionism' or a 'bundle theory'. Elaborating further, bundle theorists propose that our life is a bundle of experiences and sensations – a series of impressions tied together through memory. Accordingly, the self is an illusion; similarly life is an illusion perhaps in the same way a film appears real despite being just a series of static pictures streamed together (Bach, 1977/1998). A further argument forwarded by such bundle theorists or reductionists is that science has yet to detect the soul or spirit, the actual attribute that animates us.

However, just because science has yet to determine the existence of a metaphysical 'self', it does not mean that the self does not exist. This is similar in nature to searching for the Higgs boson particle (the 'God' particle), which was proposed 50 years ago and which was discovered in 2012 using the Large Hadron Collider. (This is a collection of scientific equipment that cost approximately €7 billion, is claimed to be the fastest racetrack on the planet and can achieve temperatures a hundred thousand times hotter than the sun, while using the world's most advanced supercomputer: (CERN, 2009).) Consequently with enough support and investment, science may one day prove the existence of the self, the thing that animates us.

In contrast to the reductionist, bundle theorists are the anti-reductionist (or holism) ego theorists who assert that the sum of the whole is greater than the parts. As an analogy, a Monet painting from a reductionist perspective would be just paint and canvas; within the holistic approach, a Monet painting is so much more. Therefore ego theorists perceive the self as a single, continuous being; that the self is an enduring structure. In other words, something or someone has thoughts and makes decisions based on these – there is a consciousness (Blackmore, 2005; Lancaster, 2004).

The psychology of consciousness is a complex area. As you may have gathered through reading to this point, there are times when psychology and philosophy tend to merge, and the area of consciousness is one such area. For example, we live in a world of quantitative phenomena in a space/time continuum: things have weight, size and shape. The laws of physics apply to everyone on this planet, we fall down and not up. Yet we also have our own personal thoughts and experiences that are subjective in nature. My experience of blue may be what another person sees as a shade of green. What is music to my ears may be mere noise to another. The slurp of the coffee I am currently drinking may be different from your experience of the taste of coffee. Indeed, such experiences are indescribable to another person: I can attempt to describe my taste of coffee, yet words would not do justice to the experience (heck, it is a great cup of coffee after all!). This relates to what Chalmers (1996) calls the 'hard problem of consciousness', which simply defined asks why we have such a richness of experience from our sensory processes and how this operates. Indeed, how do we know that we are different from what Chalmers calls 'philosophical zombies': creatures identical to humans, who operate in a prescribed way to a given stimulus but do not actually experience the stimulus in the same way as humans. Such philosophical zombies may move their hand when they touch something hot and say 'ouch' but do not actually experience the sensation of pain. They may say 'That's a lovely cup of coffee' as a given response to the stimulus of coffee, yet not subjectively experience the taste as being 'lovely'. You could assess whether you are a zombie by adding salt to coffee and tasting it, yet perhaps you are just conditioned that, when certain taste buds are stimulated in a specific way, behaviourally you go 'uugh'. The taste does not conjure up the same poetic, subjective experience of finely ground fresh coffee beans from Kenya when you have that first cup in the morning.

Where things further separate from a psychological to a philosophical basis is through the assertion by James (1890), whereby we can never have exactly the same thought more than once. By this, James suggests that, as we live in a constantly changing world, our reactions will constantly change, although we may sustain the illusion that our thoughts are the same. Such an assertion in turn distances us from philosophical zombies.

ACTIVITY   Coffee

Keep track of each cup of coffee you drink during the day. How does your perception of each cup differ? For example, are your patterns of thought the same? Is the first cup rushed first thing in the morning, with perhaps a cup later on enjoyed at a more leisurely pace?

What is your relationship with the various cups of coffee? Do they taste the same each time? Are your thought processes the same?

Does James (1890) have a valid point that our reactions constantly change although the illusion is that our thoughts remain the same?

In relation to education the most important aspect about the 'I' is that it is a subjective construct: we may perceive experience differently from others; similarly we may perceive ourselves differently from how other people see us. Of course, this is true of the learners we work with: what may work for one learner may not work for another. Learners may perceive aspects differently (as discussed in Chapter 6). Their perception of a learning experience may be different from that of other learners, or from what we originally planned.

In summary, developing an understanding of the 'self-as-I' may help us to appreciate that we are all different, something that can be overlooked within the education system in the drive to ensure a standardised approach, where all learners are expected to behave the same way, learn the same way, achieve the same attainment levels and so on. Although the self as a unique component has been introduced, the other concept of self is that we operate in a society. Through such interactions, we develop a sense of self in relation to others, which leads into the discussion of the 'self-as-me'.

8.4 THE 'SELF-AS-ME'

While the 'self-as-I' relates to our unique subjective experience, the 'self-as-me' relates to our interpersonal relationships with others. This is an aspect described by James (1890) whereby the 'me' is the object known to other people. According to Damian and Robins (2012), there are different levels on which the concept of 'me' operates (Figure 8.1). The first is similar to the 'self-as-I', which is the personal or individual self. On this level, our beliefs and values about our private self are formed. This is influenced through the second level, the relational self. At this level, we perceive ourselves as having different personal relationships with others; for example, I may perceive that I am different with friends than I am with colleagues. The social self is where we perceive ourselves in relation to general interpersonal contexts, for example, our social role as teachers and our reputation. The final level is that of the collective self, where our personal identities are considered in relation to a variety of groups, for example, nationality, ethnicity or how we are perceived as teachers. There is a parallel between the sense of 'me' and 'ecological systems theory', whereby the child is affected through various environmental systems (Bronfenbrenner, 1979).

Such environments consist of the child's direct experience with their friends, family, peers or school, known as the microsystem. This relates to Damian and Robins' relational level. An indirect environment is the mesosystem, where two microsystems connect. An example of this is where the child's parents may not hold school in high regard, with such attitudes in turn affecting the child's attitude to school. The exosystem is similarly external to the child, yet may influence the child: such an exosystem is a parent's workplace, whereby if the parent is stressed through their work such stress may manifest itself in the home environment. A parallel with the collective self is Bronfenbrenner's macrosystem, or the culture in which the child lives. The culture

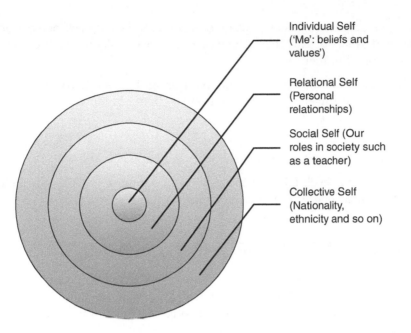

Individual Self ('Me': beliefs and values')

Relational Self (Personal relationships)

Social Self (Our roles in society such as a teacher)

Collective Self (Nationality, ethnicity and so on)

Figure 8.1 Summarising the levels of the 'me' (based on Damian and Robins, 2012)

can relate to nationality, ethnicity or socioeconomic status. Bronfenbrenner's final level is the chronosystem, which is historical in nature and evolves over time: one example is the effect of childhood illness which, as time progresses, may improve. Other examples are the immediate effect of divorce on the child and how this improves as life becomes more settled.

Taking Bronfenbrenner's model further, an analogy could be made with how a drop ripples across a pond: one small change in one area can affect a completely different area. For example, consider how the economic crisis from 2008 is still rippling and affecting the economy today: the recession may in turn have led to a tightening of available funds for an individual, who in turn spends less money on materialistic items, such as internet purchases. If enough individuals are feeling the pressure on their money, the shops will have less business, which in turn may result in a business entering administration and closing. From this, an employer/employee may have been made redundant, which increases pressure on their finances, their stress level and in turn their family, one of which is a child. Yet in a classroom of 30, with the relative pressures of the curriculum and a range of associated factors, such ripples that have affected a child may be ignored.

Consequently, from a teaching perspective, an awareness that a multitude of factors impact on the developing child and their sense of self is of fundamental importance: any one of the areas from either Bronfenbrenner or Damian and Robins' model can in turn affect a child's sense of self. How can we in turn assure that a child's sense of self is developed as best we can?

On a personal level, this may relate to ensuring the child's self-perception is realistically developed. This chapter will progress specifically to explore how this can be developed further.

On a relational level, this may relate to ensuring the child is able to form productive and successful relationships with others, understanding how to interact with others (see Chapter 7).

On a social level, this may relate to ensuring the child is aware of a sense of belonging to a group, class and school (see Chapters 9 and 13).

On a collective level, this may relate to appreciating the richness of their culture and the similar richness of other cultures.

8.5 INTEGRATION OF THE 'I' AND 'ME'

From the preceding sections in this chapter, you may have appreciated that the sense of self is paramount to psychology, yet you may also appreciate it is an area with many depths. Indeed, Klein (2012: 363) comments that 'There is no more widely used, yet less well-understood, term in psychology than the self.' How true. Part psychology, part philosophy, the concept of the self (or the self-concept) resonates across many branches of psychology. It is the interplay between these branches that can lead to the lack of clarity as they all have a certain perspective constrained by their field.

Certain psychologists have attempted to develop integrated models of the self, notably Roberto Assagioli and Ken Wilber. A brief overview of their theories is provided below, as a point of reference should you wish to explore them in further depth at a later stage.

8.6 ROBERTO ASSAGIOLI AND PSYCHOSYNTHESIS

Assagioli (1888–1974) founded the movement of psychosynthesis, having studied under both Freud and Jung. Indeed, within Assagioli's theory, the influences of Freud are apparent through the unconscious, and from Jung, the notion of archetypes. At the heart of psychosynthesis is self-realisation: understanding the true self through direct experience to develop one's greatest potential (Firman and Russell, 1993). To this extent, the focus of psychosynthesis is on developing the 'self-as-I' to access our true individuality. In relation to Jung's archetypes (alternating characters that make up our personality, or alter-egos), Assagioli viewed the self as composed of different parts, for example, the child, the parent, the critic. At different times, a different archetype comes to the fore: if our sense of self feels threatened, we can adopt one of these different roles, for example, the 'wounded child' who is defensive, or perhaps the 'parent' who says what other people should do. (Indeed, such child/parent roles similarly relate to 'transactional analysis'.)

Assagioli understood that the self is a construct of a wider collective: that it is influenced by culture, society, the physical environment, through various philosophies and religions. This parallels the work of Bronfenbrenner as previously highlighted. Yet psychosynthesis attempts to establish further the development of the self partly as a therapy or counselling (to get people to accept and understand the events in their life) and partly as a growth process or coaching (to achieve and exceed our potential). Indeed, the focus of developing personal potential, then transcending this, places Assagioli in the same field as Carl Rogers and Abraham Maslow through a humanistic or transpersonal psychology (despite Assagioli's model pre-dating both of these branches of psychology).

8.7 PSYCHOSYNTHESIS AND EDUCATION

Given the parallels with Rogers and Maslow on achieving then exceeding personal potential, psychosynthesis can be usefully applied to education, if our personal philosophy of education is to develop learners as best we can.

ACTIVITY   A reading

As you read the following quotation, identify in your mind when this may have been written.

> The poor results caused by exaggerated applications of the new educational methods have given rise to a counter-reaction, but this has not solved the problem. All attempts to return to the 'good old methods of the past' are in vain and are destined to fail, both due to the fact that those methods were not really 'good', and because their imposition has been rendered impossible given the profound changes that have occurred in the psychology of the new generation and in the environmental conditions. In the meantime, the rapid increase in the number of students, the tumultuous extension of 'mass education' in the form of compulsory education (something which is both desirable and necessary), and the resulting scarcity of competent teachers and adequate schools have created new and serious difficulties and complications. All this explains the current crisis in the field of education, where the old and the new are found in different proportions, side by side, and often, in sharp contrast with one another.

The answer is found in the next paragraph.

Assagioli specifically discussed the 'fundamental importance' of education in relation to creativity, imagination, thought and will. Assagioli (1968) also discussed that education is in a crisis (yes, nearly 50 years ago!), as he identified both that education is a process of 'imparting something from the outside' through authority and control of the teacher and curriculum, while conversely education should be learner-centred. Assagioli considers that either extreme can be harmful and that a balance needs to be found: one of developing the child's autonomy through careful guiding by the teacher, ideas central to the work of Vygotsky and other constructivist theorists.

In addition, Assagioli (1968) proposes that psychosynthesis should promote synthesis of the individual (intrapersonal development) and synthesis between individuals (interpersonal development). In relation to the former, he discussed the balance between building under-developed psychological components of the individual, and for over-developed components, how best to use them through 'wise regulation and use'. Furthermore, Assagioli examined the need to develop a child's inner identity, specifically the use of the will. In relation to interpersonal development, he highlighted the importance of cooperation rather than competition between individuals and groups, and furthermore that the science of relationships and the techniques from which to develop interpersonal skills be developed (see Chapters 7 and 13).

Psychosynthesis has continued to evolve over the past hundred years: its roots pre-date the work of Maslow and Rogers, and permeate through to today. As noted, many of the themes within psychosynthesis are relevant to education today.

8.8 KEN WILBER AND AQAL

Ken Wilber is the author of many recent books, attempting to take the theory of the self into the twenty-first century through combining the perspectives of psychology, philosophy, religion and therapy to develop the person. Some of the themes of this chapter will resonate with Wilber's work. As an example, according to Wilber (2000a, 2000b), every entity and concept can be deemed a 'holon'. A holon operates in a dual role as both a single, self-reliant unit (the whole entity) and as part of one or more other systems. As an example, a letter from the alphabet is a single, whole entity in itself, yet it can be combined with other letters to form words, words into sentences, sentences into paragraphs and pages, and so on. If we take the letter 'a', within the last sentence it featured 14 times in 11 words, the sentence being 37 words in length from about 300 or so on this page.

According to Wilber, each holon has an interior and exterior perspective, very much akin to James's (1890) concept of the self, where the 'I' is interior to the self, yet the 'me' is exterior in relation to others. In turn, this leads to a simple figure that serves as a basis for Wilber's (2000a) AQAL model (Figure 8.2).

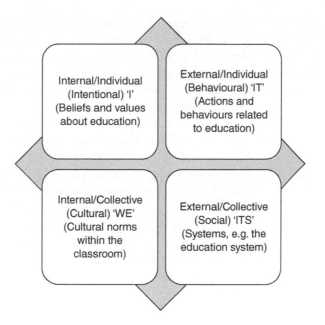

Figure 8.2 The AQAL model (adapted from Wilber, 2000a, 2007)

The internal/individual (the sense of 'I') relates to the thoughts, beliefs, emotions and values of the individual. The internal/collective (the sense of 'we') relates to the values of a specific culture. The external/individual (the sense of 'it') relates to the way the individual reacts within the world through their action and behaviour. Finally, the external/collective (the sense of 'its') relates to the external structures of the collective, for example, the education system.

In relation to this model, Wilber (2000a, 2007) asserts that, as individuals, we perceive the world through different perspectives, yet all four perspectives are complementary in nature. This is why the model is called AQAL or 'All Quadrants, All Levels'. In Figure 8.2, the quadrants are explicitly defined: implicitly, the aspect 'All Levels' indicates that we are at different stages of development within each of the quadrants. For example, we may have a developed internal/individual quadrant (in other words our thoughts, beliefs and values concerning education); however, this may be at odds with an under-developed external/collective quadrant, that the education system needs radical change. On an interpersonal level, our sense of self (the internal/individual quadrant) may not be the same as that of another person.

This model is deemed Wilber's meta-theory, from which many of his other models develop. Indeed, the AQAL model has been extended to consider 'all lines', or the different levels of skills we have and how these balance with others. For example, a person may have highly developed intellectual skills but rudimentary interpersonal skills. Furthermore, the model can also consider 'all states': the emotional states that can manifest at different levels and different lines. For example, the more we develop our skills at teaching and our thoughts about education we may become increasingly dissatisfied if the school we are working in does not reflect the same values, which in turn affects our emotions. Finally, 'all types' specifies that the quadrants, levels, lines and states affect people in different ways: there are all types of people who will be at varying points with their levels, lines and quadrants.

As teachers, what can we take from Wilber's work? At the simplest level, no two learners are the same (a perennial assertion in this chapter), and although we may all appreciate it, this chapter seeks to explain how and why we differ. Additionally, we operate through different yet complementary perspectives, and as such we need to ensure learners are aware of such perspectives in developing a healthy sense of self. There are many ideas on the self, of which only a few are highlighted here. The central concept could be summarised in one sentence: From these perspectives, the self is an organic 'thing' – being organic means that the self grows, develops and evolves to given stimuli within itself and in interaction with the environment. Although the theme of this chapter has related the self to education, the subsequent part of this chapter will bring the reader into more familiar territory about a learner's sense of self.

8.9 METACOGNITION

Socrates said, 'Know thyself'. This phrase has been philosophised since the day it was purportedly uttered. From a hermeneutic perspective, what did Socrates mean, nearly two-and-a-half thousand years ago, compared to how we may interpret the phrase today? Did he mean to develop an existential philosophy as to how we should live and make sense of our lives? Did he throw down the gauntlet for philosophers and psychologists to muse over the sense of self as a puzzle for over two millennia? Was he the true 'father of psychology' long before William James, Sigmund Freud and others? Or did he mean we should spend time understanding our personal capabilities, as Baumeister (2011) suggests?

Metacognition is defined by Flavell (1979) as cognition about cognition, although Lee et al. (2012: 23) refine this through stating, 'It is the awareness and regulation of the process of the learner's thinking.' Although many definitions of metacognition exist in relation to developing thinking skills and problem-solving skills, the quote by Lee et al. provides a broader scope: that the learner's thinking is not only about study skills, but also about themselves as learners. This self-perception of the learner is fundamental to their development: in other words, a learner's perception of their abilities can either help or hinder their development.

A range of studies have focused on metacognition within schools. For example, López-Vargas et al. (2017) investigated the effects of metacognitive scaffolding and cognitive style along with cognitive load and learning achievement, concluding that students who used metacognitive scaffolding achieved at a greater level than those who did not. Bonnett et al. (2017) conducted research where metacognitive reflection was used to increase motivation within mathematics to a positive extent to support learning. Furthermore, research by Callan and his colleagues investigated learning strategies across 65 countries. They assert that while memorisation and elaboration strategies have received significant attention, their findings refuted the correlation to higher achievement, instead advocating that metacognitive strategies enabled greater achievement (Callan et al., 2016).

Four core concepts can influence a pupil's metacognition: self-esteem, self-efficacy, self-attribution and self-determination.

8.10 SELF-IMAGE AND SELF-ESTEEM

Try a psychological thought experiment proposed by Allport (1955). While you are reading this book, saliva is continuing to accumulate in your mouth. Think about it. Think about how much more saliva is produced when thinking about lemons. Now swallow. No problem! Now, consider the same thing: saliva accumulating in one's mouth, perhaps even more so when thinking about lemons. Spit into a cup, and then swallow the contents from the cup. Allport thus discussed what is deemed as 'me' and what is not deemed as 'me' in relation to this thought experiment. Whenever our body changes in some way, so does our self-image.

Our self-image is what we personally describe as being 'ourself', what we perceive of as our body. This can come into conflict if we are affected in different ways. Perhaps we are aware of a huge pimple that has been accumulating on our nose for the past few days but appears to be all-consuming every time we pass a mirror, or see our reflection in a window: we are not the same person, as we have altered in some way. Perhaps you have had your arm in a sling, or have hobbled around on crutches after injuring your leg. Our body image is an undisputable descriptive account of ourselves, specifically in relation to our physical being.

This evaluative measure of our self can relate to a variety of dimensions: although physical appearance has been discussed previously in relation to a pimple, other dimensions consist of our scholastic competence, athletic competence, social acceptance and behaviour (Harter, 1999). If, however, we start evaluating ourselves, this is self-esteem. If we add a value label to our physical being, we are affecting our self-esteem in one way or another. In returning to the pimple, self-identity would be 'Oh, I have a pimple', while self-esteem would be 'Ugh, I look like a witch with that pimple on my nose' (negative self-esteem). Alternatively we could say, 'Wow, a beauty spot, it will make everyone look at me and see my inherent beauty' (positive self-esteem).

According to James (1890), our self-esteem can be seen as a balance between our potential versus our actual abilities: if we set a goal that is too high ('I will never be young, I will never understand psychology, nor will I ever stop drinking copious amounts of coffee'), we may never achieve this goal, yet it is when we

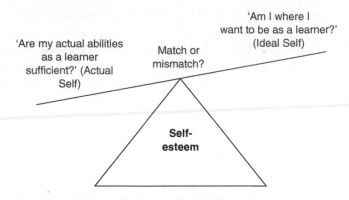
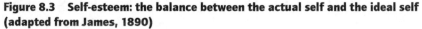

Figure 8.3   Self-esteem: the balance between the actual self and the ideal self (adapted from James, 1890)

make a conscious decision to give up on chasing this goal that we develop a lightness of heart (this is summarised in Figure 8.3).

As James comments, with each of these illusions we give up, there is one less thing to disappoint, and one less thing that gets in the way of our real self. Branden (1969) discusses how our self-esteem occurs when we live according to reason and our own principles, and our perception is central to this. Through this perception, Branden asserts that we are in control of our own destiny, although he appreciates that our emotions can affect our engagement, even when our intellect determines that we should pursue a course of action. If we cannot rationally justify a thought and instead let emotions dictate, we are limiting our self-esteem, which in turn can lead to depression, self-doubt and fear (Branden, 1969).

ACTIVITY   Quiet reflection

Set aside a few minutes for quiet reflection (literally!).

Look at yourself in a mirror. Reflect for a few moments on yourself using the W5H1 questions below:

Who are you? Who will you be in the future?

What are you? What will you be in the future?

Where are you? Where will you be in the future?

When will you know you have achieved the above?

How will you get there?

Why are you, you?

Branden (1969) also suggested that psychological pain should be seen in the same category as physical pain, and that both are survival mechanisms to stop us doing what is hurting us. From this, we should understand that psychological pain, such as guilt or anxiety, is telling ourselves that the unconscious is in an unfit state, and that we should revisit who we are as individuals in relation to our beliefs and values. Of course, in relation to our learners, their personal beliefs about their ability may need to be supported: if a learner thinks that they are hopeless at reading, they may stop engaging with trying to read, which in turn affirms their belief. Through a learner saying they are 'hopeless at reading', are they really saying they do not like reading or more specifically, they do not like reading a certain style of book? Perhaps they find it hard to understand new words and have not developed strategies to address such words when they appear on the page. Consequently, is such a learner telling us that they are 'hopeless' or are they trying to tell us something else? With such a self-fulfilling prophecy, it is us, as teachers, who need to find a way to bolster a learner's self-esteem by perhaps understanding in greater depth why they feel a certain way. Ultimately how can self-esteem be developed? What strategies can be used? We will get to that slightly later after understanding a couple of other theories about the self that can impede learning.

8.11 SELF-EFFICACY

Previously self-esteem was defined as an evaluation of our self: this is subjective in nature and may be realistic or unrealistic given the evidence. Yet, what do we personally do about this subjective evaluation of our abilities? We are characterised by the way we respond to the environment; consequently the amount of effort we devote to an activity, our motivation to complete the task and our persistence are all affected by our subjective evaluation. Indeed, research has indicated how learners with a higher self-efficacy demonstrate greater persistence, motivation and interest in their education than learners with a lower self-efficacy (Zimmerman et al., 1992).

According to Bandura (1986), there are two aspects related to self-efficacy: our actual competence (or skill) required for the task and our estimation of our competence, which is subjective in nature. Put another way, it is a balance between what the learner chooses to do and the amount of energy or effort they expend in completing a task (see Figure 8.4).

From this, Bandura identifies four factors that can affect our self-efficacy: enactive, vicarious, persuasory and emotive.

ENACTIVE

The enactive domain relates to whether a learner's action achieves a result of success or failure (or somewhere in between). From a teacher's perspective, has the

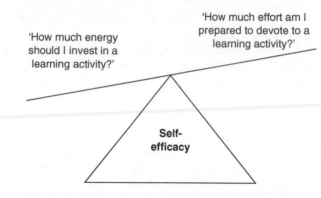

Figure 8.4   The balance of self-efficacy (adapted from Bandura, 1986)

challenge been made too easy or too hard for that particular learner? Similarly, is the learner equipped with the tools to utilise to achieve success? An analogy can be made with tools you can purchase from a hardware store. Have you purchased the right tool for the job at hand? Do you only have a screwdriver to hammer in a nail? Even if you have a hammer, is it a sledge-hammer, a mallet, a gavel (used by judges when passing sentence) or the more familiar claw hammer? If you have the right tool for the job, can you use it appropriately? Therefore, whether the learner achieves the desired result will depend on a careful balance between the challenge the teacher has set and their personal 'toolkit'. It may be that the teacher needs to indicate or develop the learner's use of the appropriate tool. Links can therefore be made to metacognition, equipping the learner to understand what tools and processes they need to engage with a task, and how to try another tool or process if they have not met with immediate success. Within this, an emotive element resides: if a learner continues to experience failure, how can we ensure that they persevere and meet with success? How can we help them to develop their emotive response to failure? This will be discussed slightly further on in the chapter in relation to self-attribution.

VICARIOUS

Within the vicarious domain, the learner compares their performance with others. Have you ever asked why you cannot do something that others find easy? Perhaps you are using the wrong tool from your toolkit as described within the enactive domain. There again, you may not see the relevance of the task and therefore have not engaged to the same extent. It may be that the person you are comparing yourself with is fantastic and naturally gifted at the specific task, yet you excel at something different. It may be due to a range of physiological aspects, such as lack of sleep or food.

In comparing our efforts and their results to others, we may start to negatively affect our self-efficacy, or our emotive belief in our ability. Consider previous exams at school you may have studied for. Across the country, no doubt learners discuss how easy or difficult they found the exam after they are released from the examination room. Learners may similarly compare their grades on an assignment, focusing solely on the grade and not the feedback that informs the learner as to their strengths and areas for future development. Consequently, although the education system may encourage comparison through league tables, standardised tests and qualifications, should learners rather be comparing their abilities against their own benchmark and how they engage with tasks? This in turn relates to process goals as opposed to performance goals (as discussed in Chapter 14). As teachers, we can help learners appreciate their abilities as individuals while appreciating that the sense of self is constantly being refined through the reaction and interaction with others (Argyle and Henderson, 1984).

PERSUASORY

Related to the previous domain, how do the statements from others affect learners' engagement? Are they encouraging? Are they discouraging and dispiriting? Such comments can be made by other learners, parents and even teachers. However, they only have an effect if they are internalised and believed to be true, or we 'introject' the information from others. Needless to say, as teachers, are we offering encouragement? Even if we are, does the learner internalise or use introjection for these words of support? Do we need to balance our guiding words with actions to help develop their enactive and vicarious domains?

One significant factor seldom discussed is the way we use self-defeating patterns of behaviour, for example, saying how useless we are at something, or continually reprimanding ourselves through saying, 'I must' or 'I shouldn't'. Such internal cognitive dialogue is discussed further in Chapter 16, specifically in relation to cognitive restructuring.

EMOTIVE

With the completion of any task, there is an emotional element ranging on a continuum from boredom to fear. Although I may have driven the same route to work over a thousand times, the task is never boring: every journey is different – from the music on the radio, the way the seasons evolve as indicated on the trees and the daylight, finding a parking space when at work and so on. However, at certain times, the task can turn to fear, especially if there is snow, ice or flooding on the road. Therefore how can we ensure that a task leads to optimal attention by a learner without leading to polar ends of the continuum?

ACTIVITY   Self-efficacy

Consider a learner you have previously worked with. Write down three points for each domain that you could implement to help develop that learner's self-efficacy.

- Enactive
- Vicarious
- Persuasory
- Emotive

As a brief review, Bandura's (1986) concept of self-efficacy is the way in which we subjectively evaluate our abilities, and this can be influenced through the enactive domain (success at a task), vicarious domain (comparison with others), persuasory domain (comments by others that we introject), and emotive domain (a continuum of boredom to fear). However, a further model can be considered that determines our reasoning for success or failure. This is known as self-attribution (Weiner, 1974).

8.12 SELF-ATTRIBUTION

Attribution theory is the process of attributing an interpretation to the outcome of a task: in other words, the explanation we provide for success or failure. Furthermore, the explanations we provide can determine our expectations of experiencing the same result at a future stage. If we perceive that we will fail again, our motivation will decrease (Weiner, 1974). Weiner (1986) extends this model through discussing whether the individual perceives the outcome as having an internal or external cause, and whether the cause is stable or unstable in nature. These are continua (the plural of continuum): the person may decide that there was a mixture to a greater or lesser extent of one cause or another. Additionally, the internal/external nature of the cause can be overlapped with its stability to provide four quadrants, as demonstrated in Figure 8.5.

Learners who are deemed to be high achievers attribute their successes to an internal and stable cause, for example, their ability. If they fail, they will attribute their results to either external/stable causes (the difficulty of the task), or internal/unstable causes (their effort) (Figure 8.6). The core aspect is that such high achievers attribute, or associate, their personal ability to success. Conversely, low achievers do not make the direct link between their ability and success, attributing any success either to an external/unstable cause, for example luck, or internal/unstable causes, such as the amount of effort they devoted. While the internal/unstable cause is attributed to effort within the high achievers, which in turn may motivate them further, for the low achievers,

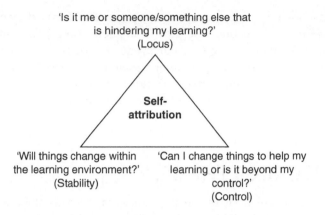

Figure 8.5   The triad of self-attribution (adapted from Dweck, 1978)

the internal/unstable cause (although similarly attributed to effort) may lead to decreased motivation as it confirms their belief (self-esteem) that they are not academically able (Dweck and Leggett, 1988). Such confirmation for low achievers is termed 'learned helplessness' where the learner believes that they have no control over their environment (Dweck, 1978).

A related aspect to self-attribution is Rotter's (1966) 'locus of control'. The locus of control discusses the relationship between the outcome of a person's behaviour

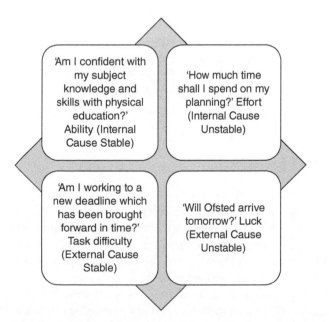

Figure 8.6   Applied example using self-attribution theory (based on Weiner, 1986)

and how they ascribe their role within that outcome. The 'locus' depends on whether the individual perceives the outcome as within their control (an 'internal locus of control', for example, their ability and perseverance), or from the environment (an 'external locus of control', for example, other people or chance). If a learner is deemed a low achiever, they can be supported through retraining their attribution by developing their metacognition and their self-efficacy and, in turn, this may enhance their self-esteem.

8.13 NURTURING THE SELF

From the moment we are born (some psychologists, such as Roberto Assagioli and Stanislav Grof, suggest even while in the womb), our sense of self is continually evolving. Careful nurturing is paramount as it could be argued that it is the most fragile component that we own. From this chapter, you will understand how the self can be threatened in so many ways yet perhaps we, as teachers, owe it to the learners we work with to ensure a healthy sense of self is developed. This can be deemed as far more important than anything on the curriculum: without a healthy sense of self, learning will be hampered.

An analogy could be made with a seed. Provided with the right components – the warmth, the nutrients, the watering – the seed becomes a seedling. The seedling requires further nurturing at its most critical stage to ensure it can continue to develop and grow, setting down firm roots, while continually reaching upwards as it grows. Additional tending will ensure that a strong foundation is provided for the seed to continue its growth process: if the seed is an acorn, it will turn into a mighty oak, a tree that can withstand a lifetime of external pressures, maintaining its solid stance. Perhaps the seed is a cherry stone with the potential to flourish and blossom, in turn nurturing many others through delighting the senses: the taste of cherries, the sight each spring of its blossom, the scent, the sound of the wind gently rustling its leaves.

8.14 CONCLUSION

This chapter has provided an overview of the self, specifically its uniqueness, the various models of the self and the associated elements of the various constructs such as self-image, self-esteem, self-efficacy and self-attribution. Although you may have dipped into this chapter to gain an understanding of a specific term, you are strongly encouraged to read in full what could be deemed the pivotal chapter of this book as it really does set the tone for the other applied aspects.

The self is perhaps the least understood concept within psychology. Klein (2012) suggests that this may be due to the way in which psychology has attempted to develop as a science, one which is independent from other subjects and is empirically driven in nature. Yet given the discussion of the self by transpersonal psychologists such as Assagioli, the self is rooted in philosophical discussion. Indeed, a core theme throughout this book has been the association between psychology and philosophy: that perhaps psychology should not ignore its conceptual origins. As Klein (2012) comments, the self has been a core puzzle of the human condition for over 2,500 years.

8.15 FURTHER READING

Baumeister, R.F. (2011) 'Self and identity: A brief overview of what they are, what they do, and how they work', *Annals of the New York Academy of Sciences*, 1234: 48–55.
This journal article provides an informed discussion of the structure of the self.

Chalmers, D. (1996) *The Conscious Mind*. New York: Oxford University Press.
A clear overview of consciousness, written in an accessible manner.

Firman, J. and Russell, A. (1993) *What Is Psychosynthesis?* Palo Alto, CA: Psychosynthesis Palo Alto.
Firman and Russell's overview of psychosynthesis is an accessible foundation of the area.

Wilber, K. (2008) *The Pocket Ken Wilber*. Boston, MA: Shambhala Publications.
Ken Wilber's work combines Eastern spirituality and Western science. He is widely respected for his discussion of the self and how it develops. This book provides an overview of his works and in turn makes his further work more accessible.

9

UNDERSTANDING SPECIAL EDUCATIONAL NEEDS AND DISABILITIES (SEND)

CHAPTER OBJECTIVES

- Develop a comprehension of some of the classifications of special educational needs.
- Identify the causes, indicators and support strategies for some of the major classifications of special educational needs.
- Appreciate the difference between inclusion as a philosophy and inclusion as a practice.

TEACHERS' STANDARDS

A teacher must:

1 Set high expectations which inspire, motivate and challenge pupils

- set goals that stretch and challenge pupils of all backgrounds, abilities and dispositions

2 Promote good progress and outcomes by pupils

- demonstrate knowledge and understanding of how pupils learn and how this impacts on teaching

5 Adapt teaching to respond to the strengths and needs of all pupils

- know when and how to differentiate appropriately, using approaches which enable pupils to be taught effectively
- have a secure understanding of how a range of factors can inhibit pupils' ability to learn, and how best to overcome these
- have a clear understanding of the needs of all pupils, including those with special educational needs; those of high ability; those with English as an additional language; those with disabilities; and be able to use and evaluate distinctive teaching approaches to engage and support them

9.1 INTRODUCTION

According to several authors, the purpose of compulsory schooling is to group and classify children (Freire, 1996, 2005; Gatto, 2002, 2011; Harber, 2009; Holt, 1995;

Howarth, 2012; Illich, 1995). Indeed, consider age-related classes, exams, reading level and ability grouping, among other things, and you can see their point: that the education sector labels children. Of course, a child may be ascribed to more than one category; alternatively a global term is used, for example that the child has Special Educational Needs (SEN) or Special Educational Needs or Disability (SEND). However, the label can actually replace the identity of the child, and alternately the child and the label can be viewed synonymously. Although this is a subtle change of reference, it is one that can become increasingly overlooked within the hectic school climate.

Indeed, the title of this chapter may perpetuate this common misconception, that the chapter will solely focus on children deemed to have SEN. However, it is important to stress the notion of the 'individual' in the title: that each child is a unique, independent, original creation – no two children are the same, not even identical twins.

Take the thought experiment of the mind/body split (Schick and Vaughn, 2013). If we could clone you completely, atom for atom, so that there was a truly identical second version of you, would that version think the same thoughts as you at that particular moment in time? Would they have been in exactly the same position, at exactly the same point in time, to experience exactly the same experiences, and interpret these experiences accordingly in the same way that you have? Even after considering this extreme thought experiment, arguably, how can any two children in the same class be the same?

Taking this further, the average time in school is approximately 6 hours a day, 5 days a week for 190 days of the year. This is roughly 1,140 hours out of 8,670, about 13 per cent of the child's year. For the other 87 per cent of the year, the child is influenced by a multitude of stimuli. So even with the same curriculum, the same teacher, in the same setting, much of what influences children and their development is external to what happens in school. The counter-issue can be raised: if no two children are the same, why do we treat them the same and teach them in the same way? The argument made here is not exactly new within education, yet aiming to balance the individual needs of one child, let alone a class of 30, is a central aspect to the art of teaching.

Consequently, this chapter will discuss the traditional way of viewing children as individuals before progressing to discuss how to enable this within the classroom. Why is this important, however? According to the Department for Education (1999/2012), there are core and specific skills that a teacher needs to be able to utilise in their career. The core skills that are required to manage SEND in the classroom, particularly for teacher training and induction periods of a teacher's career, are:

- planning and teaching for inclusion and access to the curriculum
- behaviour management, and an awareness of the emotional and mental health needs of pupils (to build their self-esteem)
- assessment for learning (learning skills)
- an understanding of when professional advice is needed and where to find it.

9.2 THE TRADITIONAL PERSPECTIVE ON INDIVIDUAL CHILDREN

What is 'normal'? What is a 'normal' child? From the introduction, if you have read this far and thought, 'Why are you asking me this?' then you will realise that there is no straightforward answer to this question. We can only develop a composite picture in our minds of a child from our sum total experience of children: those we used to play with as children, family relations, those we have taught. However, this composite picture is used to inform our perspectives to classify children, so that we can teach according to the set criteria for that group. Yet, before National Curriculum assessments in England and Wales, SATs in the USA or even IQ measures devised by Binet over a hundred years ago, humans have grouped other humans according to set criteria. Two-and-a-half thousand years ago, Plato discussed such classifications through his work on the aristocracy where men were classified as either 'gold' (philosopher-kings, the ruling class), 'silver' (the auxiliaries of the ruling class such as soldiers) and 'bronze' (everyone else) (Cahn, 2002; Plato, 2007). How does this apply in today's society? Do we have a classless society? Needless to say, with such groupings, very few are considered to be in the top tier compared with those at the bottom. Such a taxonomy (a way of grouping) is hierarchical in nature, often represented as a triangle; however, in an attempt to humanise such classifications further, the average, normal or bell-shaped distribution curve is used (Figure 9.1).

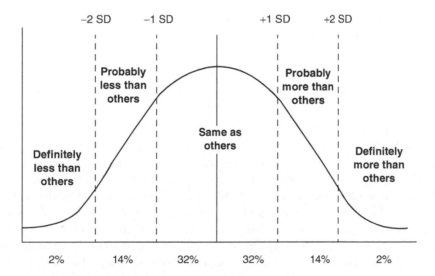

Figure 9.1   The average distribution curve, or 'Gaussian' curve

The correct name for the curve is a 'Gaussian' distribution curve – the curve being determined by ascertaining what the average is for a set of responses. From this, the standard deviation can be determined, in other words, where most of the other responses may be found. As an example, if you were to measure the shoe size of a class of children, most of the class will group round one or two different shoe sizes, a smaller number who will be about three sizes smaller or three sizes larger, and then there may be one or two who have a very small or a very large shoe size.

Of course this can be extended to include height, weight, head circumference or indeed any measurable attribute where data appears continuous, or in other words, goes up in stages. As illustrated in Chapter 5, this can relate to children's growth charts, although within a more school-based context, this could apply to test scores: some will score higher, some lower and most will be average.

Although there is nothing wrong with plotting data on a Gaussian curve, or indeed using the data to draw conclusions, what is actually done with the data is central to the themes of this book and this chapter. In other words, we can use the data to inform how we should teach the class as a whole, or perhaps as three or four groups (top, above average, below average, bottom). We can also use the data to inform how we approach each individual within the class. However, this data may have only been determined through mathematics, or English; can we say that where a child is on a chart for mathematics will allow us to make an equal assumption of where they are on a different chart? Needless to say, this would be very poor practice indeed.

At either end of the continuum, two terms are frequently ascribed to specific children: 'Special Educational Needs', and 'Gifted and Talented'. Both terms will be examined within this chapter, but it is vitally important to note that the practices discussed should be held as models of teaching for any specific child and that the themes within the entire book inform this approach.

9.3 SEND CODE OF PRACTICE

One of the most significant developments within the area has been the publication of the new *SEND Code of Practice: 0 to 25 Years* (Department for Education/Department for Health, 2015), which updated the original 2001 code. The core changes with the new Code of Practice (CoP) are that the age range it covers is extended; there is a clear focus on ascertaining the views of children and young people, and also parents, in decision-making; there is a stronger focus on raising aspirations; there is cooperation between education, health and social care services; and that there is a coordinated assessment process, which focuses on health and care as opposed to statements and learning difficulty assessments. While these areas were developed in a CoP that was released a year earlier, the 2015 version clarified the roles and responsibilities to support integrated working and record sharing between different organisations.

Specifically, for schools, there is guidance on taking a graduated approach for identifying and supporting pupils with SEN to replace the existing School Action and School Action Plus from the previous code. Furthermore, within the new code, there is a greater focus on supporting a child's successful transition into adulthood while keeping parents informed about their child's development. In addition, there is a list of legal obligations to ensure that schools must not discriminate against a child under the Equality Act (2010). Most importantly for the teacher, as outlined in Paragraph 6.1, there is clarification that all children and young people are entitled to an education that is appropriate to their needs, and which promotes high standards while enabling them to fulfil their potential.

A child with Special Educational Needs is defined as follows: 'A child or young person has SEN if they have a learning difficulty or disability which calls for special educational provision to be made for him or her' (Department for Education/Department for Health, 2015: 15). Specifically, a child of compulsory school age or young person is deemed to have a learning difficulty or disability if they have 'a significantly greater difficulty in learning than the majority of others of the same age, or … a disability which prevents or hinders him or her from making use of facilities of a kind generally provided for others of the same age in mainstream schools or mainstream post-16 institutions' (Department for Education/Department for Health, 2015: 16).

It is important to note that the child is not deemed to have a learning difficulty solely based on whether their native language is different from English.

From this definition, there are four different groups of SEND: communication and interaction; cognition and learning; behavioural, emotional and social development; and sensory and physical development. Within the primary school context, for children who receive a 'Statement' (an official entitlement to enable specific provision to enable their learning), the Department for Education (2011) provides a percentage breakdown of children with different needs:

5.1 per cent	Specific learning difficulties
16.2 per cent	Moderate learning difficulties
12.1 per cent	Behaviour, emotional and social difficulties
22.5 per cent	Speech, language and communication needs
7.2 per cent	Hearing, visual or multisensory impairment
17.6 per cent	Autistic spectrum disorder
9.7 per cent	Physical disability
9.5 per cent	Other (e.g. severe learning difficulty, or profound and multiple learning difficulty)

What is important to note here is that the above percentages relate to those children who have a Statement, not the numbers of children within the full school population.

Consequently, a child may have a learning need, but this does not necessarily equate to them receiving a Statement.

Furthermore, two additional terms are detailed for consideration, whether the learning difficulty is 'global' or whether it is 'specific'. Global learning difficulties affect all aspects of a child's learning, while specific learning difficulties are deemed to be an anomaly that only affects one aspect of the child's learning. Yet, when does a specific learning difficulty become a global learning difficulty? For example, although dyslexia is termed a specific learning difficulty, the child may experience low self-esteem, which may in turn impact on other domains of learning. However, due to the way education tends to classify learners, the different groups of SEND are detailed in the following sections.

A WORD OF WARNING ON CLASSIFICATIONS

In May 2013, version five of the *Diagnostic and Statistical Manual of Mental Disorders* (or *DSM-5*), was published. This is the core handbook developed by the American Psychiatric Association used to define and categorise various disorders. It took 13 years to update the *DSM-IV* and a number of significant changes have been incorporated. For example, Asperger's syndrome, which was defined in *DSM-IV* as a separate disorder, has been merged under autistic spectrum disorders. In relation to ADHD, the diagnostic criteria have been extended from symptoms being present under 7 years of age to symptoms being present at less than 12 years of age, or a minimum of four symptoms if aged 17 or over. A similar publication is the *ICD-10 International Classification of Mental and Behavioural Disorders*, which provides a set of internationally recognised defining criteria for specific conditions (World Health Organization, 1992/2010). (There is currently a revision being written, which is at phase two of development, so *ICD-11* is expected for publication in 2018. We will therefore refer to *ICD-11* from this point forward.) Although the *DSM-5* is an American publication, it is used globally. As part of the consultation period, the authors of the *DSM-5* invited responses: this in turn prompted 13,000 comments and 12,000 emails and letters (www.dsm5.org). One such response was a 26-page report written by the British Psychological Society (BPS), which has contributed to the debate regarding classification (Allen et al., 2011). We acknowledge this position and would ask teachers to ensure a balance between the dangers of classification and the benefits of the application of classification, in an adapted framework.

9.4 AUTISTIC SPECTRUM DISORDERS (ASD)

WHAT IS IT?

'Autism' was a word originally used in 1943 by Leo Kanner; however, since the inception of the term, the more familiar phrase 'autistic spectrum disorder' has been used

(Wing, 2003). ASD is deemed to be a complex neuro-developmental disorder, which affects an individual's social and emotional interaction with others, for example, in understanding other people's emotional state and providing what society may view as the appropriate response. To this extent, ASD affects social communication, both verbally and non-verbally. A further symptom can include social understanding, which is characterised through repetitive thoughts and behaviour, where an action or a word may be used repeatedly with the person unable to monitor their personal response to varying situations. The three symptoms are consequently referred to as the 'triad of impairments' (Terrell and Passenger, 2011).

The emphasis of ASD, however, is on the middle word, 'spectrum', which means that the symptoms will vary between individuals: one or other of the symptoms may be more or less significant than the others.

WHAT CAUSES IT?

ASD was originally deemed to be a product of nurture, in other words, the child's environment and the way they were brought up. However, recent research (Ronald et al., 2005; Silverman et al., 2002) indicates that ASD is more likely due to 'nature': in other words, the genetics of the child passed on through previous generations.

From a historical perspective, in 1998, ASD was associated with a childhood vaccination, the MMR jab (measles, mumps, rubella). Research suggested that children who had the MMR jab had a higher chance of developing ASD. This was based on a sample of 12 children and the research methods were challenged by other scientists, yet the myth was perpetuated, which in turn has resulted in children not being vaccinated and an increasing prevalence of the three diseases. As recently as the spring of 2013, unprecedented numbers of people with measles were reported in South Wales, culminating in a national vaccination programme targeting over a million children in the UK. The original article was retracted by *The Lancet* (2010) and the research has been deemed by some as the most damaging medical hoax in the last century (Flaherty, 2011).

GENERAL INDICATORS

A child with ASD tends to exhibit symptoms of the triad of impairments between the ages of two and three years. Unfortunately, however, it is very problematic to determine whether the symptoms are typical child development, or whether they are indicative of ASD (Terrell and Passenger, 2011). Repetitive play as evidenced through play schemas is part of normal childhood development, for example, putting cars or other objects in order, joining objects together or continually hiding objects. Such repetitive behaviour could in turn be deemed as one of the triads of impairment. Alternatively, the condition can go undetected for several years, especially in children who demonstrate more subtle signs of ASD.

If we take the triad of impairments individually, other indicators become prevalent. For example, in relation to social interaction, a child may not respond well to other children in the class. This may be exhibited through social isolation by other children within the class, or the child not engaging in the same way as other children. A child with ASD may be able to mimic the social responses of other children, but these may be inappropriate to the situation, for example, not knowing when a conversation has finished, or what appropriate physical contact is warranted within a situation. The child may not be able to 'read' and respond to social interactions in the same way as others from the same culture. In relation to communication, a child with ASD may not be able to express their thoughts, feelings or ideas with others, or indeed empathise with others.

The use of imagination can similarly be problematic in a child with ASD. This can be exhibited through a lack of engagement with fiction, for example, understanding a character's motivation within a story or offering their perspective on a book or a film. The impairment of imagination can also result in a fixation on a certain form of play, for example, continually playing with the same toy or repeating the same action (for example, tapping, rocking, touching specific objects). This can manifest too in the form of an attachment to a specific object, arranging objects uniformly or collecting objects. Again, it is important to note that children (and adults) can and do have attachments to different objects; for example, philatelists collect stamps, numismatists collect coins, lepidopterists collect butterflies and moths, and tegestologists collect beermats. Consequently, can all stamp collectors or children who collect football stickers be deemed as having Asperger's syndrome (a subtle form of ASD)?

Coping with change is a further symptom that can be problematic. Indeed, according to Hritz (2008), only 20 per cent of people actually like change: does this mean that 80 per cent of the population are deemed to have ASD? Yet for the child in school, subtle changes can be significant, for example, where they sit, what pencil or pen they work with, who they work with and changes to the timetable. To some extent, this is explained through the fixation of the child with ASD on certain aspects and attributes.

Other symptoms of ASD can include language disorders, difficulties with fine and gross motor coordination, extremes of mood (excitement, misery), through to psychiatric conditions such as anxiety or depression. It is important to note that, as a teacher, we are not clinicians, whether a medical doctor or psychologist; consequently, if we suspect a child is exhibiting signs of ASD and this has not been diagnosed previously, the first discussion, above all else, needs to be with the Special Educational Needs Coordinator (SENCo) who will be able to make a more informed assessment and in turn contact the relevant professionals.

SUPPORT STRATEGIES

It is important to note that ASD is lifelong: children with this condition grow into adults with this condition. It is fundamentally important, however, that the child is supported through appropriate intervention at an early stage and that this in turn enables the child to achieve their full potential. Consequently, as teachers, we can only offer support to ensure that we are enabling the child.

Generally, children with ASD tend to be visual learners; therefore providing pictorial instructions and representations (such as Makaton, or the Picture Exchange Communication System, PECS) can be helpful with certain tasks to support oral information (see Figure 9.2).

Figure 9.2   Examples of pictorial representations for communication similar to systems such as Makaton or PECS

For instance, it may be useful to make laminated lists to help the child understand what is required, where and when, so that they can understand the requirements of a specific activity. In addition, providing specific instructions to assist with group work would be beneficial: for example, indicating questions to ask others, providing written rules for working cooperatively, or through role-playing specific incidents (such as winning or losing a game), and similarly discussing appropriate conduct and the use of personal space.

There are obvious overlaps between the previous support strategies to develop the child's social understanding with communication. As a teacher, however, it is important to ensure that the child knows you are talking to them; consequently using their name before offering instructions is beneficial to ensure the child is aware that the instruction is for them specifically. Additionally, ensuring instructions are kept short and simple will enable the child to act accordingly, as opposed to inwardly digesting what could be deemed abstract information. It would be worth assessing the child's understanding of the task by getting them to repeat back the instructions, allowing you to identify whether they have or have not fully comprehended them. Open questions can similarly be problematic for the child. As a result, despite the advocacy of open questions to promote thinking, offering some closed questions for the child with ASD would be appropriate. Furthermore, use of irony or figurative speech can also be problematic for the child to understand.

ACTIVITY

Review the points in the previous paragraph to support a child with ASD:

- eye contact
- use of the child's name
- short, specific instructions
- asking them to repeat back the instructions
- use of closed questions
- avoiding figurative speech, for example, 'Grab a pencil'.

How would you encourage the child to get ready to go home at the end of the day?

Organisation can be helpful. Although visual prompts and lists have been discussed, other support strategies may include help in organising their resources for the lesson (for example, pencils, pens or books), perhaps providing a clearly identified set of resources for that particular child. In relation to organising their work, providing the child with writing frames (short visual instructions on what to do or how much to complete) would provide additional support. Sequencing thoughts and organising and communicating this through their own writing can similarly be problematic. Consequently use of a scribe (for example, a teaching assistant) to support writing their thoughts may be beneficial.

Needless to say, the strategies outlined here are very generic: the focus of this chapter is to ensure that the individual is provided with learning opportunities specifically for them, whether or not they have SEND.

9.5 DYSLEXIA OR SPECIFIC LEARNING DIFFICULTIES (SpLD)

WHAT IS IT?

Think of the actors Sir Anthony Hopkins, Sylvester Stallone, Keanu Reeves, Keira Knightly. Now consider some famous scientists such as Thomas Edison or Albert Einstein. Let's add some artists, for example, Leonardo da Vinci, Pablo Picasso or Andy Warhol; or some musicians: John Lennon, Damon Albarn, Joss Stone. How about athletes such as Sir Steve Redgrave and Muhammad Ali; or business leaders: Bill Gates, Richard Branson and Steve Jobs? The list can go on. As you have probably guessed, these are just a few of the many famous people deemed to have dyslexia (for a more comprehensive list, please refer to: www.dyslexia.com/famous.htm).

Indeed, such people can be deemed to have a 'gift', a way of envisaging something in a new way, a way of thinking, a way of working, perhaps an element of creativity: an element of 'genius'. Admittedly, while you may have heard of only a few of the names above, all have capitalised on their strengths, their unique skill-set in how they process information. Indeed, this is what dyslexia is: where information is processed differently from others. According to the British Dyslexia Association (2017), dyslexia is a combination of strengths and limitations that can affect reading, writing and spelling, and sometimes mathematical ability, although there may similarly be problems with short-term memory or sequencing due to the way information is processed differently.

As with the theme of this chapter, dyslexia is not to be viewed as a 'difficulty': it is only a difficulty if the teacher is unable to match appropriate activities with the child's specific needs. Indeed, despite dyslexia synonymously being referred to as a 'specific learning difficulty', the British Dyslexia Association would prefer to use the term 'specific learning difference' – that children with dyslexia learn differently from other children, yet as we have consistently maintained in this chapter and in this book, all children learn differently as they are all individual.

WHAT CAUSES IT?

Before answering this question, please take a few moments to engage with the following reflection.

REFLECTION

What does a butterfly look like? Indeed, ask a young child to draw a picture of a butterfly and you can almost guarantee it will look something like Figure 9.3a or Figure 9.3b. Similar features but uniquely different.

Next, consider asking two different architects to draw a house, perhaps from different countries or from different times. Would you expect their houses to look the same if you limited them to the same building materials? Would they both have four sides to the house? Would one be daring and add a couple of extra sides, or perhaps make the house triangular or even circular in shape?

Now consider what you think would be the best attributes for a tablet computer. Would you optimise it for playing games, for social interaction, for processing speed? Next take the world's most outstanding computer: our brain.

(Continued)

ca m cron

Figure 9.3a   An example of a child's drawing of a butterfly (from Cameron Buckler, aged 8, permission obtained)

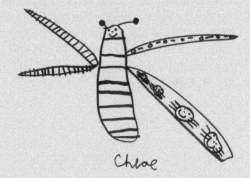

Chloe

Figure 9.3b   Another example of a child's drawing of a butterfly (from Chloe Buckler, aged 8, permission obtained)

How do you 'make' one? What bits need to be connected? What happens if you connect one bit differently to another bit in someone else's brain? Indeed, this is what dyslexia is: the neurological development of the brain forms slightly differently at the foetal stage of development within a child.

As dyslexia is perceived to be a result in such 'architecture' of the brain, information tends to be processed differently. From a psychological perspective, information is processed in four stages: input, integration, storage and output. Consequently, dyslexia may affect one or more of these processes as outlined in Table 9.1.

There is some evidence which indicates that dyslexia is inherited genetically. Despite dyslexia being identified by Oswald Berkhan in 1881, with the term developed by Rudolf Berlin in 1887 (Wagner, 1973), within your parents' generation, dyslexia

Table 9.1   Processes affected by dyslexia

Input: **where information is perceived through the senses, specifically visually or auditory**

Visually, difficulties can arise with problems in recognising the shape, position and size of items, along with sequencing.

Auditory, difficulties can arise from being unable to screen out competing sounds to focus on just one, such as the teacher.

Integration: **where the perceived input from the senses is interpreted, categorised, placed in a sequence or related to previous learning**

Students with such integration problems may be unable to tell a story in a correct sequence or memorise information such as the days of the week, multiplication tables, etc.

They may be able to understand a new idea or concept, although they are unable to relate this to previous learning.

Storage: **this relates to difficulties with the memory**

Short-term memory difficulties make it difficult to learn new material without using a lot of repetition.

Long-term memory difficulties occur when the pupil is unable to access stored information.

Output: **this relates to the way in which information comes out of the brain through either spoken words/language, or through muscle activity**

Language: difficulties such as answering a question due to problems in retrieving information, organising thoughts and putting the thoughts into words before they are spoken.

Writing: difficulties in retrieving information, organising thoughts and putting the thoughts into actions before they are written.

may have been deemed a 'trendy middle-class disease', one which didn't really exist except in the minds of parents whose children were not performing well. Consequently, some parents may not be aware of their own dyslexic tendencies even if their children have been diagnosed as dyslexic. Although the causes are still being investigated, as teachers again it is our responsibility to ensure that we enable each individual child.

GENERAL INDICATORS

Arguably, no two learners with dyslexia are the same, in the same way that no two children are the same. There may, however, be some indicative patterns that indicate dyslexia. For example, a child may be able to engage very well within a group activity through offering valuable insights and thoughts, yet there may be a problem with the child recording this in a meaningful way for the teacher, for example, in written format. If you ask a child to compose a story, the child with dyslexia may have the most developed, stunningly thought-through piece of work, yet on paper there is just a name and a date. If the stories are collected in from the class, who will be the child who receives a resounding (and proverbial) 'F' grade in thick red pen? Consequently, signs that tend to indicate dyslexia are that the child may seem as intellectually able (or even more able) than their peers, yet is unable to record this on paper. Furthermore, the child may excel in areas where there is less emphasis on writing, for example art, drama, music or sport. (Indeed, just refer to the list of names at the beginning of this section.) Although clumsiness can be associated with dyslexia, this may not be evident in the types of activity that a child with dyslexia may excel at.

The learner with dyslexia may attempt to 'make up' for their perceived limitation in what the education system deems as academic excellence in writing things down, through distraction activities (for example, by being the classroom joker or engaging in other disruptive behaviour). Alternatively, the child may appear withdrawn and isolated, which can be exacerbated through higher incidents of bullying. The learner may also have problems in processing information, especially if this is presented very quickly, or they cannot remember all of the items on a list. Furthermore, the child may easily become exhausted due to the increased effort they need to invest in their learning.

Within the early years, children with dyslexia may display signs of a lack of attention, delayed speech development and problems with naming items, getting dressed and putting shoes on correctly. Additionally, the child may enjoy listening to stories but not display any interest in learning letters or words. As the child develops, such signs may become more evident in terms of getting dressed, confusion over left and right, or remembering instructions. Although it is often perceived that the child with dyslexia may have difficulty with reading, not all have such problems. Specific signs to look for are loss of place when reading, pronouncing polysyllabic words, being hesitant with their reading, and perhaps confusion over words with similar letters such as was/saw, on/no, of/off. An additional sign may be that the child has problems understanding what they have read. Within the child's writing, perhaps the most explicit incidents are where there is a sense of disparity between the child's written and spoken language. Other signs are spelling words phonetically such as 'moor' or 'mor' as opposed to 'more', and 'fli' as opposed to 'fly'. Furthermore, there may be issues in presenting their work such as untidy handwriting or being poorly set out. As the child develops further, they may avoid using longer words or have problems planning and writing longer extracts of work. Most significantly, however, the child may have diminished confidence and self-esteem because they know they are different from other learners: they can intellectually 'stand their ground' in relation to concepts, yet they are unable to perform in a way that achieves the same academic approval due to their problems in organisation or presentation.

SUPPORT STRATEGIES

The core focus for the teacher should be on enabling the learner's personal attributes: indeed, having read through the general indicators, you may have already considered some ways in which to provide an equitable educational experience. Some of the strategies are models of good practice for any learner, for example, providing clear, explicit instructions, or indeed, being able to explain something in many different ways. Although there are specific strategies outlined in Table 9.2, it must be noted that these are not a definitive list: the emphasis should be on negotiating with the child to find a way to enhance their personal attributes.

Table 9.2   Support strategies for dyslexic learners

Writing	In relation to their writing, you may be able to challenge them intellectually and record their thoughts on a voice recorder, yet have a more reasonable expectation in what they produce as 'written work'.
	Cursive handwriting to memorise the order of letters.
	Word processing.
Marking work	Using different-coloured pens for marking may help the child understand what has been marked in relation to content, with another colour for spelling or structure. Furthermore, when going through a child's work, aim to understand how and why they may have made a mistake and target specific aspects for development in the course of your teaching (e.g. specific spelling structures).
	Credit for effort as well as achievement are both essential. This gives the pupil a better chance of getting a balanced mark. Creative writing should be marked on context.
	Spelling mistakes pinpointed should be those appropriate to the child's level of spelling. Marking should be done in pencil and have positive comments.
	Try not to use red pens to mark the dyslexic child's work. There's nothing more disheartening for the child than to have work returned covered in red ink, when they've tried harder than their peers to produce the work.
	Only ask a pupil to rewrite a piece of work that is going to be displayed. Rewriting pages for no reason at all is soul-destroying, as usually much effort will have already been put into the original piece of work.
Fatigue	As previously discussed, the child with dyslexia is likely to demonstrate greater signs of fatigue; consequently the teacher needs to consider how best to address this issue, perhaps ensuring that the child's activities are structured accordingly.
Multisensory	Multisensory approaches to learning are to be encouraged: for example, forming shapes, numbers or letters in sand so the child can develop a kinaesthetic sense of how to form their writing.
Instructions	Spending time explaining instructions to children is fundamental; however, it may also be necessary to teach specific skills to children such as how to tidy their belongings, or get dressed.
Environment	Sit near the front.
	Ensure the room and resources are appropriately organised, such as providing word banks and work screens to focus attention and so forth.
	Limit use of whiteboard as it is in the vertical plane opposed to horizontal. May be easier to present information as a photocopied transcript.
	Label resources to include not only the word but also a symbol.
Metacognition	Encourage the child to develop learning strategies relevant for them.
Organisation	Checklists.
	Stop, look, listen.
	Concept mapping.
	Drawing diagrams.
Understanding	Repeat and redefine words.
Reading	A structured reading scheme that involves repetition and introduces new words slowly is extremely important. This allows the child to develop confidence and self-esteem when reading.
	Don't ask pupils to read a book at a level beyond their current skills; this will instantly demotivate them. Motivation is far better when demands are not too high, and the child can actually enjoy the book. If they have to labour over every word they will forget the meaning of what they are reading.

(Continued)

Table 9.2   (Continued)

	Save the dyslexic child the ordeal of having to read aloud in class. Reserve this for a quiet time with the class teacher. Alternatively, perhaps give the child advanced time to read preselected reading material, to be practised at home the day before. This will help ensure that the child is seen to be able to read out loud, along with other children.
	Real books should also be available for paired reading with an adult, which will often generate enthusiasm for books. Story tapes can be of great benefit for the enjoyment and enhancement of vocabulary. No child should be denied the pleasure of gaining access to the meaning of print, even if they cannot decode it fully.
	Reading for comprehension.
	Remember reading should be fun.
Spelling	Many of the normal classroom techniques used to teach spellings do not help the dyslexic child. All pupils in the class can benefit from structured and systematic exposure to rules and patterns that underpin a language; for example, irregular words need whole-word approaches, flashcards for words with similar beginnings or endings.
	Spelling rules can be given to the whole class. Words for class spelling tests are often topic-based rather than grouped for structure. If there are one or two dyslexic pupils in the class, a short list of structure-based words for their weekly spelling test will be far more helpful than random words. Three or four irregular words can be included each week; eventually this should be seen to improve their free-writing skills.
	All children should be encouraged to proof read, which can be useful for initial correction of spellings. Dyslexic learners seem to be unable to correct their spellings spontaneously as they write, but they can be trained to look out for errors that are particular to them.
	Remember, poor spelling is not an indication of low intelligence.
Handwriting	Reasons for poor handwriting at any age can be poor motor control, tension, badly formed letters, speed, etc. A cursive joined style is most helpful to children with dyslexic problems. Encourage the children to study their writing and be self-critical. Get them to decide for themselves where faults lie and what improvements can be made, so that no resentment is built up at yet another person complaining about their written work.
	Discuss the advantages of good handwriting and the goals to be achieved with the class. Analyse common faults in writing, by writing a few well-chosen words on the board for class comment.
	Make sure a small reference chart is available to serve as a constant reminder for the cursive script in upper and lower case.
	If handwriting practice is needed, it is essential to use words that present no problem to the dyslexic child in terms of meaning or spelling.
	Improvement in handwriting skills can improve self-confidence, which in turn reflects favourably throughout a pupil's work.

ASSOCIATED ASPECTS

There are further associated terms with SpLD, such as dyspraxia or motor difficulties, and dyscalculia or difficulties with mathematics. Indeed, the prefix 'dys-' derives from the Greek word, 'badly'. Dyspraxia can often be misinterpreted as the child being 'clumsy', for example, knocking things over, difficulties in catching or kicking a ball and difficulties standing on one leg. Alternatively the child with dyspraxia may not be able to sit still and tends to fidget or play with their hands or other objects in their immediate environment.

Dyscalculia is often associated with use of mathematical operations such as confusing the addition and multiplication symbol, or the subtraction and division symbols, through to difficulties with time, measurement or space. It is estimated that approximately 90 per cent of children with dyslexia experience problems in some areas of mathematics. The child with dyscalculia may tend to confuse numbers, for example, reading 35 as 53, or not comprehending that $2 + 6 = 8$ is the same as $6 + 2 = 8$. They may similarly have problems with mathematical reasoning.

9.6 ATTENTION DEFICIT/HYPERACTIVITY DISORDER (ADHD)

WHAT IS IT?

Attention deficit/hyperactivity disorder (ADHD) is the most prevalent neurodevelopmental disorder, affecting 5 per cent of children internationally from a range of cultures and regions (Polanczyk et al., 2007; Tannock, 1998). According to the World Health Organization (1992/2010: F90), the condition is a 'hyperkinetic disorder'. ADHD predominantly affects more boys than girls at a ratio of 3:1 (Tannock, 1998). There are three associated elements of ADHD: inattention (attention deficit), hyperactivity and impulsivity (hyperactivity) (Figure 9.4). In relation to the term, you may see it written with or without the forward slash (AD/HD or ADHD); similarly you may also see the term 'attention deficit disorder' (or ADD). The current preference is, however, ADHD (American Psychiatric Association, 2013). The confusion arises when attempting to analyse the associated symptoms: the learner may be predominantly inattentive (ADHD-I), predominantly hyperactive (ADHD-H) or combined (ADHD-C) (Graetz et al., 2001).

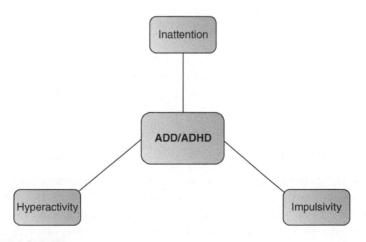

Figure 9.4   ADD/ADHD

According to Biederman et al. (1991, 1996), between 20 and 30 per cent of learners with ADHD have an associated learning disorder with reading, writing, spelling or arithmetic. Despite the impact that ADHD has on educational achievement, research indicates that learners with ADHD have increased risk of mood and anxiety disorders, poorer social and vocational outcomes, and substance misuse (Sciberra et al., 2013). Furthermore, ADHD can account for educational underachievement to a greater extent than IQ level, whereby learners perform at a lower level than would be predicted by their IQ (Barry et al., 2002; Daley and Birchwood, 2010).

Although ADHD was once viewed exclusively as a childhood disorder, it is now understood that ADHD persists into adulthood (Chronis-Tuscano and Stein, 2012). Indeed Sciberra et al. (2013) suggest that ADHD continues into adulthood for 50 per cent of children affected. The prevalence of ADHD within the adult population is likely to be increased among individuals involved with the criminal justice system: research indicates that up to two-thirds of young offenders and roughly 40 per cent of the male adult prison population have been positively screened for childhood ADHD (Ginsberg et al., 2010; Young et al., 2011).

ACTIVITY

Consider the following indicative behaviours of ADHD:

- fails to give attention to details
- difficulty sustaining attention
- difficulty organising tasks or activities
- restlessness
- excessively loud or noisy
- rushes through activities
- interrupts others.

Try and explain alternate reasons for such behaviours using your understanding of psychology, rather than just saying the behaviour is a symptom of ADHD. For example, could lack of attention be explained by factors listed in Chapter 6?

WHAT CAUSES IT?

The causes of ADHD are complex in nature and may include genetic and environmental factors (Grizenko et al., 2012). Genetically, parents who have ADHD are more likely to have children with ADHD, with estimates that 17 per cent of parents of children with ADHD met criteria for ADHD in childhood (Barkley et al., 2002; Mannuzza and Klein, 2000). In addition, neuroimaging studies of learners with ADHD have demonstrated a decreased size within the prefrontal cortex of the brain: this can affect certain executive functions such as response inhibition, which may explain the impulsivity element of ADHD and working memory, which could explain the inattention element of ADHD (Hill et al., 2002; Tannock, 1998).

In relation to environmental factors, deprivation, family dysfunction, adversity and impairments in parenting, such as parenting style and parental mood disorder, have been suggested (Biederman et al., 1995; Grizenko et al., 2012; Hinshaw et al., 2000; NCCMH, 2008). In relation to parenting style, negative, critical, over-reactive and author-itarian discipline among fathers has been suggested to similarly contribute to ADHD (Arnold et al., 1997). Further factors for the prevalence of ADHD appear to cluster around issues with pregnancy, such as maternal smoking and alcohol use, and most significantly stress during pregnancy (Grizenko et al., 2012).

GENERAL INDICATORS

Although inattention, hyperactivity and impulsivity are the indicators of ADHD, what do these terms specifically mean? For example, if a learner has slept poorly, they may lack attention during the day, yet does this warrant a label of ADHD? Alternatively a learner who is excited by a stimulating lesson may be perceived as impulsive if they are eager with their learning and call out an answer before putting their hand up.

The condition ADHD is associated with five specific criteria as identified in *DSM-5* (American Psychiatric Association, 2013): that symptoms are present before the age of 12; that symptoms are apparent in two or more settings (for example, school and home); that symptoms interfere with or reduce the quality of social, academic or occupational functioning; that symptoms are not accounted for by some other disorder; finally that six or more symptoms from either category in Table 9.3 are evident for at least 6 months (for a child under 12), or four symptoms for those aged 17 and over). Furthermore, the symptoms are not due to oppositional behaviour, defiance, hostility or a failure to under-stand instructions (American Psychiatric Association, 2013).

SUPPORT STRATEGIES

Medical interventions

As discussed in Chapters 5 and 6, the medical model of treatment for ADHD is to prescribe medication to limit the effects of the symptoms. Non-amphetamine stimu-lants (methylphenidate) include such brand names as Ritalin, or there are amphetamine stimulants (dextroamphetamine), which in turn stimulate the central nervous system. This boosts areas of the brain that attempt to seek stimulation, as ADHD is perceived as a lack of arousal in the brain, with the result that learners aim to seek more stimu-lation through their exhibited behaviours. Conversely medication that suppresses the

Table 9.3   Symptoms of ADHD as identified in the *DSM-5* (adapted from American Psychiatric Association, 2013)

Inattention	a.	Fails to give close attention to details.
	b.	Difficulty sustaining attention.
	c.	Does not seem to listen when spoken to directly.
	d.	Does not follow through on instructions.
	e.	Difficulty organising tasks and activities.
	f.	Avoids, seems to dislike and is reluctant to engage in tasks that require sustained mental effort.
	g.	Frequently loses objects necessary for tasks or activities.
	h.	Is often easily distracted by extraneous stimuli.
	i.	Is often forgetful in daily activities, chores and running errands.
Hyperactivity and impulsivity	a.	Often fidgets or taps hands or feet or squirms in seat.
	b.	Often restless during activities when others are seated.
	c.	Runs about or climbs on furniture and moves excessively in inappropriate situations.
	d.	Often excessively loud or noisy during play, leisure or social activities.
	e.	Is often 'on the go'.
	f.	Often talks excessively.
	g.	Often blurts out an answer before a question has been completed.
	h.	Has difficulty waiting his or her turn or waiting in line.
	i.	Often interrupts or intrudes on others.
	j.	Tends to act without thinking, such as starting tasks without adequate preparation or avoiding reading or listening to instructions.
	k.	Is often impatient.
	l.	Is uncomfortable doing things slowly and systematically and often rushes through activities or tasks.
	m.	Finds it difficult to resist temptations or opportunities, even if it means taking risks.

central nervous system (such as heterocyclic antidepressants) may be prescribed (Zsigmond and Benga, 2009). One explanation for the effect of medical treatment on children with ADHD is that there is a direct effect on parent–child interactions. Specifically parents were observed to be less controlling and more positive with their children when they were taking medication (Barkley and Cunningham, 1979; Barkley et al., 1985, 2002).

Other interventions

There has been an increasing level of interest in alternatives to the medical model in treating the symptoms of ADHD. Most significant is the use of cognitive behavioural therapy (CBT), which has been demonstrated to improve symptoms in both children

(NCCMH, 2008) and adults (Ramsey and Rostain, 2011; Weiss et al., 2012). Although cognitive behavioural techniques are discussed in greater detail in Chapters 11 and 13, the emphasis of the approach is on developing new ways of responding, for example, through helping the learner with planning, time management, reducing procrastination and so on.

One such approach is cognitive restructuring (as discussed in Chapter 16). This is the basis of the 'if–then' approach to enhance self-control (Gawrilow et al., 2011; Gollwitzer, 1993, 1999). The 'if–then' approach focuses on forming 'implementation intentions': a statement is made about 'if' a specific event occurs or a situation is encountered; consequently a follow-up 'then' statement is provided. The 'then' statement is related to the behaviour, the goal-directed response. For example, as opposed

Table 9.4   Intervention and support strategies (adapted from Raggi and Chronis, 2006)

Strategy	Description
Peer tutoring	A learner with ADHD is paired with a peer tutor to work collaboratively on an academic activity. The peer tutor provides one-to-one guidance and assistance to work at the learner's own pace.
Computer-assisted instruction	Specific objectives and division of content into smaller elements, along with immediate feedback in relation to response and accuracy can be facilitated through computer programs, games and so on.
Task/instructional modifications	There are several modifications that can be made for the learner with ADHD, for example, reducing task length, subdividing tasks, setting goals, using increased stimulation of the task, providing more explicit instructions and so on. Such methods increase the structure and organisation of the learner's environment, which as a result makes goals and tasks appear increasingly manageable. This in turn can reduce frustration while increasing persistence.
Visual versus auditory presentation of material	It has been suggested that learners with ADHD have difficulties in the internalisation of speech, which in turn can affect working memory. Consequently, encouraging the learner to respond orally may enable greater integration and retention of material than trying to learn information silently.
Adding structure to a task	Increasing the structure and predictability in classroom activities, for example, maintaining a clear structure to the day and providing instructions one at a time.
Choice making	Enabling the learner to take a certain level of individual decision-making and control over a task. (This relates to self-determination theory, which is covered in Chapter 10.)
Self-monitoring and self-reinforcement	Involves the learner setting goals for classwork completion and accuracy, monitoring these goals, and administering rewards upon successful completion.
Strategy training	Involves teaching the learner a specific skill so they can implement it in an academic situation, to improve their performance (metacognition link).
Homework-focused interventions	Providing guidance to parents on how they can assist with homework (for example, establishing a routine or a quiet space, providing support when required, helping to structure tasks, goal-setting).
Classroom-based functional assessment procedures	Developing an intervention specific to the learner, based on the identification and manipulation of environmental variables that initiate, maintain and/or increase the child's problematic behaviour in a particular setting: seat location, activity grouping, time of day, active/passive response, task structure, specific consequences and so on.

to saying 'I will concentrate on my work', it is better to say, 'If I am distracted by somebody talking, I will close my eyes, breathe deeply, then refocus on my work.' Further intervention and support strategies for children and adolescents with ADHD have been suggested by Raggi and Chronis (2006) as summarised in Table 9.4.

REFLECTION

Although there is a tendency to classify ADHD as part of the umbrella term of 'behavioural, emotional and social difficulties' (BESD, discussed below), we would ask you to reflect on the validity of such an association.

9.7 SPEECH, LANGUAGE AND COMMUNICATION NEEDS (SLCN)

WHAT IS IT?

As discussed in Chapter 5, language development is critical to cognitive development due to the constructivist nature of learning. To this extent, language is of fundamental importance for the child to access the full curriculum (Rose, 2006). Additionally, if the child is unable to communicate appropriately with their peers, this may impact on their ability to form friendships. As a result, children with SLCN are likely to experience academic, social or emotional difficulties. SLCN can occur owing to a number of different factors. For example, some people may have a specific difficulty with language only, without any general learning difficulties or physical or sensory impairments. This is often referred to as 'specific language impairment'.

WHAT CAUSES IT?

The nature of SLCN is predominantly due to the result of other needs, for example, autism. As both the Teacher Training Agency (1999) and the Foundation for People with Learning Disabilities (2000) highlighted, most children with SEN have difficulty with some aspect of SLCN.

GENERAL INDICATORS

A child with SLCN is likely to have other impairments that result in SLCN, for example, autism. Indicators that a child has SLCN can be exhibited through language use that is not as advanced as the child's peers. This in turn may result in a lack of understanding of what has been said, by either the teacher or other children. Similarly, the child may be unable to say exactly what they want.

SUPPORT STRATEGIES

Although a child with SLCN is likely to require additional professional support through a speech and language therapist, within the classroom context, the teacher can ensure that the child's needs are met. Indeed, what has been deemed as good educational practice throughout this book and this chapter can similarly be reiterated here, for example, adapting your use of language to ensure that instructions are kept short, simple and specific, and ensuring that the environment is effectively utilised so the child is able to both see and hear you effectively. Further environmental strategies are presented in Chapter 20. However, perhaps the most important aspect is to ensure that there is full information provided by professionals: for example, if a child has received a recent report from the speech and language therapist, this may be sent directly to the SENCo, yet it is paramount that the SENCo in turn shares this with the teacher. Similarly, if the child has moved to a new class, the information relating to the child's needs may not be automatically sent through to the teacher; thus the teacher needs to ensure that they can view any records and reports on the child that may be held by the SENCo. Such reports will detail how the school and teacher can best provide support for the child.

Additional strategies can be implemented, for example, effective targeting of the speech-processing deficit and addressing this through phonological teaching. Providing the opportunity for the child to engage with language use through developing the child's grammatical knowledge or through reading comprehension, or indeed through facilitating activities that require language to be utilised in different contexts (for example role play), can similarly be utilised.

9.8 BEHAVIOURAL, EMOTIONAL AND SOCIAL DIFFICULTIES (BESD)

WHAT IS IT?

'Behaviour, emotional and social difficulties' (BESD) is another umbrella term: a wide-ranging term where children are grouped under a specific label. As it implies, there is some difficulty with the child's interaction with others. Indeed, can a child be poorly behaved in isolation, if nobody is there to witness what they are doing? This is an analogy equated to the Zen koan, 'If a tree falls in a wood and there is nobody present, does it make a sound?' Consequently, the very presence of another person means that the child can exhibit emotions, from anger and frustration to isolation, disruptive or disturbing behaviour, which can affect what another person is doing, or social difficulties, such as being unable to interact in an appropriate way.

WHAT CAUSES IT?

BESD can be the result of nature or nurture. From a nurture perspective, the child's environment may affect the way they interact with others. Alternatively from the nature perspective, there may be a neurological deficiency, for example, depression, anxiety, ADHD, or as a result of ASD or dyslexia. Please note that behaviour is discussed in greater detail in Chapter 20 as the topic is one which is not possible to do justice to here.

GENERAL INDICATORS

Any general behaviour that affects the child's interaction with others, whether they are peers or adults, may be deemed BESD. Indeed, in Section 9.6, we asked you to question whether ADHD should be included within the category of BESD. If the exhibited behaviour is deemed to be negative, arguably the child is deemed to 'have' BESD needs: again, this is discussed further in Chapter 20.

SUPPORT STRATEGIES

In addition to the support strategies outlined in this chapter, other strategies may similarly be implemented, specifically in adhering to routine: for example, ensuring that lessons are structured appropriately, specifically in group work, where SMART goals are set (see Chapter 14). In addition, there may be opportunities to develop mentoring, where a child with BESD approaches a specific person if, and when, they need advice on handling a situation. The emphasis on mentoring is that the child speaks to someone they trust and can confide in: this may not necessarily be you, the teacher.

Given the emphasis on routine as discussed here, it is similarly worth limiting any unstructured time. However, on two or three occasions during the day, a significant period of unstructured time is provided to children: this is referred to as 'playtime' and 'lunchtime'. While teachers may escape to the sanctuary of the staffroom, they can often end up addressing incidents from their absence at the start of the next lesson. Consequently, providing structured activities that children can engage with during unstructured time can paradoxically help. In addition, providing some form of haven for a child to escape to can be of benefit: a place where a child who needs to can find a quiet place to take stock of themselves or a situation.

9.9 MODERATE LEARNING DIFFICULTIES (MLD)

WHAT IS IT?

'Moderate learning difficulties' (MLD) is a poorly defined term (Norwich and Kelly, 2005). It is hard to categorise and in the past would have been related to a child being called 'feeble-minded', 'slow', 'an idiot' or a variety of other such terms that were deemed to be perfectly acceptable within education. Indeed, Sternberg (2000) discusses how, in the past, a 'moron' was deemed to have an IQ of 51–70, an 'imbecile' an IQ of 26–50, and an 'idiot' an IQ of 0–25. Taking a more specific definition, MLD can be defined as a child with a general developmental delay, which places them approximately three years behind their peers.

Consequently, MLD is not the result of any one specific need, such as ASD or dyslexia, and indeed it may be multifaceted in nature (Fletcher-Campbell, 2005). This is why various authors question whether it should be included within the umbrella term of 'SEN'. Additionally, while certain specific needs like dyslexia affect one domain of the curriculum, for example English or mathematics, but not the child's intelligence, a child with MLD experiences low attainment across the curriculum.

WHAT CAUSES IT?

Given that the term is very poorly constructed, a working understanding would be that it is an interplay of two or more conditions.

GENERAL INDICATORS

As outlined, a child with MLD is likely to experience low attainment across the curriculum; although the early years or primary teacher may be aware of the child's access to the full curriculum, a subject-specific secondary teacher may not necessarily realise that a child is not performing equally across all the other curriculum subjects. However, there may be secondary indicators, for example, the child may have low self-esteem and motivation. Furthermore, the child may have less-refined academic attributes for successful studying, perhaps evident through poor attention within the classroom, less developed social skills and difficulties with auditory or visual memory, or they require a higher level of support with more self-directed activities (such as problem-solving) whereby they may overly rely on other children, the teaching assistant or teacher.

SUPPORT STRATEGIES

There are many strategies that the teacher can effectively utilise as discussed within this chapter and throughout the book: for example, considering a multisensory approach to learning; ensuring activities are carefully explained and structured; using visual prompts, writing frames or lists to help the child structure their work; and encouraging work to be recorded in different ways such as figures or concept maps, as opposed to an over-reliance on written prose.

9.10 GIFTED AND TALENTED

The majority of this chapter has been devoted to discussing perceived problems as a result of learning needs: needs that are not addressed by the teacher for that individual. It is easy to assume that such needs are indicative of children being lower achievers due to a range of factors. However, with the exception of MLD (which arguably is not a classification), it must equally be noted that at no point have we said that the child is of a lower ability than their peers – the child with ASD or dyslexia may actually be a higher achiever. Furthermore, a child whose needs are not challenged productively can exhibit BESD. This in turn underlines a core theme within this chapter: although the education system tends to label children, this can create many problems, and the focus of the teacher should be on ensuring each individual can meet with success at their level in a way that offers structured challenge.

Taking what people perceive as the higher end of the Gaussian curve, the term 'gifted and talented' is often attributed. The term 'gifted' is defined by Gagné (1985, 2003) as a learner whose potential is above average in one (or more) of the following domains: intellectual, social, physical or creative. Perhaps the core word here is 'potential': a child needs support and guidance to achieve their specific gifted potential. However, the term 'gifted' is more often ascribed to where a child excels in academic subjects, such as English or mathematics, while the term 'talented' is ascribed to practical subjects such as sport, music or art.

There are no set criteria in identifying a gifted child: this may be due more to intuition than an exact measure. For example, does the child tend to use language at a higher level than their peers? Do they learn quickly? Do they ask or answer lots of questions? Are they very curious? Perhaps the most fundamental question is whether the child is challenged or whether they appear bored or easily complete the work set.

Despite the differing needs of every individual child within your classroom, it can be easy to overlook the child who is either gifted or talented, at the expense of children who are perceived to be struggling more. However, in enabling full access to an inclusive curriculum, such a child is equally entitled to have their needs met. The challenge for the teacher is to ensure that the child is provided opportunity to extend their learning beyond that of the lesson in hand, perhaps through setting more challenging questions and open-ended extension tasks.

9.11 INCLUSION

Inclusion is often discussed within the educational context but it is similarly often mis-interpreted. Is inclusion something we do to ensure that everyone has equal access? Or is it something embodied in everything we do? Is it a collection of practices? Or is it a philosophy? Although these may appear to be subtle questions, there is a world of difference between inclusion as a practice and inclusion as a philosophy. For example, in relation to inclusion as a practice, this may relate to a child with dyslexia being provided with additional one-to-one support with the teaching assistant outside of the classroom. However, in relation to inclusion as a philosophy, that same child is part of the class, with all children in the classroom engaging with the lesson, utilising different resources that engage their understanding, while producing work that is a relevant, meaningful representation of their achievement. As such, throughout this book we advocate that teaching, and similarly inclusion, is a philosophy informed through research and practice (see Chapters 4 and 18).

REFLECTION

Although we may think we are being inclusive through addressing a child's specific needs, are we? We may be providing additional strategies to support their writing, but will the fact that during every lesson they go out with a specific person for additional support foster their self-esteem? Taking another example, if we introduce the lesson to the class, then focus on one child and provide them with additional instruction, again, is this inclusive? In relation to these examples, could we use the teaching assistant to play a word game with a group of children within the classroom, of which one child may have dyslexia? Could we ensure that all of our instructions to the children are presented in a clear, concise form, both orally and in writing?

Taken as a philosophical approach, can we actually see inclusion in operation, or is it just effective practice to enable all children? Alternatively we could be inclusive through providing a specific strategy for a specific child for their specific need for the entire class of children. Indeed, according to the British Dyslexia Association, 'If they don't learn the way we teach them, we must teach them the way they learn', a quote originally ascribed to Harry Chasty (British Dyslexia Association, 2016: 1). Despite this quote being written by the BDA, arguably this is a model for teaching any child.

A subtle choice of terminology has been used throughout this chapter in that at no point has the child 'got' a 'special need', or 'is special educational needs'. In returning to the use of labels, this would classify the child into a specific group. The emphasis in this chapter has been that the child 'is deemed' to have a special educational need. Subtly, this means that the child is not the label but that they have requirements which need to be considered, and that all children have their own individual needs. Consequently, such terms should never be used as an excuse, for example, 'That child has/is SEN', 'He or she has dyslexia'. Instead, a more accurate phrasing would be, 'The child experiences attributes associated with dyslexia, which in turn means that my teaching needs to be tailored to their specific learning attributes.' The 'condition' is not the cause or the blame: instead it is for us to teach in a way that ensures each individual achieves their full potential.

A FINAL REFLECTION

Although the following was written in 1997, to what extent does this relate today?

> The notion of inclusion does not set parameters … Rather it is about a philosophy of acceptance; it is about providing a framework within which all children can be valued equally, treated with respect and provided with equal opportunities at school … In short, accepting inclusion means moving away from what Roaf has called an 'obsession with individual difficulties' (Roaf, 1988: 7) to an agenda of human rights. (Thomas, 1997: 103)

9.12 A REVISED FOCUS FOR PRACTICE

Taking the variety and nature of the needs of each individual, the core focus of teaching is to move children forward from A to B while we are responsible for them. A to B is basically indicative of moving the child forward; however, one child's progression may well be different from another child's progression, for many of the reasons discussed not only within this chapter but also within the book. However, the political perspectives of our politicians set what could be argued as unrealistic levels for a percentage of children to achieve a required grade. In a world without league tables, continual assessment and targets, perhaps teachers may be allowed to do the thing that defines them: their ability to teach, although admittedly teaching does need to be informed through the teacher's assessment of the child on a specific task so that they can plan future learning activity.

9.13 CONCLUSION

What does a child look like? Are they all the same? If not, why do we tend to classify children into discrete labels? How many labels are enough within a class? Top, middle and bottom? Above average, average, below average? SEN? Does SEN equate to being below average? Consequently, are three, five, or even ten labels enough to use within a class? Whose classification are we using? Perhaps the only label we should use is the child's name, acknowledging that each is an individual with a competing range of abilities that may differ from others.

Many strategies have been presented within this chapter; although these are strategies to provide support for labelled children, alternatively could they be considered as part of the teacher toolbox – strategies that all children could benefit from? Essentially, this chapter questions how inclusive we are as teachers, whether inclusion is something we do, or whether inclusion is something we embody.

Taking these strategies forward, the next chapter will discuss how we can ensure individual success.

9.14 FURTHER READING

Frederickson, N. and Cline, T. (2016) *Special Educational Needs, Inclusion and Diversity: A Textbook* (3rd edn). Maidenhead: Open University Press.
This book provides a clear discussion of various principles and concepts from a theoretical perspective, in turn providing clear insight for effective practice.

Thompson, J. (2010) *The Essential Guide to Understanding Special Educational Needs: Practical Skills for Teachers*. Harlow: Pearson Education.
Thompson's book provides a coherent overview of the history of special educational needs, before progressing to discuss the practical skills to support a variety of needs.

10
MOTIVATION

CHAPTER OBJECTIVES

- Develop an understanding of the role of motivation within the classroom.
- Consider the differences between classical conditioning and operant conditioning in relation to educational practice.
- Recognise the difference between deficiency needs and being needs.
- Appreciate how self-determination theory can be applied within the classroom context.

TEACHERS' STANDARDS

A teacher must:

1   Set high expectations which inspire, motivate and challenge pupils

- establish a safe and stimulating environment for pupils, rooted in mutual respect
- set goals that stretch and challenge pupils of all backgrounds, abilities and dispositions

2   Promote good progress and outcomes by pupils

- guide pupils to reflect on the progress they have made and their emerging levels
- encourage pupils to take a responsible and conscientious attitude to their own work and study

4   Plan and teach well-structured lessons

- promote a love of learning and children's intellectual curiosity
- reflect systematically on the effectiveness of lessons and approaches to teaching
- contribute to the design and provision of an engaging curriculum within the relevant subject area(s)

7   Manage behaviour effectively to ensure a good and safe learning environment

- have high expectations of behaviour, and establish a framework for discipline with a range of strategies, using praise, sanctions and rewards consistently and fairly
- manage classes effectively, using approaches which are appropriate to pupils' needs in order to involve and motivate them

10.1 INTRODUCTION

The previous chapters in this part have highlighted a range of factors that affect the developing learner. Chapter 8 identified the components of the self through to discussing the way the self develops through a series of perspectives. From this, Chapter 9 discussed how education tends to classify learners in one or more ways, as opposed to appreciating the complexity and uniqueness of the individual. The diverse needs of individual learners can be attributed to a number of physical, cognitive or social aspects, which in turn can lead to the child being bracketed with a specific label such as autistic, specific learning difficulties or dyslexia.

Although psychological theory explains many of the issues surrounding the individual, a multitude of others can also affect the learner. Similarly although the past couple of chapters have discussed some support strategies to enable the individual, it is important to stress that one strategy will not suit every learner who displays, for example, low self-esteem. In returning to the core theme within this book, teaching is an 'art form': there is not necessarily one way of doing things, yet as professionals, we should continue to consider, implement, reflect on, evaluate and refine our approach.

In essence, what has been discussed up to this point provides more of an understanding of the way psychology affects the developing learner: from this point forwards, it is important to consider how psychology can be applied. In other words, what can be utilised from the psychological toolkit to ensure the learner fulfils their potential.

This next chapter therefore takes the concept of potential, identifying how this can be nurtured to enable the learner. In returning to the seed analogy, if we can ensure the right conditions for the learner, we can unleash their potential to achieve. Through providing these optimal conditions, we are enabling the inner resources of the learner to come to fruition. Such optimal conditions relate to the topic of motivation.

10.2 WHAT IS MOTIVATION?

If the optimal conditions are provided, the learner will achieve their potential. However, if you consider the analogy of a forest with a multitude of trees, what may be optimal conditions for one may not be the optimal conditions for another; for example, a willow requires a closer proximity to water than an oak. Some trees prefer shade more than others, some a different type of soil. Furthermore, some trees are deciduous and move into periods of dormancy; others are evergreen. For each one, the correct balance of conditions is required of a certain mixture of water, light, air, space and temperature. Motivation is the same: there are a number of core conditions within motivation, yet it is the balance that is essential for each individual.

Consequently, motivation is simply defined here as 'a balance of optimal conditions relevant for the individual to ensure that they achieve their potential'. Unfortunately this adds yet another definition to the already saturated area of motivation definitions.

ACTIVITY   Defining motivation

Find three definitions of 'motivation' from the internet (or journals, or books).

Copy and paste these into one document.

Highlight the core attributes for each of the definitions: what are the defining features of each?

Is there any overlap between these definitions? Do they differ?

Next, take all of the words you have highlighted and aim to utilise these in one sentence.

This 'study skills' exercise has enabled you to analyse various sources, identify their relative strengths and limitations, then synthesise the components into a new definition, which is arguably more developed than any of the definitions you originally identified.

In case you have not engaged with this activity (due to your lack of motivation!?), some sample definitions are provided below, which you can use:

- The amount of effort we are prepared to put into an activity (Brehm and Self, 1989).
- Why people act in a certain way. Such behaviour has three aspects: it has energy, direction and persistence (Santrock, 2001).
- An inner state where behaviour is prompted, directed then maintained (Sternberg and Williams, 2002).

Returning to the definition provided, that 'motivation is a balance of optimal conditions relevant for the individual to ensure that they achieve their potential', how does this compare with the others? Indeed, as this chapter progresses, we would encourage you to continually revisit and refine your own definition of motivation.

Having established a working definition of motivation, the next step is to understand the various perspectives on motivation before proceeding to discuss methods that can be applied within the classroom.

10.3 PSYCHOLOGICAL PERSPECTIVES ON MOTIVATION

Without wanting to sound too repetitive, there are many different perspectives within psychology. Motivation is no exception. Each perspective offers a different explanation for why individuals act as they do: indeed, each can make a contribution to our conception of the total person. According to Reeve (2014), who devotes a 600-page book to the topic, there are over 24 theories of motivation alone. However, due to the constraints of this chapter, the core perspectives that are often related to education will be discussed: the behaviourist approach, the humanist approach and self-determination theory.

10.4 BEHAVIOURAL PERSPECTIVE ON MOTIVATION

The behavioural perspective analyses motivation in relation to external environmental events; in other words, a stimulus (an event in the environment) occurs that elicits a specific behaviour (a response by the individual). At a very simple level, if you touch a kettle when it is hot (stimulus), you are very unlikely to touch it again (behaviour). To this extent, the process is in one linear direction: something occurs and someone does something. From this assertion, behavioural psychologists maintain that they can bring about a desired response if the right stimulus is provided. Historically, four specific theorists were at the forefront of this field: Ivan Pavlov and John Watson (classical conditioning), and Edward Thorndike and B.F. Skinner (operant conditioning).

CLASSICAL CONDITIONING

Pavlov noted that dogs drool (the behaviour) when they see food or their feeding bowl (the stimulus). The food is an 'unconditioned stimulus' while the salivating is an 'unconditioned response'. The dog will naturally salivate at the sight, smell or taste of food: they do not need to be trained to do this.

If a bell is rung at the same time as food is presented, the bell is deemed a 'conditioned stimulus': in other words, it is this stimulus that helps to ensure that the dog associates the bell with food. Normally, a dog will not salivate when a bell is rung. However, through the partnership of the bell and the food, the dog will start to associate that hearing a bell will mean food will be present. Consequently, the dog is being trained to salivate upon hearing a bell: this training is a 'conditioned response'. After being conditioned, the dog will salivate just upon hearing the bell.

Pavlov extended this further through introducing other stimuli with the sound of the bell. For example, if a black square is presented at the same time as the bell, the dog will soon be conditioned to associate the black square with the desired conditioned response – salivation. This is known as 'second-order conditioning'. To this day, such conditioning serves as the basis for dog training: if a dog responds in a prescribed way by the owner raising their hand and saying 'sit', the dog will receive a reward (a snack). After a while, the dog will no longer need the reward: the prescribed (or conditioned) response will occur on the command 'sit' or the raising of the upturned hand.

ACTIVITY Thought experiment

Can dogs train their owners?

Poppy is a collie-cross who understands the distinct sound of a rustling packet with a gorgeous smell. In this case, Poppy ventures into the kitchen to see Cameron opening a packet of chocolate digestives. Out of guilt for eating one biscuit in front of his much-loved dog, Cameron gets Poppy to sit and then throws her a small part of the biscuit.

Poppy naturally associates a rustling packet of biscuits with Cameron providing a tasty snack. The next time Cameron reaches for a biscuit, Poppy is sitting at his feet looking at him with doleful eyes. Cameron reinforces the behaviour of sitting by providing Poppy with part of the biscuit. Poppy is thus 'rewarded'. Yet who is training who? Has Poppy 'trained' Cameron by exhibiting the behaviour where she was previously rewarded? Or has Cameron elicited a prescribed response in Poppy?

Watson applied Pavlov's conditioning of dogs to humans, so was arguably the psychologist to found the field of behaviourism. The core focus for which Watson and his co-researcher are known is the conditioning of 'Little Albert'. In their study, Watson and Rayner (1920) obtained a nine-month-old baby and presented a range of stimuli (a rabbit, dog, monkey, white rat, cotton wool, masks, burning newspaper and the sound of a hammer striking a bar behind his head). It was this last stimulus that Little Albert was scared of.

A couple of months later, Watson and Rayner allowed Little Albert to play with the rat. Watson then came up behind the baby and hit the bar with the hammer. This took place on seven successive occasions over seven weeks, whereby Little Albert was conditioned to react to the rat (the conditioned stimulus) with the expression of fear (the conditioned response). Unfortunately, this conditioned response of fear similarly transferred to other items such as the dog, the rabbit, cotton wool and so on. After five days the conditioned response of fear was still evident, although it became less so after ten days, then a month.

REFLECTION

Despite the ethical concerns of this experiment by Watson and Rayner, such conditioning operates within the education system today.

Consider how a conditioned stimulus achieves a conditioned response in relation to encouraging children to raise their hands to answer a question.

(Continued)

For example, if a learner raises their hand to answer a question and they provide the right answer, the teacher is likely to provide praise, which in turn encourages the learner to attempt to answer more questions. If, however, a learner calls out an answer without raising their hand, even if it is the right answer, will such praise be offered? What if the learner raises their hand and provides a wrong answer? Are they encouraged for trying? Or something else?

OPERANT CONDITIONING

Edward Thorndike achieved psychological notoriety through developing a puzzle cage for cats. A hungry cat was placed in a cage with a latch: outside of the cage was a piece of fish. When the cat released the latch, they could exit the cage and eat the fish. After attempting to exit the cage in a random way, the cat accidentally released the latch and was freed. After each successful escape the cat was returned to the cage: in turn the cat escaped within shorter periods of time. Such trial-and-error learning occurred due to the number of errors made being reduced.

Although the reward of food was present in both Thorndike and Pavlov's work, the differences are that, for Pavlov, a reward was provided to elicit behaviour, although this can be used with a 'negative reinforcement', as in the case of Little Albert where something not wanted is provided to elicit a prescribed response. Indeed, think of how a speed camera can result in a ticket being issued to a speeding driver, which may in turn reduce their speed in the future. However, in relation to Thorndike's work, the behaviour results only from reward (in the above example, being released from a cage), while if the behaviour does not elicit the reward, the behaviour ceases. This is known as the 'law of effect'. If you consider how this applies to the classroom context, the phrase 'catch them being good' resounds: this is where the learner is praised when they are engaged with their work, exhibiting all the desired learning behaviours the teacher wants, while if they are not displaying these learning behaviours, they are ignored at the expense of others who have been praised.

B.F. Skinner extended Thorndike's work further through the use of rats and pigeons, adapting this slightly where the relationship between pressing a lever and receiving a food pellet was at the mercy of the experimenter. This way the experimenter could reward different behaviours (such as a pigeon turning around in a circle before pressing the lever). Such operant conditioning is similarly used within the education context, specifically by managing learner behaviour, through the A, B, C approach: antecedents, behaviours, consequences. If you consider Learner A who has turned around and poked Learner B with their pencil, Learner B may verbally protest, which in turn catches the teacher's attention. A 'consequence' is then applied (for example, Learner A being told off, or kept in at playtime). The behaviour has warranted a consequence. (This is discussed further in Chapter 20.) However, what actually caused this behaviour by Learner A in the first place? Are they a habitual 'pencil poker' unable to control their action, or did something occur to Learner A to warrant that response? Perhaps Learner B kicked Learner A under the table. Perhaps Learner B had previously poked Learner A with their pencil. Indeed, it is only when we understand the antecedent that causes the behaviour (which in turn elicits the consequence), that we can fully understand how and why learners behave the way they do. Given that there are typically four hours of learning in the school day (having taken out breaks and assemblies), do we, as teachers, realistically know what has happened in the remaining 20 hours leading up to a behaviour being exhibited? Perhaps the learner is upset because their pet hamster had died that morning, internalising their grief until a moment when it is exhibited.

To summarise the behavioural approach to this point, behaviour can be modified through reinforcement. This could occur as a result of positive reinforcement, where something is provided that the person wants (typically a reward); alternatively the person may avoid a negative reinforcement (in this case, the person avoids something not wanted, for example, being moaned at continually to always wear the correct uniform). Punishment is where something is given that the person does not want (as opposed to where they avoid something, as in negative reinforcement).

LEARNED HELPLESSNESS

As an aside, it is interesting how psychologists develop over the years. For example, the father of positive psychology (Martin Seligman) originally developed the area of 'learned helplessness' (Seligman et al., 1968). Within the education context, learned helplessness relates to a learner who faces repeated failure, where no matter what they try, they are unable to achieve, so in turn they give up trying. However, this concept stems from Seligman's work on giving electric shocks to dogs for a period of 50 seconds. Dogs were trained to experience learner helplessness through being strapped in a harness and shocked. Later on, they were placed in a cage where a buzzer sounded prior to a shock being delivered. The dog could avoid the shock if they jumped over a barrier. The dogs that had previously experienced the shock in a helpless state did not try to escape the shock through jumping the barrier, while dogs that had not previously been shocked soon discovered what to do. According to Seligman, some dogs had to be pushed over the barrier a couple of hundred times before their learned helplessness receded. In a later study, Miller and Seligman (1975) used human participants (thankfully not with shocks, but inescapable noise with depressed and non-depressed college students). From their research, their conclusion indicated that a person can become depressed when they have no control over a situation.

Given the previous reflection about Poppy, the biscuit-snaffling dog, an interesting case study occurs from a transpersonal psychology perspective as to Seligman's original motivation for his experiment, then how he progressed to form positive psychology.

The model of learned helplessness subsequently became refined in relation to self-attribution (see Chapter 8), where a person questions why they are helpless, trying to identify the cause (Abramson et al., 1978, 1980). From learned helplessness, Seligman has progressed to the field of optimism and has developed the dominating force of positive psychology (see Chapter 2).

REFLECTION

Through learned helplessness, Martin Seligman evolved his theory from one that may be deemed negative (unavoidable shocks to dogs) through to positive psychology, which in turn is helping many people to develop. However, from your personal perspective, is such a journey valid, where harm is caused to a smaller number of beings to serve the purpose of the majority? This leads to the thought experiment below.

As noted time and again in this book, psychology overlaps with the subject it originated from – philosophy. Similarly, there are no right answers for every situation: we are informed through our experience, which in turn informs our perspectives. If you reconsider how the behaviourist approach is used within education, at a simple level it involves a teacher getting a learner to do (or stop doing) something, through offering the learner something they want (such as a reward, or positive reinforcement, for writing a fantastic piece of work), or a learner avoiding something they do not want (they know they need to complete their work, otherwise they will be moaned at or kept in to complete the work, a negative reinforcement). It would be easy to note that this relates purely to the reinforcement or punishment arising from the external authority of somebody in control. By this, if you get caught speeding on the motorway, you may get stopped and receive a fine or points on your licence (a punishment), which in turn is likely to lessen speeding in the future. The punishment of the fine or points may also be seen as a reason not to speed in the first place. If your passenger continually moans at you for speeding, the moaning may cease when you slow down – an example of a negative reinforcement where something is avoided. However, if you continually obey the speed limit, what reward do you experience? Indeed, this line of reasoning can be applied within the education context. How many learners who get on with their work are overlooked at the expense of ensuring those less enamoured with the education system fall in line? Furthermore, if learners are continually rewarded, what happens when they venture into the 'outside world' and realise that rewards are limited in relation to negative reinforcements or punishments?

ACTIVITY   Rewards and sanctions in school

Consider rewards within the education system (some examples include: reward charts, 'praise' assemblies, stickers, 'golden time').

Consider whether rewards focus learners on the actual reward itself, as opposed to the learning experience.

Consider whether the rewards are age dependent: would a 13-year-old be as motivated for a sticker as a 5-year-old?

Using your understanding of psychology, consider their relative strengths and limitations in relation to this section of the book.

THE CARROT OR THE STICK?

In 2004 a three-part documentary appeared on Channel 4 (UK television) called 'The Carrot or the Stick'. It took 12 men and separated them into two teams for a variety of military challenges. For one team, all they ever had was the 'stick'. No matter how hard they tried, their leader could only punish them (or they would avoid punishment if they did well: in other words, negative reinforcement). For the 'carrot' team, all they ever experienced was praise and reward. Throughout the series, both teams were equally matched in the number of challenges they won, although the final challenge went to the stick team. What did the programme reveal? In essence, the military leaders of both teams (both from army backgrounds) commented that a balance needs to be achieved: that both the carrot and the stick are needed.

Perhaps the best example of classical conditioning in relation to humans is in the book *A Clockwork Orange* (Burgess, 1962/2011), where the delinquent character Alex is subjected to aversion therapy by being forced to view images while listening to Beethoven (his favourite music), yet also being given emetics (nausea-inducing drugs). As a result, whenever he heard Beethoven, or considered violence, he felt nauseous. The summary of the story is that such aversion therapy can have dramatic consequences. Indeed such aversion therapy has previously used emetics or electric shocks for substance abuse, although more recently covert sensitisation has replaced such overt sensitisation. Covert sensitisation occurs when a nausea- or anxiety-inducing image is presented with an image of the undesirable behaviour (Cautela and Kearney, 1986). For example, if you wanted to wean yourself off the biscuit tin in the staffroom, you would imagine walking into the staffroom with an increasing sense of nausea, which gets worse as you reach for the tin, vomiting before you can take a biscuit. For ethical reasons, please remember that this is an illustration of covert sensitisation summarised in a couple of sentences, without the presence of a covert sensitisation therapist present – do not try this at home! On a more subtle (and more pleasant) basis, consider how advertising can condition us to buy a certain brand of chocolate, coffee or perfume.

10.5 HUMANISTIC PERSPECTIVE

Ask most teachers to name a theory of motivation and one name will repeatedly be mentioned: Maslow's hierarchy of needs. Year in, year out, the hierarchy of needs is used through a multitude of degree courses: teaching, nursing, psychology, sociology and business studies among others. Furthermore, many psychology-based textbooks similarly provide a superficial page or two on his theory before progressing to a new topic. Indeed, this is true of the way in which many psychologists are summarised to one or two core ideas at the expense of their lifetimes' work.

Maslow's hierarchy of needs has previously been discussed in Chapter 1 where an overview was provided of the model. In this chapter, the hierarchy of needs is discussed in relation to motivation. As tempting as it is to present the standard triangular diagram shown in Figure 1.5 (which any textbook on psychology would similarly represent), the model was never presented in any of Maslow's work in this way: he only discussed the model as a hierarchy, which others then translated into the triangular form. A hierarchy is a way of structuring items in relation to other such items to depict either importance (as in the structure of a company, with fewer managing directors above the larger proportion of administrators), or chronology (for example, a family tree). Furthermore hierarchies can be presented vertically or horizontally (such as in the order of tennis players in a tournament), although other forms could be presented such as a tree map, or a radial map (a series of concentric circles, see Figures 10.1a and 10.1b).

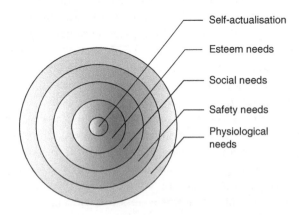

Self-actualisation

Esteem needs

Social needs

Safety needs

Physiological needs

Figure 10.1a   Maslow's hierarchy of needs: one alternative vision?

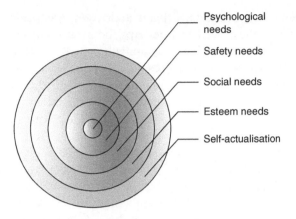

- Psychological needs
- Safety needs
- Social needs
- Esteem needs
- Self-actualisation

Figure 10.1b Maslow's hierarchy of needs: another alternative vision?

REFLECTION

Refer to Figures 10.1a and 10.1b.

Which makes more sense to you: that physiological needs are peripheral to the development of all needs (10.1a) or that physiological needs are the central component (10.2b)? Explain your reasons.

Could you consider an alternative way of demonstrating the hierarchy of needs (for example, through a Venn diagram)?

According to Maslow, humans are motivated to satisfy a series of needs (or motivations) where lower-order, or deficiency, needs (D-Needs) have to be satisfied before progressing to the higher-order, or being, needs (B-Needs). The former D-Needs relate to aspects we need to gain in order to survive, while the latter B-Needs relate to becoming the best we can become. Conceptually, this makes perfect sense: a person needs to satisfy basic physiological needs of hunger, thirst and warmth, before then satisfying the need to feel safe and secure. Safety and security relate not only to personal safety (not being at risk) but also to health and wellbeing; financial security, for example, means having enough money to satisfy the core physiological needs of food, shelter and water. Progressing further up the hierarchy, the person then needs to feel a sense of belonging through developing a sense of friendship, through the family or through intimacy. From this, a sense of esteem can be developed, which relates to developing confidence, respect, independence or freedom, and competence or mastery. This can be achieved through engaging productively with work or through hobbies.

Once the aforementioned needs have been addressed, the person can progress to self-actualisation: the highest need and perhaps the most confusing to understand.

'Self-actualisation' is a term that was initially used by Goldstein (1939/1995) whereby an organism realises, or actualises, its inherent capacities and capabilities. In other words, the organism achieves its potential. Although this term is quite vague, one way of looking at it is through the previously used analogy of how an acorn has the potential to grow into a mighty oak tree if provided with the right conditions. Goldstein's definition of self-actualisation was adopted by Rogers (1961), although Maslow's own definition varied throughout his work (Daniels, 1988, 2005; Engler, 2006; Heylighen, 1992; Leclerc et al., 1998; Weiss, 1987). Perhaps the most developed definition is that self-actualisation is 'the apex of personal growth, in which we become freed from basic needs and deficiency motivation' (Maslow, 1996: 206). The difference between Maslow's definition and that of Rogers and Goldstein is that Maslow envisaged self-actualisation as only being achieved once deficiencies have been overcome, a somewhat negative view, while Rogers and Goldstein's perspective was more positive in nature, that self-actualisation is inherent in everyone as long as the right conditions are met to allow it to be released and expressed.

Although many attempts have been made to refine what is meant specifically by self-actualisation, its defining feature is reported to be the peak experience (Maslow, 1971/1993; Rowan, 1983). Peak experiences are reported to be the happiest moments in life, yet also consist of being absorbed in the present through being engaged in work, reading a book or watching a film (Maslow, 1971/1993). While the hierarchy of needs has been presented in relation to just five levels of needs, various interpretations of Maslow's work have produced six, seven and even eight levels of the hierarchy, the subsequent levels being subdivisions of previous levels. It must also be noted that Maslow (1954/1987) indicated that the levels overlap and are not abruptly separated, indicating that a person may need to put their personal safety first before then acquiring food. As an example, if you have broken down on the motorway a couple of miles before you were going to pull into a service station for a tasty, nutritious treat to satisfy your hunger, you are probably going to put your personal safety first by standing on the embankment of the motorway while waiting for rescue as opposed to walking a couple of miles for that sumptuous treat.

However, this overlooked, overlapping aspect that Maslow (1954/1987) had previously identified is where many of the criticisms of the hierarchy of needs have originated. Neher (1991) noted that artists or scientists can be so caught up with their work that they go without eating or meaningful relationships for lengthy periods (of course, this can apply to anyone caught up with their work). Saul (1993) highlighted the way in which dancers place themselves at physiological risk in the name of creative expression or aesthetic needs. Anyone who has injured themselves through a physical activity should allow their body to fully recover (safety and security needs) before engaging again with their aesthetic needs (which may similarly relate to belonging, as in team sports, or esteem needs). Likewise, a number of authors have reported that peak experiences can be achieved through depriving lower-level needs (Neher, 1991). Take for example the periods of fasting, which several religions engage with: the basic physiological need of hunger is ignored for spiritual development. And also there is the hermit who forgoes the need to engage with others at the expense of pursuing spiritual development is another example of depriving the lower-level needs of belonging and love. Furthermore Battista (1996) reports that personal growth can come from painful or difficult confrontations, an aspect Maslow (1962/1999) previously reported through the 'nadir experience'.

Several authors have raised the issue too that chasing peak experiences places self-actualisation as a deficiency need (Daniels, 2005; Rowan, 1999). The person is pursuing something they do not have, in the same way they would with food, shelter, safety or esteem. Indeed, this is an aspect Maslow (1970) had previously reported (alongside 11 other criticisms of self-actualisation), which culminated in Maslow stating that the hierarchy of needs was no longer fit for purpose. Let me repeat that: back in 1970, Maslow reported that the hierarchy of needs was no longer fit for purpose, suggesting that all future research in the area is directed towards self-transcendence, as characterised by the plateau experience (Buckler, 2011b).

So why do we continue to see the hierarchy of needs in print? At a base level, it makes conceptual sense. For example, if a learner is hungry, feeling ill or feels that they do not belong, they are unlikely to engage satisfactorily with their learning. Indeed, at a deeper level, through reading the previous two chapters, we can understand why the hierarchy of needs is conceptually valid. As an example from Chapter 8, learning potential is limited when a learner has a weakened sense of self; furthermore if we do not have a developed relationship with peers or the teacher (as discussed in Chapters 14 and 20), our learning potential will similarly be limited. Consequently, the hierarchy of needs can be synthesised along with other models of the self or motivation, which in turn has assured its place in psychology textbooks probably for many more years to come.

10.6 SELF-DETERMINATION THEORY

In 1979 a book, *Fifteen Thousand Hours*, was published that discussed the amount of time children spend in compulsory schooling and the effect this has through the domains of achievement, attendance, behaviour and delinquency (Rutter et al., 1979). The book detailed how secondary schools with the same sociodemographic background (specifically, inner London) differed considerably across the four domains. Through their research, it was shown that schools were more successful across the domains that had clear expectations and regulations. Further attributes for successful schools included a core focus on academic study along with music and art, being well resourced, having high levels of learner participation, while also offering vocational work experience and extra-curricular activities. This led to the conclusion that schools which promoted high self-esteem, while developing the academic and social capabilities of learners, reduced behavioural and emotional problems. Although the book discussed secondary schooling, from the previous chapters it is clear that the themes within it are as relevant today and apply across age phases: self-esteem should be developed, along-side intra- and interpersonal skills, while developing the whole learner. Taking the approximate amount of time learners spend in school (six to six-and-a-half hours per day), the number of school days per academic year (190), and the number of years of compulsory schooling (12 years from Reception to Year 11), the figure 15,000 is quite close (14,820 based on a 6.5 hour day, if you have not yet worked it out).

How on earth does this historical overview of a classic educational work relate to motivation? According to Deci et al. (1991), schools are a primary socialising influence on people and in turn society: schools that promote enthusiasm for education while enabling students to feel involved with the process provide optimal learning experiences. These in turn enable the student to develop at a conceptual level along-side others and such conditions also enable personal growth. Indeed, this provides a foundation from which self-determination theory operates. There are three strands to self-determination theory: competence, relatedness and autonomy (Figure 10.2). Indeed, each of these strands has parallels with other areas of psychological theory discussed in the previous chapters, although self-determination theory unites these in one model. For example, competence relates to the ability to utilise one's skills to accomplish an outcome – in other words, metacognition (see Chapter 8). Relatedness refers to the development of secure, satisfying connections with others (an aspect dis-cussed in Chapters 7, 8 and 20). Autonomy relates to a sense of choice or, in other words, self-initiating and self-regulating one's actions (Deci et al., 1991). This last aspect similarly relates to Chapter 20.

Schools are fundamental contexts for children's development due to the amount of time children spend there, along with the degree to which children's experiences are influenced. In order for a school to be considered as a positive psychological environment, it should exert a positive influence facilitated through the construct of self-determination theory (Deci and Ryan, 1985). The three strands of the model are:

1. Learners should have a degree of choice within their learning (autonomy).
2. Learners should perceive themselves as competent in their various learning activities (competency).
3. Learners should be able to relate well with their peers and adults while learning (relatedness).

If these three strands are suitably addressed in the classroom environment, the learner can grow as they take control of personal challenges. To illustrate self-determination theory and how it can operate, consider your planning and delivery of a lesson. A teacher who is able to discuss their planning with others and who feels that they have been able to discuss honestly and openly the content of the lesson will experience relatedness. From their planning, the teacher exerts a degree of freedom in deciding how to put the planning into action, in turn experiencing autonomy. The teacher then utilises their planning through their teaching ability, ensuring that the lesson capitalises on their personal strengths to captivate learners in an engaging manner (competency). By working through a typical example of lesson planning and delivery, the three strands are united: of course, the key is to then develop these strands with the learners you work with. Provided below are some suggestions for developing each of the strands with your learners.

Figure 10.2   An applied example of the self-determination theory triad for teachers (adapted from Deci and Ryan, 1985)

AUTONOMY

At the start of a new block of work, ask the learners what they want to learn about the subject. This could be facilitated through preparing a concept map, or learners posing questions they want to be addressed through the subsequent lessons.

Encourage learners to plan their learning by setting their own goals, then planning how to achieve these goals. Such planning may conform to SMART targets (specific, measureable, achievable, realistic and time-restricted).

Encourage self-reflection for learners to consider how they could make subsequent improvements with their learning.

COMPETENCY

Ensure learners understand their individual abilities and their personal strengths and limitations, their specific needs, their specific interests and their learning preferences. If learners are aware of such issues, they can utilise their strengths to help engage with their own learning.

Equip learners with problem-solving skills, which in turn will help them to identify and define a problem before they generate possible solutions.

RELATEDNESS

Ensure learners have the ability to discuss honestly and openly with one another, perhaps encouraging the less dominant to write their thoughts down initially before sharing them with those they are working with.

Ensure positive learning relationships are developed within the classroom, perhaps through establishing a classroom code of conduct.

Promote time to listen attentively to one another, perhaps through circle-time or other such PSHE (Personal, Social, Health and Economic) Education activities.

If the three strands of self-determination theory are balanced, this in turn promotes intrinsic motivation, a form of motivation that people engage with out of interest, from free choice, with a sense of personal control, while not requiring any material rewards from the activity (Deci and Ryan, 1985). Compare this to the behaviourist approach to motivation, which is extrinsically motivated, where the rewards or punishments are provided by an external source.

Deci and Ryan (1985) do, however, discuss how extrinsic motivation can lead to intrinsic motivation through the four stages of regulation: external, introjected, identified and integrated regulation. These four forms of regulation are based on the concept of internalisation; in other words, initially a learner may be motivated only by external reward or punishment, yet through internalisation the learner regulates their relationship with the learning, and the motivation becomes internal in nature. As an example, a learner may first need to be externally motivated (or externally regulated) for learning to read through the use of rewards or punishments, yet in time the learner may internalise the motivation to read, thus reading for their own enjoyment in their own time (intrinsic motivation).

Taking this example of reading further, the other stages of regulation can be illustrated. As discussed above, the learner may need initial coercion (external regulation) to learn to read: they receive praise, perhaps a sticker, for taking a book home to read with a parent. From this, the learner may appreciate that they have to read, that there is a pressure to learn to read as everybody else is doing it. Through acting on this, the learner understands and internalises the need to take their reading book home, even if they do so reluctantly: that taking their book home is not really a choice; it is something they have to do to avoid negative feelings. Such internal coercion can be deemed introjected regulation.

When the learner values the specific behaviour of taking their reading book home, which in turn will ensure they develop their reading ability, they have identified that the behaviour is deemed useful (identified regulation). From this, the learner may appreciate that learning to read is a personally important value, one which will enable them to meet with success at school: they therefore read because it develops their sense of self through the values, needs and identity that reading provides (integrated regulation). Deci et al. (1991) highlight that the subtle difference between integrated regulation and intrinsic motivation is that the latter is pursued due to interest in the activity itself, as opposed to integrated regulation, which is deemed important for a valued outcome.

ACTIVITY   Your intrinsic relationship to subjects

Consider your personal journey as a learner. Think of a subject you have found difficult and whether you progressed to intrinsic motivation, or remained at a previous level of regulation.

Think of yourself as a teacher. Are there any subject(s) that you are not intrinsically motivated to teach? How could you develop your relationship with such subject(s)? Is your relationship with the subject affected by your previous experience as a learner?

Self-determination theory has collected momentum in terms of research where a positive correlation has been demonstrated between intrinsic motivation and positive emotions within the classroom, such as enjoying work and school, and through greater achievement (Brouwer, 2012; Daniels and Perry, 2003; Gottfried, 1990; Guay et al., 2010).

In returning to the three strands of self-determination theory, competence, autonomy and relatedness, how can we develop an environment to foster such self-determination and, in turn, intrinsic motivation? Deci et al. (1991) suggest that, for learners to feel actively engaged, they must value learning, achievement and accomplishment across all subjects. Consequently for teachers, ensuring learners understand: how subjects relate in terms of cross-curricular links; how skills from one subject can correspond to another (such as using mathematical skills in different subjects or using problem-solving skills); and the personal utility of the lesson, through relating to a real context and providing explicit objectives, providing learners with a choice of activity and acknowledging learners' perspectives – all are important to assure self-determination. This sounds easier said than done. However, a lesson is detailed below where all of these elements are combined.

ACTIVITY

Read through the following lesson:

A typical lesson with seven-year-old learners in science relates to the optimum conditions for growing seeds. A typical lesson may involve setting up seeds in the same pots, providing the same amount of water, but placing the pots in locations that have different light intensity. This way, the variables are kept the same except for the light intensity. The seeds can be measured over time in relation to their height. Of course, a different variable could be changed: for example, the amount of water each pot has, while all other variables are kept the same.

The problem with this lesson is that there is little autonomy from the learner: they are purely following their teacher's directions. The lesson can be altered slightly to ensure a more self-determined focus.

The teacher could introduce the lesson about seeds growing through a variety of ways, perhaps relating this to the story of 'Jack and the Beanstalk', or through making bread in Design and Technology. The teacher can then ask the learners to help with an investigation to see what helps seeds to grow as they will need to grow some food for a later lesson (for example, decorating a salad, sandwich or pizza).

Two labels are then presented on the board: 'What we could change' and 'What we could measure'. The learners are asked to list as many ideas as possible under each of these headings. As an example, under 'What we could change', learners may suggest water, soil, pots, location or temperature. Under 'What we could measure' learners may suggest height of plant or number of leaves.

Once the choices are saturated, learners can be grouped and encouraged to choose one word from each list. One group may choose to change the amount of water, while measuring the number of leaves; another group may choose to change the soil type while measuring the height of the plant. It is important to note that all of the other variables under 'What we could change' are kept the same to ensure fair testing. Not only have the learners collaborated to select the experiment they want to conduct; they can also plan how the experiment can proceed.

Through conducting the lesson this way, the learners have been encouraged to think about how the experiment may relate to other subjects (such as English or Design and Technology), and how skills from other subjects may help in conducting the experiment (in this example, problem-solving, measuring). Furthermore, the experiment could be related to a real context if, for example, the learners were to grow some food that they could use for cooking. A choice has been presented in how they conduct the experiment by selecting the variable and measure and, through this choice, the learners have been encouraged to collaborate, developing their relationship with others in a group. Similarly, they have developed a relationship with the teacher who has trusted the learners to construct their own experiment.

Consider how such an approach could be adapted for a different curriculum subject.

From the above lesson, various aspects can be adopted no matter what the age or ability of the learner, or the lesson content. What has been provided is a basis to explore learning where there is a symbiotic level of trust between the teacher and learner, the learner and other learners, also the learner and the curriculum (relatedness); the activity promotes learning but in a way directed by the learner where there is a level of structured choice (autonomy); finally there is some control where the learner is able to utilise their established skill-set to engage with the learning (competence). A parallel may further be made between competence and a theory discussed in Chapter 2 on flow, whereby the experience of flow can be facilitated through ensuring that the skills of the learner are matched with a suitably challenging activity, an activity that is neither too demanding (which will result in anxiety), nor too easy (resulting in boredom).

So where does this leave self-determination theory as a model for education? Deci et al. (1991) highlighted that the theory is at odds with the education system in general. Indeed, they note that there is a balance to be addressed between a teacher's behaviour being either controlling or supportive of autonomy. Furthermore, research indicates that when a teacher feels pressured or controlled by others, such as the school, community, society or by the education system in general, they are more likely to be controlling with their learners. Consequently, if teachers are made to feel accountable for achievement of their learners, this is counterproductive as it leads teachers to be more controlling, which can limit learners' conceptual understanding and their personal growth (Deci et al., 1991). There has, however, been increasing attention directed towards self-determination theory in recent years. For example, Fretz (2015) discussed the contribution to creating optimal learning environments, while Wilding (2015) discussed how self-determination theory could be used for disaffected students and Anderson (2016) used the theory to develop a 'Learning Incentive Programme' (LIP) to enhance learning-relevant student outcomes through the development of formative quizzes. Research also extends to discuss how self-determination theory relates to teacher wellbeing with Canadian schools (Collie et al., 2016) while Emery et al. (2015) investigated how the theory can be used to support pupils exhibiting depressive symptoms. Such themes about teacher and pupil wellbeing will be discussed in the next part of the book.

10.7 CONCLUSION

Motivation relates to the energy and direction devoted to complete a task. Although teachers can influence motivation, it is not something we can give: it is something teachers can facilitate within each learner to ensure they utilise their inherent energy and direct this into an educational activity.

Teachers can use a variety of reinforcers or punishments to encourage a learner to engage, although this is deemed as extrinsic motivation and is demonstrated to not be as effective as fostering intrinsic motivation, where an activity is engaged with because it is inherently interesting.

It is important to note that the models of motivation within this chapter relate to many other psychological theories within this book, for example, in developing self-esteem and fostering relationships. Motivation is an applied perspective, which is multi-dimensional in nature.

Perhaps the most significant aspect of this chapter is appreciating that, if the optimum conditions are provided, a learner can achieve their potential (the humanistic perspective). One way to achieve such potential is through ensuring that the learner has a sense of autonomy and choice in their learning, that they understand their skills (or know how to develop them), and also that they can work with others, both peers and teachers: in other words, the three components of self-determination theory.

10.8 FURTHER READING

Deci, E., Koestner, R. and Ryan, R. (2001) 'Extrinsic rewards and intrinsic motivation in education: Reconsidered once again', *Review of Educational Research*, 71 (1): 1–27.
This journal article provides an informed discussion of self-determination theory in relation to education, providing a detailed update on Deci and Ryan's original 1985 publication.

Gilbert, I. (2013) *Essential Motivation in the Classroom* (2nd edn). London: Routledge.
Gilbert's book provides a wonderful discussion on how motivation affects the teaching, learning and thinking of children. Gilbert writes in an engaging style and the book has many practical suggestions to enhance motivation.

Watson, J.B. and Rayner, R. (1920) 'Conditioned emotional reactions', *Journal of Experimental Psychology*, 3: 1–14.
Watson and Rayner's seminal paper on classical conditioning discusses the case of 'Little Albert' in depth.

11

INTEGRATING PSYCHOLOGY IN THE CLASSROOM

CHAPTER OBJECTIVES

- Consider the interplay of themes related to the self, SEN and motivation.
- Demonstrate how the interplay of themes can be applied on a class and an individual level.
- Develop strategies to promote positive engagement with learners.
- Evaluate the components of a solution-focused approach and how this may be applied within learners.

TEACHERS' STANDARDS

A teacher must:

1   Set high expectations which inspire, motivate and challenge pupils
   - establish a safe and stimulating environment for pupils, rooted in mutual respect
   - set goals that stretch and challenge pupils of all backgrounds, abilities and dispositions
   - demonstrate consistently the positive attitudes, values and behaviour which are expected of pupils

2   Promote good progress and outcomes by pupils
   - guide pupils to reflect on the progress they have made and their emerging levels
   - encourage pupils to take a responsible and conscientious attitude to their own work and study

5   Adapt teaching to respond to the strengths and needs of all pupils
   - know when and how to differentiate appropriately, using approaches which enable pupils to be taught effectively
   - have a secure understanding of how a range of factors can inhibit pupils' ability to learn, and how best to overcome these

7   Manage behaviour effectively to ensure a good and safe learning environment
   - manage classes effectively, using approaches which are appropriate to pupils' needs in order to involve and motivate them
   - maintain good relationships with pupils, exercise appropriate authority and act decisively when necessary

11.1 INTRODUCTION

Many different theories and perspectives have been provided in this part and at times it is difficult to understand how they all relate to each other. Indeed, you may appreciate the need to strengthen children's self-esteem, yet with the competing demands of the curriculum and the pressure to achieve results, individual children can be overlooked. Consequently, how are these theories put into practice within the classroom context so that each individual can benefit?

The sense of self can be harmed in different ways, and additionally our sense of self can be labelled if we experience problems with learning in the same way as others. Most motivation comes from avoiding punishments while seeking rewards; furthermore we operate to satisfy specific needs. This raises two questions: How do the themes relating to the individual overlap (a macro- or wide-ranging perspective)? And how can we affect individuals on a positive level (at the micro-perspective)?

11.2 THE MACRO-PERSPECTIVE: AN OVERLAP OF THEMES

Various themes have been highlighted from the past three chapters, yet looking at each chapter holistically, the way in which they progressed can be summarised succinctly. In Chapter 8, the individual as a 'self' was explored with discussion as to how we ascribe a value to our sense of self (self-esteem), the way we view our abilities (self-efficacy) and the causes we ascribe to certain events (self-attribution). Chapter 9 explored how individuals can differ further through physical, cognitive or environmental aspects, which can affect learning in various ways, specifically discussing the way we can apply labels for certain categories of learning need. Yet the chapter asserted that we should look beyond the classical view of the learner having the 'problem': instead, it is the education system that needs to find ways to enable each learner, no matter what their ability or perceived limitation. If the sense of self is limited, perhaps through a learning need, as teachers we need to find a way to encourage learners to achieve their potential, as discussed in Chapter 10 on motivation. Although the education system classically uses behaviourist approaches as the predominant motivator through rewards and sanctions, other forms of motivation could be utilised, such as encouraging learners to understand their competencies and seek autonomy, while relating to others effectively (self-determination).

In developing your own educational philosophy, the following activity encourages you to review the various themes from the last three chapters.

ACTIVITY

Consider the following questions:

- How would you define the 'self'?
- What can inhibit the self from healthy development?
- How would you define 'inclusion'?
- Do you see inclusion as a practice or a philosophy?
- What is your perspective on the use of rewards and sanctions in the classroom?
- How could you apply self-determination theory within one lesson?

In considering the themes from the past three chapters, Figure 11.1 demonstrates one way in which they can be synthesised. For example, if competence is analysed, this relates to our own abilities and is one of the components of self-determination theory. Within competence is our valuing of our abilities, or our self-esteem: we may have the skills but think we are not any good at using them. A second component of self-determination is the amount of autonomy we have; or in other words, do we have a choice or do we feel coerced? On the left, outside edge of the triangle, the link between competence and autonomy is control, an aspect of self-attribution theory. If we think our abilities are limited, we may feel out of control given the demands of a situation. Furthermore, if we feel that we have no autonomy in a situation, we may feel that we are being controlled.

Figure 11.1   A synthesis of perspectives

Autonomy also relates to the way in which we relate to others: are we acting under our own volition (our own choice), or are we working under the direction of others? If our relationship is strong with our peers, we will feel part of the learning community and will be able to negotiate the way we work. If the relationship is based on mutual trust, the working relationship is stronger all round. On the bottom edge of the triangle is another component of self-efficacy: stability. This relates to the way we feel that a cause is stable or unstable: whether no matter what we do, things will stay the same, or whether we can change the outcome. This links to both autonomy and relationships in that, if we feel we have a choice – a sense of control that we can negotiate with others – then the stability is within our control. If, however, we feel threatened by the relationship or we perceive we have limited autonomy, we are likely to feel unstable, which is a weak foundation from which to operate. There is a link between the self-determination components of competence and relationships: that of the locus of control or whether we perceive there is an internal or external cause. If we believe that we do not have the competence to engage with an activity, we have a choice to develop this competence, therefore the locus is internal. If we believe that, no matter what we do, our actions will result in failure in the eyes of another person, this is an external locus, or an external cause.

Ultimately, if we can ensure that learners are realistically aware of their own abilities and how to develop these (competence); that learners have a sense of choice or control in their learning (autonomy); that learners have developed learning relationships with their peers and their teachers; that children understand that events can be controlled through their own abilities – then we would have taken many actions to enable their success and to help direct their energy in a positive, conducive way. We have influenced their motivation through developing a greater sense of self.

ACTIVITY

The following lesson integrates all of the components from the previous paragraph. Can you identify where and how the various components are located?

The lesson is to make a newspaper bridge.

Learners can test their ideas and contribute them to a discussion, perhaps using a range of relevant resources to investigate bridges, for example, the internet, books and so forth.

Learners can contribute to a group discussion about how best to proceed with the available resources of newspaper: whether each sheet is folded or rolled.

Learners can decide on the design of the bridge to maximise structural integrity and test this through weight.

(Continued)

In some way, the bridge is recorded. This could be through drawings, photographs, written instructions or through some other way.

At a later stage, they are encouraged to make a second bridge that is stronger than their first bridge.

As an extension activity, design a lesson of your own that integrates the components you have identified.

Having engaged with the previous activity, you may be able to appreciate how one lesson can be structured to engage each learner at their own ability. The outcome is not whether they can make the best bridge in the class but whether they can refine their ideas on a subsequent occasion. To this extent, they are competing against their own abilities while continually enhancing and refining their skills. If the various components of the bridge-building lesson can be adapted to a different context, then learning and motivation will continue to be enhanced.

11.3 THE MICRO-PERSPECTIVE: AFFECTING INDIVIDUALS ON A POSITIVE LEVEL

STARTING FROM THE INDIVIDUAL

If you perceive the purpose of education is to provide a generic, prescribed, rigid curriculum, for at least 12 years and expect each to come out of the education system with the required number of grades, please read no further. In fact return this book to whomever or wherever you got it and our apologies for taking your precious time: your philosophy would probably resonate better in an Orwellian context. However, please do not let us force our own educational philosophy onto you as a reader: remember you need to take ownership of your educational philosophy before somebody else does. This paragraph could have been made considerably shorter just through using those two words uttered by Socrates, 'Know thyself'.

Just as you have developed as an individual, perhaps the central component of teaching is to develop the individual abilities and potential abilities of the learners we work with. If you consider the learners you have worked with previously, either as a learner or as a teacher, who stands out in your mind and why? What was unique about them? If you devote the average 40 years to the teaching profession with an average class size of 30, you are likely to work with 1,200 children throughout your career. Of course this may increase if you become a headteacher. How can you ensure that each child is remembered as a unique individual in the same way you would like to be known as a unique individual now? Indeed, what would you have been remembered for by your teachers?

ACTIVITY   School report

Part of being a successful teacher is the ability to evaluate and reflect upon your performance. The run of inspections, observations and so on help facilitate this process. However, how often have you considered what your old school reports said about you? Even if you cannot find your reports from yesteryear, cast your mind back to how you would view yourself from a teacher's perspective.

- What were your strengths?
- What were your interests?
- What were your limitations?
- What made you unique in your class?
- What prospective career would you have been advised to pursue?
- How could you make the most of your potential?
- What would you be remembered for?

If the previous school reports of notable people are considered, one of Einstein's teachers is reported to have said that 'He will never get anywhere', while John Lennon's school report is alleged to have said, 'certainly on the road to failure' (Hurley, 2002). In addressing graduating Yale students, President George W. Bush said, 'To those of you who received honours, awards and distinctions, I say well done. And to the C students, I say you too may one day be President of the United States.' As teachers, do we really know what learners will become? Would our teachers be surprised we have followed in their footsteps?

REFLECTION

'Imagine you're a tree!' How we love that phrase. How many teachers up and down the country have used that phrase for drama lessons or physical education? It is a classic phrase and we just had to use it here!

Seriously though, consider the variety of trees:

- those that grow straight and tall, staying green all year round, such as a Scots pine
- those that may be a bit gnarled yet sturdy, weathering any storm, such as an oak
- those that bring a delicate scent and beauty, such as a magnolia
- those that bring blossom and fruit
- those that are gently tussled by the wind, adapting to their environment, such as the willow.

(Continued)

In Chapters 9 and 10, the analogy was used where each child could be viewed as a different seed requiring a balance of various elements to grow into their specific tree. Indeed, will any two identical seeds produce exactly the same tree or will the conditions affect how it grows? Applying this analogy to yourself, what tree have you become?

Furthermore, what elements helped you to become the tree that represents you? Was your potential always to become that tree, or have there been events that have affected the way your tree has developed?

11.4 POSITIVE AND NEGATIVE

According to Seligman (2011), we spend too much time focusing on the aspects that have gone wrong in our lives as opposed to considering the aspects that have worked well. Learners can spend an inordinate amount of time concerned about their shortcomings. As teachers, we can spend sleepless nights or anxious weekends contemplating the outcome of an incident, or something that may potentially happen. Focusing on the negative aspects of life has been a survival process for humans: as Seligman discusses, we have needed to consider threats and risks in order to survive. However, given the perceived risk to our survival on a day-to-day basis where our base physiological and safety needs are addressed, Seligman asserts that we should focus more on the positive. This is easier said than done: accordingly, if we are presented with two pieces of information, one positive and one negative, the negative information will form a stronger impression, a theory known as 'negativity bias' (Baumeister et al., 2001). Our emotions are affected for a longer time period by negative events than positive events (Baumeister et al., 2001).

Relating such negativity bias to teaching, how often do we consider the negative aspects rather than the positive during the day? After a day in the classroom, are we more likely to head home continually replaying the negative elements of the day as opposed to those moments of success with our learners? Furthermore, if we are more attuned to negativity, when we receive feedback on our teaching, we are more likely to ignore the many positive elements, selectively focusing on the negative.

ACTIVITY   Teacher clichés

The journal article 'Bad is stronger than good' (Baumeister et al., 2001) indicates that we are more selectively attuned to negative events and experiences than positive ones.

Consider how this affects the learners you work with.

How can you rephrase a negative comment into a positive? For example, the phrase, 'Sit down and stop talking' could be rephrased as 'It would be great to see how well you can sit down as quietly as possible.'

Try rephrasing the following teacher clichés:

- 'Stop talking and look this way.'
- 'You've forgotten your homework again!'
- 'Wrong answer!'
- 'If I've told you once, I've told you a hundred times: stop exaggerating!'

Taking this further, how many messages do our learners hear and pay attention to? Given the discussion in Chapter 8 on self-esteem, if learners only hear and concentrate on the negative, how can we redress the balance?

11.5 SOLUTION-FOCUSED APPROACHES

Although negativity bias can cause people to dwell on problems, a relatively new approach predominantly focuses on solutions: solution-focused therapy. The central concept of solution-focused approaches is that individuals are resilient and can utilise their personal strengths and competencies to resolve problems, as opposed to being encouraged to develop new approaches. In this way, the focus is on solution-building, not problem-solving (Iveson, 2002).

Solution-focused approaches have developed over the past 20 years through theoretical development, research and clinical practice (Trepper et al., 2010). Given the focus on solutions (as opposed to problems), the solution-focused approach is clearly suited to the field of positive psychology. Central to this approach is a series of principles or tenets, summarised below (adapted from Cepeda and Davenport, 2006; Trepper et al., 2010):

- The focus is on the desired future, as opposed to the past problems.
- The individual has the inherent strengths and resources to initiate change.
- Solutions are not necessarily related to the identified problem.
- The individual is encouraged to increase the frequency of their useful behaviours.
- Problems do not occur all of the time: there are exceptions, for example, when a problem could have happened but did not.
- Individuals are encouraged to find alternative approaches to their current thoughts, behaviours or interactions.
- A small change can lead to larger changes, which in turn can initiate a solution.

- If something does not work, stop doing it and do something different.
- If something works, do more of it.
- The future is created and negotiated.

According to De Jong and Berg (2008), there are five core stages within the solution-focused approach, as demonstrated in Figure 11.2.

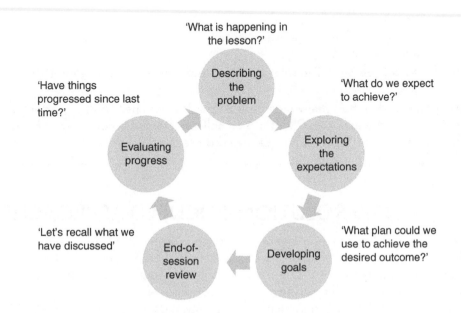

Figure 11.2   An applied example of the five stages of the solution-focused approach (adapted from De Jong and Berg, 2008)

Through these five stages, a conversation can be structured that includes the following components.

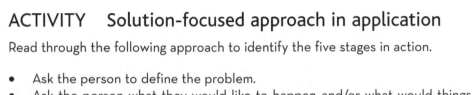

ACTIVITY   Solution-focused approach in application

Read through the following approach to identify the five stages in action.

- Ask the person to define the problem.
- Ask the person what they would like to happen and/or what would things look like when the problem is resolved.
- Ask them to score on a scale of 1–10 where they are at the moment.
- Ask them to say why they are already at that level and not lower.

- Ask what small steps they could take to start moving up the scale.
- Ask what signs they would see to indicate initial success and/or that things have changed for the better.
- Ask them how they would like to be different when they're a 10 on the scale.
- Ask them to turn these into affirmations – positive statements that serve as a reminder.

Central to the conversation is to ensure that a positive approach is maintained, whereby solutions are sought through asking a series of engaging questions to focus the individual on the future, as opposed to the past. The emphasis on the questioning ensures that the conversation is not being directed. In ensuring a positive approach, compliments are provided when the person indicates solutions and approaches that are working well, although at times, the person can also be encouraged to do more of what is working. The focus of the conversation should be on solution-focused goals that the person has identified through the questioning, goals that they similarly scale and where they identify a level that would be satisfactory.

ACTIVITY   The 'miracle question'

One of the potential difficulties with the solution-focused approach is in ensuring the person can actually identify what the problem is, or what they want to have changed. One way to help the person is to ask them the 'miracle question'. This is a question that helps promote their thinking further about how things would look in a different context, as presented below (adapted from Berg and Dolan, 2001: 7; De Jong and Berg, 2008: 85).

> I am going to ask you a rather strange question [pause]. The strange question is this [pause]:
>
> After we finish our conversation, I would like you to picture yourself continuing with your day-to-day activities, going home, having a meal, perhaps watching some television, then going to bed. You drift off into a deep, refreshing sleep. In the middle of the night, a miracle happens, which makes your problem disappear. However, because this happened while you were asleep, you have no way of knowing that the miracle occurred and solved the problem.

(Continued)

When you wake up in the morning, what small change will you notice that will make you say, 'Wow, something has happened: my problem has gone'?
What else will you notice?

According to Taylor (2009), the miracle question invites the person to project what life will be like without the problem, whereby the answer to the question becomes the focus to the solution.

Consider other types of miracle question.

From your understanding of self-determination theory, such a solution-focused approach encourages the person to realise their competencies about what is working and what they can do more of. There is a sense of autonomy that the person is in control of the solution. Furthermore, given that the solution-focused approach is a mutual conversation, as opposed to the 'therapist' providing directives on what the individual could and should do, such a mutual conversation ensures a better sense of relationship, the third component of self-determination theory.

ACTIVITY   Personal solution-focused approach audit

It may be difficult to find someone to engage with for a solution-focused conversation; however, the following activity may help stimulate your thoughts.

- What is my problem?
- What would I like to happen?
- How will things appear when this occurs?
- Where am I at the moment? (From 1-10, where 1 = worst possible scenario, 10 = fully achieved the goal.)
- Why am I at this level and not any lower?
- What am I doing already to stop myself going any lower?
- What can I do more of? What small steps can I take?
- What would be the signs that improvements are happening?
- Where would I feel sufficiently satisfied? (6, 7 or 8?)
- How will I be different when I am a 10 on the scale?
- What affirmation(s) or statement(s) of intent can I make?

According to several authors, solution-focused approaches are effective with children and adolescents, as well as adults (Corcoran, 2006; Franklin et al., 2001; Nims, 2007). Although the samples used have been relatively small, solution-focused approaches are being used more frequently in schools, specifically in the United States (Gingerich and Wabeke, 2001). In a review of available research, or a meta-analysis, solution-focused approaches were deemed to be more effective with internalising problems such as anxiety, depression or low self-esteem; the solution-focused approaches were less effective with externalising problems such as behaviour and conduct problems or aggression (Kim, 2008).

In using solution-focused approaches with children, kinaesthetic resources can be used to help the child focus, as discussed by Nims (2007). As an example, a child could draw a picture of what they would like to talk about, their present situation, or something they would like to change. Similarly, a sand tray could be used to draw a picture or to record a number in the sand in relation to the scale previously discussed. Alternatively, a puppet could be used to vocalise the child's thoughts. With a little thought, the activity could be employed with learners of different ages, for example, with different faces to indicate success (see Figure 11.3).

Figure 11.3   An alternative solution-focused scale

11.6 COGNITIVE BEHAVIOURAL THERAPY

As discussed in Section 1.11, a cognition is a thought, an idea, a concept, a belief or an attitude. The central idea behind cognitive behavioural therapy (CBT) is that our behaviour is governed to a large extent by our thought processes: if our thought processes are maladaptive (not adequate or appropriate to the situation), this can result in maladaptive behaviour. One way of illustrating this is to consider the well-known saying of Descartes (see Section 1.5), *cogito ergo sum* (I think, therefore I am).

In terms of CBT, if we think something, it certainly can happen. If I think I am going to have a rotten day, I most probably will. In essence, our thoughts, emotions and behaviours affect one another.

As an example, we may not look forward to teaching a specific class or a specific subject and our thought process may be along the lines of, 'Oh no, I've got to teach (fill in the missing blank) today.' As such, we have already provided a value to the thought: that of fear. In turn, our behaviour may be fearful in nature: if you think you are not going to enjoy something, you probably will not. By changing the value ascribed to the thought or the cognition, our behaviour can in turn change. So, for example, we could say, 'I'm ready to teach ... today: it will go well because I have planned it to.'

CBT is an approach to analysing specific difficulties through a sequential process. One such approach is the ABC model, which is interrelational in nature (Bernard and Wolfe, 2000; Ellis, 2001):

A is the activating agent (a real external event that has occurred, or a future event that you think may occur, an internal event).

B is your beliefs (thoughts and meaning).

C is the consequence (emotions, behaviours, physical sensations).

In returning to the example about the perceived fear of teaching a class, the ABC model would be:

A: You imagine that the lesson will not go well.

B: You believe that the lesson will not go smoothly.

C: You experience nervousness, which may manifest as an emotion (anxiety), in turn leading to physical tension and mental/cognitive tension.

Needless to say, being anxious and physically and mentally tense will not result in you teaching at an optimum level. Arguably the solution-focused approach discussed in 11.5 is an adaptation of CBT. Furthermore, many of the strategies in Chapter 12 are cognitive behavioural related.

11.7 KEEPING TO THE POSITIVE

As discussed within this chapter, it is all too easy to focus on the negative, as opposed to the positive: although the mind is an organic, evolving entity, it can be very lazy indeed. It is sometimes easier to keep doing what we do as a protection strategy, rather than confronting change. However, this section has demonstrated that there are ways we can encourage the mind to make changes. From a cognitive perspective, the way in which the brain changes as a response to our experience of the environment is called 'neuroplasticity': that we can change how we think and respond to the environment (Arden, 2010; Begley, 2009; Doidge, 2007; Pascual-Leone et al., 2005).

The focus of positive psychology consequently encourages the individual to rewire their brain, focusing on the positive to a greater extent. Although some strategies have been provided within this chapter and throughout the book, Seligman (2011) has developed a simple acronym to summarise the five components of wellbeing: PERMA, or Positive emotion, Engagement, positive Relationships, Meaning and Accomplishments.

At a simple level, the various elements of the PERMA model can be described as follows. Positive emotion relates to authentic happiness and life satisfaction, or positive moods and feelings, which make us feel uplifted. Engagement refers to engaging in personally meaningful activities in which we experience a sense of flow (discussed in Chapter 2). Forming positive relationships relates to our engagement with other people, or our interpersonal connections. Ensuring that we have a clear sense of direction and engagement with elements we find important is the focus of meaning. Finally accomplishment is our sense of achieving what we have set out to achieve; to meet with success while progressing towards the goals we have set ourselves (Grenville Cleave, 2012).

REFLECTION

Consider Seligman's PERMA model and how it relates to the components of self-determination theory. Are they similar in nature?

11.8 CONCLUSION

The focus of this chapter was to combine the various themes from the preceding chapters in this part so that you can appreciate how these can be used within the classroom. The activities and reflections are provided to enable you to develop a sense of ownership over the various theories and models, considering how you could apply these within your professional context and how these could similarly be applied to facilitate your professional development.

The associated areas related to the individual are numerous; however, having engaged to this point you should have a firm foundation from which to explore aspects that are personally interesting and relevant.

REFLECTION   Three things

- What three aspects stand out the most for you from this part of the book?
- What three aspects would you like to find out more about?
- What three aspects will you apply within your classroom context?

11.9 FURTHER READING

Gatto, J.T. (2011) *Weapons of Mass Instruction: A Schoolteacher's Journey Through the Dark World of Compulsory Schooling*. Gabriola Island, Canada: New Society Publishers.
Gatto's work provides a critical and engaging discussion of conventional education to encourage the reader to think about the purpose of schooling.

Illich, I. (1995) *Deschooling Society* (new edn). London: Marion Boyars.
This book is similar to Gatto's work critiquing compulsory education.

Seligman, M.E.P. (2011) *Flourish: A New Understanding of Happiness and Well-Being and How to Achieve Them*. London: Nicholas Brealey Publishing.
Martin Seligman's update on many of the themes within positive psychology.

Trepper, T.S., McCollum, E.E., De Jong, P., Korman, H., Gingerich, W. and Franklin, C. (2010) 'Solution-focused therapy treatment manual for working with individuals', Research Committee of the Solution Focused Brief Therapy Association. www.sfbta.org/research.pdf (accessed 20 September 2017).
This article provides a clear discussion of solution-focused therapy and how it can be used.

Part 4
MENTAL HEALTH, WELLBEING AND RESILIENCE

Mental health and wellbeing (MHWB or MWB) has emerged as perhaps the most significant issue in this decade, gathering pace considerably since 2015. While concerns about MWB have been building over a number of years and much research has been conducted, a global MWB pandemic is upon us, or at least in Westernised societies. The Improving Access to Psychological Therapies (IAPT) programme has developed in the UK in recent years, in response to the increasing challenges to the mental health of a significant proportion of patients presenting at their GPs with symptoms of anxiety, stress and depression (see Kuhn, 2011). In the educational context, schools, colleges and universities are experiencing issues of this nature and are only now equipping themselves to deal with the challenge. Developing resilience is at the heart of the solution and this part examines MWB in the context of both the 'resilient teacher' and the 'resilient student'.

Note: we have chosen to adapt the term, by dropping the word 'health' from the acronym MHWB. Rather, we prefer to acknowledge implicitly the health element, but wish to reduce the stigma associated with the notion that the opposite of health is illness, which then gives rise to the inappropriate term 'mental illness'. Society is moving away from this notion. We would be grateful if you adopt 'mental wellbeing' (MWB) as a non-stigmatising concept.

12

MENTAL WELLBEING

CHAPTER OBJECTIVES

- Outline the wide range of MWB sources available to the teacher.
- Understand the need to develop personal MWB and facilitate development in the classroom.
- Differentiate between a range of support systems and their integration into the wider educational system.

TEACHERS' STANDARDS

A teacher must:

4   Plan and teach well-structured lessons

- reflect systematically on the effectiveness of lessons and approaches to teaching
- contribute to the design and provision of an engaging curriculum within the relevant subject area(s)

5   Adapt teaching to respond to the strengths and needs of all pupils

- demonstrate an awareness of the physical, social and intellectual development of children, and know how to adapt teaching to support pupils' education at different stages of development
- have a clear understanding of the needs of all pupils, including those with special educational needs; those of high ability; those with English as an additional language; those with disabilities; and be able to use and evaluate distinctive teaching approaches to engage and support them

8   Fulfil wider professional responsibilities

- take responsibility for improving teaching through appropriate professional development, responding to advice and feedback from colleagues
- communicate effectively with parents with regard to pupils' achievements and wellbeing

12.1 INTRODUCTION

Mental wellbeing is becoming an increasingly prevalent challenge to people of all ages. The pace of daily life is so fast nowadays that keeping up with it is difficult, to say the least. Individuals require skills, strategies and understanding of themselves in order to cope with the pressures they face, and these skills, strategies and underlying understanding are usually developed over the lifespan. But is the pace of life too fast for this development to be effective? Do we need to acquire a skill-set far earlier in life nowadays, compared to 50 years ago? Indeed, what chances are there for our young people to acquire the necessary skill-set from the outset, during childhood, so that they are prepared for adulthood and are able to meet the demands of primary, secondary and tertiary education? Are our young people more or less able to cope in today's societies and what can we do as educators to assist them during these difficult, formative years? This chapter offers an insight into the psychological issues that lie within a clinical spectrum or classification system. Practitioners working in this area subscribe to the view that proactive early intervention is preferable to reactive treatment and also that an element of education in self-help facilitates progress by engendering a sense of personal control. Teachers would welcome such an approach, but may also need to consider the role that they must play in this process.

12.2 NHS CHILD AND ADOLESCENT MENTAL HEALTH SERVICES (CAMHS)

Mental health provision, administered by the National Health Service (NHS), must be diverse in its reach, available to all, from birth to old age and across all walks of life. As a result of this wide remit, it may be sub-categorised into the following distinct, yet interrelated services: child and adolescent services; learning disability services; adult services; older adult services; substance misuse services; forensic services. For the purposes of this chapter, however, we will focus on Child and Adolescent Mental Health Services (CAMHS) in relation to child and adolescent services (perhaps with an element of overlap with learning disability services and substance misuse services). Nevertheless, since we are dealing with education as a process beyond childhood and adolescence, we also consider elements of mental health in university students (which of course all teachers will have been, before embarking on their teaching positions) and we would also urge the reader to consider the material presented here in relation to MWB for teaching and support staff, who are equally an important part of the equation.

In respect of child and adolescent services, CAMHS is an umbrella term covering the various services who work with young people and children experiencing emotional or behavioural issues that are impacting on their MWB. This service also extends to parents and carers in order to provide appropriate support where it is needed most. Beyond generic support offered by local authorities, NHS Trusts or schools, for example, there is provision for specialist support through a network of multidisciplinary teams, comprising psychologists and psychological therapists, such as family therapists and play therapists, occupational therapists, psychiatrists, nurses, social workers and specialists in substance misuse. The website for NHS England offers a springboard for further exploration, and having an awareness of it in the first instance provides a useful resource, should it be needed (www.nhs.uk/NHSEngland/AboutNHSservices/mental-health-services-explained).

Access to support would normally be from a GP referral, although it may come from a school headteacher acting on behalf of concerned staff. Although a referral is the usual route to mental health services support, there are situations involving alcohol and drug issues where support can be gained without being referred by one's GP. The NHS website provides further links for those wishing to pursue them. The fact that there are a number of 'parties' involved, such as child, school, GP and social worker, ensures that the issue remains within focus and the child is not simply left without support. It is worth pointing out, however, that with the current trend towards economic cuts, the NHS is no different. As a result of government cuts, funding in CAMHS has experienced a net loss in excess of £50 standard million in England. It is perhaps little coincidence that CAMHS do not have the capacity to provide support for the approximately one in four children and young people referred to them.

If this resource does indeed act as a springboard for further exploration, the CAMHS link to the Youth Mental Health Hub is also worth exploring (www.nhs.uk/Livewell/youth-mental-health/Pages/Youth-mental-health-help.aspx). Written for young people, it offers self-help guidance on issues such as depression, anxiety, stress (including exam stress), eating disorders, bullying (including cyber-bullying), panic attacks, low self-esteem, addiction, bereavement, relationship abuse and drugs, alongside other issues faced by young people nowadays.

12.3 DEFINING MENTAL WELLBEING

In providing a definition of mental wellbeing, we have explored some of the prominent organisations, whose aims are to promote mental wellbeing within society. The World Health Organization (WHO) provides the following definition, with a *caveat* that debate remains regarding all possible elements: 'Concepts of mental health include subjective wellbeing, perceived self-efficacy, autonomy, competence, inter-generational dependence and recognition of the ability to realize one's intellectual and emotional potential' (World Health Organization, 2003: 7). It has also been defined as a state of wellbeing whereby individuals:

> recognize their abilities, are able to cope with the normal stresses of life, work productively and fruitfully, and make a contribution to their communities. (World Health Organization, 2009: 10)

In wider Western society, MWB has become a prominent feature of daily life. Indeed, the World Health Organization (Europe) acknowledges this as a major public health challenge affecting more than 30 per cent of the population and requiring an appropriate action plan to improve health and wellbeing across the European region (World Health Organization, 2013), in line with and contributing towards 'Health 2020', the European policy frame for health and wellbeing. The WHO lists a variety of psychosocial factors that adversely influence MWB, which are worth mentioning here, since they have implications for teachers, trainee teachers and children alike: income, unemployment, substance misuse, crime and educational achievement are important and it is high-lighted that often these form in clusters rather than existing in isolation (World Health Organization, 2013). For the purpose of this chapter, we will not explore these in detail, as they would draw attention away from our remit. Nevertheless, as teachers, we have a pastoral role to play and this role is more effective when available data is accessible and our awareness of the signs is heightened. We will return to this in Section 12.4 below. It is worth pointing out here that the WHO do propose a set of actions across the lifespan, taking into account the needs of children, adults and the elderly alike. Within the remit of this chapter, one of the WHO action points refers to 'best start', which promotes support for appropriate family life and parenting, encouraging parents to emphasise the importance of the home as a suitable learning environment and reducing detrimental childhood experiences. In order to do this, there is an increased emphasis on promoting mental health in schools, awareness of identifying emotional issues, along with actions targeting bullying inside or outside of schools (World Health Organization, 2013). This is an excellent, chronologically 'bottom up' strategy that aims to equip children with the necessary resilience skills required to enter adulthood and lead a successful life, in MWB terms.

Of course, this leads us nicely on to the notion of 'society'. In this section, we are discussing Western society; however, this is extremely broad and highlights that the educational system is itself a society. Indeed, primary, secondary and tertiary education are distinct 'societies' within the educational society, and in operational terms, each school, college or university is equally a distinct society. It is important to acknowledge this notion, because MWB has no boundaries and is not, or indeed should not be, per-ceived as being irrelevant within whichever 'educational society' the reader chooses to operate. We all have a certain responsibility to promote MWB in the domains within which we operate. It is important that we communicate with other like-minded profes-sionals, who perhaps operate outside of our 'societies' but who share an element of overlap, or whose expertise we require because there is a line that, professionally, should not be crossed. We are thinking here especially of situations where a teacher with no formal psychiatric specialism may encounter a student experiencing severe mental health difficulties. We will discuss 'referring on' elsewhere in this chapter.

Within the higher education context, where aspiring undergraduates train to become teachers, there is an increasing level of concern in terms of the number of students who may be experiencing issues of mental wellbeing. The Royal College of Psychiatrists has acknowledged the heightened risk, such that 'Student service manag-ers, counsellors and mental health advisors report increasing numbers of clients and an increase in the severity of the problems that trouble them' (Royal College of Psychiatrists,

2011: 20). This has been complemented by Universities UK, who produced a Student Mental Wellbeing in Higher Education (MWBHE) good practice guide (Universities UK, 2015), aimed at facilitating the integration and embedding of student mental wellbeing within higher education institutions, in line with review and potential revision of internal policies and procedures. It has been estimated by the chair of the MWBHE working group that there are approximately 115,000 students currently in higher education who have reported MWB issues. Elements of training in terms of mental health awareness and reporting protocols are recommended within this report, which has been widely adopted across the higher education sector. The 'Healthy Universities' initiative, established by the University of Central Lancashire (UCLAN) in 2006, was set up with the intention of offering a facilitative and supportive environment for the development of a whole university approach to health and wellbeing. As of 2017 it has attracted 87 affiliated UK higher education institutions (www.healthyuniversities. ac.uk). Internally, higher education institutions have further developed their existing structures and protocols for dealing with these challenges. We say 'challenges' because one might argue that such institutions are not 'specialist mental health services' and therefore it is not within their remit to provide such support. Nevertheless, higher education institutions are communities and, in some respects, they are self-contained, which makes it important for some element of MWB provision. Historically, this has been the domain of university counselling services, although more recently some of the lower-level non-counselling (yet pastoral) issues that personal academic tutors now have to deal with mean that an element of awareness of MWB issues is available to academic staff. Indeed, some institutions, such as the University of Worcester, are beginning to address the increasing number of students entering higher education with MWB issues (see Musiat et al., 2014).

12.4 WITHIN SCHOOLS

The World Health Organization report that approximately 50 per cent of mental disorders emerge before 14 years of age (WHO, 2013). The cycle of mental wellbeing model (World Health Organization, 2013: 18) incorporates socioeconomic, psychosocial and political elements that influence and are influenced by mental disorders, risk factors and available health provision. It is a useful source of reference, perhaps to print off and pin on the school noticeboard, as it provides a succinct, effective reminder of the complex issues that surround mental wellbeing. While one might initially consider it to be a model for the adult world, children are still subject to its elements. Although it is not always a good thing to compartmentalise children or adults into 'boxes', we live in a society that operates on the basis of classification systems. Indeed, this is evident specifically in terms of the clinical classification of mental disorders, using *DSM-5* and *ICD-11* mentioned elsewhere in this chapter. Children are classified in terms of stages of development, Key Stages and SATS results among many other forms of classification.

The model is shown in Figure 12.1. Our advice would be to examine the model in two ways: firstly, 'from the outside inwards', i.e., look at each box and consider how it relates to other boxes, how it relates to the systems in place within schools; and secondly, by starting with the signs presented by a child in school and then use the boxes in the model to make associations. This can be seen in the case study that follows.

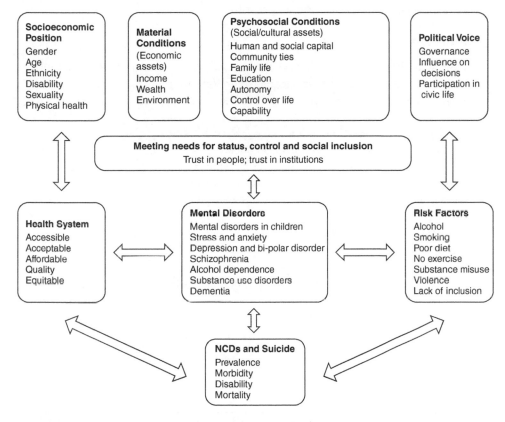

Figure 12.1   Adaptation of the cycle of wellbeing model (adapted from World Health Organization, 2013)

CASE STUDY   James

James is a 7-yearold from a single-parent family, living in a high-rise tower-block in an inner city. His father was imprisoned just before James was born, after being convicted of an offence involving firearms; now out of prison, he is not

(Continued)

permitted to have contact with his wife as a result of long-term violence issues towards her. This means that James does not have any contact with his father.

His 25-year-old mother is a drug addict, currently undergoing a heroin rehabilitation programme. She receives unemployment benefit and has not worked since leaving school without any qualifications at 16, although she appears to have funded her drug habit through prostitution.

Comments

In looking at the cycle of wellbeing model again (Figure 12.1), it becomes more apparent where the model is applicable to anyone helping James.

Factors from the model that should stand out to the reader are:

- *Socioeconomic position*: gender, age, physical health.
- *Material conditions*: income, wealth (lack of), environment.
- *Psychosocial conditions*: human and social capital, family life, education (hampered), autonomy (lack of), control over life (lack of), capability.
- *Risk factors*: poor diet, no exercise, potential for future substance misuse, potential for future violence.
- *Mental disorders*: potential for stress, anxiety, depression, alcohol dependence, substance use.

Of course, it must be stressed that we cannot be certain that James will experience poor MWB issues at all. That is not the point. Rather, teachers and students alike should be made aware of the potential mediating factors, the risk factors and the relationships between them. On this basis, the model helps to direct attention.

ACTIVITY

In taking the case study of James a step further, we would suggest that you perhaps visualise different scenarios of what James would look like and the ways in which he may behave in school, if you manipulate the mix of factors in the model. This will help you to establish some patterns of physical appearance and behaviour, i.e., the signs to look out for in the classroom and the playground (see Section 12.6 below).

It should not be difficult to write a series of 5–10 case studies of your own. Indeed, this might be an excellent group activity for all staff to participate in during a training session, so that a wider series of examples can be produced. A loose structure might be:

- Brief background information on the child.
- Brief outline of signs and symptoms displayed.
- Brief outline of the course of action that you might recommend, including other parties who should be informed.

In effect, there should be a protocol in place in school already that you report to the Head or Head of Department. We are suggesting that you have an awareness of the role played by GPs, educational psychologists and clinical psychologists as part of your own continuing professional development. This will also enable you to direct your own pastoral care in a manner that we would hope leads in to and complements the help of other agencies at a later date.

12.5 OBSERVING AND IDENTIFYING 'SIGNS AND SYMPTOMS'

In no particular order of priority, here is a list of possible indicators of a change in a student's personal circumstances outside of school that may impact on activities, performance and behaviour within school:

- A change in previous cleanliness or tidiness of school uniform beyond the accepted 'norm'.
- A change in apparent hygiene, i.e., unkempt hair and a 'ripe odour' emanating from the student.
- Appearance of dark rings or bags under the eyes indicating lack of sleep, along with falling asleep in lessons.
- Difficulties in concentration and focus on tasks during lessons.
- Increased lateness for registration.
- Stealing of or begging for food from peers during the school day, indicating a change in diet and nutrition at home.
- Increased agitation or aggressive behaviour, towards either teaching staff or peers.

Criticism has been levelled at attempts to define wellbeing in terms of the culmination of constituent parts, rather than in terms of generic themes (Dodge et al., 2012). These authors propose the existence of a wellbeing 'set point' or fulcrum reflecting a state of homeostasis, which is influenced by fluctuating resources and challenges. For them, wellbeing is defined as 'the balance point between an individual's resource pool and the challenges faced' (2012: 230). They go on to say that stability or homeostasis occurs 'when individuals have the psychological, social and physical resources they need to meet a particular psychological, social or physical challenge. When individuals have more challenges than resources, the see-saw dips, along with wellbeing, and vice versa' (2012: 230).

Others would argue perhaps that this state of equilibrium equates to the term 'flourishing' (Ramachandram, 2016; Seligman, 2011), referring to 'the experience of life going well' (Huppert and So, 2013: 838). Huppert and So refer to research suggesting that flourishing, which they argue is synonymous with wellbeing, is linked to enhanced learning, increases in both productivity and creativity, effective relationships and increases in pro-social behaviour, improved health and extended life expectancies (Huppert and So, 2013: 838). The aim of Huppert and So's research was to examine the symptoms of depression and anxiety, in accordance with international classification (see Section 12.7 on classification below), and identify the mirror opposites of their symptoms. Ten features reflecting hedonic (H) and eudemonic (E) dimensions, i.e., positive feelings and positive functioning, were established: competence, emotional stability, engagement, meaning, optimism, positive emotion, positive relationship, resilience, self-esteem and vitality. Ranking of each of these elements in relation to three European regions and 22 European countries can be found in Huppert and So (2013) and is well worth examining. It shows, for example that those living in Denmark are ranked 1st for positive emotion, positive relationships, resilience and emotional stability, whereas those living in the UK are ranked 10th, 3rd, 6th and 19th respectively on the same features. Indeed, the UK does not rank 1st on any of these features.

12.6 MENTAL WELLBEING ORGANISATIONS

Society loves to classify, code and compartmentalise objects, ideas, concepts and phenomena, in order to provide a suitable and standardised understanding of them (as we will see in Section 12.8 below). With the extreme variation in quality of information available electronically these days, through a wide range of social media and internet sources, it is important to establish the suitability of material. For example, if we choose to set up a wiki page, stating that the world is flat, with slightly curled up edges to stop boats and people falling over the edge, there is nothing to stop us doing it and inevitably there will be people who access the material and believe us entirely because we are 'qualified' and are 'experts'. While such naivety may be slightly alarming, there is a grey area when one examines the available resources on MWB. With this in mind, the resources we have selected in this chapter (and indeed throughout the book in general) have been deemed to be of an appropriate standard. Professional bodies, such as the British Psychological Society (BPS) or the Royal College of Psychiatrists (RCP), are governed by professional and ethical principles and are therefore deemed to be 'safe'. Equally, the websites chosen below have, wherever possible, been selected because they have been certified by NHS England and have achieved the status of satisfying the 'Information Standard', which is committed to raising the quality of health and care information that is accessible by the public, patients and practitioners in the health and care professions (www.england.nhs.uk/tis/about/the-info-standard).

The Health and Care Professions Council is another quality provider that governs various health and care professions. Registered practitioners practise under its auspices and are governed by its rules, regulations and disciplinary procedures, and so members of the public using its services receive an appropriate level of protection, commensurate with the expectations of the professions within its remit. Often, practitioner psychologists will be chartered members of the British Psychological Society as well as members of the Health and Care Professions Council. Psychiatrists will have trained in medicine and specialised in psychiatry and it is the medical training that distinguishes them from clinical psychologists. For the purposes of this chapter we would not wish to exclude the Royal College of Psychiatry as an important source of information, with a considerable element of overlap with psychology in terms of MWB.

Another organisation that sits under the certification of the Information Standard is Mind (mind.org.uk), a registered charity whose aim is to provide advice and support to empower people experiencing mental health difficulties. Since the production of their 2012 strategy document, Mind acknowledge the amelioration in public perception towards mental health, which has led to their producing a new strategy for 2016–2021, 'Building on Change' (Mind, 2016). In this document, six fundamental challenges remain: one in four people will experience a mental health issue in any year; approximately 25 per cent of people experiencing mental health issues receive support in a given year; 57 million prescriptions for antidepressants have been prescribed, equating to a 46 per cent increase since 2012; a reduction in funding for mental health services in England alone by 8.25 per cent has been seen during the last parliament; 50 per cent of people have to wait over three months before starting 'talking therapies' and in excess of 105,000 people were hospitalised as a result of their mental health; there has been an increase in suicide in England and Wales in 2013, compared to 2012, with approximately 5,140 people taking their own lives.

Other examples include the Mental Health Foundation and the Charlie Waller Memorial Trust, which are charities set up along similar lines to address mental health, providing support for children and adults alike. The Mental Health Foundation (www.mentalhealth.org.uk) has been conducting pioneering research in this field over the past 60 years and has recently, for example, explored the concept of 'digital mental health' or 'e-mental health' as a platform for providing assistance to a society that spends large amounts of time online in both adults (Musiat et al., 2014) and children (Stallard et al., 2010). Although e-therapies are increasing, both studies represent and reflect the caution its users perceive towards it, a situation certainly highlighted in Stallard et al.'s paper, in which 49 per cent of 8–17-year-old participants reportedly preferred face-to-face contact, as opposed to e-support. Capp (2015) calls for a mental health 'presence' to be integrated into school communities, rather than being 'accessed off-site', suggesting again the preference for face-to-face contact. We will, however, consider digital mental health in more detail elsewhere in this chapter.

The Charlie Waller Memorial Trust aims to offer support for young people relating to mental wellbeing and specifically the signs of depression. An e-learning package consisting of six 20-minute sessions has been designed for those people working with students; it is available online, free of charge (www.learning.cwmt.org.uk), and allows users to work through it at their own pace. Guidance is provided on: key principles in supporting students in order to provide effective support within the realms of one's professional role; awareness of the signs of deterioration in mental health and what to do in such instances; the skill-set required in order to support a student who presents in a distressed state, or who becomes increasingly distressed during a period of support; transitional issues from home to university, in the case of students entering higher education; support in crisis-intervention where students are taking risks, either with their own mental health or that of others; integrating skills from sessions 1–5 into a key summary for helping students, along with an example of good practice. In each of these sessions, there is a useful set of case-study-type scenarios and a self-test element to check the viewers' understanding. An associated Charlie Waller Memorial Trust project has facilitated the creation of 'Students Against Depression', a website that offers clinically validated information, strategies and resources for students facing issues such as low mood, depression and suicidal thoughts (www.studentsagainstdepression.org). Significantly, it offers stories from students who have experienced these issues and how these challenges were overcome. Depression is seen as something requiring a campaign against it and the aim is to kickstart the campaign against depression. Cleverly and in keeping with student-relevant terminology, the organisers provide a set of ten modules for students to work through on their campaign. Each module has a downloadable workbook for recording notes, providing evidence and a sense of what is being focused on, along with their acting as a monitoring and reflection tool. There is certainly a benefit in being able to look back on one's journey and see how far one has come. The module series is structured as per Table 12.1 below.

Table 12.1   Summary of steps in a student's personal campaign against depression

1	Creating a safety plan
2	Establishing a support network
3	Taking those difficult first steps
4	Establishing a healthier daily routine
5	Increasing one's understanding of depression
6	Changing thinking patterns
7	Developing skills for living well
8	Viewing depression from a different perspective
9	Making efforts to continue working on overcoming depression
10	Writing a personal reflective account of winning the campaign to overcome depression

Source: adapted from www.studentsagainstdepression.org/take-action/take-action-in-your-own-life/

Although aimed primarily at undergraduate-level students, much of the material can be easily transferred to secondary school and college-level students, along with post-graduate students, all of whom are equally susceptible to depression at some point in their student lives (and beyond). The key element that must be adhered to is that progress builds on solid foundations, so with this in mind, we propose that it is useful to see Table 12.1 in terms of a series of incremental and related steps. Modules 1–3 are concerned with the immediacy of the situation, and on this basis they sit together nicely. This is rather like planning ahead for the short-term future (also, see Prochaska and DiClemente's stages of change model in Chapter 14) (Prochaska and DiClemente, 1982). Modules 4–6 focus on increasing understanding of depression and the ways in which one might change one's thinking about it, while also beginning to make changes. This is rather like working on it in the present: it concerns action rather than planning and focuses the person on actively changing their patterns of activity. Module 7 starts with the present and then, in combination with Modules 8 and 9, begins to adopt a longer-term, future approach to living well, recognising and acknowledging one's emotions, how these should be expressed, what society expects and how to remain true to one's own (and probably newly restructured) perspectives on mental health. This is rather like the transition to the 'next level' of the campaign. Again, we can draw appropriate parallels with the stages of change model here. Finally, Module 10 requires reflection on the past, the campaign and the level of success achieved.

There are two things to notice here. Firstly, beginning the sentence with 'Finally' is not really appropriate. It is not 'final'. It is the start of the rest of one's life and as with stages of change, is in need of constant monitoring and adaptation as necessary. This, however, is not a burden, but rather is satisfying, motivating and self-confidence building. It is in effect a 'campaign for life', with depression entering the campaign as a part of the richness of that life. Secondly, by embarking on a package such as this, or indeed any similarly structured package of mental health support, it would be nigh on (if not) impossible to be at the same point at the end as the starting point. Obtaining appropriate guidance, creating a support network and working through the challenge foster a sense of control, which by its very nature would appear to be the inverse of that experienced by someone with depression.

Since there are numerous other organisations we could have included here, there comes a point at which one needs to finish off, so we will do so with two additional charities: Young Minds and Heads Together. We have not excluded others on any basis other than restricted space in the pages of this chapter, but what we have attempted to do is provide an 'e-journey' or 'paper-trail'. You will notice that among the collective resources here, there is a synergy between many of these links.

Young Minds (www.youngminds.org.uk) is a leading charity, established in 1993, aimed at improving the health and wellbeing of children and young people, with a specific early-intervention approach. Heads Together (www.headstogether.org.uk) is a campaign established by their Royal Highnesses the Duke and Duchess of Cambridge along with Prince Henry of Wales (Prince Harry), and in synergy with partners such as Young Minds, serves to raise awareness of and reduce the stigma associated with underlying, unresolved mental health issues that are creating significant difficulties to individuals and the societies within which they live.

12.7 A COLLECTIVE FOCUS?

Collectively, two common themes emerge from these sources. Firstly, the stigma that has been inappropriately linked with mental ill-health has been challenged in recent years and continues to diminish (e.g., Murman et al., 2014; Yau et al., 2011). There is still progress to be made; however, young people appear to be far more at ease and open with discussing issues that would have remained hidden 30 years ago. Fostering this de-stigmatisation through the agencies outlined here, along with the countless others which we have not been able to mention but which share this collective focus, is vital in perpetuating the momentum that exists. Secondly, early awareness is a key element in helping people to overcome their mental health challenges. In the context of this book, this is especially the case for children, which is why there has been an increasing emergence of MWB-related programmes introduced into schools, both in the UK and abroad. An extremely short article in the *Education Journal* (2017) highlights how this is being tackled in Wales, since 2012, through the use of 'young champions', although there is no other information available. Early awareness by staff is a vital element in ensuring the MWB of children in the education system. Naturally, additional training is always a favoured approach and this is no exception in terms of MWB in schools. Of course, we are not advocating that you train to become a professional counsellor (unless you have a desire to change your profession at this point). There are, however, important and extremely beneficial courses that can be taken, with a little investment of time from you, which you can take back into school and share with colleagues, where you are the 'named member of staff'. One such course operating currently is Mental Health First Aid (MHFA), which was originally developed in Australia in 2000; it is internationally recognised in 23 countries and was implemented in the UK in 2007, by the Department of Health's National Institute of Mental Health in England (NIMHE) as one element of a national approach to improving public mental health. MHFA is aimed at a wide variety of people and professions, particularly where contact with the public is a primary feature. It is certainly of benefit to teachers, especially those working in secondary education, where mental health issues are frequently seen, and has been evaluated favourably, in terms of using educational psychologists to deliver the MHFA-YP (young people) programme through NHS Scotland (Currie and Davidson, 2015). This has been echoed in the MHFA country of origin, with similar favourable results in Australia (Hart et al., 2016), and in relation to the Wellbeing in Secondary Education (WISE) study in the UK, which examines MHFA for wellbeing in students and teachers alike (Kidger et al., 2016).

MHFA aims to provide support in the first instance, using principles applicable to physical first aid. Participants on the course are taught to recognise the warning signs associated with diminishing mental health. Training is also given on how to talk directly with someone who is expressing an issue, what might help them, how to remain or become calm and what not to say or do, depending on the presenting signs and symptoms. A toolkit, entitled 'Take 10 Together' and developed for World Mental Health Day 2016 has been adapted by MHFA England for year-round use (https://mhfaengland.org/mhfa-centre/resources/take-10-together). There is also a school

Table 12.2 Adaptation of MHFA infographic 'Take 10 Together'

Provide a 'safe' space	• The classroom may be intimidating, so use a neutral area outside of the classroom, such as a pastoral support room.
	• Ensure that you sit down, which will foster a more relaxed approach to the conversation.
	• Allow plenty of time. You are not restricted to 10 minutes.
How to ask questions	• Use a non-confrontational style and body language.
	• Keep them positive and encouraging.
	• Show empathy and take the questions (and their answers) seriously.
	• Avoid irrelevant advice, such as 'Cheer up'.
	• Make eye-contact while being mindful of potential cultural differences.
Types of question to ask	• 'How are you feeling at the moment?'
	• 'How long have you felt like this? Is it an ongoing issue?'
	• 'Who do you feel you can go to for support?'
	• 'What kind of support do you think might help you?'
	• 'Are there any factors outside of school or the classroom that are contributing to the way you are feeling?'
	• 'How can I help you?'
How to listen	• Pay full attention without interrupting or being distracted while the student speaks. Focus on their choice of words, their tone of voice and any signs of body language for cues.
	• Respect the student's attitudes, values, beliefs and feeling as important, even if they differ from your own.
	• Show genuine concern by avoiding making any moral judgement or criticism of what they say.
	• Establish a rapport by placing yourself in their position, displaying empathy for what they are saying.
What to do next	• Ensure that the conversation continues until you feel that you have both determined the next course of action.
	• Make a note to follow up within a period of time (this may be an hour, a day or a few days, depending on the severity of the issue).
	• Provide reassurances regarding your support along with the support of other staff (subject to confidentiality and your assessment of any risk). Ensure that the student is aware of the school counselling service, the school nurse and their family GP.
	• Report through usual school protocols as appropriate.

Source: adapted from MHFA (2017) 'Take 10 Together at School'

version for use with young people and it is this version that we will discuss here, although we would direct teachers to the adult version for their own MWB. Readers will be aware of the day-to-day pressures surrounding modern school life, such as bullying, academic pressures and increasingly challenging concerns based on social media technologies, along with those issues of daily life experienced outside of school, so it is not surprising that MWB issues are increasing in young people. These issues are perhaps an inescapable element of modern Western societies, and young people will only benefit from resolving issues if they are provided with adequate support. As inferred by the title of the toolkit, the starting point for this may be as simple as taking ten minutes with a student, in a non-confrontational way, to explore their mental health. 'Back in the day' we would have called this 'a chat', which of course, it still is. The difference is the underlying purpose, which structures the questions one might ask and the way in which those questions probe specific mental health issues. There is a downloadable infographic on the MHFA England site for use in the staff room, although the information has been adapted for inclusion in Table 12.2 (which we believe is less attractive but succinctly condensed as a quick reference).

12.8 MENTAL WELLBEING IN A CLINICAL CONTEXT

Classification enables us to assess something against an agreed set of criteria and, in this sense, ensures accuracy and replication, subject to the suitability of the criteria of course. While mental wellbeing issues are perhaps less tangible than concrete, physical items, there are still elements of consistency that enable us to classify human behaviour in a way that provides insight and facilitates appropriate interventions. Of course, from a philosophical perspective, there is an argument against the classification of mental health in this way. Such classification may be seen as trying to fit behaviour into a specific category, purely because the category and its associated label exists. There will inevitably be elements of confusion in which a child with something non-clinical, such as a behaviour-management problem, is categorised into something more serious because a classification exists. For the purpose of this chapter, we adopt the former position and use classification in a positive light. Regardless of any standpoint against classification, classification exists, is in use and will continue to be used. No doubt refinements will be made over time, in line with cutting-edge thinking, and this provides an element of protection for all. Two major classification systems exist: *Diagnostic and Statistical Manual of Mental Disorders (DSM-5)*, written on behalf of the American Psychiatric Association; and the *International Classification of Mental and Behavioural Disorders (ICD-11)*, written on behalf of the World Health Organization and used across Europe. Chapter 7, entitled 'Mental and Behavioural Disorders', has received 310 proposed revisions, of which 286 have been successfully actioned as of February 2016.

We refer to the *ICD-11* as a clinical source of reference, in guiding the reader through clinical descriptions and diagnostic guidelines. It is important to bear in mind that this source is used in primary health care settings and general medical practice, but nevertheless it is important for us, our colleagues and you, the reader, to have an understanding of these descriptions and guidelines in order to inform our own courses of action, when needs arise. The *caveat* that we must impress on you is the issue of where to draw the line in terms of the support you are able to offer students without overstepping the professional boundaries requiring counselling or clinical qualifications. This is a grey area, so if in doubt, do not go beyond areas of pastoral support that you would be expected to provide as a teacher. For more guidance, it is worth looking at webpages of the British Association for Counselling & Psychotherapy (www.bacp.co.uk, www.itsgoodtotalk.org.uk), the British Psychological Society's Division of Clinical Psychology (www.bps.org.uk/networks-and-communities/member-microsite/division-clinical-psychology) and the Royal College of Psychiatrists (www.rcpsych.ac.uk/). Each of these contains a diverse array of resources that may guide your intuitive thinking and help you to balance the issue of providing support with that of duty of care.

The UK National Health Service (NHS) offers five generic steps to aid mental wellbeing: connect, be active, keep learning, give to others, be mindful (NHS Choices – www.nhs.uk/Conditions/stress-anxiety-depression/Pages/improve-mental-wellbeing.aspx). Each of these are based on sound underpinning research literature and indeed apply to children and adults alike. Connecting with people – building and developing relationships with colleagues, peers, family and friends – helps to provide a support network (Ponce-Garcia et al., 2015). Finding a form of physical activity that is personally enjoyable provides physical and psychological benefits that are well documented and multifaceted (e.g., Christie and Cole, 2017; McNaughton and Meldrum, 2017; Thum et al., 2017). Learning new skills or developing knowledge in new areas provides motivation, confidence and a sense of achievement. Giving to others can be as simple as smiling at someone, or holding a door open for them, or be more structured as in the example of volunteering. Regardless of what it entails, this is an element of altruistic behaviour that provides personal satisfaction and a good feeling for the altruist. Mindfulness, or spending time in the present, rather than pondering on the past or thinking about the future all of the time, enables people to take stock or 'stop the merry-go-round' for a while and is linked to states of relaxation (e.g., Zeidan et al., 2014). There is of course an element of overlap between these steps. For example, learning new skills through participation in a sporting or exercise activity increases physical fitness, but more than likely involves other like-minded participants and hence increases connectedness and enhances support networks. It may be that one offers a lift to a fellow participant and thus is an act of giving. While participating, the future or past are of little significance and hence a sense of mindfulness is fostered. Readers who walk, run or cycle as a preferred form of physical activity will perhaps readily identify with this final point (we will return to mindfulness in Chapter 17)

12.9 MEASURING MENTAL WELLBEING

As we discussed above, MWB can be measured in adults using the 14-item Warwick-Edinburgh Mental Well-Being Scale (WEMWBS) (Tennant et al. 2007). This has strong construct validity against the Positive and Negative Affect Scale (PANAS) (Watson et al., 1988) and the Scale of Psychological Well-Being (SPWB) (Ryff and Keyes, 1995), against which it was compared. Where depression may be suspected as an underlying issue during a visit to one's GP, MWB can be measured using the nine-item Patient Health Questionnaire-9 (PHQ-9) (Kroenke et al., 2001), which is widely available to health professionals and acts as a quick and efficient screening tool for depression along with potential suicide risk.

Difficulties associated with any questionnaire that should be borne in mind are validity and reliability. Validity refers to whether the questionnaire measures what it purports to measure, i.e., whether it is accurate and precise. It also refers to the appropriateness of the data generated and whether it has been measured correctly. Reliability refers to the repeatability of data generated, i.e., is the measure consistent in producing similar results over multiple occurrences (Denscombe, 2010)? To use an analogy, a tin of baked beans labelled 'baked beans' should contain baked beans. If it contains baked beans it shows strong validity, but if it contains peas it shows poor validity! If one opens ten tins of baked beans and each one contains baked beans, it shows a high level of reliability, but if seven of those tins (this is simply a subjective choice of number here) contain peas it shows poor levels of reliability (see Chapter 19 on validity and reliability).

The questionnaires outlined above have been peer-reviewed, which acts as a quality assurance mark concerning their validity and reliability. As with many questionnaires, refinements tend to be made over time: new ways of thinking promote new (and one would hope better) questionnaires. We would like to think that avid readers are beginning to anticipate a serious potential difficulty in respect of the questionnaires highlighted. They are all aimed at an adult population and as a result may be neither valid nor reliable for use with children. In real terms, this raises the question not of when to use them, but rather how far down the chronological age scale one is able to go before the questionnaire becomes inappropriate. Is it 16? Is it 14? Is it 12? And so forth. Equally, there is an issue regarding the type of language used in questionnaires that may give an indication about whether it is suitable for children of a particular age. Of course, as a teacher, you should have become adept at assessing the level at which pieces of prose, instructions, guidelines, rules, etc. need to be 'pitched' for your specific audience, whether it is a class of 8-year-olds or a class of 14-year-olds. Some language may render the information prohibitive and one's judgement is a good indicator of appropriateness. However, this is not enough. Do not simply assume that a questionnaire is inappropriate for children if it has been designed for use with adults. A quick search engine query usually establishes this, and some follow-up research using a

Table 12.3 Example 'search' query form

Search Engine	Search Term	Sample result and our comments
Google	Can the PHQ-9 be administered to children?	Severity Measure for Depression, Child Age 11 to 17:
		www.psychiatry.org/psychiatrists/practice/dsm/educational-resources/assessment-measures. Click on 'Disorder-Specific Severity Measures' and then 'Severity Measure for Depression, Child Age 11 to 17 (PHQ-9 modified for Adolescents [PHQ-A], Adapted)'
		Used to monitor progress through the treatment. Administered at initial session and then as a monitoring tool. Further background information provided in DSM-5. Adapted from PHQ-9 A (Johnson et al., 2002), which can be used with children aged 11–17.
		Subtle differences in phrasing, more specific to 'school' rather than 'work'.
		Original PHQ-9 can be used with clients aged 13 years and above.
		As PHQ-9 A also examines suicide risk, a 'Life Satisfaction' measure may be appropriate, such as the Students' Life Satisfaction Scale (SLSS) (Huebner, 1991a, 1991b, 1991c), a 7-item self-report scale, which assesses overall life satisfaction for students aged 8–18. (cf. Proctor et al., 2009)
Google	Strengths and Difficulties Questionnaire	The Strengths and Difficulties Questionnaire (SDQ):
		www.sdqinfo.com/a0.html
		A 25-item behavioural screening questionnaire about 3–16-year-olds. There are numerous versions in different languages and for different age groups. To be completed by a child, teacher and/or a parent, on the basis of observed behaviours (see discussion below on triangulation).
		An 'early years' version exists for 3–4-year-olds, which is completed only by parents and/or teachers. We are certain that it is not necessary that we explain the reason for this here!

variety of journal articles can be used to provide academic support for one's findings. The examples below highlight how efficient this process can be.

Once you have established whether a questionnaire is appropriate for your requirements, it is then important to consider who may be eligible to complete it. Of course, the child should be able to complete a self-report version if the language and terminology are adequate. This, however, only provides part of the available picture. In transferring the concept of triangulation, adopted in sport psychology, for example, the picture can be 'enhanced' (e.g., Thelwell and Maynard, 2002). In sport, there are generally three stakeholders in relation to the performer, or client: the performer themselves, family/partner/spouse, coach/trainer. By obtaining data from each of these stakeholders, it becomes clear whether an element of agreement exists regarding the data. For example, you might hold certain maladaptive beliefs about your competence that are not shared by your coach or your partner. Equally, you may hold maladaptive beliefs that you are more competent than you actually are, whereas the coach perceives your competence in a more realistic manner. The ability to triangulate the data and look for similarities or differences provides a far richer picture than without triangulation. So, in transferring this concept to the school environment, different stakeholders exist: the child, the teacher, the parent or carer (see Handley and McAllister, 2017). Rather than looking for similarities, we would suggest that one looks for discrepancies in the triangulated data, simply because adopting a mindset where one is looking for discrepancies seems to set thinking in terms of asking the question: why would X (child/parent/teacher) think this when the other stakeholders do not?

12.10 A WORD ON EMOTICONS OR 'EMOJIS'

In recent years, there has been a novel emergence of the use of the emoji as a child-friendly equivalent to the widely used Likert-scale form of psychometric measurement. In this sense, communication is enhanced as a result of considering the simplicity with which it takes place (Hickson, 2013). Depending on the child's age, a standard Likert-scale version of a questionnaire may appear to be a daunting and confusing document; however, the incorporation of emojis in the form of 'smiley faces' can transform the same document. Indeed, the same principle applies to adults and is not restricted to psychometric measures, as illustrated when we were travelling towards a small village in Worcestershire recently. The mandatory 30mph speed limit sign was prominently displayed and of course we began to slow down in order to adhere to it. A car that was a little distance ahead of us did not appear to slow down sufficiently and, just after this sign, another sign suddenly illuminated with a red

Figure 12.2   Use of emojis in the environment

Source: iStock.com/vladru

'frownie face' representing a speed in excess of 30mph. For us, the sign illuminated with a green 'smiley face' representing an appropriate speed for the village, as depicted in the example images below. Apart from this appearing to be a great success on our part, we also perceived that 'society', or at least the villagers, were 'pleased' with our commitments to road safety. The point here is that the emoji served a practical purpose, but also seemed to relate nicely to our emotional feelings associated with the activity at that point.

In terms of MWB, emojis would seem, therefore, to be powerful in the message underlying them. Look at the example 'emoji Likert scale' below and rate how you feel at this particular point in time. Can you go one step further and put a percentage to this feeling? In the true sense of Likert scales, you should choose one box only, so the scale is perhaps not very accurate. Can you identify why? As we were writing this subsection, we were feeling happy but also the topic was somewhat amusing. In this situation, one would need to consider the primary feeling, which for us was happiness. The research methods chapter (Chapter 18) will help you to avoid anomalies such as this when designing or using pre-existing emoji-based measures.

Figure 12.3   Example emoji-based Likert scale

There is evidence in the literature regarding the psychology of emoticons/emojis and their possible underlying mechanisms. In this age of digital technology, electronic communication is often criticised for lacking emotional expression, or for expression being misinterpreted. The use of emoticons has been explored as a way of expressing emotions, reinforcing messages and in the expression of humour, and it has been argued that emoticons incorporate everyday facial expression into this form of computer-mediated communication (Derks et al., 2008). It has also been pointed out that internet users have become increasingly familiar with this type of computer-mediated communication and are adept in its use (Lo, 2008). In the nine years since this research, one would be safe in assuming that the generation of younger people who have known nothing other than this type of daily communication would feel perfectly 'at home' with emoticons as a language-form. Differences in usage between males and females exist, with more usage in females compared to males, although the sample population examined was 18+ (Fullwood et al., 2013).

As a result of a study examining brain activation in relation to a happiness emoticon, it is suggested that the underlying mechanism relates to the configuration of shapes, assembled in a configuration of their well-known form (i.e., a face) rather than their constituent parts (e.g., colon + semi-parentheses) (Churches et al., 2014). This provides some neuroscientific evidence to support the plethora of examples within perception, where humans create objects, faces, etc. in relation to perceptual constancy, figure-ground, illusory contours (edge detection) and object ambiguity.

12.11 MENTAL WELLBEING IN A SCHOOL CONTEXT

In combination with the *ICD-11* it becomes possible to consider mental wellbeing in schools, which in essence mirror institutions and businesses in the adult world, but with a different set of members. With this in mind, one might consider the pastoral role played by teachers and dedicated support workers within the counselling side of the school care system. Each school will have a member of staff, or a team, dedicated to fulfilling this role and there will be a policy in place to guide staff through the process (Roffey, 2015). It is essential that all staff familiarise themselves with school policy as a minimum requirement, not least because, unfortunately, it is necessary in this age of litigation to protect oneself against potential disciplinary procedures. Having said this, it is also hugely rewarding to help guide a young person through some of the challenges they face and which appear insurmountable to them at the time, but which they can conquer, with your assistance. Adolescents and young adults are an 'at risk' group for problems as serious as suicide (e.g., Zanus et al., 2017), and it would appear that school is the place where serious psychological issues incubate and indeed show themselves (Onieal, 2017). It is vital, therefore, that we all consider the ways in which we can best help young people before they arrive at this 'at risk' group, or indeed, create a new, younger 'at risk' group, which is something we suspect is already beginning to emerge.

12.12 ANNUAL SCHOOL CYCLES: SEASONAL PATTERNS?

Humans are subject to internal biorhythms or cycles, which dictate (physiologically speaking) how we operate. Sleep–wake cycles dictate our patterns over a 24-hour period. Within sleep, 90-minute 'ultradian' rhythms dictate how deeply we are sleeping at given points throughout the night (or day); body temperature fluctuates rhythmically over a 24-hour period, as does protein synthesis, which acts to repair our bodies before, during and after the daily challenges we face. Excretion of faecal material follows a similar pattern as indeed you already know when you need to rid yourself of a previous meal. Casting the eye further, fluctuations in MWB follow seasonal patterns. For example, seasonal affective disorder (SAD) or 'winter depression' is, as one may expect, more prevalent during the winter months, when light levels are low, sunshine is a rare occurrence and what would appear to be '50 shades of grey' fill the skies, before darkness sets in far too early for our liking.

The academic school year is no different, containing what we would describe as shared 'pinch points': certain generic periods in the school year that are commonly anxiety and stress inducing. Certainly, we see this in higher education, where anxiety and stress increases around November time. The academic year starts in September, yet from an MWB perspective, it is relatively quiet for counselling staff until November, which generally tends to be synonymous with the first set of assessment deadlines. The same can be said around April/May with an increase especially in final-year students – whose final dissertation deadline looms large – requesting support from counselling services. In order to provide common 'pinch points' for primary, secondary and tertiary education, Table 12.4 below offers some insight into this phenomenon. We have specifically left some cells blank, which may not have 'pinch points', or for you to insert your own.

There will of course be variation within this table, in terms of exact timings. However, the principle remains the same and we would advise that you create a bespoke version of your own, which is appropriate to your own school, bearing in mind that there may be differences between the state sector and private or independent sector, or differences if you are teaching (or intending to teach) in a different country. The main thing is that you ask the question and establish an awareness, so that you can be alert to issues when they inevitably arise. Of course, there will also be situations that do not fit neatly into such a table, but this does not matter, since your focus towards identifying issues will now be heightened.

A NOTE ON 'BLUE MONDAY'

'Blue Monday' is a term that seems to be endearing to the media. It is the notion that the third Monday in January is the most depressing day of the year, at least in the northern hemisphere anyway. The day is short (although not the shortest); there is usually a greyness to the day; it is cold, miserable and dank; Christmas and New Year celebrations are well and truly over, with no holiday period in sight; and the bills start to arrive, signalling how much debt the festivities have cost. Little to cheer about then! Why wouldn't this be the most depressing day of the year? Despite this accumulation of doom and gloom, there is no evidence to support the claims. The second or fourth Monday could be equally as bad. Some journalists even cite the last Monday in January as Blue Monday, as seen in a newspaper article printed in the *Times Educational Supplement* in 2008 (Frankel, 2008), in which advice is provided for teachers on how to beat the Blue Monday blues. There is just as much likelihood that

Table 12.4   Generic 'pinch points' throughout the education system

Month	Primary Schools	Secondary Schools	Higher Education
September	New start, new class, sometimes a new school	New start, new class, sometimes a new school Beginning of 2-year GCSE subjects for Years 10 and 11	New start in a completely new environment (and possibly city), with new systems Possible feelings of social anxiety
October			
November		Mock GCSE examinations	First assignment deadlines
December	Winter Festival Productions		
January	'Blue Monday' (see note in text)	Deadline for university applications (sixth form only) 'Blue Monday' (see note in text)	'Blue Monday' (see note in text)
February	Teacher assessments Key Stage 1		Return to campus Readjustment period
March		GCSE coursework BTEC coursework	
April		GCSE coursework BTEC coursework	Final year dissertation deadline
May	SATs	Revision for examinations	Final year dissertation deadline Revision for examinations Examinations and assessments including A level students in further education
June	Report writing	Examinations, especially for GCSE students and A level students within sixth form Report writing	Examinations and assessments, including A level students in further education
July	Transition period for Year 6 students, leaving primary and moving on to secondary school	Departure of final year students	Results made available, determining future courses and beginning of career progression
August	n/a	n/a	n/a

the second day of August, the fourth of September or even Christmas day could be equally depressing. The key element is that depression does not adhere to a calendar or schedule. So, avoid adding it to your annual list of 'pinch points' and question the validity of the message by seeking out evidence to support or refute it. A quick search of academic databases using the terms 'depression' and 'Blue Monday' swiftly revealed no peer-reviewed, data-driven research articles at all. It is important, however, that we do not confuse Blue Monday with 'winter depression', or seasonal affective disorder, to give it its correct term, which is a very real phenomenon, related to the time of year in a far wider sense and related to low levels of melatonin production as a partial consequence of lack of available daylight. A similar search of the academic databases will throw up a vast amount of peer-reviewed, data-driven research articles to support it, along with potential interventions or solutions to assist in reducing its deleterious effects.

12.13 THE NATIONAL CURRICULUM AND MENTAL HEALTH

In contextualising this section, the new National Curriculum was largely introduced in September 2014. English and Mathematics became operational a year later for Year 2, 6 and 10 students, while for Year 11 students this was the case from September 2016. The new curriculum for Personal, Social, Health and Economic Education (PSHE) was published in September 2013. As a non-statutory subject the publication maintains that 'Schools should seek to use PSHE education to build, where appropriate, on the statutory content already outlined in the national curriculum, the basic school curriculum and in statutory guidance on: drug education, financial education, sex and relationship education (SRE) and the importance of physical activity and diet for a healthy lifestyle (Department for Education, 2013). One might expect that MWB is embedded within this; however, while there is an underlying link, it is not made explicitly.

With this is mind, there was a call for MWB to be incorporated into the National Curriculum formally. Indeed, a petition was created online in July 2015, which aimed to introduce education in mental health into schools in order to equip children with the skills required to face the challenges that life might present to them, while reducing the stigma associated with mental ill-health at the same time (https://petition.parliament.uk/petitions/104545). As with all government petitions, this ran for a period of six months, closing in January 2016, and as is the norm, required 100,000 signatures in order for it to trigger a debate by members of parliament. It achieved 51,234 and thus failed to do so. While this would appear to be a missed opportunity, the Department for Education did provide funding to the PSHE Association, which provides dedicated support, resources, training and guidance for PSHE education professionals, to produce guidance on how to embed MWB into the curriculum (PSHE Association, 2015). This document provides advice on mental health and emotional wellbeing in each of the Key Stages. Table 12.5 below is an adapted representation of the four, much larger separate tables found in the original document. It appears here purely as an example and taster and we would recommend that you access the original as appropriate. You will note that what students should learn in later Key Stages is based on the premise that earlier Key Stages are used to provide stable foundations for development.

Table 12.5   Example guidance provided in PSHE Association Teacher Guidance Document on Mental Health

	Health and wellbeing	Relationships	Living in the wider world
	Students should have the opportunity to learn about:	Students should have the opportunity to learn about:	Students should have the opportunity to learn about:
Key Stage 1	Positive and negative feelings, how to describe those feelings and simple strategies for dealing with those feelings.	Communicating feelings with other people, recognising the feelings of other people and discovering appropriate ways to respond to the feelings of other people.	The needs of other people and other living things, along with the responsibilities to meet those needs by everyone.
Key Stage 2	Expanding their understanding of their feelings by increasing the vocabulary used to explain the variety and intensity of those feelings.	Identifying the constituents of positive healthy relationships, including how to develop and maintain them.	Health and wellbeing in society, by examining debates, challenges, topical issues and making recommendations about these.
Key Stage 3	The relationships between confidence, self-esteem and attitudes, personal qualities, achievements, acquired skills and how these may be interpreted by other people.	Developing and maintaining relationships by enhancing essential communication skills, such as active listening, providing and obtaining constructive feedback and assertiveness skills.	Developing an appreciation and understanding of similarities, differences and their impacts on societies, by examining sex, gender identity, culture and ethnicity, stereotyping and prejudice, discrimination and bullying.
Key Stage 4	Causes and characteristics of mental health, along with the development of effective management strategies, e.g., for anxiety, stress, depression, self-harm and suicide.	Developing an awareness of bullying, harassment and exploitation in relationships and effective strategies for responding to these, including cyber-bullying and abuse within relationships.	Approaches for evaluating personal strengths and challenges, through intervention strategies such as goal-setting.

Source: adapted from PSHE Association, (2015) : 6–10

12.14 WHEN TO 'REFER ON'?

When deciding whether or not to refer a student, there are two recommendations we would offer here and these are perhaps two sides of the same coin. Firstly, remain within the realms of your professional qualifications and, secondly, use what can only be described as a highly subjective, yet intuitively effective sense of your 'comfort zone'. We will discuss this latter point first, simply because it may seem controversial. Whether we use the term 'comfort zone', 'gut-feeling' or 'instinct' does not matter. What we are talking about here is whether you feel that you are acting within the realms of your (perceived) capabilities or whether you feel totally out of your depth. As a rule of thumb either of these can act as an indicator of whether you should refer on and, crucially, you should do so quickly. Let us illustrate with a case study illustrated in Table 12.6. Rather than using three different case studies, which would be rather straightforward, we have chosen to show how the referral process may operate with increasing levels of symptoms. Our student is 14 years old and has just entered the first year of GCSEs.

Table 12.6   Considerations for referring a student presenting to staff

	Presenting Issues	Comments	Refer On
1	Difficulties with social group at school. Continually falling out over minor 'differences of opinion'. Performance on schoolwork has started to drop. No other signs or areas of concern shown.	For the student's age group is this a common adolescence issue? Is performance dropping in all subjects? Check with relevant staff. Is this a 'bullying' case? (N.B. we are presenting it as non-bullying.)	No. Provide pastoral support to student. Involve other staff only as appropriate.
2	Difficulties with social group at school. Continually falling out over minor 'differences of opinion' and X is becoming increasingly isolated from social group, peers and friends outside of school. Performance on schoolwork has shown a marked drop across all subjects, homework is not being handed in and X is absent from lessons more than one day per week.	See above and: Invite student into office for a personal tutorial to discuss any issues. Consider speaking to all members of the social group to ascertain their perspective on the situation. Invite parent(s) into school to discuss the situation.	Yes. Inform Head or Head of Department and school counsellors. Inform Educational Psychologist of concerns if necessary.
3	Completely isolated from social group at school. X is absent from lessons most days per week and, when in attendance, shows signs of self-harm on arms and legs. Tells certain teachers that 'there is no point being alive anymore' and when confiding in them is frequently in tears. Physical appearance has changed, in terms of lack of hygiene, dirty clothing, little pride in appearance. Often overheard vomiting in the toilets.	See above and: Make contact with and assemble a support team as a matter of urgency. Provide the student with contact telephone numbers, or offer to make telephone calls on their behalf.	Yes. Inform GP, Educational Psychologist, Clinical Psychologist as a matter of urgency.

It is your professional qualifications that ultimately act as your level of protection. Remaining within professional boundaries will provide this protection (assuming you have conducted yourself appropriately of course), should you need it (*Teachers' Standards*, Department for Education, 2013). In terms of continuing professional development (CPD), there are of course areas where expertise may be lacking that you can then target for development, which will naturally enable you to extend your capabilities and in turn widen your skill-set. The consequence of this would usually be that you create a wider, broader or deeper 'comfort zone'.

We like to keep a simple phrase in mind, when MWB cases emerge:

'Whatever you do, do something'

Or even just

'Act!'

This serves as an opportunity to assess the student and his or her issue, assess your pastoral support role and where it ends, assess your capabilities to deal with the issue and finally assess 'relevant others' who may need to be made aware of the issue. There is of course an element of confidentiality here, if a student has told you something in confidence, but equally there is an element of responsibility, on your behalf, to report issues where threat of harm (to the student or others) is a possibility.

Each of these questions deals with the 'what' of what to do, but not the 'when' element. It may be that referring on to someone with the appropriate level of expertise to help has been established, but in the short term ('short term' is determined by your own judgement and on a case-by-case basis) the student may benefit from your pastoral support in helping them to take the next step of seeing someone else. It may be that you ask to be included in the process as it progresses, or where this is not possible for professional or confidentiality reasons, that you are provided with some form of updates, with whatever information can be made available to you. This is certainly the case within counselling, where you would be suggesting to a student that they sign a 'freedom to disclose information' form, which would enable the counsellor to keep you updated on progress. In our experience, we are noticing a trend for students in higher education to see no reason not to sign such a form, since there appears to be far less of a stigma attached to MWB issues than say, 20 years ago.

12.15 DIGITAL OR E-MENTAL HEALTH: BENEFITS, CHALLENGES AND IMPLICATIONS

As we mentioned earlier in this chapter, both adults and children are spending what appears to be increasing amounts of time on digital media, to the extent that it is now seen as commonplace. Indeed, this is evident in higher education every day of the working week. It is common for lecturing staff to stand at the lectern and be faced with a sea of laptops or tablets in the audience, almost to the point where an A4 pad and a pen are seemingly redundant as a form of note-taking. This phenomenon was unheard of even five years ago and would, previously, have been frowned upon as a distraction away from the lecture and the speaker, rather than as an aid to learning. Of course, we are aware that social media platforms are being accessed during lectures, which of course is not conducive to learning, but there is certainly an acceptance that technology cannot be removed from the learning environment. It is quite common in the classroom for adventurous teachers to make use of e-technology within sessions in order to retain focus, motivation, entertainment and to foster learning. Access to downloadable journal articles and books, specific to MWB, can be almost immediate and this certainly helps to facilitate learning. In staff meetings, the tablet is now increasingly more popular and has similar benefits in terms of efficiency-saving, information-providing resource acquisitions. Equally, in the classroom at primary and secondary level, the use of tablets has increased, to the extent where children in some regions have what we would argue is the privilege and luxury of having tablets allocated to them in the longer term, compared to 'the good old days' (e.g., Kim et al., 2016; Korenova, 2015; Van Hove et al., 2017). As an anecdote, we recall the days when accessing journal articles not held in the university library necessitated completing an inter-library loan form, which required a signature of approval, waiting up to two weeks for it to arrive, before being able to read and work on it, along with no more than six other requests. This involved much planning ahead and frustration during the waiting period. In contrast, a search on the library databases, or even a generic search engine, usually provides a multitude of options and opportunities with great ease. There is no waiting, no forward planning and perhaps most efficiently – if the article turns out to be less relevant than originally thought, there is little time wasted.

In this respect, digital technology goes far beyond providing information at the click of a mouse. In relation to MWB, it provides materials, support platforms and *fora* (as in the plural of 'forum') almost as if it were a personal e-assistant. We highlighted evidence earlier to suggest that people are somewhat reluctant to use digital technology as a replacement for face-to-face support. There is something comforting in knowing (or perceiving that one knows) the person providing the support. A 'virtual practitioner' is just not the same. While this may be the perception of older adults (we are not specifying a particular age range here), advances in technology, through video-conferencing platforms, enable people to communicate while seeing each other face-to-face. As a learner, I (Paul Castle) take regular 'remote' French language lessons with my teacher, Olivia, who lives 360 miles away in Brussels. We both sit at our laptops in the comfort of our respective homes and finish one hour later. For me, there is nowhere to hide! Each lesson is so challenging and exhausting, yet so rewarding and confidence inspiring. Broadband speeds are efficient and the connection is predictable and usually consistent (ironically and with a little humour, 'buffering' would offer a few seconds of respite but this rarely happens). As a practitioner psychologist, i.e., with the shoe on the other foot, I have taken the knowledge acquired through using such straightforward video technology and applied it to my consultancy work. In embracing this technology, I have been able to provide support on MWB to clients far further away than without using it. The beauty is that multiple information sources can be accessed; copy and paste can be used to send material, images and worksheets directly or by email; and a transfer of completed materials can be returned, frequently even for discussion during a session. There is something satisfying about this and it fosters a sense of working in the present, while providing material for the future. In this way, both client and practitioner work on the challenge as a unit. For instance, they might work on a questionnaire, which appears on both computer screens at the same time, so that it becomes more like a conversation, rather than a questionnaire. Results are obtained immediately, along with a summary piece of prose explaining what the results mean. An example of this can be seen with a robust personality questionnaire I have completed (both in English and in French) from www.16personalities.com (see Cattell et al., 1993), which sets the tone for further discussions on MWB with clients.

The *caveat* of course is to remember that face-to-face interaction was discussed earlier as being preferred to 'remote', e-interaction. The question is, however, whether video-conferencing is perceived by the interlocutors as 'remote'. It goes without saying that an e-mental health platform is not recommended for teachers to use with students, but rather that it is a potential tool for personal MWB.

12.16 CONCLUSION

We have established the importance of MWB in this chapter, through a wide variety of sources. Significant opportunities have been provided for you to explore your own MWB needs and we have suggested how you may incorporate this experiential learning into the classroom, in order that your students may develop similar strengths. In the following chapter, we explore the topics of positive coaching psychology and the development of resilience. In the absence of developing MWB strengths, resilience would be difficult in the extreme. When taken in the context of developing these strengths, resilience is more likely to emerge and this is the challenge we face in the next chapter.

12.17 FURTHER READING

For information on the IAPT programme currently in operation within England please visit www.england.nhs.uk/mental-health/adults/iapt/ (accessed 6 October 2017). *The Psychologist*, 22 (5) contains two additional papers that are relevant to the IAPT programme and are worth reading in conjunction with the Marzillier and Hall papers (2009a and 2009b).

Roffey, S. (2015) 'Becoming an agent of change for school and student well-being', *Educational & Child Psychology*, 32 (1): 21–30.
This paper explores the role of educational psychologists and additional support in enhancing MWB in schools. It is also linked to the next chapter, on developing resilience.

NB: We would recommend that in the first instance, your reading results from accessing the web links provided. Follow the areas that interest you personally, or share the reading load with your peers in order to build up a collective knowledge-base in your school.

13

COACHING PSYCHOLOGY AND DEVELOPING RESILIENCE

CHAPTER OBJECTIVES

- Understand the different ways of defining and conceptualising resilience.
- Understand the relationship between MWB and resilience in a variety of contexts, and relate knowledge of these to the classroom.

TEACHERS' STANDARDS

A teacher must:

5   Adapt teaching to respond to the strengths and needs of all pupils

- demonstrate an awareness of the physical, social and intellectual development of children, and know how to adapt teaching to support pupils' education at different stages of development
- have a clear understanding of the needs of all pupils, including those with special educational needs; those of high ability; those with English as an additional language; those with disabilities; and be able to use and evaluate distinctive teaching approaches to engage and support them

8   Fulfil wider professional responsibilities

- take responsibility for improving teaching through appropriate professional development, responding to advice and feedback from colleagues
- communicate effectively with parents with regard to pupils' achievements and well-being

13.1 INTRODUCTION

Having considered MWB in the previous chapter, it is now possible in this chapter to explore the links between MWB, developing resilience and the role of coaching psychology in this process. In the following section, we will explore applied techniques from the realms of psychological skills training to provide guidance on the 'how to…' element of this section.

13.2 CONTEXTUALISING RESILIENCE

Drop-out rates in the teaching profession have become an internationally recognised problem. It has been reported that 70 per cent of Canadian teachers leave within the first five years and 50 per cent within the first two years of service (see Carsenti and Collin, 2013). Carsenti and Collin contrast this with findings elsewhere, showing that 46 per cent of teachers in the USA leave within the first five years, while the attrition rate in the UK is 40 per cent within the first three years, with rates in France and Germany being significantly less, postulated to be due to the non-accountability of teachers for their failing pupils (cf. Carsenti and Collin, 2013). Findings such as these are now being mirrored at the beginning of the process, in the UK, where government-set recruitment targets have not been met in the last five years (House of Commons Education Committee, 2017). Female teachers between the ages of 30 and 39 are most likely to leave within two years of training, falling far short of the 5 and 8 years required to develop into an 'experienced' teacher (Newton, 2016).

On the flipside of the coin, 92 per cent of students entering higher education have reported experiencing what has been termed 'mental distress', with 20 per cent disclosing mental health issues (Macintosh and Shaw, 2017). Not only is this of concern to all higher education institutions: it is a sign of the times and perhaps provides some insight into just how resilient our early career personnel might be as they enter our challenging profession. We pick this up in more detail elsewhere in the chapter.

13.3 THE ORIGINS OF COACHING PSYCHOLOGY

As the discipline of psychology has evolved since its inception, so too have its sub-disciplines established themselves more widely. In the UK, the Special Group in Coaching Psychology (SGCP) emerged in 2004 from the previous Coaching Psychology Forum (CPF), which aimed to improve and promote standards within the profession. The SGCP provides a platform for the sharing and dissemination of research and practice in all aspects of the psychology of coaching for coaching psychologists and for those coaches who wish to use psychology in their coaching. It is one of eight internationally recognised professional coaching psychology bodies (British Psychological Society, 2017). Examples of recent research within the SGCP can be seen in the June 2017 edition of the *Coaching Psychologist*, which includes: an article on mindfulness in coaching (Passmore, 2017); an article on 'conversational mapping', which aims to simplify theory in a non-technical way, in order to facilitate effective communication between coach and client (Grant, 2017); an article on the role that coaching practitioners adopt in working with mental health issues (Corrie, 2017); followed by a book review on Gestalt coaching (Laughlin, 2017). Links have been made to show that emotion coaching as a strategy for promoting MWB in schools helps to develop empathy in the adult–child relationship, by having an awareness of a child's emotions, recognising emotion-based opportunities for teaching, utilising empathic listening, normalising emotions and providing safe boundaries within which to operate (Gus et al., 2015).

In adopting a coaching psychology approach, we now have clarity, yet at the same time we have overlap. Or is it perceived overlap? If there is overlap, where should one draw the line? That is, at what point does a topic that is firmly within the realm of one sub-discipline become the 'property' of another? Let's put it another way using the example of the following case study.

CASE STUDY   John

John is a 13-year-old student who has recently told his friends that he feels 'really low, down and depressed'. He has felt like this for around three months but hasn't mentioned it until now. He has slipped back at school and is no longer performing to his ability, according to his teachers, in most subjects. His friends have mentioned that 'he is sick a lot', which you now know means that he often vomits in the toilets after eating. He has started to isolate himself at school in the last two weeks and you have noticed that his appearance is more unkempt than it used to be.

Should one enlist the support of a clinical psychologist, an educational psychologist, a coaching psychologist, a health psychologist, a sport and exercise psychologist, a social psychologist or a cognitive (neuro) psychologist? The correct answer, in an ideal world, would be to enlist as many of these as is appropriate! Of course, we do not operate in an ideal world and so our guidance would be to enlist as many of these as is expedient, given the constraints of any budget. Multidisciplinary working is always more effective than working in isolation. Let us assume, at this juncture, that John is not experiencing any neurological or neuropsychological deficits. A key factor will be the point at which one becomes aware of John's symptoms and his ensuing needs. A clinical psychologist would not be appropriate and indeed would not be available, if John was in the early stages of his situation. Similarly, an educational psychologist would only be called on at a particular point, where the school becomes increasingly concerned about John's welfare. A sport and exercise psychologist may be available to offer guidance on MWB through the realms of sport or physical activity, and there is a wealth of research to suggest potential ways that this could help.

A brief literature search on the relationship between depression and neurotransmitters in the brain reveals a significant body of work; among these, we discovered a meta-analysis of studies examining effects of probiotic supplements on the two-way communication channel between the central nervous system and the gastrointestinal tract, known commonly as the 'gut–brain axis' (Wallace and Milev, 2017). Would John benefit from an intervention that adopts this approach to his issues? Would specialists in other disciplines of psychology even be aware that probiotic supplements may ameliorate symptoms of depression? How would we reconcile this with John being sick in the toilets? Alternatively, a search on the antidepressant effect of physical activity can be found, for example, in systematic review articles examining type of activity and amount or 'dosage' (Nyström et al., 2015). We will return to Nyström et al. (2015) in the section on physical activity elsewhere in this chapter.

Coaching psychology was borne out of a need to offer expertise that was not strictly clinical, i.e., it did not require the expert knowledge of psychological disorders. It acts perhaps as the preventative measure before issues become clinical. This is reflected in the findings that 98 per cent of coaching psychologists in a recent survey stated the importance of being able to detect poor mental health in clients and 88 per cent had a desire to receive additional training related to mental health issues (Corrie, 2017). In terms of this chapter, MWB is not positive/negative, on/off, good/bad. It is a fluctuating state and every one of us will move along or around different points at different times of our lives, or even within a single day. Using the analogy of wakefulness, some days we feel more awake than others, or more awake at a certain point in one day than another point. Interestingly, even during sleep, we are all more asleep at some points during the sleep cycle than others (search engine term: 'ultradian rhythms'). MWB is conceptually similar, insofar as neither is it possible to have none!

13.4 INTEGRATION OF COACHING PSYCHOLOGY WITH COUNSELLING, CLINICAL AND EDUCATIONAL PSYCHOLOGY

As there would seem to be a significant area of overlap between these sub-disciplines of psychology, pointed out above, one must consider how each sub-discipline can enmesh itself with its counterparts, in order to provide solutions to challenges. In aiming to facilitate an element of 'protection' or 'protective layer', through knowledge acquisition, one can understand how the term 'resilience' has emerged, especially in the realms of sport, business and in the military. We now move on to begin exploring resilience in a thematic manner, focusing on resilience as an overarching theme, followed by an exploration of resilience in teaching, in students training to become teachers and in children who are required to build resilience skills. The common factor in each of these groups is that the rigours of day-to-day life require resilience. Without it, challenges become struggles, struggles become fatiguing and ultimately there is a danger of being unable to cope, with an ensuing sense of 'drowning' in one's problems.

13.5 WHAT EXACTLY IS RESILIENCE?

Such a simple question! Unfortunately, it does not have a simple answer, but then we imagine that you already knew this would be the case. Resilience means many different things to many different people. Is it being hardened to the pressures experienced in daily life? Is it being able to continue in the face of adversity? Is it taking on more and more roles and responsibilities without 'cracking'? Is it stamina, endurance and the sheer determination to succeed? Is it the ability to bounce back after a challenge that was too large? Is it dealing with failure in a positive way? We will explore definitions shortly, but in short, yes, perhaps it is all of these, or any combination of these things. This leads us to ask the question: who is resilient, or is more resilient than other people? Elite athletes and sports performers? Military personnel in life-threatening environments and/or situations? Medical professionals carrying out life-saving procedures on patients? Business people, chasing financial rewards or securing the big deal? Teachers facing challenges linked to the education of our future adults? Did you just stop reading and wonder why the word 'teachers' was included in this list? If you did, you are perhaps correct in questioning its inclusion. Nevertheless, we would argue that there are huge similarities among them, to some extent or other. For instance, who spends long hours, day in, day out, constantly striving to operate at their best? Any of these groups! Who performs or adopts a role that they have trained for and who must overcome the issues faced by those who are at the other end of the performance? Any of these groups! The important point here is that there are shared qualities in each of these professions, along with many more professions (we did not wish to labour the point by creating an exhaustive list); and often, teachers do not see these qualities in themselves. If you did not possess these qualities, you would not have got to where you are today.

13.6 FACING MENTAL WELLBEING CHALLENGES BY DEVELOPING RESILIENCE

In exploring definitions of resilience, we will offer a variety, from the various fields mentioned above, in order to establish similarities, along with any nuanced differences among them. Having made the professional transition from student to qualified teacher, the following definition seems to be rather practical and useful to bear in mind. Madewell and Ponce-Garcia suggest that resilience is: 'The capacity of an individual to maintain normative, or positive, development in the presence of risk' (Madewell and Ponce-Garcia, 2016: 250). This infers that an element of equilibrium is necessary when choice means taking 'risks'. Gu and Day (2013) couch their definition in terms of experiencing resilience as it relates to capacity; hence the experience of resilience is 'perceived as being closely allied to their [teachers'] everyday capacity to sustain their educational purposes' and 'successfully manage the unavoidable uncertainties which are inherent in the practice of being a teacher' (Gu and Day, 2013: 22).

A report produced by Unite Students, in collaboration with YouGov and YouthSight, in 2017, based on 2016 data, explored key non-academic elements of student life that impact on higher education students' studies (Macintosh and Shaw, 2017). While this report would view resilience as an element, rather than an umbrella term, it does identify both positive and negative contributory features related to life satisfaction, which are pertinent. Positive elements include confidence and support networks, i.e., friends, family and support from the university, through its support services, tutors, counsellors, etc. Acting against these positive elements are feelings of isolation and desperation, social life stress, university (study) life stress and any pre-existing MWB issues. The authors call for further urgent exploration of resilience in higher education and the implementation of a series of practical steps: embedding resilience into everyday interactions with students; creating a 'Resilience Toolkit', to be adopted across all higher education institutions; exploring all potential areas where resilience can be developed, such as teachers, parents, peers, the living and learning environment, as well as the more obvious teaching and support services mentioned earlier; and adopting an integrated approach that takes place in synergy with approaches developing in primary and secondary education, in order to promote resilient adults, as we outlined in Chapter 13.

The resilient student 'embodies a set of identified characteristics ("internal factors") and makes use of them in order to bounce back from setbacks and difficult situations' (Macintosh and Shaw, 2017: 8). An interplay between internal and external factors exists, whereby self-management and emotional control (internal) cohabit the space with social integration, social support and support networks. The ability to bounce back emerges from the complex interplay between these factors, with willpower and self-control emerging, from the report, as noteworthy elements.

The Unite Students report acknowledges the fact that its data was concerned with non-academic issues related to student life, in a wider sense, and that little by way of literature exists that has explored the development of resilience external to the classroom context. It seems that we may all have been looking in the wrong place, or, at the very least, should explore the interplay between the academic and non-academic. The report recommends that we adopt a new perspective on resilience, and indeed this is something that has been happening at the University of Worcester in recent years (see Section 13.11 below).

Lawton-Smith (2017) provides an excellent and articulate exposition of resilience in the context of a study which combines resilience, coaching psychology and leadership. The study in itself is fascinating and provides insight into the semantics used by 'resilient senior leaders' and how resilience integrates into existing leadership and organisational frameworks. It is worth spending time discussing this paper here.

Smith argues that it is difficult to define and pinpoint resilience, unless one is clear about the nuances in current literature, which would appear to align with three distinct approaches: asset approach, systemic approach and developmental approach. This is helpful in directing the reader to identify the type of approach adopted, when searching for relevant journal articles. The asset approach, perhaps the most commonly perceived and once intuitively favoured approach, sees resilience as a list, rather like a list of ingredients in making a cake, such as a Black Forest gateau. If all of the ingredients are present, the final outcome will be as intended. If the kirsch is missing, it becomes a simple matter of ensuring that kirsch is added next time. Similarly, any missing resilience ingredients can be identified, e.g., self-esteem, and can then be instilled or installed so that the gap has been filled. While this would seem to be a rational idea, it is actually less than ideal, insofar as it fails to take a wide range of internal and external factors into account. Resilience is more than simply acquiring a list of attributes. Equally, it is misleading to assume that, having acquired the attributes, that they are enduring and useable at any given point in time. In resilience terms, there must be something more. The systemic approach addresses this need to move away from assets, in the direction of dynamics, by taking internal, psychological and biopsychological factors and integrating these with exogenous factors, such as social support, Smith suggests. The developmental approach is an extension of the systemic approach, but is seen as 'relative, emerging and changing in transaction with specific circumstances and challenges' (Lawton-Smith, 2017: 10). What Smith is referring to here is that the person not only adapts to new challenges, but also learns to become more adaptable with each challenge. It is the learning element that takes centre stage, rather than simply adaptation. In this way, resilience is perhaps akin to flexibility in different circumstances, and flexibility leads to learning how to use transferable skills to enhance this, which then promotes ease of adaptation.

13.7 RESILIENCE IN SPORT AND BUSINESS RESEMBLES RESILIENCE IN EDUCATION

In business, resilience is perceived to be about bouncing back after setbacks and doing so with a positive mindset. This is equally the case in sport, where athletes and performers learn from failure in order to become mentally stronger in future competitions and events. People in these spheres of life talk in terms of 'being knocked down and getting back up again' – there is a 'never give up' mindset. Challenges do not sap resources, rather they fuel resources. Any student teacher or newly qualified teacher should be able to identify with this mindset, or at least should do, now that we have drawn parallels. As the equivalent to an endurance athlete, you do have the resources to deal with the challenge. Knowing how best to allocate those resources is the key to ongoing development and, ultimately, to success. We will examine these areas briefly and also delve into the literature on military psychology relating to resilience, in order to help us formulate a clearer picture of themes that emerge in each of these spheres.

13.8 RESILIENCE IN BUSINESS

In business, resilience is the domain of the individual, yet equally there is a notion of 'organisational resilience' (Chen, 2016), which relates to the adaptability of an organisation to the challenges it faces. This embodies a sense of personification in companies that gives them a life-force of their own. In an ideal world, educational establishments bear a strong resemblance to businesses and one would hope that the metaphor would operate equally well. Chen identified five factors of organisational resilience in R&D (research and development) teams: shared vision, willingness to learn, adaptation ability, cooperation awareness and work enthusiasm. Each of these map onto primary, secondary and tertiary education appropriately. These factors combine to produce organisational resilience and, as Chen highlights, resemble self-evaluations from individual members, contributing to the overall team (Chen, 2016). Unsurprisingly, in line with our positive attitude towards the importance of resilience, resilience training has emerged in a recent systematic review of workplace resilience training, as being beneficial to mental health, as personal resilience develops (Robertson et al., 2015).

The theme of workplace resilience emerges and there is an element of commonality among the external factors of social support, social relationships and social integration, where everyone involved is in it together. Think in terms of Seligman's 'learned help-lessness' (Seligman, 1973) and you will be misunderstanding our point. It is not a case of everyone experiencing what are perceived to be the overwhelming demands of the job, but rather a shared appreciation and understanding of the job that is required of us. Accordingly, the very people we work with are important in providing support because they understand too. A support network of this type is a significant contribution to resilience-building and sits nicely with the dual nature of resilience and relationships proposed by the relational coordination theory, from social psychology, which pairs up the psychosocial elements associated with support, alongside the technical elements associated with the role of the job (Gittell, 2016). It is not uncommon these days for companies in the corporate sector to employ a 'Wellbeing Director' or 'Head of Wellbeing' and this concept is being trialled by Nuffield Health Care, in the education sector (Paton, 2015).

A noteworthy study that examined the effectiveness of different resilience training delivery formats discovered that one-to-one delivery was more effective than group delivery sessions, which in turn were more effective than train-the-trainer or computer-based resilience programmes (Vanhove et al., 2016).

Wood (2016) advises that a little caution is aired while considering exactly how much 'scaffolding' should be put in place by institutions as support, highlighting that students of today are different from those in the past, the stressors for students have changed and that providing too much support does not necessarily help students to establish resilience and indeed independence. While this is a controversial point, we can understand that a framework of support, which facilitates flexibility for self-discovery and self-help, may better promote resilience. Wood's notion of a supportive learning environment echoes what many of us would argue to be of huge importance in the business of education prevalent today.

13.9 RESILIENCE IN SPORT AND PHYSICAL ACTIVITY

Sport is perhaps the most common place where one would expect to find resilience. We hear of professional sports people 'pushing the limits', winning gold, achieving new world records, performing feats of endurance previously unheard of and so forth. Equally, recreational sports people display levels of resilience, perhaps not to the same extent, but certainly of a similar kind. The recreational jogger who only started six months ago shows resilience in completing a half marathon. The cardiac rehabilitation patient who has taken up cycling to help with the recovery programme shows resilience. The child struggling with an obesity issue and has started using a Nintendo Wii Fit shows resilience, as does the teacher trying to balance work-life with exercise in order to keep going until the end of term.

Russell (2015) argues that resilience is a central virtue both in sport and in life. In understanding resilience, Russell suggests that the contribution of sport to wellbeing and culture becomes apparent. In adopting a philosophical perspective, he suggests that resilience is reflected in a particularly arduous, challenging and adverse set of circumstances. His paper refers to several sporting anecdotes of teams or individuals bouncing back from the significant setbacks, and it is well worth a read for those readers who may take more of a philosophical interest in this perspective on resilience. Russell highlights nine elements of adversity that help to foster resilience: training skills, performance, competitive strategy, destructive emotions, coordinating teamwork, injuries, bad luck, losses and pain, and waning capacities (2015: 168). Experiencing challenge in or through each of these serves to make the individual stronger psychologically. Resilience, Russell argues, begins in failure. Such a statement is certainly transferable to education, for students and for teachers, and should be borne in mind during times of adversity. A practical mantra is perhaps, 'This will make me stronger, this will make me stronger', and links nicely with the material discussed on positive psychology, in this chapter. A paper by Secades et al. (2016) echoes this, in stating that in the absence of adversity and of adaptation (coping) to adversity in a positive way, resilience cannot be expected to develop. This would suggest that seeking out adversity is a worthwhile exercise. In one sense, there is little difference between this and the fundamental principles of inoculation against disease, or even Stress Inoculation Training (SIT) (Meichenbaum, 1977) for that matter.

Gabana (2017) provides an excellent piece of advice, in saying that those people who wish to develop resilience in their sport might seek to develop it in their life.

Equally those people wishing to develop resilience in their lives might seek to use sport as a vehicle to do so. The transferable nature of skills is mutually inclusive, rather than exclusively domain-specific. Similarly, Roncaglia (2017) acknowledges the role of sport psychology, not only in helping athletes, but also in the transferable skills that it can offer to other groups, in her study examining Seligman's PERMA model (Seligman, 2011) in children with autistic spectrum conditions (ASCs). Seligman's model refers to a set of 'flourishing domains' relating to positive wellbeing: positive emotions, engagement, relationships, meaning and accomplishment. Roncaglia shows how the case studies detailed in her paper have benefited from the integration of sport psychology with positive psychology for use within an educational psychology setting.

Readiness to change and engagement in training have been postulated as key elements of strengths-based approaches both in sport and in the military, with mental toughness, positive emotion, learned optimism, resilience, post-traumatic growth, and self- and emotion regulation being significant attributes of operating in extreme sporting or military situations (Wagstaff and Leach, 2015). The authors highlight the growing interest in looking to both sport psychology and military psychology for commonality. It must be pointed out that in sport psychology the favoured term previously was 'mental toughness', as seen in various works (e.g., Connaughton et al., 2011; Gucciardi and Gordon, 2011) and which developed in different stages of a sports performer's career. Previously, Daniel Gucciardi had examined mental toughness in cricketers, developing the Cricket Mental Toughness Inventory (CMTI) (Gucciardi and Gordon, 2009), followed by examining mental toughness profiles of adolescent Australian and New Zealand cricketers (Gucciardi and Jones, 2012). It is now widely considered that resilience is an ingredient of mental toughness. In reality, the term 'resilience' far better sums up the concept than the more nebulous umbrella term 'mental toughness'. Interestingly, the emerging issue of sports officiating, where dropout rates among referees, umpires, etc. have risen and are a global trend, has led to research into resilience, motivation and perceived levels of support in this sports group. Alongside moderate to high resilience levels, thematic analysis suggested that officials' resilience was a key factor in their effectiveness in the role, highlighting the importance of experience and support from fellow officials in bolstering resilience (Livingston and Forbes, 2017). A strong support shone through as a theme, and the protective factors necessary to undertake the role were similar to those discussed in this chapter.

Resilience in exercise, or physical activity, which for the purposes of this chapter we view as an umbrella term encapsulating all forms of non-sedentary activity, can perhaps best be inferred by examining factors that impede resilience. One such factor is depression. Arguably, an individual who is experiencing high levels of resilience will not be experiencing depression. Equally, an individual who is experiencing depression will not be feeling very resilient. In addressing the issue of depression, one should be able to establish higher levels of resilience. This subsection focuses, therefore, on physical activity and its indirect relationship with resilience. In doing so, we have chosen to consider recent systematic reviews, which, in our opinion, hold a considerable amount of important information that can be used by teachers in a number of different ways, whether this is from a self-help perspective, or from a helping-others perspective.

Nyström et al. (2015), mentioned at the beginning of this chapter, carried out a systematic review of the literature in physical activity, examining the type of activity and the amount required (the 'dosage') to have an effect on reducing depression. Aerobic activities, such as walking or jogging and cycling were the most common respectively, with weightlifting among the only two anaerobic activities. The authors discovered that 30–45-minute sessions were most common, during a period of 12–16 weeks. Interestingly, they found that sessions lasting 90 minutes did not ameliorate the effects of depression any more than the shorter sessions. This is excellent news for busy teachers, who frequently say that they do not have the time for exercise. It is not about quantity! We would recommend this journal article for the reader who wishes to discover a little more about the findings outlined in this review. Rebar et al. (2015) point out that many reviews have explored depression in clinical populations. As a result, their systematic review of non-clinical populations showed that physical activity has a moderate effect in ameliorating the effects of depression, along with a less strong effect on reducing anxiety. In a separate, specific, systematic review, physical activity has also been found to have low to moderate effects on depression in cardiac rehabilitation patients, for whom depression is a potential consequence of coronary artery events (Janzon et al., 2015).

Finally, we discovered an interesting review by Li et al. (2016), who examined the literature in relation to the concept of physical activity and computer-game technology, with the enticing title: 'Effect of exergames on depression'. The underlying message contained in this review of the literature is twofold. Firstly, exergames are a young person's technology and can be used to improve physical activity levels, compared to baseline. Secondly, the older generation can make more use of exergames as a means of overcoming a sedentary lifestyle, or where lack of local facilities, or safety concerns, restrict or prohibit exercise. Each of these reviews has one common factor. Exercise or physical activity is beneficial in ameliorating depression and, while doing so, equally fosters a sense of resilience and a sense of wellbeing; not to mention the social support, relationships and social integration involved in many types of physical activities, with the possible exception of exergaming (although even this could possibly be linked to the multi-player idea of social integration).

13.10 RESILIENCE IN MILITARY SETTINGS

One might wonder whether there is a need to include a section on military settings in a text on psychology for teachers. We would argue that, while there are few similarities between the classroom and 'theatres of war', conceptually, the protective factors that link the two are remarkably similar. We will not provide an exhaustive literature review here, but merely offer some examples that support our intentions, while at the same time perhaps asking us all to consider whether the challenges we face are indeed that big an issue in the grand scheme of things.

Resilience training is imperative in the military, in order to ensure that personnel are able to operate effectively under extremely adverse circumstances. They are trained rigorously to acquire the necessary skills before entering operational duties. The American military have implemented the Comprehensive Soldier Fitness Program (CSF) (Casey, 2011), which is based in part on the Global Assessment Tool (GAT); an internet-based psychometric tool designed to test one million respondents per annum (Peterson et al., 2011), to which we will return in the section on education; alongside the Connor–Davidson Resilience Scale (CD-RISC) (Connor and Davidson, 2003), which measures five factors: personal competence, standards and tenacity; trust, tolerance of negative affect and stress; acceptance of change and strong relationships; control; and spirituality. This psychometric tool has recently been revised for use with Chinese military personnel, for whom the original version was culturally inappropriate, leading to the formation of three factors instead of five – competency, toughness, adaptability – and showing favourable validity and reliability (Xie et al., 2016). For an alternative and extremely thought-provoking perspective on the efficacy of the CSF, we would draw your attention to an article, previously rejected for a special issue of the *American Psychologist* in 2011 but now published elsewhere in the interests of parity (Pilisuk and Mahr, 2015).

Cacioppo et al. (2015) highlight the focus of studies being on individual resilience, while neglecting social resilience – the development of resilience through positive relationships and camaraderie that exist in the military. Social Resilience Training (SRT) aims to reduce inappropriate social cognitions and reduce feelings of isolation and loneliness. Cacioppo et al. (2015) found that SRT did indeed improve social cognitions, increasing empathy, hardiness, adopting perspectives, belief in social skills and their use along with reduced feelings of isolation and loneliness. Each of these elements readily transfers to other occupations to some degree or other. There is much to be learned from exploring the literature involving military studies, and transfer of findings to other domains would appear to be significantly worth the foray into this fascinating field of psychology. Bryan and Heron (2015) discuss the importance of belongingness, in the context of reducing depression in military personnel. A cohesive group with common, shared goals is achieved in part through social support and this is beneficial for fostering individual resilience and social resilience.

The importance of family support under differing conditions of threat while on deployment is highlighted wonderfully in the following statement from a paper examining self-efficacy, family support and threat engagement: 'During deployment, service members are confronted with a range of stressors. The encounter with enemy troops, incoming mortar fire, roadside bombs, and other life-threatening situations are the most conspicuous situations that come to mind. However, service members also have to deal with boredom, restricting rules of engagement, separation from the home front and organizational bureaucracy when on deployment' (Delahaij et al., 2016: 78). While 'enemy troops, incoming mortar fire, roadside bombs and other life-threatening situations' have no place in the world of the teacher, if one considers them as metaphors for education, then reinterpretation becomes rather intriguing. Delahaij et al. discovered that it is advantageous to retain high levels of self-efficacy under conditions of extreme stress, that family support is a factor in achieving this and that work-engagement (being more productive) is enhanced. This is yet another message from our foray into the military that is transferable for our needs in education. If you are single, have little or no family support, don't worry. Our advice would be to reinterpret the term 'family support' to suit your own set of circumstances and create or access a support network that functions appropriately for your needs. Let's face it: the entire teaching profession would crumble if we – none of us – was party to the 'sharing society' that we have created as teachers. One only needs to look at the internet to see electronic examples of this in operation.

In a qualitative study examining psychosocial adjustment to the loss of limbs in female military personnel, several protective factors were deemed to play a role in fostering resilience: positive attitude; social support, especially within a military context (similar to Wood's (2016) comment within the medical profession); recognition of what could have happened; sense of humour; and establishing meaning from their loss (Cater, 2012). Adaptive, situation-appropriate coping strategies can be developed through self-reflection practices. Systematic self-reflection practices have been postulated as an important strategy in Australian military recruits and is viewed not as a drain on an individual's psychological resources, but rather as something that facilitates growth and development in the individual experiencing adversity (Crane and Boga, 2017). They propose five systematic self-reflection practices: recollection of critical incidents; coping values and goals; evaluation of effectiveness; analysis of why/why not effective; approach to future stressors. By reflecting in this systematic manner, individuals should become more resilient as they deal with adverse situations and 'engaging in self-reflection of this type is also proposed to influence the motivational system in a way that encourages stressor engagement' (Crane and Boga, 2017: 32). There are similarities from this that one can readily transfer into the educational domain, simply be redefining what is meant by 'recollection of critical incident'.

An interesting paper by Courtney (2015) grabbed our attention, insofar as it introduced the concept of HeartMath, an approach to stress-resilience by balancing the body's emotional and physiological responses to stressful situations. Essentially, by changing heart rate variability, coherence is achieved as change in the body's physiology enables stability in thinking, as emotions reach equilibrium. The aspect that struck us as interesting was mention of the need to move between 'theatres of war' and 'civilian life' in the most effective/least-destructive manner psychologically. In education, this echoes the need to transition between work-life and home-life, or between term-time and vacation-time, in order to maximise the recovery period in readiness for the next stint of duty. Courtney suggests that the concept should be adopted by agencies outside of the military. The education setting would seem to be the perfect opportunity to embrace this.

In finishing this section, we opted to include a paper examining the perceived barriers to initiating and continuing mental health treatment in an army cohort where a risk and resilience programme is in operation (Naifeh et al., 2016). Naifeh et al. explored perceived need, structural reasons and attitudinal reasons as perceived barriers to support. Perceived need was seen, as one might expect, as whether a need to seek support existed in participants. We would perhaps see this as analogous to a 'burying one's head in the sand' approach. Structural reasons were seen as more day-to-day issues, such as appointment scheduling or financial constraints. Attitudinal reasons were seen as having negative perceptions of mental health support or a perceived stigma associated with needing or accessing it. The authors found that 70 per cent of 744 respondents perceived no need to seek support. Equally, of those 208 participants who did perceive a need, 80.7 per cent cited an attitudinal reason for not seeking support and 62.7 per cent reported a structural reason. In short, barriers prevented the participants from accessing the appropriate level of support and this is largely related to the stigma associated with mental health. As teachers, we should be aware of articles that highlight the barriers to us and we should then seek ways to overcome those barriers so that the support that is available can be used to help us on our journey through our educational careers.

13.11 RESILIENCE IN EDUCATION

Within education, it is acknowledged that resilience training is necessary in facilitating MWB, by providing adaptive coping strategies that children can use on their progress through education. The SPARK Resilience programme (Boniwell and Ryan, 2009), which also examines depression, is one such programme that has been further examined recently by Pluess et al. (2017). Participants comprised 438 girls from 11 to 13 years old, with the sample taken from among the most deprived and challenging neighbourhoods in London, deemed to be at high risk for incidences of depression. The intervention aims to combine cognitive behavioural therapy (CBT) with positive psychology over the course of 12 one-hour sessions, delivered by class teachers who had undergone two days of intensive training in SPARK. Using hypothetical scenarios, children are taught a skills-based coping strategy, based on the SPARK acronym: Situation, Perception, Autopilot, Reaction, Knowledge. Accordingly, automatic emotional responses are triggered by the child's perceptions of a situation, which require them to gain knowledge from the behavioural response to the automatic emotional response. In keeping with a context-specific element targeting this age group, the metaphor of a parrot is used and the parrot has many guises, resembling blame, pessimism, judgement; always being right; catastrophising. The parrot is 'put on trial' and evidence is examined in support or to refute explanations. Strategies such as relaxation and deep breathing are adopted in acting as distractions. All of these cover the elements of CBT contained within the 'hot cross bun' concept where emotional, behavioural and physiological responses interact in a given situation. Significant and persistent improvements in resilience scores were observed post-intervention, at 6-month follow-up and at 12-month follow-up, with similar decreases in depression scores between pre- and post-intervention, but with increases shown at both 6-month and 12-month follow-up (Pluess et al., 2017).

It is worth mentioning at this point that the SPARK Resilience programme should not be confused with the health-related physical activity, Sports, Play and Active Recreation for Kids (SPARK) programme of the late 1990s in the USA and Canada (Marcoux et al., 1999; Sallis et al., 1997). A literature search revealed no other journal articles on either programme, so we eagerly await more findings from Pluess et al., along with any additional research ideas SPARK may spark (we couldn't resist the opportunity here!).

Chris Peterson's work in positive psychology, as applied to military settings and discussed earlier, has filtered through to education, as we postulated above. White and Waters (2015) contributed a tribute to Peterson, in a memorial edition of the *Journal of Positive Psychology*, applying Peterson's approach to a large Australian school as a case study. The researchers focused on 'enabling institutions' and 'character strengths' in their case study. An enabling institution builds academic excellence, but equally builds character, morals and wellbeing, and these should be inherent not only in individuals within the institution, but also as part of the fabric of the institution as a collective. Character strengths are those inherent qualities that one would wish to possess on one's journey through life, such as wisdom, knowledge, love, forgiveness, humility, perseverance and honesty. These examples can be explored in more detail by looking at Peterson and Seligman's (2004) text on character strengths and virtues. By introducing a positive education curriculum into the school, character strengths can be built across curricula, depending on the needs of each child, who equally must reflect on his strengths and those of his peers and teachers (it was a private boys' school). White and Waters (2015: 75) describe what this journey might look like for a typical boy under the positive education curriculum, and is well worth reading, although it must be borne in mind that they do not provide any data beyond simple description.

César Dias and Cadime (2017) examined the effect of school, home, community and peers (i.e., externally-driven, protective factors) on the development of self-regulation and resilience in secondary school children, finding that higher resilience levels were found in girls and in students who were on non-vocational courses.

Kotzé and Niemann (2013) examined the psychological resources possessed by 789 industrial psychology students in higher education and their academic achievement in the first year, finding that optimism did not predict success, but three factors of resilience were significant: positive interpretation, facing adversity, and religion. It must be mentioned that the authors state that the use of the Adult Resilience Indicator (ARI) (cf. Kotzé and Niemann, 2013) was designed for use within South Africa and perhaps may be culturally specific to the South African university system.

In exploring resilience in teaching staff, Pareek and Rathore (2016) examined the character strengths and virtues, postulated by Peterson and Seligman (2004), in 60 faculty members in an Indian higher education institution using the Values in Action Inventory of Strengths (VIA-IS) (Peterson and Seligman, 2004). They found that a gender difference existed, insofar as female faculty members displayed higher character strengths and virtues, compared to their male colleagues. The VIA-IS is a 240-item questionnaire, resulting in 24 character strengths and 6 virtues. From the perspective of brevity, we have taken each of these and adapted them in Table 13.1, which also includes a practical task for you to spend a little time reflecting on.

Table 13.1   Summarising Peterson and Seligman's character strengths and virtues

Virtue	Character Strength	Virtue	Character Strength
Wisdom and Knowledge	Creativity	Justice	Teamwork
	Curiosity		Leadership
	Love of learning		Fairness
	Perspective	Temperance	Forgiveness
	Judgement		Humility
Courage	Bravery		Self-regulation
	Perseverance		Prudence
	Honesty	Transcendence	Appreciation of beauty and excellence
	Zest		Gratitude
Humanity	Love		Hope
	Kindness		Humour
	Social intelligence		Spirituality

Source: adapted from Peterson and Seligman, 2004

ACTIVITY

Look down the list of character strengths and for the purposes of brevity, rate yourself out of ten on each one. Go with your intuitive feeling for what each character strength refers to, or alternatively, if you wish to obtain a definition of each characteristic, this can be viewed online at www.viacharacter.org/www/Character-Strengths/VIA-Classification. This will give you a subjective approximation of how

(Continued)

you see yourself. If you have a spare 15 minutes, we would recommend that you take the free online survey available from this link. There are 'pay options' should you wish to obtain a detailed report. The site is the shopfront for Peterson and Seligman's VIA-IS and so is a trustworthy source. If you take the test, you will be able to see how accurately your original self-report was.

Next, look at your scores and consider how to develop some of the character strength where you scored lower than others. This is a perfect opportunity to explore and establish some short-term, mid-term and long-term goals. In doing so, you will be further developing resilience skills. Remember, this may be a reasonably long process, so do not expect to be resilient by the weekend!

We finish this section of the chapter by considering students as 'professionals of the future'. In a longitudinal study at the University of Worcester examining resilience in undergraduate students, Barber et al. (2017) have mapped the five internal and external domains from Macintosh and Shaw (2017) with the four protective factors from Ponce-Garcia et al. (2015). Preliminary findings were presented at the university's Learning and Teaching Conference in June 2017 and reflect a reduced level of resilience in incoming students compared to the sample used in the Ponce-Garcia et al. study, which focused on students in two North American universities. This issue is not restricted to our university and is an area of increasing concern in the higher education sector globally (e.g., for India: see Balgiu, 2017; for Romania: see Patil and Adsul, 2017; for Malaysia: see Narayanan and Weng Onn, 2016; for cross-cultural comparisons between USA, China and Taiwan: see Li and Yang, 2016).

Barber et al.'s study is part of a longitudinal project, tracking students as they progress through their respective degree programmes, and we aim to extend the study to PGCE cohorts of the future, by establishing strategies for embedding developmental resilience into our *curricula* at all levels. Of course, our natural next step will be to focus attention on developmental resilience in the education system in schools.

Table 13.2   Resilience: combining domains with factors

Internal Domain	Internally driven protective factor	External Domain	Externally driven protective factor
Emotional control	Goal-efficacy	Social integration	Social support
Self-management	Planning and prioritising	Social relationships	Social skills
		Support networks	

If we consider that resilience domains and factors are akin to the ingredients in a recipe, then building these provides the teacher with a set of resilient assets. To provide an asset-type flavour of what each cell may comprise, we discuss examples below. Internally, emotional control includes an ability to move on and not become fixated on problems. Similarly, it involves an ability to remain calm and composed in adverse situations, in order to maintain rational thought processes. The goal remains in focus throughout, hence goal efficacy is protected. Self-management both reflects persistence in pursuing and completing a task and requires goal-setting, for example, as a strategy for achieving the intended aims. This in essence is what we commonly talk about when we mention someone who is 'driven'. Externally, social integration is the perceived ability to become part of, in this instance, a new group of students. It is, in essence, a perceived measure of a 'good fit', i.e., how well do I actually fit into this group of people? This can be considered in terms of other students on a degree programme, flatmates or housemates, and members of clubs and societies. The principle is similar with younger students, with the obvious exception of accommodation. Social relationships play an important part in successful integration and therefore are interrelated. Family and existing friends aid resilience, as does the formation of newly emerging friendship groups. Social skills are developed and refined as a result of this interaction, and support networks become important, especially in times of emotional hardship. Indeed, the longstanding idiom, 'A problem shared is a problem halved', would certainly appear to ring true in this instance.

The issue of capability versus capacity seems to be clearer now. Asset approaches focus on capabilities, lists of characteristics, ingredients, etc. and this is indeed both admirable and necessary. Capacity both is considered by researchers adopting systemic and development approaches and is an indicator of the ability to utilise capabilities at different points in time, which continually fluctuate. Lawton-Smith's (2017) analogy of a Formula 1 car works really well in illustrating this. The car has all the necessary 'ingredients', all the technological advances and has been designed, constructed and driven with the ultimate goal of winning in mind. Yet it needs to come into the pits for fuel, without which it is unable to operate in the conditions for which it was designed. Viewing resilience as 'fuel' provides us with a totally different perspective. Do we conserve? Do we accelerate harder? When do we come in to the pits? Are we getting low on fuel? The list goes on. This essentially is a capacity issue. Now remove the Formula 1 analogy and replace it with the school calendar. How should we use our resilience resources or 'fuel' wisely to get us through each term, until we reach the finishing line at the end of the year? Should we hold something back? Should we pace ourselves? What happens if we begin to run out of resources? You get the picture here. We would concur with Smith, in terms of recommending that capacity should not be overlooked when considering resilience.

13.12 CONCLUSION

We are sadly mistaken if we consider resilience as a 'have it/don't have it' attribute. Reflecting on the associated issues of one's daily life should be factored in, as should fluctuations in the academic year, energy levels, sleeping patterns, nutrition and hydration, along with physical activity levels and current or recent stressors. Assembling a strong support network and relationships with family, friends and colleagues, in combination with self-management strategies, clear goals and an ability to develop emotional control skills, will provide some of the ingredients required. The research literature from the wide array of fields discussed in this chapter also suggests that it would be prudent to actively seek out challenges that will test us, and this may lead to failures. It is these failures that help to build resilience. One may need to lose some battles in order to win the war!

13.13 FURTHER READING

Gus, L., Rose, J. and Gilbert, L. (2015) 'Emotion coaching: A universal strategy for supporting and promoting sustainable emotional and behavioural well-being', *Educational & Child Psychology*, 32 (1): 31–41.
This paper highlights the way in which emotion coaching may be used in schools with students, and is worth reading.

Macintosh, E. and Shaw, J. (2017) *Student Resilience: Exploring the Positive Case for Resilience. Unite Students Insight Report.* Bristol: Unite Students.
This report is primarily aimed at tutors in higher education, in relation to helping students develop resilience. It is thus relevant to those currently on PGCE courses as well as newly or fully qualified teachers, since it provides an insight into tertiary education. By fostering resilience at an earlier age, those entering tertiary education will have been guided and aided by you, having read the report in conjunction with this chapter. Early intervention is the key.

Part 5
PSYCHOLOGICAL SKILLS TRAINING

This part provides applied psychology strategies to enable and empower the teacher. In turn, this should ensure that life in the classroom is an enjoyable experience for both teacher and learners. The techniques available to the teacher include goal-setting, mental imagery, self-talk/cognitive restructuring and relaxation. Knowing how to use these techniques is important. However, knowing this alone is not enough. A teacher must also know when to use these techniques. Consequently, an element of time and effort is required by teachers if they are to benefit fully from these techniques. The investment will pay off in the longer term. In practical terms, our intention in this part is to provide effective techniques to develop MWB and resilience. These can also be used to develop leadership. The strategies will be related to chapters elsewhere in this book where applicable.

14

GOAL-SETTING

CHAPTER OBJECTIVES

- To understand the importance of goal-setting and how it relates professionally.
- To distinguish between outcome, process and performance goals.
- To consider the strategies for setting relevant SMART/SMARTER goals.

TEACHERS' STANDARDS

1 Set high expectations which inspire, motivate and challenge pupils

- set goals that stretch and challenge pupils of all backgrounds, abilities and dispositions

2 Promote good progress and outcomes by pupils

- be accountable for pupils' attainment, progress and outcomes
- be aware of pupils' capabilities and their prior knowledge, and plan teaching to build on these.
- guide pupils to reflect on the progress they have made and their emerging needs.
- encourage pupils to take a responsible and conscientious attitude to their own work and study.

6 Make accurate and productive use of assessment

- make use of formative and summative assessment to secure pupils' progress.
- use relevant data to monitor progress, set targets, and plan subsequent lessons.

14.1 INTRODUCTION

As teachers, we tend to be experts as setting goals for our students … yet how often do we apply the same goal-setting to our professional life to ensure we continue to strive for success? While the Teachers' Standards specifically identify the need for effective goal-setting, the standards, and indeed teacher training, seldom provide the psychological context for setting goals. To this extent, the predominant factor within the education sector is that of management, which relates to setting goals and monitoring others' progress towards achieving these.

Setting goals is an ideal way of progressing in teaching. Goal-setting formalises a paper-trail of intent and provides opportunities for personal progress monitoring. Moreover, it plots a course towards goal achievement, or the desire to display competence through the attainment of goals (Nicholls, 1989). There is debate regarding whether such a linear approach to goal-setting is detrimental to goal achievement and if one should think more in terms of charting a course towards achievement (see Grant, 2012). Nevertheless, we retain the current label here, for convenience.

In our experience, teachers often report setting goals that are either unrealistic or overly vague, or are so distant that they become demotivating. Goal-setting is a technique used to assist people in meeting targets at some point in the future. It is a 'how-to-get-there' resource, which can, for example, help teachers to set targets in order to reach a certain level of expertise. Examples of such goals include: 'I want to complete all my weekly planning over the holidays', or 'I want to write all my reports this morning.' Setting appropriate, specific goals helps to improve performance and enables levels of motivation in achieving these goals to continue. Essentially, then, it is target setting. We must clear up one issue at this point. Goal-setting involves setting one's own targets and is very effective in helping us to achieve these. In reality of course, other people may set targets for us. Often we are unable to negotiate or change these targets, so we have to find ways of achieving them. Goal-setting is a way of moving closer to achieving those targets. You might not like the target set for you, but need to find a solution to achieving it. Goal-setting offers that solution.

Consequently, in this chapter, we discuss the psychological context that underpins effective goal-setting, in turn providing advice and guidance for establishing these.

14.2 EDUCATION AND GOAL-SETTING

In-part, a chapter solely devoted to goal-setting may appear a waste of pages given that teaching, throughout the ages, has utilised goals to measure performance and set targets for pupils. Recent research demonstrates that goal-setting is still being investigated as to the positive impact it has. For example, several studies have used goals for developing social skills (e.g. Buckle and Walsh, 2013; Ginsburg, 2016; Rodkin et al., 2013). Weedon et al. (2016) developed goal-setting strategies for class-wide behaviour intervention strategies for students with emotional and behavioural difficulties. Different types of goal-setting approaches, which are discussed as this chapter progresses, have been used within research. For example, King and McInerney (2016) used outcome goals for developing metacognitive learning strategies (enabling pupils to establish and monitor their own learning through goal-setting). Torrence et al. (2015) used process goals to significantly increase time-on-task for developing pupils' writing ability. Further research into goal-setting for developing writing for students with learning needs has been investigated by Gillespie and Graham (2014).

Within the educational context, this demonstrates that goal-setting is still an area of research interest to ensure that such goals are effective in nature. What the research has, however, indicated is the importance of ensuring that goals are relevant (e.g., Peterson et al., 2013), and similarly that pupils are involved in setting goals (Hart and Brehm, 2013). Specifically, Hart and Brehm (2013) have used the motivation approach of self-determination theory related to goal-setting for children with individual educational plans. The area of self-determination theory is explicitly discussed in Chapter 10.

14.3 WHAT IS GOAL-SETTING?

As previously discussed, goal-setting is an approach to help people meet future targets. Setting appropriate, specific goals helps to improve performance and enables levels of motivation in achieving these goals to continue. Essentially then, it is target setting. We must clear up one issue at this point. Goal-setting involves setting one's own targets and is very effective in helping us to achieve the goals we set. In reality of course, other people may set targets for us as discussed in Chapter 10. Often we are unable to negotiate or change these targets, so we have to find ways of achieving them. Goal-setting is a way of moving closer to achieving those targets. You might not like the target set for you, but need to find a solution to achieving it. Goal-setting offers that solution.

ACTIVITY

Before reading any further, list five or so targets that you would like to achieve, or have been advised that you must achieve in the next academic year. These are your goals. Keep this list safe. You will need to refer to it later in the chapter.

14.4 WHICH PERSPECTIVE: OUTCOME, PERFORMANCE OR PROCESS GOALS?

Within psychology, psychologists differentiate between three different types of goal.

OUTCOME GOALS

As you might expect, outcome goals are based on the end product of a performance: on its outcome. By the very nature of outcome goals, the frame of reference is a comparison between your performance against targets, or ensuring your students reach their targets, or perhaps comparing yourself with another teacher's performance, etc. You are comparing yourself on outcomes, outcomes that may well be beyond your control. In teaching, outcome goals are prevalent in terms of reaching targets. A teacher who may have set their class the target of all achieving a required grade and who is teaching effectively may still fail to reach their set goal. Not only is this demotivating but also it does not take into account any success that has been achieved, for example, a student who has made exceptional progress from their starting point, yet who may still not have achieved the set target.

The use of outcome goals has given rise to an area known as outcome-based education (OBE) (Tam, 2014). In this approach, pupils are provided with continuous assessment to meet specific outcomes, with the perspective that this provides clear goals to the pupil, flexibility for the teacher to structure appropriate learning opportunities, the ability to compare a pupil within a school and also compare performance to other schools; furthermore this involves the student in taking responsibility for their own learning (Malan, 2000; Tam, 2014). However, the approach has been widely criticised and is being phased out in Australia (Donnelly, 2007) and also in South Africa (Allais, 2007). Reasons for such criticism relate to the interpretation of outcomes and also the concern that the approach makes learning reductionist (Tam, 2014).

PERFORMANCE GOALS

Performance goals may be seen as diluted versions of outcome goals. In essence, they are related to a teacher's performance regardless of the outcome. The comparison is between your performance now and your performance last week, or last month. An example of a performance goal might be to ensure all work is completed within the school week, so that the teacher has their weekends free to get refreshed (something that was perhaps unachievable a month ago). We would argue that performance goals are preferable to outcome goals, since they relate directly to a teacher's development. So, we may be the worst teachers in the school, yet if our performance is improving, we are achieving success! As such, a good use of setting performance goals is to modify an existing performance goal to see if you can push that little bit further.

Within the educational context, how often are pupils provided with a measure of their previous performance and their current performance? While teachers tend to focus on outcome goals for assessment purposes and record keeping, to what extent does the pupil feel involved with their learning, if they are unable to ascertain how their performance has fared to a previous performance?

PROCESS GOALS

Arguably the most appropriate kind of goal-setting involves examining the process of teaching and the 'flow' needed to get students learning in an effective, smooth manner.

Process goals are, therefore, about how it feels. Think of a time when everything was working well in the classroom, a time when you were in your element, where the lesson was effortless, enjoyable and exceptional. Consider why this was the case. What did you do to facilitate this successful scenario?

For every element of teaching, it should be possible to set a process goal so that you can get the most out of, yet expand, your teaching experience. You can do this by working out what information you will need to perform the process successfully. For example, you may have utilised a new teaching technique from a staff develop-ment session, or tried a new technique for getting the class in order. Perhaps you have adopted a new method of planning or assessing. Essentially, it is something that just feels right. The key is to strive for the correct feel and to take this knowledge into each aspect of your career. So, you should aim to set goals on the basis of doing the job rather than on the end product or outcome. If you take care of the process the outcome will take care of itself.

Such process goals relate to the field of flow theory discussed in Chapter 2, whereby if the conditions are right, things will seem natural and work at their optimal level. It is a case of balancing an individual's existing skill-set and ensuring an appropriate level of challenge. With pupils, while outcome goals are more measurable, consider whether within your teaching there is scope for process goals.

Despite this overview of the different types of goals, a careful blend is required to respond to different contexts with different pupils.

14.5 PSYCHOLOGICAL PRINCIPLES BEHIND GOAL-SETTING

Knowledge of how goal-setting may exert its effect on performance will help you to understand how to set effective goals and how goal-setting can be utilised in directing your attention, channelling effort and persistence and developing new strategies of learning how to overcome challenges. We will explore each of these in turn.

DIRECTING OR FOCUSING ATTENTION

It is important to direct attention towards a specific goal. Teachers who do not focus on specific goals usually find themselves floundering and their attention easily dis-tracted from the task at hand. You will perhaps have experienced the feeling of, 'So many things to do ... which one first?' and you end up failing to complete any of them in a particularly focused manner. This might include not paying adequate atten-tion to the timing and pace of your lesson. If attention is directed at ensuring a steady pace and ensuring you leave time for a plenary and clearing away before the bell, the teacher can focus on this as a goal. Essentially, the teacher is breaking down the overall task of teaching into small, manageable chunks, which can be developed with practice – a sort of, 'I need to do X and Y if I want to do Z' approach.

In relation to pupils, how many goals or learning objectives are set for each lesson, and realistically how many can a pupil attune to?

CHANNELLING EFFORT

Having focused your attention on a specific goal, as in the example above, you then need to make a concerted effort to achieve that goal. On its own, therefore, directing attention is not enough. Active effort is also required in achieving the goal. You need to evaluate how you are going to achieve the goal.

PERSISTENCE

Having directed attention and mobilised effort in pursuit of the goal, the next step in the process is persistence. In attempting to achieve the goal, it is of no benefit for a teacher to direct attention and mobilise effort for the first few lessons of the day. It is not enough to persist for the first three days of the week. Persistence means having the stamina to keep going for the duration of the week. It is the endurance element in order to reach the set goals that enables a teacher to achieve success.

DEVELOPING NEW STRATEGIES OF LEARNING TO OVERCOME CHALLENGES

Having directed attention, mobilised effort and persisted in the activity, you are finally able to develop new strategies of learning. This ensures that you do not become stale and shows adaptation to the ever-changing circumstances. Think of this as being similar to evolution. No species remains the same but, rather, constantly adapts to the changing environment. A teacher should be striving to adapt to different situations, take opportunities when they emerge and look for the most appropriate strategy for the situation.

Whether you achieve your goals may also depend on the following.

ABILITY

We have hinted at ability above. Your ability is an obvious point for considering whether you can actually complete the task successfully. Do you have the relevant knowledge, experience or resources to hand? Perhaps identifying a learning mentor to discuss such issues will help improve your ability on a particular aspect.

Avoid setting goals that are beyond your ability. Be aware, however, that as you develop, your ability may also increase.

COMMITMENT

It is vital for a teacher to be committed to achieving the goals that he or she sets. If commitment is absent, there is very little chance that the goals will be achieved, at least in part because the desire must also be missing. This is more difficult when targets have been set for you. We like the idea of differentiating between targets (set by others) and goals (set by ourselves to meet others' targets). In differentiating in this way, you can take ownership because you are striving to achieve your own goals, which will, in turn, meet others' targets.

FEEDBACK

Feedback is a vital element of goal-setting. Feedback provides the teacher with a way of evaluating whether or not the goal has been achieved. Of course, there are objective measurements that are of use in establishing whether a goal has been achieved, such as discussions with others, observations, etc. We would also argue that subjective information is relevant in terms of feedback, but only if it can be quantified. For instance, we might ask you to rate the 'feel' or 'success' of a particular lesson on a scale of 1 to 10, where 1 is poor and 10 is excellent, as discussed below.

As an example, imagine that a teacher has been asked, 'On a scale of 1 to 10, how did the lesson on introducing the concept of gravity go?' Let's assume the answer is a 3, and of course, this is unique to that particular teacher on that particular occasion. We would then ask the teacher to explore ways in which they might approach this task in a different manner, in order to improve on the 3 rating. This could be through ascertaining what students already know about gravity through using concept maps, perhaps discussing why things fall down (as opposed to up) in greater detail, or additional practical activities on dropping different-sized objects, etc. Although this is subjective, it does offer a way in which a teacher can measure their performance.

TASK COMPLEXITY

The complexity of the task may influence the effectiveness of the goal. Setting a particular goal of completing all your short-term planning for the term may be unrealistic as you will have to be flexible and accommodating to your students' needs as they develop: your planning may be aimed at the wrong level. It is important therefore, when setting goals, that they are realistic, given the complexity of the task.

The setting of inappropriate outcome goals can lead to problems with self-confidence, anxiety and satisfaction. The more confident you are, the greater the likelihood of achieving the goal. Psychologists call this 'self-fulfilling prophecy' (Merton, 1948). If you believe that you will fail, you will fail. If you are confident that you will achieve, then you will. Additionally, each performance has a certain amount of anticipated satisfaction attached to it. When goals are achieved, satisfaction increases, confidence grows and motivation to achieve the next goal remains strong.

Regardless of the theoretical perspective one adopts, goal-setting remains one of the most important techniques in psychology in helping teachers to develop skills and achieve success. The effective use of goal-setting is imperative in this development and it is to this that we will now turn.

REFLECTION

Consider a time when you may have set a personal or professional goal. Did you achieve it? We tend to remember the goals we achieve and forget the ones we don't. As such, if you can remember a goal you didn't achieve, was this due to your ability, commitment, lack of feedback on progress, or the complexity in achieving the goal?

Perhaps consider a goal you may currently be working on. Do you think it will need revising in light of what has been covered so far in this chapter?

14.6 EFFECTIVE USE OF GOAL-SETTING

From our experience in working with teachers, it is apparent that a lack of appreciation and understanding of goal-setting has led teachers to set inappropriate goals, or to think about their performance in the classroom in the wrong way. This is quite normal. When asking teachers what their personal goals are, we tend to find that they do not set personal goals; rather their goals are linked in some way to the outcome of the class. We frequently get responses such as 'to ensure all my students reach level X in subject Y'. In itself, this is all very well. The difficulty, however, is that not all factors are controllable for your students in order for them to achieve a set target. By approaching goal-setting from a different perspective, the attainment of others is not as important as the process of achieving personal and professional growth, which ultimately will ensure attainment as a by-product. Once a teacher understands this, their performance should improve and students will make the required target as a consequence of the process. In our opinion, this is implicit in the way inspirational teachers approach their lessons. Telling teachers not to focus on student outcome is among the hardest things we do. Telling you that improving your own performance through setting appropriate goals is like putting money into a savings account; at some point in the future it will provide you with everything you need.

14.7 GUIDELINES FOR ESTABLISHING GOALS

Various types of goal-setting systems exist in psychology. However, most involve three logical, progressive stages: preparation and planning, education and acquisition, and implementation and review or follow-up.

PREPARATION AND PLANNING

It is important for you to assess your abilities and needs. For us, a teacher's input is essential and will guide our assessment. A useful method of keeping motivation levels high is to set wide-ranging goals, so that you can work on different elements at different times. It is important to plan to help achieve the strategies you have put in place, so that you are aware of whether progress is being made. For example, we may agree to use goal-setting to:

- overcome motivational or confidence problems
- aid the development of teaching technique and/or mental preparation
- help you through a programme of injury rehabilitation
- assist you in recovering from staleness or burnout.

EDUCATION AND ACQUISITION

When carrying out a goal-setting strategy, it is necessary to organise regular meetings with another person, such as a mentor, to monitor performance in relation to the set goals. Some people advocate working on a single goal at one time although we would suggest that you may be in a position to work on more than one goal during a particular period. Again, the responsibility for appropriate goal-setting rests on collaboration between the teacher and the mentor.

After initial preparations, it becomes possible to observe and monitor progress and overall confidence in a teacher's ability. As goal progression or goal achievement data is collected, a picture builds up and this may serve to motivate you to continue with the programme.

ACTIVITY

Set a deadline for the future. This may be a week, a month or a term, depending on the goals you have listed. Identify what types of evidence you need to collect in order to assess your progress towards meeting the goal.

IMPLEMENTATION AND REVIEW

It is important that you identify relevant procedures for the assessment of goals. If you do not know how the procedures work, there is little chance of success. Throughout the process, the mentor should provide appropriate support and encouragement wherever progress towards goal achievement is taking place. You should set a date for the review of goals set; it is important to reflect on progress, achievement or reasons for not meeting set goals.

In setting a date, it is necessary to be mindful of the time frame associated with different goals. Goals may be short-, mid-, or long-term. Of course, this distinction is specific to each teacher. What we consider is a mid-term goal for one teacher may be a long-term goal for another. We will now outline each type of goal below.

ACTIVITY

Reassess your progress at the deadline, or review date. Mark off the goals that have been achieved. If any goals have not been met, reflect on why this might be and consider revising the goal for a follow-up review.

LONG-TERM GOALS

These are your ultimate goals, the things you desire most from your career. Long-term goals can cover a single year, or your entire career. You set the boundaries yourself and your long-term goals relate to your own perspective on time. However, this poses a problem in terms of keeping the motivation alive for the duration of the goal period.

MID-TERM GOALS

Mid-term goals act as a way of keeping motivation levels alive. They serve as a focus at a closer point in the future. How do you know whether you are progressing towards your long-term goal? You know because you have set and achieved a mid-term goal. Mid-term targets should be clear and should be set in relation to long-term goals. For example, if you have set a long-term goal linked to the end of a year, then your mid-term goal will perhaps be after a term. If, however, your long-term goal is a five-year plan, then the mid-term goal might be assessed at some point during the third year.

SHORT-TERM GOALS

Short-term goals are again relative to mid- and long-term goals. They serve as a focus point in the near future. You do not have to wait for too long before a short-term goal can be assessed for progress. In keeping motivation levels high, short-term goals should provide manageable, regular opportunities to achieve success. In setting a personal target, rather than an outcome-based goal, you can concentrate on your own strategy, rather than becoming a pawn in others' games. Having achieved this short-term goal, you should then consider setting a new short-term goal for the next time frame (see Prochaska and DiClemente, 1982).

14.8 COMMON GOAL-SETTING PROBLEMS

Without appropriate guidance, it is easy to fall into the trap of failing to achieve the goals that have been set. If progress is not monitored, as we have mentioned, there will be an increasing likelihood that goals will not be achieved. Indeed if goals are not achieved, motivation may diminish and performance may be impaired as a result. Not only should goals be monitored, but also they should be revised or readjusted as necessary. If you have not achieved the goal set, then refocus, or dilute it so that you can achieve it. It may be that the original steps towards the goal were simply too large. Keep this statement in your mind: 'If I chip away at my performance, I will get where I want to be at some point.'

It may be that the goals set are too general or not measurable. If you are unable to measure achievement towards the goal, how do you know whether or not you have reached it? We will discuss these points in greater depth, under the section on SMART targets. Similarly, if you set too many goals, you may not be able to achieve all (or any) of them in the timescale you have set for yourself.

Finally, individual differences play a role in goal-setting problems. We would not ask you to compare your fingerprint with ours and tell us which one is the best. In the same way, the goals that you set for yourself should not be related to what other people are doing or can do. We would, however, expect you to set a goal that might ultimately send you on the route to success ... which indeed is among our foremost for writing this book!

14.9 SMART GOAL-SETTING

SMART (Raia, 1965) is an acronym for a technique that helps psychologists and teachers set appropriate goals. It stands for Specific, Measurable, Action-oriented, Realistic and Time-phased. We shall take each element in turn. It is important when goal-setting that you identify exactly what goal you wish to achieve. It is no use saying, 'I want to be a good teacher.' This is too general, and arguably immeasurable. Instead, you might wish to ensure that all your lessons utilise an effective plenary. Depending on your definition of the word 'effective', this goal is specific. Having set a specific goal, it is vital that some form of measurement is used to evaluate whether or not the goal has been attained. This is perhaps the most awkward aspect to set in terms of identifying an appropriate measure. Think of a piece of string. If we ask you to measure the string without using a ruler, the likelihood is that you will over- or under-estimate its length. If you use a ruler, there is an absolute measure that can be relied on. Absolute measures are not always possible in goal-setting. Nevertheless, the aim is to strive towards precise, observable measurement wherever it is available. A measurable goal is therefore quantifiable and, as such, acts to tell the teacher whether it has been reached. In our 'effective plenary session' goal, producing a 1–10 or even 1–3 rating scale may suffice. It is quantifiable, if defined appropriately.

As one might anticipate, action-oriented goals are goals that highlight something that needs to be achieved. An action-oriented goal is not thinking about doing something, but rather it is about actively doing it. Setting unrealistic goals will generally result in goal failure and this in turn may diminish motivation and impair performance. Setting a realistic goal will provide a light at the end of the tunnel, something that is within your grasp and will assist you in getting to where you desire to be. However, setting goals that are too easily reached renders them meaningless. This highlights the importance of setting realistic yet challenging goals. Setting goals without a deadline for review is an equally fruitless activity. This essentially is what we mean by the term 'time-phased'. A time-phased goal must be accomplished by a particular deadline, or target date. Again, if you set a deadline that is too short, the goal may not be achievable, so it is important to remain realistic about your expectations for accomplishing it. Of course you may have different goals with different deadlines. So you may have a time-phased goal linked to performance during the forthcoming lesson, but you might also have a time-phased goal of achieving consistency over a number of lessons this half-term. There is, therefore, an element of crossover with target dates.

REFLECTION

Start to consider SMART goals for your development. Just make a mental note of these at the moment as we will come back to setting them shortly.

14.10 ADDITIONAL PRACTICAL GUIDANCE ON SETTING GOALS

The psychology literature gives additional practical advice for effective goal-setting. Issues include: setting performance and process goals, setting goals for complementary areas, recording goals, and goal commitment and support. We will briefly outline each issue below.

SETTING PERFORMANCE AND PROCESS GOALS

It is good practice to set both performance and process goals. Indeed, it is acceptable to set outcome goals, but these should be of secondary importance. Performance and process goals should provide you with the necessary requirements to achieve the desired outcome. You should concentrate on your own performance and the process you go through to achieve that performance.

SETTING GOALS FOR COMPLEMENTARY AREAS

It is quite common for teachers to set goals only for the day-to-day job. We would, however, advocate that you set goals for all aspects of life that relate to your teaching. As teaching is likely to take a considerable chunk out of your week, ensuring you are able to balance other dimensions of your life is crucial! You should also consider whether to set goals in relation to themes discussed elsewhere in this book. So you might have a National Curriculum-based set of goals on one sheet of paper, a set of exercise/physical activity goals on another sheet of paper, a set of confidence-related tasks/goals on a third, a set of time management goals on a fourth and … the list is almost endless.

RECORDING GOALS

Recording goals is vital to progress. The academic year is long: if we ask you in May to cast your mind back to a lesson in January, could you remember all aspects of what happened? This is unlikely! Consequently, we would encourage you to keep a personal log relating to your goals. What were the goals for each week? Did you achieve them? If not, why? What were the readjusted goals? Did you achieve them? It then becomes possible to look back over the year, review progress and reflect on the implications in advance of next year. Examples of ways in which to record goals can be found later in this chapter.

GOAL COMMITMENT AND SUPPORT

It is important that teachers buy in to the idea of goals and their effectiveness in improving performance. The teacher must show commitment to achieve. All people associated with the teacher are in a position to foster that commitment by providing support wherever possible. It is of no use whatsoever for the mentor and teacher to work on a goal-setting programme, only for the headteacher to override the programme and instead set unrealistic outcome goals. If everyone is aware of the goals, achievement becomes more likely.

FEEDBACK

As we have pointed out elsewhere, feedback is a vital element in goal-setting. The mentor is responsible for evaluating progress on the goal-setting programme and providing feedback where appropriate. Feedback may sometimes be seen as criticism, depending on how it is delivered. However, it should be viewed as a means of communication that enables the teacher to refine their performance.

ACTIVITY

Having reached the end of this chapter you should now be able to set your own SMART goals. These may vary considerably from the way in which you wrote down the goals in the earlier activities in this chapter. Your task is to put these newly acquired skills into operation.

14.11 CONCLUSION

Effective goal-setting is a fundamental skill in order to progress successfully within teaching. To this extent, it is important to focus on the type of goal you are aiming for. Is it one or more of the following?

Outcome – focusing on the end product.

Performance – focusing on your actual performance.

Process – focusing on how it feels.

Setting goals is useful as it helps direct and focus your attention, in turn channelling your effort and ensuring persistence. As a product of achieving the goal, you may have also developed new strategies for learning to overcome challenges. However, any goal is dependent on your ability to achieve the goal, your commitment, obtaining feedback so you know how well you're progressing, and finally task complexity: if the task is too complex, can it be divided into smaller goals?

The key message is that a written goal somehow becomes formal. It is there for you to see (and others if you wish). You have therefore committed yourself to set about achieving it. Setting SMART goals is perhaps the best way to proceed.

14.12 FURTHER READING

Grant, A.M. (2012) 'An integrated model of goal-focused coaching: An evidence-based framework for teaching and practice', *International Coaching Psychology Review*, 7 (2): 146–65.
Grant's journal article discusses in further depth the use of goals, providing evidential support for their effectiveness in teaching.

15
MENTAL IMAGERY

CHAPTER OBJECTIVES

- Understand the difference between visualisation and imagery.
- Appreciate how imagery works and how it can help you professionally.
- Recognise the differences between internal and external imagery.
- Develop effective imagery skills for a specific purpose.
- Plan and write your own imagery script.

TEACHERS' STANDARDS

A teacher must:

4   Plan and teach well-structured lessons

- reflect systematically on the effectiveness of lessons and approaches to teaching
- contribute to the design and provision of an engaging curriculum within the relevant subject area(s)

5   Adapt teaching to respond to the strengths and needs of all pupils

- have a secure understanding of how a range of factors can inhibit pupils' ability to learn, and how best to overcome these
- demonstrate an awareness of the physical, social and intellectual development of children, and know how to adapt teaching to support pupils' education at different stages of development

7   Manage behaviour effectively to ensure a good and safe learning environment

- manage classes effectively, using approaches which are appropriate to pupils' needs in order to involve and motivate them

15.1 INTRODUCTION TO VISUALISATION AND IMAGERY

Visualisation is seeing a picture of an event in your mind. Mental imagery takes this picture and converts it into a sequence similar to mentally streaming a movie. At a simple level, visualisation may simply involve the storage of a single picture or basic moving image, e.g., of a classroom. In contrast, mental imagery is an active, dynamic process, in which the image is continuously modified as if it were an enhanced video recording. You may already use this technique. Many teachers believe that they know the classroom in their minds. The question you should ask yourself is, 'Are you able to see a *picture* or a *moving sequence*?' You may have a visual image of the classroom, but there is so much more that you could include to make it real. In achieving this, other senses may be included to enhance the quality of the internal experience. When we talk of mental imagery, we are therefore concerned with so much more than just the visual system. In order to avoid any misleading or confusing subtleties in terminology, we favour the term 'mental rehearsal' to encompass all aspects of acquiring, developing and refining a mental representation of a forthcoming lesson. The idea that other senses can be incorporated into mental imagery is not surprising. The human brain comprises many systems and sub-systems, all of which communicate in some way with each other, whether this is directly or indirectly. Indeed, if you look out of the window at this very moment and see a vehicle go past, you will more than likely also hear that vehicle. The brain does not store these pieces of information as two separate perceptions. Rather, they are combined. Why not, therefore, use the senses to your advantage when creating a mental image? The more detail you can add, the more realistic the experience.

As we have said elsewhere, humans are visually dominant. If you take the time to reflect on how important sight is to your own daily life and, indeed your passion for teaching, you can understand why there is such a heavy reliance on the visual sense. Nevertheless, this leaves a wealth of untapped information provided by other sensory systems that can be incorporated into visualisation to provide a higher-quality experience. This is where mental imagery goes a step further.

15.2 INTERNAL VERSUS EXTERNAL IMAGERY

People tend either to create imagery where they see themselves in the situation (an external perspective) or they see the situation as if it were from their own eyes (an internal perspective) (Libby et al., 2011). Moran et al. (2012) offer the notion of 'first person' and 'third person' perspectives. Yuwei et al. (2014) give the example of imagining a red Ferrari approaching along a beach road, as opposed to imagining driving the red Ferrari along the same beach road. As they quite correctly point out, the experience of imagining each of these will be very different and will elicit different thoughts, feelings and emotions. While Yuwei et al. discuss their example in relation to goal-driven, consumer behaviour, our working example below is contextualised to the classroom and equally highlights these differences in thoughts, feelings and emotions.

CASE STUDY   Tom and Sally

Read the following case study:

Tom and Sally sat in one of our CPD workshops on mental imagery. As an NQT, Tom said that he suffered from a lack of confidence in the classroom and felt that the children were able to 'see through to my soul and, thus, expose my weaknesses as a teacher' (Tom's words). Sally, on the other hand, also an NQT, said that her lack of confidence was related to 'not feeling confident in progressing the lesson to the bell [signalling the end of the lesson]'. The issue with both Tom and Sally is undoubtedly confidence, but adopting the same perspective would not work equally well for each of them.

We asked Tom to adopt an external imagery perspective:

Imagine a perspective looking through the classroom window into the room, where you see the learners sitting at their desks, together with displays and resources. You see the teacher's desk, the board and someone standing at the front of the room. You see the person speaking, turning to the board, then back to the learners. You see the person work confidently, moving around the class as required. Of course, the person you are looking at is yourself, Tom, a confident teacher. You are not transparent: nobody can see through you.

We asked Sally to adopt an internal imagery perspective:

Imagine a perspective from behind your own eyes, looking out of and around the classroom, where you see the learners, the board and the resources. You monitor the class and bring the learners to attention; you turn to the board and highlight the lesson objectives; you move around the room confidently monitoring learners' engagement. You look at the lesson plan on your desk, look at the clock, and segment the lesson into smaller chunks. Teach, check the time, questions, check the time, learners on task, check the time, final plenary, check the time (this is an abridged version of Sally's detailed lesson plan), pack away, learners lead out; deep, relaxing sigh, job done ... successfully.

Both Tom and Sally achieved their desired outcomes, yet they adopted different perspectives. The paper by Libby et al. (2011) relates internal and external perspectives to high or low self-esteem, and this paper is worth reading before you decide on which perspective to adopt for yourself.

ADOPTING A PERSPECTIVE

The perspective you should adopt will inevitably depend upon the underlying reasons for using imagery. For example, if you need to rehearse your routine mentally, in order to familiarise yourself with the lesson, reduce potential stressors and such like, then it may be preferable to adopt an internal perspective. Imagery has been found to enhance performance in various areas, including preoperative preparations for orthopaedic trauma surgery (Ibrahim et al., 2015), olfactory training in oncology students (Tempere et al., 2014), autobiographical and episodic memory in multiple sclerosis patients (Ernst et al., 2015), academic learning arithmetic in 9–11-year-olds (Pirrone and Di Nuovo, 2014), learning of a forearm pass in volleyball (Ay et al., 2013) and using guided imagery for trainee counsellors in the classroom (Kress et al., 2014).

If, on the other hand, you need to boost self-confidence, then adopting an external perspective would enable you to 'see' yourself performing successfully in the situation.

QUESTIONING YOUR IMAGERY POTENTIAL

It is helpful to carry out an 'imagery audit' or 'needs assessment' to establish your imagery potential. Do you use all senses? If not why not? If you do, then are you including the level of detail covered in this chapter? You should then develop and refine your goals wherever possible.

In practical terms, it is possible to use mental imagery in three different, yet complementary, ways, as explained on p. 338.

Effective use of mental imagery in preparation for teaching is based on belief, lucidity (or vividness) and control. A theoretical model known as the PETTLEP model, applied to sport, highlights the component parts of successful imagery (Holmes and Collins, 2001). Physical, Environmental, Task, Timing, Learning, Emotional, and Perspective elements are necessary, in order to achieve as realistic an imagery sequence as possible. The Holmes and Collins paper is worth a read, although we do cover each of the elements throughout this chapter.

It is vital to recognise that mental imagery will only aid preparation for an event if you believe in it. Let's face it, if we ask you to do something that you don't believe you can do, it is unlikely to work at all. Equally, a lucid piece of mental imagery contains high-quality, detailed information of varying levels of significance. It is as close to the real thing as one can be but is in the mind. Control is a vital yet sometimes overlooked aspect of mental imagery. It is imperative that you are able to control the imagery to your advantage. It will help you to visualise the outcome that you want. So, if you feel your pace is wrong part-way through the imaginary lesson, incorporate a change into the imagery by controlling it. In effect, you are rehearsing worst-case scenarios and learning how to control what happens next.

15.3 MECHANISMS FOR IMAGERY

The exact mechanism behind imagery remains elusive. Nevertheless, imagery seems to convince your brain that imagining a situation is synonymous with reality, rather akin to Aristotle's notion of 'phantasia' (Roumbou, 2017). This is conveniently illustrated through dreaming. For example, you may have had the fairly common 'I'm late' dream. You have an important event/appointment/lesson-observation tomorrow and you suddenly wake up in a cold sweat during the night, because you have been dreaming about missing the alarm clock, getting up late, vehicle not starting, being stuck in traffic and not getting there on time. This, of course, is all taking place in your subconscious mind. Nevertheless, it is sufficiently 'real' to elicit physiological changes in your autonomic nervous system, such that you wake in a panic. Essentially therefore, *the events in your mind are 'real'* until your conscious mind wakes and evaluates the reality of the situation, i.e., it is in fact 2 a.m. and you have plenty of time. Psychologists are not entirely certain exactly how imagery works and many theories exist. It may be that an examination of computational simulations in artificial models – that is, simulating a neural network that 'learns' mental imagery – offers an element of hope in establishing underlying mechanisms (McKinstry et al., 2016).

15.4 OPERATIONALISING IMAGERY

In practical terms, it is possible to use mental imagery in three different but complementary ways:

1. Learning and developing physical skills. The physical elements of any skill can be rehearsed mentally if the necessary information is available.
2. Developing psychological skills, such as reducing anxiety or 'psyching up'. This ought to be useful in situations where you need to deal with pressure.
3. Developing and refining perceptual skills, such as monitoring the class for understanding and engagement with the lesson.

ACTIVITY

In your journal note down the differences between internal and external imagery. Consider which of these you would find easier to work with. Why is this?

15.5 USING ALL OF THE SENSES TO ENHANCE IMAGERY

As mentioned above, humans are a visually dominant species. As a result, one might argue that we have become rather complacent. If the information you receive from your visual system is sufficient for you to do the job, then why use valuable time and energy in acquiring information from other senses? Of course, this is not strictly the case. The human brain constantly receives information from all sensory systems. However, it does not necessarily process all of the incoming information at the same level or in the same depth. Nevertheless it is possible, with practice, to train the brain in processing information that is relevant to the task in hand. This can be seen in the example of 'auditory imagery', which can be used as an inner representation of sound and activity in combination with visual imagery by musicians, in performing memorised pieces of music (Saintilan, 2014).

In short, the more useable information one has, the easier, and indeed more appropriate, the decision becomes. The only time that this situation becomes detrimental is when the information is meaningless and, if this happens, an inappropriate decision is made.

So what information might the other senses provide? The next time you are in the classroom, start to become aware of what your senses are telling you. What can you see? You should be able to see the students, the classroom, how they act with one another, with the subject content, with the teacher: all contextually relevant pieces of information. What can you hear? You may be able to hear students talking about a task, and whether the talk is constructive to the outcome; you may hear noise from other classes; perhaps you can hear noise from the playground or sports field, etc. What can you feel physically? You may feel the texture of the floor as you walk around the classroom from the carpeted area to the wooden/tiled areas. What is the temperature – too hot or cold? What can you smell!? (See the following Activity.) The gustatory, or taste, sense plays little if any role in providing information in a teaching environment. However, you might notice the 'dry mouth' sensation that some teachers get before a lesson. A dry mouth is quite natural and is part of the human body's defence mechanism: 'fight-or-flight', a readiness to do, or react to a situation. As you read this, you may identify with any, most or all of these examples. If they have happened in reality, then why not incorporate them into mental imagery?

As this section highlights, if a teacher incorporates information provided by various senses into their mental imagery, the imagery should be vivid and of high quality. This is hardly surprising, given that, although the human brain comprises many systems, it is also a part of a system. Consequently, the brain processes information from a variety of interdependent sub-systems, such as the senses, the endocrine system (responsible for hormone release), cardiovascular system (responsible for fluctuations in heart rate) and autonomic nervous system (responsible for the stress response), to name but a few (Kolb and Whishaw, 2015). This interdependence also operates for psychological skills techniques. For example, combining mental imagery with relaxation can be extremely powerful. Indeed, a study by Veena and Alvi (2016) has explored guided imagery (GI) as a tool for anxiety reduction in adolescents, finding that reductions in both state and trait anxiety were observed post-intervention. In combination with relaxation and/or cognitive restructuring, the effects may be enhanced, and further research aims to examine these interventions further.

15.6 WRITING AN IMAGERY SCRIPT

Before beginning to help you to write an imagery script, it is important to establish how successfully you can create a mental image at the moment. Again, there are psychometric measurements in place to establish imagery ability, such as the Plymouth Sensory Imagery Questionnaire (Psi-Q) (Andrade et al., 2014), which measures imagery ability across different sensory modalities, and the Movement Imagery Questionnaire (MIQ-RS) (Gregg et al., 2010) and the Test of Ability in Movement Imagery (TAMI) (Madan and Singhal, 2013), both of which measure movement imagery. If you are not inclined to complete these formally and then transfer the knowledge into the classroom context, you should respond to the following statements and then revisit them after you have developed your imagery technique. You will then be able to assess your progress.

ACTIVITY

Tick the box on the right if your answer to each statement is 'yes'. The more boxes you are able to tick, the more successful you are at mental imagery. Remember to be honest!

I can see myself in the classroom	☐
I can feel the classroom atmosphere	☐
I can see the students actively learning	☐
I can feel myself getting 'psyched up' for the lesson	☐
I can make up new teaching responses and strategies in my head	☐

I can see myself successfully following my lesson plan	☐
I can imagine myself being in control in difficult situations	☐
I can see myself successfully overcoming challenging situations	☐
I can see myself giving 100% during the lesson	☐
I can imagine myself appearing self-confident in front of the class	☐
I can hear the sounds of the classroom	☐
I can hear the sounds outside of the classroom	☐
I can smell the odour of the classroom	☐
I can smell the odour outside of the classroom	☐

Use this chapter to help you develop your imagery for any boxes left un-ticked. You may also use the chapter to help in enhancing the vividness and clarity of your mental imagery. In doing so, you will be recreating and practising these situations in your mind – remaining calm, focused and in control of your thoughts/feelings. Having explored your existing level of imagery ability, this information can be used to help develop an imagery script. It would be unwise, however, to launch straight into writing the imagery script before we have given you an idea of what is and is not important in the environment. To do this, we would like you to start by taking a mental journey around your living room at home.

Try to picture the shape of the room, the location of the furniture, television, fireplace, tables, etc. Then picture the colour of the walls, the location of mirrors, prints or photographs. Picture the location of any windows or doors and the view through these. A basic representation of your living room should now be emerging in your mind. When you are happy that you can picture the scene, it is necessary to add increasing levels of detail. Picture the colour of the carpet or floor covering. Has the sun faded it in patches? Are there any stains on it and is it frayed anywhere? If you are unable to answer these questions, have a look the next time you are in the living room, check them and incorporate the new information into the image. You can also add the colour of the walls, damaged areas, position of light switches and perhaps radiators. Next might be the visual texture of the walls and whether the prints or photographs are hanging straight or skewed. Your mental image is now beginning to build to a high degree of complexity. If you build the picture in this way, it becomes possible to take this to the finest level of detail. The point is to show you how powerful the technique can be as you pick up more and more information from the environment. We tend to concentrate only on the visual system for the living room example and pay less attention to other senses.

Now that you are ready to move on to mental imagery for the classroom, we can include your other senses. An example might include asking you to 'feel' how comfortable your seat is at your desk when marking. How does the pen feel in your hand?

How far can you reach up the board to write something? What does it feel like to walk around the classroom – is there easy access? Now think about a lesson you have taught previously – one you are happy with and know very well. Start to build up a mental imagery sequence of the lesson. The example provided in Table 15.1 highlights this.

Table 15.1   Sample imagery script

The class is lining up outside in the playground. I am already there, ready to bring them to order and ensure they walk calmly into the class.

I tell the students exactly what I want them to do when they go into the class. After removing their coats, they need to sit quietly at their desks with their individual whiteboards.

I tell the students to write down five mathematics questions to give to the person sitting next to them.

I monitor the students as they come into the room, ensuring everyone is doing as requested, reminding them they need their boards.

All the students are writing down their questions and calmly passing their boards to one another, then they are answering the questions.

I set the timer on the board for two minutes then monitor the students to keep them on task.

The two minutes pass and I tell the students to return their boards so their partner can check their answers. I set the timer for another two minutes.

I give the students one minute to feed back to their partner on how they did and any mistakes.

Once the time has expired, I ask the class to focus on the board again, where the lesson objectives are displayed.

I ask them to check their understanding of the words in order to ensure they focus on the key concepts of the lesson.

If you are familiar with starting a lesson as in the example script above, we would like to think that you are able to picture each element as it relates to the class you work with. (Of course you may not actually teach mathematics so feel free to adapt!) Naturally, not all of the information you need will be in the script. For example, the script above takes place at the start of a new year and students may not be used to the routine that is being established. Is it the first or last lesson of the day? How will this affect the students? The weather conditions may affect the students: it may be a very hot summer's day or cold and wet.

Having produced a script of the kind shown above it should be used to get a grasp for the intricacies of the lesson and become imprinted on your mind. You can then reduce it to something more practical to remind yourself of the stages, as shown in Table 15.2.

You can see how this script has been created from the previous one. It is not the words that make the script. Rather it is the visual imagery in your mind that brings the script to life. If these words don't allow you to 'see' the lesson, then you need to adapt them until the lesson is brought to life. Keep practising until it appears for you!

A correctly designed mental imagery sequence can be used to rehearse even the finest of detail, to the point where it becomes second nature. As pointed out earlier,

Table 15.2   Sample abbreviated imagery script

Be outside as they line up

Sit at desks, whiteboards out

Five questions then swap

Two minutes on timer

Hand board back. Mark partner's work

Feedback to partner

Lesson objectives

Check understanding

Table 15.3   Example mental imagery script template

Phase 1: Basic Awareness	Phase 2: Inclusion of Details		Phase 3: Refinement of Detail
	Descriptors	*Actions and Emotions*	
1: Preparing for the lesson.	Confident, excited, aware of the time until the start.	Feel full of energy, confident in my ability. I can hear the students outside.	I am preparing for the start of the lesson. I am feeling energised, confident and ready to teach.
2: Meet and greet.	Greet students outside. Instructions as to the next lesson.	I go out and greet the students. I stand confidently and call them to attention. I feel alert and enthused.	I go outside pre-empting the bell so I am there before the students. I stand confidently; this is my classroom and it is my lesson. I will enjoy it with the students. I can hear the bell and see the students coming to line up. I tell them the instructions for entering the classroom and settling themselves.
3: Transition.	Position in classroom. Monitoring.	Position myself so I can monitor what is happening and be seen.	I enter the classroom first and wait by the door so I can monitor the students settling. I remind them what they need.
4: Focusing students' attention.	Move to front of class. Ensure attention. Inform students of the first task.	I feel my heart rate increasing but this inspires me with confidence: this is my adrenaline to ensure I am on top form for the lesson. I move with confidence to the front of the class.	I walk comfortably and confidently to the front of my class. I face the students and ask for everyone to look forward. I am alert for those who may be distracted and call them to attention. I ask the students to write five questions on their whiteboards.
5: Introductory task.	Students complete task. Start timer on board.	I am relaxed yet focused on the students. I am aware of what I want to ask them next.	All of the students are actively engaged with writing their questions. I start the timer on the board. I monitor their engagement. I will ask students to swap boards with a partner when the time is up.

this should free up available mental resources for strategy. Table 15.3 can be used as a template for writing an imagery script. It contains details for that act as a mental rehearsal for the events leading up to the start of the lesson outlined above. See if you can identify with it. The script can easily be adapted to suit any lesson for any subject.

> ### ACTIVITY
>
> Reviewing the last section of this chapter, specifically Table 15.3, consider developing your own imagery script.

15.7 PRACTISING IMAGERY BEFORE THE EVENT

Mental practice is essential. After deciding on whether to use internal or external imagery, you should consider another aspect of imagery, related to the job that you want imagery to help you with. You need to decide whether your imagery needs to be a general or specific sequence. Then you need to decide whether you need it for cognitive or motivational reasons. If it is to do with teaching strategy, it will be cognitive. If it is to do with boosting confidence, for example, it will be motivational. Table 15.4 will help you in deciding which type of mental imagery you may need.

Table 15.4   Different types of mental imagery (adapted from Paivio, 1985)

	Cognitive/Instructional	Motivational
General	Strategic planning	Arousal
	Example: imaging a strategy to gain students' attention and maintain for the start of the lesson.	Example: imaging increases or decreases in heart rate before the lesson.
Specific	Skills practice	Goal response
	Example: imaging the fine balance between helping individuals and monitoring the class.	Example: imaging students achieving the lesson outcomes and ending the lesson on time in a calm manner.

Having decided which imagery to use, you are now ready to practise. This is where we must return to the issue of controlling the mental imagery sequence. We would ask you to return to the living room sequence discussed earlier, but this time, to imagine a friend or colleague sitting on one of the chairs. We would then make suggestions about that person: Are they smiling? Drinking a cup of coffee? How are they sitting? And so on. Next, we would ask you to imagine the person getting up and walking over to switch on the television. You should be able to control what is happening within the imagery sequence. In developing control, it is then necessary, for example, for you to imagine an anxiety-evoking situation from your teaching. This might be a situation such as the moments leading up to the start of a lesson. Perhaps you may focus on the feelings of anxiety: tension in the shoulders and neck, increased heart rate, dry mouth, clammy hands. We would then take each of these and ask you to imagine the shoulders and neck becoming more relaxed, the speed of the heart beat reducing, saliva beginning to return in the mouth, and perspiration on the hands beginning to dry. If you have been able to focus on these things returning to normal, *you* have controlled all the things causing heightened anxiety and are now ready to focus on the lesson. The power of verbalising the situation will prepare you for the lesson when it happens in reality. Your imagery practice should enhance your positive emotions (McCarthy, 2009). As we have pointed out throughout this chapter, the key word of course is 'PRACTISE'!

15.8 PRACTISING IMAGERY AFTER THE EVENT

Although this seems rather strange, practising imagery sequences after a lesson is a useful technique. It can act as a kind of debrief to ensure that the imagery used before the event was appropriate. If you find that certain things didn't go according to plan, or there were unexpected situations that arose, then now is the time to incorporate this new information before it gets forgotten. Is it for cognitive/instructional or motivational reasons? This will enhance your store of information about this particular situation for next time.

REFLECTION

Consider an event that happened which you would like to revisit. Replay the event in your mind, bringing it to the conclusion you wish to have achieved.

15.9 IMAGERY SCRIPTS

Having developed your first written imagery script, you might now be considering variations on it, to cover different situations within the same lesson. Perhaps the students had more trouble understanding the concept. Perhaps they completed their work before you had envisaged. What would you then do? You will begin to build up an actual set of electronic or paper copies of your sequences. Keep them together in a file for reference purposes and for review if you need to return to them to refresh your memory. Think of this file as being a recipe book of lessons, or strategies to incorporate for different scenarios.

15.10 CONTEXTUAL SETTING

Wherever possible, you should aim to carry out your mental imagery sequence in a contextually appropriate setting, such as in the classroom. Of course such an enriched environment will also serve to be motivational (Beadle, 2008). This will provide an element of reality. Research in psychology reveals that recall from memory works well if it takes place in the same environment in which it was learned, known as context-dependent memory (Godden and Baddeley, 1975). The same applies to the state that you are in when you learn (Baddeley, 1982). If you are relaxed when you learn, you will remember more if you are relaxed when tested, but if you are tense, you will not be able to remember as much. We flippantly tell our students that if they revise for an examination when they are drunk, the theory suggests that they should remember more in the examination if they are drunk! Of course, we swiftly move on to point out the obvious flaw in this argument. In psychology, there are always exceptions to the rule.

15.11 CONTEXTUAL PROPS

If you are unable to carry out your mental imagery sequence at the school, perhaps because you are developing it before you even get there, then there are things that you can do to enhance the sequence (e.g., recall our comment about odour-evoked memories). For example, you may have a different wardrobe for teaching than from your casual clothes. Put your teaching clothes on and run through the mental imagery sequence in your mind. We're sure you will agree that it feels so much more real. Other contextual props could be identified but we would rather you consider what is significant for your own script.

15.12 CONCLUSION

Imagery is a powerful tool in the armoury of the teacher for a variety of reasons, as discussed. Once a certain level of skill is achieved, imagery can be used in a multitude of situations. Equally, developing this technique in your students can be effective, not only in enhancing their learning, but also in enhancing their resilience. The next time your class has been given a piece of creative writing to do, why not take them on a mental journey through the topic using imagery? Or the next time you wish to cover fractions in maths, why not use imagery associated with a cherry pie to enable them to understand parts of the whole? And the next time you have a student with a self-confidence or anger management issue, why not use imagery as part of the solution to their challenges?

15.13 FURTHER READING

Ibrahim, E.F., Richardson, M.D. and Nestel, D. (2015) 'Mental imagery and learning: A qualitative study in orthopaedic trauma surgery', *Medical Education*, 49 (9): 888–900.
Although this may seem to be a strange suggestion for further reading, we have included it to enable you to ask the question, 'How can I make it work in the classroom?' As researchers in orthopaedic trauma surgery, the authors would have asked a similar question (obviously related

to the operating theatre rather than the classroom) when they delved into the sports science literature, which has an abundance of material on mental imagery in sport.

Joffe, V.L., Cain, K. and Maric, N. (2007) 'Comprehension problems in children with specific language impairment: Does mental imagery training help?', *International Journal of Language & Communication Disorders*, 42 (6): 648–64.
This paper explores the use of mental imagery in helping children who are struggling with comprehension and reading. The findings show that using mental imagery is effective in boosting the story comprehension of children with specific language impairment.

Libby, L.K., Valenti, G., Pfent, A. and Eibach, R.P. (2011) 'Seeing failure in your life: Imagery perspective determines whether self-esteem shapes reactions to recalled and imagined failure', *Journal of Personality and Social Psychology*, 101 (6): 1157–73.
This journal article examines internal and external imagery in relation to high and low self-esteem.

McCarthy, P.J. (2009) 'Putting imagery to good affect: A case study among youth swimmers', *Sport and Exercise Psychology Review*, 5 (1): 27–38.
This paper explores how imagery can be used to enhance positive emotions.

Selcuk Haciomeroglu, E. and LaVenia, M. (2017) 'Object-spatial imagery and verbal cognitive styles in high school students'. *Perceptual & Motor Skills*, 124 (3): 689–702.
This paper examines the object imagery and spatial imagery in relation to cognitive style and various performance indicators. While it is heavily theoretical and underpinned by extensive research literature, it remains accessible if you delve in at a depth you feel comfortable with.

Taktek, K., Zinsser, N. and St-John, B. (2008) 'Visual versus kinaesthetic mental imagery: Efficacy for the retention and transfer of a closed motor skill in young children', *Canadian Journal of Experimental Psychology*, 62 (3): 174–87.
This paper compares the effects of visual versus kinaesthetic mental imagery and physical practice on the retention and transfer of throwing a ball (with the non-dominant hand) at a target in young children.

16

SELF-TALK AND COGNITIVE RESTRUCTURING

CHAPTER OBJECTIVES

- Understand how self-talk may be utilised in a variety of situations.
- Consider personal and specific self-talk expressions for a variety of occasions.
- Understand how to retrain thought processes through cognitive restructuring.

TEACHERS' STANDARDS

A teacher must:

5   Adapt teaching to respond to the strengths and needs of all pupils

- have a secure understanding of how a range of factors can inhibit pupils' ability to learn, and how best to overcome these
- demonstrate an awareness of the physical, social and intellectual development of children, and know how to adapt teaching to support pupils' education at different stages of development

8   Fulfil wider professional responsibilities

- develop effective professional relationships with colleagues, knowing how and when to draw on advice and specialist support
- take responsibility for improving teaching through appropriate professional development, responding to advice and feedback from colleagues

16.1 INTRODUCTION

This chapter is based around the concept of mind-to-muscle techniques, whereby the brain (mind) focuses on activity that effects a change in the body (muscle). Techniques such as these may be used to reduce anxiety, worry and tension. An awareness of one's state of arousal in a positive, productive manner is important in helping to overcome the symptoms associated with these challenges. In order to do this, two applied techniques are available: self-talk – the internal 'voice'; and cognitive restructuring – a 're-framing' of thought patterns. As is familiar now, we will draw upon literature from various domains outside of education and will, where possible, explore education-specific literature. Self-talk and cognitive restructuring can be thought of as two sides to the same coin: self-talk can only be successful if the thoughts in a teacher's head are positive. If those thoughts are negative, they can be changed, or restructured to become positive. This, in essence, is what cognitive restructuring aims to do.

16.2 WHAT IS SELF-TALK AND WHEN SHOULD IT BE USED?

Self-talk is mental activity that occurs whenever an individual thinks and allows perceptions and beliefs to become conscious. It is an internal dialogue, which is sometimes verbalised, but is not intended to elicit a verbal response from someone else (Hardy et al., 2001). Self-talk helps you to stay focused on strategic elements of your teaching. In practice, you might use the word 'focus' to signify the exact moment you feel your concentration slipping when engaged with your planning, preparation or assessment. It is the equivalent of hitting the 'turbo mode', narrowing your focus, providing a shot of energy and leading to successfully completing the task at hand.

Although self-talk is commonly regarded as being positive or negative (Zourbanos et al., 2014), an additional distinction to be aware of is that self-talk can be instructional or motivational. An earlier paper by Zourbanos (2013) highlights the difference between instructional and motivational self-talk for a basketball free-throw, for use by PE students. This paper is worth reading, since it will enable you to understand how to apply it in PE lessons, but equally it will enable you to reflect on which other areas of the curriculum may benefit from your teaching this technique to your students. Similarly, a paper by Cutton et al. (2015) offers the notion that teachers and educators should possess a self-talk repertoire, based on awareness, reflection and action. This repertoire may be rather diverse. Self-talk has been found to be used by 33 per cent of athletes in injury-rehabilitation (Arvinen-Barrow et al., 2015). Interestingly, this paper also revealed that 47 per cent used goal-setting, 32 per cent used mental imagery and 24 per cent used relaxation techniques in their rehabilitation, suggesting that these techniques are commonplace and benefit those who adopt them. An extreme example of negative self-talk is the notion of 'fat talk', whereby individuals endorse the 'value' of thinness by verbalising beliefs about the 'ideal body' (Cruwys et al., 2016), and this perhaps is an area where cognitive restructuring, to be discussed later, would be of benefit in the classroom, before 'fat talk' becomes deeply ingrained from childhood. It is worth noting at this point that while one might intuitively consider negative self-talk to be detrimental, in a systematic review of the sport literature, this has not been shown to be the case (Tod et al., 2011). This may indeed be specific to the sporting arena, but we felt it necessary to provide a more balanced picture than intuition might suggest.

Self-talk can be used to correct bad habits, to build self-confidence and to reduce anxiety and when controlling effort and refocusing.

CORRECTING BAD HABITS

This is rather like self-coaching or self-instruction. Here, self-talk is used to question how you are presenting yourself in the classroom, your confidence, scanning the class for students who may be experiencing difficulties, the pace and progress of your lesson, etc. Self-talk may be used to make corrections when you are learning a new skill and need to develop and refine it, for example, using a new software package, or for checking your understanding of a concept you are to teach (Cutton et al., 2015). Through the learning experience the 'whispering self' enables teachers to shape their perceptions and their behaviour as they develop (Chohan, 2010).

ACTIVITY

Select a phrase that will keep you focused on the present, something to bring your attention back if it starts to wander. Next, consider a song that helps to motivate or stimulate you in some way. You may even want to make your own playlist of such motivational songs.

BUILDING SELF-CONFIDENCE AND REDUCING ANXIETY

Self-confidence and reduced anxiety are vital elements of successful performance. Teachers who lack self-confidence are immediately disadvantaged and face an uphill battle. If you are lacking in self-confidence you may enhance it, indirectly, through self-talk. Moreover, it is second-person self-talk (you) that may facilitate this more so than first-person self-talk (I), since it may resemble advice and guidance given by others previously (Dolcos and Albarracin, 2014). It is prudent also to mention the distinction between first-person singular (I) and first-person plural (we) self-talk, of which the latter is preferable when focusing on the capabilities of groups (Son et al., 2011). Similarly, anxiety reduction can be achieved through a reinterpretation of one's current physiological state, through the use of self-talk (Wood et al., 2009). Essentially it is used to control your arousal level depending on how nervous you are and whether the level of arousal is facilitative or debilitative. This also depends on how you perceive that excitement or arousal and is linked to your changes in mood and different 'emotional internal interlocutors' (Puchalska-Wasyl, 2015). If you do not feel in the right frame of mind to teach, you can use self-talk to alter your present mood state. Find out what the problem is through accurately defining the problem, seek the solution, and then use self-talk, in combination with appropriate language, to confirm that you are moving towards that solution (Kross et al., 2014).

CONTROLLING EFFORT AND REFOCUSING

Having focused on the task in hand, it is important that teachers 'stay in tune'. Self-talk can be used to keep the level of effort high, avoiding any lapses in performance and concentration. Indeed, the phrases 'stay in tune' or 'stay on the pace' are good examples that help to control effort levels (although feel free to take ownership over your own similar phrase). As a safety net, refocusing should be used if effort does falter too much. A problem may occur, however, when somebody else tells you to put in more effort as this can make you frustrated if you are already committing 100 per cent. Such requests are irritating! A good self-talk response would be something like, 'I will put in the effort that feels right for me.'

Cue words and statements such as 'be here', 'here and now' and any others you feel comfortable with are useful for bringing you back to the reality of now (Cutton et al., 2015).

You might have lyrics from favourite songs that may help you here, or you may want to find inspirational lyrics through a search website (e.g. www.songlyrics.com). For example, a line from Toni Braxton's song 'Let It Flow' has the lyrics, 'Just let go … And let it flow… Everything's gonna work out right.' From this the lyrics 'Just let go … And let it flow' could mean to stop struggling against something, relax, let what happens happen – good advice if you're worrying over something! Another is, 'While everyone's lost, the battle is won … With all these things that I've done', by The Killers. Be careful in your selection. 'Help!' by the Beatles would not go down too nicely!

16.3 FACILITATING SELF-TALK IN THE CLASSROOM

We will outline some methods for using self-talk in teaching. You should decide which one works best for you, or whether a combination of methods provides a useful variation on the theme. Once you feel comfortable with each one, consider how you will facilitate the acquisition of self-talk in the classroom, in order to develop resilience in your students.

Think back to very good and not-so-good performances. Try to recall your pre- and post- thoughts and feelings. It is important to remember, however, that using recall methods can lead to distorted and inaccurate incidents. Psychologists know from research that our memory is not always as accurate as we think it is. If you start to keep a log or journal, you can use this information in the future when you need to 'look back'. If we ask you to recall events from a particular time three years ago, you may struggle. If you kept records, you can give us all the information we need. A recent study by Arnold et al. (2016) found a solution to the retrospection issue in a study with golfers, by comparing verbalised self-talk, via portable microphone recordings, with retrospective accounts, finding large discrepancies between the two. The study highlights the need to utilise technology to capture the moment in the best way possible, despite extraneous constraints.

Keeping daily logs is a common form of monitoring and has been used, for instance, in active recording of sleep diaries (Mairs and Mullan, 2015), monitoring multiple aspects of athlete training programmes (Saw et al., 2015) and monitoring food intake (Mujcic and Oswald, 2016). Keeping daily records of any self-talk that you have carried out and making a note of what the situation was when you carried out that self-talk will provide a monitoring tool. This also helps you to assess whether you are pre-dominantly positive or negative in your self-talk.

It is essential that you identify patterns of self-talk before you can develop the technique for personal use. Several methods exist for you to use, including: thought stopping, visual cues and physical signals. It is possible to use a thought or cue to interrupt those unwanted thoughts as they occur (Wolpe, 1958). You can quickly say out loud 'stop' as soon as you know you are saying or thinking an undesirable thought (Wilde, 2008). It is important that you consider the thought, if there is time. Evaluate and reflect on it, but then you need to insert another, more positive thought in its place. You can use a visual cue, such as a mental picture of a red traffic light, representing 'stop'. Again, you will need quickly to insert another more positive thought in its place and then change the red traffic light to green. Alternatively, consider using a sad-faced emoji to represent 'stop'. Whatever works for you! You can use physical movements, such as snapping your fingers to represent 'stop'. Yet again, you need quickly to insert another more positive thought in its place.

16.4 SELF-TALK SHOULD BECOME AUTOMATIC OR SECOND NATURE

If a teacher thinks too much about what they are doing, these very thought processes may distract him or her from the task, by disrupting the automatic performance. However, self-talk is about key words or phrases. It is mentally economical and it feeds into teaching. As soon as you begin to focus too much on exactly the task at hand, concentrating excessively much on one element, your attention will be diverted and you will begin to make mistakes. You should be aiming to be able to use self-talk automatically rather than having to over-think it. However, paradoxically, in order to achieve this, you have to go through the process of overthinking the task in hand. An example of this is midway through a lesson and you get caught up thinking about the next lesson. Automatically a bellowing voice comes from inside, 'Focus!' In a single word, you have given yourself the guidance on monitoring the class, monitoring the development of the lesson, being clear and calm and not getting distracted from an incident that may be escalating. This takes practice ... Take the challenge!

16.5 COGNITIVE RESTRUCTURING: HOW TO GET THE MOST FROM YOUR INNER VOICE

Arguably, none of us 'see' the world as it really is. Instead, we perceive the world. We see it as we think it exists for us. It is all a matter of perspective! Think about each student in your class – they have a different view of the room, the board, you. Our perspective is shaped by the way we think, our attitudes, beliefs, superstitions, stereotypes, etc. Cognitive restructuring is derived from a psychotherapy technique, known as Rational Emotive Behavioural Therapy (REBT), developed back in the 1960s by Albert Ellis, which remains in use today (Ellis, 1962; 2011). It aims to direct us towards modifying self-defeating, irrational and anxiety-provoking cognitions or thoughts. It can be used to restructure these thoughts and to alter irrational or 'bad' thoughts. It is relatively easy to spot negative thoughts and substitute them with positive thoughts before they get too serious. With practice, you will stop negative thoughts before they emerge. There should be nothing negative in your head when you are teaching, regardless of what is happening. Instead, you will have plenty of things to keep your focus. A combination of cognitive restructuring with self-talk can be used to provide self-reward and to increase your effort.

16.6 WHEN TO USE COGNITIVE RESTRUCTURING

Cognitive restructuring can be used in various situations. For example, it is effective in reducing anxiety and increasing levels of coping under adverse conditions (Hope et al., 2010). It is also useful in increasing self-confidence, as well as motivation (see Hanton et al., 2008). If you have trouble in making a start on your marking, then perhaps cognitive restructuring can help you to think differently about how you approach it.

16.7 STAGES IN DEVELOPING COGNITIVE RESTRUCTURING

Cognitive restructuring is not as difficult as it may initially appear. It typically comprises four stages. You need to be aware that your beliefs, perceptions and assumptions influence emotional arousal. Consider the perceptions of a day-to-day occurrence, yours and your line manager/head. If they have just asked you to complete an additional task, you may feel frustration. You should identify underlying thoughts to recognise any potential irrational, self-defeating foundations you may have, such as

'I am always given extra responsibilities: they must not like me' or 'When will I have time to do this?' Once you have identified these irrational thoughts, you need actively to criticise them (your thoughts, *not* your line manager/head!), replacing them with thoughts that prevent or reduce maladaptive anxiety. For example, in the situation of being given extra responsibility, you could replace the thoughts with 'They must think I do a good job and can handle the extra responsibility.' Finally, you should practise and rehearse new thoughts, applying them to relevant situations.

ACTIVITY

The task below will help you to identify where cognitive restructuring may help you. Follow the instructions below, decide how many of them are in your control and work on putting positive statements in place to overcome any challenges you have identified.

Instruction

1 Recall some aspect of your teaching experience in which you felt you could have produced a more successful performance. This could be working with students, or planning, preparation and assessment time.

2 Write down what you did, what you felt and what you said. Look critically at your narrative for negative thoughts. How could you change some of the negative thoughts? Are there some areas where you are thinking positively? Try not to punish yourself for these; give yourself some credit!

3 List ten of your most common thoughts when you are engaged with teaching.

4 Look at the list you have produced. Have you focused on issues outside of your control? Have you been unduly negative?

5 For every thought write a positive statement or a self-focused alternative.

6 All you need to do now is to recognise when this occurs and insert the new positive thought in its place!

CASE STUDY   Jane

Having established that some thoughts may be irrational or distorted, Jane set out to produce a list of negative thoughts that might be interfering with her performance. Jane sat down the following evening to focus on writing the positive, self-enhancing substitute thoughts. After checking their 'authenticity', Jane has now rehearsed them and is able to bring them to mind when/if the self-defeating thoughts emerge.

(Continued)

Self-Defeating Thought	Self-Enhancing Thought
I have the term's planning to complete.	Planning takes time but if done properly now, it will make the term easier.
That was stupid of me!	Ease off. Everyone makes mistakes.
	Shrug it off and put your mind on what you want to do.
I have no time to do this!	I can arrange my time more efficiently to ensure I can fulfil all my tasks.
I can't concentrate.	I will go for a walk or get some exercise then I will be invigorated to get back on with the task.
I don't want to take the additional role of maths coordinator, because of my existing workload.	I have many things to focus on. My workload will change if I take the maths coordinator role and negotiate reductions elsewhere.

This section has provided examples of self-enhancing thoughts that you may use during sessions to fend off self-defeating thoughts before they happen. If any creep in, you must address them rationally in relation to other things that are working positively. Your anxiety levels should remain comfortable. It is imperative that you believe these new thoughts. Anything less than total belief will be met with failure. We would also ask you to identify key words or phrases that will help you to keep focused and motivated during your teaching. These might include: 'Come on!', 'Yes!', 'That was good', 'I can do it', 'Smooth!', 'Calm' … as opposed to 'Oh, damn!' or 'Breathe'.

16.8 CONCLUSION

Self-talk and cognitive restructuring are intimately interlinked. We have seen how self-talk can be positive, but is quite often negative. We have seen how self-defeating thoughts can be reframed, or restructured, with practice and a little consideration about the type of thought as a preferred substitute. We have discussed the need to take ownership and hold a belief in the restructured thoughts. Your interpretation of this chapter, in relation to your own specific needs, will facilitate the direction you will take next.

16.9 FURTHER READING

Ellis, A. and Ellis, D.J. (2011) *Rational Emotive Behaviour Therapy* (2nd edn). Washington, DC: American Psychological Association.
An essential primer, outlining the history, theory, research and application of REBT, from which cognitive restructuring is derived. Well worth a read.

Hamilton, R.A., Scott, D. and Macdougall, M.P. (2007) 'Assessing the effectiveness of self-talk interventions on endurance performance', *Journal of Applied Sport Psychology*, 19: 226–39.
This paper explores different types of self-talk on endurance (in this case cycling), but contains relevant, transferable information. Don't be put off by the 'academic nature' of the paper. Take what you need from the introduction and discussion.

Helmstetter, S. (2015) *365 Days of Positive Self-Talk*. Florida: Park Avenue Press.
This 'pop psychology' paperback provides a positive self-talk statement for every day of the year. What more could you want!? Although overly simplified for a (very) general audience, if you strip away the 'tinsel and decoration', this book is based on the published self-talk literature. An easy read, if the style doesn't irritate, but if it does, then there must be a positive affirmation to replace your maladaptive thought. Just be mindful that the statement of the day might not fit with your schedule!

17
RELAXATION

CHAPTER OBJECTIVES

- To define relaxation and understand the differences between physical and mental tension.
- To understand that relaxation requires engagement to produce the required effects.
- To identify how anxiety, stress, attention and concentration relate to relaxation.
- To develop and practise some relaxation strategies.

TEACHERS' STANDARDS

None of the Teachers' Standards relate to this topic ... but there should be one!

17.1 INTRODUCTION

Teacher wellbeing has never been so central to discussions about the sustainability of the workforce. Perhaps one day, this last sentence will become a main headline: for now it is a mere prediction. We are frequently aware of the inordinate number of hours worked during the week and at weekends. Holidays are a time when teachers can work without going into school. However, when it comes to a time to be able to switch off, it can be extremely difficult. Combined with this, as discussed in Chapter 12, pupils' MWB has increasingly worsened. With the range of academic pressures, along with physical and emotional maturation, the overemphasis on achieving results through continual testing is causing immeasurable longer-term problems.

In teaching, the implications of not being relaxed are potentially severe, culminating in excessive stress loads or potentially leading to an instantaneous poor decision with personal and professional repercussions. So the general advice would be to do just that: 'Relax'. Yet very few people are ever taught how to relax properly. To dispel a common myth, relaxation is not simply about taking a few moments to unwind, listening to some music, taking a walk and so forth; it involves a conscious engagement to relax. Various techniques exist and we will discuss these in this chapter. It is important to note that relaxation training should not be thought of as a simple technique that can be learned quickly. Rather, it may take somewhat longer than teachers anticipate. The key to success is that it should be carried out in a systematic, progressive manner.

Through understanding and embodying principles to help relax, these in turn can be utilised with pupils. As this chapter is being written, a local denominational first school in Worcestershire is engaging with a wellbeing week where some of the principles in this chapter are being shared with children. Arguably, however, such techniques and principles ought to be included daily within the curriculum.

17.2 AVOIDING BURNOUT

'Burnout' is a term that has been defined as a combination of depersonalisation, emotional exhaustion and reduced personal accomplishment that has resulted from prolonged work-related stress (Maslach et al., 2001; O'Brennan et al., 2017). Contributory factors include a lack of clarity about roles, aims and the content of work (Schaufelli and Baker, 2004). Furthermore, as Maslach and Leiter (1999) reported in their research, teacher burnout contributes to both teachers' and pupils' behaviour and experience: that teacher behaviour as a result of burnout decreases classroom preparation and classroom involvement, which in turn impacts on pupils and their behaviour. Further research demonstrates the impact of teacher burnout on pupil motivation as reported by Shen et al. (2015). Teacher burnout is evident not just in the UK but in India (Seth, 2016), Sweden (Arvidsson et al., 2016), the United States (O'Brennan et al., 2017), China (Zhang et al., 2016), Lithuania (Bernotaite and Malinauskiene, 2017) and New Zealand (Blanchi et al., 2016), among many other countries.

Can it really be that teaching is a profession that globally affects the MWB of its staff? With such high prevalence, why would anyone enter into teaching? Of course the answer to this is multi-dimensional, although at some level, intrinsic motivation (discussed in Chapter 10) would be fundamental to the answer. Consequently, something appears to happen once an individual is within the teaching profession, such as factors already mentioned of exhaustion, depersonalisation and reduced personal accomplishment. An additional factor that has received increased attention is compassion fatigue, a term first used by Joinson (1992) – defined as the physical, social, emotional and spiritual exhaustion that overwhelms a person, causing a pervasive decline in their ability, desire and energy to care for others (Merriman, 2015). Compassion fatigue has been discussed predominantly through many caring professions such as nursing, although we would assert that over the coming years, it will increasingly be reported within education.

One way of visualising burnout is putting your car in first gear, then increasing the speed to 30 miles per hour. The needle on the rev counter will enter the red zone as the engine strains. The signs and signals warn you not to maintain this. This is similarly portrayed through the Yerkes–Dodson inversed curve, where some level of stress is required to initially motivate the person (Yerkes and Dodson, 1908). As the level increases to the pinnacle, the individual experiences eustress, or positive stress. Further increase of pressure will move the individual into the de-stress zone, which can be maintained for a while, yet not excessively. Indeed, given the discussion in Chapter 13, operating in the de-stress zone can help develop resilience; but there is a time to ease off. Bakusic et al. (2016) report that there are no diagnostic criteria for burnout; however, there is a need for further longitudinal research to explore the cause and effect relationship between work stress, burnout and depression. We would argue that searching for a causal link may not be the most prudent approach to take, given the intricate interplay between each of these complex issues.

From this initial discussion about the causes of tension, we can progress to considering what relaxation is: as such, it is the reduction of tension mentally and physically, which directly facilitates emotional relaxation.

17.3 HOW DOES RELAXATION WORK?

When considering relaxation, the core is to identify what the cause of the tension is: whether a person is experiencing somatic anxiety (physical tension) or cognitive anxiety (mental tension). Although they relate to each other, establishing the cause can ensure correct guidance for either somatic relaxation or cognitive relaxation. The differences between somatic and cognitive relaxation are distinct. They can be categorised as muscle-to-mind relaxation and mind-to-muscle relaxation, respectively.

PHYSICAL TENSION: SOMATIC OR 'MUSCLE-TO-MIND' RELAXATION

The premise underlying somatic relaxation is that the mind cannot be anxious in the absence of muscle tension. So, if there is no tension in the muscles, then the messages going back into your brain must be saying that there is no need for anxiety. If you reduce tension in your muscles, the signals returning to the brain will tell you that you are no longer tense. The key here is that you need to know what signs to look for and we will cover these shortly when we outline four basic yet really effective relaxation techniques.

MENTAL TENSION: COGNITIVE OR 'MIND-TO-MUSCLE' RELAXATION

Cognitive relaxation acts in the opposite direction. Rather than the muscles providing the mind with information about tension, it is negative thoughts that are causing anxiety and these thoughts may then lead to muscle tension. If the teacher trains his or her mind to relax, then the muscles in turn will become relaxed.

An analogy is in flipping a coin: it cannot fall on both sides at the same time. If a person is relaxed mentally, they cannot be anxious.

ACTIVITY

- List as many indicators as you can think of which would indicate physical (somatic) tension.
- List as many indicators as you can think of which would indicate mental (cognitive) tension.

17.4 THE IMPORTANCE OF BREATHING

Breathing is fundamental to our existence, and one of the easiest and most predominant forms of relaxation is that of breathing (Jerath et al., 2015; Klainin-Yobas et al., 2015; Panda, 2014; Smith and Norman, 2017; Van Diest et al., 2014). All of the techniques mentioned below involve mastery of breathing. It is not enough to simply outline these techniques out of context. Rather, it is important to understand that appropriate breathing is a necessary requirement, and to receive guidance in correct breathing techniques. This may sound strange, given that breathing just happens – a newborn baby can breathe without being taught. As such, breathing is a function of the autonomic nervous system and is controlled without thinking. Indeed, if we ask you now to hold your breath for as long as possible, we will not have to tell you when to start breathing again, it will simply happen after a while. Consequently, the type of breathing required for relaxation techniques is rather more formal and structured, yet equally simple with practice.

During daily life, many of us use thoracic or chest breathing. It is superficial and shallow, generally only utilising the upper section of the respiratory system. Chest breathing is fairly rapid and is associated with the rigours of daily life. In contrast, abdominal or deep breathing is rhythmic, slow and, as expected, deep. It utilises the full capacity of the respiratory system. You can feel the difference as you read this section. Does your breathing feel shallow and irregular? Now, if we ask you to take a breath, fill your chest with air, then fill some more and finally take one extra breath to fill your lower abdomen, you will understand the difference in capacity. When you have filled this extra space, hold for the count of three and then slowly and gently release the inspired air to the count of five. Do this properly three times and we guarantee that you will feel more relaxed than you did before starting the task. Having shown that there seems to be an immediate difference, it is now possible to practise deep breathing to feel the benefits.

ACTIVITY

Think of the lungs as having three compartments: shallow, middle, deep. As you breathe in, fill each section in turn *before* you exhale.

17.5 COMMON RELAXATION PROCEDURES

To recap, the distinction between somatic and cognitive relaxation should be remembered as a quick and effective way of establishing preliminary information about tension and anxiety. We will now discuss four common techniques used to elicit relaxation: progressive muscle relaxation, self-suggestion (or autogenic training), meditation and listening to your body (or biofeedback). We will then conclude by introducing the idea of an enhanced relaxation procedure, using psychological principles to provide what can perhaps be described as a 'supercharged' method due to its links with mental imagery techniques discussed in Chapter 15.

17.6 PROGRESSIVE MUSCLE RELAXATION

Progressive muscle relaxation, or PMR, is a muscle-to-mind technique, originally developed by Jacobson (1938). It has been used in a variety of contexts globally, for example with elderly patients in Iran (Hassanpourt-Dehkordi and Jalali, 2016), cancer treatment in Cyprus (Charalambous et al., 2016), footballers in Malaysia (Sharifah Maimunah and Hashim, 2016), among many other contexts. Essentially, this technique involves tensing and then relaxing different muscle groups. If all of the muscle groups are relaxed, then there can be no tension in the body. As a consequence, any tension in the mind should disappear. It is important that the teacher knows the difference between these two opposing states. Awareness of muscular tension will act as the trigger for the teacher to begin the relaxation technique. Table 17.1 provides practical instructions for PMR. Follow each step, by tensing and relaxing each muscle group in turn. You should pay attention to the difference between tense and relaxed muscles. Each step should take approximately 10 seconds. It may help to transfer the instructions into audio format, so that you can play it back and follow the verbal instructions it gives.

When you have mastered PMR, you can dispense with the tension part of the technique. By this, we mean that you can go straight to the relaxation steps, because you have already identified tension. This is where the benefits occur. If you are standing in the classroom, with tense shoulders and one minute to go before the morning bell, there will not be enough time to run through the whole technique. Instead, you

Table 17.1   Instructions for progressive muscle relaxation

Step	Instruction
1	Make yourself comfortable in a quiet environment. Remove or loosen any restrictive clothing. Breathe in deeply, hold and exhale. Do this two more times. You should begin to feel more relaxed.
2	If you hear any noises, do not ignore them, but focus on inhaling and exhaling slowly.
3	Begin by tensing the muscles of your lower left leg and foot by pointing your toes. Hold this tension for five seconds and then relax. You can feel the difference between tension and relaxation in your calf and foot. Repeat this procedure once more. Do this for the left leg and then twice for the right leg and foot.
4	Move on to tensing the left thigh and buttocks. Tense the left thigh muscle and buttocks by pushing down into the floor. Hold this tension for five seconds and then relax. You can feel the difference between tension and relaxation in your left thigh and buttocks. Repeat this procedure once more. Do this for the left leg and then twice for right thigh and buttocks.
5	Next, tense and relax the left forearm. Do this by bending at the elbow. Hold this tension for five seconds and then relax. You can feel the difference between tension and relaxation in your left bicep. Repeat this procedure once more. Do this for the left bicep and then twice for the right bicep.
6	Next, tense and relax the left bicep. Do this by making a fist. Hold this tension for five seconds and then relax. You can feel the difference between tension and relaxation in your left forearm. Repeat this procedure once more. Do this for the left forearm and then twice for the right forearm.
7	Move on to tensing and relaxing the muscles in your back. Do this by arching your back. Hold this tension for five seconds and then relax. You can feel the difference between tension and relaxation in your back muscles. Repeat this procedure once more.
8	Next, tense and relax the muscles in your stomach and chest. Do this by inhaling, holding and releasing. Hold this tension for five seconds and then relax. You can feel the difference between tension and relaxation in your stomach and chest. Repeat this procedure once more.
9	Next, tense and relax the muscles in your neck and shoulders. Do this by shrugging your shoulders. Hold this tension for five seconds and then relax. You can feel the difference between tension and relaxation in your neck and shoulder muscles. Repeat this procedure once more.
10	Move on to tensing and relaxing the muscles in your face and forehead. Do this by clenching your jaw and frowning. Hold this tension for five seconds and then relax. You can feel the difference between tension and relaxation in your facial muscles. Repeat this procedure once more.
11	Mentally scan your whole body for any tension. If there is any, release it by tensing and relaxing.
12	Finally, focus on the relaxed feelings your muscles are now giving you. You are calm and relaxed.
13	Before getting up, it is important to return to a greater degree of conscious awareness. Count slowly, from 1 to 7, exhaling on every count. As you get closer to 7, you will feel more and more alert.
14	You should now feel completely relaxed and rejuvenated.

should simply feel the tension in your shoulders and run through the relaxation step for these muscles. Within a matter of seconds, you should find that the tension dissipates and is replaced with relaxed shoulder and neck muscles.

17.7 AUTOGENIC TRAINING (OR SELF-SUGGESTION)

Autogenic training is a mind-to-muscle technique, originally developed in the 1930s by Schultz (Luthe and Schultz, 1969). The underlying concepts of autogenic training are the physical sensations of 'heaviness' and 'warmth'. Mental effort is directed towards a particular body part and a sensation of heaviness is produced in that body part. For example, we might instruct you to imagine your right calf becoming extremely heavy. We would then ask you to imagine the right calf losing its heaviness and becoming warm and sun-kissed. After successful practice, we would progress by directing your attention towards 'coolness' in your forehead. The remaining element of this technique is to direct attention towards having a rhythmic breathing pattern and strong, stable heart rate. This technique is akin to self-hypnosis and rests on verbal instruction or internal thought processes, for example: 'My right calf is heavy; my right calf is relaxed and warm; my heart rate is slow and calm; my breathing is strong and rhythmic; and my forehead is cool.' This technique takes a long time to develop to a high standard and, given that teachers' schedules are usually rather hectic, is not ideal. However, it is available and may prove useful, so the message is to give it a try.

Autogenic training continues to be used in a variety of settings. For example, Kiba et al. (2017) have successfully used the process for patients with functional somatic syndrome, while others have demonstrated the effectiveness on sufferers with chronic migraine (Peper et al., 2016), or improved performance with athletes (Mikicin and Kowalczyk, 2015). Specifically, Kuhlmann et al. (2015) have used such a programme with students experiencing excessive stress.

17.8 MEDITATION AND MINDFULNESS

In the first edition of this book, we discussed whether mindfulness should be included given that it was being treated as a fad, despite our extensive research into the area. Mindfulness has now become commonplace – appearing on the front cover of *Time* magazine, and featuring on various popular television and radio programmes. The school discussed in Section 17.1 is utilising mindfulness techniques for its well-being week. Consequently, mindfulness appears to have become the Western world's acceptable face of meditation, which is still perceived as somewhat esoteric in nature. Arguably both meditation and mindfulness are the same: they both involve focused concentration on one element at a time, for example, breathing, chanting, physical activity and so forth.

According to Germer (2013), the definition of mindfulness originates from the Buddhist philosophical language of 'Pali', specifically the word 'Sati' which translates as 'awareness', 'clear headedness', or 'joy'. Germer et al. (2013: xi) provide a new interpretation, that mindfulness is 'being aware of where your mind is from one moment to the next, with gentle acceptance'. Conversely, Gunaratana (2002) argues that mindfulness cannot be fully captured with words because it is a subtle, non-verbal experience.

The Chinese character for mindfulness encompasses the notion that it concerns undivided attention and is an interplay of the senses, specifically the eyes and ears, combined with the heart through feeling, and the mind through thinking. This is demonstrated in Figure 17.1.

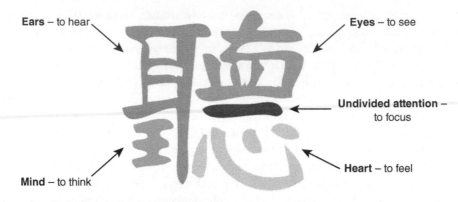

Ears – to hear

Eyes – to see

Undivided attention – to focus

Heart – to feel

Mind – to think

Figure 17.1 Chinese character for mindfulness

Within mindfulness, there are three levels: focused attention, open monitoring and compassion (Salzberg, 2011). Focused attention is the area that most people consider mindfulness: it is the aspect of concentrating on one thing, fully, at that moment, whether this is through movement, postures, breathing, chanting, mandalas, eating or any practice that involves heightening one's senses. As such, the focus is on concentration. However, true mindfulness is at the second level of practice, that of open monitoring. This is where there is an awareness of thinking, specifically being aware of thoughts and feelings without attachment or a judgement of them. The third level of mindfulness is that of compassion, or loving kindness.

Taking these further, activities that help focus attention are global in nature, for example, the use of prayer beads, or mala, is common within many faith traditions such as Islam, Hinduism, Buddhism, Christianity, or Judaism, and consist of using beads to activate the memory and count recitations of prayers, or a mantra. Many such prayer beads consist of 108 beads (or 27 for a wrist mala). One mantra is 'Om Mani Padme Hum' (Sanskrit: ॐ मणिपद्मे हुम्). The six-syllable invocation translates as 'O jewel in the lotus blossom', or 'O, thou jewel in the lotus, hail.' The meaning of a mantra is often irrelevant, as the sound is more important: indeed, the sounds of the mantra can lie beyond meaning. The mantra is the most widely used in Mahayana Buddhism but also widely in East Asia (Tibet, Mongolia, China, Korea, Japan, Burma, Vietnam, Thailand).

Open monitoring meditation involves a non-reactive monitoring of the moment-to-moment content of experience. This helps the individual to become reflectively aware of the nature of emotional and cognitive patterns. The aim of the practice is to develop a non-judgemental awareness of sensory, cognitive and affective fields of experience in the present moment. One such practice adapted from Siegel (2011) is listed below.

- Start by sitting comfortably in a dignified posture. Notice the sensations of sitting in the chair. Eyes can be closed or softly open.
- Take a few breaths, letting go of any burdens you might be carrying. Stay with your breath, the sounds around you, or the sensations in your hands for a few minutes until you can focus and gather your attention.

- Picture an image of a wheel and bring your attention to the hub. Then expand the image to include the spokes going out to the rim of the wheel.
- Now place yourself in the hub of the wheel. Give yourself a few moments to feel anchored and steadied.
- Place the things in your life that may be upsetting or distracting you on the rim of the wheel. The distance between the hub and the rim is up to you. Allow as much space as you need – a few feet or yards, or even a football field. Give yourself a few moments to find the space you need. Allow yourself this respite.
- When you're reading, see if you can venture out on a spoke and begin to investigate one of the items on the rim. Start with something that is manageable, not the most difficult problem that you face.
- See what arises as you begin to bring your attention to this issue. What do you notice in your body? What emotions arise? If you start to feel overwhelmed, return to the hub and allow yourself to steady and ground. Experiment with going back and forth between the hub and the rim. Go slowly. (Pollack, 2013: 144)

One of the most powerful open monitoring meditations we have used with clients is outlined below.

THE PEBBLE MEDITATION

Close your eyes gently ... Settle yourself in your chair ... Focus on your breathing ... As you breathe in, say in your mind the word 'calm' ... As you breathe out, say in your mind the word 'relax' ... Continue to breathe naturally, as you breathe in, 'calm' ... as you breathe out, 'relax'.

(Allow about a minute for the person to focus on their breathing.)

Imagine being at the edge of a beautiful pond ... The sun is shining and you can see some of its rays reflected in the water ... There are water lilies, and blue and green dragonflies circling ... Maybe you hear a frog croaking ... Perhaps you can hear the rustling of leaves gently blowing in the wind ... Can you feel the gentle breeze on your skin? ... Allow yourself to visualise this pond in all its glory and add any image or sound to the picture that you create in your imagination.

Now see yourself picking up a small, flat pebble ... Take the pebble in your hand. Feel the texture ... is it smooth or rough ... is it cold, or is it warming up within your hands? How did the pebble get to be where it is?

Imagine throwing the pebble gently into the water ... See the concentric ripples dancing on the surface from where the pebble entered the water ...

(Continued)

Watch the pebble sink a little ... Notice what thoughts, feelings and sensations you are experiencing right now ... Allow the pebble to sink deeper and see whether any sensations, images or feelings change.

Let the pebble settle at the bottom of the pond. You may even be able to see where it has settled ... What do you feel, sense, or think now? ... Are there any messages arising from your consciousness that you need to hear or bring to your awareness?

Stay a little longer and just breathe, from moment to moment ... taking care of the here and now.

Source: adapted from Collard, 2014: 38–9.

In relation to compassion, a loving-kindness meditation (or 'metta bhavana') is provided below.

A LOVING-KINDNESS MEDITATION

- **Mindful breathing with gratitude**

  o Begin by feeling your natural breathing with a sense of affection. Feel thankful that you're breathing, nourishing your body with lovely oxygen.

- **Well-wishing towards someone you find it easy to show affection to**

  o Choose someone with whom you have a simple, unconditionally loving relationship. Visualise the person, and in your mind, say to yourself several times, slowly and thoughtfully: '*May you be well, may you be happy, may you be healthy, may you be free from suffering.*'
  o Say it with kindness and affection.

- **Well-wishing towards yourself**

  o Now transfer the same sense of well-wishing to yourself. Visualise yourself and wish yourself a sense of wellbeing. Say to yourself, several times: '*May I be well, may I be happy, may I be healthy, may I be free from suffering.*'
  o Feel the words coming out of your heart area. Feel as if you're absorbing any pleasant feelings that arise.

- **Well-wishing towards someone neutral**
  - Now think of someone to whom you have neither particularly positive nor negative feelings – perhaps a ticket seller at the railway station or the assistant at your local shop. As before say: *'May they be well, may they be happy, may they be healthy, may they be free from suffering.'*
  - Visualise the person and wish them well, as best you can.

- **Well-wishing towards someone difficult**
  - Think of someone who you don't particularly like; perhaps someone who irritates or annoys you – essentially someone with whom you have a difficult relationship but whom you're willing to work with today. Say: *'May they be well, may they be happy, may they be healthy, may they be free from suffering.'*
  - Notice what emotions arise for you as you do this.
  - Remember, you're not condoning any inconsiderate behaviour: you're just wishing them a sense of wellbeing rather than holding a grudge against them.
  - The meditation makes no difference to the difficult person, but you may feel a weight coming off your shoulders as you let go of a sense of frustration with them.

- **Well-wishing for all four or you together**
  - Imagine yourself, your loved one, your neutral person and your difficult person all together. See if you can wish everyone a sense of wellbeing together, in equal measure.

- **Well-wishing to everyone on the planet**
  - In this final stage, zoom out to the planet as a whole. Think about all the human beings in all of the different countries around the world, all the families and friends, all the children and elderly people. Think of all the animals, all the creatures in the oceans, lakes and rivers. Wish them all wellness. Use the words, *'May we all be well, may we all be happy, may we all be healthy, may we all be free from suffering.'*

- Note that you can change the wording of the sentences to whatever resonates with you.

There are potential concerns with any such practice, specifically in relation to whether it is being conducted correctly, although negative effects, or contraindications, are limited (Pollack, 2013). The core guidance is that the person leading the mindfulness session should have experience before leading such a session (Davis and Hayes, 2011). However, mindfulness is not just a meditation technique: instead, 'It is a lifelong endeavour to embody awareness, compassion, and ethical behaviour in one's life' (Pollack, 2013: 135).

17.9 BIOFEEDBACK

Biofeedback is a mind–body, self-regulation process for improving performance and health (Ratanasiripong et al., 2015), which has been used successfully within the school setting (e.g., Edwards, 2016; Kassel, 2015). It is a way of using signs and signals from your body to check whether your strategies are working in your favour or against you. In order to do this, you need to be made aware of what to look for, to recognise the correct signs. In a laboratory setting, this would be achieved, for example, by recording an electromyogram (EMG), skin conductance response (SCR) and heart rate (HR). Yet, such measurement techniques are largely inaccessible to teachers. However, biofeedback devices are readily accessible to us all – cheap (and expensive) heart rate monitors are available in many sports shops, or through internet retailers. Indeed, we have delivered lectures and classes using these devices, out of curiosity about what our heart rate does during such sessions. Nowadays, we can attune to our breathing and to our heart rate. If we feel tension in our chest as we breathe or if we are not breathing slow deep breaths, then we are probably tense. If we feel our hearts pounding rapidly, then equally we are not that relaxed.

REFLECTION

Try each of the methods above. Does one stand out as being more suitable for you than the others? In your journal note down the following:

- What method is it?
- Why do you think this method is more suitable for you than the others?
- How can you incorporate this into your everyday schedule?
- When will you set aside time to practise this method?
- Where will you be able to practise this method?
- Who could you get in contact with to learn more about this technique?

17.10 WHEN SHOULD RELAXATION TECHNIQUES BE USED?

As highlighted earlier, relaxation techniques should be used to combat muscular anxiety (somatic) or mental anxiety (cognitive). It is vital that you explore your optimal levels of arousal for peak performance. Imagine sitting in the staffroom, prior to the start of the day. You are running through a deep relaxation exercise and are now in such a state of relaxation that you are no longer ready to carry out the task in hand. As such, we would suggest finding out what level of arousal you need to perform successfully. This can be explored through discussion and concentrating on how you feel during the course of the day. If, after a day of teaching you felt you were unable to retain focus or were 'having an off day', we may infer that the relaxation technique was employed at an inappropriate time. We would have to adopt a calculated, although somewhat trial-and-error method of finding the most opportune time to employ the technique. For this very reason, you should be practised in using relaxation techniques before you need to use them for that all-important visit by the inspectors/tutor/mentor!

It is, however, possible to keep an eye on proceedings during teaching in order to identify when problems begin to emerge. Psychologists are often experts in using observational techniques, which will enable them to pinpoint various occasions where tension and anxiety manifest themselves through a teacher's behaviour. We observed a teacher gently tapping their hand on the desk waiting for their pupils to quickly tidy up after an art lesson. This sign of tension led to an increasing sense of frustration as the teacher obviously wanted the lesson to end so that the pupils could finish on time. The teacher was running behind schedule and this was making the pupils late finishing the lesson. If this teacher had been successfully practised in relaxation techniques, they would have refocused on what actually needed doing, restoring an organised and methodical clear-up, in turn reducing any tension and ending the day in a calm, relaxed way. This is the essence of relaxation techniques. If you only have a matter of seconds to prepare, then you need to be able to use a technique that can be adapted to suit the situation. It is common, among trainee teachers we have worked with, for them to practise relaxation techniques during the days leading up to a teaching practice and during teaching practice so that they are mentally and physically prepared for a successful and stimulating experience. The message is quite simple: identify when it is necessary to relax and find the time and place to carry it out. Relaxation is an important part of a teacher's preparation. If it is left out or a half-hearted attempt is made, there can be no guarantees that performance will be successful. If, however, time and effort are allocated, the possibilities are limited only by the teacher's confidence and ability. Next, we would expect you to feel the change to relaxation as you run through the PMR or autogenic technique. We would expect your heart rate to be reduced through your awareness of biofeedback, but we certainly would not expect you to enter a 20-minute meditative state just before the pupils come into the classroom.

CASE STUDY   Enhanced relaxation training (ERT)

This section acts as a link between relaxation and mental imagery techniques, outlined in Chapter 15. John King, a psychiatrist from Worcestershire, developed a technique for use with patients who were referred to him suffering from depression. The technique, which he called enhanced relaxation training (ERT), aimed to reduce the symptoms of depression, by providing patients with a mental simulation of a seaside environment. Essentially, this clever technique involved sounds and smells of the coast, combined with the feel of sunshine, provided by heat lamps. King used mental imagery to underpin these stimuli, by talking his patients through a mental sequence of visual events at the sea-side. The result was a mental imagery sequence that was life-like for his patients. The technique rested on simple, yet effective theory. In the main, people go on holiday to relax, unwind, recover from the stresses of daily life and return feeling refreshed.

King assembled all of the relevant props to provide the context for a holiday in the privacy and safety of his consulting room and was able to manipulate the environment such that he could introduce feelings of calmness and relaxation in his patients. He was then able to make suggestions about how the sea-side seemed to be improving their mood and emotional feelings, thus providing these patients with a dilemma: if my mood has improved, how can I be depressed? You will recall a similar argument earlier in the chapter regarding anxiety and relaxation. Of course, we have simplified the situation considerably. However, it is only necessary to highlight the concept of what King was attempting to do.

The message is simply that if you wish to get into the mindset of relaxation, you should put as many props in place as possible. Of course, we do not want you to think that combining mental imagery and relaxation training is only useful for combating depression. Rather, the use of mental imagery may be used to induce relaxation quickly and easily, with the power of verbal persuasion.

ACTIVITY

From the case study outlined above, what would your ideal escape consist of? What memories are evoked from a time or place where you felt relaxed? Make a note of these in your journal.

- Consider a series of multisensory props you could collect.
- Consider how you could collect these props (whether you need to download a sound file of waves crashing, or use an audio recorder to record such sounds, etc.).

17.11 CONCLUSION

While relaxation may appear to be a luxury for many teachers, worldwide research indicates that the profession is reaching crisis-point leading to burnout. With reduced efficiency and effectiveness, smaller issues within schools gain momentum, in turn adding to the overall pressure. This cyclic process needs to be broken: how this is achieved requires an interplay of factors such as ensuring effective leadership is in place, that resilience is more openly discussed (Chapter 13), that teachers' MWB is addressed (Chapter 12), while educating teachers about strategies for relaxation and engaging the workforce at all levels in the debate.

17.12 FURTHER READING

Fontana, D. (1999) *Learn to Meditate: Find Deep Relaxation, Relieve Stress and Anxiety, Enhance Creativity*. London: Duncan Baird Publishers.
This book was written by Professor David Fontana who had an extensive career in academically researching a range of therapeutic techniques. He was one of the founders of the Transpersonal Psychology Section in the British Psychological Society.

Lovewell, K. (2012) *Every Teacher Matters: Inspiring Well-Being through Mindfulness*. St Albans: Ecademy Press.
This is a clearly accessible book aimed directly at teachers.

Part 6
EVIDENCE-BASED TEACHING

Throughout this book, our intention has been to make psychological theory accessible while providing advice on how it is applicable within the classroom context. We have supported every aspect with a range of literature from relevant journal articles and books, ensuring that these are as recent as possible. While some theories that have been provided are 'classical' in nature and may appear dated, their inclusion sets the foundation for more recent research. Consequently, as this book is now in its second edition, we have not only written new sections and chapters based on being proactive to the emerging themes and needs within education, but have also updated areas where new research has been conducted.

Indeed, only through engaging with research, through being informed of the latest research findings, making sense of these, then embedding them within our own teaching and research, can we move forwards. Additionally, our respective research interests have progressed, which continually occurs throughout an academic's career. While our research may not have been earth-shattering, each time we engage, we enhance our perspectives at both a micro and macro level, enabling us to support students with their research interests. By developing the research community, collectively we can continue to evolve education.

Thankfully, research engagement has now been recognised as a core feature of the teaching profession through the new standard related to continuing professional development (CPD). Chapter 19 discusses the new standard, while also providing an overview of the research process, specifically how to find a research focus, working within an ethical framework, then engaging with research. Chapter 20 progresses to discuss the analysis of research. Importantly, through understanding both the research process and research analysis, when you are reading additional journal articles on psychological research applied to education, or educational research more generally, you will have a clearer understanding of what has been conducted and the relevance of the findings.

18
DOING RESEARCH

CHAPTER OBJECTIVES

- To understand the importance of effective CPD.
- To be able to use an analogy to establish a research focus.
- To understand how to research within an ethical framework.
- To understand the relationship between reading, research and the development of a reasoned argument.
- To locate and use literature effectively.

TEACHERS' STANDARDS

3   Demonstrate good subject and curriculum knowledge

- demonstrate a critical understanding of developments in the subject and curriculum areas, and promote the value of scholarship

4   Plan and teach well-structured lessons

- reflect systematically on the effectiveness of lessons and approaches to teaching
- contribute to the design and provision of an engaging curriculum within the relevant subject area(s)

6   Make accurate and productive use of assessment

- Use relevant data to monitor progress, set targets, and plan subsequent lessons

8   Fulfil wider professional responsibilities

- take responsibility for improving teaching through appropriate professional development, responding to advice and feedback from colleagues

18.1 INTRODUCTION

Throughout the book, we have advocated that teaching is a profession: as your career develops, so do you. We have also advocated that teaching is a philosophy – not a set of practices. We both agree that year-by-year, our experience has continued to evolve, and as such, we have yet to say we have achieved everything. It is what drives academics forwards in the same way as any professional – keeping focused by asking three questions daily: What am I doing? Why am I doing it? And how am I doing it?

While initial teacher-training providers focus on evidencing the Teachers' Standards, our first edition of this book advocated engaging with continuing professional development (CPD). Thankfully the government has now appreciated this by the development of the Chartered College of Teaching, through to the Framework of Core Content for Initial Teacher Training (ITT) (a Department for Education report commissioned following the Carter Review (Department for Education, 2016a)). Specifically, the fourth core finding states, 'Initial teacher training is precisely that: INITIAL', while the fifth core finding states, 'High-quality professional development is of the utmost importance.' In relation to this latter point, the report states, 'It is essential for all providers to emphasise the importance of continuing training and development as a career-long process for teachers' (Department for Education, 2016a: 8).

Furthermore, our first edition similarly advocated the need for teachers to develop their philosophy, which thankfully has similarly been acknowledged in the seventh core finding, 'The moral purpose of education should be emphasised in high-quality ITT' (Department for Education, 2016a: 9). We would therefore encourage you to revisit Chapter 4 on developing your philosophy, and Chapter 21 on the 'ideal' teacher.

While the existing Teachers' Standards do allude to such professional development (specifically 8d, 2d, 3a, 4d, 6a), there has been a new standard developed – the *Standard for Teachers' Professional Development* (Department for Education, 2016b). The actual standard states:

1. Professional development should have a focus on improving and evaluating pupil outcomes.
2. Professional development should be underpinned by robust evidence and expertise.
3. Professional development should include collaboration and expert challenge.
4. Professional development programmes should be sustained over time.

And all this is underpinned by, and requires that:

5. Professional development must be prioritised by school leadership. (Department for Education, 2016b: 6)

18.2 CONTINUING PROFESSIONAL DEVELOPMENT

According to Robinson et al. (2009), promoting and participating in professional learning has the largest effect size of all on the outcomes of learners. An effect size is a quantitative measure of difference between two groups and is presented as a decimal fraction. The effect size was developed by Cohen who provided values to indicate the size of the effect: 0.2 or below indicated a small effect size, 0.5 equated to a medium effect size, and 0.8, a large effect size (Cohen, 1988). Robinson and colleagues reported an effect size of 0.84, i.e., that professional learning has the largest effect size on the outcomes of learners. This was twice the size of the next most effective contribution, that of planning, coordinating and evaluating teaching, with an effect size of 0.42. Let us reiterate that teacher CPD has twice the impact on learning than planning, coordinating and evaluating teaching.

Such findings are equally highlighted by Garet et al. (2001), who found that sustained, intensive professional engagement has a greater effect on instructional change than shorter professional development programmes, such as an in-service training, or teacher training days.

With the recent development of the Chartered College of Teaching and the teachers who have flocked to join their ranks, along with the British Education Research Association's (BERA) widely discussed findings in schools across the country, there have (and are) developing opportunities for teachers to engage in high-quality professional learning. Indeed, BERA is over 40 years old, while the Chartered College of Teaching has existed under different guises since 1846, achieving a royal charter in 1849 when it became the College of Preceptors.

The previous chair of BERA, Professor Ian Menter, proposed four paradigms for teacher development. At the lower level is the concept of the effective teacher. This is where the focus is on skills, knowledge and competencies, technical accomplishment and accountability. The next level is that of the reflective teacher, based on the concepts of Dewey (1933), Schön (1987) and Pollard (2014), where the teacher reflects on their practice to ensure informed decision-making. The enquiring teacher is the next highest level, whereby the teacher engages with systematic research into developing classroom practice as a form of professional development. Finally there is the transformative teacher, where the teacher is responsible for contributing to social change and preparing pupils to contribute to change in society (Menter et al., 2010).

According to McLaughlin (2013: xvii), there are many challenges ahead if teachers' learning is to continue to be rich, purposeful and effective, at classroom, school and network level. Further issues relate to coordination with inconsistent, unevenly distributed development. As such, the poor coordination may be the result of a lack of strategic planning and identification of learning needs. Furthermore, there are issues of the quality of such CPD within education as stated by the Department for Education (2015) and Storey (2009).

Furthermore, from a psychological perspective, Opfer and Pedder (2013) discuss the notion of change creating a disequilibrium (what Festinger (1957) termed 'cognitive dissonance'), between the beliefs a teacher may have about learning and their actual practice. Such a psychological challenge can result from questioning one's practice and, sometimes, finding it lacking. McLaughlin (2013) notes that such dissonance that accompanies 'real learning' can be especially painful in a climate of inspection, target-setting and performance management.

There are, however, two core themes as to how effective CPD can be facilitated. The first is enquiry-oriented learning. Schleicher (2012) suggests that teachers need to be agents of innovation, something he discusses as being critically important for generating new sources of growth through improved efficiency and opportunity. This relates to what Doyle (2003) and Becher (1999) discuss in solving real problems in the natural cycle of one's work as being rewarding. This is not a new concept: arguably, Laurence Stenhouse's concept of 'extended professionalism' originally raised the issue that teachers should engage with lifelong learning and research, specifically researching their own practice (Stenhouse, 1975).

Secondly is the area of collaboration. Authors such as Cordingley (2013) and McLaughlin (2013) highlight the importance of collaborative work, and as Kennedy (2011) states, such collaborative CPD has been shown to have the most impact on teaching and learning, and was also shown to encourage teacher commitment and ownership of CPD. Such collaboration is specifically noted between schools and universities as discussed by Opfer and Pedder (2013), and recently the Department for Education (2015) in the consultation on the College of Teaching.

Consequently, as Ofsted reported in 2006, there needs to be an emphasis to ensure that effective CPD matches the needs of the teacher. Twelve years on, perhaps schools may start taking note of this.

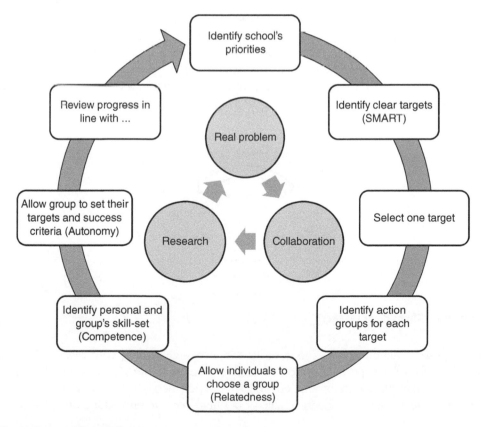

Figure 18.1   CPD model

In weaving this discussion to a conclusion, we propose that to develop effective CPD, at the core, there needs to be an enquiry-oriented collaborative development, where a real problem is addressed through effective collaboration and research with colleagues, in a clearly structured manner as demonstrated in Figure 18.1.

18.3 RESEARCH-BASED TEACHING AND ITS SYNONYMS

Many terms are currently circulating about teachers engaging with research, either through reading research or engaging with their own research. Terms such as research-based teaching, research-informed teaching, evidence-based teaching, research-led teaching, classroom-based research and so forth are currently being used. Identifying the nuances between these can be an exercise in futility. Each will have their own adherents: each will assert that they are the favoured approach. Each will have strengths, each will have limitations. In essence, this can be reduced to two perspectives: do you read information about a strategy, then implement? Alternately, do you engage with research, then find how this relates to literature?

The former informs your research, the latter develops from a hunch, which is then developed into an effective investigation. However, this approach is akin to asking what was the best thing before sliced bread, or metaphysical debates about the evolution of chickens. In simplifying the process, and given we are discussing education, we advocate the three Rs of research: reading, research, reasoned argument (Figure 18.2).

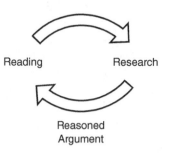

Reading   Research

Reasoned
Argument

Figure 18.2   Three Rs of research

The purpose of encompassing the three Rs is that of establishing your focus. What are your intentions? What specifically are you reading or researching? This is often overlooked and – as we both have seen through our collective experience – is the least-developed factor when students, whether undergraduate or postgraduate, are embarking on research.

These three areas operate through a constant interplay: no single one can be used in isolation. You could collect research findings but what does this mean to others and why should they change their practice based on your research alone? You could read hundreds of journal articles on effective teaching and summarise the core themes, yet without a clear context in which to apply this, or how, again your work would be limited. Consequently, only through providing a reasoned argument does the reading or research come to life.

18.4 FOCUS

Within education there are things that interest you and things that do not. The key to any research is that you have a passion for the area: a passion to prove or disprove something (although technically in research, we would argue that there is no such thing as 100 per cent certainty – researchers are, however, happy if there is a 95 per cent or 99 per cent certainty). Indeed, refer to the discussion on intrinsic motivation for further information (see Chapter 10).

Yet such freedom can also be limiting: with so much choice, what do you focus on? Our advice would be to nurture a couple of ideas until one becomes more prevalent. Similarly, you will need to make sure there is a focus to limit the scope of your area to make it manageable. But given the breadth and depth you could explore in relation to any focus, this can be limiting, if not metaphorically paralysing. Consequently, being able to narrow your focus from the outset will ensure you can keep the research manageable.

One of the best techniques for this comes from Buckler and Walliman (2016) through the forest analogy. If you consider the UK, there are numerous forests with their own names and identity. In relating this to education, one forest could be a curriculum subject, another could be motivation, a different forest could be special educational needs. They are related, yet you will need to choose one.

From identifying a forest, you have numerous trees. Take the forest of 'English': within this forest are trees, one of which is reading, another is writing, another is speaking and listening, and so forth. Take the tree labelled 'reading'. This mighty oak has umpteen main branches: for our working example, take the branch of reading preference. Each main branch has dozens of smaller branches, through to twigs, and then leaves. If we focus on one such sub-branch, we could look at gender, then progress to age groups. Bringing this together, your focus has developed into analysing reading preferences in relation to gender and age.

From identifying the focus for your research, the next step is to formulate a definitive statement of intent: in other words, your overarching aim. In one sentence, can you define what your research aim is? Following on from the example above, the aim could be written as: To identify whether there are gender and age determinants to reading preference.

While your aim provides the frame for the research, it does not detail how this will be achieved: this is where the objectives come in. Objectives are sub-statements that detail components of the research, focusing on the 'what' and the 'how'; for example: To analyse reading preference (the what) by distributing a questionnaire to Year 9 pupils (the how).

An example from Buckler and Walliman (2016: 64) is:

- Aim

  o   An investigation into after-school provision at a large rural primary school.

- Objectives

  o   To systematically explore the issue of after-school provision through conducting an extensive, critical review of the literature.
  o   To critically analyse the needs of parents through a paper-based questionnaire.
  o   To investigate the perspectives of children in relation to after-school provision, through conducting a focus-group with Year 5 and 6 children.
  o   To examine the resource implications of after-school provision through conducting semi-structured interviewing with the senior management team.
  o   To synthesise differing perspectives from staff, children and parents on after-school provision in an attempt to propose feasible solutions.

From the aim and objectives, Bucker and Walliman (2016: 64) highlight that the process develops a clear argument structure, which they summarise as:

- According to the background research there is a problem, an issue, a lack of information, or an unanswered question about such-and-such. This provides the necessary motive for defining the aim.
- The first objective expands on the aim, stating that a literature review will be conducted to explore the theoretical and research literature background to the topic.
- Subsequent objectives specify the data to be collected, detailing *what* you intend to find out, the *how* you intend to collect the data (your method), and from *where* or from *whom* (your sample, for example, Year 7 pupils).

It is important to note that your aim and objectives will continue to evolve as you progress with your research. They will never stay exactly the same as when you first wrote them; however, they will provide a framework, which can be enhanced. An area that will influence their development relates to the background information you have read, which leads us to the next part of the chapter.

18.5 READING

As previously discussed, through reading you are able to help refine your research focus. This is important so that you use previous research to ensure that you build upon what has gone before, as opposed to wasting time reiterating what somebody else has already found. A lot of time can be spent looking for sources that specifically relate to your focus; consequently the following advice should help.

EFFECTIVE SEARCHING

If you are a student, you will have a range of ways for obtaining information such as your university library, online journal databases and so forth. If you are an established teacher, you can still use such resources, often for a small fee each year; alternatively with the open-access resources available, there is an ever-increasing range from which you can find information. The key, however, is finding relevant information of a sufficiently good quality. Relying on an internet search engine or a collaborative online encyclopaedia is not enough. Similarly, relying on websites is insufficient.

USING KEY SEARCH TERMS

Before turning on your computer, sit down with a plain sheet of paper and make a list of your search terms. From this, make a list of synonyms for the terms/words that are similar in nature. For example, you may have used the word 'pupil', yet 'student' or 'learner' may equally apply. Review your list of search terms and consider whether there are alternate spellings. For example, the word 'behaviour' may limit your search results to UK data, whereas using 'behavior' may help broaden your search. Indeed, you could use 'wildcards' in a search engine: these are symbols that are placed after the root of the word, such as an asterisk. For example, 'behav*' will return results such as behave, behaved, behaviour, behavioural, behaviourism, behaviourist, and of course any instances where the 'u' is dropped.

From your list of words, keep a note of the search terms you have used where you have combined different words for your search, for example, if you have used 'behaviour' and 'classroom', or 'behaviour' and 'learning'. Recording your permutations of search terms will save you repeating exactly the same searches at a later stage.

When you have various sources you have identified, consider how you will file these. Will you keep a separate folder in your internet browser's bookmarks? Will you download and save the file to a folder on your computer, or will you print off or photocopy relevant information?

EVALUATING SOURCES

Take for example the 'Thrive Approach', which has been developing widely in schools. While the intentions of Thrive are commendable, and we daresay the results, on what theoretical grounding has the programme been developed? Having requested information previously, while invited to attend the course (and pay the significant fee), no information was forthcoming about the theoretical background for the development of Thrive. In addition, while there may be case studies which support the approach, to what extent has lasting change been significantly evidenced?

This is not to dismiss Thrive in the slightest, yet professionally we can end up doing something because others are. Such an example relates to a study by Milgram et al. (1969) where, at a signal from a sixth-floor window of an office building, a group stopped and looked at the window. They maintained their gaze for 60 seconds, after which they were signalled to disperse. The group size who were primed to gaze consisted of varying sizes: 1, 2, 3, 5, 10 and 15 people. When one person was gazing at the window, only 4 per cent of pedestrians stopped and similarly gazed. When the group of 15 gazed, this increased to 40 per cent of pedestrians stopping. Milgram and his colleagues concluded that the size of the gazers affects the proportion of other pedestrians.

Such experiments led to the development of social impact theory, a theory that outlines how individuals can be either sources or targets of social influence. In summarising some key themes from this theory, if an individual is perceived to have a higher status, and where the action is more immediate, greater numbers of others will follow (Latané, 1981). Additionally, as with the Milgram et al. (1969) experiment, the higher the number of sources, the greater are those that are influenced. Social impact theory resonates in today's society where the world of tweets, Facebook 'likes' and other social media can go viral in a short space of time (e.g., Ding et al., 2017; Perez-Vega et al., 2016).

Consequently, within education there are times when ideas become accepted wisdom due to the lack of critical reasoning. Indeed, several books have been written about the area in relation to education, for example, Christodoulou's *Seven Myths About Education* (2014), De Bruyckere et al.'s *Urban Myths About Learning and Education* (2015) and Didau's *What If Everything You Knew About Education Was Wrong?* (2016). For evaluating sources, whether books, websites or even journals, the framework in Table 18.1 can be used to assist you.

When you have saturated your searching and identified several core sources, your next task is to make notes of the information. You would have developed your own approach in your previous studies, for example, using different coloured highlighting pens for different elements in a source (e.g., pink for the most important sentences, yellow for key information, green for explanations). Alternatively, you may keep a table of information where you copy core material from each source. Such an example is demonstrated in Table 18.2.

Table 18.1 Evaluating sources framework (adapted from Buckler and Walliman, 2016: 89–90)

Is it accurate? Is information provided to explain where the research has come from? Are there other sources that may be compared to this? If the sources of data differ, is there an explanation for this?

What authority is it based on? Who are the authors? Do they have a reputable background, ascertained through their qualifications and other publications? Have other publications cited their work? What organisation do they work for?

Is it biased? Many pressure groups and commercial organisations promote their ideas and products, and present information in a one-sided way. Can you detect a vested interest in the subject on the part of the author? What is the motive for the publication? Is the information self-published for financial gain or to share knowledge and understanding?

How detailed is the information? Is the information so general that it is of little use, or so detailed and specialised that it is difficult to understand? Are there lapses of information in relation to the subject, where only the core findings are discussed to 'tell the story' the authors want you to hear? Do they acknowledge their limitations?

Is it out of date? Consider when the source was published. Is the work 'seminal', in other words has it left an outstanding contribution to research whereby subsequent research still advocates the original source? Alternately, have things moved on? If the source cites references, are these references current? By current, this could mean in the last year to the last 20 years depending on the context and whether anyone has furthered the research. Indeed, it is worth checking the references to similarly assess for the questions listed here.

Have you cross-checked? Compare the contents with other sources of information such as books, articles, official statistics and other websites. Does the information tally with or contradict these? If the latter, can you see why?

Has the source been peer-reviewed? If the research is cited in a journal, does this adhere to a strict peer-review process where other experts analyse the research to ensure it is credible, valid and reliable? If it is a book, has this been published by a reputable academic publisher who similarly engage with the peer-review process?

Table 18.2 An example record form

Author:	Buckler, S. and Walliman, N.	
Title:	*Your Dissertation in Education*, Sage Publications	
Year:	2016	
Page	Quote	Notes
128	Your literature review should comment on specific articles and arguments raised by others, assessing parallels of differences between articles, leading towards a conclusion ...	
128	... there needs to be a definitive introduction, development and conclusion.	

WRITING A LITERATURE REVIEW

Once you have compiled your notes, you then need to structure them in a way so that you can make a summary of the research which informs your focus, leading to a definitive argument. Furthermore, through engaging with the literature and looking for how sources relate to or refute one another, the process helps to develop your thinking, while highlighting gaps in existing knowledge. The focus of the literature review consists of three components: an introduction, where you explain your focus while highlighting your approach to reviewing literature; the development, where you explore sources in detail and how they relate to each other; and finally a conclusion, which summarises the key elements you have discussed. Ideally the conclusion should then be linked to explain why your aim and objectives have been developed.

There are different ways to structure a literature review, although we will focus on two, the inverted triangle approach and the Venn diagram approach. The inverted triangle provides a series of layers where the focus can be continually narrowed. This approach works well when there is a definitive structure that can be narrowed. Such an approach would work well when you have a key concept, such as motivation. The top layer could consist of defining the term, the subsequent layers then narrow further: for example, classical theories of motivation, modern theories of motivation, self-determination theory (SDT) overview, SDT related to reading engagement strategies, specific studies of reading engagement strategies that have used an SDT approach, strengths and limitations of such studies, conclusion.

An alternative is that of the Venn diagram approach (Rudestam and Newton, 2014). With this method, the key concepts or core variables are placed in the outer circles, for example, 'motivation', 'reading engagement', 'secondary pupils'. While each of these terms alone would generate thousands of sources, it is the area where any two overlap which establishes the focus and provides the core search term when looking for sources. Consequently, searching for 'motivation *and* reading engagement' will provide a narrower range of sources, as will the term 'reading engagement *and* secondary pupils', or 'secondary pupils *and* motivation'. Each of the areas will provide distinct

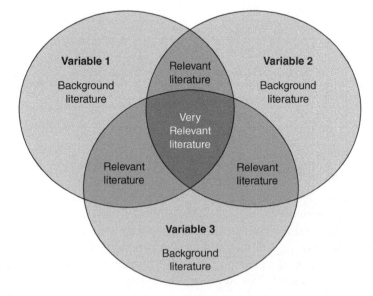

Figure 18.3   Venn diagram

sources, yet they will be more explicitly linked to your focus. Of course, when all three terms are combined, you will find a few core sources to really concentrate on. Indeed, the bulk of your literature review should target this central area, less so where two overlap, and a limited amount for each key term in the circle (see Figure 18.3).

As Buckler and Walliman (2016) suggest, you may want to present the Venn diagram at the start of the literature review to explain to readers your process. Furthermore, the circles of the Venn diagram can be made different sizes to emphasise which of the concepts is the most important to your literature review.

The Venn diagram is a better model than the inverted triangle in that the concepts you discuss within your literature review are more likely to overlap in a themed approach and not lend themselves as neatly to a sequential discussion. You may even want to present the Venn diagram within the introduction to your literature review chapter to explain to the reader how you have framed the literature.

ANALYSIS AND SYNTHESIS

The key to a successful review of literature is to be able to utilise effective synthesis and analysis. Analysis is the deconstruction of a component, for example, critiquing a source through explaining whether the research is dated, or has been conducted in a specific context, and so forth (see Table 18.1 above for further guidance). Additional analysis may be developed through comparing one source against others to explore similarities and differences, for example, if two or more sources came to the same conclusion, or whether there is an ongoing debate. This can be represented by Figure 18.4 where sources A, B and C are compared.

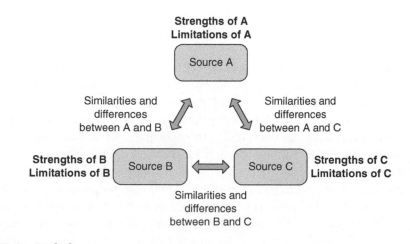

Figure 18.4   Analysis

Synthesis relates to the ability to construct new meaning from the sources you have previously analysed, through taking the component parts and combining to make a more articulate explanation. By extending the previous figure, this may be represented in Figure 18.5 where components of sources A, B and C are used to make D.

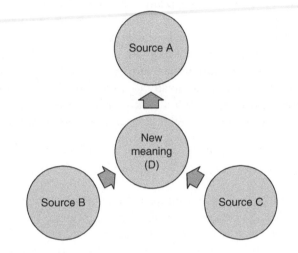

Figure 18.5   Synthesis

To illustrate how this could be developed, please refer to the following example.

EXAMPLE

Three different quotes on social exclusion are listed below:

1. The dynamic process of being shut out, fully or partially, from any of the social, economic, political and cultural systems which determine the social integration of a person in society. (Walker and Walker, 1997: 8)
2. Social exclusion is a broader concept than poverty, encompassing not only low material means but the inability to participate effectively in economic, social, political and cultural life and in some characterisations alienation and distance from mainstream society. (Duffy, 1995: 33)
3. Social exclusion is a complex and multi-dimensional process. It involves the lack or denial of resources, rights, goods and services, and the inability to participate in the normal relationships and activities, available to

the majority of people in a society, whether in economic, social, cultural or political arenas. It affects both the quality of life of individuals and the equity and cohesion of society as a whole. (Levitas et al., 2007: 25)

Analysis

- From the quotes, highlight the important words or phrases that stand out in relation to defining social exclusion.
- Next structure the component parts into a short paragraph comparing and contrasting how the authors' works relate to one another. (Note, the direct quotes below are highlighted in bold and italics, which is not normal referencing convention: they have been provided this way to make them stand out in the paragraph.)

Duffy (1995: 33) states that social exclusion is '*a broader concept than poverty, encompassing not only low material means but the inability to participate effectively in economic, social, political and cultural life and in some characterisations alienation and distance from mainstream society*'. Walker and Walker (1997: 8) define social inclusion as '*the dynamic process of being shut out, fully or partially, from any of the social, economic, political and cultural systems which determine the social integration of a person in society*'.

According to Levitas et al. (2007: 25) '*social exclusion is a complex and multi-dimensional process*'. Indeed, social exclusion is an evolving term that has no single definition. For example, Duffy (1995: 33) explains that it is '*a broader concept than poverty*', which prevents people effectively engaging in '*economic, social, political and cultural life*', a view that is shared by Walker and Walker (1997). Levitas et al. (2007: 25) additionally comment that, fundamentally, it is the '*lack or denial of resources, rights, goods and services*' that prevents successful engagement within the various domains.

Good phrases to use for analysis include:

- according to AUTHOR (Year)
- a view shared by AUTHOR (Year)
- AUTHOR (Year) explains that/states that/comments that/defines
- similarly/which is also explained by AUTHOR (Year)
- conversely/a different perspective is provided by AUTHOR (Year)
- additionally/furthermore.

(Continued)

Synthesis

- From the direct quotes, these three sentences appear to define social exclusion the best:

  '*social exclusion is a complex and multi-dimensional process*'

  '*a broader concept than poverty*', which prevents people effectively engaging in '*economic, social, political and cultural life*'

  '*lack or denial of resources, rights, goods and services*' that prevent successful engagement within the various domains.

- In order to synthesise the quotes consider rewriting all three into one sentence, and at the end of the sentence, list the authors (with dates) alphabetically from whom the quotes derived:

  From synthesising these various definitions, a new definition can be provided, that social exclusion is a complex, multi-dimensional process that affects people engaging effectively in economic, social, political and cultural life through the lack of or denial of resources, rights, goods and services (Duffy, 1995; Levitas et al., 2007; Walker and Walker, 1997).

The literature review should have provided direction in which to take your research. This may involve reframing your aim and objectives to align more coherently; however this leads to the next component, that of the actual research.

18.6 RESEARCH

Simply put, research is finding out something that you either did not know about before, or that you want to find out more about. It could consist of just reading articles through to engaging with practical research. Arguably teachers informally research on a day-to-day basis, for example, evaluating lessons and making changes to subsequent lessons. However, when considering anything beyond this, we strongly assert that you discuss any research intentions with your line manager prior to starting. It must also be noted that this chapter will only cover a superficial orientation to research, given the limitations of word count and so forth.

Before progressing with some pointers about engaging with research, and before you start planning, it is important to review the ethical considerations.

ETHICS

According to Buckler and Walliman (2016), ethics relates to moral principles and rules of conduct: in other words, the 'right' and 'wrong' way of achieving things. It is also worth noting that, over time, these principles and rules evolve. They provide (2016: 29) the 'four P' framework in which to operate:

- *Proposal*: What are your intentions? What is the purpose of your research and why are you conducting it?
- *Potential*: What are the potential benefits of your research? What are the potential risks?
- *Permission*: Whom do you need to gain access from? How will you achieve this?
- *Protection*: How will you ensure that research participants and/or the organisation will be protected? How will you ensure that you are protected?

There are further established ethical protocols for teachers, for example, the British Education Research Association's 'Ethical Guidelines for Educational Research' (BERA, 2011). Generally the core areas to consider are listed below.

- *Inform people*: how will you explain to the 'gatekeepers' (such as parents, line management), or indeed the pupils, your research intentions so that they can make an informed decision as to whether the research should proceed, or whether they want to be involved?
- *Ask permission*: once participants have been informed, they have a right to decide whether or not they want to engage with research. If you were conducting research on one of your lessons, it may involve allowing pupils to still engage but their data is not used in your analysis. Furthermore, participants have the right to withdraw from the research at any point – this includes when you are collecting data, or even after you have collected the data – so their data will need destroying. Additionally, those who do not wish to engage should not be penalised.
- *Anonymity*: at no point during your research, or when analysing and sharing your research, should anyone be identified explicitly or implicitly. Depending on the nature of the research, this may also mean the school should not be identified.
- *Fairness*: if you are researching the intervention of one approach over another, with different classes, those with the intervention may benefit. As such, you will need to ensure that the other group will similarly be entitled to the intervention so that they are not disadvantaged.

- *Scientific honesty and subjectivity*: while unscrupulous researchers throughout time have either 'fudged' their results (massaging or making up data), or 'dry-labbed' (reporting on experiments that were never conducted), researchers need to be scrupulously honest throughout the research process. Even if your experience tells you something should work out, yet your research proves negative, this is still as important to acknowledge in your research. Indeed, you may have found out how not to do something, which is as important as how to do something.

Again, we would stress that it is important to check with your school about the processes and permissions required before embarking on research, while also discussing your intentions. Once you have identified a focus and worked through the ethical considerations, you can start planning your research.

RESEARCH PARADIGM

A research paradigm is a way of looking at the world. While there are many different terms for these paradigms, in essence they can be summarised as whether you see the world working to a set of laws, or whether you see the world as a more complex and nuanced relationship between factors. The former tends to lend itself to finding a definitive answer, predominantly through collecting data numerically, while the latter is more illustrative, providing descriptions and looking for links between themes.

The world of numbers is hence deemed quantitative, while the world of words is qualitative. While quantitative data answers questions such as 'how many?' or 'how often?', it does not provide the answer to 'why?' Conversely, qualitative data answers questions such as 'why?' but lacks the generalisability to answer 'how many?' Consequently, a developing theme in the research world has been mixed methodology, which utilises both quantitative and qualitative data.

In determining the best paradigm for your research, the next consideration relates to the selection of appropriate data collection methods.

DATA COLLECTION METHODS

Most educational research is relatively small-scale in nature, tending to rely on one or more of the core data collection methods such as interview, focus group, observation, questionnaire or analysis of documents such as pupils' work. Each of these will be discussed briefly in turn.

- *Interview*: an interview is the process of asking questions to another person. The format may be structured where everyone is asked the same list of questions, semi-structured where the standard questions are asked but there is room to ask follow-up questions, or unstructured, which in essence is a conversation about an area. The interview could be audio-recorded and at a later stage transcribed; alternatively just the key points are taken.

- *Focus group*: a focus group is a group interview where the researcher stimulates discussion between the group.
- *Observation*: observations may adhere to a formal, structured schedule, for example where specific points are made on a preformatted table; alternatively it could consist of writing notes as the researcher observes what is happening.
- *Questionnaire*: a questionnaire can ask questions in a variety of ways, such as: selecting a single choice from a list; multiple choices from a list; ranking things in order of preference such as 1st, 2nd, 3rd; highlighting a preference on a scale such as 'strongly disagree' to 'strongly agree', and also open-ended text boxes.
- *Documentary analysis*: this involves collating copies of documents, such as pupils' work, then annotating the work with comments to identify themes.

RELIABILITY AND VALIDITY

Two key terms are central with any research, whether quantitative or qualitative. These are reliability and validity. Reliability as its name implies is whether the research is actually reliable in nature, or the extent that the data is trustworthy. In other words, are the results obtained from one sample likely to be similar to results collected from a similar sample? Validity refers to whether the data collected is representative in nature to make an informed decision. Take for example a tape measure. It is a valid measure of length. It is also reliable in that the demarcations do not alter. However, if you had a tape measure made out of rubber, while still valid in measuring length, it would not be reliable as it could be stretched.

To ensure research is reliable, a measure is required that does not change, for example, where the same interview questions are asked to different participants. There are statistical measures discussed in Table 19.2 to assess reliability.

In relation to validity, there are two key distinctions: whether the research has internal validity or external validity. Internal validity is the extent to which a measure can assess the cause and effect between two different variables. By this, will changing one variable directly influence another variable? To what extent is there a correlation between the cause and effect? External validity relates to whether the results from a group can be generalised to other similar groups, assuming that the sample is representative in nature.

There are a number of other forms of validity that you may read about in research. The core forms are content validity, whereby an instrument must demonstrate that all the aspects it claims to assess are comprehensively covered, in other words, the content. For example, a science test would need to test all aspects of the curriculum in order to provide a fair portrayal of a pupil's ability within the subject. In essence, both depth and breadth are required so that the pupil can demonstrate not only that they are aware of the different components, but also that they can utilise these at a specific level. Another form of validity is construct validity, which relates to the actual element that is being measured and whether the measure is appropriate. For example, measuring the circumference of a person's head is not a valid measure of intelligence if the assumption that a larger circumference means a larger brain, which in turn is a measure of intelligence. Construct validity can be assured through developing a measure and ensuring that it either correlates with other measures, or is based upon theoretical perspectives through the literature.

A further form of validity is concurrent validity where the data from one measure is used to correlate against the data from another. If, for example, you were developing a measure to assess mathematical ability, those pupils who score highly on your new measure should similarly score highly on different tests.

In terms of ensuring both reliability and validity, although these can be addressed in the planning stage of research, one core term that helps to assure both is triangulation. There are four different approaches to triangulation, which have been identified by Denzin and Lincoln (2011). These are: data, investigator, theoretical and methodological. Data triangulation relates to the sample used within the research. In terms of sample, the more respondents who engage with the research, the more comprehensive the results. If only one respondent was asked to engage with the research, the findings would only relate to that one person. A further consideration is where the sample is derived. If there are three classes in a year group, would it be sufficient just to conduct research with one of the classes? How about using a different class of the same year group in a different school? Although this would allow for comparison, if three classes were used from different locations, a more comprehensive perspective would be developed, assuming that time and access were not an issue.

Investigator triangulation relates to using more than one researcher to capture the data. If you consider an Ofsted inspection, it is highly unlikely that just one inspector will visit. With one inspector, all forms of bias could be evident in the report, especially if the inspector does not agree with the ethos of the school. A team of inspectors is therefore used to gain their respective perspectives, which are then collaboratively discussed to provide a more informed report.

Theoretical triangulation refers to using more than one approach to interpret your data. Although you may have conducted four interviews, could you say how many of the group agreed with a response to a question? Although the permutations of this would be either all agreed, all disagreed, an even split or three-quarters expressed a specific preference, such an approach would be limited in not providing the richness of responses. Consequently, could themes be explored in more detail, illustrating a richer discussion with quotes from the respondents?

In relation to methodological triangulation, this is where more than one method is used to collect results, for example, using both interviews and questionnaires or observations.

18.7 REASONED ARGUMENT

Engaging with the two components of reading and research are integrated through developing a reasoned argument to provide the coherent whole. Your research would have evolved around a core theme, which has culminated in a conclusion and recommendations based on the evidence. However, it is only through structuring a reasoned argument that you can link your research findings to your conclusion. While Buckler and Walliman (2016) discuss arguments thoroughly in Chapter 11 of their book, a condensed overview is provided here.

TYPES OF ARGUMENTS

There are three central ingredients to an argument: a statement that is reasoned for, evidence to support the statement, and an indication that an argument is being conducted through a conclusion, which uses terms such as 'therefore', 'hence', 'thus', and 'implies that'.

There are two different types of arguments: deductive arguments and inductive arguments. Deductive arguments make a general statement, then provide an example related to this. At a simple level, the following argument provides an example: All dogs are animals. Poppy is a dog. Therefore, Poppy is an animal. An inductive argument provides greater flexibility through use of logic; however, the conclusion only indicates probability. For example: Chloe is rich and drives a large car. Kianna is rich and drives a large car. Cameron is rich and drives a large car. Therefore, rich people probably drive large cars.

There are four inductive argument structures. Arguments by example provide instances to support a generalisation. Arguments by analogy provide parallels between two different examples, which may share similar characteristics. Arguments by authority are based on expert testimony: the assumption that the expert knows about what they are saying. Finally, arguments about causes are based on a correlation between different causes and events.

Deductive argument structures use logic to make inferences such as modus ponens (the mode of putting), modus tollens (the mode of taking), hypothetical syllogism, disjunctive syllogism and dilemma. The previous argument about Poppy being an animal is an example of modus ponens, which is characterised through logical terms: *If P then Q. P. Therefore Q.* The other forms of deductive argument similarly adhere to such logic sentences in slightly different ways.

You may use arguments in different ways, for example, providing a particular perspective, proposing a new way of working, dismissing another perspective, drawing together contrasting positions and so forth. Indeed, through structuring your research, you need to consider the arguments from other people's perspectives, question such perspectives, then provide your perspective ensuring that it is stronger through supporting evidence.

18.8 CONCLUSION

This chapter has highlighted the importance of engaging with your own classroom-based research, while providing a framework in which to operate. From understanding the importance of CPD and how this contributes to teacher effectiveness, through to establishing a research focus, developing an aim and objectives, locating and utilising literature effectively, through to planning and engaging your own ethical research, the chapter has provided an orientation which, we hope, will encourage you to develop educationally changing research.

18.9 FURTHER READING

Buckler, S. and Walliman, N. (2016) *Your Dissertation in Education* (2nd edn). London: Sage Publications.
This book, while written for students, is accessible to anyone engaging with school-based research. It expands on many of the themes within this chapter.

Thomas, G. (2013) *How to Do Your Research Project* (2nd edn). London: Sage Publications.
This book similarly takes the reader through the various research stages.

19

ANALYSING DATA

CHAPTER OBJECTIVES

- To review the difference between quantitative and qualitative research paradigms.
- To understand how to process quantitative data.
- To be able to determine a correct statistical test depending on the data collected.
- To understand how to process qualitative data through open and axial coding.
- To consider different ways of presenting qualitative data analysis.

TEACHERS' STANDARDS

3   Demonstrate good subject and curriculum knowledge

- demonstrate a critical understanding of developments in the subject and curriculum areas, and promote the value of scholarship

4   Plan and teach well-structured lessons

- reflect systematically on the effectiveness of lessons and approaches to teaching
- contribute to the design and provision of an engaging curriculum within the relevant subject area(s)

6   Make accurate and productive use of assessment

- use relevant data to monitor progress, set targets, and plan subsequent lessons

8   Fulfil wider professional responsibilities

- take responsibility for improving teaching through appropriate professional development, responding to advice and feedback from colleagues

19.1 INTRODUCTION

In Chapter 18, the focus was on finding research articles, journals and books, so that these could inform your research. While aspects such as effective literature searching and being able to analyse and synthesise were included within the chapter, often you will find an article that is full of charts, tables and numbers. Although you can read through the article and understand the conclusion, an analogy is being blindfolded at the start of a journey with the blindfold taken off just as you reach the end. The array of information can be confusing especially when the nuances of the analysis are discussed. The purpose of this chapter is to provide a working overview of data analysis for two purposes: explicitly, so that you can analyse your own data when you have conducted research, and implicitly, so that you can understand other people's research.

19.2 A RETURN TO RESEARCH PARADIGMS

From the previous chapter, the terms 'quantitative' and 'qualitative' data were introduced in relation to being paradigms. As we discussed, a research paradigm is a way of looking at the world, whether you see it as adhering to a set of laws such as cause and effect (quantitative research), or whether you see it as more complex and nuanced (qualitative research). The strengths and limitation of both were similarly discussed in that quantitative research provides answers to questions such as 'how many?', or 'Is there a relationship between X and Y?'; however, quantitative research does not say 'why'. On the other hand, qualitative research provides the explanations to 'why?', yet it does not enable conclusions to be drawn on the 'how many?'-type questions. Consequently, research is now progressing to combine both quantitative and qualitative approaches through mixed methodology (which confusingly can also be called 'mixed methods' research).

Mixing methodologies relates to combining different approaches and can be used at different research stages. For example, at the data collection stage a qualitative interview can be used to generate themes, then a quantitative questionnaire can be used to ascertain how often these themes are reported. Alternatively, the mixing of methodologies can be used when analysing data. A different way of mixing data can be developed where the same data collection instrument (such as a questionnaire) asks for both qualitative responses (such as 'Why do you … ?') and quantitative responses through providing closed-questions (such as yes/no). Mixed methods research relates to using two or more data collection techniques, for example, developing a questionnaire while also conducting observations. Ultimately though, data analysis falls into two categories: qualitative and quantitative.

The results of a survey, experiments, archival studies, or whatever methods are used to collect data about a subject are of little use if they are merely presented as raw data. It should not be the duty of the reader to try to make sense of them: it is up to the researcher to use the information collected to make a case for arriving at some conclusions.

The data you have collected might be recorded in different ways that are not easy to read or to summarise. Perhaps it is contained in numerous questionnaire responses, in handwritten reports, recorded speech, as a series of photographs or observations in a journal. It can be difficult even for the researcher to make sense of it all, let alone someone who has not been involved in the research. Consequently, some form of analysis is required.

19.3 QUANTITATIVE ANALYSIS

Quantitative analysis deals with numbers and uses mathematical operations to investigate the properties of data. The levels of measurement used in the collection of the data (that is, nominal, ordinal, interval and ratio) are an important factor in choosing the type of analysis that is applicable, as is the numbers of cases involved.

Most surveys result in quantitative data, such as numbers of people who believed this or that, how many children of what age do which sports, levels of family income, etc. However, not all quantitative data originates from surveys. For example, content analysis is a specific method of examining records of all kinds. A checklist is made to count how frequently certain ideas, words, phrases, images or scenes appear in order to be able to draw some conclusions from the frequency of their appearance.

One of the primary purposes of doing research is to describe the data and to discover relationships among events in order to describe, explain, predict and possibly control their occurrence. Statistical methods are a valuable tool to enable you to present and describe the data and, if necessary, to discover and quantify relationships. And you do not even have to be a mathematician to use these techniques, as user-friendly computer packages (such as Excel and Statistical Package for the Social Sciences, SPSS) will do all the presentation and calculations for you. However, you must be able to understand the relevance and function of the various displays and tests in relationship to your own sets of data and the kind of analysis required.

The most straightforward process is to describe the data in the form of tables, graphs and diagrams. For this, a spreadsheet program such as Excel is quite sufficient. This will order and display the data in a compact form so that you can make comparisons, detect trends and measure amounts and combinations of amounts. If you do not know how to use a spreadsheet for this, attend a course of instruction or find a handbook to guide you.

If you need to do more sophisticated analysis, then there is a wide range of statistical techniques that you can employ using SPSS. Many tests have exotic names such as Kruskal's gamma, Kendall's coefficient of concordance, Guttman's lambda and chi-square and Kolmogorov–Smirnov tests. However, do not be put off by these, as you will only be required to use the most common ones and there are simple rules as to when and how they should be applied. Even so, it is always advisable to consult somebody with specialist statistical knowledge in order to check that you will be doing the right thing before you start. Also, attend a course, usually made available to you by your university, in the use of SPSS or any other program that is available to you.

Another factor to be taken into account when selecting suitable statistical tests is the number of cases about which you have data. Generally, statistical tests are more reliable the greater the number of cases. Usually, more than about 30 cases are required to make any sense of the analysis, though some tests are designed to work with less. Always consult the instructions on this issue for the particular tests you want to use. It may affect your choice.

Although there are a range of statistical procedures that can be used with quantitative research, as previously noted, this book will not attempt to explain these in depth: instead a general description of some of the aspects within statistical research is given below.

19.4 PARAMETRIC AND NON-PARAMETRIC STATISTICS

The two major classes of statistics are parametric and non-parametric statistics. You need to understand the meaning of a parameter in order to appreciate the difference between these two types. A parameter of a population (that is, the things or people you are surveying) is a constant feature that it shares with other populations. The most common one is the 'bell' or 'Gaussian' curve of a normal frequency distribution.

This parameter reveals that most populations display a large number of more or less average cases along with extreme cases tailing off at each end. For example, most people are of about average height, with those who are extremely tall or small being in a distinct minority. The distribution of people's heights shown on a graph would take the form of the normal distribution curve, or Gaussian curve (Figure 19.1).

Although the shape of this curve varies from case to case (for example, flatter or steeper, lopsided to the left or right), this feature is so common among populations that statisticians take it as a constant: a basic parameter. Calculations of parametric statistics are based on this feature.

Not all data is parametric, where populations sometimes do not behave in the form of a Gaussian curve. Data measured by nominal and ordinal methods will not be organised in a curve form. Nominal data tends to be in the dichotomous form of either/or (for example, this is a cow or a sheep or neither), while ordinal data can be displayed in the form of a set of steps (such as the 1st, 2nd and 3rd positions on a winners' podium). For those cases where this parameter is absent, non-parametric statistics may be applicable.

Non-parametric statistical tests have been devised to recognise the particular characteristics of non-curve data and to take into account these singular characteristics by specialised methods. In general, these types of test are less sensitive and powerful than parametric tests: they need larger samples in order to generate the same level of significance.

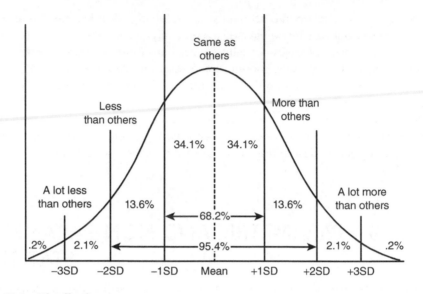

Figure 19.1   Distribution curve

STATISTICAL TESTS: PARAMETRIC

The two classes of parametric statistical tests are descriptive and inferential.

Descriptive statistics

Descriptive statistics provide a method of quantifying the characteristics of the data, where its centre is, how broadly it spreads and how one aspect of the data relates to another aspect of the same data. The 'centre of gravity' of the data, its point of central tendency, can be determined by finding the mode or the median and any one of several means. These measures have their own characteristics and applications and should be chosen with regard to the data being analysed.

The measure of the dispersion (or spread) of the data – how flat or steep the Gaussian curve appears – is an indication of how much of the data closely resemble the mean. The flatter the curve, the greater is the amount of data that deviates from the mean, that is, the fewer the values that are close to the average. The horizontal length of the curve also gives an indication of the spread of values and the extent of the extremes represented in the data, while the occurrence of a non-symmetrical curve indicates a skewness in the data values.

Apart from examining the qualities of a single set of data, the main purpose of statistical analysis is to identify and quantify relationships between variables.

This is the type of research called correlation research. However, it is important to remember that the mere discovery and measurement of correlations is not sufficient on its own to provide research answers. It is the interpretation of these discoveries that provides the valuable knowledge that will give answers to your research question.

The technical term for the measure of correlation is the coefficient of correlation. There are many types of these, the Pearson r being the most common. It is possible to measure the correlation between more than two variables if you use the appropriate tests. However, be wary about assuming that, because a strong statistical correlation between variables can be demonstrated, there is necessarily a causal bond between the variables. It may be purely chance or the influence of other factors that, say, leads to areas of high-density development in cities having high crime rates. You must carefully question the assumptions on which such a causal assertion is made, and review the facts to examine if such causality is verifiable in other ways.

Inferential statistics

Inferential statistical tests go beyond describing the characteristics of data and the examination of correlations between variables. As the name implies, they are used to produce predictions through inference, based on the data analysed. This entails making predictions about the qualities of a total population on the basis of the sample and how far a specific case, group or person deviates from the 'norm'.

In comparing to the norm, the term 'standard deviation' is used. This is the degree to which any result on a Gaussian curve is the same as, or different from, the average, represented by the highest point on the curve.

In terms of standard deviation, it is measured as 1SD, 2SD or 3SD (see Figure 19.1). If a result is to 1SD, this means that the result is pretty close to the average: 34.1 per cent either above or below the highest point on the curve. This is where most of the results within a population occur (68.2 per cent). Consequently, within 1SD, just over two-thirds of the population are included. If a result is to 2SD, this includes an extra 13.6 per cent above or below the previous standard deviation. In other words, a further 27.2 per cent of cases are within 2SD. This means that 95.8 per cent of results are within 2SD. This is why, when statistics are reported, the figure of 95 per cent certainty is reported as being significant. This is represented as a 'p value'. If you see the statistic $p < 0.05$ (or $p < .05$), this means that there is a 95 per cent certainty of statistical significance. If a result is to 3SD, this accounts for the remaining 2.1 per cent at either end of the curve (or 99.6 per cent of the whole population).

As with all predictions made from samples, the representative quality of the sample is crucial to accuracy; the sample must be as typical as possible of the whole.

STATISTICAL TESTS: NON-PARAMETRIC

Statistical tests built around discovering the means and standard deviations of the typical characteristics of a Gaussian curve are clearly inappropriate for analysing non-parametric data. Hence, non-parametric data cannot be statistically tested in the above ways.

There are tests that can be used to compare the qualities of two or more groups or samples, to analyse the rankings made by different judges, or to compare the data from observed and theoretical sources. Detailed information about which tests to use for particular data sets can be obtained from specialised texts on statistics and your own expert statistical adviser.

In order to avoid producing reams of impressive looking but meaningless analytical output, it is up to you to ensure that the tests are appropriate for the type of data you have. Figure 19.2 will help you determine which statistical approach is appropriate given the data collected.

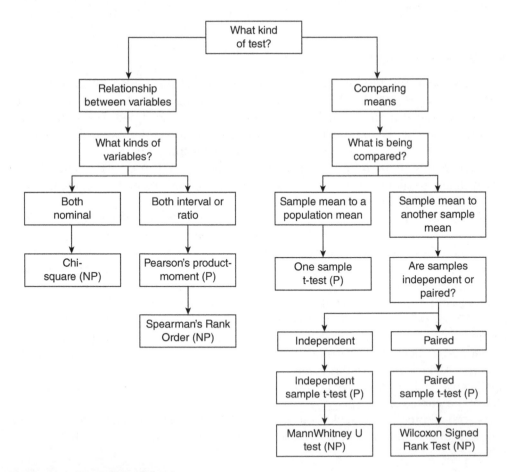

Figure 19.2   Stats flow diagram

If we work through Figure 19.2, the first question at the top leads you in one of two directions. To the left, the 'relationship between variables' relates to when you want to compare one measurement against another. Here four terms need distinguishing: nominal, ordinal, interval and ratio.

Nominal data is also known as categorical data: it is where something is labelled, named or categorised one way or another. Such nominal variables include gender (male/female), yes/no responses, form of transport taken to university and so on.

An ordinal variable is where something is rated, for example, a score from one to ten, or the extent to which a respondent agrees with something ('strongly agree', 'agree', 'neither agree nor disagree', 'disagree', 'strongly disagree').

Interval data is also known as continuous data: it is where results feature on a scale. By this, age is continuous and increases by one year. Measurements such as distance or time are also continuous as they are demarcated by set intervals: seconds, centimetres, etc.

Ratio data is a form of interval data, where the value of zero is clearly defined as an absence of that measure. It is unlikely within educational research that you will ever use ratio data, as opposed to the frequency with which you may use nominal, ordinal or interval data.

If you have data that compares two sets of nominal variables, for example, you are comparing gender (male/female) versus dropout rates (yes/no), the test that you would use is the chi-square. This has the letters 'NP' to indicate it is a non-parametric test. If you have two interval variables, for example, age versus test scores, the flow diagram would lead you to use either Pearson's product-moment coefficient, which is a parametric test (indicated by the 'P'), or Spearman's rank order test (non-parametric).

On the right side of the flow diagram, the core question asks what means are being compared. By this, a score on a test could be compared to scores from a wider population to determine the extent to which the results relate. Here, you would use the one sample t-test, a parametric test. If, however, you are comparing a test score against another test score using the same group, the next choice is to determine whether they are independent or paired. By independent, this would enable two different groups of people to have their scores on the same test compared for differences. For example, reading confidence would be compared between males and females through the independent sample t-test. For paired samples, this is where you would compare results on 'before and after' tests, where the same measure is given twice. As such, the paired sample t-test would be used.

Although further statistical tests are available, if you can understand the difference between those in Figure 19.2, understanding further tests such as ANOVAs and so on will be a relatively straightforward progression.

Although you may understand the type of statistical test needed, detailed guidebooks are available that will take you through the correct way to run the test through the computer program SPSS and how to interpret the results. Julie Pallant's most recent version of the *SPSS Survival Manual* (2016) is highly recommended.

19.5 PRESENTING QUANTITATIVE DATA

Both spreadsheet and statistical programs will produce very attractive results in the form of charts, graphs and tables that you can integrate into your research to back up your argument. The important issue is that you have carried out the appropriate analysis related to what you want to demonstrate or test. Explain what data you have collected, perhaps supplying a sample to show its form; give the reasons for doing the particular tests for each section of the investigation; and then present the results of the tests.

Graphs, tables and other forms of presentation always need to be explained. Do not believe that the reader knows how to read them and that they are self-explanatory in relation to your argument. Interpret the main features of the results and explain how these relate to the parts of the sub-problems or sub-questions that you are addressing. Now draw conclusions. What implications do the results have? Are they conclusive or is there room for doubt? Mention the limitations that might affect the strength of the result, for example, limited number of responses, possible bias or time constraints. Each conclusion will only form a small part of the overall argument, so you need to fit everything together like constructing a jigsaw puzzle. The full picture should clearly emerge at the end. It is best to devote one section or chapter to each of the sub-problems or sub-questions. Leave it to the final chapter to draw all the threads together in order to answer the main issue of the research.

Computer programs provide you with enormous choice when it comes to presenting graphs and charts. It is best to experiment to see which kind of presentation is the clearest. Consider whether you will be printing in monochrome or colour, as different coloured graph lines will lose their distinctiveness when reduced to shades of grey. It is also a good idea to set up a style that you maintain throughout the research.

19.6 INTERPRETING STATISTICAL DATA

Now you have a working overview of quantitative analysis, the most common statistical tests will provide different results in complex sentences. These sentences appear to be written in a code with each component part meaning something different. Take for example the following sentence:

> An independent samples t-test was conducted to compare the stress level scores for females and males. There was no significant difference in scores for females (M = 3.86, SD = 1.66) and males (M = 4.5, SD = 1.38; t (20) = −.83, p = .42).

What on earth does this actually mean? While you can decode the meaning that stress levels were pretty much the same for males and females, the numbers at first can seem gobbledegook. While the sentence may at first appear complicated, the core statement 'there was no significant difference' is the most important. The statistical output supports this, with the relevant numbers in the tables (see Table 19.1) inserted into the sentence. By this, the Mean (M) and Standard Deviation (SD) come from the first table. The t-test (t) number is the total in the population (14 females, 6 males = 20). Finally the −.83 comes from the row 'Equal variances assumed', and the .42 from the same row under the 'Sig. (2-tailed)' column. Please note that the numbers have been rounded, so −.831 becomes −.83 (see Table 19.1).

Table 19.1 Example statistical output

Group Statistics

	Gender	N	Mean	Std. Deviation	Std. Error Mean
Stress level	Female	14	3.86	1.657	.443
	Male	6	4.50	1.378	.563

Independent Samples Test

		Levene's Test of Equality of Variances		t-test for Equality of Means					95% Confidence Interval of the Difference	
		F	Sig.	t	df	Sig. (2-tailed)	Mean Difference	Std. Error Difference	Lower	Upper
Stress Level	Equal variances assumed	.462	.505	−.831	18	.417	−.643	.773	−2.268	.982
	Equal variances not assumed			−.898	11.429	.388	−.643	.716	−2.212	.926

In essence, there are only a few numbers that you will need to be familiar with when interpreting statistics. These are listed in Table 19.2.

19.7 QUALITATIVE ANALYSIS

Qualitative research is based more on information expressed in words: descriptions, accounts, opinions, feelings and so on. This approach is common whenever people are the focus of the study, particularly small groups or individuals. Frequently it is not possible to determine precisely what data should be collected as the situation or process is not sufficiently understood. Periodic analysis of collected data provides direction to further data collection.

Table 19.2   Interpreting four different types of statistical output

Type	Description	Test Name	Notes
Significance	To test the probability of a result occurring due to chance.	p value	A test is deemed significant if the p value is less than or equal to 0.05
Reliability	To test the internal consistency of a scale or questionnaire.	Cronbach's alpha	Values over 0.7 are deemed acceptable. Values over 0.8 are, however, preferable.
Correlation	To test the strength of the relationship between two variables.	Pearson's correlation coefficient (r), or Spearman's rank order correlation (rho).	The output will range between −1 to +1. A positive correlation would be +1, a negative correlation −1. The closer the result is to either −1 or +1, the stronger the correlation. Small correlation r = .1 to .29 Medium correlation r = .3 to .49 Large correlation r = .5 to 1.0
Effect size	To test the level of difference between groups.	ETA squared	Small effect size = .01 Moderate effect size = .06 Large effect size = .14

The essential difference between quantitative analysis and qualitative analysis is that with the former, you need to have completed your data collection before you can start analysis, while with the latter, analysis is carried out concurrently with data collection. With qualitative studies, there is a constant interplay between collection and analysis that produces a gradual growth of understanding. You collect information, review it, collect more data based on what you have discovered, then analyse again what you have found. This is quite a demanding and difficult process, and is prone to uncertainties and doubts. At the level of an undergraduate research, you will have to be careful not to be too ambitious, as the restricted time you have does not allow for lengthy delving and pondering. Keep the study focused and limited in scope so that you can complete the process. The important criteria for the examiner will be whether you have correctly used the methods and whether your conclusions are based on evidence found in the data collected.

Bromley (1986: 26) provides a list of ten steps in the process of qualitative research, summarised as follows:

1. Clearly state the research issues or questions.
2. Collect background information to help understand the relevant context, concepts and theories.
3. Suggest several interpretations or answers to the research problems or questions based on this information.
4. Use these to direct your search for evidence that might support or contradict these. Change the interpretations or answers if necessary.

5. Continue looking for relevant evidence. Eliminate interpretations or answers that are contradicted, leaving, hopefully, one or more that are supported by the evidence.
6. 'Cross-examine' the quality and sources of the evidence to ensure accuracy and consistency.
7. Carefully check the logic and validity of the arguments leading to your conclusions.
8. Select the strongest case in the event of more than one possible conclusion.
9. If appropriate, suggest a plan of action in the light of this.
10. Prepare your report as an account of your research; in this case present your research.

According to Robson and McCartern (2016), the core focus within qualitative analysis is that the analyst requires clarity in their thinking: as such, the analyst is being tested as much as the data they are testing. Although it has been the aim of many researchers to make qualitative analysis as systematic and as 'scientific' as possible, there is still an element of 'art' in dealing with qualitative data. However, in order to convince others of your conclusions, there must be a good argument to support them. A good argument requires high-quality evidence and sound logic. In fact, you will be acting rather like a lawyer presenting a case, using a quasi-judicial approach such as used in an enquiry into a disaster or scandal.

Qualitative data, represented in words, pictures and even sounds, cannot be analysed by mathematical means such as statistics. So how is it possible to organise all this data and be able to come to some conclusions about what it reveals? Unlike the well-established statistical methods of analysing quantitative data, qualitative data analysis is still in its early stages. The certainties of mathematical formulae and determinable levels of probability are not applicable to the 'soft' nature of qualitative data, which is inextricably bound up with human feelings, attitudes and judgements. Also, unlike the large amounts of data that are often collected for quantitative analysis, which can readily be managed with the available standard statistical procedures conveniently incorporated in computer packages, there are no such standard procedures for codifying and analysing qualitative data.

However, there are some essential activities that are necessary in all qualitative data analysis. Miles and Huberman (1994: 10–12) suggested that there are three concurrent flows of action:

- data reduction
- data display
- conclusion drawing/verification.

The activity of data display is important. The awkward mass of information that you will normally collect to provide the basis for analysis cannot be easily understood when presented as extended text, even when coded, clustered, summarised and so on. Information in text is dispersed, sequential (rather than concurrent), bulky and difficult to structure. Our minds are not good at processing large amounts of information, preferring to simplify complex information into patterns and easily understood configurations. Consequently, if you use suitable methods to display the data in the form of matrices, graphs, charts and networks, you not only reduce and order the data, but also can analyse it.

19.8 CODING DATA

As the data accumulates, a valuable step is to organise the shapeless mass of data by building typologies and taxonomies. These are technical words for the nominal level of measurement, that is, ordering by type or properties, thereby forming subgroups within the general category.

Even the simplest classification can help to organise seemingly shapeless information and to identify differences in, say, behaviour or types of people. For example, children's behaviour in the playground could be divided into 'joiners' and 'loners', or people in the shopping centre into 'serious shoppers', 'window shoppers', 'passers through', 'loiterers' and so on. This can help you to organise amorphous material and to identify patterns in the data. Then, noting the differences in terms of behaviour patterns between these categories can help you to generate the kinds of analysis that will form the basis for the development of explanations and conclusions.

This exercise in classification is the start of the development of a coding system, which is an important aspect of forming typologies. Codes are labels or tags used to allocate units of meaning to the collected data. Coding helps you to organise your piles of data (in the form of notes, observations, transcripts, documents) and to provide a first step in conceptualisation, and helps to prevent data overload resulting from mountains of unprocessed data in the form of ambiguous words.

Codes can be used to label different aspects of the subjects of study. Lofland (1971: 14–15), for example, devised six classes on which you could devise a coding scheme for 'social phenomena':

1. Acts
2. Activities
3. Meanings
4. Participation
5. Relationships
6. Settings.

The process of coding is analytical, and requires you to review, select, interpret and summarise the information without distorting it. Normally, you should compile a set of codes before doing the fieldwork, based on your background study, and then refine it during the data collection.

There are two essentially different types of coding, one that you can use for the retrieval of text sequences, the other devised for theory generation. The former refers to the process of cutting out and pasting sections of text from transcripts or notes under various headings. The latter is a more fluent coding system used as an index for your interpretive ideas: reflective notes or memos, rather than merely bits of text.

What unites both these forms of coding is that you are seeking to reduce the data into a meaningful chunk or ascribe a meaningful label, where you actually assign meaning to the information you have. Such chunks are referred to as open coding.

OPEN CODING

Open coding is where one or more words are noted next to a sentence or paragraph of text. For example, you could transcribe an interview into a table with each row representing a different sentence. These rows can be numbered. From this, one or two words could be used to summarise the sentence as demonstrated in Table 19.3. Here you can see how open codes have been used to summarise the teacher's responses.

Table 19.3a   An example of open coding of an interview (Teacher A)

Line	Person	Response	Open code
1	Interviewer	Why did you decide to become a teacher?	
2	Teacher A	I didn't know what to do when I finished school so I started helping out at my local primary school, the one I used to go to.	helping out
3	Teacher A	At first I started listening to readers and working with one child at a time.	individuals
4	Teacher A	Then once I became more confident, I worked with smaller groups.	confidence improved
5	Teacher A	After a couple of months I was asked if I wanted to help with a school residential on Dartmoor.	residential
6	Teacher A	I really enjoyed it ... it was an excellent experience as I love the outdoors.	excellent experience/ enjoyment
7	Teacher A	During the week, I was taking more responsibility in organising team games, an orienteering exercise around the site, and running some evening activities.	responsibility
8	Teacher A	A teacher then said to me, 'You could get paid for doing this', and that was when the lightbulb lit.	teacher comment
9	Teacher A	I can still remember that moment now 30 years on.	core memory
10	Teacher A	I then had the focus to get the grades needed at A level and applied for a place on a course.	focus
11	Teacher A	I have never looked back since.	no regrets
12	Interviewer	So would you say that it happened by chance?	
13	Teacher A	I don't think anything ever happens by chance ... I think it was something within me I didn't realise I had and just needed the right environment to bring this out.	nothing by chance/ right environment/ latent ability

Table 19.3b   An example of open coding of an interview (Teacher B)

Line	Person	Response	Open code
1	Interviewer	Why did you decide to become a teacher?	
2	Teacher B	From a young age it is all I wanted to do.	lifelong aspiration
3	Teacher B	I have always loved working with children and wanted a job where I could continue to work and support them.	loved working with children
4	Teacher B	It was only when I did work experience at school that I realised it was the job for me.	work experience

If there were two or three interviews asking the same questions, there may be a pattern emerging where the open codes are similar for different responses to specific questions. This leads into looking for patterns, or axial coding, which will be discussed shortly.

Several computer programs used for analysing qualitative data also have facilities for filing and retrieving coded information. They allow codes to be attached to the numbered lines of notes or transcripts of interviews, and for the source of the information/opinion to be noted. This enables a rapid retrieval of selected information from the mass of material collected. However, it does take quite some time to master the techniques involved, so take advice before contemplating the use of these programs.

AXIAL CODING (LOOKING FOR THEMES)

The next stage of analysis requires you to begin to look for patterns and themes between the open codes you have ascribed initially. As this develops, you will start to develop explanations of why and how these themes occur. This requires a method of pulling together the coded information into more compact and meaningful groupings. Axial coding can do this by reducing the data into smaller analytical units such as themes, causes/explanations, relationships among people and emerging concepts, to allow you to develop a more integrated understanding of the situation studied and to test the initial explanations or answers to the research issues or questions. This will generally help to focus later fieldwork and lay the foundations for cross-case analysis in multicase studies by identifying common themes and processes.

Miles and Huberman (1994: 70–1) describe three successive ways that pattern codes may be used:

1. The newly developed codes are provisionally added to the existing list of codes and checked out in the next set of field notes to see whether they fit.
2. Next, the most promising codes are written up in a memo (described below) to clarify and explain the concept so that it can be related to other data and cases.
3. Finally, the new pattern codes are tested out in the next round of data collection.

Actually, you will find that generating pattern codes is surprisingly easy, as it is the way by which we habitually process information. However, it is important not to cling uncritically onto initially developed patterns but to test and develop, and if necessary, reject them as your understanding of the data develops, and as new waves of data are produced. One way that you could present axial coding is through developing a concept map as demonstrated in Figure 19.3.

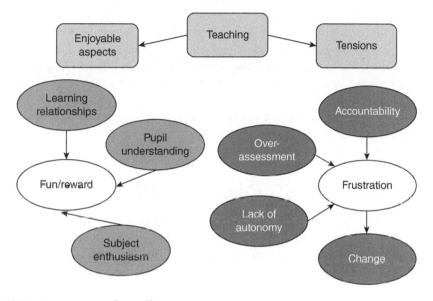

Figure 19.3   Concept map for coding

With the concept map, explicit links can be made between the open codes you have generated from the table approach.

A different approach is to compile memos to explore links between data and to record and develop intuitions and ideas. You can do this at any time but it is best done when the idea is fresh. Remember that memos are written for you, so the length and style are not important, but it is necessary to label a memo so that it can be easily sorted and retrieved. You should continue the activity of memoing throughout the research project. You will find that the ideas become more stable with time until saturation point – the point where you are satisfied with your understanding and explanation of the data – is achieved.

It is a very good idea, at probably about one-third way through the data collection, to take stock and seek to reassure yourself and your supervisors by checking:

- the quantity and quality of what you have found out so far
- your confidence in the reliability of the data
- the presence and nature of any gaps or puzzles that have been revealed
- what still needs to be collected in relation to your time available.

This exercise should result in the production of an interim summary – a provisional report a few pages long. This report will be the first time that everything you know about a case will be summarised, and presents the first opportunity to make cross-case analyses in multicase studies and to review emergent explanatory variables.

Remember, however, that the nature of the summary is provisional. Though it is perhaps sketchy and incomplete, it should be seen as a useful tool for you to reflect on the work done, for discussion with your colleagues and supervisors, and for indicating any changes that might be needed in the coding and in the subsequent data collection work. In order to check on the amount of data collected about each research question, you will find it useful to compile a data accounting sheet. This is a table that sets out the research questions and the amount of data collected from the different informants, settings, situations and so on. With this you will easily be able to identify any shortcomings.

Although we have looked at the notion of coding, different ways of structuring the analysis at a deeper level are provided below.

19.9 CONDUCTING QUALITATIVE ANALYSIS

Traditional text-based reports tend to be lengthy and cumbersome when presenting, analysing, interpreting and communicating the findings of a qualitative research project. Not only do they have to present the evidence and arguments sequentially, they also tend to be bulky and difficult to grasp quickly because information is dispersed over many pages.

This presents a problem for you, the writer, as well as for the final reader, who rarely has time to browse backwards and forwards through masses of text to gain full information. Graphical methods of data display and analysis can largely overcome these problems and they are useful for exploring and describing as well as explaining and predicting phenomena. They can be used equally effectively for single case and cross-case analysis.

Graphical displays fall into two categories: matrices and networks.

Matrices or tables

The two-dimensional arrangement of rows and columns can summarise a substantial amount of information. You can easily produce these informally in a freehand fashion to explore aspects of the data, to any size. You can also use computer programs in the form of databases and spreadsheets to help in their production. You can use matrices to record variables such as time, levels of measurement, roles, clusters, outcomes and effects. If you want to get really sophisticated, latest developments allow you to formulate three-dimensional matrices.

Networks

A network is made up of blocks (nodes) connected by links. You can produce these maps and charts in a wide variety of formats, each with the capability of displaying different types of data:

- *Flowcharts* are useful for studying processes or procedures. Not only helpful for explanation, their development is a good device for creating understanding.
- *Organisation charts* display relationships between variables and their nature, e.g., formal and informal hierarchies.
- *Causal networks* are used to examine and display the causal relationships between important independent and dependent variables, causes and effects.

These methods of displaying and analysing qualitative data are particularly useful when you compare the results of several case studies, as they permit a certain standardisation of presentation, allowing comparisons to be made more easily across the cases.

You can display the information in the form of text, codes, abbreviated notes, symbols, quotations or any other form that helps to communicate compactly. The detail and sophistication of the display can vary depending on its function and on the amount of information available. Displays are useful at any stage in the research process.

Ordering information in displays

The different types of display can be described by the way that information is ordered in them.

Time-ordered displays record a sequence of events in relation to their chronology. A simple example of this is a project programme giving names, times and locations for tasks of different kinds. The scale and precision of timing can be suited to the subject. Events can be of various types, such as tasks, critical events, experiences, stages in a programme, activities, decisions and so forth.

Some examples of types of time-ordered displays are:

- *Events lists or networks*: showing a sequence of events, perhaps highlighting the critical ones, and perhaps including times and dates.
- *Activity records*: showing the sequential steps required to accomplish a task.
- *Decision models*: commonly used to analyse a course of action employing a matrix with yes/no routes from each decision taken.

Conceptually ordered displays concentrate on variables in the form of abstract concepts related to a theory, and the relationships between these. Examples of such variables are motives, attitudes, expertise, barriers, coping strategies, etc. They can be shown as matrices or networks to illustrate taxonomies, content analysis, cognitive structures, relationships of cause and effect or influence.

Here is a selection of different types of conceptually ordered displays:

- *Conceptually or thematically clustered matrix*: helps to summarise the mass of data about numerous research questions by combining groups of questions that are connected, either from a theoretical point of view, or as a result of groupings that can be detected in the data.
- *Taxonomy tree diagram*: useful to break down concepts into their constituent parts or elements.
- *Cognitive map*: a descriptive diagrammatic plotting of a person's way of thinking about an issue; useful to understand somebody's way of thinking or to compare that of several people.
- *Effects matrix*: plots the observed effects of an action or intervention, a necessary precursor to explaining or predicting effects.
- *Decision tree modelling*: helps to make clear a sequence of decisions, by setting up a network of sequential yes/no response routes.
- *Causal models*: used in theory building to provide a testable set of propositions about a complete network of variables with causal and other relationships between them, based on a multicase situation. A preliminary stage in the development of a causal model is to develop causal chains, linear cause/effect lines.

Role ordered displays show people's roles and their relationships in formal and informal organisations or groups. A role defines a person's standing and position by assessing their behaviour and expectations within the group or organisation. These may be conventionally recognised positions, for example, headteacher, teacher, teaching assistant, parent/guardian, student; or more abstract and situation dependent, for example, leader, motivator, objector. People in different roles tend to see situations from different perspectives. A role ordered matrix will help to systematically display these differences or can be used to investigate whether people in the same roles are unified in their views.

Partially ordered displays are useful in analysing 'messy' situations without trying to impose too much internal order on them. For example, a context chart can be designed to show, in the form of a network, the influences and pressures that bear on an individual from surrounding organisations and persons when making a decision to act. This will help to understand why a particular action was taken.

Case-ordered displays show the data of cases arranged in some kind of order according to an important variable in the study. This allows you to compare cases and note their different features according to where they appear in the order.

If you are comparing several case studies, you can combine the above displays to make 'meta' displays that amalgamate and contrast the data from each case. For example, a case-ordered meta-matrix does this by simply arranging case matrices next to each other in the chosen order to enable you to simply compare the data across the meta-matrix. The meta-matrix can initially be quite large if there are a number of cases. A function of the analysis will be to summarise the data in a smaller matrix, giving a summary of the significant issues discovered. Following this a contrast table can also be devised to display and compare how one or two variables perform in cases as ordered in the meta-matrix.

19.10 CONCLUSION

The purpose of this chapter has been to provide an understanding to how qualitative and quantitative research can be analysed, supplying different approaches for each. It must be noted that this is just an overview of the processes; however, it should enable you to access more complex research methodology books if considering conducting your own research. Furthermore, when reading research reports, you should understand how the researchers have reached their conclusions.

19.11 FURTHER READING

Pallant, J. (2016) *SPSS Survival Manual: A Step by Step Guide to Data Analysis Using IBM SPSS* (6th edn). Maidenhead: Open University Press.
This book is very popular in explaining statistical processes through analysis software. It breaks down the process into easy progressive stages.

Miles, M.B., Huberman, A.M. and Saldana, J. (2013) *Qualitative Data Analysis: A Methods Sourcebook* (3rd edn). Thousand Oaks, CA: Sage Publications.
This is perhaps the most comprehensive book available on qualitative analysis.

Part 7
CLASSROOM PRACTICE

In combination with Part 4, this part acts as a goldmine of information to help teachers use psychology to inform their day-to-day classroom activities, and to create pleasant, creativity-inspiring learning environments (Chapter 20), within which they and their learners can achieve their full potential. The part is also experimental in the sense that a teacher may need to adapt the guidance to suit their specific requirements. We do not see this as a bad thing. Rather, it is exactly this approach that leads to an evolution in one's teaching (Chapter 21). Chapter 22 draws each of these strands together.

20
THE LEARNING ENVIRONMENT

CHAPTER OBJECTIVES

- Identify the factors affecting the learning environment.
- Consider the teacher's role in influencing the learning environment.
- Develop an understanding of how behaviour is related to perspective.
- Critically evaluate approaches to influencing behaviour positively.

TEACHERS' STANDARDS

A teacher must:

1 Set high expectations which inspire, motivate and challenge pupils

- establish a safe and stimulating environment for pupils, rooted in mutual respect
- demonstrate consistently the positive attitudes, values and behaviour which are expected of pupils

2 Promote good progress and outcomes by pupils

- demonstrate knowledge and understanding of how pupils learn and how this impacts on teaching

4 Plan and teach well-structured lessons

- impart knowledge and develop understanding through effective use of lesson time
- promote a love of learning and children's intellectual curiosity

5 Adapt teaching to respond to the strengths and needs of all pupils

- have a secure understanding of how a range of factors can inhibit pupils' ability to learn, and how best to overcome these

7 Manage behaviour effectively to ensure a good and safe learning environment

- have clear rules and routines for behaviour in classrooms, and take responsibility for promoting good and courteous behaviour both in classrooms and around the school, in accordance with the school's behaviour policy
- have high expectations of behaviour, and establish a framework for discipline with a range of strategies, using praise, sanctions and rewards consistently and fairly

- manage classes effectively, using approaches which are appropriate to pupils' needs in order to involve and motivate them
- maintain good relationships with pupils, exercise appropriate authority and act decisively when necessary

8 Fulfil wider professional responsibilities

- make a positive contribution to the wider life and ethos of the school

20.1 INTRODUCTION

Simply defined, the learning environment is where learning takes place. Yet such an environment is multifaceted in nature. If you consider the environment where you are currently reading this page, how would you describe it? Are you at home, in a library or sitting on a train? Are you comfortable where you are sitting, assuming you are seated? How would you describe your current location to another person? If you are on a train, you may not even be sitting. Perhaps the person next to you is rustling a newspaper, distracting your attention. Maybe there is the underlying base sound of whatever they are listening to on their MP3 player. It is very unlikely that you are reading this paragraph in a formal context, for example in a classroom, lecture hall or so on. Ultimately is the place where you are reading this paragraph conducive to your learning or are you being distracted in some way?

The environment where learning occurs can therefore be one of many places. Even within a school, learning occurs in many different contexts: the hall, the playground, the classroom and so on. Yet what actually contributes to the development of an effective learning environment?

> ## ACTIVITY   The classroom environment
>
> What contributes to the classroom environment?
>
> Make a list of at least ten factors that contribute to the classroom environment.
>
> Can any of the items on your list be grouped in different ways?

Your response to the previous activity would probably have included aspects relating to the physical environment. Your response may have included the climate: the temperature, the lighting. Some of the attributes may include social or emotional elements, for example the 'warmth' on a personal level: how welcoming the classroom feels. According to Creemers and Reezigt (1999), the classroom environment consists of the physical and social domains, also its atmosphere, norms and values. Furthermore, the classroom environment is one of the most important predictors of learner achievement (Brophy and Good, 1986). In reviewing your list, how many of the factors are within your control? How can you affect the environment? This chapter will discuss the way in which psychology can be applied to create your ideal learning environment.

In an ideal world, you would be able to design your very own classroom, with the luxury of resourcing the room with whatever you deem appropriate. Yet the harsh reality of the place you are working in may be somewhat different. Throughout our careers as teachers, we will rarely be placed in the absolutely ideal classroom, yet we can take control of what we have been given, and work with what we have.

Within our educational careers, we will find ourselves working in different environments. From mobile classrooms that feel like an oven in the summer, through to cold, dark classrooms that have no direct sunlight; classrooms that are air-conditioned with triple-glazed windows because the school is under the flight path of Heathrow Airport, through to schools next to motorways with the constant rumbling sound of traffic; schools that were built over a hundred years ago, those built in the late 1960s, to those that are a couple of years old. Educational establishments have changed significantly over the last hundred years. Classrooms of the Victorian era, for example, were dour, drab places, where learning was imposed through harsh means. With the advent of modern academies, sponsored by industry, the classroom of today is a far cry from its earlier incarnations and is in many instances unrecognisable. Bright, airy classrooms, adequately lit, painted in appropriate colours (see Section 20.4 for more on this topic) and with modern equipment and resources, provide a pleasant context for learning to take place. In psychological terms, this is the essence of motivational climates (Ames, 1992; Pintrich, 2003). A plethora of evidence across many different domains suggests that motivational climates improve performance. No matter where we teach or what physical rooms we are provided with, we can still ensure that the learning environment is the best we can provide for our learners.

REFLECTION

Consider the various classrooms you have previously worked in. What are the best components of each that you would like to take to equip your ideal classroom?

20.2 THE PSYCHOLOGY OF CLASSROOM LAYOUTS

Walking into classrooms today provides us with an insight into the mindset of the teacher whose classroom it is. There is of course an initial *caveat* to bear in mind:

classroom layout may be determined by a directive from management. If this is the case, there is perhaps little flexibility. However, if there is no directive and the teacher has free reign, the question of which layout is best begins to emerge. We would argue that there is no best layout. Rather, a classroom layout is an ingredient of the way that a teacher wishes to interact with his or her environment. Furthermore, this layout may change to suit differing needs or even differing seasons. What we can say is that certain layouts may not be as effective as others in terms of classroom discipline or harmony, but this again is a subjective comment that is dependent upon teaching style and preferences.

Figure 20.1 provides a sample layout. Some will suit your needs, others will not. Our advice would be to sketch out the classroom on a sheet of paper, cut out paper shapes to resemble groups of desks, preferably to an approximate scale, and experiment by moving the shapes around. At the very least, this method will provide guidance on which layout will not fit into the space available, especially when one takes into account health and safety issues, fire exit-route issues and other operational matters associated with your own classroom. Following on from this, we mentioned mental imagery in Chapter 15. Once you have established a potential layout on paper, it is possible to visualise it in your mind, by embarking on a mental tour of the classroom. Imagine walking in through the door of the classroom and around the desks; turn, look around; assess how effective the layout is and see if it works for you. Taking this a step further, you might even visualise which children will occupy which desks, as individuals, or more beneficially for you as groups. In this way, it becomes possible to establish how certain layouts may be more effective than others in maintaining discipline.

In Figure 20.1, the clusters of desks may work well if a large open area is required (for example, the blue mat for younger children). This can be contrasted with the photo in Figure 20.2, which has a completely different feel to it.

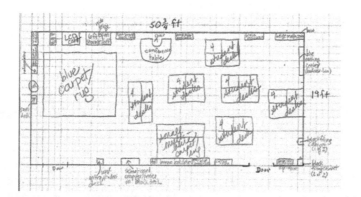

Figure 20.1   A classroom outline plan

Figure 20.2   A contrasting classroom

Source: iStock.com/quizbiz

20.3 AGE AND GENDER DIFFERENCES

It goes without saying that a classroom should match the needs of its inhabitants. With this in mind, the issue of age is significant when determining how the classroom should be designed. For example, a primary school classroom needs to be something of a 'Jack/Jill-of-all-trades', but also needs to focus on having, for example, a literacy wall and a numeracy wall. In contrast, a secondary school geography classroom will focus on areas of the curriculum to match the level of study. Understanding the psychology underpinning the acquisition and display of information is therefore important if a teacher is to maximise the impact of their display space.

20.4 THE PSYCHOLOGY OF COLOUR

If a classroom is to match the needs of its occupants, there are a host of strategies that can be employed to enhance the classroom in order to provide the necessary stimulation. If we take visual stimulation as our starting point, there is evidence to show that adequate classroom lighting, or luminance, influences concentration in a positive way (Sleegers et al., 2013). Luminance is a prerequisite to colour perception and is essential in providing dynamism and vibrancy, while also providing areas that may be needed to portray calmness and tranquility. If luminance of the room itself is taken into account, colour may potentially produce a different effect from that perceived by the teacher when designing his or her environment (Tuncer et al., 2012). Although, in reality, poor colour–luminance relationships will not necessarily be detrimental to the physical wellbeing of the room's inhabitants, they may do little to foster psychological wellbeing.

Teachers should be mindful that colour is not restricted to walls, displays and models. The use of coloured filters in helping dyslexic children to read and understand instructions, worksheets or homework tasks is a simple yet effective way of facilitating their progress (Northway et al., 2010). This method of reducing visual noise or stress enables a child to focus on the meaning present in the visual array, rather than being overloaded by it (Wilkins et al., 2009).

20.5 THE PSYCHOLOGY OF TYPEFACES

Typeface and its size are important factors to consider when designing displays, PowerPoint presentations, documents and such like. It is worth reminding oneself that a preferred typeface, style or size may not be the most effective when seen through the eyes of a child. Let us provide a simple example here. In Chapter 6, we discussed the fact that depth perception develops to maturity over a period of time. Consequently, younger children lack depth perception, when compared to older children. Evidence suggests, for example, that children show a preference for larger font sizes (Arial 5mm) over smaller font sizes (Arial 4.2mm) if given a choice (Wilkins et al., 2009). In the same study children were able to read and search the font Verdana more quickly for information compared with Sassoon Primary.

While the selection of a suitable typeface enhances letter identification (Fiset et al., 2008) and readability (Gump, 2001), from which it may be possible to infer an improvement in decision-making and understanding, there are wider implications of typeface selection. Typefaces have been linked to emotion and consequently are seen to affect how people feel. Simon Jarvis provides an interesting essay, 'To the letter', elaborating an insight into the effects of typefaces on the reading of poetry (Jarvis, 2011). One should reflect on the issue of how to use typefaces effectively in order to convey emotion beyond that provided by the printed word alone. If a typeface is capable of altering emotions or influencing moods, then it is indeed a powerful tool in a teacher's resource kit. At a neurophysiological level, the typeface is exerting an influence on the visual system but also on the limbic system in the brain. The limbic system, as we saw in Chapters 5 and 7, is responsible for emotions and is integrated into cognitive processing. By this, we mean that there is an interplay between the printed matter and the feelings associated with the way in which that printed matter is presented. In practical terms, this means that, if attention is paid to the design of educational material, including displays, it may be possible to achieve beneficial results by approaching the emotions evoked, rather than the content. One possible consequence of this is that a child's confidence may be boosted as a result of their engagement with the material at a higher level. A teacher operating at this level of attention to detail is indeed making full use of the psychology of typefaces, not only to facilitate learning, but also to enhance the nature of that learning experience.

ACTIVITY

Take a walk through a shopping mall or local high street and pay attention to the commercial signage on display. Ask yourself whether the typeface has been chosen at random, or whether it has been chosen carefully to portray a particular type of message to the consumer. Next, ask yourself how the signage makes you feel about the shop and how well, if at all, the signage has achieved its purpose. If you have never done this as an exercise, it will certainly start your mind racing with the possibilities of what can be achieved in your own 'commercial' environment, the classroom.

In essence, what we have been discussing thus far in this chapter is a way of using psychology to provide order and structure in an appropriate, considered manner, by paying attention to details that other people may not have considered before. If the classroom environment is sufficiently well designed, the opportunities for children to want to be in that classroom increase. This equates to the notion of 'ownership', which we consider below.

20.6 LEARNING STYLES, PERSONALISED LEARNING, OR THE QUALITY OF THE TEACHER

Learning styles can be deemed as the way in which the person concentrates on, processes, internalises and remembers new information, based on the biological and developmental characteristics of the individual and how they tend to respond to the learning environment (Keefe, 1979). It could be argued that this section appears in the wrong place in the book because it is used to convey the stable individual characteristics that the individual learner predominantly uses. Consequently, this section could have appeared equally in Chapters 6 or 7 (thus demonstrating that material should be used to suit your own learning requirements).

According to Franklin (2006), the term 'learning styles' has become a byword in a drive to raise educational standards, citing how learning styles (specifically VAK: Visual, Auditory, Kinaesthetic) have become popularised through the government and various initiatives. Pashler et al. (2009) similarly highlight the prevalence of learning styles.

The fundamental reason for identifying learning styles is that the educational environment can be structured in such a way as to ensure it is tailored to the needs of the student. This popularity may be explained through the appeal of personalised learning, where the student is deemed an individual with a unique approach to their studies, and that effective outcomes can be promoted if suitable instruction is provided that adheres to their unique style. Conversely, if a student is not succeeding, it is likely to be more comforting to consider that the education system, and not the student, is responsible (Pashler et al., 2009). According to Coffield et al. (2004), there are at least 71 learning styles, which they categorised under five areas: constitutionally based learning styles and preferences, cognitive structure, stable personality type, 'flexibly stable' preferences, and learning approaches and strategies.

While current research still indicates that children have learning preferences, for example within science (Kant and Singh, 2015), there has been an increasing debate about their relevance. While learning styles became a prevalent area of focus in schools during the mid-2000s with schools following government advice, Coffield et al. (2004) had already highlighted the problematic nature of labelling, instead advocating that a more personalised approach is required, whereby the pupil uses their metacognition strategies for learning. Of course, this depends on metacognitive strategies being facilitated with pupils. Indeed, towards the latter part of the 2000s, there was a move towards personalised learning in schools, following the Gilbert Review (2007). However, with the change of government in 2010, the focus was moved back into the quality of the teacher, specifically in recruiting effective people, improving teacher training, and also improving professional development. With the focus being returned to the actual teacher, the concept of teacher effectiveness is similarly relevant, as discussed in Chapter 3.

20.7 STRUCTURE, ORDER AND OWNERSHIP

An ordered classroom is not only a pleasant environment for all to work in, including the teacher; it also facilitates efficiency through its structure. In practical terms, this means that everything has a place and everything is generally in its place. Children know where to look for helpful guidance and are being exposed to orderliness, which they will tend to adopt in their own approach to learning – you will notice this through the neatness of exercise books of some children within the class. A teacher who fosters and nurtures this orderliness will be contributing to the child's sense of ownership. By this, we mean that the classroom becomes the children's classroom, a place where pride is fostered, as the children become protective over 'their' space. This sense of positive ownership may act as a motivational aid in striving to achieve individual and class goals. A consequence of children taking positive ownership of the classroom environment has, for example, been associated with helping to reduce violence in the classroom (Johnson, 2009).

20.8 LEARNING CLIMATES

As a teacher, you have the wonderful ability of being in control of the learning climate. How can you ensure that your classroom is a welcoming place? After all, learners will be spending approximately 190 days each year in that location. What is it that you want learners to feel as they enter their domain: a safe, comfortable, inclusive learning environment, or one where they are scared, feel unwelcome or feel that they are trespassing? How can you as the teacher establish the climate you want to foster to make sure that life is equally pleasant for anyone who steps over the threshold into your classroom?

This book has encouraged you to develop your own philosophy so that it can be embodied in practice within your teaching, and that includes taking control of the place where the teaching occurs. As a teacher, you are the conductor of the orchestra of learning that occurs minute-by-minute in your domain, a domain you share with your learners. Although this book has provided information on the individual learner, specifically how psychology can be applied to support their learning, as soon as there are more than two learners in the classroom, a balancing act needs to be maintained. How can you ensure that the optimal learning conditions are provided for each of these? How can you ensure the environment and climate are appropriate? With one learner, you will have the ability to guarantee they are sitting in an ideal location, that they are comfortable, that you can provide exactly the right amount of encouragement and motivation, and that you can help when help is required. Yet with the addition of one extra learner, your attention is divided. Now add seven more learners into the equation. Perhaps some of these have had an argument prior to entering your classroom. Perhaps others are keen to share their opinion on the latest release by their favourite group. Perhaps a learner is feeling unwell; another did not get enough sleep last night due to their baby brother or sister keeping them awake. Perhaps one is scared of a dental appointment immediately after school. Now add another 20 and your meticulously planned lesson may go awry.

The competing demands we need to provide for each learner are of paramount importance: if we get this right, learning progresses in an enjoyable climate. If we get this wrong, that same climate could change. It is all too easy to discuss this change in climate as being due to the learner: but is the manifestation of the inappropriate learning behaviour a result of an inappropriate learning environment? We have passed on the responsibility of the behaviour to the learner – someone who is younger and less experienced than we are as the teacher.

In returning to a theme in Chapter 9, it is all too easy to label a learner as the one with the problem, whether this is with a learning need we have not addressed, or with their behaviour. In Chapter 10, the motivational climate was discussed in relation to positive reinforcement (rewards) and negative reinforcement (punishments) as a way of ensuring a specific behaviour is engaged with. Yet surely, as teachers, it is our responsibility to establish an appropriate educational environment for each learner and, through doing this, limiting the opportunities for poor behaviour to manifest itself? This leads the chapter to one of the most significant areas perceived by teachers: learner behaviour.

20.9 BEHAVIOUR 'MANAGEMENT'?

Often, when discussing behaviour in the classroom, the term 'behaviour management' is used. This term implies that behaviour occurs spontaneously and is managed by the teacher. Even if behaviour management is perceived as those components that can be implemented to diminish undesirable behaviour, in order to maximise the positive attributes of learning, the emphasis still focuses on the misbehaviour of the learner. Whether we react to unwanted exhibited behaviour or are proactive in diminishing it, the emphasis is on controlling or limiting certain aspects. However, this section does not view misbehaviour as maladaptive: it views behaviour in relation to contextual issues in the learner's current circumstances.

REFLECTION

What in your mind contributes to unwanted behaviour in your classroom?

Now consider yourself as a learner, whether you are a student teacher in a lecture or a teacher engaged with a professional development session.

Have you always engaged with an appropriate learning behaviour, or have you whispered to another colleague or learner, checked your phone for a text message, made a shopping list, had off-task discussions or not been completely engaged with the task at hand?

Now imagine that we live in a world where the learner is in control. What behaviours would they see as unwanted behaviours in you?

Managing behaviour is part of the teaching profession that every teacher has to develop a relationship with. This is not the same as behaviour management in the traditional sense. Rather, it is the management of whatever behaviour the teacher is currently faced with. Overcoming this is a concern for everyone across the teaching profession, whether they are a student, newly qualified or experienced. It is perhaps the most important aspect that affects the enjoyment of teaching, even despite the flood of directives and paperwork that come a close second or third. Yet as teachers, our relationship to the behaviour is perhaps the single most significant element. How do we react to different behaviours? What behaviours cause the most concern? What behaviours take the most time to address?

Swinson and Harrop (2012: 53) identify three different types of unwanted behaviour: non-disruptive off-task behaviour; disruptive off-task behaviour, such as talking; and severe disruptive behaviour that prevents the class from functioning. According to Elton (1989), it is the high-frequency, low-level disruptive behaviour that is of most concern to teachers and indeed may be contributing to the high level of stress resulting in teachers leaving the profession (NASUWT, 2010; NUT, 2012).

ACTIVITY

Some unwanted behaviours are listed below:

- Calling out in class
- Talking to another learner while the teacher is talking
- Fidgeting
- Disturbing another learner who is on task
- Not getting on with set work
- Appearing uninterested in the lesson
- Other

Now prioritise the behaviours in order from the most to the least disruptive. For each of the behaviours, consider the W5H1 questions:

- Why do you think this behaviour has occurred?
- Who is affected by the behaviour?
- What is the behaviour?
- Where does the behaviour occur?
- When is this behaviour exhibited?
- How could this behaviour be dealt with?

From an historical perspective, in a report by Rutter et al. (1979), teacher disapproval and reprimands were twice as evident as teacher praise within the UK (an area we will further discuss in this chapter), although from a psychological perspective Brophy (1981) suggested that it was the actual quality of the feedback that influenced children's behaviour, not just whether it was praise or a reprimand. Furthermore, a core report into behaviour was conducted in 1989: the Elton Report (Elton, 1989). This sought to define what was meant by good behaviour and discipline (and their opposites) within the school context, while also investigating the causes and extent of discipline problems in school, in turn suggesting how good behaviour could be promoted. Indeed, the issue of behaviour has been reviewed more recently by the Steer Report (Steer, 2009), a government-commissioned report that made 47 recommendations. Such recommendations identify that there is no single solution and that a combination of inseparable elements are needed: effective learning, teaching and behaviour management through a whole-school approach.

STRATEGIES

Although there are many strategies for promoting positive learning behaviour, the significant element is to ensure that the approach is consistent so that learners are aware of what is required and what is not deemed acceptable. This consistent approach needs to be developed as a whole school to avoid conflicting messages for learners. Furthermore, there also needs to be consistency in the way teachers make use of the approach. For example, our recommendation that physical education be tailored to facilitate concentration is one possible way to alleviate behavioural issues (as discussed in Chapter 6). However, one teacher alone cannot effect change: all teachers would need to subscribe to a physical education intervention to ensure consistency.

A FOUR-STEP MODEL

A current model based upon positive psychology has been developed by Swinson and Harrop (2012). Their four-stage model is illustrated in the following activity.

ACTIVITY   Example based on Swinson and Harrop

Read through the four-step process below, while considering how you could adapt it for your classroom context.

Step One

The first step is to ensure instructions and directions are absolutely clear. By this, Swinson and Harrop suggest using simple, unambiguous instructions. Furthermore instructions should be limited in number, to a maximum of three at any one time. The instructions should indicate the expected behaviour, for example, working by themselves/in pairs/groups, noise level and also the materials needed to engage with the task.

(Continued)

Step Two

The second step is to follow any instruction or direction by looking for those learners who are doing as they have been asked and acknowledging them. By this, identify learners who are engaged with your instructions and praise them for the behaviour: for example, 'Well done table three for putting your materials away quietly. Well done Amy for sitting there quietly after you have tidied up.' Naming the individual or a group reinforces to others what is required.

Step Three

The third step is to frequently acknowledge learners when they are doing whatever they have been requested to do. Within moments of receiving an instruction, the learners may become engrossed in the activity, or else their attention may have been distracted, or something in between. Consequently, it is important to reinforce the initial instructions through identifying those engaged with the task. Importantly, the feedback should be individual, again using a name to highlight a person or group engaged with the activity. The feedback should be specific and descriptive, related to the task or instruction that has been requested; furthermore it should be sincere and appropriate to the age. An example could be, 'It is great to see you so engaged with tidying up quickly and quietly, James.'

Step Four

The final step is to always know exactly what to do to deal with inappropriate behaviour. Ensure a consistent approach is adopted for each of the specific categories of behaviour. From the non-disruptive off-task behaviour through to severe disruptive behaviour, the teacher should have a set of developed strategies that they can consistently use. For example, the comment could be made: 'Claire, you have been asked to tidy up quickly and quietly: would you prefer to do this now, or after the rest of the class are at play?' By providing a choice, the learner can decide whether to engage with the instruction or to engage with the resulting consequence. The consequence is directly related to the behaviour, an aspect discussed further on in this chapter.

THE ABC OF BEHAVIOUR

Although the behaviourist perspective has been discussed in Chapters 1 and 10, a further strategy often advocated is the ABC of behaviour. As a reminder of the approach, generally when teachers see undesirable learning behaviour (B) within their classrooms, they tend to convey a consequence (C). For example, a learner continues to talk when we ask for everyone's attention (B), and as a result, the learner is spoken to by name and reminded of your request (C). Alternatively a learner kicks another under a table, resulting in some form of protest from the injured party (B), with the resultant action of the perpetrator being reprimanded in some way (C).

What is missing from both examples is the antecedent (A): in other words, what actually motivated the exhibited behaviour (B), which led to the consequence (C). Could the talker have been caught up in their learning and about to make a break-through in their cognitive process in relation to the task, only to be stifled by the teacher's interruption? Could the kicker have been kicked previously, on purpose or by accident, by another learner?

Given the number of learners within the class, can we really be aware of every antecedent? Consequently, we tend to deal with the behaviours: any protest from the learner about the injustice of the situation is likely to be seen as a threat to our author-ity and can escalate the situation further as we try to maintain order. It is this understanding of behaviour that is fundamental to many behavioural support strate-gies: what is actually the motivation behind the behaviour? This leads us into a further strategy outlined below.

FOUR MOTIVATORS OF BEHAVIOUR

Rudolf Dreikurs was a psychologist influenced by the theories of Alfred Adler. Dreikurs et al. (1972/2004) suggest that there are four motivators for misbehaviour, which are based on the learner's maladaptive logic in their motivation to gain status or approval. The four motivators, or goals, were identified by Dreikurs through many observations of children, and any exhibited example of unwanted behaviour can fall into one of the categories. The motivating goals are: to get attention, to get power, to get revenge and to purposefully display inadequacy. Each of these is explained in turn in Table 20.1.

REFLECTION

Consider examples of unwanted behaviour within your classroom.

To what extent do you agree that the 'four-goal technique' explains such incidents?

From the four motivators, or goals, a framework of intervention is advocated where the learner is questioned about each motivator. This brings attention to the underlying reasons for the behaviour. (The intervention is explained in Table 20.2.)

Table 20.1   The 'four-goal technique' of behaviour (adapted from Dreikurs et al., 1972/2004: 40–5)

To get attention

If the learner is deprived of the opportunity to gain status through useful contributions, they can seek evidence of their status through gaining attention, thinking, 'Only if people pay attention to me do I belong in this classroom.' The learner is unaware that gaining attention through exhibiting expected behaviour will not develop self-confidence. Instead, the learner develops an 'insatiable appetite for attention', requiring increased amounts of attention in a misguided attempt to belong.

To get power

If correct methods are not used to prevent the demands for undue attention, the learner can become a 'power-seeker': the learner wants to become the leader based on the 'faulty logic' that 'I only count when you do what I want.'

To get revenge

If the teacher implements a range of discipline strategies to address the previous aspect, the learner may decide to retaliate in order to get revenge. The motivation is that others have hurt them, so they will hurt others in order to find their place.

To purposefully display inadequacy

As a result of the sequence of the three previous escalating motivations, the learner who displays inadequacy has given up trying to belong, only expecting failure and defeat.

Table 20.2   Example intervention conversation (adapted from Dreikurs et al., 1972/2004: 49–50)

Teacher	Do you know what you did (whatever the behaviour was)?
Learner	No. (*The learner has probably provided an honest answer, not understanding why they had reacted in a specific way.*)
Teacher	I have some suggestions as to why you may have (describe the behaviour). Would you be willing to consider if any of these apply? (Or words to that effect. *This has provided a sense of autonomy to the learner by presenting some options.*)
Learner	OK.
Teacher	(*Each of the following questions is proposed by the teacher in a non-judgemental, unemotional manner, inviting a response from the learner after each one.*)
	Could it be that you want special attention?
	Could it be that you want your own way?
	Could it be that you feel hurt by others?
	Could it be that you want to be left alone?

Once the motivator of the behaviour has been identified by the learner, Dreikurs et al. advocate what they refer to as a natural consequence. By natural consequence, the learner is requested to engage with an activity appropriate to the exhibited behaviour. If, for example, a learner is not engaged with tidying up at the end of the lesson, once their behaviour has been explored through the intervention conversation, the natural consequence is that the learner will need to tidy up in their own time. Such an approach may be deemed 'restorative' in nature, where a chance is provided to make amends.

This restorative approach relates to 'restorative justice'. Restorative justice is an approach that involves the active participation of the victim and perpetrator, with a focus on resolving relationships through empowerment, communication and forgiveness (Hopkins, 2004; Lynch, 2010). The aim of restorative justice is to facilitate a process where the perpetrator comes to a realisation about the effect of their behaviour, and so remorse will be felt (or shown), in turn reducing the likelihood of their repeating the behaviour (Macready, 2009). One suggestion for why this approach is beneficial is due to the autonomy within the situation, whereby both the perpetrator and the victim share their thoughts and feelings, and ownership of resulting decisions is established. Specifically Ahmed and Braithwaite (2006) discuss the need for empathy within the approach, which in turn should lead to a heartfelt apology, which is not shamed or coerced from the perpetrator: only then will there be a reduction in reoffending.

Ultimately, the way in which the teacher relates to behaviour will affect the learning climate in their classroom: do you see yourself in a constant battle against unwanted behaviour, or do you see yourself as an active agent in control, orchestrating a stimulating learning environment?

20.10 TO PRAISE OR NOT TO PRAISE?

One extrinsic motivator which has been discussed in depth is that of praise. Praise is used in many different ways within the school context, from verbal recognition (for example, 'That is a great question' or 'Well done for working so quietly') through to stickers for younger children and certificates of some other recognition of effort. Praise can be explained through the research of Dinkmeyer and Dreikurs (2000) who suggested that such forms of encouragement help to focus effort rather than achievement: in turn, this provides positive attention for learners to increase their motivation more than not praising the learner.

REFLECTION
- How do you respond to praise?
- How do you use praise?

Further research by Henderlong-Corpus and Lepper (2007), however, indicates that praise can similarly be applied for achievement: the actual outcome or product of a learner's effort. They note that praise can be of the inherent skills of the child. Such praise of the person, process or product diminishes as the child grows: by the age of nine, praise only has limited effects on the learner. This age-related factor is explained by Boekaerts (2002), who noted that less importance is placed by the learner on their effort to explain success: instead, they attribute their success to their experience and the experience of their peers, which in turn promotes a fixed belief of their performance capability.

A further explanation for the diminished response to praise is suggested by Dweck (2007), whereby the learner may appreciate that their outcome is not in line with their personal expectations, even if they have been praised for their effort. As a consequence, the learner may feel demotivated and their response to future praise may be diminished.

REFLECTION

You are working with a group of 11-year-olds on the production of a class news report. They have worked very hard; however, they are starting to become distracted. You want to encourage them for their effort but realise from the previous discussion that praise for effort may be devalued. How can you intervene to maintain their motivation so that they will feel very pleased with the result?

Despite the previous assertion by Dweck, further research indicates that praising the learner's effort (the process) can help to maintain focus on a task (Dreikurs et al., 1972/2004, 1998; Dweck and Master, 2009).

Despite behaviourist approaches such as praise, rewards and even punishments being used in schools as a predominant motivator, the approach by Rudolf Dreikurs was different. Dreikurs (1897–1972) developed a model of social discipline, suggesting that misbehaviour is the result of feeling a lack of belonging to one's group and that all behaviour (whether wanted or not) is orderly, purposeful and directed towards achieving social approval. However, it is the perception of the individual and how they choose to behave in a certain way to achieve this approval that is fundamental to why behaviour may be wanted or not (Dreikurs et al., 1998, 1972/2004).

As discussed, Dreikurs did not adhere to rewards or punishments: instead he promoted the process of encouragement in preventing discipline problems, asserting that a learner who misbehaves is a discouraged learner and that encouragement enables them to gain approval in a legitimate way. The difference between encouragement and praise, as Dreikurs comments, was that the former focuses on effort, the latter on achievement. Dreikurs suggested that praise indicates to a learner that they have satisfied the demands of others, and therefore it can be patronising, with the person offering the praise being in a superior position. Furthermore, Dreikurs noted that praise can promote competition and, in turn, selfishness. (For a further insight into the work of Dreikurs, we would strongly suggest a read of Kohn's 1993 book, *Punished by Rewards*.)

This discussion of Dreikurs' work (which dates back to the early 1960s) can be seen as relevant today, specifically in relation to the current thrust of interest in self-determination theory. The research of Deci et al. (2001) indicates that rewards can demotivate learners due to their sense of autonomy being threatened by an external source.

20.11 CONCLUSION

When seen as a motivational climate, or environment, the classroom itself is a power-ful tool in facilitating learning. Equally, it is a powerful tool in enabling children to feel comfortable within the educational setting, something that will inevitably foster a sense of relaxation and in turn lead to more effective, pleasant learning. The emo-tional wellbeing of children in such an environment will enable them to explore and develop, academically, emotionally and socially (also see Chapters 7, 9 and 10). The teacher's role in designing and developing a setting in which this can take place is therefore of paramount importance. In poorly designed classroom environments the teacher will immediately face an uphill battle if the underlying principles of psychol-ogy outlined in this chapter are not employed as an aid. While teachers may indeed enjoy a challenge, there are times when minimising that challenge allows for more time to be spent in other areas of the curriculum. Through establishing an effective learning environment, our relationship with behaviour also needs to be identified so we can ensure the climate is one in which everyone feels welcome.

20.12 FURTHER READING

Coffield, F., Moseley, D., Hall, E. and Ecclestone, K. (2004) *Learning Styles and Pedagogy in Post-16 Learning: A Systematic and Critical Review*. London: Learning and Skills Research Centre.

Despite the discussion of learning styles within this report being based on post-16 learning, the overview and detailed critique of a number of such learning styles, along with the recommen-dations, should be core reading for every education course.

Creemers, B.P.M. and Reezigt, G.J. (1999) 'The role of school and classroom climate in elementary school learning environments', in H.J. Freiberg (ed.), *School Climate: Measuring, Improving and Sustaining Healthy Learning Environments*. London: Falmer Press, pp. 30–47.

The chapter by Creemers and Reezigt provides a greater depth on the way in which an effective learning environment can be established.

Dreikurs, R., Grunwald, B.B. and Pepper, F.C. (1998) *Maintaining Sanity in the Classroom: Classroom Management Techniques* (2nd edn). London: Taylor & Francis.
This work should be read with a critically open mind as it provides an informed discussion of a coherent approach, which has been diluted over the years within education.

Kohn, A. (1993) *Punished by Rewards: The Trouble with Gold Stars, Incentive Plans, A's, Praise, and Other Bribes*. Boston, MA: Houghton Mifflin.
Kohn's book provides a fascinating insight into how counterproductive rewards can be, although you are encouraged to read this through a critical lens.

21

THE 'IDEAL' TEACHER

CHAPTER OBJECTIVES

- Reconsider the qualities of an ideal teacher.
- Appreciate the role of the teacher's personality.
- Revisit reflection and how this enhances professional practice.

TEACHERS' STANDARDS

A teacher must:

1   Set high expectations which inspire, motivate and challenge pupils

- demonstrate consistently the positive attitudes, values and behaviour which are expected of pupils

8   Fulfil wider professional responsibilities

- make a positive contribution to the wider life and ethos of the school
- make effective professional relationships with colleagues, knowing how and when to draw on advice and specialist support
- take responsibility for improving teaching through appropriate professional development, responding to advice and feedback from colleagues

21.1 INTRODUCTION

It has taken 13 chapters to reach this point in the book, yet the various complexities of the development of the learner and their differing needs, combined with an understanding of differing psychological perspectives, have enabled you to understand a little more clearly the praxis of the book: teaching and learning. Indeed, the educational term 'praxis' is where the combined theories are put into use or put into practice – how you have used psychology to inform what you do in the classroom.

Through the various chapters, you have been encouraged to consider your personal educational philosophy by combining the models presented. It has involved merging various themes alongside your thoughts, reflections and actual classroom experience in order to develop your personal approach as a teacher. Furthermore, through engaging with the activities and considering how the various teaching standards relate to the psychological perspectives, you can justify your teaching approach and how it relates to theory.

It would be wonderful to think that you have read the chapters in an appropriate order (for you to have engaged with each activity and reflection as they have been presented), read the recommended texts, and had the time to immerse yourself in the pages of this book without any other distractions. Perhaps you have shared your thoughts and reflections, in the spirit of best practice, with others who have similarly read the book. Maybe you have been directed to read various chapters by tutors, or perhaps you have just dipped into the information you have required at a specific point in time while reading numerous other texts. Whatever way you have used this book, somehow and in some way, you would have developed your learning.

REFLECTION

Read the last paragraph again. Consider how you have approached this book and how it has developed your learning.

From considering how you have utilised the information:

- How does this relate to you as a learner?
- How does this relate to learning in general?

It is unlikely that you have read each chapter sequentially without any disruption. Does learning occur in a linear manner? Or is learning more complicated, where you piece together information that you internalise and make sense of? Was your learning dictated by another or did you get the information you required at a specific moment for a specific purpose? Were you fully engaged with whatever piece of information you were reading, or did you find it hard to concentrate and have to revisit the information? Did you have to read other sources to deepen your understanding? Did you use the information directly within the classroom context? Did you have to speak to others to develop your knowledge? This chapter encourages you to consider yourself as a learner in the constant interplay of learning and teaching, or teaching and learning.

REFLECTION

Do you prefer the term 'learning and teaching' or do you prefer 'teaching and learning'? Why? Does the order matter or does it depend on the context in which they are used? Can one occur without the other? What is the most important word of the two? Why? How do your responses compare with another person?

21.2 THE RELATIONSHIP BETWEEN TEACHING AND LEARNING

From the previous reflection, you may appreciate that there is a symbiotic relationship between the two terms: you cannot have one without the other, both are harmonious in nature (Figure 21.1).

Specifically within compulsory education such a symbiotic relationship exists. Learners go to school, where their teacher facilitates learning, ensuring that the curriculum is covered and that the learner has advanced with their learning. Teaching can therefore be seen as a directed activity by a more experienced person who develops the learning in someone less experienced. However, 'directed activity' can vary significantly in nature from the teacher passing on their direct knowledge, through to knowledge being constructed between the learners as demonstrated in Figure 21.2.

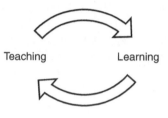

Teaching   Learning

Figure 21.1   The dynamic interplay of the teaching and learning relationship

Teacher-centred   **Learner-centred**
Passive learning   Active learning
Formal   Informal
Didactic   Dialectic
Traditional   Progressive
                                     Constructivist

Figure 21.2   Teacher-centred versus learner-centred continuum

From the continuum, the emphasis is on the amount of direct control over the experience that either the teacher or the learner has. At the traditional end of the continuum, learning is directed, for example, a teacher may tell a learner exactly what they need to do and how. The traditional perspective can also be called a 'didactic' approach: a specific way to encourage the learner to engage with learning, the spotlight being on what the teacher does. In this way, the focus is teacher-centred. At the contemporary end of the continuum, learners are encouraged to develop their own learning through engaging with each other. This contemporary perspective relates in part to the 'dialectic' approach where reasoned discussion occurs between two or more learners:

a constructivist approach where learning is actively developed between learners. In this way, the focus is student-centred. These two approaches are discussed by Bennett (1976) and summarised in Table 21.1.

Table 21.1   Teacher-centred versus student-centred approach

Teacher-centred	Student-centred
• Focused on covering the curriculum.	• Focused on developing the learner.
• Driven by the ability of the learner to meet standards.	• Driven by a constructivist approach to learning.
• Traditional approach.	• Progressive approach.
• Encourages a breadth to learning.	• Encourages a depth to learning.
• Subjects are covered in isolation.	• Subjects are integrated through a themed approach.
• Rote knowledge: learning of prescribed previous knowledge.	• Experiential knowledge: learning through experience.
• Extrinsically motivated.	• Intrinsically motivated.
• Regular assessment of learning.	• Little assessment of learning.
• Competitive approach where learners are compared against standards and/or each other.	• Cooperative approach where learners are encouraged to develop their learning mutually.

The opposing ends of the continuum were originally discussed in relation to primary maths and English (reading and creative writing) in a detailed piece of research conducted by Bennett (1976). In his report, Bennett demonstrated that the traditional, teacher-centred approach enabled learners to perform better than the contemporary or 'progressive' approach. However, Bennett's research also demonstrated that the contemporary approach promoted creativity, initiative and risk taking and, although learners did not exceed the high scores of the teacher-centred approach, they still produced good scores.

REFLECTION

Where are you on the continuum? Would you prefer to ensure learners had high scores through a traditional approach? Or would you prefer learners to develop their creativity and problem-solving skills? Is it simply a case of being at one end of the continuum or the other? Are you exactly midway between the two, or more towards one than the other? Alternatively, is it context-dependent? Does it depend on the subject, the lesson, the objectives, whether you are being observed and so on?

Although such reflective activities throughout this book have encouraged you to consider your personal philosophy, how does your developing philosophy compare against research that indicates the qualities of an effective teacher? Does your developing philosophy resonate with available research within this area?

21.3 THE QUALITIES OF AN 'IDEAL' TEACHER

ACTIVITY   Dr Frankenstein's teacher

If you were Dr Frankenstein, what components from different teachers would you combine to form your ideal teacher? You could consider this in relation to the teachers you have experienced in both formal and informal contexts, teachers you have worked with, your peers and so on.

This activity encourages you to consider the attributes of your ideal teacher, yet what is meant by 'ideal'? Is it the ability to ensure all learners are motivated, engaged and are actively learning to the best of their abilities? If so, how do the actual attributes and qualities of your teacher ensure this can happen? As opposed to the word 'ideal', would a different word such as 'effective' be more applicable?

There are different ways of considering the qualities of the ideal teacher, viewing teachers through different perspectives or lenses (Brookfield, 1995). According to Brookfield, the four lenses are the autobiographical (self-reflection), the learners' eyes (learner feedback), colleagues' experiences (peer assessment) and theoretical literature (through both reading and writing, such as assignments). In relation to the autobiographical, the various reflections in this book have encouraged you to consider your personal approach to teaching. You would similarly have developed your self-reflection through analysing and evaluating your role within the classroom, how a lesson progressed and so on. However, self-reflection also encompasses the other three lenses, whereby you consider how the dynamic interplay of the learner response, discussions with other teachers and your engagement with theory inform and develop your professional approach. It is not enough to merely engage with learner feedback or discussions with colleagues: there has to be a practical component where you synthesise the information from the various lenses and examine this in practice, while continually refining your approach to teaching. One way of presenting a model of Brookfield's lenses is provided in Figure 21.3, where the autobiographical lens, or the lens of the 'self', is central.

This book integrates all four lenses: predominantly the book is theoretical in nature; if you have engaged with the various reflections, then the autobiographical lens is also being used; if you have explored the themes from this book within your practice, the learner's lens would be utilised; finally if you have discussed any element of this book with colleagues, the peer lens has been used.

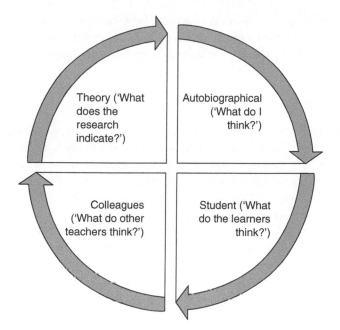

Figure 21.3   Critical lenses (adapted from Brookfield, 1995)

ACTIVITY

By yourself, make a list of the qualities of an ideal teacher.

Ask your learners what makes an ideal teacher, perhaps through a discussion or through a questionnaire.

Discuss your list of ideal teacher qualities with colleagues to see if they share your thoughts.

21.4 THEORETICAL PERSPECTIVES ON THE IDEAL TEACHER: A REVIEW

It is necessary to be critical about writings on the ideal teacher. For example, have perspectives changed since the work was produced, or are the findings still relevant today? Do any of the findings overlap with other findings, or do they contradict each other? How many of the findings actually resonate with your Dr Frankenstein creation, or those from learners and other teachers? Much of the following discussion is phenomenological in nature and comes from research into educational practice. The research discussed here spans 30 or so years and is from various countries, although it is only indicative of many hundreds of publications on teacher effectiveness, as any search through an electronic journal catalogue will indicate. What is important is the way some themes continue to resonate through the literature, themes that have previously been discussed in Chapter 3, although they are summarised below.

ENVIRONMENT

A frequent component of the effective teacher is the ability to create a stimulating learning environment. Specifically, researchers discuss the need to establish a relaxed, enjoyable atmosphere (Brown and McIntyre, 1993). Such an atmosphere can be developed through the teacher relating well to the learners at their level on both an individual and class basis (Check, 1986; Rutter et al., 1979), and also where the teacher actually seems to enjoy teaching both the subject and their learners (Ruddick et al., 1996; Santrock, 2001). Furthermore, the atmosphere is one that is supportive and cooperative (Langlois and Zales, 1992), where the teacher consistently praises learners for their achievement (Rutter et al., 1979), while monitoring and controlling behaviour and helping learners with difficulties (Brown and McIntyre, 1993; Santrock, 2001). Respect is a core attribute in establishing the environment (Ramsden, 1992; Santrock, 2001; Ursano et al., 2007).

WORK FOCUS

Many authors discuss the need to ensure that the actual work within the classroom is interesting and engaging, which in turn ensures that learners are motivated (Brown and MacIntyre, 1993; Langlois and Zales, 1992; Ramsden, 1992; Ruddick et al., 1996, 1979; Santrock, 2001; Ursano et al., 2007).

ORGANISATION

Related to the work focus is the teacher's level of organisation of the classroom and preparation of lessons, specifically lessons that maximise learning time through a variety of pace and activity (Check, 1986; Langlois and Zales, 1992; Ruddick et al., 1996; 1979; Rutter et al., 1979).

CLEAR EXPECTATIONS

As Check (1986) discussed, it is necessary to understand the learners' abilities and, from this, it is possible to have a clear expectation about what they can achieve, through establishing high academic standards that are intellectually challenging with clear goals – goals being important so that appropriate assessment and feedback can be provided to the learner (Brown and McIntyre, 1993; Langlois and Zales, 1992;

Polk, 2006; Ramsden, 1992; Ursano et al., 2007). At a further level, learners can raise expectations of their own ability and identify what needs to be learned, and how (Brown and McIntyre, 1993; Ursano et al., 2007).

TEACHER KNOWLEDGE

A lesson can only be structured to facilitate learning if the teacher has a good understanding of the subject and how this can be effectively communicated (Check, 1986; Polk, 2006; Santrock, 2001).

From the identified themes, you will probably appreciate how they overlap (Figure 21.4). For example, teacher knowledge permeates the other themes: the teacher has to know how to construct an effective, organised learning environment, which has a work focus with clear expectations. Similarly, if the teacher establishes an explicit work focus, there will be clear expectations on what needs to be achieved.

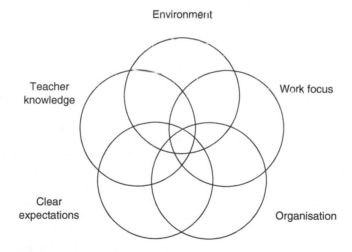

Figure 21.4   Ideal teacher themes

ACTIVITY

Review the five identified themes of teacher effectiveness.

For each, identify how psychological theory relates to each theme. For example, in relation to the theme of clear expectations, possible psychological links could be made with motivation, goal-setting, metacognition, self-determination theory and self-efficacy.

In bringing the discussion about teacher effectiveness up to date, the Teaching and Learning Research Programme (TLRP) was a UK-funded meta-project managed by the Economic and Social Research Council (ESRC), which aimed to identify how educational research could enhance learning across different educational sectors (James and Pollard, 2006). As a meta-project, the TLRP consisted of a number of smaller coordinated projects. Through the research, ten principles were developed as applicable to all learners, no matter what their context (Table 21.2). The TLRP uses 'pedagogy' as an inclusive term to replace the phrase 'teaching and learning': although pedagogy is often referred to as the learning of children, the TLRP assert that the phrase can equally be used as a lifelong term (TLRP, 2013).

Table 21.2   Ten principles of effective pedagogy (TLRP, 2013)

Principle	Effective pedagogy	Explanation
1	Equips learners for life in its broadest sense.	Pedagogy should develop intellectual, personal and social resources to enable the individual to participate as an active citizen in a diverse, changing society.
2	Engages with valued forms of knowledge.	Learners should engage with a variety of learning processes across a variety of contexts, while understanding what constitutes quality, standards and expertise.
3	Recognises the importance of prior experience and learning.	Pedagogy should take into account what the learner already knows at an intellectual level, along with the individual's personal and cultural experiences.
4	Requires learning to be scaffolded.	Those engaged with facilitating the learning of others should provide activities, cultures and structures to promote intellectual, social and emotional support to move learners forward with their learning.
5	Needs assessment to be congruent with learning.	Assessment should be designed and implemented to ensure the learning outcomes and learning processes have been achieved.
6	Promotes the active engagement of the learner.	The promotion of learner independence and autonomy, through developing positive learning dispositions and the confidence to become an agent in their own learning.
7	Fosters both individual and social processes and outcomes.	Learners should be encouraged to develop learning relationships with others for the mutual construction of knowledge and to enable learners to have a voice in their own learning.
8	Recognises the significance of informal learning.	Learning that takes place outside of the formal context of school or the workplace should be recognised to be as significant as formal learning, and similarly valued and appropriately utilised in formal learning.
9	Depends on the learning of all those who support the learning of others.	The people responsible for facilitating the learning of others should also engage in a continual process to develop their knowledge and skills to adapt and develop their roles, through practice-based enquiry.
10	Demands consistent policy frameworks with support for learning as their primary focus.	At all levels, there needs to be recognition about the fundamental importance of continual learning.

Although at first the TLRP principles appear different from the themes of effective teaching previously identified, there are areas of overlap, for example, in relation to the continued emphasis on the teacher developing their professional knowledge (Principle 9), the development of learning relationships (Principle 7), enabling the learner to be autonomous and confident with their learning (Principle 6), that learning should take place in a variety of contexts (Principle 2), and that learning should start from the learner (Principle 3).

REFLECTION

In returning to Brookfield's lenses, how have the themes identified through the theoretical perspective compared to your autobiographical lens?

21.5 TEACHER PERSONALITY

Although the themes of an effective teacher have been discussed, how do these relate to the individual teacher in the classroom? In other words, although a prescriptive checklist of the qualities a teacher needs can be provided either through the literature, or indeed through the teacher's standards, what would the world be like if all teachers were the same? In a futuristic society, would it be possible to envisage an army of cloned, ideal teachers? Would you want to be a learner in that future society? What would distinguish a cloned staffroom from Chalmers' 'philosophical zombies' as discussed in Chapter 8? Should teachers all teach the same way, or should we still ensure that teachers are animated with their own personality?

Personality was discussed in Chapter 7, in terms of the learner perspective, by which we mean 'child' in this instance. We would now like you to consider personality from the teacher, or teacher-as-learner, perspective. Although the term is used in everyday language when describing others, from a psychological perspective the term is difficult to define, as personality is multifaceted in nature with many various components (Engler, 2006). Additionally personality can be analysed through the variety of psychological perspectives from the psychodynamic to the behavioural, the cognitive to the humanist approach. As a working definition of personality, it could be viewed as the way in which we engage with the world: in other words, how we behave in response to a given stimulus, our interests, our values, our motivation, our attitudes and so on. In essence, our personality is the external component of the self – the outward manifestation of the way our self responds to a given stimulus. Our self may be quite positive and this will be characteristic of being more optimistic than pessimistic. Perhaps our sense of self is somewhat fragile: this may manifest in being overly aggressive or defensive.

Psychologists perceive personality as either an enduring, stable characteristic of the person (a trait), or a changeable, unstable element, which differs according to the environmental situation (a state, or a situational, approach). In relation to this 'situationism', the way in which we perceive the situation affects our emotional response to it (Mischel, 1973).

Another dimension of personality that separates psychologists is whether personality attributes can be grouped into types, whereby people have a similar collection of characteristics or traits; or alternatively whether we are unique, differing as individuals, or the idiographic approach. Despite Part 3 of this book discussing how we are individual, no doubt you are aware of the similarities that exist among people.

ACTIVITY

According to psychologists, personality is constructed through social interaction (for example, Cooper, 2010; Mahoney, 2011). You are an eminent psychologist who has constructed a theory about other people based on their personality.

What personality types would you suggest based on your earthly experience with other people?

Classifying people according to their personality has a long tradition. From a classical perspective, the Greek physician Galen suggested that illness is caused through an imbalance of bodily fluids (Strathern, 2005). These fluids were classified as blood, phlegm, black bile and yellow bile. Each of these fluids related to a specific element, and in turn gave rise to specific characteristics as described in Table 21.3.

Table 21.3   The four humours: from Galen to today

Humour	Name	Characteristics	Teacher traits
Blood	Sanguine	Optimistic, enthusiastic	Positive, enthused approach
Phlegm	Phlegmatic	Calm, strong, unemotional, relaxed	Confident, unfazed, in control
Yellow bile	Choleric	Excitable	Outgoing, animated approach
Black bile	Melancholic	Introverted, thoughtful	Methodical, measured approach

In Chapter 7, the four temperaments were discussed in relation to learner personality, although Steiner (2008) also suggested that teachers must consider their own temperament and be prepared to work with it positively. Furthermore, the four humours were used as a basis for Eysenck's model of personality types (Eysenck and Eysenck, 1975), where people were viewed along two continua: stable–unstable (neuroticism) and extroverted–introverted. As we mentioned in Chapter 7, Eysenck developed a psychological questionnaire, or a psychometric test (or measure), to assess these personality characteristics. A different way of classifying people was proposed by Cattell (1946) who identified a series of 16 personality factors: each factor could be seen as a separate continuum; for example, in relation to the factor of 'warmth', a person could be on a continuum between outgoing or reserved. Cattell's personality factors have stood the test of time, with different versions of the test developed over the years (Russell and Darcie, 1995). In more recent years, further versions of the psychometric test have been developed, which also measure 'the Big Five' personality characteristics: groups of characteristics from various psychometrics that fall into the five broad categories of neuroticism, extroversion, openness to experience, agreeableness and conscientiousness (McCrae and Costa, 1987; see Chapter 7).

A psychometric test that combines Cattell's personality factors and 'the Big Five' is the 15FQ+. The psychometric test has been used across many populations to assess whether groups share similar characteristics, for example, within different occupations. Psychometric tests are used for a number of purposes within occupational psychology, for example in providing career advice or as part of a process for recruitment and selection.

Although there is a readily available series of psychometric tests available online or through the pages of various magazines, caution has to be noted about their use. Can a person really be described through answering 20 questions, 50 questions or even 200? When a psychologist uses a psychometric test this is just one part of the process. The psychologist should use the results as a basis for lengthy discussion with the client in order to gain further insight and information, perhaps asking whether they agree with the results and for examples from the client's experience. Additionally, psychologists have to be qualified to administer psychometric tests and have a further advanced qualification to interpret the results: after qualification, the psychologist has to be registered with the British Psychological Society's 'Register of Competence in Test Use'.

Within the UK, there has been discussion and consultation about using psychometric tests as part of the selection process to recruit students onto teacher education courses. In this context, what would you consider to be the ideal qualities of a teacher?

ACTIVITY   Adapted personality profile for teachers

As part of the process of identifying potential students for teacher education courses, a team of psychologists need to consider the 'ideal' traits of a teacher based on a 1–10 scale. For example, would it be better for a teacher to be

(Continued)

introverted or extroverted, or somewhere in between, for example in the region of 6–8 for extroversion?

Introverted	1	2	3	4	5	6	7	8	9	10	Extroverted

Consider the 'ideal' profile for the following factors: these factors are related specifically to the Teachers' Standards and are underpinned by the Big Five, the 15FQ+ and Cattell's 16PF. Shade a range of three numbers for each of the factors.

Inflexible to change	1	2	3	4	5	6	7	8	9	10	Adaptive to change
Unassuming	1	2	3	4	5	6	7	8	9	10	Authoritative
Low anxiety	1	2	3	4	5	6	7	8	9	10	High anxiety
Self-directed	1	2	3	4	5	6	7	8	9	10	Requires direction
Reflective	1	2	3	4	5	6	7	8	9	10	Confident
Solo	1	2	3	4	5	6	7	8	9	10	Team-player
Other	1	2	3	4	5	6	7	8	9	10	Other

What other factors would you include within this profile?

REFLECTION

What are the potential problems with using psychometrics to assess the potential of future teachers?

Would you expect the factors to differ as a person progresses through their career?

Although many psychometrics exist to assess a range of human conditions, psychometrics have to be used with caution due to the ethical issues in administering and interpreting tests. In the book *The Psychopath Test* (Ronson, 2012), the author investigates how a psychometric can be used to identify psychopaths. His journey takes him to Broadmoor Psychiatric Hospital where he meets a man who faked a psychological disorder to avoid being sent to prison. He then remained at Broadmoor despite his assertions to psychiatrists that he was sane. In another chapter, Ronson discusses the 20-item Hare PCL-R (Hare, 2003) psychometric, which assesses psychopathological traits, for example, item 4 (pathological lying) and item 13 (lack of realistic long-term goals). Considering just these two, how many parents perpetuate the myth of 'Santa

Claus' or the 'tooth fairy'? Does this mean parents are psychopaths? In relation to item 13, as teachers, do we have long-term goals when the curriculum changes approximately every three to four years and governmental initiatives land in the school's letterbox on a week-by-week basis? Perhaps as a profession, teachers are psychopaths? Indeed, Ronson starts identifying with many of the 20 attributes on a personal level.

There are psychometric measures developed for the teaching profession, for example, the Teaching Styles Questionnaire (TSQ) (Evans, 2004). The TSQ consists of a 34-item questionnaire that has a strong reliability (meaning the results are consistent over time). From responding to a five-item Likert scale, it is possible to determine if a teacher is a 'Wholistic' or an 'Analytic'. Wholistics are characterised as being informal, flexible, spontaneous, concerned with the global aspects of learning and learning processes. Analytics are more formal in their approach, controlling, structured and attentive to details (Evans et al., 2008).

Another psychometric measure that has been developed is the Teacher Personality Disorder, which assesses whether teachers are affected by recurrent self-sacrifice for the perceived benefit of others, low self-concept and a high degree of tolerance for the behaviour of others (Marlowe and Page, 2004). From their questionnaire, Marlowe and Page identify different categories of teacher, for example, those with 'Affective Sheep Syndrome' – who have an inability to think for themselves and a rigid adherence to governmental directives. The questionnaire consists of such items as, 'Do you do whatever your principal tells you to do without discussion or question?' and 'Do you wish you didn't have to spend so much time preparing your students for standardised tests?' (Marlowe and Page, 2004: 30).

Needless to say, this last psychometric measure is a tongue-in-cheek perspective on what it means to be a teacher. Ultimately, however, do we need psychometric measures to determine our qualities as a teacher? In returning to a theme from Chapter 8, surely the person who understands us the most is our 'self' or ourselves. As a professional occupation, the emphasis should be on continually questioning our teaching in order to strive to make it the best we can. As discussed in this chapter, one way of analysing our abilities is by looking through different lenses as determined by Brookfield (1995). Yet, there are other forms of analysis, or reflection, on our abilities, as previously discussed in Chapter 4 and revisited below.

21.6 TEACHER REFLECTION

If you have obtained your driver's licence, you may have heard the advice that 'You only start to learn to drive after passing your test.' Once you are free to roam the highways, you do not have an experienced driver sitting with you acting as a second pair of eyes or to advise you as to when to enter a junction to join moving traffic. It is your experience as an individual driver that in turn enables you to develop and enhance your skills further. When you run out of petrol for the first time, you vow never to run your car 'on empty'. If your car has broken down and you do not have roadside assistance, you may decide to spend some additional money on a yearly basis to save a costly call-out charge. Such self-imposed, self-regulating behaviour is known as 'reflection'. It is reflection that is central to any professional occupation, where we learn from what has worked well and, perhaps, what has not (what would you do next time?). In learning to drive, you most likely started on quiet roads to develop your confidence and understanding of the control of the car before progressing to busier roads.

Similarly in teaching, you no doubt started working with individuals or small groups of children before progressing to larger groups and whole classes. With both driving and teaching, there are moment-to-moment decisions to consider; likewise there are competing aspects for our attention. Most of the time, our training will ensure that things progress smoothly both on the road and in the classroom; however, there will be times when we experience something new. In teaching, it may be the first time a dog wanders into your classroom. No amount of training can prepare you for such moments: you draw upon your experience and address the situation as best you can. Afterwards you consider whether you handled the situation appropriately. Consequently, reflection is paramount to a teacher's professional practice (Marcos et al., 2009; Poulsen et al., 2006); indeed, it is possible to ask: if such a professional stops reflecting on and questioning their practice, can they still be called a 'professional'?

There are many models of reflection, yet in essence they have similar attributes: What? So what? Now what? (Rolfe et al., 2001). Taking this to a further level, the 'what?' relates to the situation, in other words, what has happened; the 'so what?' relates to making sense of what has happened, drawing upon theoretical, practical and experiential knowledge; finally, the 'now what?' relates to how the situation can be improved currently or in the future (Figure 21.5).

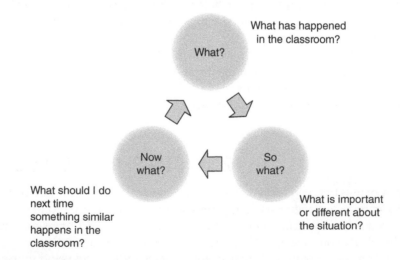

Figure 21.5   A triad of reflection (adapted from Rolfe et al., 2001)

One model often discussed in relation to reflection is Kolb's cycle of experiential learning (as previously introduced in Chapter 4). Experiential learning relates to learning from experience through a dynamic interplay of experiencing, reflecting, thinking and acting (Kolb, 1984). Kolb specifically discusses the way in which knowledge consists of 'grasping' an experience then 'transforming' this experience. The first stage of the cycle is that a concrete experience happens, which in turn promotes the individual to engage with reflective observation of that experience. The person considers how the experience relates to their understanding and whether there are any inconsistencies between their understanding and the concrete experience. Such inconsistencies between experience and understanding relate to Piaget's concept of equilibrium (Piaget, 1955, 1964), where imbalance results in the learner assimilating or accommodating new information (see Chapter 5). From this, the person engages with abstract conceptualisation, where through reflection, new concepts or ideas are either considered, or existing concepts and ideas are modified. Finally, there is a process of active experimentation where the thoughts and reflections of the person are put into practice. And through putting the experience into practice, a new cycle is engaged with.

Kolb suggested that, although all four processes are required for effective learning to occur, learners tend to emphasise one of the dimensions more than the others, which he related to learning styles. Divergers prefer to use concrete experience and reflective observation, resulting in their use of imagination and their ability to view differing perspectives. Assimilators prefer reflective observation and abstract conceptualisation to create theoretical models through their inductive reasoning. Convergers tend to favour abstract conceptualisation and active experimentation through using deductive reasoning to develop practical ideas, while accommodators prefer active experimentation and concrete experience to put ideas into practice, preferring to try things out rather than thinking or studying the issues.

If Kolb's cycle is compared to the model of Rolfe et al. (2001), there are direct links between considering what has happened (which relates to Kolb's concrete experience), making sense of the experience (the 'so what?' relating to reflective observation), then considering the next course of action (the 'now what?' relating to both abstract conceptualisation and active experimentation).

Although the models by Rolfe et al. and Kolb relate to reflecting upon actual experience, when does such reflection occur? The time factor is not considered: how quickly does a cycle of reflection last? If we burn ourselves on a hot oven, we have had a concrete experience. We make sense of the experience through reflective observation, muttering words to the effect of 'Ouch! That hurt!' From this, we use abstract conceptualisation to consider the effect of the throbbing pain as a result of touching an exceedingly hot surface and probably vow to be careful around hot items in the future so as not to burn ourselves again (active experimentation). Such a cycle is brief in nature, maybe a couple of seconds. Related to the classroom context, a short-lived cycle of reflection may consist in using your professional knowledge and experience the first time there is a power cut in the middle of a lesson. You adapt to the situation and carry on promoting learning according to your plan, as opposed to being paralysed by this situation you have never experienced before.

If, however, you realise that, for example, when the learners are working in the classroom there is quite a lot of noise, you are likely to reflect on what an appropriate working level is and how to ensure that the noise is kept to a productive, and not disruptive, level. This may involve continually monitoring the conversations to ensure learners are on task, while discussing the issue with other teachers, perhaps reading around the area to develop strategies to establish a functional level, and then trying out different strategies over subsequent lessons. A different example would be to continually revisit your teaching approach to guarantee that you embody the qualities of your ideal teacher, which may span your entire career. Consequently, reflection can be relatively short-lived; alternatively it may be the start of a very long process. Furthermore, such reflection can occur as the experience unfolds, or 'reflecting in action' (Schön, 1983); in contrast you may reflect upon the experience after it has occurred, or 'reflecting on action' (Schön, 1987). Indeed, there are many different models of reflection that encompass or develop upon the themes discussed in this chapter.

REFLECTION

Consider the various models of reflection.

Can you identify other models from the literature? Can you identify where the models are similar?

Can you develop your own model of reflection that encompasses elements of two or more of these models?

Reflection is undoubtedly at the heart of the teaching profession, whether as individual teachers reflecting on their lessons, as colleagues perhaps in collaborative planning, as a school through self-evaluation, or indeed as a profession. Although reflection is an aspect we engage in due to our inquisitive nature as humans, through understanding and applying approaches to reflection, we can ensure that we do not just castigate ourselves over something we did or did not do: we can take steps to consider what to do next time. As a student, teacher and lifelong learner, you are encouraged to reflect through discussion with your peers and discussion with more experienced others, alongside your internal dialogue and personal reflection, to guarantee that you can continue to be the teacher you want to be.

21.7 CONCLUSION

This chapter has encouraged you to consider yourself not only as a teacher but also as a learner, and the constant interplay between these two attributes. From identifying what you think contributes to an ideal teacher, through to the theoretical perspectives about the qualities of an effective teacher, perhaps the most important attribute any teacher can develop is that of reflection.

REFLECTION

What do you see in the mirror when you look at yourself as a teacher? Which of the following sentences resonates most with you?

- Mirror, mirror, on the wall, who is the greatest teacher of them all?
- Mirror, mirror, on the wall, how can I be the greatest teacher of them all?

21.8 FURTHER READING

Cottrell, S. (2017) *Critical Thinking Skills: Developing Effective Analysis and Argument* (Palgrave Study Skills) (3rd edn). London: Palgrave Macmillan.
Stella Cottrell's book provides practical suggestions and activities to enhance critical thinking, an element that has been encouraged throughout this book.

Ronson, J. (2012) *The Psychopath Test*. London: Picador.
If you have had enough of the more academic books, Jon Ronson's exploration of psychopaths is very engaging. Specifically, the book highlights the issues with classification criteria.

Ronson, J. (2004) *The Men Who Stare at Goats*. London: Picador.
Ronson also wrote this intriguing book exploring how psychology and parapsychology was investigated for use by the military.

22
REFLECTIVE POSITION: INTEGRATING THE STRANDS OF THIS BOOK

CHAPTER OBJECTIVES

- Appreciate the relationship between psychology and education.
- Consider the future partnership of psychology and education.
- Develop a critically enquiring approach to new initiatives.

22.1 INTRODUCTION

In pulling the strands of this book together four generic issues have emerged. The main consequence from reading this book, we hope, has been a learning experience, whereby you have extended your own knowledge of psychology for teaching. Equally, you should reflect on why psychology matters for teachers, on how psychology can be used to enhance the skills of the learner (including yourself as learner) and on how knowledge of psychology can improve your employability. We will look at each of these in turn below.

22.2 WHY DOES PSYCHOLOGY MATTER FOR TEACHERS?

As we mentioned at the beginning of this book, psychology is an inescapable element of our daily lives. From the clothes we wear to the food we eat, the activities we take part in, the career paths we choose and the homes, cars and other purchases we make are all influenced by psychology, whether this is our own psychology, or the psychology implemented by others to 'help us' in our choices. In teaching, the same rules of engagement apply. Our thoughts, feelings and actions provide others with a 'window' on ourselves. Sometimes, we may be suffering from issues of self-confidence, yet we disguise them well; on other occasions we fail miserably to do so. We try to understand colleagues and learners on the basis of our perceptions of them. Sometimes we are correct, at other times we also fail miserably. Indeed, 'failing miserably' appears to happen when we are at our lowest ebb, when we are fatigued or when the term has yet to reach its conclusion.

If psychology is inescapable, we should embrace it rather than fight against it. Psychology is not a bad thing. Rather it is there to support us through our lives. An analogy that fits nicely here is that of Plato's Cave. Plato's Cave is an allegory – a story that symbolises specific concepts. Imagine a group of cave dwellers who have only ever known the inside of a cave, prisoners of their own existence. The only source of illumination is a small fire, which casts dancing shadows on the wall. The fire is too bright to stare at, so the troglodytes (cave dwellers) only watch these dancing shadows. These shadows are deemed to be alive: the troglodytes perceive the shadows as reality.

One troglodyte decides to break away from the rest of the group, daring to seek out what else lurks in the cave. They venture further away from their group: their group calls them 'insane' as they are breaking away. 'Surely you will get lost and never find your way back!' and 'You will come to harm as you don't know what hides in the darkness!' they shout. The lone troglodyte ventures further and falls over a rocky crevice, causing the group to laugh and say, 'We told you so!' The troglodyte dusts herself off and continues to walk further away from the group. Eventually a small glimmer of light appears: a light that isn't the same as the fire. The light increases in brightness as the troglodyte approaches it, and they are astonished by the source of this light and what it illuminates. The troglodyte has reached the mouth of the cave

Figure 22.1   Plato's cave

Source: iStock.com/dulancristian

and stares in wonder at the golden orb in the sky that enables everything below it to reflect their respective colours. When the troglodyte returns to the group with tales of wonder of this fire, so bright that it hurts the eyes, that the dark dancing shadows are replaced by a living vibrancy, the group think the other has gone insane.

Indeed, the concept of the shadow is a very powerful metaphor: it is one of Carl Jung's archetypes, a representation of part of us, yet the shadow is a hidden component we would rather not face. We see our shadow in other people, traits they portray that remind us of ourselves, yet when we see such traits, we are appalled. In embracing our shadow, we can function more fully, understanding the depth of ourselves, the hidden aspects we need to confront. Indeed, both teaching and psychology promote such introspection: both get us to confront our true selves. As reiterated throughout this book, the sense of reflection is paramount in our professional identity where we confront ourselves on a daily basis. Consequently, your new level of knowledge and experience of using applied psychology to inform your practice should place you ahead of the game (or closer to blue-sky thinking as depicted on the cover of this book).

22.3 MAINTAINING A CRITICAL MIND

Within this book, it has been our intention to bring you up to date with the way in which psychological perspectives and education relate to ensure best practice. However, how can you be sure that what has been presented is of relevance and not just the musings of two academics? In principle, we 'practise what we preach'. All of the methods, theories and ideas shared through these pages have been implemented within our own practice, or used to enhance the practice of others. Secondly, the research that has informed this book has been critically evaluated from our respective academic disciplines and our forays into each other's worlds. It is this critical evaluation that is a central tenet of this book, and an aspect we would advocate for any teacher. Where we have cited research to support the different sections of this book, the research has followed a robust, scientific approach to the issue.

During your studies, you may have engaged with primary research: research where you have investigated an approach within the classroom context to inform, and perhaps improve, your practice. Such classroom-based research would be expected to conform to a variety of ethical protocols, as well as maintaining validity (that you were measuring what you claim to measure) and being reliable (that the research would likely provide similar results if you, or another person, adopted the same approach elsewhere). Similarly, the research cited in this book has conformed to this same standard. Peer-reviewed, academic journals have informed the majority of the work, or are based on *a priori* knowledge (derived from philosophical reasoning: that the theory can be derived through reason alone). At times, the information has been presented in order to provide the necessary background to a discussion (the references to the 'father' of psychology, William James, being a case in point). At other times, the information may appear dated. We prefer to use the term 'classical' as it is still fundamental to theoretical perspectives today (for example, the classical behaviourist approach is still a model implemented in schools through 'zone boards').

Yet despite research being current, this will not prevent initiatives that appear to be a 'good idea at the time' being introduced within schools. One such case has been illustrated through the discussion of 'Brain Gym®' (Chapter 6). Although we have discussed issues such as learner hydration (Chapter 5), or the use of physical exercise before lessons (Chapter 6), there is a paucity or lack of peer-reviewed, robust research to support the use of 'Brain Gym®'. There may be testimonials about the advantages of the approach, but how common are such findings within a sample of one hundred teachers? An acceptable level would be that at least 95 per cent of the teachers could report that incorporating 'Brain Gym®' activities had a significant impact on the learners compared with not using the approach. Consequently, the next time an initiative is promoted within the education system or the school, it might be worth asking for evidence before you blindly accept it – unless, of course, the initiative is being trialled and you can help to inform the research through your monitoring. In other words, do not be afraid to question policy or practice.

22.4 SOLUTIONS TO PREDICAMENTS

Do you view life from a 'glass is half empty' or 'glass is half full' perspective? Did you view this any differently before reading Chapter 13 on resilience? If you view it from a half-empty perspective you are adopting a pessimistic attitude, whereas if you view it from a half-full perspective, you are adopting an optimistic attitude. We would rather have two half-full glasses than two half-empty glasses. Daily life is littered with negative things, things that make life worse. However, if these negative things are viewed as predicaments sent to challenge us, they no longer have negative connotations. Remember in an earlier chapter we spoke of problem-focused coping strategies. In this sense, a predicament is a straightforward issue that we find ourselves faced with. The evidence regarding the situation is available to us and our role, using psychology, is to find solutions to the predicament. A non-challenging example can be used here to illustrate our point. In writing this book, we have incorporated a predicament–solution focus to 'spell-check and grammar-check' in the word-processing software. Whenever an issue of spelling or grammar presents itself for changing, we endeavour to 'beat it' without using the software to correct it. This becomes the challenge to the problem. Of course, the easy solution would be to use the software, but then where is the fun in that?

Take the concept that we outline here and apply it to more important aspects of your daily life. Of course, the consequences may be more serious, but the process remains the same. You will minimise your 'problems' and maximise your 'challenges'.

For example, you might like to explore behaviour management. As a student teacher, or a teacher in the early stages of your career, learners' behaviour can become all-consuming at the expense of your detailed lesson planning. Instead of focusing solely on the manifestation of behaviour you fixate on the negative aspects of behaviour management. A predicament–solution-focused approach would require you to focus on the delivery of the content, taken from your lesson plan, which in turn would ensure the learners are engaged with your planned content, negating unwanted behaviour.

22.5 EMPLOYABILITY

An understanding of psychology will shine through at interview, during teaching prac-tice, in so-called 'pressure situations' such as an observation during a school inspection and indeed throughout the day in the classroom with your learners. Equally, an under-standing of psychology will help you to understand your colleagues and their approaches to dealing with the rigours associated with teaching as a profession. In adopting a developmental approach to psychology, your knowledge will set you apart from others who have less familiarity with this discipline. If successful, you will be viewed as the 'calm, controlled member of staff who is seemingly unflappable'. This in turn becomes your reputation and it is this reputation that enhances your employabil-ity. Opportunities for promotion will become challenges rather than anxiety-evoking barriers to overcome.

Furthermore, the applied psychology discussed throughout this book will enable you to remain motivated, while using mental imagery and cognitive restructuring to ensure you maintain a positive perspective when applying for jobs and attending interviews, making presentations or working under the spotlight. Indeed, you may even be in a position to share your insights with others as you progress through your teaching career and help with their continuing professional development.

The links to the Teachers' Standards at the start of each chapter (excluding this one) will similarly enable you to identify how your teaching and understanding of psychol-ogy can be used to meet these criteria, no matter what stage of your career.

22.6 MAINTAINING A WORK–LIFE BALANCE

Maintaining a critical mind while finding suitable solutions to problems is likely to increase your employability; however, none of this is possible without establishing a healthy work–life balance. MWB will act as the springboard for you to achieve this. Your starting point will tend to be, 'I don't have time for a work–life balance.' Therein lies the dilemma. Making the time will pay dividends in the long-term and will enable you to achieve your goals and sustain your health. There is always time! Start off looking for small 'pockets of time' and use Chapters 12–14, with 15–17, to help you.

22.7 FINAL WORDS

Most of all, this book has encouraged you to develop your psychological 'toolkit'; or perhaps a better analogy for teachers would be a psychological 'pencil case', where, through engaging with the reflections and the activities, you not only have developed strategies to assist with your teaching, but also have the understanding of why such strategies work – embodying these through your educational philosophy. We hope that you have so much enjoyment in both the teaching profession and the depth of psychology as a subject that you will continue to be rewarded with each new perspective.

REFERENCES

Abramson, L.Y., Garber, J. and Seligman, M.E.P. (1980) 'Learned helplessness in humans: An attributional analysis', in J. Garber and M.E.P. Seligman (eds), *Human Helplessness*. New York: Academic Press, pp. 3–35.

Abramson, L.Y., Seligman, M.E. and Teasdale, J.D. (1978) 'Learned helplessness in humans: Critique and reformulation', *Journal of Abnormal Psychology*, 87: 49–74.

Agay, N., Yechiam, E., Carmel, Z. and Levkovitz, Y. (2010) 'Non-specific effects of methylphenidate (Ritalin) on cognitive ability and decision-making of ADHD and healthy adults', *Psychopharmacology*, 210 (4): 511–19.

Ahmed, E. and Braithwaite, V. (2006) 'Forgiveness, reconciliation, and shame: Three key variables in reducing school bullying', *Journal of Social Issues*, 62 (2): 347–70.

Allais, S. (2007) 'Education service delivery: The disastrous case of outcomes-based qualifications framework', *Progress in Development Studies*, 7 (1): 65–78.

Allen, C.A., Kinderman, P., van Scoyoc, S., Harper, D., Pilgrim, D., Bentall, R., Johnstone, L., C de C Williams, A. and James, P. (2011) *Response to the American Psychiatric Association: DSM-5 Development*. Leicester: British Psychological Society.

Allport, G.W. (1927) 'Concepts of trait and personality', *Psychological Bulletin*, 24: 284–93.

Allport, G. (1955) *Theories of Perception and the Concept of Structure*. New York: Wiley.

Allport, G.W. and Odbert, H.S. (1936) 'Trait-names: A psycho-lexical study', *Psychological Monographs*, 47: 1–171.

American Psychiatric Association (2013) *Diagnostic and Statistical Manual of Mental Disorders* (5th edn) (*DSM-5*). Arlington, VA: American Psychiatric Publishing.

Ames, C.A. (1992) 'Classrooms: Goals, structures, and student motivation', *Journal of Educational Psychology*, 84: 261–71.

Ametepee, L.K., Chitiyo, M. and Abu, S. (2009) 'Examining the nature and perceived causes of indiscipline in Zimbabwean secondary schools', *British Journal of Special Education*, 36 (3): 155–61.

Anderson, J.E. (2015) 'Brain development in adolescents: New research – implications for physicians and parents in regard to medical decision making', *Issues in Law & Medicine*, 30 (2): 193–6.

Anderson, J.R. (2016) 'Student engagement and the Learning Incentive Program: Evidence and applications', *Sensoria: A Journal of Mind, Brain & Culture*, 12 (1): 28–37.

Andrade, J. (2009) 'What does doodling do?', *Applied Cognitive Psychology*, 24 (1): 100–6.

Andrade, J., May, J., Deeprose, C., Baugh, S. and Ganis, G. (2014) 'Assessing vividness of mental imagery: The Plymouth Sensory Imagery Questionnaire', *British Journal of Psychology*, 105 (4): 547–63.

Aoyama, S., Toshima, T., Saito, Y., Konishi, N., Motoshige, K., Ishikawa, N. and Kobayashi, M. (2010) 'Maternal breast milk odour induces frontal lobe activation in neonates: A NIRS study', *Early Human Development*, 86 (9): 541–5.

Arden, J.B. (2010) *Rewire your Brain: Think your Way to a Better Life*. Hoboken, NJ: John Wiley & Sons.

Argyle, M. and Henderson, M. (1984) 'The rules of friendship', *Journal of Social and Personal Relationships*, 1: 211–37.

Arnold, E.H., O'Leary, S.G. and Edwards, G.H. (1997) 'Father involvement and self-report parenting of children with attention deficit-hyperactivity disorder', *Journal of Consulting and Clinical Psychology*, 65 (2): 337–42.

Arnold, T., Baltzell, A. and Hayden, L. (2016) 'Exploring accuracy and impact of concurrent and retrospective self-talk among golfers', *Journal of Multidisciplinary Research (1947–2000)*, 8 (3): 41–56.

Arvidsson, I., Hakansson, C., Karlson, B., Bjork, J. and Persson, R. (2016) 'Burnout among Swedish school teachers: A cross-sectional analysis', *BMC Public Health*, 16 (823): 1–11.

Arvinen-Barrow, M., Clement, D., Hamson-Utley, J., Zakrajsek, R., Sae-Mi, L., Kamphoff, C., Lintunen, T., Hemmings, B. and Martin, S. (2015) 'Athletes' use of mental skills during sport injury rehabilitation', *Journal of Sport Rehabilitation*, 24 (2): 189–97.

Assagioli, R. (1968) *Notes on Education*. Psychosynthesis and Research Foundation. http://synthesiscenter.org/articles/0321.pdf (accessed 27 September 2017).

Atkinson, R.C. and Shiffrin, R.M. (1968) 'Human memory: A proposed system and its control processes', in K.W. Spence and J.T. Spence (eds), *The Psychology of Learning and Motivation: Advances in Research and Theory*, vol. 2. New York: Academic Press, pp. 89–195.

Audet, K. and Mare, L. (2011) 'Mitigating effects of the adoptive caregiving environment on inattention/overactivity in children adopted from Romanian orphanages', *International Journal of Behavioral Development*, 35 (2): 107–15.

Ay, K.M., Halaweh, R.S. and Al-Taieb, M.A. (2013) 'The effect of movement imagery training on learning forearm pass in volleyball', *Education*, 134 (2): 227–39.

Bach, R. (1977/1998) *Illusions: The Adventures of a Reluctant Messiah*. London: Arrow Books.

Baddeley, A.D. (1982) 'Domains of recollection', *Psychological Review*, 89: 708–29

Baddeley, A.D. (2002) 'Is working memory still working?', *European Psychologist*, 7 (2): 85–97.

Baker, J.A., Dilly, L.J., Aupperless, J.L. and Patil, S.A. (2003) 'The development context of school satisfaction: Schools as psychologically healthy environments', *School Research Quarterly*, 18 (2): 206–21.

Bakker, A.B. and Demerouti, E. (2007) 'The job demands-resources model: State of the art', *Journal of Managerial Psychology*, 22: 309–28.

Bakusic, J., Schaufeli, W. and Claes, S. (2016) 'Stress, burnout and depression: A systematic review on DNA methylation mechanisms', *Journal of Psychosomatic Research*, 92: 34–44.

Balgiu, B.A. (2017) 'Self-esteem, personality and resilience. Study of a students' emerging adults group', *Journal of Educational Sciences & Psychology*, 7 (1): 93–9.

Bandettini, P.A. (2009) 'Seven topics in functional magnetic resonance imaging', *Journal of Integrative Neuroscience*, 8 (3): 371–403.

Bandura, A. (1986) *Social Foundations of Thought and Action: A Social Cognitive Theory*. Englewood Cliffs, NJ: Prentice-Hall.

Bandura, A. (1999) 'Moral disengagement in the perpetration of inhumanities', *Personality and Social Psychology Review*, 3 (3): 193–209.

Barber, L., Castle, P.C., Roberts, C.-M. and Breeze, N. (2017) 'How resilient are undergraduate students?', University of Worcester Annual Learning and Teaching Conference 'Beyond Boundaries', 15 and 16 June.

Barbu, S., Cabanes, G. and Le Maner-Idrissi, G. (2011) 'Boys and girls on the playground: Sex differences in social development are not stable across early childhood', *PLOS ONE*, 6 (1): 1–7.

Bar-David, Y.Y., Urkin, J.J., Landau, D.D., Bar-David, Z.Z. and Pilpel, D.D. (2009) 'Voluntary dehydration among elementary school children residing in a hot arid environment', *Journal of Human Nutrition and Dietetics*, 22 (5): 455–60.

Barkley, R. (2004) 'Adolescents with attention-deficit/hyperactivity disorder: An overview of empirically based treatments', *Journal of Psychiatric Practice*, 70 (1): 39–56.

Barkley, R.A. and Cunningham, C. (1979) 'The effects of methylphenidate on the mother–child interactions of hyperactive children', *Archives of General Psychiatry*, 36 (2): 201–8.

Barkley, R.A., Fischer, M., Smallish, L. and Fletcher, K. (2002) 'The persistence of attention-deficit/hyperactivity disorder into young adulthood as a function of reporting source and definition of disorder', *Journal of Abnormal Psychology*, 111: 279–89.

Barkley, R.A., Karlsson, J., Pollard, S. and Murphy, J.V. (1985) 'Developmental changes in the mother–child interactions of hyperactive boys: Effects of two dose levels of Ritalin', *Journal of Child Psychology and Psychiatry*, 26 (5): 705–16.

Barry, T.D., Lyman, R.D. and Klinger, L.G. (2002) 'Academic underachievement and attention-deficit/hyperactivity disorder: The negative impact of symptom severity on school performance', *Journal of School Psychology*, 40: 259–83.

Bass, C. (1985) 'Running can modify classroom behaviour', *Journal of Learning Disabilities*, 18 (3): 160–1.

Battista, J.R. (1996) 'Abraham Maslow and Roberto Assagioli: Pioneers of transpersonal psychology', in B.W. Scotton, A.B. Chinen and J.R. Battista (eds), *Textbook of Transpersonal Psychiatry and Psychology*. New York: Basic Books, pp. 52–61.

Baumeister, R.F. (2011) 'Self and identity: A brief overview of what they are, what they do, and how they work', *Annals of the New York Academy of Sciences*, 1234: 48–55.

Baumeister, R.F., Bratslavsky, E. and Finkenauer, C. (2001) 'Bad is stronger than good', *Review of General Psychology*, 5 (4): 323–70.

Beadle, P. (2008) *Could Do Better! Help Your Kid Shine at School*. London: Transworld.

Beaver, B.R. (2008) 'A positive approach to children's internalizing problems', *Professional Psychology: Research and Practice*, 39 (2): 129–36.

Becher, T. (1999) *Professional Practices: Commitment and Capability in a Changing Environment*. New Brunswick, NJ: Transaction Publishers.

Bechtel, W. and Abrahamsen, A. (1990) *Connectionism and the Mind: An Introduction to Parallel Processing in Networks*. Cambridge, MA: Blackwell.

Begley, S. (2009) *The Plastic Mind*. London: Constable & Robinson.

Behrmann, M. and Plaut, D.C. (2015) 'A vision of graded hemispheric specialization', *Annals of the New York Academy of Sciences*, 1359: 30–46.

Bell, L.G. (2009) 'Mindful psychotherapy', *Journal of Spirituality in Mental Health*, 11: 126–44.

Bennett, N. (1976) *Teaching Styles and Pupil Progress*. London: Open Books.

Benton, D. (2010) 'The influence of dietary status on the cognitive performance of children', *Molecular Nutrition and Food Research*, 54: 457–70.

BERA (British Education Research Association) (2011) *Ethical Guidelines for Educational Research*. www.bera.ac.uk/researchers-resources/publications/ethical-guidelines-for-educational-research-2011 (accessed 20 September 2017).

Berg, I.K. and Dolan, Y. (2001) *Tales of Solutions: A Collection of Hope-Inspiring Stories*. New York: Norton.

Bergen, D. (2016) 'Play, toys, learning, and understanding', *American Journal of Play*, 8 (2): 145–56.

Bernard, M.E. and Wolfe, J.L. (2000) *The REBT Resource Book for Practitioners* (2nd edn). New York: Albert Ellis Institute.

Bernotaite, L. and Malinauskiene, V. (2017) 'Workplace bullying and mental health among teachers in relation to psychosocial job characteristics and burnout', *International Journal of Occupational Medicine and Environmental Health*, 30 (3): 629–40.

Bezrukikh, M.M. and Terebova, N.N. (2009) 'Characteristics of the development of visual perception in five- to seven-year-old children', *Human Physiology*, 35 (6): 684–9.

Biederman, J., Farone, S., Milberger, S., Guite, J., Mick, E., Chen, L., Mennin, D., Marrs, A., Oullette, C., Moore, P., Spencer, T., Norman, D., Willens, T., Kraus, I. and Perrin, J. (1996) 'A prospective 4-year follow-up study of attention-deficit hyperactivity and related disorders', *Archives of General Psychiatry*, 53: 437–46.

Biederman, J., Milberger, S., Faraone, S.V., Kiely, K., Guite, J., Mick, E., Ablon, S., Warburton, R. and Reed, E. (1995) 'Family environment risk factors for attention-deficit hyperactivity disorder: A test of Rutter's indicators of adversity', *Archives of General Psychiatry*, 52 (6): 464–70.

Biederman, J., Newcorn, J. and Sprich, S. (1991) 'Comorbidity of attention deficit hyperactivity disorder with conduct, depressive, anxiety, and other disorders', *American Journal of Psychiatry*, 148: 564–77.

Black, P.E. and Plowright, D. (2010) 'A multi-level model of reflective learning for professional development', *Reflective Practice*, 11 (2): 245–58.

Blackburn, S. (1999) *Think*. Oxford: Oxford University Press.

Blackmore, S. (2005) *Consciousness: A Very Short Introduction*. Oxford: Oxford University Press.

Blanchi, R., Verkuilen, J., Brisson, R., Schonfeld, I.S. and Laurent, E. (2016) 'Burnout and depression: Label-related stigma, help-seeking, and syndrome overlap', *Psychiatry Research*, 24: 591–8.

Boekaerts, M. (2002) 'Motivation to learn', *Educational Practices*, 10: 2–27.

Bogartz, R.S., Shinskey, J.L. and Schilling, T.H. (2000) 'Object permanence in five-and-a-half-month-old infants?', *Infancy*, 1 (4): 403–28.

Boniwell, I. (2006) *Positive Psychology in a Nutshell: A Balanced Introduction to the Science of Optimal Functioning*. London: PWBC.

Boniwell, I. and Ryan, L. (2009) *SPARK Resilience: A Teacher's Guide*. London: University of East London.

Bonnett, V., Yuill, N. and Carr, A. (2017) 'Mathematics, mastery and metacognition: How adding a creative approach can support children in maths', *Educational & Child Psychology*, 34 (1): 83–93.

Boothman, N. (2008) *How to Make People Like You in 90 Seconds or Less*. New York: Workman Publishing.

Boud, D. and Walker, D. (1998) 'Promoting reflection in professional courses: The challenge of context', *Studies in Higher Education*, 23 (2): 191–206.

Bova, S.M., Fazzi, E., Giovenzana, A., Montomoli, C., Signorini, S.G., Zoppello, M. and Lanzi, G. (2007) 'The development of visual object recognition in school-age children', *Developmental Neuropsychology*, 31 (1): 79–102.

Bowlby, J. (1969) *Attachment*. New York: Basic Books.

Bradley, M.M., Miccoli, L., Escrig, M.A. and Lang, P.J. (2008) 'The pupil as a measure of emotional arousal and autonomic activation', *Psychophysiology*, 45 (4): 602–7.

Branden, N. (1969) *The Psychology of Self-Esteem*. New York: Bantam.

Brehm, J.W. and Self, E.A. (1989) 'The intensity of motivation', *Annual Review of Psychology*, 40: 109–31.

Brigham, J.C., Verst, M. and Bothwell, R.K. (1986) 'Accuracy of children's eyewitness identifications in a field setting', *Basic and Applied Social Psychology*, 7 (4): 295–306.

British Dyslexia Association (2016) 'Statement: British Dyslexia Association concerned about DFE announcement on further testing for under-11-year-olds on times tables', 5 January. www.bdadyslexia.org.uk/common/ckeditor/filemanager/userfiles/News/DfE_introduce_further_testing_for_time_tables_-_5_Jan_2016.pdf (accessed 17 October 2017).

British Dyslexia Association (2017) 'Definitions'. www.bdadyslexia.org.uk/dyslexic/definitions (accessed 17 October 2017).

British Psychological Society (2017) 'The British Psychological Society: Home'. www.bps.org.uk (accessed 30 July 2017).

Broadbent, D.E. (1958) *Perception and Communication*. London: Pergamon Press.

Bromley, D.B. (1986) *The Case-Study Method in Psychology and Related Disciplines*. Chichester: Wiley.

Bronfenbrenner, U. (1979) *The Ecology of Human Development: Experiments by Nature and Design*. Cambridge, MA: Harvard University Press.

Brookfield, S.D. (1995) *Becoming a Critically Reflective Teacher*. San Francisco, CA: Jossey-Bass.

Brophy, J. (1981) 'Teacher praise a functional analysis', *Review of Educational Research*, S1, 3–52.

Brophy, J.E. and Good, T.L. (1986) 'Teacher behaviour and pupil achievement', in M.C. Wittrock (ed.), *Handbook of Research on Teaching*. New York: Macmillan, pp. 328–75.

Brouwer, K.L. (2012) 'Writing motivation of students with language impairment', *Child Language Teaching and Therapy*, 28 (2): 189–210.

Brown, S. and McIntyre, D. (1993) *Making Sense of Teaching*. Buckingham: Open University Press.

Bryan, C. and Heron, E. (2015) 'Belonging protects against post-deployment depression in military personnel', *Depression & Anxiety*, 32 (5): 349–55.

Buckle, M.E. and Walsh, D.S. (2013) 'Teaching responsibility to gang-affiliated youths', *Journal of Physical Education, Recreation and Dance*, 84 (2): 53–8.

Buckler, S. (2011a) 'Transpersonal education: An educational approach for the twenty-first century?', in C.A. Shoniregun and G.A. Akmayeva (eds), *London International Conference on Education (LICE-2011)*. London: Infonomics Society, pp. 296–300.

Buckler, S. (2011b) *The Plateau Experience: Maslow's Unfinished Theory*. Saarbrücken, Germany: Lambert Academic Publishing.

Buckler, S. (2012) 'An international investigation into the validity of "transpersonal education"', in C.A. Shoniregun and G.A. Akmayeva (eds), *London International Conference on Education (LICE-2012)*. London: Infonomics Society, pp. 52–7.

Buckler, S. (2014) 'Transpersonal education: A 360° mixed-methodological investigation into the validity of the construct', *International Journal for Cross-Disciplinary Subjects in Education*, 4 (4): 1284–91.

Buckler, S. and Walliman, N. (2016) *Your Dissertation in Education*. London: Sage Publications.

Burgess, A. (1962/2011) *A Clockwork Orange* (reissue edn). London: Penguin Books.

Bütün Ayhan, A., Mutlu, B., Aki, E. and Aral, N. (2015) 'A study of conceptual development and visual perception in six-year-old children', *Perceptual & Motor Skills*, 121 (3): 832–9.

Butzer, B., Ahmed, K. and Khasla, S.B.S. (2016) 'Yoga enhances positive psychological states in young adult musicians', *Applied Psychophysiological Biofeedback*, 41: 191–202.

Cacioppo, J., Lester, P., Thomas, J., Adler, A., McGurk, D., Hsi-Yuan, C. and Cacioppo, S. (2015) 'Building social resilience in soldiers: A double dissociative randomized controlled study', *Journal of Personality & Social Psychology*, 109 (1): 90–105.

Cahn, S. (2002) *Classics of Political and Moral Philosophy*. Oxford: Oxford University Press.

Callan, G.L., Marchant, G.J., Finch, W.H. and German, R.L. (2016) 'Metacognition, strategies, achievement, and demographics: Relationships across countries', *Educational Sciences: Theory & Practice*, 16 (5): 1485–1502.

Campbell, J. (1949/2012) *The Hero with a Thousand Faces (Collected Works of Joseph Campbell)* (3rd edn). Novato, CA: New World Library.

Capp, G. (2015) 'Our community, our schools: A case study of program design for school-based mental health services', *Children & Schools*, 37 (4): 241–8.

Carlson, N.R. (2012) *The Physiology of Behaviour* (11th edn). New York: Pearson.

Carlson, N.R. and Birkett, M.A. (2017) *The Physiology of Behaviour* (12th edn). New York: Pearson.

Carlson, N.R., Martin, G.N. and Buskist, W. (2004) *Psychology* (2nd edn). Harlow: Pearson.

Carr, A. (2011) *Positive Psychology: The Science of Happiness and Human Strengths* (2nd edn). Hove: Routledge.

Carsenti, K. and Collin, T. (2013) 'Why are new teachers leaving the profession? Results of a Canada-wide survey', *Education*, 3 (3): 141–9.

Carslaw, H. (2011) 'Developmental coordination disorder', *Innovait*, 4 (2): 87–90.

Casey, G.W. (2011) 'Comprehensive soldier fitness: A vision for psychological resilience in the US Army', *American Psychologist*, 66: 1–3.

Castle, P.C. and Buckler, S.R. (2009) *How to Be a Successful Teacher: Strategies for Personal and Professional Development*. London: Sage Publications.

Castle, P.C., Van Toller, S. and Milligan, G.J. (2000) 'The effect of odour priming on cortical EEG and visual ERP responses', *International Journal of Psychophysiology*, 36: 123–31.

Cater, J.K. (2012) 'Traumatic amputation: Psychosocial adjustment of six Army women to loss of one or more limbs', *Journal of Rehabilitation Research & Development*, 49 (10): 1443–55.

Cattell, R.B. (1946) *The Description and Measurement of Personality*. Yonkers-on-Hudson, NY: World Book Co.

Cattell, R.B. (1956a) 'Personality and motivation theory based on structural measurement', in J.L. McCary (ed.), *Psychology of Personality*. New York: Logos, pp. 63–121.

Cattell, R.B. (1956b) 'A shortened "basic English" version (Form C) of the 16 P.F. Questionnaire', *Journal of Social Psychology*, 44: 257–8.

Cattell, R.B. (1956c) 'Validation and intensification of the Sixteen Personality Factor Questionnaire', *Journal of Clinical Psychology*, 12: 205–14.

Cattell, R.B. (1956d) 'Second-order personality factors in the questionnaire realm', *Journal of Consulting Psychology*, 20: 411–18.

Cattell, R.B., Cattell, A.K. and Cattell, H.E.P. (1993) *16PF Fifth Edition Questionnaire*. Champaign, IL: IPAT.

Cautela, J. and Kearney, A. (1986) *The Covert Conditioning Handbook*. New York: Springer.

Cepeda, L.M. and Davenport, D.S. (2006) 'Person-centred therapy and solution-focused brief therapy: An integration of present and future awareness', *Psychotherapy: Theory, Research, Practice, Training*, 43 (1): 1–12.

CERN (2009) *CERN FAQ: LHC The Guide*. Geneva: CERN Communication Group: CERN-Brochure-2009-003-Eng.

César Dias, P. and Cadime, I. (2017) 'Protective factors and resilience in adolescents: The mediating role of self-regulation', *Psicologia Educativa*, 23 (1): 37–43.

Chalmers, D. (1996) *The Conscious Mind*. New York: Oxford University Press.

Charalambous, A., Guannakopoulou, M., Bozas, E., Marcou, Y., Kitsios, P. and Paikousis, L. (2016) 'Guided imagery and progressive muscle relaxation as a cluster of symptoms management intervention in patients receiving chemotherapy: A randomized control trial', *PLoS ONE*, 11 (6): e0156911.

Check, J.F. (1986) 'Positive traits of the effective teacher: Negative traits of the ineffective one', *Education*, 106 (3): 326–34.

Chen, S. (2016) 'Construction of an early risk warning model of organizational resilience: An empirical study based on samples of R&D teams', *Discrete Dynamics in Nature & Society*, 1–9. DOI: 10.1155/2016/4602870

Child, I.L. (1968) 'Personality in culture', in E.F. Borgatta and W.W. Lambert (eds), *Handbook of Personality Theory and Research*. Chicago, IL: Rand McNally, pp. 82–145.

Chinen, A.B. (1996) 'The emergence of transpersonal psychiatry', in B.W. Scotton, A.B. Chinen and J.R. Battista (eds), *Textbook of Transpersonal Psychiatry and Psychology*. New York: Basic Books, pp. 9–20.

Chohan, S.K. (2010) 'Whispering selves and reflective transformations in the internal dialogue of teachers and students', *Journal of Invitational Theory & Practice*, 16: 10–28.

Christie, M. and Cole, F. (2017) 'The impact of green exercise on volunteers' mental health and wellbeing: Findings from a community project in a woodland setting', *Journal of Therapeutic Horticulture*, 27 (1): 17–33.

Christodoulou, D. (2014) *Seven Myths About Education*. London: Routledge.

Chronis-Tuscano, A. and Stein, M.A. (2012) 'Pharmacotherapy for parents with Attention-Deficit Hyperactivity Disorder (ADD): Impact on maternal ADHD and parenting', *CNS Drugs*, 26 (9): 725–32.

Churches, O., Nicholls, M., Thiessen, M., Kohler, M. and Keage, H. (2014) 'Emoticons in mind: An event-related potential study', *Social Neuroscience*, 9 (2): 196–202.

Coffield, F., Moseley, D., Hall, E. and Ecclestone, K. (2004) *Learning Styles and Pedagogy in Post-16 Learning: A Systematic and Critical Review*. London: Learning and Skills Research Centre.

Cohen, J. (1988) *Statistical Power Analysis for the Behavioural Sciences* (2nd edn). London: Routledge.

Collard, P. (2014) *The Little Book of Mindfulness: 10 Minutes a Day to Less Stress, More Peace*. London: Gaia Books.

Collie, R.J., Shapka, J.D., Perry, N.E. and Martin, A.J. (2016) 'Teachers' psychological functioning in the workplace: Exploring the roles of contextual beliefs, need satisfaction, and personal characteristics', *Journal of Educational Psychology*, 108 (6): 788–99.

Connaughton, D., Thelwell, R. and Hanton, S. (2011) 'Mental toughness development: Issues, practical implications and future directions', in D. Gucciardi and S. Gordon (eds), *Mental Toughness in Sport: Developments in Research and Theory*. Abingdon: Routledge, pp. 135–162.

Connor, K.M. and Davidson, J.R. (2003) 'Development of a new resilience scale: The Connor-Davidson resilience scale (CD-RISC)', *Depression and Anxiety*, 18: 76–82.

Cooper, C. (2010) *Individual Differences and Personality* (3rd edn). London: Hodder Education.

Corcoran, J. (2006) 'A comparison group study of solution-focused therapy versus "treatment as usual" for behaviour problems in children', *Journal of Social Science Research*, 33: 69–81.

Cordingley, P. (2013) 'The role of professional learning in determining the profession's future', in C. McLaughlin (ed.), *Teachers Learning Professional Development and Education* (the Cambridge Teacher Series). Cambridge: Cambridge University Press, pp. 21–31.

Coren, S., Ward, L.M. and Enns, J.T. (2004) *Sensation and Perception* (6th edn). Hoboken, NJ: Wiley.

Corrie, S. (2017) 'SGCP Research Network: What role do coaching practitioners have in working with mental health issues? Results of a survey', *Coaching Psychologist*, 13 (1): 41–8.

Costa, P.T., Jr and McCrae, R.R. (1985) *The NEO Personality Inventory Manual*. Odessa, FL: Psychological Assessment Resources.

Cottrell, S. (2017) *Critical Thinking Skills: Developing Effective Analysis and Argument* (Palgrave Study Skills) (3rd edn). London: Palgrave Macmillan.

Courtney, J. (2015) 'The war on stress: Resilience in the military', *Occupational Health*, 67 (12): 18.

Covey, S. (2004) *The Seven Habits of Highly Effective People*. London: Simon & Schuster.

Cowen, E.L. (2000) 'Now that we all know that primary prevention in mental health is great, what is it?', *Journal of Community Psychology*, 28: 5–16.

Craig, E. (2005) 'Philosophy', in N. Warburton (ed.), *Philosophy: Basic Readings* (2nd edn). Abingdon: Routledge, pp. 5–10.

Crane, M. and Boga, D. (2017) 'A commentary: Rethinking approaches to resilience and mental health training', *Journal of Military & Veterans' Health*, 25 (1): 30–3.

Creemers, B.P.M. and Reezigt, G.J. (1999) 'The role of school and classroom climate in elementary school learning environments', in H.J. Freiberg (ed.), *School Climate: Measuring, Improving and Sustaining Healthy Learning Environments*. London: Falmer Press, pp. 30–47.

Crews, F.T. (2008) 'Alcohol-related neurodegeneration and recovery', *Alcohol Research and Health*, 31 (4): 377–88.

Cruwys, T., Leverington, C. and Sheldon, A. (2016) 'An experimental investigation of the consequences and social functions of fat talk in friendship groups', *International Journal of Eating Disorders*, 49 (1): 84–91.

Csikszentmihalyi, M. (1988) 'The future of flow', in M. Csikszentmihalyi and I. Csikszentmihalyi (eds), *Optimal Experience: Psychological Studies of Flow in Consciousness*. Cambridge: Cambridge University Press, pp. 364–83.

Csikszentmihalyi, M. (1993) *The Evolving Self: A Psychology for the Third Millennium*. New York: Harper Perennial.

Csikszentmihalyi, M. (1996) *Creativity: Flow and the Psychology of Discovery and Invention*. New York: Harper Perennial.

Csikszentmihalyi, M. (2000) *Beyond Boredom and Anxiety: Experiencing Flow in Work and Play*. San Francisco, CA: Jossey-Bass.

Csikszentmihalyi, M. (2002) *Flow: The Classic Work on How to Achieve Happiness*. London: Rider.

Csikszentmihalyi, M. and Csikszentmihalyi, I. (eds) (1988) *Optimal Experience: Psychological Studies of Flow in Consciousness*. Cambridge: Cambridge University Press.

Cunningham, P.F. (2006) 'Transpersonal education: Problems, prospects and challenges', *International Journal of Transpersonal Studies*, 25: 62–8.

Currie, R. and Davidson, K. (2015) 'An evaluation of the initial impact of using educational psychologists to deliver NHS Scotland's "Scottish Mental Health First Aid: Young People" training programme', *Educational & Child Psychology*, 32 (1): 42–8.

Cutton, D., Killion, L. and Burt, D. (2015) 'Self-talk repertoire of physical education teachers: Awareness, reflection and action', *JOPERD: The Journal of Physical Education, Recreation & Dance*, 86 (8): 22–6.

Daley, D. and Birchwood, J. (2010) 'ADHD and academic performance: Why does ADHD impact on academic performance and what can be done to support ADHD children in the classroom?', *Child: Care, Health and Development*, 36 (4): 455–64.

Damian, R.I. and Robins, R.W. (2012) 'Investigations into the human self: A naturalist perspective', *Social Cognition*, 30 (4): 431–48.

Daniels, D.H. and Perry, K.E. (2003) '"Learner-centred" according to children', *Theory into Practice*, 42 (2): 102–8.

Daniels, M. (1988) 'The myth of self-actualization', *Journal of Humanistic Psychology*, 28 (1): 7–38.

Daniels, M. (2005) *Shadow, Self, Spirit: Essays in Transpersonal Psychology*. Exeter: Imprint Academic.

Daniels, M. (2011) 'Retrospective and challenges for transpersonal psychology', Keynote paper given at the British Psychological Society Transpersonal Psychology Section 15th Annual Conference, Cober Hill, Scarborough, 17 September.

Danner, D., Snowdon, D. and Friesen, W. (2001) 'Positive emotion in early life and longevity: Findings from the nun study', *Journal of Personality and Social Psychology*, 80: 804–13.

Darwin, C.R. (1859) *The Origin of Species.* London: Macmillan.

Davis, D.M. and Hayes, J.A. (2011) 'What are the benefits of mindfulness? A practice review of psychotherapy-related research', *Psychotherapy*, 48 (2): 198–208.

Dawes, J., Dolley, J. and Isaksen, I. (2005) *The Quest: Exploring a Sense of Soul.* Ropley, Hants: O-Books.

Day, C., Stobart, G., Sammons, P. and Kington, A. (2007) 'Variations in the work and lives of teachers: Relative and relational effectiveness', *Teachers and Teaching: Theory and Practice*, 12 (1): 169–92.

De Bruyckere, P., Kirschner, P.A. and Hulshof, C.D. (2015) *Urban Myths About Learning and Education.* London: Academic Press.

Deci, E.L. and Ryan, R.M. (1985) *Intrinsic Motivation and Self-Determination in Human Behaviour.* New York: Plenum.

Deci, E.L. and Ryan, R.M. (2000) 'The "what" and "why" of goal pursuits: Human needs and the self-determination of behavior', *Psychological Inquiry*, 11: 227–68.

Deci, E., Koestner, R. and Ryan, R. (2001) 'Extrinsic rewards and intrinsic motivation in education: Reconsidered once again', *Review of Educational Research*, 71 (1): 1–27.

Deci, E.L., Vallerand, R.J., Pelletier, L.G. and Ryan, R.M. (1991) 'Motivation and education: The self-determination perspective', *Educational Psychologist*, 26 (3–4): 325–46.

Deco, G. and Rolls, E.T. (2003) 'Attention and working memory: A dynamical model of neuronal activity in the prefrontal cortex', *European Journal of Neuroscience*, 18: 2374–90.

Deco, G., Rolls, E.T. and Horwitz, B. (2004) '"What" and "where" in visual working memory: A computational neurodynamical perspective for integrating fMRI and single-neuron data', *Journal of Cognitive Neuroscience*, 16 (4): 683–701.

De Jong, P. and Berg, I.K. (2008) *Interviewing for Solutions* (3rd edn). Belmont, CA: Thomson Brooks/Cole.

Delahaij, R., Kamphuis, W. and van den Berg, C. (2016) 'Keeping engaged during deployment: The interplay between self-efficacy, family support, and threat exposure', *Military Psychology* (American Psychological Association), 28 (2): 78–88.

Delle Fave, A. and Bassi, M. (2009) 'Sharing optimal experiences and promoting good community life in a multicultural society', *Journal of Positive Psychology*, 4 (4): 280–9.

Dennison, P.E. and Dennison, G.E. (1994) *Brain Gym® Teacher's Edition* (revised). Ventura, CA: Edu-Kinesthetics.

Denscombe, M. (2010) *The Good Research Guide: For Small-Scale Social Research Projects* (4th edn). Glasgow: Oxford University Press.

Denzin, N.K. and Lincoln, Y.S. (2011) *The SAGE Handbook of Qualitative Research* (4th edn). London: Sage Publications.

Department for Education (1999/2012) *National Special Educational Needs Specialist Standards.* London: Teacher Training Agency.

Department for Education (2010) *The Importance of Teaching: The Schools White Paper 2010.* London: The Stationery Office.

Department for Education (2011) *Special Educational Needs in England: January 2011.* London: The Stationery Office.

Department for Education (2013) *Teachers' Standards* (rev. edn). London: The Stationery Office.

Department for Education (2015) *A World-Class Teaching Profession: Government Consultation Response*. www.gov.uk/government/consultations/developing-the-teaching-profession-to-a-world-class-standard (accessed 3 July 2017).

Department for Education (2016a) *A Framework of Core Content for Initial Teacher Training*. www.gov.uk/government/uploads/system/uploads/attachment_data/file/536890/Framework_Report_11_July_2016_Final.pdf (accessed 27 September 2017).

Department for Education (2016b) *Standard for Teachers' Professional Development: Implementation Guidance for School Leaders, Teachers, and Organisations that Offer Professional Development for Teachers*. www.gov.uk/government/publications/standard-for-teachers-professional-development (accessed 27 September 2017).

Department for Education/Department for Health (2015) *Special Educational Needs and Disability Code of Practice: 0 to 25 Years*. Statutory guidance for organisations which work with and support children and young people who have special educational needs or disabilities. www.gov.uk/government/uploads/system/uploads/attachment_data/file/398815/SEND_Code_of_Practice_January_2015.pdf (accessed 14 July 2017).

Derks, D., Bos, A.E. and von Grumbkow, J. (2008) 'Emoticons in computer-mediated communication: Social motives and social context', *Cyberpsychology & Behavior*, 11: 99–101.

Dewey, J. (1933) *How We Think*. New York: D.C. Heath.

Didau, D. (2016) *What If Everything You Knew About Education Was Wrong?* Bancyfelin, Camarthen: Crown House Publishing.

Dimova, Y. and Loughran, J. (2009) 'Developing a big picture of understanding of reflection in pedagogical practice', *Reflective Practice*, 10 (2): 205–17.

Ding, C., Cheng, H.K., Duan, Y. and Jin, Y. (2017) 'The power of the "like" button: The impact of social media on box office', *Decision Support Systems*, 94: 77–84.

Dinkmeyer, D.C. and Dreikurs, R. (2000) *Encouraging Children to Learn*. Abingdon: Routledge.

Dodge, R., Daly, A., Huyton, J. and Sanders, L. (2012) 'The challenge of defining wellbeing', *International Journal of Wellbeing*, 2(3): 222–35.

Doidge, N. (2007) *The Brain that Changes Itself: Stories of Personal Triumph from the Frontiers of Brain Science*. London: Penguin Books.

Dolcos, S. and Albarracin, D. (2014) 'The inner speech of behavioral regulation: Intentions and task performance strengthen when you talk to yourself as a You', *European Journal of Social Psychology*, 44 (6): 636–42.

Dolezal, B.A., Neufeld, E.V., Boland, D.M., Martin, J.L. and Cooper, C.B. (2017) 'Interrelationship between sleep and exercise: A systematic review', *Advances In Preventive Medicine*, 2017: 1–14.

Donaldson, M. (1978) *Children's Minds*. Glasgow: Fontana/Collins.

Donaldson, S. and Ko, I. (2010) 'Positive organizational psychology, behaviour, and scholarship: A review of emerging literature and evidence base', *Journal of Positive Psychology*, 5 (3): 177–91.

Donnelly, K. (2007) 'Australia's adoption of outcomes based education: A critique', *Issues in Educational Research*, 17 (2): 183–206.

Doyle, C. (2003) 'Occupational and organisational psychology', in R. Bayne and I. Horton (eds), *Applied Psychology: Current Issues and New Directions*. London: Sage, pp. 134–41.

Dreikurs, R., Cassel, P. and Dreikurs-Ferguson, E. (1972/2004) *Discipline without Tears Revised: How to Reduce Conflict and Establish Cooperation in the Classroom* (rev. edn). Etobicoke, ON: John Wiley & Sons Canada.

Dreikurs, R., Grunwald, B.B. and Pepper, F.C. (1998) *Maintaining Sanity in the Classroom: Classroom Management Techniques* (2nd edn). London: Taylor & Francis.

Duffy, K. (1995) *Social Exclusion and Human Dignity in Europe*. Strasbourg: Council of Europe.

Dweck, C.S. (1978) 'Achievement', in M.E. Lamb (ed.), *Social and Personality Development*. New York: Holt, Rinehart & Winston, pp. 268–76.

Dweck, C.S. (2007) 'The perils and promises of praise', *Educational Leadership*, 65 (2): 34–9.

Dweck, C.S. and Leggett, E.L. (1988) 'A social-cognitive approach to motivation and personality', *Psychological Review*, 95: 256–73.

Dweck, C.S. and Master, A. (2009) 'Self theories and motivation: Students' beliefs about intelligence', in K. Wentzel and A. Wigfield (eds), *A Handbook of Motivation at School*. Abingdon: Routledge, pp. 123–40.

Dyke, M. (2006) 'The role of the "other" in reflection, knowledge formation and late modernity', *International Journal of Lifelong Education*, 25 (2): 105–23.

Dymoke, S. and Harrison, J. (2008) *Reflective Teaching and Learning*. London: Sage Publications.

Education Journal (2017) 'Welsh schools' mental health scheme to tackle stigma', 303: 12.

Edwards, L. (2016) 'Combining biofeedback and mindfulness in education', *Biofeedback*, 44 (3): 126–9.

Egbert, J. (2003) 'A study of flow theory in the foreign language classroom', *Modern Language Journal*, 87 (4): 499–518.

Eich, E. and Macaulay, D. (2000) 'Are real moods required to reveal mood-congruent and mood dependent memory?', *Psychological Science*, 11 (3): 244–8.

Eich, J.M. (1980) 'The cue-dependent nature of state-dependent retrieval', *Memory and Cognition*, 8 (2): 157–73.

Ellis, A. (1962) *Reason and Emotion in Psychotherapy*. New Jersey: Lyle Stuart.

Ellis, A. (2001) *Overcoming Destructive Beliefs, Feelings, and Behaviors*. Amherst, MA: Prometheus Books.

Ellis, A. (2011) 'Rational Emotive Behaviour therapy', in R.J. Corsini and D. Wedding (eds), *Current Psychotherapies* (9th edn). Florence, KY: Cengage Learning, pp. 196–233.

Ellis, A. and Ellis, D.J. (2011) *Rational Emotive Behaviour Therapy* (2nd edn). Washington, DC: American Psychological Association.

Elton, R. (1989) *Discipline in Schools: Report of the Committee of Enquiry Chaired by Lord Elton*. London: HMSO.

Emery, A., Toste, J. and Heath, N. (2015) 'The balance of intrinsic need satisfaction across contexts as a predictor of depressive symptoms in children and adolescents', *Motivation & Emotion*, 39 (5): 753–65.

Engler, B. (2006) *Personality Theories: An Introduction* (7th edn). Boston: Houghton Mifflin.

Engler, B. (2013) *Personality Theories: International Edition*. Belmont, CA: Wadsworth Publishing.

Ernst, A., Blanc, F., De Seze, J. and Manning, L. (2015) 'Using mental visual imagery to improve autobiographical memory and episodic future thinking in relapsing-remitting multiple sclerosis patients: A randomised-controlled trial study', *Restorative Neurology & Neuroscience*, 33 (5): 621–38.

Evans, C. (2004) 'Exploring the relationship between cognitive style and teaching style', *Educational Psychology*, 2 (3): 509–30.

Evans, C., Harkin, M.J. and Young, J.D. (2008) 'Exploring teaching styles and cognitive styles: Evidence from school teachers in Canada', *North American Journal of Psychology*, 10 (3): 567–82.

Eveland-Sayers, B.M., Farley, R.S., Fuller, D.K., Morgan, D.W. and Caputo, J.L. (2009) 'Physical fitness and academic achievement in elementary school children', *Journal of Physical Activity and Health*, 6 (1): 99–104.

Everts, R., Lidzba, K., Wilke, M., Kiefer, C., Wingeier, K., Schroth, G. and Steinlin, M. (2010) 'Lateralization of cognitive functions after stroke in childhood', *Brain Injury*, 24 (6): 859–70.

Eysenck, H.J. and Eysenck, S.B.G. (1975) *Manual of the Eysenck Personality Questionnaire*. London: Hodder & Stoughton.

Eysenck, M.W. (2009) *Fundamentals of Psychology*. Hove: Psychology Press.

Fadda, R., Rapinett, G., Grathwohl, D., Parisi, M., Fanari, R., Calò, C.M. and Schmitt, J. (2012) 'Effects of drinking supplementary water at school on cognitive performance in children', *Appetite*, 59 (3): 730–7.

Fellin, T. (2009) 'Communication between neurons and astrocytes: Relevance to the modulation of synaptic and network activity', *Journal of Neurochemistry*, 108 (3): 533–44.

Ferrer, J.N. (2002) *Revisioning Transpersonal Theory: A Participatory Vision of Human Spirituality* (SUNY Series in Transpersonal and Humanistic Psychology). Albany, NY: State University of New York Press.

Festinger, L. (1957) *A Theory of Cognitive Dissonance*. Stanford, CA: Stanford University Press.

Firman, J. and Russell, A. (1993) *What Is Psychosynthesis?* Palo Alto, CA: Psychosynthesis Palo Alto.

Fiset, D., Blais, C., Éthier-Majcher, C., Arguin, M., Bub, D. and Gosselin, F. (2008) 'Features for identification of uppercase and lowercase letters', *Psychological Science* (Wiley-Blackwell), 19 (11): 1161–8.

Fish, D. (1998) *Appreciating Practice in the Caring Profession*. Oxford: Blackwell Science.

Flaherty, D.K. (2011) 'The vaccine–autism connection: A public health crisis caused by unethical medical practices and fraudulent science', *Annals of Pharmacotherapy*, 45 (10): 1302–4.

Flavell, J.H. (1979) 'Metacognition and cognitive monitoring: A new area of cognitive-developmental inquiry', *American Psychologist*, 34 (10): 906–11.

Fletcher-Campbell, F. (2005) 'Moderate learning difficulties', in A. Lewis and B. Norwich (eds), *Special Teaching for Special Children*. Maidenhead: Open University Press, pp. 180–91.

Flower, J. (1999) 'In the mush', *Physician Executive*, 25 (1): 64–6.

Fontana, D. (1999) *Learn to Meditate: Find Deep Relaxation, Relieve Stress and Anxiety, Enhance Creativity*. London: Duncan Baird Publishers.

Fontana, D. (2003) *Psychology, Religion, and Spirituality*. Leicester and Oxford: BPS Blackwell.

Fontana, D. (2005) 'The development and meaning of transpersonal psychology', *Transpersonal Psychology Review*, special issue, Winter: 3–6.

Fontana, D. and Slack, I. (2005) 'The need for transpersonal psychology', *Transpersonal Psychology Review*, special issue, Winter: 7–11.

Fostick, L., Bar-El, S. and Ram-Tsur, R. (2012) 'Auditory temporal processing and working memory: Two independent deficits for dyslexia', *Psychology Research*, 2 (5): 308–18.

Foundation for People with Learning Disabilities (2000) *Learning Disabilities: The Fundamental Facts*. London: Mental Health Foundation.

Frankel, H. (2008) 'Monday, Bluesday', *TES: Times Educational Supplement*, 18 January (4771): 32–3.

Franklin, C., Biever, J., Moore, K., Clemons, D. and Scarmardo, M. (2001) 'The effectiveness of SF therapy with children in a school setting', *Research on Social Work Practice*, 11: 411–34.

Franklin, S. (2006) 'VAKing out learning styles: Why the notion of "learning styles" is unhelpful to teachers', *Education 3–13: International Journal of Primary, Elementary and Early Years Education*, 34 (1): 81–7.

Frederickson, N. and Cline, T. (2016) *Special Educational Needs, Inclusion and Diversity: A Textbook* (3rd edn). Maidenhead: Open University Press.

Freire, P. (1996) *Pedagogy of the Oppressed* (2nd rev. edn). London: Penguin Books.

Freire, P. (2005) *Education and Critical Consciousness*. London: Continuum.

Fretz, J.R. (2015) 'Creating optimal learning environments through invitational education: An alternative to control-oriented school reform', *Journal of Invitational Theory & Practice*, 21: 23–30.

Friedman, H. (2002) 'Transpersonal psychology as a scientific field', *International Journal of Transpersonal Studies*, 21: 175–87.

Friedman, H.L. and Hartelius, G. (2013) *The Wiley-Blackwell Handbook of Transpersonal Psychology*. Chichester: John Wiley & Sons.

Frisch, M.B. (1999) 'Quality of life assessment/intervention and the Quality of Life Inventory (QOLI)', in M.R. Maruish (ed.), *The Use of Psychological Testing for Treatment Planning and Outcome Assessment*. Hillsdale, NJ: Lawrence Erlbaum, pp. 1227–331.

Fullwood, C., Orchard, L.J. and Floyd, S.A. (2013) 'Emoticon convergence in Internet chat rooms', *Social Semiotics*, 23 (5): 648–62.

Fung, Y.L. (1976) *A Short History of Chinese Philosophy: A Systematic Account of Chinese Thought from its Origin to the Present Day*. New York: Free Press.

Gaab, J. (2011) 'The Berlin Wall at fifty: Crossing borders at the wall since 1989', *International Journal of Interdisciplinary Social Sciences*, 6 (3): 297–306.

Gabana, N. (2017) 'A strengths-based cognitive behavioral approach to treating depression and building resilience in collegiate athletics: The individuation of an identical twin', *Case Studies in Sport & Exercise Psychology*, 1 (1): 4–15.

Gable, S.L. and Haidt, J. (2005) 'What (and why) is positive psychology?', *Review of General Psychology*, 9 (2): 103–10.

Gagné, F. (1985) 'Giftedness and talent: Re-examining a re-examination of the definitions', *Gifted Child Quarterly*, 29: 103–12.

Gagné, F. (2003) 'Transforming gifts into talents. The DMGT as a developmental theory', in N. Colangelo and G.A. Davis (eds), *Handbook of Gifted Education* (3rd edn). Boston, MA: Allyn & Bacon, pp. 60–74.

Gallahue, D.L. and Ozmun, J.C. (2011) *Understanding Motor Development: Infants, Children, Adolescents, Adults* (7th edn). Boston, MA: McGraw-Hill.

Galton, M., Simon, B. and Croll, P. (1980) *Inside the Primary Classroom*. London: Routledge & Kegan Paul.

Garet, M., Porter, A., Desimone, L. Birman, B. and Yoon, K. (2001) 'What makes professional development effective? Analysis of a national sample of teachers', *American Education Research Journal*, 38 (4): 915–45.

Gatto, J.T. (2002) *The Hidden Curriculum of Compulsory Schooling* (2nd edn). Gabriola Island, Canada: New Society Publishers.

Gatto, J.T. (2011) *Weapons of Mass Instruction: A Schoolteacher's Journey through the Dark World of Compulsory Schooling*. Gabriola Island, Canada: New Society Publishers.

Gawrilow, C., Gollwitzer, P.M. and Oettingen, G. (2011) 'If-then plans benefit delay of gratification performance in children with and without ADHD', *Cognitive Therapy and Research*, 35: 442–55.

Geake, J.G. (2009) *The Brain at School: Educational Neuroscience in the Classroom*. Glasgow: McGraw-Hill.

Gebrewold, M.A., Enquselassie, F., Teklehaimanot, R. and Gugssa, S.A. (2016) 'Ethiopian teachers: Their knowledge, attitude and practice towards epilepsy', *BMC Neurology*, 16: 167.

Germer, C.K. (2013) 'Mindfulness: What is it? What does it matter?', in C.K. Germer, R.D. Siegel and P.R. Fulton (eds), *Mindfulness and Psychotherapy* (2nd edn). New York: Guilford Press, pp. 3–35.

Germer, C.K., Siegel, R.D. and Fulton, P.R. (2013) 'Preface', in C.K. Germer, R.D. Siegel and P.R. Fulton (eds), *Mindfulness and Psychotherapy* (2nd edn). New York: Guilford Press, pp. xi–xvi.

Geschwind, N. and Levitsky, W. (1968) 'Left–right asymmetry in temporal speech region', *Science*, 161: 186–7.

Ghaye, T. (2010) *Teaching and Learning through Reflective Practice: A Practical Guide for Positive Action* (2nd edn). Abingdon: Routledge.

Ghaye, T. and Lillyman, S. (2000) *Reflective: Principles and Practice for Healthcare Professionals*. Salisbury: Mark Allen Publishing.

Gibson, E.J. and Walk, R.D. (1960) 'The "visual cliff"', *Scientific American*, 202: 64–71.

Gibson, J.J. (1966) *The Senses Considered as Perceptual Systems*. Boston, MA: Houghton Mifflin.

Gibson, J.J. (1979) *The Ecological Approach to Visual Perception*. Boston, MA: Houghton Mifflin.

Gilbert, I. (2013) *Essential Motivation in the Classroom* (2nd edn). London: Routledge.

Gilbert Review (2007) *2020 Vision: Report of the Teaching and Learning in 2020 Review Group*. London: DfES.

Gillespie, A. and Graham, S. (2014) 'A meta-analysis of writing interventions for students with learning disabilities', *Exceptional Children*, 80 (4): 454–73.

Gillham, J.E., Reivich, K. and Shatté, A. (2002) 'Positive youth development, prevention, and positive psychology: Commentary on "Positive Youth Development in the United States"', *Prevention and Treatment*, 5: article 18.

Gingerich, W.J. and Wabeke, T. (2001) 'A solution-focused approach to mental health intervention in school settings', *Children and Schools*, 25: 33–47.

Ginnis, P. (2001) *Teacher's Toolkit: Raise Classroom Achievement for Every Learner*. Bancyfelin, Camarthen: Crown House Publishing.

Ginsburg, J. (2016) 'Four simple steps to social skills success', *The Asha Leader*, May: 30–1.

Ginsberg, Y., Hirvikoski, T. and Lindefors, N. (2010) 'Attention Deficit Hyperactivity Disorder (ADHD) among longer-term prison inmates is a prevalent, persisting and disabling disorder', *BMC Psychiatry*, 10 (112): 1–13.

Gittell, J.H. (2016) 'Rethinking autonomy: Relationships as a source of resilience in a changing healthcare system', *Health Services Research*, 51 (5): 1701–5.

Godden, D.R. and Baddeley, A.D. (1975) 'Context-dependent memory in two natural environments: On land and under water', *British Journal of Psychology*, 66: 325–31.

Gold, E., Smith, A., Hopper, I., Herne, D., Tansey, G. and Hulland, C. (2010) 'Mindfulness-based stress reduction (MBSR) for primary school teachers', *Journal of Child and Family Studies*, 19: 184–9.

Goldstein, K. (1939/1995) *The Organism: A Holistic Approach to Biology Derived from Pathological Data in Man*. New York: Zone Books.

Gollwitzer, P.M. (1993) 'Goal achievement: The role of intentions', in W. Stroebe and M. Hewstone (eds), *European Review of Social Psychology* (Volume 4). Chichester: Wiley, pp. 141–85.

Gollwitzer, P.M. (1999) 'Implementation intentions: Strong effects of simple plans', *American Psychologist*, 54: 493–503.

Goodwin, D.W., Powell, B., Bremer, D., Hoine, H. and Stern, J. (1969) 'Alcohol and recall: State-dependent effects in man', *Science*, 163 (3873): 1358–60.

Gottfried, A.E. (1990) 'Academic intrinsic motivation in young elementary school children', *Journal of Educational Psychology*, 82: 525–38.

Graetz, B.W., Sawyer, M.G., Hazell, P.L., Arney, F. and Baghurst, P. (2001) 'Validity of DSM-IV ADHD subtypes in a nationally representative sample of Australian children and adolescents', *Journal of the American Academy of Child and Adolescent Psychiatry*, 40: 1410–17.

Grant, A.M. (2012) 'An integrated model of goal-focused coaching: An evidence-based framework for teaching and practice', *International Coaching Psychology Review*, 7 (2): 146–65.

Grant, A.M. (2017) 'Conversational mapping: Coaching others (and ourselves) to better have difficult conversations', *Coaching Psychologist*, 13 (1): 34–40.

Greenspoon, P.J. and Saklofske, D.H. (2001) 'Toward an integration of subjective well-being and psychopathology', *Social Indicators Research*, 54: 81–108.

Gregg, M., Hall, C. and Butler, A. (2010) 'The MIQ-RS: A suitable option for examining movement imagery ability', *Evidence-Based Complementary and Alternative Medicine*, 7: 249–57.

Gregory, R.L. (1980) 'Perceptions as hypotheses', *Philosophical Transactions of the Royal Society London*, B290: 181–97.

Grenville-Cleave, B. (2012) *Positive Psychology: A Practical Guide*. London: Icon Books.

Grizenko, N., Fortier, M.E., Zadorozny, C., Thakur, G., Schmitz, N., Duval, R. and Joober, R. (2012) 'Maternal stress during pregnancy, ADHD symptomatology in children and genotype: Gene–environment interaction', *Journal of the Canadian Academy of Child and Adolescence Psychiatry*, 21 (1): 9–15.

Grof, S. (1985) *Beyond the Brain: Birth, Death and Transcendence in Psychotherapy*. Albany, NY: State University of New York Press.

Gross, R. (2015) *Psychology: The Science of Mind and Behaviour* (7th edn). London: Hodder Education.

Gu, Q. and Day, C. (2013) 'Challenges to teacher resilience: conditions count', *British Educational Research Journal*, 39 (1): 22–44.

Guay, F., Chanal, J., Ratelle, C.F., Marsh, H.W., Larose, S. and Boivin, M. (2010) 'Intrinsic, identified, and controlled types of motivation for school subjects in young elementary school children', *British Journal of Educational Psychology*, 80: 711–35.

Gucciardi, D. and Gordon, S. (2009) 'Development and preliminary validation of the Cricket Mental Toughness Inventory (CMTI)', *Journal of Sports Sciences*, 27 (12): 1293–310.

Gucciardi, D.F. and Gordon, S. (2011) *Mental Toughness in Sport: Developments in Research and Theory*. Abingdon: Routledge.

Gucciardi, D. and Jones, M. (2012) 'Beyond optimal performance: Mental toughness profiles and developmental success in adolescent cricketers', *Journal of Sport & Exercise Psychology*, 34 (1): 16–36.

Gump, J.E. (2001) 'The readability of typefaces and the subsequent mood or emotion created in the reader', *Journal of Education for Business*, 76 (5): 270–3.

Gunaratana, B. (2002) *Mindfulness in Plain English*. Somerville, MA: Wisdom.

Gus, L., Rose, J. and Gilbert, L. (2015) 'Emotion coaching: A universal strategy for supporting and promoting sustainable emotional and behavioural well-being', *Educational & Child Psychology*, 32 (1): 31–41.

Haibach, P.S., Reid, G. and Collier, D.H. (2011) *Motor Learning and Development*. Champaign, IL: Human Kinetics.

Hamilton, R.A., Scott, D. and Macdougall, M.P. (2007) 'Assessing the effectiveness of self-talk interventions on endurance performance', *Journal of Applied Sport Psychology*, 19: 226–39.

Hamzelou, J. (2010) 'Why teenagers find learning a drag', *New Scientist*. www.newscientist.com/article/dn18678-why-teenagers-find-learning-a-drag.html (accessed 30 April 2012).

Handley, C. and McAllister, M. (2017) 'Elements to promote a successful relationship between stakeholders interested in mental health promotion in schools', *Australian Journal of Advanced Nursing*, 34 (4): 16–25.

Hannaford, C. (1996) 'Smart moves', *Learning*, 25 (3): 66–8.

Hanton, S., Wadey, R. and Mellalieu, S.D. (2008) 'Advanced psychological strategies and anxiety responses in sport', *Sport Psychologist*, 22 (4): 472–90.

Haralambos, M. and Holborn, M. (2008) *Sociology: Themes and Perspectives* (7th edn). London: Collins Educational.

Harber, C. (2009) *Toxic Schooling: How Schools Became Worse*. Nottingham: Education Heretics.

Hardy, J., Gammage, K. and Hall, C. (2001) 'A descriptive study of athlete self-talk', *Sport Psychologist*, 15 (3): 306–18.

Hare, R.D. (2003) *Manual for the Revised Psychopathy Checklist* (2nd edn). Toronto: Multi-Health Systems.

Harlow, J.M. (1848) 'Passage of an iron rod through the head', *Boston Medical and Surgery Journal*, 39: 389–93.

Harlow, J.M. (1868) 'Recovery from the passage of an iron bar through the head', *Publications of Massachusetts Medical Society*, 2: 327–47.

Harris, D.V. and Harris, B.L. (1984) *The Athlete's Guide to Sport Psychology: Mental Skills for Physical People*. New York: Leisure Press.

Hart, J.E. and Brehm, J. (2013) 'Promoting self-determination: A model for training elementary students to self-advocate for IEP accommodations', *Teaching Exceptional Children*, 45 (5): 40–8.

Hart, K.E. and Sasso, T. (2011) 'Mapping the contours of contemporary positive psychology', *Canadian Psychology*, 52 (2): 82–92.

Hart, L., Mason, R., Kelly, C., Cvetkovski, S. and Jorm, A. (2016) '"Teen Mental Health First Aid": A description of the program and an initial evaluation', *International Journal of Mental Health Systems*, 10: 1–18.

Hartelius, G., Caplan, M. and Rardin, M.A. (2007) 'Transpersonal psychology: Defining the past, divining the future', *The Humanistic Psychologist*, 35 (2): 135–60.

Harter, S. (1999) *The Construction of the Self: A Developmental Perspective*. New York: Guilford Press.

Hashim, H.A., Freddy, G. and Rosmatunisah, A. (2012) 'Relationships between negative affect and academic achievement among secondary school students: The mediating effects of habituated exercise', *Journal of Physical Activity and Health*, 9 (7): 1012–19.

Hassanpourt-Dehkordi, A. and Jalali, A. (2016) 'Effect of progressive muscle relaxation on the fatigue and quality of life among Iranian aging persons', *Acta Medica Iranica*, 54 (7): 430–6.

Hayes, N. (2010) *Understand Psychology*. London: Hodder Education.

Haywood, K.M. and Getchell, N. (2014) *Lifespan Motor Development* (6th edn). Champaign, IL: Human Kinetics.

Heider, F. (1958) *The Psychology of Interpersonal Relations*. New York: John Wiley & Sons.

Held, B.S. (2002) 'The tyranny of the positive attitude in America: Observation and speculation', *Journal of Clinical Psychology*, 58: 965–91.

Hellige, J.B. (2006) 'Evolution of brain lateralization in humans', *Cognitie, Creier, Comportament/ Cognition, Brain, Behavior*, 10 (2): 211–34.

Helmstetter, S. (2015) *365 Days of Positive Self-Talk*. Florida: Park Avenue Press.

Hemker, L., Granrud, C.E., Yonas, A. and Kavšek, M. (2010) 'Infant perception of surface texture and relative height as distance information: A preferential-reaching study', *Infancy*, 15 (1): 6–27.

Henderlong-Corpus, J. and Lepper, M. (2007) 'The effects of person versus performance praise on children's motivation: Gender and age as moderating factors', *Educational Psychology: An International Journal of Experimental Educational Psychology*, 27 (4): 487–508.

Hergenhahn, B.R. (2009) *An Introduction to the History of Psychology* (6th edn). Belmont: Wadsworth.

Heyes, C. (2010) 'Where do mirror neurons come from?', *Neuroscience and Biobehavioral Reviews*, 34 (4): 575–83.

Heylighen, F. (1992) 'A cognitive-systemic reconstruction of Maslow's theory of self-actualization', *Behavioural Science*, 37 (1): 39–57.

Hickson III, M. (2013) 'The largest whale penis in the jungle and other big things: Toward simpler messages', *A Review of General Semantics*, 70 (4): 395–404.

Hill, D.A., Yeo, R.A., Campbell, R.A., Hart, B., Vigill, J. and Brooks, W. (2002) 'Magnetic resonance imaging correlates of attention-deficit/hyperactivity disorder in children', *Neuropsychology*, 17: 496–506.

Hillier, Y. (2009) *Reflective Teaching in Further and Adult Education* (2nd edn). London: Continuum.

Hinshaw, S.P., Owens, E.B., Wells, K.C., Kraemer, H.C., Abikoff, H.B., Arnold, L.E., Conners, C.K., Elliott, G., Greenhill, L.L., Hechtman, L., Hoza, B., Jensen, P.S., March, J.S., Newcorn, J.H., Pelham, W.E., Swanson, J.M., Vitiello, B. and Wigal, T. (2000) 'Family processes and treatment outcome in the MTA: Negative/ineffective parenting practices in relation to multimodal treatment', *Journal of Abnormal Child Psychology*, 28 (6): 555–68.

Hohnen, B. and Murphy, T. (2016) 'The optimum context for learning: Drawing on neuroscience to inform best practice in the classroom', *Educational and Child Psychology*, 33 (1): 75–90.

Holland, J.N. and Schmidt, A.T. (2015) 'Static and dynamic factors promoting resilience following traumatic brain injury: A brief review', *Neural Plasticity*, 2015: 1–8.

Holmes, P. and Collins, D. (2001) 'The PETTLEP approach to motor imagery: A functional equivalence model for sport psychologists', *Journal of Applied Sport Psychology*, 13: 60–83.

Holt, J. (1995) *How Children Fail*. New York: DaCapo Press.

Honderich, T. (ed.) (2005) *The Oxford Companion to Philosophy* (new edn). Oxford: Oxford University Press.

Honey, P. and Mumford, A. (2000) *The Learning Styles Helper's Guide*. Maidenhead: Peter Honey Publications.

Hope, D.A., Burns, J.A., Hayes, S.A., Herbert, J.D. and Warner, M.D. (2010) 'Automatic thoughts and cognitive restructuring in cognitive behavioral group therapy for social anxiety disorder', *Cognitive Therapy and Research*, 34 (1): 1–12.

Hopkins, B. (2004) *Just Schools: A Whole School Approach to Restorative Justice*. London: Jessica Kingsley Publishers.

Houdé, O., Rossi, S., Lubin, A. and Joliot, M. (2010) 'Mapping numerical processing, reading, and executive functions in the developing brain: An fMRI meta-analysis of 52 studies including 842 children', *Developmental Science*, 13 (6): 876–85.

House of Commons Education Committee (2017) *Recruitment and Retention of Teachers: Fifth Report of Session 2016–17*. https://publications.parliament.uk/pa/cm201617/cmselect/cmeduc/199/199.pdf (accessed 6 October 2017).

Howarth, R.H. (2012) *Anarchist Pedagogies: Collective Actions, Theories and Critical Reflections on Education*. Oakland, CA: PM Press.

Hritz, C. (2008) 'Change model: Three stages to success', *Leadership Excellence*, May: 14.

Huajin, T., Haizhou, L. and Rui, Y. (2010) 'Memory dynamics in attractor networks with saliency weights', *Neural Computation*, 22 (7): 1899–926.

Huebner, E.S. (1991a) 'Correlates of life satisfaction in children', *School Psychology Quarterly*, 6 (2): 103–11.

Huebner, E.S. (1991b) 'Further validation of the Students' Life Satisfaction Scale: The independence of satisfaction and affect ratings', *Journal of Psychoeducational Assessment*, 9 (4): 363–8.

Huebner, E.S. (1991c) 'Initial development of the Students' Life Satisfaction Scale', *School Psychology International*, 12 (3): 231–240.

Huebner, E.S. and Gilman, R. (2003) 'Toward a focus on positive psychology in school psychology', *School Psychology Quarterly*, 18 (2): 99–102.

Huppert, F.A. and So, T.T.C. (2013) 'Flourishing across Europe: Application of a new conceptual framework for defining well-being', *Social Indicators Research*, 110 (3): 837–61.

Hurley, C. (2002) *Could Do Better: School Reports of the Great and the Good*. London: Pocket Books.

Hyatt, K.J. (2007) 'Brain Gym®: Building stronger brains or wishful thinking?', *Remedial and Special Education*, 28 (2): 117–24.

Ibrahim, E., Richardson, M. and Nestel, D. (2015) 'Mental imagery and learning: A qualitative study in orthopaedic trauma surgery', *Medical Education*, 49 (9): 888–900.

Iivonen, S.S., Sääkslahti, A.A. and Nissinen, K.K. (2011) 'The development of fundamental motor skills of four- to five-year-old preschool children and the effects of a preschool physical education curriculum', *Early Child Development and Care*, 181 (3): 335–43.

Illich, I. (1995) *Deschooling Society* (new edn). London: Marion Boyars.

Iveson, C. (2002) 'Solution-focused brief therapy', *Advances in Psychiatry*, 8: 149–56.

Jacobson, E. (1938) *Progressive Relaxation*. Chicago, IL: University of Chicago Press.

James, M. and Pollard, A. (eds) (2006) *Improving Teaching and Learning in Schools: A Commentary by the Teaching and Learning Research Programme*. London: TLRP.

James, W. (1890) *The Principles of Psychology* (volumes 1 and 2). New York: Henry Holt.

James, W. (1902/1999) *The Varieties of Religious Experience: A Study in Human Nature*. London: Penguin Random House.

Jankowski, P.J. (2002) 'Postmodern spirituality: Implications for promoting change', *Counseling & Values*, 74 (1): 69–79.

Janzon, E., Abidi, T. and Bahtsevani, C. (2015) 'Can physical activity be used as a tool to reduce depression in patients after a cardiac event? What is the evidence? A systematic literature study', *Scandinavian Journal of Psychology*, 56 (2): 175–81.

Jarvis, P. (1995) *Adult and Continuing Education: Theory and Practice* (2nd edn). London: Routledge.

Jarvis, S. (2011) 'To the letter', *Textual Practice*, 25 (2): 233–43.

Jerath, R., Crawford, M.W., Barnes, V.A. and Harden, K. (2015) 'Self-regulation of breathing as a primary treatment for anxiety', *Applied Psychophysiological Biofeedback*, 40: 107–15.

Johnson, D. and Cannizzaro, M.S. (2009) 'Sentence comprehension in agrammatic aphasia: History and variability to clinical implications', *Clinical Linguistics and Phonetics*, 23 (1): 15–37.

Johnson, J.G., Harris, E.S., Spitzer, R.L. and Williams, J.B.W. (2002) 'The Patient Health Questionnaire for Adolescents: Validation of an instrument for the assessment of mental disorders among adolescent primary care patients', *Journal of Adolescent Health*, 30: 196–204.

Johnson, S. (2009) 'Improving the school environment to reduce school violence: A review of the literature', *Journal of School Health*, 79 (10): 451–65.

Johnston Molloy, C.C., Gandy, J.J., Cunningham, C.C. and Glennon Slattery, C.C. (2008) 'An exploration of factors that influence the regular consumption of water by Irish primary school children', *Journal of Human Nutrition and Dietetics*, 21 (5): 512–15.

Joinson, C. (1992) 'Coping with compassion fatigue', *Nursing*, 22 (4): 118–19.

Jokic, C.S. and Whitebread, D. (2011) 'The role of self-regulatory and metacognitive competence in the motor performance difficulties of children with developmental coordination disorder: A theoretical and empirical review', *Educational Psychology Review*, 23 (1): 75–98.

Jordi, R. (2011) 'Reframing the concept of reflection: Consciousness, experiential learning, and reflective learning practices', *Adult Education Quarterly*, 61 (2): 181–97.

Judas, M. and Cepanec, M. (2007) 'Adult structure and development of the human fronto-opercular cerebral cortex (Broca's region)', *Clinical Linguistics and Phonetics*, 21 (11–12): 975–89.

Judelson, D.A., Maresh, C.M., Anderson, J.M., Armstrong, L.E., Casa, D.J., Kraemer, W.J. and Volek, J.S. (2007) 'Hydration and muscular performance', *Sports Medicine*, 37 (10): 907–21.

Kabat-Zinn, J. (2001) *Full Catastrophe Living: How to Cope with Stress, Pain and Illness Using Mindfulness Meditation*. London: Piatkus Books.

Kabat-Zinn, J. (2004) *Wherever You Go, There You Are*. London: Piatkus Books.

Kant, R. and Singh, M.D. (2015) 'Relationship between learning styles and scientific attitude of secondary school students and their achievement in science subject', *Journal of Educational Sciences and Psychology*, 5 (67): 1–10.

Kantor, R. (1975) 'The affective domain and beyond', in T.B. Roberts (ed.), *Four Psychologies Applied to Education: Freudian, Behavioural, Humanistic, Transpersonal*. Cambridge, MA: Schenkman Publishing, pp. 406–16.

Kassel, S.C. (2015) 'Stress management and peak performance crash course for ninth graders in a charter school setting', *Biofeedback*, 43 (2): 90–3.

Katzir, T. and Paré-Blagoev, J. (2006) 'Applying cognitive neuroscience research to education: The case of literacy', *Educational Psychologist*, 41 (1): 53–74.

Kavšek, M., Yonas, A. and Granrud, C.E. (2012) 'Infants' sensitivity to pictorial depth cues: A review and meta-analysis of looking studies', *Infant Behavior and Development*, 35 (1): 109–28.

Keefe, J.W. (1979) 'Learning style: An overview', in NASSP, *Student Learning Styles: Diagnosing and Prescribing Programs*. Reston, VA: National Association of Secondary School Principals, pp. 1–17.

Kennedy, A. (2011) 'Collaborative continuing professional development (CPD) for teachers in Scotland: Aspirations, opportunities and barriers', *European Journal of Teacher Education*, 34 (1): 25–41.

Kenrick, D.T. (2001) 'Evolutionary psychology, cognitive science and dynamical systems: Building an integrative paradigm', *Current Directions in Psychological Science*, 10: 13–17.

Kiba, T., Abe, T., Kanbara, K., Kato, F., Kawashima, S., Saka, Y., Yamamoto, K., Mizuno, Y., Nishiyama, J. and Fukunaga, M. (2017) 'The relationship between salivary amylase and the physical and psychological changes elicited by continuation of autogenic training in patients with functional somatic syndrome', *Biopsychosocial Medicine*, 11: 17.

Kibby, M.Y. and Cohen, M.J. (2008) 'Memory functioning in children with reading disabilities and/or attention deficit/hyperactivity disorder: A clinical investigation of their working memory and long-term memory functioning', *Child Neuropsychology*, 14: 525–46.

Kidger, J., Evans, R., Tilling, K., Hollingworth, W., Campbell, R., Ford, T., Murphy, S., Araya, R., Morris, R., Kadir, B., Fernandez, A., Bell, S., Harding, S., Brockman, R., Grey, J. and Gunnell, D. (2016) 'Protocol for a cluster randomised controlled trial of an intervention to improve the mental health support and training available to secondary school teachers: The WISE (Wellbeing in Secondary Education) study', *BMC Public Health*, 16 (1): 1–13.

Kim, H.J., Park, J.H., Yoo, S. and Kim, H. (2016) 'Fostering creativity in tablet-based interactive classrooms', *Educational Technology & Society*, 19 (3): 207–20.

Kim, J.S. (2008) 'Examining the effectiveness of solution-focused brief therapy: A meta-analysis', *Research on Social Work Practice*, 18 (2): 107–16.

King, R.B. and McInerney, D.M. (2016) 'Do goals lead to outcomes or can it be the other way around? Causal ordering of mastery goals, metacognitive strategies, and achievement', *British Journal of Educational Psychology*, 86: 296–312.

Kington, A., Sammons, P., Regan, E., Brown, E., Ko, J. and Buckler, S. (2014) *Effective Classroom Practice*. Maidenhead: Open University Press.

Kinsella, E.A. (2009) 'Professional knowledge and the epistemology of reflective practice', *Nursing Philosophy*, 11: 3–11.

Kirschenbaum, H. (1975) 'What is humanistic education?', in T.B. Roberts (ed.), *Four Psychologies Applied to Education: Freudian, Behavioural, Humanistic, Transpersonal*. Cambridge, MA: Schenkman Publishing Co., pp. 327–9.

Klainin-Yobas, P., Oo, W.N., Yew, P.Y.S. and Lau, Y. (2015) 'Effects of relaxation interventions on depression and anxiety among older adults: A systematic review', *Aging and Mental Health*, 19 (12): 1043–55.

Kleim, J.A. and Jones, T.A. (2008) 'Principles of experience-dependent neural plasticity: Implications for rehabilitation after brain damage', *Journal of Speech, Language and Hearing Research*, 51 (1): S225–S239.

Klein, S.B. (2012) '"What is the Self?" Approaches to a very elusive question', *Social Cognition*, 2 (4): 363–6.

Knifong, J.D. (1974) 'Logical abilities of young children: Two styles of approach', *Child Development*, 45 (1): 78–83.

Kohn, A. (1993) *Punished by Rewards: The Trouble with Gold Stars, Incentive Plans, A's, Praise, and Other Bribes*. Boston, MA: Houghton Mifflin.

Kolb, B. and Gibb, R. (2011) 'Brain plasticity and behaviour in the developing brain', *Journal of the Canadian Academy of Child and Adolescent Psychiatry*, 20 (4): 265–76.

Kolb, B. and Whishaw, I.Q. (2011) *An Introduction to Brain and Behaviour* (3rd edn). New York: Worth.

Kolb, B. and Whishaw, I.Q. (2015) *Fundamentals of Human Neuropsychology* (7th edn). New York: Worth.

Kolb, D.A. (1976) *The Learning Style Inventory: Technical Manual*. Boston, MA: McBer.

Kolb, D.A. (1984) *Experiential Learning: Experience as the Source of Learning and Development*. Englewood Cliffs, NJ: Prentice Hall.

Kolb, D.A. and Fry, R. (1975) 'Toward an applied theory of experiential learning', in C. Cooper (ed.), *Theories of Group Process*. London: John Wiley, pp. 33–58.

Korenova, L. (2015) 'Mobile learning in elementary and secondary school mathematics in Slovakia', *Electronic Journal of Mathematics & Technology*, 9 (3): 259–68.

Korunka, C., Kubicek, B., Schaufeli, W. and Hoonakker, P. (2009) 'Work engagement and burnout: testing the robustness of the Jobs Demands-Resources model', *Journal of Positive Psychology*, 4 (3): 243–55.

Kotzé, M. and Niemann, R. (2013) 'Psychological resources as predictors of academic performance of first-year students in higher education', *Acta Academica*, 45 (2): 85–121.

Kramer, M. (2011) 'The demise of the Soviet Bloc', *Europe-Asia Studies*, 63 (9): 1535–90.

Kress, V., Paylo, M., Adamson, N. and Baltrinic, E. (2014) 'Teaching diagnosis in context: Guided imagery as a contextually sensitive pedagogical technique', *Journal of Creativity in Mental Health*, 9 (2): 275–91.

Kroenke, K., Spitzer, R.L. and Williams, J.B. (2001) 'The PHQ-9: Validity of a brief depression severity measure', *Journal of General Internal Medicine*, 16: 606–13.

Kross, E., Bruehlman-Senecal, E., Park, J., Burson, A., Dougherty, A., Shablack, H., Bremner, R., Moser, J. and Ayduk, O. (2014) 'Self-talk as a regulatory mechanism: How you do it matters', *Journal of Personality & Social Psychology*, 106 (2): 304–24.

Kuhlmann, S.M., Bürger, A., Esser, G. and Hammerle, F. (2015) 'A mindfulness-based stress prevention training for medical students (MediMind): Study protocol for a randomized controlled trial', *Trials*, 16 (1): 40–50.

Kuhn, P. (2011) 'Improving access to psychological therapies: Systemic therapy in the Newham pilot site', *Journal of Family Therapy*, 33 (4): 400–14.

Kyriacou, C. (2014) *Effective Teaching in Schools: Theory and Practice* (4th edn). Oxford: Oxford University Press.

Lancaster, B.L. (2004) *Approaches to Consciousness: The Marriage of Science and Mysticism*. London: Palgrave Macmillan.

The Lancet, editors (2010) 'Retraction: Illeal-lymphoid-nodular hyperplasia, non-specific colitis, and pervasive developmental disorder in children', *The Lancet*, 375 (9713).

Langlois, D.E. and Zales, C.R. (1992) 'Anatomy of a top teacher', *Education Digest*, 57 (5): 31–4.

Latané, B. (1981) 'The psychology of social impact', *American Psychologist*, 36: 343–56.

Laughlin, P. (2017) 'Contact and context: New directions in Gestalt coaching', *Coaching Psychologist*, 13 (1): 50–2.

Lawton-Smith, C. (2017) 'Coaching for leadership resilience: An integrated approach', *International Coaching Psychology Review*, 12 (1): 6–23.

Lazarus, R.S. (1991) *Emotion and Adaptation*. New York: Oxford University Press.

Lazarus, R.S. (1999) *Stress and Emotion: A New Synthesis*. London: Free Association.

Leclerc, G., Lefrancois, R., Dube, M., Hebert, R. and Gaulin, P. (1998) 'The self-actualization concept: A content validation', *Journal of Social Behaviour and Personality*, 13 (1): 69–84.

Lee, C.B., Koh, N.K., Cai, X L, and Quek, C.L. (2012) 'Children's use of meta-cognition in solving everyday problems: Children's monetary decision-making', *Australian Journal of Education*, 56 (1): 22–39.

Lee, J., Semple, R.J., Rosa, D. and Miller, L. (2008) 'Mindfulness-based cognitive therapy for children: Results of a pilot study', *Journal of Cognitive Psychotherapy: An International Quarterly*, 22 (1): 15–28.

Leisman, G., Mualem, R. and Mughrabi, S.K. (2015) 'The neurological development of the child with the educational enrichment in mind', *Psicologia Educativa*, 21 (2): 79–96.

Leonard, C.M. and Eckhart, M.A. (2008) 'Asymmetry and dyslexia', *Developmental Neuropsychology*, 33 (6): 663–81.

Leontiev, D. (2006) 'Positive personality development: Approaching personal autonomy', in M. Csikszentmihalyi and I.S. Csikszentmihalyi (eds), *A Life Worth Living: Contributions to Positive Psychology*. New York: Oxford University Press, pp. 49–61.

Leung, P.W., Chan, J.Y., Chen, L.H., Lee, C.C., Hung, S.F., Ho, T.P. and Swanson, J.M. (2017) 'Family-based association study of DRD4 gene in methylphenidate-responded attention deficit/hyperactivity disorder', *PLoS ONE*, 12 (3): 1–11.

Levitas, R., Pantazis, C., Fahmy, E., Gordon, D., Lloyd, E. and Patsios, D. (2007) *The Multi-Dimensional Analysis of Social Exclusion*. London: Department for Communities and Local Government (DCLG).

Levitin, D.J., MacLean, K., Mathews, M., Chu, L. and Jensen, E. (2000) 'The perception of cross-modal simultaneity (or "the Greenwich Observatory Problem" revisited)', *AIP Conference Proceedings*, 517 (1): 323.

Li, J., Theng, Y., and Foo, S. (2016) 'Effect of exergames on depression: A systematic review and meta-analysis', *CyberPsychology, Behavior & Social Networking*, 19 (1): 34–42.

Li, M. and Yang, Y. (2016) 'A cross-cultural study on a resilience-stress path model for college students', *Journal of Counseling & Development*, 94 (3): 319–32.

Libby, L.K., Valenti, G., Pfent, A. and Eibach, R.P. (2011) 'Seeing failure in your life: Imagery perspective determines whether self-esteem shapes reactions to recalled and imagined failure', *Journal of Personality and Social Psychology*, 101 (6): 1157–73.

Linley, P.A. and Joseph, S. (2004) *Positive Psychology in Practice*. Hoboken, NJ: John Wiley & Sons.

Linley, P.A., Joseph, S., Harrington, S. and Wood, A.M. (2006) 'Positive psychology: Past, present, and (possible) future', *Journal of Positive Psychology*, 1 (1): 3–16.

Livingston, L. and Forbes, S. (2017) 'Resilience, motivations for participation, and perceived organizational support amongst aesthetic sports officials', *Journal of Sport Behavior*, 40 (1): 43–67.

Lo, S. (2008) 'The nonverbal communication functions of emoticons in computer-mediated communication', *Cyberpsychology & Behavior*, 11 (5): 595–7.

Lofland, J. (1971) *Analysing Social Settings: A Guide to Qualitative Observation and Analysis*. Belmont, CA: Wadsworth.

Lopez, S.J., Pedrotti, J.T. and Snyder, C.R. (2014) *Positive Psychology: The Scientific and Practical Explorations of Human Strengths* (3rd edn). Thousand Oaks, CA: Sage Publications.

López-Vargas, O., Ibáñez-Ibáñez, J. and Racines-Prada, O. (2017) 'Students' metacognition and cognitive style and their effect on cognitive load and learning achievement', *Journal of Educational Technology & Society*, 20 (3): 145–57.

Loubser, A., Pienaar, A.E., Klopper, A. and Ellis, S. (2016) 'The effect of a learner-support intervention on perceptual-motor skills of kindergarten learners from deprived environments', *Australasian Journal of Early Childhood*, 41 (1): 54–63.

Lourenco, O. (2003) 'Children's appraisals of antisocial acts: A Piagetian perspective', *British Journal of Developmental Psychology*, 21 (1): 19.

Lovewell, K. (2012) *Every Teacher Matters: Inspiring Well-Being through Mindfulness*. St Albans: Ecademy Press.

Luthe, W. and Schultz, J.H. (1969) *Autogenic Therapy*. New York: Grune & Stratton.

Lynch, N. (2010) 'Restorative justice through a children's rights lens', *International Journal of Children's Rights*, 18 (2): 161–83.

Lyubomirsky, S., King, L.A. and Diener, E. (2005) 'The benefits of frequent positive affect: Does happiness lead to success?', *Psychological Bulletin*, 131: 803–55.

Macintosh, E. and Shaw, J. (2017) *Student Resilience: Exploring the Positive Case for Resilience. Unite Students Insight Report*. Bristol: Unite Students.

Macready, T. (2009) 'Learning social responsibility in schools: A restorative practice', *Educational Psychology in Practice*, 25 (3): 211–20.

Madan, C. and Singhal, A. (2013) 'Introducing TAMI: An objective test of ability in movement imagery', *Journal of Motor Behavior*, 45 (2): 153–66.

Madewell, A. and Ponce-Garcia, E. (2016) 'Assessing resilience in emerging adulthood: The Resilience Scale (RS), Connor–Davidson Resilience Scale (CD-RISC), and Scale of Protective Factors (SPF)', *Personality and Individual Differences*, 97: 249–55.

Mahoney, B. (2011) *Personality and Individual Differences* (Critical Thinking in Psychology series). Exeter: Learning Matters.

Mairs, L. and Mullan, B. (2015) 'Self-monitoring vs. implementation intentions: A comparison of behaviour change techniques to improve sleep hygiene and sleep outcomes in students', *International Journal of Behavioral Medicine*, 22 (5): 635–44.

Majorek, M., Tlichelmann, T. and Heusser, P. (2004) 'Therapeutic eurythmy-movement therapy for children with attention deficit disorder (ADHD): A pilot study', *Complementary Therapies in Nursing and Midwifery*, 10 (1): 46–54.

Malan, S.P.T. (2000) 'The "new paradigm" of outcomes-based education in perspective', *Tydskrif vir Gesinsekologie en Verbruikerswetenskappe*, 28: 22–8.

Malina, R., Bouchard, C. and Bar-Or, O. (2003) *Growth, Maturation and Physical Activity* (2nd edn). Champaign, IL: Human Kinetics.

Mannuzza, S. and Klein, R.G. (2000) 'Long-term prognosis in attention deficit/hyperactivity disorder', *Child and Adolescent Psychiatric Clinics of North America*, 9 (3): 711–12.

Mansur, D.I., Shrestha, A., Sharma, K., Mehta, D.K., Shakya, R. and Timalsina, B. (2015) 'A study on pattern of growth in height among children of Dhulikhel municipality', *Journal of Nepal Paediatric Society*, 35 (3): 209–17.

Marcos, J.J.M., Migual, E.M. and Tillema, H. (2009) 'Teacher reflection on action: What is said (in research) and what is done (in teaching)', *Reflective Practice*, 10 (2): 191–204.

Marcoux, M., Sallis, J., McKenzie, T., Marshall, S., Armstrong, C. and Goggin, K. (1999) 'Process evaluation of a physical activity self-management program for children: SPARK', *Psychology & Health*, 14 (4): 659.

Marlier, L. and Schaal, B. (2005) 'Human newborns prefer human milk: Conspecific milk odor is attractive without postnatal exposure', *Child Development*, 76 (1): 155–68.

Marlowe, B. and Page, M. (2004) 'The good news about Teacher Personality Disorder', *ENCOUNTER: Education for Meaning and Social Justice*, 17 (1): 28–30.

Martin, R.C. (2006) 'The neuropsychology of sentence processing: Where do we stand?', *Cognitive Neuropsychology*, 23 (1): 74–95.

Marzillier, J. and Hall, J. (2009a) 'The challenge of the Layard initiative', *The Psychologist*, 22 (5): 396–9.

Marzillier, J. and Hall, J. (2009b) 'Alternative ways of working', *The Psychologist*, 22 (5): 406–8.

Maslach, C. and Leiter, M.P. (1999) 'Teacher burnout: A research agenda', in R. Vandenberghe and A.M. Huberman (eds), *Understanding and Preventing Teacher Burnout: A Sourcebook of International Research and Practice*. Cambridge: Cambridge University Press, pp. 295–304.

Maslach, C., Schaufeli, W.B. and Leiter, M.P. (2001) 'Job burnout', *Annual Review of Psychology*, 52: 397–422.

Maslow, A.H. (1954/1987) *Motivation and Personality* (3rd edn). Delhi: Pearson Education.

Maslow, A.H. (1962/1999) *Toward a Psychology of Being* (3rd edn). Chichester: John Wiley & Sons.

Maslow, A.H. (1966) *The Psychology of Science: A Reconnaissance*. New York: Harper & Row.

Maslow, A.H. (1970) *Religions, Values, and Peak-Experiences*. New York: Penguin Compass.

Maslow, A.H. (1971/1993) *The Farther Reaches of Human Nature*. London: Penguin Books.

Maslow, A.H. (1996) 'Critique on self-actualization theory', in E. Hoffman (ed.), *Future Visions: The Unpublished Papers of Abraham Maslow*. Thousand Oaks, CA: Sage Publications, pp. 26–32.

Mavroveli, S. and Sánchez-Ruiz, M. (2011) 'Trait emotional intelligence influences on academic achievement and school behaviour', *British Journal of Educational Psychology*, 81 (1): 112–34.

McCarthy, P.J. (2009) 'Putting imagery to good affect: A case study among youth swimmers', *Sport and Exercise Psychology Review*, 5 (1): 27–38.

McClelland, J.L. and Rummelhart, D.E. (1981) 'An interactive activation model of context effects in letter perception: Part 1. An account of basic findings', *Psychological Review*, 88: 375–407.

McCrae, R.R. and Costa, P.T. (1987) 'Validation of the five-factor model of personality across instruments and observers', *Journal of Personality and Social Psychology*, 52: 81–90.

McCrae, R.R. and Costa, P.T. (1990) *Personality in Adulthood*. New York: Guilford Press.

McDermott, R. (ed.) (2010) *The New Essential Steiner: An Introduction to Rudolf Steiner for the 21st Century*. Great Barrington, MA: Lindisfarne Books.

McDonald, M. and O'Callaghan, J. (2008) 'Positive psychology: A Foucauldian critique', *The Humanistic Psychologist*, 36: 127–42.

McIntosh, P. (2010) *Action Research and Reflective Practice: Creative and Visual Methods to Facilitate Reflection and Learning*. Abingdon: Routledge.

McKinstry, J.L., Fleischer, J.G., Chen, Y., Gall, W.E. and Edelman, G.M. (2016) 'Imagery may arise from associations formed through sensory experience: A network of spiking neurons controlling a robot learns visual sequences in order to perform a mental rotation task', *PLoS ONE*, 11 (9): e0162155.

McLaughlin, C. (2013) 'Editor's Introduction', in C. McLaughlin (ed.), *Teachers Learning Professional Development and Education* (Cambridge Teacher Series). Cambridge: Cambridge University Press, pp. ix–xix.

McNaughton, J. and Meldrum, J. (2017) 'Dreams of social inclusion: True experiences of street soccer through fictional representation', *Creative Approaches to Research*, 10 (1): 52–70.

Meichenbaum, D.H. (1977) *Cognitive Behavior Modification: An Integrative Approach*. New York: Plenum.

Menter, I., Hulme, M., Elliott, D. and Lewin, J. (2010) *Literature Review on Teacher Education in the 21st Century*. Edinburgh: Scottish Government.

Mercugliano, M. (1995) 'Neurotransmitter alterations in attention deficit/hyperactivity disorder', *Mental Retardation and Developmental Disabilities Research Reviews*, 1 (3): 220–6.

Merriman, J. (2015) 'Enhancing counsellor supervision through compassion fatigue education', *Journal of Counseling & Development*, 93: 370–8.

Merton, R.K. (1948) 'The self-fulfilling prophecy', *The Antioch Review*, 8 (2): 193–210.

Meyer, D.K. and Turner, J.C. (2006) 'Re-conceptualizing emotion and motivation to learn in classroom contexts', *Educational Psychology Review*, 18: 377–90.

MHFA (2017) *Resources*. Available at: https://mhfaengland.org/mhfa-centre/resources/take-10-together/ (accessed 19 January 2018).

Mikicin, M. and Kowalczyk, M. (2015) 'Audio-visual and autogenic relaxation alter amplitude of alpha EEG band, causing improvements in mental work performance in athletes', *Applied Psychophysiological Biofeedback*, 40 (3): 219–27.

Miles, A.N. and Berntsen, D. (2011) 'Odour-induced mental time travel into the past and future: Do odour cues retain a unique link to our distant past?', *Memory*, 19 (8): 930–40.

Miles, M.B. and Huberman, A.M. (1994) *Qualitative Data Analysis: An Expanded Sourcebook*. London: Sage Publications.

Miles, M.B., Huberman, A.M. and Saldana, J. (2013) *Qualitative Data Analysis: A Methods Sourcebook* (3rd edn). Thousand Oaks, CA: Sage Publications.

Milgram, S., Bickman, L. and Berkowitz, L. (1969) 'Note on the drawing power of crowds of different size', *Journal of Personality and Social Psychology*, 13 (1): 79–82.

Miller, A. (2008) 'A critique of positive psychology – or "the new science of happiness"', *Journal of Philosophy of Education*, 42 (3–4): 591–608.

Miller, C. (1991) 'Self-actualization and the consciousness revolution', *Behaviour and Personality*, 6 (5): 109–26.

Miller, G.A. (1956) 'The magical number seven plus or minus two: Some limits on our capacity for processing information', *Psychological Review*, 63: 81–97.

Miller, W.R. and Seligman, M.E.P. (1975) 'Depression and learned helplessness in man', *Journal of Abnormal Psychology*, 84: 228–38.

Mind (2016) 'Building on Change: Mind's 2016–2021 Strategy'. Available at https://www.mind.org.uk/media/4205494/building-on-change_booklet_final_pdf_21march16.pdf (accessed 22 January 2018).

Minnis, H. and Bryce, G. (2010) 'Maltreated children: Finding the right attachment relationship', *Educational and Child Psychology*, 27 (3): 51–8.

Mischel, W. (1973) 'Toward a cognitive social learning reconceptualization of personality', *Psychological Review*, 80: 252–83.

Mischel, W. (1984) 'Convergences and challenges in the search for consistency', *American Psychologist*, 39: 351–64.

Moore, T.W. (1975) 'Transpersonal education: A preview', *Journal of Education*, 157 (4): 24–39.

Moran, A., Guillot, A., MacIntyre, T. and Collet, C. (2012) 'Re-imagining motor imagery: Building bridges between cognitive neuroscience and sport psychology', *British Journal of Psychology*, 103 (2): 224–47.

Moustakas, C. (1990) *Heuristic Research: Design, Methodology, and Applications*. Newbury Park, CA: Sage Publications.

Muckli, L. (2010) 'What are we missing here? Brain imaging evidence for higher cognitive functions in primary visual cortex V1', *International Journal of Imaging Systems and Technology*, 20 (2): 131–9.

Mujcic, R. and Oswald, A. (2016) 'Evolution of well-being and happiness after increases in consumption of fruit and vegetables', *American Journal of Public Health*, 106 (8): 1504–10.

Mukherjee, S., Ting, J.L.C. and Fong, L.H. (2017) 'Fundamental motor skill proficiency of 6- to 9-year-old Singaporean children', *Perceptual and Motor Skills*, 124 (3): 584–600.

Mulrine, C.F., Prater, M.A. and Jenkins, A. (2008) 'The active classroom: Supporting students with attention deficit hyperactivity disorder through exercise', *Teaching Exceptional Children*, 40 (5): 16–22.

Murdock, B.B. (1962) 'The serial position effect on free recall', *Journal of Experimental Psychology*, 64: 482–8.

Murman, N., Buckingham, K., Fontilea, P., Villanueva, R., Leventhal, B. and Hinshaw, S. (2014) 'Let's Erase the Stigma (LETS): A quasi-experimental evaluation of adolescent-led school groups intended to reduce mental illness stigma', *Child & Youth Care Forum*, 43 (5): 621–37.

Musiat, P., Conrod, P., Treasure, J., Tylee, A., Williams, C. and Schmidt, U. (2014) 'Targeted prevention of common mental health disorders in university students: Randomised controlled trial of a transdiagnostic trait-focused web-based intervention', *PLoS ONE*, 9 (4): 1–10.

Musiat, P., Goldstone, P. and Tarrier, N. (2014) 'Understanding the acceptability of e-mental health: Attitudes and expectations towards computerised self-help treatments for mental health problems', *BMC Psychiatry*, 14 (1): 1–16.

Myers, D.G. (2000) 'The funds, friends, and faith of happy people', *American Psychologist*, 55: 56–67.

Myers, D. (2010) *Psychology* (9th edn). New York: Worth.

Nagel, T. (1987) *What Does it All Mean? A Very Short Introduction to Philosophy*. Oxford: Oxford University Press.

Naifeh, J., Colpe, L., Aliaga, P., Sampson, N., Heeringa, S., Stein, M., Ursano, R., Fullerton, C., Nock, M., Schoenbaum, M., Zaslavsky, A. and Kessler, R. on behalf of the Army STARRS Collaborators (2016) 'Barriers to initiating and continuing mental health treatment among soldiers in the Army Study to Assess Risk and Resilience in Servicemembers (Army STARRS)', *Military Medicine*, 181 (9): 1021–32.

Narayanan, S. and Weng Onn, A. (2016) 'The influence of perceived social support and self-efficacy on resilience among first year Malaysian students', *Kajian Malaysia: Journal of Malaysian Studies*, 34 (2): 1–23.

NASUWT (2010) *Teachers' Mental Health: A Study Exploring the Experiences of Teachers with Work-Related Stress and Mental Health Problems*. Redhill: NASUWT.

NCCMH (National Collaborating Centre for Mental Health) (2008) *Attention Deficit Hyperactivity Disorder: Diagnosis and Management of ADHD in Children, Young People, and Adults* (National Clinical Practice Guideline, 72). London: NCCMH.

Neher, A. (1991) 'Maslow's theory of motivation: A critique', *Journal of Humanistic Psychology*, 31: 89–112.

Neisser, U. (1976) *Cognition and Reality*. San Francisco, CA: W.H. Freeman.

Newell, K.M. (1986) 'Constraints on the development of coordination', in M.G. Wade and H.T.A. Whiting (eds), *Motor Development in Children: Aspects of Coordination and Control*. Dordrecht: Martinus Nijhoff, pp. 341–61.

Newton, G. (2016) 'Why do teachers quit and what could help them to stay?', British Educational Research Association Conference, University of Warwick, 15 November. www.bera.ac.uk/blog/why-do-teachers-quit-and-what-could-help-them-to-stay (accessed 10 October 2017).

Nicholls, J.G. (1989) *The Competitive Ethos and Democratic Education*. Cambridge, MA: Harvard University Press.

Niedenthal, P.M., Krauth-Gruber, S. and Ric, F. (2006) *Psychology of Emotion*. Hove: Psychology Press.

Nims, D.R. (2007) 'Integrating play therapy techniques into solution-focused brief therapy', *International Journal of Play Therapy*, 16 (1): 54–68.

Noddings, N. (2003) *Happiness and Education*. New York: Cambridge University Press.

Northway, N., Manahilov, V. and Simpson, W. (2010) 'Coloured filters improve exclusion of perceptual noise in visually symptomatic dyslexics', *Journal of Research in Reading*, 33 (3): 223–30.

Norwich, B. and Kelly, N. (2005) *Moderate Learning Difficulties and the Future of Inclusion*. London: Routledge-Falmer.

Nowicka, A. and Tacikowski, P. (2011) 'Transcallosal transfer of information and functional asymmetry of the human brain', *Laterality*, 16 (1): 35–74.

NUT (2012) 'Teacher stress: NUT guidance to divisions and associations'. www.teachers.org.uk/node/12562 (accessed 1 April 2013).

Nutbrown, C. (2011) *Threads of Thinking: Schemas and Young Children's Learning*. London: Sage Publications.

Nyström, M., Neely, G., Hassmén, P. and Carlbring, P. (2015) 'Treating major depression with physical activity: A systematic overview with recommendations', *Cognitive Behaviour Therapy*, 44 (4): 341–52.

O'Brennan, L., Pas, E. and Bradshaw, C. (2017) 'Multilevel examination of burnout among high school staff: Importance of staff and school factors', *School Psychology Review*, 46 (2): 165–76.

O'Brien, C. (2008) 'Sustainable happiness: How happiness studies can contribute to a more sustainable future', *Canadian Psychology*, 49 (4): 289–95.

Ofsted (2006) *The Logical Chain: Continuing Professional Development in Effective Schools*. London: Ofsted.

Onieal, M. (2017) 'More than "teen angst": What to watch for', *Clinician Reviews*, 27 (3): 14–28.

Opfer, V.D. and Pedder, D. (2013) 'Teacher change and changing teachers via professional development', in C. McLaughlin (ed.), *Teachers Learning Professional Development and Education* (Cambridge Teacher Series). Cambridge: Cambridge University Press, pp. 93–118.

Orden, A.B. and Apezteguía, M.C. (2016) 'Weight and height centiles of Argentinian children and adolescents: A comparison with WHO and national growth references', *Annals of Human Biology*, 43 (1): 9–17.

Ortmann, M., Zwitserlood, P., Knief, A., Baare, J., Brinkheetker, S., am Zehnhoff-Dinnesen, A. and Dobel, C. (2017) 'When hearing is tricky: Speech processing strategies in prelingually deafened children and adolescents with cochlear implants having good and poor speech performance', *PLoS ONE*, 12 (1): 1–27.

Paivio, A. (1985) 'Cognitive and motivational functions of imagery in human performance', *Canadian Journal of Applied Sport Sciences*, 10: 225–85.

Pallant, J. (2016) *SPSS Survival Manual: A Step by Step Guide to Data Analysis Using IBM SPSS* (6th edn). Maidenhead: Open University Press.

Palmer, S.E. and Ghose, T. (2008) 'Extremal edges: A powerful cue to depth perception and figure ground organization', *Psychological Science* (Wiley-Blackwell), 19 (1): 77–84.

Panda, S. (2014) 'Stress and health: Symptoms and techniques of psychotherapeutic management', *Indian Journal of Positive Psychology*, 5 (4): 516–20.

Panebianco-Warrens, C. (2014) 'Exploring the dimensions of flow and the role of music in professional ballet dancers', *Journal of Music Research in Africa*, 11 (2): 58–78.

Pareek, S. and Rathore, N.S. (2016) 'Gender differences in character strengths and virtues of teachers in higher education', *Indian Journal of Positive Psychology*, 7 (3): 312–17.

Parfit, D. (1984) *Reasons and Persons*. Oxford: Oxford University Press.

Park, N. and Peterson, C. (2003) 'Early intervention from the perspective of positive psychology', *Prevention and Treatment*, 6: article 35.

Parr, G.D., Montgomery, M. and DeBell, C. (1998) 'Flow theory as a model for enhancing student resilience', *Professional School Counselling*, 1 (5): 26–31.

Pascual-Leone, A., Amedi, A., Fregni, F. and Merabet, L.B. (2005) 'The plastic human brain cortex', *Annual Review of Neuroscience*, 28: 377–401.

Pashler, H., McDaniel, M., Rohrer, D. and Bjork, R. (2009) 'Learning styles: Concepts and evidence', *Association of Psychological Science*, 9 (3): 105–19.

Passmore, J. (2017) 'Mindfulness in coaching: A model for coaching practice', *Coaching Psychologist*, 13 (1): 27–30.

Patil, A. and Adsul, R. (2017) 'A correlational study on resilience and well-being among college adolescents in Kolhapur city', *Indian Journal of Positive Psychology*, 8 (1): 83–6.

Paton, N. (2015) 'Evolution of occupational health 4: Making health a work priority', *Occupational Health*, 67 (12): 11–13.

Payne, V.G. and Isaacs, L.D. (2011) *Human Motor Development: A Lifespan Approach* (8th edn). Boston, MA: McGraw-Hill.

Pederson, N.L., Plomin, R., McClearn, G.E. and Friberg, I. (1988) 'Neuroticism, extraversion and related traits in adult twins reared apart and reared together', *Journal of Personality and Social Psychology*, 55: 950–7.

Pellis, M. and Pellis, V.C. (2007) 'Rough-and-tumble play and the development of the social brain', *Current Directions in Psychological Science*, 16 (2): 95–8.

Peper, E., Miceli, B. and Harvey, R. (2016) 'Educational model for self-healing: Eliminating a chronic migraine with electromyography, autogenic training, posture, and mindfulness', *Biofeedback*, 44 (3): 130–7.

Perez-Vega, R., Waite, K. and O'Gorman, K. (2016) 'Social impact theory: An examination of how immediacy operates as an influence upon social media interaction in Facebook fan pages', *The Marketing Review*, 16 (3): 299–321.

Peterson, C., Park, N. and Castro, C.A. (2011) 'Assessment for the US Army Comprehensive Soldier Fitness program: The Global Assessment Tool', *American Psychologist*, 66: 10–18.

Peterson, C. and Seligman, M.E.P. (2004) *Character Strengths and Virtues: A Handbook and Classification*. New York: Oxford University Press.

Peterson, L.Y., Burden, J.P., Sedaghat, J.M., Gothberg, J.E., Kohler, P.D. and Coyle, J.L. (2013) 'Triangulated IEP transition goals: Developing relevant and genuine annual goals', *Teaching Exceptional Children*, 45 (6): 46–57.

Piaget, J. (1955) 'Perceptual and cognitive (or operational) structures in the development of the concept of space in the child', *Acta Psychologica*, 11: 41–6.

Piaget, J. (1964) *The Child's Conception of Number.* London: Routledge & Kegan Paul.

Piccolo, L.R., Merz, E.C., He, X., Sowell, E.R. and Noble, K.G. (2016) 'Age-related differences in cortical thickness vary by socioeconomic status', *PLoS ONE*, 11 (9): e0162511.

Pilisuk, M. and Mahr, I. (2015) 'Psychology and the prevention of war trauma', *Journal for Social Action in Counseling & Psychology*, 7 (1): 122–42.

Pinel, J.P.J. (2010) *Biopsychology* (8th edn). Englefield Cliffs, NJ: Prentice-Hall.

Pinel, P. and Dehaene, S. (2010) 'Beyond hemispheric dominance: Brain regions underlying the joint lateralization of language and arithmetic to the left hemisphere', *Journal of Cognitive Neuroscience*, 22 (1): 48–66.

Pintrich, P.R. (2003) 'A motivational science perspective on the role of student motivation in learning and teaching contexts', *Journal of Educational Psychology*, 95: 667–86.

Pirrone, C. and Di Nuovo, S. (2014) 'Can playing and imagining aid in learning Mathematics?', *BPA – Applied Psychology Bulletin (Bollettino Di Psicologia Applicata)*, 62 (271): 30–9.

Plato (2007) *The Republic.* London: Penguin Books.

Plomin, R., DeFries, J.C., McClearn, G.E. and McGuffin, P. (2008) *Behavioural Genetics* (5th edn). New York: Worth.

Pluess, M., Boniwell, I., Hefferon, K. and Tunariu, A. (2017) 'Preliminary evaluation of a school-based resilience-promoting intervention in a high-risk population: Application of an exploratory two-cohort treatment/control design', *PLoS ONE*, 12 (5): 1–18.

Plutchik, R. (2003) *Emotions and Life: Perspectives from Psychology, Biology, and Evolution.* Washington, DC: American Psychological Association.

Polanczyk, G., de Lima, M.S., Horta, B.L., Biederman, J. and Rhode, L.A. (2007) 'The worldwide prevalence of ADHD: A systematic review and metaregression analysis', *American Journal of Psychiatry*, 164: 942–8.

Polk, J.A. (2006) 'Traits of effective teachers', *Arts Education Policy Review*, 107 (4): 23–9.

Pollack, S. (2013) 'Teaching mindfulness in therapy', in C.K. Germer, R.D. Siegel and P.R. Fulton (eds), *Mindfulness and Psychotherapy* (2nd edn). New York: Guilford Press, pp. 133–47.

Pollard, A. (2014) *Reflective Teaching in Schools* (4th edn). London: Bloomsbury Academic.

Ponce-Garcia, E., Madewell, A.N. and Kennison, S.M. (2015) 'The development of the scale of protective factors: Resilience in a violent trauma sample', *Violence and Victims*, 30 (5): 735–55.

Popkin, B., D'Anci, K. and Rosenberg, I. (2010) 'Water, hydration, and health', *Nutrition Reviews*, 68 (8): 439–58.

Poulsen, A.A., Rodger, S. and Ziviani, J.M. (2006) 'Understanding children's motivation from a self-determination theoretical perspective: Implications for practice', *Australian Occupational Therapy Journal*, 53: 78–86.

Prochaska, J.O. and DiClemente, C.C. (1982) 'Transtheoretical therapy: Toward a more integrative model of change', *Psychotherapy Research and Practice*, 20: 161–73.

Proctor, C., Linley, P.A. and Maltby, J. (2009) 'Youth life satisfaction measures: A review', *Journal of Positive Psychology*, 4 (2): 128–44.

PSHE Association (2015) *Teacher Guidance: Preparing to Teach About Mental Health and Emotional Wellbeing.* https://www.pshe-association.org.uk/system/files/Mental%20health%20guidance_0.pdf (accessed 25 September 2017).

Psytech International (2013) 'Clients'. www.psytech.com/clients.php (accessed 1 April 2013).

Puchalska-Wasyl, M.M. (2015) 'Self-talk: Conversation with oneself? On the types of internal interlocutors', *Journal of Psychology*, 149 (5): 443–60.

Purdy, L., Molnar, G., Griffiths, L. and Castle, P.C. (2014) 'Ilona: "Tweeting" through cultural adjustments', in K. Armour (ed.), *Pedagogical Cases in Physical Education and Youth Sport.* London: Routledge, pp. 222–34.

Qualter, P., Gardner, K.J., Pope, D.J., Hutchinson, J.M. and Whiteley, H.E. (2012) 'Ability emotional intelligence, trait emotional intelligence, and academic success in British secondary schools: A 5 year longitudinal study', *Learning and Individual Differences*, 22 (1): 83–91.

Raggi, V.L. and Chronis, A.M. (2006) 'Interventions to address the academic impairment of children and adolescents with ADHD', *Clinical Child and Family Psychology Review*, 9 (2): 85–111.

Raia, A.P. (1965) 'Goal setting and self-control: An empirical study', *Journal of Management Studies*, 2 (1): 34–53.

Ramachandram, V. (2016) 'Positive education and higher achievers role of positive psychology', *Indian Journal of Health & Wellbeing*, 7 (8): 848–50.

Ramsden, P. (1992) *Learning to Teach in Higher Education*. New York: Routledge.

Ramsey, J.R. and Rostain, A.L. (2011) 'CBT without medications for adult ADHD: An open pilot study of five patients', *Journal of Cognitive Psychotherapy: An International Quarterly*, 25 (4): 277–86.

Ratanasiripong, P., Kaewboonchoo, O., Ratanasiripong, N., Hanklang, S. and Chumchai, P. (2015) 'Biofeedback intervention for stress, anxiety, and depression among graduate students in public health nursing', *Nursing Research and Practice*, 1–5.

Rebar, A., Stanton, R., Geard, D., Short, C., Duncan, M. and Vandelanotte, C. (2015) 'A meta-meta analysis of the effect of physical activity on depression and anxiety in non-clinical adult populations', *Health Psychology Review*, 9 (3): 366–78.

Reber, A.S, Allen, R.A. and Reber, E.S. (2009) *The Penguin Dictionary of Psychology*. Harmondsworth: Penguin Books.

Reed, J.A., Maslow, A.L., Long, S. and Hughey, M. (2013) 'Examining the impact of 45 minutes of daily physical education on cognitive ability, fitness performance, and body composition of African American youth', *Journal of Physical Activity and Health*, 10 (2): 185–97.

Reeve, J. (2014) *Understanding Motivation and Emotion* (6th edn). Hoboken, NJ: John Wiley & Sons.

Reynolds, C. and Horton, A.M. (2008) 'Assessing executive functions: A life-span perspective', *Psychology in the Schools*, 45 (9): 875–92.

Rich, G.J. (2001) 'Positive psychology: An introduction', *Journal of Humanistic Psychology*, 41 (1): 8–12.

Roaf, C. (1988) 'The concept of a whole school approach to special needs', in O. Robinson and G. Thomas (eds), *Tackling Learning Difficulties*. London: Hodder and Stoughton.

Robbins, B.D. (2008) 'What is the good life? Positive psychology and the renaissance of humanistic psychology', *Humanistic Psychologist*, 36: 96–112.

Roberts, J.D., Roberts, R.D. and Barsade, S.G. (2008) 'Human abilities: Emotional intelligence', *Annual Review of Psychology*, 59 (1): 507–36.

Roberts, T. and Clark, F.V. (1976) 'Transpersonal psychology in education', in G. Hendricks and J. Fadiman (eds), *Transpersonal Education: A Curriculum for Feeling and Being*. Englewood Cliffs, NJ: Prentice-Hall, pp. 3–23.

Robertson, I.T., Cooper, C.L., Sarkar, M. and Curran, T. (2015) 'Resilience training in the workplace from 2003 to 2014: A systematic review', *Journal of Occupational & Organizational Psychology*, 88 (3): 533–62.

Robinson, V., Hohepa, M. and Lloyd, C. (2009) *School Leadership and Student Outcomes: Identifying What Works and Why*. Wellington, NZ: University of Auckland.

Robson, C. and McCartern, K. (2016) *Real World Research* (4th edn). Chichester: John Wiley & Sons.

Rodkin, P.C., Ryan, A.M., Jamison, R. and Wilson, T. (2013) 'Social goals, social behaviour, and social status in middle childhood', *Developmental Psychology*, 49 (6): 1139–50.

Roffey, S. (2015) 'Becoming an agent of change for school and student well-being', *Educational & Child Psychology*, 32 (1): 21–30.

Rogers, C.R. (1961) *On Becoming a Person: A Therapist's View of Psychotherapy*. London: Constable & Robinson.

Rolfe, G., Freshwater, D. and Japer, M. (2001) *Critical Reflection in Nursing and the Helping Professions: A User's Guide*. Basingstoke: Palgrave Macmillan.

Ronald, A., Happé, F. and Plomin, R. (2005) 'The genetic relationship between individual differences in social and nonsocial behaviours characteristic of autism', *Developmental Science*, 8 (5): 444–58.

Roncaglia, I. (2017) 'The role of wellbeing and wellness: A positive psychological model in supporting young people with ASCs', *Psychological Thought*, 10 (1): 217–26.

Ronson, J. (2004) *The Men Who Stare at Goats*. London: Picador.

Ronson, J. (2012) *The Psychopath Test*. London: Picador.

Rose, J. (2006) *Independent Review of the Teaching of Early Reading*. Nottingham: DfES Publications.

Rose, R. and Anketell, C. (2009) 'The benefits of social skills groups for young people with autism spectrum disorder: A pilot study', *Child Care in Practice*, 15 (2): 127–44.

Rothberg, D. (2005) 'Transpersonal issues at the millennium', *Transpersonal Psychology Review*, special issue, Winter: 81–102.

Rotter, J.B. (1966) 'Generalized expectancies of internal versus external control of reinforcements', *Psychological Monographs*, 80 (1) (whole no. 609).

Roumbou, S. (2017) 'Aristotle's concept of mental imagery in sports', *Psychological Thought*, 10 (1): 49–59.

Rowan, J. (1983) 'The real self and mystical experiences', *Journal of Humanistic Psychology*, 23 (2): 9–27.

Rowan, J. (1999) 'Ascent and descent in Maslow's theory', *Journal of Humanistic Psychology*, 39: 125–33.

Rowan, J. (2005) *The Transpersonal: Spirituality in Psychotherapy and Counselling* (2nd edn). London: Routledge.

Royal College of Psychiatrists (2011) *Mental Health of Students in Higher Education*. College Report CR166. www.rcpsych.ac.uk/files/pdfversion/CR166.pdf (accessed 6 October 2017).

Ruddick, J., Chaplain, R. and Wallace, G. (1996) *School Improvement: What Can Pupils Tell Us?* London: David Fulton.

Rudestam, K.E. and Newton, R.R. (2014) *Surviving Your Research: A Comprehensive Guide to Content and Process* (4th edn). London: Sage Publications.

Russell, J. (2015) 'Resilience', *Journal of the Philosophy of Sport*, 42 (2): 159–83.

Russell, M.T. and Darcie, L.K. (1995) *The UK Edition of the 16PF5: Administrator's Manual*. Windsor: ASE.

Russell, S.T. and Heck, K.E. (2008) 'Middle school dropout? Enrolment trends in the California 4-H Youth Development Program', *Applied Developmental Science*, 12 (1): 1–9.

Russell, W.D. (2009) 'A comparison of exergaming to traditional video games on children's mood, attention, and short-term memory', *Missouri Journal of Health, Physical Education, Recreation and Dance*, 19: 77–88.

Rutter, M., Maughan, B., Mortimore, P., Ouston, J. and Smith, A. (1979) *Fifteen Thousand Hours: Secondary Schools and their Effects on Children*. Cambridge, MA: Harvard University Press.

Ryan, T. and Panettini, D. (2011) 'The interdependence of physical fitness and academic achievement', *International Journal of Sport and Society*, 2 (3): 21–34.

Ryff, C.D. and Keyes, C.L.M. (1995) 'The structure of psychological well-being revisited', *Journal of Personality and Social Psychology*, 69: 719–27.

Saintilan, N. (2014) 'The use of imagery during the performance of memorized music', *Psychomusicology: Music, Mind & Brain*, 24 (4): 309–15.

Sallis, J., McKenzie, T., Alcaraz, J., Kolody, B., Faucette, N. and Hovell, M. (1997) 'The effects of a 2-year physical education program (SPARK) on physical activity and fitness in elementary school students', *American Journal of Public Health*, 87 (8): 1328–34.

Salmanian, M., Tehrani-Doost, M., Ghanbari-Motlagh, M. and Shahrivar, Z. (2012) 'Visual memory of meaningless shapes in children and adolescents with autism spectrum disorders', *Iranian Journal of Psychiatry*, 7 (3): 104–8.

Salmond, C.H., Ashburner, J.J., Connelly, A.A., Friston, K.J., Gadian, D.G. and Vargha-Khadem, F.F. (2005) 'The role of the medial temporal lobe in autistic spectrum disorders', *European Journal of Neuroscience*, 22 (3): 764–72.

Salovey, P. and Mayer, J.D. (1990) 'Emotional intelligence', *Imagination, Cognition, and Personality*, 9: 185–211.

Salzberg, S. (2011) *Real Happiness: The Power of Meditation. A 28-Day Program*. New York: Workman Publishing Company.

Sammons, P., Day, C., Kington, A., Gu, Q., Stobart, G. and Smees, R. (2007) 'Exploring variations in teachers' work, lives and their effects on pupils: Key findings and implications from a longitudinal mixed methods study', *British Educational Research Journal*, 33 (5): 681–701.

Santrock, J. (2001) *An Introduction to Educational Psychology*. London: McGraw-Hill.

Saul, H. (1993) 'Dying swans?', *Scientific American*, December: 25–7.

Saw, A., Main, L. and Gastin, P. (2015) 'Impact of sport context and support on the use of a self-report measure for athlete monitoring', *Journal of Sports Science & Medicine*, 14 (4): 732–9.

Schaal, B., Montagner, H., Hertling, E., Bolzoni, D., Moyse, R. and Quichon, R. (1980) 'Les stimulations olfactives dans les relations entre l'enfant et la mère' (Olfactory stimulations in mother–infant relationships), *Reproduction, Nutrition, Développement*, 20: 843–58.

Schachter, S. and Singer, J.E. (1962) 'Cognitive, social and physiological determinants of emotional state', *Psychological Review*, 69: 379–99.

Schaufelli, W.B. and Baker, A.B. (2004) 'Job demands, job resources and their relationship with burnout and engagement: A multi-sample study', *Journal of Organisational Behavior*, 25: 293–315.

Schick, T. and Vaughn, L. (2013) *Doing Philosophy: An Introduction through Thought Experiments*. London: McGraw-Hill.

Schleicher, A. (ed.) (2012) *Preparing Teachers and Developing School Leaders for the 21st Century: Lessons from Around the World*. Paris: OECD Publishing.

Schön, D. (1983) *The Reflective Practitioner: How Professionals Think in Action*. New York: Basic Books.

Schön, D. (1987) *Educating the Reflective Practitioner*. San Francisco, CA: Jossey-Bass.

Sciberra, E., Efron, D., Schilpzand, E.J., Anderson, V., Jongeling, B., Hazell, P., Ukomunne, O.C. and Nicholson, J.M. (2013) 'The Children's Attention Project: A community-based longitudinal study of children with ADHD and non-ADHD controls', *BMC Psychiatry*, 13 (18): 1–11.

Secades, X., Molinero, O., Salguero, A., Ruiz Barquin, R., de la Vega, R. and Márquez, S. (2016) 'Relationship between resilience and coping strategies in competitive sport', *Perceptual & Motor Skills*, 122 (1): 336–49.

Seligman, M.E. (1973) 'Fall into helplessness', *Psychology Today*, 7 (1): 43–8.

Seligman, M.E.P. (2011) *Flourish: A New Understanding of Happiness and Well-Being and How to Achieve Them*. London: Nicholas Brealey Publishing.

Seligman, M.E.P. and Csikszentmihalyi, M. (2000) 'Positive psychology: An introduction', *American Psychologist*, 55: 5–14.

Seligman, M.E.P., Maier, S.F. and Greer, J. (1968) 'The alleviation of learned helplessness in dogs', *Journal of Abnormal Psychology*, 73: 256–62.

Seth, A. (2016) 'Study of mental health and burnout in relation to teacher effectiveness among secondary school teachers', *Indian Journal of Health and Wellbeing*, 7 (7): 769–73.

Sharifah Maimunah, S.M.P. and Hashim, H.A. (2016) 'Differential effect of 7 and 16 groups of muscle relaxation training following repeated submaximal intensity exercise in young football players', *Perceptual and Motor Skills*, 122 (1): 227–37.

Sheldon, K.M. and King, L. (2001) 'Why positive psychology is necessary', *American Psychologist*, 56: 216–17.

Shen, B., McCaughtry, N., Martin, J., Garn, A., Kulik, N. and Fahlman, M. (2015) 'The relationship between teacher burnout and student motivation', *British Journal of Educational Psychology*, 85: 519–32.

Shernoff, D.J., Csikszentmihalyi, M., Schneider, B. and Shernoff, E.S. (2003) 'Student engagement in high school classrooms from the perspective of low theory', *School Psychology Quarterly*, 18 (2): 158–76.

Siegel, D.J. (2011) 'The proven benefits of mindfulness', in B. Boyce and Shambhala Sun (eds), *The Mindfulness Revolution: Leading Psychologists, Scientists, Artists, and Meditation Teachers on the Power of Mindfulness in Daily Life*. New York: Random House Publications, pp. 136–9.

Siegel, M. (1999) 'Language and thought: The fundamental significance of conversational awareness for cognitive development', *Developmental Science*, 2 (1): 1.

Silverman, J., Smith, C., Schmeidler, J., Hollander, E., Lawlor, B. and Fitzgerald, M. (2002) 'Symptom domains in autism and related conditions: Evidence for familiality', *American Journal of Medical Genetics*, 114: 64–73.

Singh, I. (2008) 'ADHD, culture and education', *Early Child Development and Care*, 178 (4): 347–61.

Skinner, B.F. (1938) *Behaviour of Organisms*. New York: Appleton-Century-Crofts.

Skinner, B.F. (1953) *Science and Human Behaviour*. New York: Macmillan.

Sleegers, P., Moolenaar, N., Galetzka, M., Pruyn, A., Sarroukh, B. and van der Zande, B. (2013) 'Lighting affects students' concentration positively: Findings from three Dutch studies', *Lighting Research and Technology*, 45 (2): 159–75.

Smith, K.E. and Norman, G.J. (2017) 'Brief relaxation training is not sufficient to alter tolerance to experimental pain in novices', *PLoS ONE*, 12 (5): e0177228.

Son, V., Jackson, B., Grove, J. and Feltz, D. (2011) '"I am" versus "we are": Effects of distinctive variants of self-talk on efficacy beliefs and motor performance', *Journal of Sports Sciences*, 29 (13): 1417–24.

Spironelli, C. and Angrilli, A. (2009) 'Developmental aspects of automatic word processing: Language lateralization of early ERP components in children, young adults and middle-aged subjects', *Biological Psychology*, 80: 35–45.

Springer, S. and Deutsch, G. (1993) *Left Brain, Right Brain*. New York: Freeman.

Stallard, P., Velleman, S. and Richardson, T. (2010) 'Computer use and attitudes towards computerised therapy amongst young people and parents attending child and adolescent mental health services', *Child & Adolescent Mental Health*, 15 (2): 80–4.

Steer, A. (2009) *Learning Behaviour: Lessons Learned. A Review of Behaviour Standards and Practices in Our Schools*. Nottingham: DCSF Publications.

Steiner, R. (2008) *The Four Temperaments*. Forest Row, East Sussex: Sophia Books.

Stenhouse, L. (1975) *Introduction to Curriculum Research and Development*. London: Heinemann.

Sternberg, R.J. (2000) *Handbook of Intelligence*. Cambridge: Cambridge University Press.

Sternberg, R.J. and Williams, W.M. (2002) *Educational Psychology*. New York: Pearson.

Stoicea, N., Scharre, D., Abduljalil, A., Knopp, M., Petra, S., Simona, G., Alice, G. and Narayanan, A. (2011) 'fMRI and SAGE test evaluation of pre-Mild Cognitive Impairment (pre-MCI)', *Acta Medica Marisiensis*, 57 (5): 511–15.

Storey, A. (2009) 'How fares the New Professionalism in schools? Findings from the State of the Nation project', *Curriculum Journal*, 20 (2): 121–38.

Strangroom, J. (2006) *Little Book of Big Ideas: Philosophy*. London: A. & C. Black.

Strathern, P. (2005) *A Brief History of Medicine: From Hippocrates to Gene Therapy*. London: Robinson.

Sun, J., Kuo, C.-Y., Hou, H.-T. and Lin, Y.-Y. (2017) 'Exploring learners' sequential behavioral patterns, flow experience, and learning performance in an anti-phishing educational game', *Educational Technology and Society*, 20 (1): 45–60.

Sundararajan, L. (2005) 'Happiness donut: A Confucian critique of positive psychology', *Journal of Theoretical and Philosophical Psychology*, 25 (1): 35–60.

Swarbrick, N., Eastwood, G. and Tutton, K. (2004) 'Self-esteem and successful interaction as part of the Forest School project', *Support for Learning*, 19 (3): 142–6.

Swinson, J. and Harrop, A. (2012) *Positive Psychology for Teachers*. London: Routledge.

Tam, M. (2014) 'Outcomes-based approach to quality assessment and curriculum improvement in higher education', *Quality Assurance in Education*, 22 (2): 158–68.

Tannock, R. (1998) 'Attention deficit hyperactivity disorder: Advances in cognitive, neurobiological, and genetic research', *Journal of Child Psychology and Psychiatry, and Allied Disciplines*, 39: 65–99.

Tarullo, A.R., Balsam, P.D. and Fifer, W.P. (2011) 'Sleep and infant learning', *Infant and Child Development*, 20 (1): 35–46.

Taylor, E.R. (2009) 'Sandtray and solution-focused therapy', *International Journal of Play Therapy*, 18 (1): 56–68.

Teacher Training Agency (1999) *National Special Educational Needs Specialist Standards*. London: HMSO.

Tempere, S., Hamtat, M., Bougeant, J., Revel, G. and Sicard, G. (2014) 'Learning odors: The impact of visual and olfactory mental imagery training on odor perception', *Journal of Sensory Studies*, 29 (6): 435–49.

Tennant, R., Hiller, L., Fishwick, R., Platt, S., Joseph, S., Weich, S., Parkinson, J., Secker, J. and Stewart-Brown, S. (2007) 'The Warwick-Edinburgh mental well-being scale (WEMWBS) development and UK validation', *Health Quality Life Outcomes*, 5 (63).

Terrell, C. and Passenger, T. (2011) *Understanding Autism, Dyslexia and Dyspraxia* (rev. edn). Poole: Family Doctor Publications.

Thelen, E. (1985) 'Developmental origins of motor coordination: Leg movements in human infants', *Developmental Psychobiology*, 18: 1–22.

Thelen, E. (1995) 'Motor development: A new synthesis', *American Psychologist*, 50: 79–95.

Thelwell, R. and Maynard, I. (2002) 'A triangulation of findings of three studies investigating repeatable good performance in professional cricketers', *International Journal of Sport Psychology*, 33 (3): 247–68.

Theodoulou, P., Avraamidou, L. and Vrasidas, C. (2015) 'Flow and the pedagogical affordances of computer games: A case study', *Educational Media International*, 52 (4): 328–39.

Thomas, G. (1997) 'Inclusive schools for an inclusive society', *British Journal of Learning Support*, 24 (3): 103–7.

Thomas, G. (2013) *How to Do Your Research Project* (2nd edn). London: Sage Publications.

Thompson, J. (2010) *The Essential Guide to Understanding Special Educational Needs: Practical Skills for Teachers*. Harlow: Pearson Education.

Thum, J., Parsons, G., Whittle, T. and Astorino, T. (2017) 'High-intensity interval training elicits higher enjoyment than moderate intensity continuous exercise', *PLoS ONE*, 12 (1): 1–11.

TLRP (Teaching and Learning Research Programme) (2013) *TLRP: Ten Principles*. www.tlrp.org/themes/themes/tenprinciples.html (accessed 30 January 2013).

Tod, D., Hardy, J. and Oliver, E. (2011) 'Effects of self-talk: A systematic review', *Journal of Sport & Exercise Psychology*, 33 (5): 666–87.

Torrence, M., Fidalgo, R. and Robledo, P. (2015) 'Do sixth-grade writers need process strategies?' *British Journal of Educational Psychology*, 85: 91–112.

Tortella, P., Haga, M., Loras, H., Sigmundsson, H. and Fumagalli, G. (2016) 'Motor skill development in Italian pre-school children induced by structured activities in a specific playground', *PLoS ONE*, 11 (7): 1–15.

Towne, B., Williams, K.D., Blangero, J., Czerwinski, S.A., Demerath, E.W., Nahhas, R.W., Dyer, T.D., Cole, S.A., Lee, M., Choh, A.C., Duren, D.L., Sherwood, R.J., Chumlea, W.C. and Siervogel, R.M. (2008) 'Presentation, heritability, and genome-wide linkage analysis of the mid-childhood growth spurt in healthy children from the Fels longitudinal study', *Human Biology*, 80 (6): 623–36.

Treisman, A.L. (1960) 'Contextual cues in selective listening', *Quarterly Journal of Experimental Psychology*, 12: 242–8.

Trepper, T.S., McCollum, E.E., De Jong, P., Korman, H., Gingerich, W. and Franklin, C. (2010) 'Solution-focused therapy treatment manual for working with individuals', Research Committee of the Solution Focused Brief Therapy Association, 1–10. www.sfbta.org/research.pdf (accessed 27 September 2017).

Trinies, V., Chard, A., Mateo, T. and Freeman, M. (2016) 'Effects of water provision and hydration on cognitive function among primary-school pupils in Zambia: A randomized trial', *PLoS ONE*, 11 (3): 1–14.

Trivers, R.L. (1971) 'The evolution of reciprocal altruism', *Quarterly Review of Biology*, 46 (1): 35–57.

Tuncer, M., Bal, S., Özüt, A. and Köse, N. (2012) 'Evaluation of several learning environment variables at secondary institutions', *University of Gaziantep Journal of Social Sciences*, 11 (1): 85–101.

Tyler, R.W. (1949) *Basic Principles of Curriculum and Instruction*. Chicago, IL: University of Chicago Press.

Universities UK (2015) *Student Mental Wellbeing in Higher Education: Good Practice Guide*. London: Universities UK.

Upton, P. and Taylor, C.E. (2014) *Educational Psychology*. London: Pearson.

Ursano, A.M., Kartheiser, P.H. and Ursano, R.J. (2007) 'The teaching alliance: A perspective on the good teacher and effective learning', *Psychiatry*, 70 (3): 187–94.

Van Diest, I., Verstappen, K., Aubert, A.E., Widjaja, D., Vansteenwegen, D. and Vleminex, E. (2014) 'Inhalation/exhalation ration modulates the effect of slow breathing on heart rate variability and relaxation', *Applied Psychophysiological Biofeedback*, 39: 171–80.

Vanhove, A., Herian, M., Perez, A., Harms, P. and Lester, P. (2016) 'Can resilience be developed at work? A meta-analytic review of resilience-building programme effectiveness', *Journal of Occupational & Organizational Psychology*, 89 (2): 278–307.

Van Hove, S., Vanderhoven, E. and Cornillie, F. (2017) 'The tablet for second language vocabulary learning: Keyboard, stylus or multiple choice', *Comunicar*, 25 (50): 53–62.

Veena, D. and Alvi, S. (2016) 'Guided imagery intervention for anxiety reduction', *Indian Journal of Health & Wellbeing*, 7 (2): 198–203.

Venetsanou, F. and Kambas, A. (2010) 'Environmental factors affecting preschoolers' motor development', *Early Childhood Education Journal*, 37 (4): 319–27.

Voelkl, J., Ellis, G. and Walker, J. (2003) 'Go with the flow: How to help people have optimal recreation experiences', *Parks and Recreation*, August: 20–9.

Vygotsky, L.S. (1978) *Mind in Society: The Development of Higher Psychological Processes*. Cambridge, MA: MIT Press.

Wagner, R. (1973) 'Rudolf Berlin: Originator of the term "dyslexia"', *Annals of Dyslexia*, 23 (1): 57–63.

Wagstaff, C. and Leach, J. (2015) 'The value of strength-based approaches in SERE and sport psychology', *Military Psychology* (American Psychological Association), 27 (2): 65–84.

Wajuihian, S.O. (2012) 'Neurobiology of developmental dyslexia part 1: A review of evidence from autopsy and structural neuro-imaging studies', *Optometry and Vision Development*, 43 (3): 120–30.

Walker, A. and Walker, C. (eds) (1997) *Britain Divided: The Growth of Social Exclusion in the 1980s and 1990s*. London: CPAG.

Wallace, C. and Milev, R. (2017) 'The effects of probiotics on depressive symptoms in humans: A systematic review', *Annals of General Psychiatry*, 16: 1–10.

Wallace, D. and Gorman, D. (2001) *Are You Dave Gorman?* London: Ebury Press.

Walsh, R. (1999) 'Asian contemplative disciplines: Common practices, clinical applications, and research findings', *Journal of Transpersonal Psychology*, 31 (2): 83–107.

Warburton, N. (2004) *Philosophy: The Basics* (4th edn). Abingdon: Routledge.

Watson, D., Clark, L.A. and Tellegen, A. (1988) 'Development and validation of brief measures of positive and negative affect: The PANAS scales', *Journal of Personality and Social Psychology*, 6 (54): 1063–70.

Watson, J.B. (1930) *Behaviorism*. New York: Norton.

Watson, J.B. and Rayner, R. (1920) 'Conditioned emotional reactions', *Journal of Experimental Psychology*, 3: 1–14.

Weedon, M., Wills, H.P., Kottwitz, E. and Kamps, D. (2016) 'The effects of a class-wide behaviour intervention for students with emotional and behavioural disorders', *Behavioral Disorders*, 42 (1): 285–93.

Weiner, B. (1974) *Achievement and Attribution Theory*. Morristown, NJ: General Learning Press.

Weiner, B. (1986) *An Attribution Theory of Motivation and Emotion*. New York: Springer-Verlag.

Weiss, A. (1987) 'Shostrom's Personal Orientation Inventory: Arguments against its basic validity', *Personal Individual Differences*, 8 (6): 895–903.

Weiss, M., Murray, C., Wasdell, M., Greenfield, B., Giles, L. and Hechtman, L. (2012) 'A randomized controlled trial of CNT therapy for adults with ADHD with and without medication', *BMC Psychiatry*, 12 (30): 1–8.

Whalen, S.P. (1998) 'Flow and the engagement of talent: Implications for secondary schooling', *NASSP Bulletin* (National Association of Secondary School Principals), 82 (595): 22–37.

White, M.A. and Waters, L.F. (2015) 'A case study of "The Good School": Examples of the use of Peterson's strengths-based approach with students', *Journal of Positive Psychology*, 10 (1): 69–76.

WHO (2013) 'RC63 fact sheet on mental health', WHO Regional Office for Europe. www.euro.who.int/__data/assets/pdf_file/0004/215275/RC63-Fact-sheet-MNH-Eng.pdf (accessed 6 October 2017).

Wilber, K. (2000a) *A Brief History of Everything* (rev. edn). Boston, MA: Shambhala Publications.

Wilber, K. (2000b) *Sex, Ecology, Spirituality: The Spirit of Evolution* (new edn). Boston, MA: Shambhala Publications.

Wilber, K. (2007) *Integral Spirituality: A Startling New Role for Religion in the Modern and Postmodern World*. Boston, MA: Integral Books.

Wilber, K. (2008) *The Pocket Ken Wilber*. Boston, MA: Shambhala Publications.

Wilde, J. (2008) 'Rational-emotive behavioral interventions for children with anxiety problems', *Journal of Cognitive & Behavioral Psychotherapies*, 8 (1): 133–41.

Wilding, L. (2015) 'The application of self-determination theory to support students experiencing disaffection', *Educational Psychology in Practice*, 31 (2): 137–49.

Wilf, M., Ramot, M., Furman-Haran, E., Arzi, A., Levkovitz, Y. and Malach, R. (2016) 'Diminished auditory responses during NREM sleep correlate with the hierarchy of language processing', *PLoS ONE*, 11 (6): 1–21.

Wilgus, J. and Wilgus, B. (2009) 'Face to face with Phineas Gage', *Journal of the History of the Neurosciences*, 18 (3): 340–5.

Wilkins, A., Cleave, R., Grayson, N. and Wilson, L. (2009) 'Typography for children may be inappropriately designed', *Journal of Research in Reading*, 32 (4): 402–12.

Wing, L. (2003) *The Autistic Spectrum* (2nd rev. edn). London: Constable and Robinson.

Wisner, B.L., Jones, B. and Gwin, D. (2010) 'School-based meditation practices for adolescents: A resource for strengthening self-regulation, emotional coping, and self-esteem', *Children and Schools*, 32 (3): 150–9.

Wolpe, J. (1958) *Psychotherapy by Reciprocal Inhibition*. Stanford, CA: Stanford University Press.

Wong, P.T.P. (2011) 'Positive Psychology 2.0: Towards a balanced interactive model of the good life', *Canadian Psychology*, 52: 69–81.

Wood, D.F. (2016) '*Mens sana in corpore sano*: Student well-being and the development of resilience', *Medical Education*, 50 (1): 20–3.

Wood, J.V., Perunovic, W.Q. and Lee, J.W. (2009) 'Positive self-statements: Power for some, peril for others', *Psychological Science*, 20 (7): 860–6.

World Health Organization (1992/2010) *ICD-10 Classification of Mental and Behavioural Disorders: Clinical Descriptions and Diagnostic Guidelines*. Geneva: World Health Organization.

World Health Organization (2003) *Investing in Mental Health*. Geneva: World Health Organization. www.who.int/mental_health/media/investing_mnh.pdf (accessed 6 October 2017).

World Health Organization (2009) *Mental Health, Resilience and Inequalities*. Geneva: World Health Organization. www.euro.who.int/__data/assets/pdf_file/0012/100821/E92227.pdf (accessed 6 October 2017).

World Health Organization (2013) *The European Mental Health Action Plan 2013–2020*. Geneva: World Health Organization. www.euro.who.int/__data/assets/pdf_file/0020/280604/WHO-Europe-Mental-Health-Acion-Plan-2013-2020.pdf (accessed 6 October 2017).

Wray, D., Medwell, J., Fox, R. and Poulson, L. (2000) 'The teaching practices of effective teachers of literacy', *Educational Review*, 53 (1): 75–84.

Wu, K., Chan, S.K., Leung, P.L., Liu, W., Leung, F.T. and Ng, R. (2011) 'Components and developmental differences of executive functioning for school-aged children', *Developmental Neuropsychology*, 36 (3): 319–37.

Wundt, W. (1896) *Lectures on Human and Animal Psychology*. New York: Macmillan.

Xiao, Y., Brauer, J., Lauckner, M., Zhai, H., Jia, F., Margulies, D.S. and Friederici, A.D. (2016) 'Development of the intrinsic language network in preschool children from ages 3 to 5 years', *PLoS ONE*, 11 (11): 1–19.

Xie, Y., Peng, L., Zuo, X. and Li, M. (2016) 'The psychometric evaluation of the Connor–Davidson Resilience Scale using a Chinese military sample', *PLoS ONE*, 11 (2): 1–10.

Yau, S., Pun, K. and Tang, J. (2011) 'Outcome study of school programmes for reducing stigma and promoting mental health', *Journal of Youth Studies*, 14 (1): 30–40.

Yen, J. (2010) 'Authorizing happiness: Rhetorical demarcation of science and society in historical narratives of positive psychology', *Journal of Theoretical and Philosophical Psychology*, 30: 67–78.

Yerkes, R.M. and Dodson, J.D. (1908) 'The relation of strength of stimulus to rapidity of habit-formation', *Journal of Comparative Neurology and Psychology*, 18: 459–82.

Young, S.J., Adamou, M., Bolea, B., Gudjonsson, G., Müller, I., Pitts, M., Thome, J. and Asherson, P. (2011) 'The identification and management of ADHD offenders within the criminal justice system: A consensus statement from the UK Adult ADHD Network and criminal justice agencies', *BMC Psychiatry*, 11 (32): 1–14.

Yuwei, J., Adaval, R., Steinhart, Y. and Wyer Jr., R. (2014) 'Imagining yourself in the scene: The interactive effects of goal-driven self-imagery and visual perspectives on consumer behavior', *Journal of Consumer Research*, 41 (2): 418–35.

Zanus, C., Battistutta, S., Aliverti, R., Montico, M., Cremaschi, S., Ronfani, L., Monasta, L. and Carrozzi, M. (2017) 'Adolescent admissions to Emergency Departments for self-injurious thoughts and behaviors', *PLoS ONE*, 12 (1): 1–15.

Zeidan, F., Martucci, K., Kraft, R., McHaffie, J. and Coghill, R. (2014) 'Neural correlates of mindfulness meditation-related anxiety relief', *Social Cognitive & Affective Neuroscience*, 9 (6): 751–9.

Zeki, S.M. (2003) 'Improbable areas in the visual brain', *Trends in Neurosciences*, 26 (1): 23–6.

Zhang, J., Zhou, M. and Zhang, J. (2016) 'The interactive effects of personality and burnout on knowledge sharing among teachers', *Social Behavior and Personality*, 44 (8): 1267–80.

Zhang, Y. and Fishbach, A. (2010) 'Counteracting obstacles with optimistic predictions', *Journal of Experimental Psychology*, 139 (1): 16–31.

Zimmerman, B.J., Bandura, A. and Martinez-Pons, M. (1992) 'Self-motivation for academic attainment: The role of self-efficacy beliefs and personal goal setting', *American Educational Research Journal*, 29: 663–76.

Zinke, K., Fries, E., Altgassen, M., Kirschbaum, C., Dettenborn, L. and Kliegel, M. (2010) 'Visuospatial short-term memory explains deficits in tower task planning in high-functioning children with autism spectrum disorder', *Child Neuropsychology*, 16 (3): 229–41.

Zourbanos, N. (2013) 'The use of instructional and motivational self-talk in setting up a physical education lesson', *JOPERD: The Journal of Physical Education, Recreation & Dance*, 84 (8): 54–8.

Zourbanos, N., Papaioannou, A., Argyropoulou, E. and Hatzigeorgiadis, A. (2014) 'Achievement goals and self-talk in physical education: The moderating role of perceived competence', *Motivation & Emotion*, 38 (2). 235–51.

Zsigmond, M.Z. and Benga, I. (2009) 'Treatment options in ADHD', *Clujul Medical*, 82 (4): 484–7.

Zuvela, F., Bozanic, A. and Miletic, D. (2011) 'POLYGON: A new fundamental movement skills test for 8-year-old children. Construction and validation', *Journal of Sports Science and Medicine*, 10 (1): 157–63.

INDEX